Concordance
to *The Science of Mind*

Concordance

to
The Science of Mind

Compiled by
Martha Ann Stewart, RScF
and Albert G. Lowe, PhD

Science of Mind Publishing
Burbank, California

*Dedicated as a guidebook
to fellow travelers in the
virtually unexplored realm
of Mind and mind.*

*Appreciation is expressed to
Dr. and Mrs. Reginald C. Armor
for their encouragement and kindness.*

Published by Science of Mind Publishing
2600 West Magnolia Boulevard
Burbank, California 91505

Design: Randall Friesen

Printed in the United States of America
ISBN13: 978-0-9727184-7-9
ISBN: 0-9727184-7-8

This concordance displays a word, the page and paragraph where the word is located, and a part of the context in which it appears. The number preceding the hyphen represents the page number. The number following the hyphen is the paragraph in which the word is located.

Notification of errors is appreciated.

The sorting and arrangement of the words has been performed by a third generation computer and its supporting equipment. This technology is God expressing in and through the mind of man.

A

ABANDON	254 - 3	I ABANDON MYSELF TO THE LIFE
ABANDON	283 - 1	WITH A COMPLETE ABANDON
ABANDONMENT	323 - 2	WITH A COMPLETE ABANDONMENT
ABANDONMENT	358 - 3	ABANDONMENT INTO THE VERY CENTER
ABANDONMENT	440 - 4	COMPLETE ABANDONMENT TO IT
ABHORS	459 - 6	LOVES SINCERITY AND ABHORS DECEIT
ABIDE	150 - 6	AND MY WORDS ABIDE IN YOU
ABIDE	313 - 4	IF YE ABIDE IN ME
ABIDE	481 - 2	ABIDE IN ME AND MY WORDS
ABIDE	481 - 5	ABIDE IN THE SPIRIT OF TRUTH
ABIDING	242 - 3	THE ABIDING PLACE OF THIS LIFE
ABIDING	440 - 6	ABIDING IN THE CONVICTION
ABIDING IN HIM	151 - 1	ABIDING IN HIM MEANS HAVING NO
ABILITY	046 - 4	ITS ABILITY TO DO FOR US
ABILITY	073 - 1	HIS ABILITY TO THINK
ABILITY	082 - 1	ONLY ITS OWN ABILITY
ABILITY	118 - 2	ITS OWN ABILITY TO DO
ABILITY	142 - 3	MAN'S ABILITY AND RIGHT TO MAKE
ABILITY	174 - 3	DEMONSTRATE BEYOND OUR ABILITY
ABILITY	176 - 3	PERSISTENT ABILITY TO USE THE LAW
ABILITY	261 - 4	ABILITY TO MEET EVERY SITUATION
ABILITY	271 - 3	LEVEL OF OUR ABILITY TO KNOW
ABILITY	306 - 2	LIMIT OF OUR ABILITY TO DEMONSTRATE
ABILITY	401 - 3	ABILITY TO KNOW AND TO UNDERSTAND
ABILITY	500 - 5	BOTH THE ABILITY AND THE DESIRE
ABLE	040 - 1	ONLY AS WE ARE ABLE
ABLE	073 - 1	ALWAYS BEEN ABLE TO THINK
ABLE	086 - 3	WE SHOULD BE ABLE
ABLE	201 - 2	ABLE TO SEE ONLY PERFECTION
ABLE	371 - 1	ABLE TO SEE AND BE SEEN
ABLE	394 - 4	ABLE TO CONCEIVE OF ITS DOING
ABLE	439 - 2	NO LONGER ABLE TO CONTAIN THE NEW
ABNORMAL	144 - 3	ABNORMAL MENTAL STATE EXPRESSES ITS
ABNORMAL	200 - 4	ABNORMAL ABSENCE OF A NORMAL
ABNORMAL	440 - 4	ABNORMAL AND UNHAPPY
ABNORMAL	476 - 6	COST OF THE OTHERS IS ABNORMAL
ABNORMAL	481 - 5	EVIL IS ABNORMAL
ABODE	124 - 2	ABODE OF OUR MORBID IMAGINATIONS
ABOUNDING	159 - 4	HAVE ABOUNDING CONFIDENCE
ABOVE	160 - 1	THOUGHT RISES ABOVE A BELIEF
ABOVE ALL	191 - 4	ABOVE ALL WE CERTAINLY BELIEVE
ABOVE ALL	459 - 6	ABOVE ALL ELSE THE TRUTH IS WISE
ABSENT	208 - 2	THROUGH ABSENT TREATMENT
ABSENTS	239 - 2	GOD ABSENTS HIMSELF
ABSENT TREATMENT	171 - 3	THERE IS NO ABSENT TREATMENT AS OPPOSED
ABSOLUTE	036 - 5	SO ABSOLUTE THE DOMAIN OF LAW
ABSOLUTE	036 - 5	ABSOLUTE THE DOMAIN OF LAW THROUGH IT
ABSOLUTE	066 - 3	BELIEVE IN AN ABSOLUTE INTELLIGENCE
ABSOLUTE	074 - 2	SCIENCE IS ABSOLUTE KNOWLEDGE
ABSOLUTE	100 - 2	SPIRIT IS THE ABSOLUTE BEING
ABSOLUTE	128 - 4	ABSOLUTE WITH WHICH WE ARE DEALING
ABSOLUTE	148 - 4	SEED OF THOUGHT IN THE ABSOLUTE

ABSOLUTE	169 – 3	TURNS TO THE ABSOLUTE
ABSOLUTE	176 – 1	ABSOLUTE AND EQUAL OBJECTIVE FACT
ABSOLUTE	187 – 2	ALREADY EMBODIED IN THE ABSOLUTE
ABSOLUTE	188 – 3	THE ABSOLUTE WITH WHICH YOU ARE DEALING
ABSOLUTE	221 – 2	ABSOLUTE IT WILL NOT
ABSOLUTE	274 – 4	IS UNCOMPROMISING AND ABSOLUTE
ABSOLUTE	274 – 4	WE ENTER THE ABSOLUTE
ABSOLUTE	274 – 4	THE TREATMENT IS NOT IN THE ABSOLUTE
ABSOLUTE	275 – 2	TREATMENT MUST BECOME ABSOLUTE
ABSOLUTE	276 – 1	THE LAW IS ABSOLUTE
ABSOLUTE	284 – 4	PRINCIPLE IS ABSOLUTE
ABSOLUTE	300 – 2	THE RELATIVE AND THE ABSOLUTE
ABSOLUTE	300 – 2	FOR THE LAW IS ABSOLUTE
ABSOLUTE	315 – 3	WE ENTER THE ABSOLUTE
ABSOLUTE	405 – 3	CANNOT CONTRACT THE ABSOLUTE
ABSOLUTE	406 – 3	ABSOLUTE AND THE RELATIVE
ABSOLUTE	406 – 4	TO THINK IN THE ABSOLUTE
ABSOLUTE	417 – 2	MEANT BY ENTERING THE ABSOLUTE
ABSOLUTE	444 – 4	ABSOLUTE AND THE RELATIVE
ABSOLUTENESS	277 – 4	WE DEAL WITH ABSOLUTENESS
ABSOLUTENESS	488 – 4	GOD PROVES HIS ABSOLUTENESS
ABSORB	272 – 4	ABSORB THAT MEDIUM
ABSORB	480 – 3	DOES NOT ABSORB THE DIVINE NATURE
ABSTAIN	143 – 1	ABSTAIN FROM WRONG THINKING
ABSTAIN	455 – 4	ABSTAIN FROM THE OLD
ABSTAINING	442 – 3	ABSTAINING FROM EATING
ABSTRACT	026 – 5	SOMETHING THAT IS TOO ABSTRACT
ABSTRACT	040 – 3	ABSTRACT ESSENCE OF BEAUTY
ABSTRACT	076 – 3	UNIVERSAL AND ABSTRACT
ABSTRACT	088 – 4	MERELY THINK OF AN ABSTRACT PRINCIPLE
ABSTRACT	334 – 4	MISTAKE TO SO ABSTRACT THE PRINCIPLE
ABSTRACT	392 – 2	MIND IN AN ABSTRACT
ABSTRACT	397 – 1	IT IS MIND IN THE ABSTRACT
ABSTRACT	405 – 2	GOD GIVES IN THE ABSTRACT
ABSTRACT	444 – 4	JOIN THE ABSTRACT WITH THE CONCRETE
ABSTRACTING	088 – 4	BE VERY CAREFUL IN ABSTRACTING
ABSTRACTION	309 – 5	METAPHYSICAL ABSTRACTION
ABSTRACTION	396 – 3	MIND AS LAW IS AN ABSTRACTION
ABSTRACTS	255 – 4	WHICH ABSTRACTS CERTAIN MATERIALS
ABSURD	380 – 2	QUITE ABSURD TO SUPPOSE
ABSURD	486 – 1	ABSURD DOCTRINE IS WORSE THAN IGNORANCE
ABSURDIY	373 – 1	TO SUPPOSE AN ABSURDITY
ABSURDITY	380 – 2	THAN ONE IN IT IS AN ABSURDITY
ABSURDITY	473 – 3	THE POINT OF ABSURDITY
ABUNDANCE	025 – 3	WE SEE ABUNDANCE IN THE UNIVERSE
ABUNDANCE	164 – 2	ABUNDANCE HAS ALWAYS BEEN OURS
ABUNDANCE	263 – 2	ABUNDANCE IN THE LIFE OF THOSE
ABUNDANCE	263 – 5	HAVE AN ABUNDANCE OF MONEY
ABUNDANCE	264 – 1	HAVE THIS IDEA OF ABUNDANCE
ABUNDANCE	264 – 2	I HAVE ABUNDANCE
ABUNDANCE	264 – 2	I AM ABUNDANCE
ABUNDANCE	288 – 2	THROUGH POVERTY THAN ABUNDANCE
ABUNDANCE	288 – 2	GREATER ABUNDANCE OF EVERY GOOD
ABUNDANCE	403 – 4	THOUGHTS OF ABUNDANCE MANIFEST
ABUNDANCE	412 – 1	WITH ABUNDANCE AND WITH SUCCESS

ABUNDANCE	416 - 4	WE THINK ABUNDANCE
ABUNDANCE	449 - 6	SHALL HAVE MORE ABUNDANCE
ABUNDANCE	459 - 2	GOD'S LAW OF ABUNDANCE
ABUNDANCE	467 - 3	CALF REPRESENTS THE ABUNDANCE
ABUNDANCE	488 - 4	DEMONSTRATION OF ABUNDANCE
ABUNDANT	188 - 4	EXPRESS A MORE ABUNDANT LIFE
ABUNDANT	246 - 4	WITH GOD'S ABUNDANT LIFE
ABUNDANT	262 - 3	THE MORE ABUNDANT LIFE
ABUNDANTLY	082 - 4	THEY MIGHT HAVE LIFE ABUNDANTLY
ABUNDANTLY	431 - 3	BLESS US ABUNDANTLY
ABUSE	253 - 1	ABUSE GOD'S GIFT BY BECOMING
ABUSED	410 - 3	THIS POWER WAS ABUSED
ACCELERATE	249 - 4	THERE IS NOTHING TO ACCELERATE
ACCELERATION	144 - 3	ACCELERATION OF THE HEART
ACCENTUATE	319 - 2	ACCENTUATE THE STATE OF CONSCIOUSNESS
ACCENTUATED	121 - 3	A POINT WHERE INDIVIDUALITY IS ACCENTUATED
ACCEPT	027 - 4	WILLING TO ACCEPT
ACCEPT	032 - 1	ACCEPT THIS POSITION RELATIVE
ACCEPT	033 - 3	ACCEPT THE FACT THAT NATURE'S TABLE
ACCEPT	036 - 3	GIFT THAT WE DO NOT ACCEPT
ACCEPT	039 - 2	HOW MUCH CAN WE ACCEPT
ACCEPT	039 - 5	ACCEPT TODAY MORE GOOD
ACCEPT	058 - 5	WE MUST ACCEPT AND BELIEVE
ACCEPT	075 - 1	WILLING TO ACCEPT
ACCEPT	092 - 2	BOUND TO ACCEPT AND TO ACT
ACCEPT	092 - 3	IT MUST ALWAYS ACCEPT
ACCEPT	096 - 3	ITS OWN NATURE TO ACCEPT
ACCEPT	188 - 2	NOT MERELY ACCEPT IT WITH YOUR INTELLECT
ACCEPT	198 - 2	ITS NATURE TO ACCEPT
ACCEPT	221 - 5	ACCEPT WHAT YOU SAY
ACCEPT	241 - 3	PATIENT MUST ACCEPT THIS CONSCIOUSNESS
ACCEPT	251 - 4	MERELY TO ACCEPT FULLY
ACCEPT	266 - 3	ACCEPT THIS INTELLECTUALLY
ACCEPT	315 - 2	THE MIND MUST ACCEPT
ACCEPT	315 - 2	MIND MUST UNQUALIFIEDLY ACCEPT
ACCEPT	388 - 2	ACCEPT THIS AND BEGIN TO LIVE
ACCEPT	390 - 2	MAY ACCEPT OR REJECT
ACCEPT	398 - 3	MENTALLY ACCEPT MONEY
ACCEPT	399 - 2	ACCEPT THE WHOLE THING
ACCEPT	399 - 3	WE DO NOT HOPE WE ACCEPT
ACCEPT	405 - 1	MUST LEARN TO ACCEPT THIS
ACCEPT	405 - 1	OUR PRIVILEGE TO ACCEPT THE GIFT
ACCEPT	405 - 3	ALL WE CAN DO IS TO ACCEPT
ACCEPT	498 - 2	ACCEPT ONLY THAT WHICH IS TRUE
ACCEPTANCE	138 - 1	A BELIEF IN AND AN ACCEPTANCE
ACCEPTANCE	152 - 2	BE AN ACTIVE ACCEPTANCE
ACCEPTANCE	159 - 1	BELIEF ACCEPTANCE AND TRUST
ACCEPTANCE	159 - 5	ACCEPTANCE OF A CONCEPT
ACCEPTANCE	161 - 4	MOLD OF ACCEPTANCE IS THE MEASURE OF OUR
ACCEPTANCE	173 - 4	A STATE OF REALIZATION AND ACCEPTANCE
ACCEPTANCE	175 - 1	ACCEPTANCE AND OUR WILLINGNESS
ACCEPTANCE	180 - 2	TRANSMUTED INTO ACCEPTANCE
ACCEPTANCE	246 - 4	ACCEPTANCE UNTIL IT IS FILLED
ACCEPTANCE	267 - 1	ACCEPTANCE MUST BECOME
ACCEPTANCE	274 - 2	AT A PLACE OF ACCEPTANCE

ACCEPTANCE	275 - 2	MIND AS A COMPLETE ACCEPTANCE
ACCEPTANCE	278 - 4	A DEFINITE CONCRETE ACCEPTANCE
ACCEPTANCE	280 - 2	OF FAITH CONVICTION AND ACCEPTANCE
ACCEPTANCE	280 - 3	PRAYER IS FAITH AND ACCEPTANCE
ACCEPTANCE	280 - 3	LAW OF FAITH AND ACCEPTANCE
ACCEPTANCE	285 - 3	MENTAL ACCEPTANCE BY THE ONE
ACCEPTANCE	318 - 1	BELIEF, ACCEPTANCE, CONVICTION
ACCEPTANCE	321 - 2	SHOULD BE A DEFINITE ACCEPTANCE
ACCEPTANCE	385 - 3	JUSTIFIES A COMPLETE ACCEPTANCE
ACCEPTANCE	397 - 5	COMPLETE MENTAL ACCEPTANCE
ACCEPTANCE	398 - 2	ACCEPTANCE AND REALIZATION
ACCEPTANCE	398 - 3	MENTAL ACCEPTANCE OF OUR DESIRES
ACCEPTANCE	399 - 5	OTHER IS A MENTAL ACCEPTANCE
ACCEPTANCE	401 - 3	ACCEPTANCE ON OUR PART
ACCEPTANCE	431 - 3	BELIEF AND ACCEPTANCE
ACCEPTANCE	439 - 6	ACCEPTANCE OF HIS ABILITY TO DO
ACCEPTANCE	440 - 6	ULTIMATE ACCEPTANCE OF TRUTH BY ALL
ACCEPTANCE	458 - 5	REACH A POINT OF ACCEPTANCE
ACCEPTANCE	462 - 1	ACCEPTANCE WAS FILLED FROM
ACCEPTANCES	164 - 3	ACCEPTANCES AND REALIZATIONS OF PEACE
ACCEPTANCES	398 - 4	ACCEPTANCES SHOULD BE FILLED WITH
ACCEPTED	030 - 3	IDEA IS ACCEPTED AND POURED
ACCEPTED	042 - 4	NOT YET ACCEPTED THE GREATER GIFT
ACCEPTED	044 - 4	MUST BE ACCEPTED INTO OUR MIND
ACCEPTED	074 - 4	GRADUALLY BECOMES ACCEPTED
ACCEPTED	241 - 3	MUST BE ACCEPTED AS A PRESENT
ACCEPTED	443 - 1	MUST BE ACCEPTED ON FAITH ALONE
ACCEPTING	266 - 3	WHILE ACCEPTING BETTER ONES
ACCEPTS	196 - 6	ACCEPTS THESE IMAGES OF THOUGHT
ACCEPTS	198 - 5	ACCEPTS THE IMAGES OF
ACCEPTS	234 - 4	IT ACCEPTS OUR THOUGHT
ACCEPTS	258 - 2	AS MAN EXPECTS AND ACCEPTS
ACCEPTS	273 - 3	ACCEPTS THIS STATEMENT AS BEING
ACCEPTS	283 - 4	WHICH SO COMPLETELY ACCEPTS IT
ACCESS	227 - 2	HAVE CONSCIOUS ACCESS TO IT
ACCESS	273 - 5	ACCESS TO THE INTELLIGENCE
ACCESS	339 - 1	COMPLETE ACCESS TO IT
ACCESS	394 - 5	ACCESS TO THE ORIGINAL CREATIVE
ACCESS	482 - 2	EACH HAS ACCESS TO THE ALL
ACCESSIBLE	151 - 2	GOD IS ACCESSIBLE TO ALL PEOPLE
ACCIDENT	295 - 2	NO ACCIDENT NO TROUBLE NO CONFUSION
ACCIDENT	374 - 4	DISEASE DECAY OR ACCIDENT
ACCOMPANIED	047 - 1	ACCOMPANIED BY AN UNQUALIFIED
ACCOMPANIED	436 - 1	ACCOMPANIED BY A POSITIVE RECEPTIVITY
ACCOMPANY	264 - 5	PEACE AND JOY ACCOMPANY ME
ACCOMPANYING	346 - 2	ACCOMPANYING THE METHOD
ACCOMPLISH	044 - 4	ACCOMPLISH THE DESIRED RESULT
ACCOMPLISH	054 - 1	IT WILL ACCOMPLISH AND NOTHING
ACCOMPLISH	418 - 1	ACCOMPLISH ANYTHING WORTH WHILE
ACCOMPLISH	496 - 4	ACCOMPLISH BECAUSE OF OUR OWN INNER
ACCOMPLISHED	178 - 5	HEALING IS ACCOMPLISHED THROUGH
ACCOMPLISHED	180 - 2	IS ALREADY AN ACCOMPLISHED FACT
ACCOMPLISHED	338 - 3	DIVINE REALITY IS ACCOMPLISHED
ACCOMPLISHED	487 - 1	ACCOMPLISHED BY CORRECT KNOWING
ACCOMPLISHED	489 - 6	ACCOMPLISHED BY THE SPIRIT OF GOD

ACCOMPLISHES	155 - 3	ACCOMPLISHES FAR MORE THAN
ACCOMPLISHMENT	477 - 2	CONTEMPLATION TO ACCOMPLISHMENT
ACCORD	046 - 3	ACCORD WITH DIVINE LAW
ACCORD	047 - 3	ACCORD WITH THE PRINCIPLE
ACCORD	054 - 1	ACCORD WITH THIS PERFECT LAW
ACCORD	054 - 3	ACCORD WITH ULTIMATE REALITY
ACCORD	070 - 1	IN ACCORD WITH LAW
ACCORD	194 - 2	ACCORD WITH WELL KNOWN
ACCORD	393 - 3	IN ACCORD WITH LAW
ACCORD	432 - 1	IN ACCORD WITH DIVINE HARMONY
ACCORD	437 - 4	EVER IN ACCORD WITH THE DIVINE MIND
ACCORDANCE	130 - 1	ACCORDANCE WITH HER LAWS
ACCORDING	034 - 1	ACCORDING TO OUR BELIEF IN IT
ACCORDING	052 - 5	ACCORDING TO THE PRINCIPLE
ACCORDING	175 - 1	RECEIVES ACCORDING TO HIS BELIEF
ACCORDING	177 - 1	ALWAYS ACCORDING TO LAW
ACCORDING	383 - 1	ACCORDING TO THE USE WE MAKE OF IT
ACCORDING	439 - 6	ACCORDING TO YOUR FAITH
ACCORDING	481 - 4	ANSWERED ACCORDING TO LAW
ACCOUNT	067 - 2	THE ACCOUNT OF CREATION
ACCOUNTABLE	449 - 3	ACCOUNTABLE FOR THE VERY WORDS WHICH
ACCRETION	235 - 4	ACCRETION WHICH TAKES PLACE
ACCUMULATE	115 - 1	ACCUMULATE THE RIGHT KIND OF EXPERIENCES
ACCUMULATE	349 - 4	HARD STUDY COULD NOT ACCUMULATE
ACCUMULATED	349 - 1	THE ACCUMULATED SUBJECTIVE EXPERIENCES
ACCUSTOMED	384 - 4	ACCUSTOMED TO OUR NEW SURROUNDINGS
ACCUSTOMED	402 - 2	SO ACCUSTOMED TO THE THOUGHT
ACHIEVEMENT	451 - 1	POSITIVE THOUGHTS OF ACHIEVEMENT
ACIDITY	260 - 2	ANY ACIDITY IF WE ARE GOVERNED
ACKNOWLEDGING	231 - 3	NOT ACKNOWLEDGING IT AS AN ENTITY
ACORN	186 - 2	PLANET AS AN ACORN
ACQUAINT	040 - 1	INTELLIGENCE CAN ACQUAINT US
ACQUAINT	185 - 2	ACQUAINT ITSELF WITH GOD
ACQUAINT	292 - 2	ACQUAINT THE CONSCIOUSNESS WITH THIS IDEA
ACQUAINTING	264 - 3	ACQUAINTING THE MIND WITH
ACQUIESCENCE	159 - 5	ACQUIESCENCE OF THE MIND
ACQUIESCENCE	395 - 2	UNIFICATION AND ACQUIESCENCE
ACQUIRE	306 - 4	ACQUIRE A GREATER MENTAL EQUIVALENT
ACQUISITION	032 - 3	THE ACQUISITION OF NEW POWERS
ACQUISITION	282 - 2	ACQUISITION OF GREATER AND STILL GREATER
AQUISITIVE	232 - 4	MAN IN HIS ACQUISITIVE HABITS
ACQUISITIVENESS	232 - 5	UNDUE ACQUISITIVENESS
ACT	064 - 2	BE AN ACT OF CONSCIOUSNESS
ACT	064 - 5	ACT WITHIN HIMSELF
ACT	083 - 2	COMPELLED ALSO TO ACT UPON IT
ACT	092 - 2	IT IS BOUND TO ACCEPT AND TO ACT
ACT	105 - 2	ONLY ACT AS INSTRUCTED
ACT	118 - 1	ACCEPT THAT THOUGHT AND ACT UPON IT
ACT	126 - 2	ACT BELIEVE IN FEEL
ACT	131 - 3	IT IS COMPELLED TO ACT
ACT	147 - 3	ACT AS THOUGH I AM AND I WILL BE
ACT	178 - 6	ACT OF INDUCING RIGHT CONCEPTS
ACT	198 - 4	TREATMENT IS THE ACT THE ART
ACT	229 - 1	INTO INTELLIGENCE AND LETS IT ACT
ACT	269 - 3	EVERY ACT IN THE LIFE OF THE INDIVIDUAL

ACT	273 – 4	ACT OF THE DIVINE PROJECTING
ACT	290 – 2	WHEN TO ACT AND HOW TO ACT
ACT	290 – 2	ACT WITH PERFECT ASSURANCE
ACT	296 – 1	THE ACT AND THE ACTOR ARE ONE
ACT	302 – 2	ACT AS THOUGH IT WERE TRUE
ACT	304 – 5	DIRECT ACT OF BECOMING THE THINGS
ACT	307 – 3	'ACT AS THOUGH I AM AND I WILL BE'
ACT	323 – 2	ACT, BELIEVE AND KNOW THAT YOU ARE A CENTER
ACT	323 – 3	ACT AS THOUGH I AM AND I WILL BE
ACT	355 – 2	ACT THROUGH THE CREATIVE MEDIUM
ACT	392 – 3	CANNOT ACT UNTIL IT IS SET
ACT	416 – 2	TO ACT UPON THIS THOUGHT
ACT	421 – 5	ACT OF READING SUBJECTIVE THOUGHT
ACT	449 – 3	THOUGHT BEFORE THERE CAN BE AN ACT
ACT	466 – 3	ACT AS THOUGH I AM
ACTED	116 – 1	IS AT ONCE ACTED UPON
ACTED	140 – 4	ACTED UPON BY OUR THOUGHT
ACTING	131 – 5	ACTING UPON SOUL
ACTING	237 – 3	ACTING THROUGH A THOUGHT FORCE
ACTING	397 – 4	MIND ACTING AS LAW
ACTION	029 – 2	ALL MENTAL LAW AND ACTION
ACTION	047 – 4	THROUGH OUR THOUGHT AND ACTION
ACTION	056 – 4	GUARDED INTO RIGHT ACTION
ACTION	056 – 4	CONTINUOUS RIGHT ACTION
ACTION	058 – 3	TREATMENT FOR RIGHT ACTION
ACTION	068 – 4	ACTION UPON ITSELF
ACTION	078 – 1	LAW OF MENTAL ACTION
ACTION	080 – 1	LAW AND ACTION
ACTION	082 – 3	SPIRIT'S ONE MODE OF ACTION
ACTION	083 – 2	THOUGHT, POWER AND ACTION OF SPIRIT
ACTION	084 – 3	ACTION OF SPIRIT AS LAW
ACTION	087 – 5	ACTION OF THIS CONSCIOUSNESS BEING IDEA
ACTION	092 – 3	ALL LAW IS MIND IN ACTION
ACTION	095 – 1	MEDIUM FOR PHYSICAL ACTION
ACTION	095 – 1	THE MEDIUM FOR MENTAL ACTION
ACTION	126 – 2	CONSTANT ACTION ON THE SUBJECTIVE SIDE
ACTION	130 – 6	CAUSING A CORRESPONDING ACTION
ACTION	167 – 4	A SENSE OF RIGHT ACTION
ACTION	176 – 1	FOR EVERY ACTION THERE IS ALWAYS
ACTION	188 – 3	ACTION TAKES PLACE IN INFINITE
ACTION	222 – 4	LOOSES ENERGY INTO ACTION
ACTION	231 – 5	NO INACTION NO LIMITED ACTION
ACTION	232 – 1	FREE ACTION OF THE LIFE FORCES
ACTION	240 – 2	ACTION OF THE HEART IS
ACTION	240 – 2	HEART IS REFLEX ACTION
ACTION	242 – 1	THERE IS REAL LIFE AND ACTION
ACTION	242 – 1	QUICKENING IT INTO LIFE AND ACTION
ACTION	242 – 1	LIFE OF THE BOUNDLESS ACTION
ACTION	242 – 2	LIFE OR ACTION APART FROM GOD
ACTION	247 – 3	AND NO INADEQUATE ACTION
ACTION	247 – 3	ACTION BEING SPIRITUAL
ACTION	251 – 4	EVERY RIGHT ACTION AT THE RIGHT TIME
ACTION	251 – 4	NO OBSTRUCTION TO RIGHT ACTION
ACTION	252 – 1	CARE OF PERFECTION IN ACTION
ACTION	255 – 1	NOR IS THERE ANY WRONG ACTION

ACTION	255 - 1	ITS ACTION IS COMPLETE HARMONIOUS
ACTION	256 - 5	BROUGHT INTO PERFECT ACTION
ACTION	263 - 4	I AM SURROUNDED BY RIGHT ACTION
ACTION	274 - 4	RIGHT ACTION ALREADY IS
ACTION	289 - 4	ULTIMATE RIGHT ACTION IS NOW TODAY
ACTION	322 - 2	THROUGH RIGHT MENTAL ACTION
ACTION	390 - 3	LAW OF MIND IN ACTION
ACTION	409 - 3	ACTION OF SPIRIT UPON THE MIND
ACTION	415 - 3	INDEPENDENT OF ANY INDIVIDUAL ACTION
ACTION	433 - 3	ACTION PRODUCES AN EFFECT IN HIS LIFE
ACTION	466 - 3	RECIPROCAL ACTION BETWEEN THE UNIVERSAL
ACTION	477 - 2	SWING FROM INSPIRATION TO ACTION
ACTIONS	043 - 1	ONLY OF SPONTANEOUS ACTIONS
ACTIONS	244 - 5	ACTIONS OF LIFE ARE HARMONIOUS
ACTIVE	047 - 3	PRODUCE AN ACTIVE DEMONSTRATION
ACTIVE	067 - 2	CONSCIOUS, AWARE, AND ACTIVE
ACTIVE	073 - 3	MEMORY WAS AN ACTIVE THING
ACTIVE	073 - 6	MEMORY IS ACTIVE
ACTIVE	081 - 4	SPIRIT IS THE ACTIVE
ACTIVE	083 - 4	THE ONLY ACTIVE PRINCIPLE IS SPIRIT
ACTIVE	118 - 3	ACTIVE CONDITION FOR GOOD OR EVIL
ACTIVE	143 - 1	ACTIVE RIGHT THINKING
ACTIVE	152 - 2	BE AN ACTIVE ACCEPTANCE
ACTIVE	165 - 1	AS ACTIVE CONSCIOUSNESS
ACTIVE	216 - 2	EVER-PRESENT AND ACTIVE
ACTIVE	219 - 4	SPIRIT IS AN ACTIVE PRESENCE
ACTIVE	240 - 4	INACTIVE NOR IS IT TOO ACTIVE
ACTIVE	255 - 1	SPIRIT IS NOW ACTIVE THROUGH ME
ACTIVE	278 - 1	WE NEED NOT BE ACTIVE
ACTIVE PRINCIPLE	306 - 4	THE ACTIVE PRINCIPLE OF OUR LIVES
ACTIVITIES	096 - 1	ACTIVITIES OF CONSCIOUSNESS
ACTIVITY	059 - 3	ACTIVITY OF THE TRUTH
ACTIVITY	059 - 4	HAPPINESS, ACTIVITY, AND POWER
ACTIVITY	100 - 2	ETERNAL ACTIVITY OF SPIRIT WITHIN ITSELF
ACTIVITY	216 - 1	ACTIVITY OF TRUTH
ACTIVITY	233 - 4	RESPOND TO ITS HEALING ACTIVITY
ACTIVITY	235 - 4	ACTIVITY OF PERFECT PRINCIPLE
ACTIVITY	240 - 1	ACTIVITY WITHIN US
ACTIVITY	256 - 5	PERFECTLY TO ITS HEALING ACTIVITY
ACTIVITY	291 - 3	BUSINESS IS BAD THERE IS NO ACTIVITY
ACTIVITY	291 - 4	ACTIVITY WHICH IS PERFECT
ACTIVITY	295 - 1	BY THE ACTIVITY OF OUR THOUGHT
ACTIVITY	300 - 5	IF WE WERE TREATING FOR ACTIVITY
ACTIVITY	307 - 2	THINK SEE AND FEEL ACTIVITY
ACTIVITY	358 - 1	ACTIVITY OF THIS ONE
ACTIVITY	384 - 2	SHALL WE ENGAGE IN ACTIVITY
ACTIVITY	384 - 4	A HEREAFTER WITHOUT ACTIVITY
ACTOR	057 - 4	IT IS THE INVISIBLE ACTOR
ACTOR	129 - 2	SPIRIT AS THE GREAT ACTOR
ACTOR	169 - 5	A LAW WHICH IS THE ACTOR
ACTOR	188 - 3	MIND IS THE ACTOR
ACTOR	198 - 2	ACTOR IN THE UNIVERSE
ACTOR	208 - 3	FOR IT IS THE ACTOR
ACTOR	210 - 2	WITH LAW IT IS THE ACTOR
ACTOR	279 - 1	MIND IS THE ONLY ACTOR

ACTOR	296 - 1	ARRIVES AT THE POINT OF THE TRUE ACTOR
ACTOR	296 - 1	THE ACT AND THE ACTOR ARE ONE
ACTORS	349 - 3	WORLD'S ORATORS ACTORS AND WRITERS
ACTS	124 - 3	IT ACTS ACCURATELY
ACTS	199 - 2	THOUGHT AND ACTS UPON IT
ACTS	216 - 1	IT ONLY ACTS
ACTS	234 - 4	OUR THOUGHT AND ACTS UPON IT
ACTS	263 - 1	ACTS IS TO PROVE
ACTS	436 - 2	HIS ACTS WILL FALL INTO ERROR
ACTUAL	163 - 3	ACTUAL MANIFESTATION THE HEALTH
ACTUAL	332 - 3	ACTUAL BROTHERHOOD OF MAN
ACTUAL	436 - 2	BY ITS WORTH IN ACTUAL LIVING
ACTUALITY	085 - 3	ASSUME THE ACTUALITY
ACTUALITY	203 - 2	ACTUALITY OF ITS EXPERIENCE
ACTUALITY	490 - 8	MOLD IT INTO A PRESENT ACTUALITY
ACTUALLY	051 - 2	ANYONE ACTUALLY DEMONSTRATES
ACTUALLY	121 - 3	HE ACTUALLY IS A SPIRIT
ACTUALLY	387 - 2	THEY ACTUALLY DO BELIEVE
ADAM	310 - 4	ADAM AND THE GARDEN OF EDEN
ADAM	310 - 4	AS IN ADAM ALL DIE
ADAM	410 - 3	ADAM WAS PERMITTED TO NAME
ADAM	473 - 3	ADAM MEANS MAN IN GENERAL
ADAM	473 - 5	FROM A RIB OF ADAM
ADAM AND EVE	473 - 2	ADAM AND EVE OUT OF THE GARDEN
ADAM AND EVE	473 - 6	ADAM AND EVE ARE POTENTIAL IN
ADEQUATE	268 - 3	AN ADEQUATE SUBJECTIVE IMAGE
ADD	309 - 5	ADD TO THIS THAT INTELLIGENCE
ADDED	116 - 3	NOTHING CAN BE ADDED TO
ADDED	427 - 4	ADDED THE SPIRITUAL STRENGTH OF DIVINE
ADDED	490 - 1	ALL ELSE WILL BE ADDED
ADDING	410 - 2	ADDING THE SPIRIT TO THE LETTER
ADDRESSED	153 - 1	ADDRESSED TO THIS PRESENCE IN US
ADHESION	094 - 2	ADHESION AND COHESION
ADJUST	248 - 4	ADJUST HIMSELF TO THE UNDESIRABLE
ADJUSTED	254 - 2	ADJUSTED TO THEIR NATURAL
ADJUSTMENTS	316 - 3	WRONG ADJUSTMENTS TO LIFE
ADMISSION	400 - 1	ADMISSION THAT THOUGHT IS POWER
ADMIT	175 - 2	WE SHOULD NEVER ADMIT
ADMIT	213 - 3	WE ADMIT THE FACT
ADMIT	382 - 1	EVER ADMIT ANY MENTAL IMPRESSIONS
ADMIT	501 - 3	ADMIT THE LIGHT IT COMES IN
ADMITTING	173 - 3	ADMITTING THEM AS A CONDITION
ADMITTING	192 - 4	ALSO ADMITTING
ADMONITION	238 - 4	THAN HIS ADMONITION
ADOPTED	484 - 5	ADOPTED BY THE SUPREME SPIRIT
ADORATION	405 - 4	TO THE OBJECT OF ITS ADORATION
ADORED	080 - 1	WHOM WE HAVE ADORED
ADVANCE	052 - 3	RESPONDS TO OUR ADVANCE
ADVANCE	271 - 4	ADVANCE ONLY BY GOING FROM HERE
ADVANCE	402 - 4	EVERY ADVANCE IN ANY SCIENCE
ADVANCE	407 - 2	ALL ADVANCE IN SCIENCE
ADVANCE	498 - 2	ALL ADVANCE MUST COME
ADVANCEMENT	385 - 1	ADVANCEMENT OF THE SOUL
ADVANCEMENT	412 - 3	IN OPPOSITION TO THE ADVANCEMENT
ADVENT	415 - 2	MAKE ITS ADVENT THROUGH

ADVENTURE	271 - 4	GREAT ADVENTURE TO MAKE CONSCIOUS USE
ADVENTURE	404 - 4	THE GREATEST ADVENTURE OF THE MIND
ADVERSARIES	430 - 4	AGREE WITR OUR ADVERSARIES QUICKLY
ADVERSE	194 - 2	ADVERSE SUGGESTION AND BRING UPON
ADVERSE	232 - 3	EVERY ADVERSE THOUGHT IS CRUEL
ADVERSITY	147 - 2	ADVERSITY MELT BEFORE THE SHINING RADIANCE
ADVERSITY	488 - 6	ADVERSITY BUT THINK PLENTY
ADVISABILITY	315 - 1	ADVISABILITY OF USING POSSESSIONS
AFAR	366 - 2	NOT LOOK AFAR TO SEE THE CHRIST
AFFAIRS	054 - 3	THROUGH HIM AND INTO ALL HIS AFFAIRS
AFFAIRS	055 - 2	INTO THE BEING OF HIS AFFAIRS
AFFAIRS	056 - 4	AFFAIRS ARE DIVINELY GUIDED
AFFAIRS	074 - 1	RE-MOLD HIS AFFAIRS
AFFAIRS	119 - 3	TAKE PLACE IN THE WORLD OF AFFAIRS
AFFAIRS	120 - 1	PRODUCED IN OUR EXTERNAL AFFAIRS
AFFAIRS	130 - 7	AFFAIRS ARE PRIMARILY A THING OF THOUGHT
AFFMRS	140 - 4	LARGER WORLD OF OUR AFFAIRS
AFFAIRS	183 - 3	THE BODY OF ONE'S AFFAIRS
AFFAIRS	217 - 2	BODY, MIND OR AFFAIRS
AFFAIRS	257 - 1	LET GO OF THE AFFAIRS OF THE DAY
AFFAIRS	305 - 1	MY AFFAIRS ARE IN ITS HANDS
AFFAIRS	394 - 3	BODY AND AFFAIRS ARE FLUENT
AFFAIRS	399 - 2	CONTROL OF AFFAIRS IS FROM WITHIN OUT
AFFAIRS	490 - 6	AFFAIRS OF EVERYDAY LIFE
AFFECTION	298 - 2	FULL OF LOVE AND AFFECTION
AFFECTIONS	225 - 3	CENTERED AROUND THE AFFECTIONS
AFFINITY	414 - 2	A LAW AS IS CHEMICAL AFFINITY
AFFIRM	102 - 3	WE AFFIRM ITS CAUSE
AFFIRM	147 - 2	AFFIRM THE DIVINE PRESENCE WITHIN US
AFFIRM	161 - 5	AFFIRM THE DIVINITY OF ALL PEOPLE
AFFIRM	217 - 1	AFFIRM THE PRESENCE OF GOD
AFFIRM	244 - 4	AFFIRM THAT THOUGHT MAY HELP
AFFIRM	260 - 4	AFFIRM FREEDOM NOT BONDAGE
AFFIRM	298 - 2	AFFIRM THIS WHEREVER YOU GO
AFFIRM	303 - 3	AFFIRM THIS UNTIL IT IS A VERY PART
AFFIRMATION	033 - 1	BY CONFLICT BY AFFIRMATION AND DENIAL
AFFIRMATION	157 - 4	BY ITS OWN AFFIRMATION
AFFIRMATION	220 - 4	AFFIRMATION DWELLING ON ITS MEANING
AFFIRMATION	275 - 2	OF GREATER AFFIRMATION
AFFIRMATION	277 - 2	A POSITIVE AFFIRMATION
AFFIRMATION	283 - 4	CONTRADICTS OUR OBJECTIVE AFFIRMATION
AFFIRMATION	304 - 1	MAKING SUCH AN AFFIRMATION
AFFIRMATION	372 - 4	BOLD AFFIRMATION OF ITS REALITY
AFFIRMATIONS	055 - 3	REVERSE HIS PREVIOUS AFFIRMATIONS
AFFIRMATIONS	159 - 2	AFFIRMATIONS AND DENIALS
AFFIRMATIONS	173 - 4	SERIES OF AFFIRMATIONS AND DENIALS
AFFIRMATIONS	401 - 3	AFFIRMATIONS OF LIFE AND HEALTH
AFFIRMATIONS	499 - 6	THOSE WHO SHOUT AFFIRMATIONS
AFFIRMATIVE	053 - 4	TOWARD AN AFFIRMATIVE ATTITUDE OF MIND
AFFIRMATIVE	155 - 2	OUR PRAYER IS AFFIRMATIVE
AFFIRMATIVE	156 - 2	AFFIRMATIVE MENTAL APPROACH TO REALITY
AFFIRMATIVE	160 - 3	AFFIRMATIVE SIDE OF THE UNIVERSE
AFFIRMATIVE	217 - 2	AN AFFIRMATIVE ATTITUDE OF MIND
AFFIRMATIVE	235 - 4	AFFIRMATIVE OUTLOOK OF FAITH
AFFIRMATIVE	284 - 2	IT SPEAKS AN AFFIRMATIVE LANGUAGE

AFFIRMATIVE	304 - 5	ON THE AFFIRMATIVE
AFFIRMATIVE	437 - 3	FAITH ANSWERED BY AN AFFIRMATIVE
AFFIRMATIVE	455 - 4	FROM A MORE AFFIRMATIVE ANGLE
AFFIRMATIVE	493 - 5	FAITH IS AN AFFIRMATIVE MENTAL ATTITUDE
AFFIRMATIVE	497 - 1	ON THE AFFIRMATIVE SIDE OF LIFE
AFFIRMATIVELY	110 - 1	USE THE LAW AFFIRMATIVELY
AFFIRMATIVELY	188 - 4	ANSWER THESE QUESTIONS AFFIRMATIVELY
AFFIRMATIVELY	322 - 3	HAVE IT WORK AFFIRMATIVELY FOR HIM
AFFIRMED	168 - 1	AFFIRMED AS A PART OF HIS EVERYDAY
AFFIRMING	034 - 1	AFFIRMING OF IT WILL NEVER MAKE IT
AFFIRMS	284 - 4	FAITH AFFIRMS THIS AND DENIES
AFFIRMS	492 - 3	EFFECT LOUDLY AFFIRMS
AFFLUENT	287 - 4	SUDDENLY BECOME AFFLUENT
AFFLUENTLY	287 - 4	THINKS AFFLUENTLY HE DOES BEGIN
AFFORD	185 - 2	CANNOT AFFORD TO BELIEVE IN
AFFORD	299 - 1	WE CANNOT AFFORD TO FIND FAULT
AFFORD	431 - 4	AFFORD TO HOLD PERSONAL ANIMOSITIES
AFFRONT	175 - 4	AFFRONT THE INTELLIGENCE OF ANY SANE
AFRAID	161 - 2	NOT AFRAID TO BELIEVE THEIR PRAYERS
AFRAID	168 - 5	GOD IS NEVER AFRAID
AFRAID	173 - 3	DO NOT BE AFRAID OF THIS
AFRAID	383 - 3	AFRAID OF GOD
AFRAID	479 - 1	HE WAS NOT AFRAID
AFRICA	278 - 4	PERSON WAS IN THE CENTER OF AFRICA
AGAINST	146 - 2	WHO CAN BE AGAINST US
AGAINST	329 - 6	AGAINST WHICH LESSER LAWS MEANT
AGAINST	433 - 4	OPERATE AGAINST THE ONE WHO SETS IT IN
AGAINST	470 - 3	UNIVERSE HOLDS NOTHING AGAINST US
AGAINST	486 - 2	WHO CAN BE AGAINST
AGAINST	486 - 2	NO POWER PRESENCE OR LAW AGAINST
AGAINST	494 - 6	AGAINST SUCH THERE IS NO LAW
AGE	032 - 2	THINKERS OF EVERY AGE
AGE	059 - 2	NO RECOGNITION OF AGE
AGE	158 - 4	UNCONFINED TO AGE OR STATION
AGE	180 - 4	AGE IS AN ILLUSION
AGE	239 - 3	THOUGHT OF AGE
AGE	272 - 4	RUN THROUGH EVERY AGE AND RACE
AGE	342 - 1	NO MATTER IN WHAT AGE
AGE	363 - 4	APPEAR IN ONLY ONE AGE
AGELESS	239 - 3	AGELESS SPIRIT
AGELESS	250 - 5	GOD IS AGELESS DEATHLESS
AGE-LONG	111 - 3	AGE-LONG DISCUSSION OF THE PROBLEM
AGENCIES	063 - 2	AGENCIES DID IT WORK
AGENCIES	379 - 1	ARGUMENT AGAINST SPIRIT AGENCIES
AGENCIES	473 - 3	ITS AGENCIES AT HIS COMMAND
AGENCY	377 - 3	AGENCY USED IS EITHER A MENTAL BODY
AGENCY	378 - 2	AGENCY OF THE PHYSICAL EYE
AGENCY	392 - 4	ONLY CREATIVE AGENCY
AGENT	138 - 1	LEGITIMATE AND USEFUL HEALING AGENT
AGENT	433 - 3	A FREE AGENT IN THIS LAW
AGES	027 - 2	THOUGHT OF ALL AGES
AGES	069 - 2	THE MYSTICAL SECRET OF THE AGES
AGES	155 - 3	A POWER THROUGHOUT THE AGES
AGES	190 - 1	PEOPLE THROUGHOUT THE AGES
AGES	359 - 2	ALL PEOPLE IN ALL AGES

AGES	396 - 2	FOR COUNTLESS AGES
AGES	460 - 3	LOVED THROUGHOUT THE AGES
AGGREGATION	373 - 4	MATTER IS AN AGGREGATION
AGGRESSIVE	277 - 2	AGGRESSIVE MENTAL MOVEMENT
AGGRESSIVE	279 - 1	POSITIVE AGGRESSIVE MENTAL ATTITUDE
AGITATION	247 - 1	IRRITATION, AGITATION NOR INFLAMMATION
AGITATION	248 - 2	NO INNER AGITATION
AGITATION	249 - 1	INNER AGITATION IS NOW WIPED
AGONIZING	109 - 3	AGONIZING DEITY ALL OF WHICH SEEM UNTRUE
AGREE	430 - 4	AGREE WITH OUR ADVERSARIES
AGREEMENT	395 - 2	NOT BY FORCE BUT BY AGREEMENT
AGREEMENT	458 - 5	UNDISPUTED PLACE OF AGREEMENT
AID	130 - 7	AID IN THE CONTROL OF THEIR AFFAIRS
AID	256 - 3	AID TO ASSIMILATION
AIM	337 - 3	THE AIM OF EVOLUTION IS TO PRODUCE A MAN
AIM	338 - 2	THE AIM OF EVOLUTION IS TO PRODUCE A MAN
AIM	417 - 3	THE WHOLE AIM OF EVOLUTION
AIR	025 - 3	AIR IS VIBRANT WITH POWER
AIR	072 - 4	CONQUERED THE AIR
AIRPLANE	340 - 3	ON TO THE AUTOMOBILE AND THE AIRPLANE
ALIENS	158 - 2	FLIGHT ARMIES OF ALIENS
ALIGNMENT	152 - 2	PUT OURSELVES IN ALIGNMENT WITH IT
ALIKE	200 - 3	CAN BE TREATED ENTIRELY ALIKE
ALIKE	368 - 1	SPIRIT COMES TO ALL ALIKE
ALIVE	067 - 2	THE SPIRIT IS ALIVE
ALIVE	407 - 4	THE UNIVERSE IS ALIVE
ALL	032 - 2	ALL MEN SEEK SOME RELATIONSHIP
ALL	041 - 2	IT GIVES ALIKE TO ALL
ALL	050 - 2	ALL OF IT
ALL	081 - 5	IT IS ABSOLUTE AND ALL
ALL	094 - 1	ALL THOUGHT IS CREATIVE
ALL	100 - 2	CANNOT CHANGE BEING ALL
ALL	104 - 2	COMES ALIKE TO ALL
ALL	113 - 2	ALL ARE SPIRITUAL FACULTIES
ALL	128 - 2	ALL ARE EFFECTS
ALL	146 - 1	ALL WORDS HAVE POWER
ALL	153 - 2	AND SPIRIT BEING ALL
ALL	172 - S	GOD IS ALL THERE IS
ALL	188 - 3	ALL THERE REALLY IS IS GOD
ALL	203 - 2	WE CO-OPERATE WITH ALL
ALL	203 - 5	GOD IS ALL THERE IS
ALL	204 - 2	GOD IS ALL
ALL	253 - 4	FOR GOD IS ALL IN ALL OVER ALL
ALL	258 - 5	COMPLETE UNITY WITH ALL
ALL	259 - 1	I LOVE ALL
ALL	263 - 1	PROVE THAT GOD IS ALL
ALL	264 - 2	ALL THAT THE FATHER HATH
ALL	265 - 1	IN ALL, OVER ALL AND THROUGH ALL
ALL	284 - 2	IN ALL AND THROUGH ALL
ALL	286 - 1	MATTER OF IT IS ALL SPIRIT
ALL	292 - 2	GOD IS ALL THERE IS
ALL	367 - 1	ALL ARE DIVINE AT THE CENTER
ALL	383 - 3	ALL WILL BE RIGHT WITH OUR SOULS
ALL	397 - 2	LIKE ALL OTHER LAWS OF NATURE
ALL	398 - 5	GOD IS ALL IN ALL

ALL	405 - 1	GOD IS ALL THERE IS
ALL	406 - 1	ALL OF SPIRIT IS WHEREVER
ALL	407 - 4	SPIRIT THEN IS ALL THERE IS
ALL	407 - 5	ITSELF SINCE IT IS ALL
ALL	413 - 5	GOD IS ALL IN ALL
ALL	434 - 1	ALL ARE ON THE ROAD
ALL	451 - 3	SPIRITUAL CONVICTIONS COME ALL ELSE
ALL	468 - 7	ALL THAT I HAVE IS THINE
ALL	469 - 3	ALL IS LOVE AND YET ALL IS LAW
ALL	486 - 1	ALL SHALL BE SONS OF GOD
ALL	501 - 2	ALL IS LOVE BUT ALL IS LAW
ALLAYING	251 - 1	EFFECTIVE IN ALLAYING FEVER
ALL-BEING	062 - 2	ALL-BEING MOVED
ALLEGED	379 - 2	ALLEGED COMMUNICATIONS ARE REAL
ALLEGORICALLY	461 - 2	ALLEGORICALLY DENOTE THE TWO STATES
ALLEGORY	064 - 3	FORM OF AN ALLEGORY
ALLEGORY	410 - 3	THE ALLEGORY OF EDEN
ALL ELSE	133 - 2	ALL ELSE ACTS AS AUTOMATIC LAW
ALL-EMBRACING	415 - 3	AS ONE ALL-EMBRACING MIND
ALL GOOD	039 - 1	GOOD IS NOW MINE ALL GOOD
ALL GOOD	263 - 6	ALL GOOD IS NOW MINE
ALLIANCE	252 - 3	ALLIANCE WITH LIFE
ALLIANCE	463 - 4	NO TRUE ALLIANCE APART FROM LIFE
ALL-IMPORTANT	186 - 1	ALL-IMPORTANT POINT IN TREATING
ALL IN ALL	103 - 2	GOD IS ALL IN ALL
ALL-INCLUSIVE	067 - 2	PURE SPIRIT ALL-INCLUSIVE
ALL-INCLUSIVE	408 - 2	MIND IS ALL-INCLUSIVE AND ALL-PERVADING
ALL IS GOOD	158 - 5	SEE THAT ALL IS GOOD
ALL-KNOWING	066 - 2	IS OMNISCIENT ALL-KNOWING
ALL MEN	162 - 1	ALL MEN ARE THE SONS OF GOD
ALLNESS	398 - 5	MORE COMPLETE ALLNESS
ALLOW	046 - 4	CONSCIOUSLY ALLOW IT TO DO SO
ALLOW	109 - 2	ALLOW HIM TO AWAKEN
ALLOW	159 - 1	ALLOW NOTHING TO ENTER
ALLOW	399 - 4	THINK CLEARLY AND ALLOW THE IMAGE
ALLOW	418 - 1	NOT ALLOW OURSELVES TO THINK
ALLOW	489 - 3	ALLOW REALITY TO MANIFEST
ALLOWED	110 - 1	EXPERIENCE WHICH WE ARE ALLOWED
ALLOWS	125 - 3	HE ALLOWS TO ENTER HIS INNER
ALLOWS	166 - 2	ALLOWS THE FLOW OF LIFE THROUGH
ALL-PERVADING	408 - 2	MIND IS ALL-INCLUSIVE AND ALL-PERVADING
ALL POWER	410 - 2	PRESENCE OF THE ALL POWER
ALL-SEEING EYE	459 - 6	REPRESENTS THE ALL-SEEING EYE
ALL THINGS	162 - 5	DIVINE LAW ALL THINGS ARE POSSIBLE
ALMIGHTY	056 - 4	THE LIVING SPIRIT ALMIGHTY
ALMIGHTY	160 - 1	THE ALMIGHTY HAS SPOKEN
ALMIGHTY	216 - 1	WHICH IS ALMIGHTY WHICH IS GOD
ALMIGHTY	358 - 4	ALMIGHTY GOD WITHIN ME
ALMIGHTY	492 - 7	ENDLESS CREATION OF THE ALMIGHTY
ALMS	430 - 6	ALMS BEFORE MEN TO BE SEEN
ALONE	108 - 1	ALONE TO MAKE THE GREAT DISCOVERY
ALONE	238 - 1	UNTIL HE CAN STAND ALONE
ALONE	273 - 4	ALONE TO THE ALONE
ALONE	369 - 1	WALKS LIFE'S ROAD ALONE
ALONE	391 - 4	IT BELONGS TO MAN ALONE

ALONE	391 - 4	MAN ALONE IS ABLE TO CONSCIOUSLY
ALONE	400 - 4	OBJECTIVE MIND ALONE MAY
ALONE	409 - 1	CONSCIOUS OF PERFECTION ALONE
ALONE	414 - 2	IS DONE IN MIND ALONE
ALONE	422 - 3	JESUS STANDS ALONE AS A MAN
ALONE	478 - 2	WHICH ALONE CAN MAKE FREE
ALPHA AND OMEGA	144 - 2	ALPHA AND OMEGA AND ALL THAT COMES
ALPHA AND OMEGA	289 - 2	'I AM ALPHA AND OMEGA'
ALREADY	046 - 2	WE ALREADY DO KNOW
ALREADY	117 - 2	WHICH IS ALREADY GIVEN
ALREADY	187 - 2	ALREADY BEING AN ACCOMPLISHED FACT
ALREADY	187 - 2	ALREADY EMBODIED IN THE ABSOLUTE
ALREADY	203 - I	ALREADY AN ACCOMPLISHED FACT
ALREADY	250 - 3	SPIRIT IS ALREADY IN HIS PATIENT
ALREADY	355 - 2	SEES THE THING AS ALREADY DONE
ALREADY	399 - 3	IT HAS ALREADY HAPPENED
ALREADY	409 - 4	AS ALREADY DIVINE AND PERFECT
ALREADY	472 - 3	HEAVEN UNLESS HE IS ALREADY THERE
ALREADY	472 - 4	IS ALREADY IN HEAVEN
ALREADY	489 - 1	ARE DOING AS BEING ALREADY DONE
ALREADY	498 - 3	WHAT WE BELIEVE WE ALREADY HAVE
ALREADY	498 - 3	BELIEVE WE ALREADY HAVE THE ANSWER
ALTAR	285 - 4	BRING THY GIFT TO THE ALTAR
ALTAR	335 - 4	BURDENS ON THE ALTAR OF LOVE
ALTAR OF FAITH	430 - 3	ALTAR OF FAITH IS APPROACHED
ALTAR OF FAITH	501 - 4	OFFER THEM ON THE ALTAR OF FAITH
ALTER	108 - 4	DOES NOT ALTER THE FACT THAT
ALTER	202 - 3	DOES NOT ALTER THE FACT
ALTER	429 - 2	CANNOT ALTER NOR EXPERIENCE DESTROY
ALTERING	401 - 2	ALTERING OUR THOUGHT RELATIONSHIP
ALTERNATIVE	118 - 3	IT HAS NO ALTERNATIVE
ALTERNATIVE	131 - 3	NO ALTERNATIVE OTHER THAN TO OBEY
ALTITUDES	243 - 2	HIGHER ALTITUDES OF CONSCIOUSNESS
ALTRUISTIC	440 - 4	FIND SOME ALTRUISTIC PURPOSE
ALWAYS	169 - 2	ALWAYS IN HIS OWN THOUGHT
ALWAYS	206 - 2	ALWAYS THINKING INTO MIND
ALWAYS	213 - 3	FIND THAT IT WAS ALWAYS THERE
ALWAYS	224 - 4	ALWAYS COME TO A COMPLETE CONCLUSION
ALWAYS	322 - 3	IT IS ALWAYS WORKING
ALWAYS	338 - 4	ALWAYS THE IDEA OF PERFECTED
ALWAYS	342 - 1	THE OTHER IS ALWAYS TRUE
ALWAYS	406 - 2	ALWAYS RESPONDING TO OUR THOUGHT
AMERICA	272 - 3	IN AMERICA WHERE PEOPLE ARE CHRISTIANS
AMISS	150 - 5	NO LONGER ASK AMISS
AMISS	481 - 4	WE CANNOT ASK AMISS
AMPLE	385 - 3	GIVEN US AMPLE EVIDENCE
ANAEMIC	247 - 3	SPIRIT IS NEVER ANAEMIC
ANALYSIS	091 - 3	FINAL ANALYSIS OF MATTER
ANALYSIS	096 - 2	IT IS A PROCESS OF ANALYSIS
ANALYSIS	096 - 3	INDUCTIVE REASONING IS AN ANALYSIS
ANALYSIS	199 - 4	DOWN TO ITS LAST ANALYSIS
ANALYSIS	204 - 1	ANALYSIS OF ULTIMATE REALITY
ANALYSIS	237 - 1	ANALYSIS OF THE SOUL
ANALYSIS	434 - 4	STUDY OF SOUL ANALYSIS
ANALYZE	027 - 6	PRAYER LET US ANALYZE THIS

ANALYZE	054 – 3	LET US ANALYZE THIS
ANALYZE	079 – 4	WHICH WE CAN SOMEWHAT ANALYZE
ANALYZE	086 – 2	CAN TAKE HOLD OF AND ANALYZE
ANALYZE	092 – 3	IT CANNOT ANALYZE DISSECT OR DENY
ANALYZE	096 – 3	BECAUSE IT COULD ANALYZE
ANALYZE	116 – 2	ANALYZE THE BODY AND FIND
ANALYZE	156 – 3	LET US ANALYZE THE FEARS
ANALYZE	193 – 4	THE WILL MUST FIRST ANALYZE
ANALYZE	283 – 3	WHEN YOU ANALYZE FAITH
ANALYZE	288 – 2	ONE SHOULD ANALYZE HIMSELF
ANALYZE	372 – 1	ANALYZE AND DISSECT EVERY ATOM
ANALYZED	372 – 3	REACTIONS CAN BE ANALYZED
ANALYZED	372 – 3	INCARNATED IN US CANNOT BE ANALYZED
ANATHEMAS	383 – 3	THE ANATHEMAS OF THEOLOGY
ANCESTORS	158 – 3	ANCESTORS BELIEVED THESE RECORDS
ANCESTORS	352 – 3	ANCESTORS WHILE THEY WERE ON EARTH
ANCIENT	295 – 4	ONE OF THE ANCIENT SAYINGS
ANCIENT OF DAYS	429 – 4	ANCIENT OF DAYS ONLOOKS ETERNITY
ANCIENTS	078 – 2	ANCIENTS TAUGHT THAT THERE IS
ANDROGYNOUS	449 – 5	GOD IS THE ANDROGYNOUS
ANEW	160 – 1	ANEW INTO CREATION
ANEW	482 – 2	GOD GOES FORTH ANEW
ANGEL	306 – 4	THE ANGEL OF GOD'S PRESENCE
ANGELS	391 – 4	LITTLE LOWER THAN THE ANGELS
ANGELS	491 – 4	BE ENTERTAINING ANGELS
ANGER	255 – 3	FILLED WITH THOUGHTS OF ANGER
ANGER	255 – 3	ANGER CAN BE TURNED INTO
ANGLE	100 – 1	PSYCHOLOGICAL OR METAPHYSICAL ANGLE
ANGLICAN	341 – 4	THINKER IN THE ANGLICAN CHURCH
ANGUISH	110 – 1	ANGUISH OF THE HUMAN RACE
ANIMAL	342 – 2	INTELLIGENCE IN AN ANIMAL
ANIMATE	164 – 3	TO ANIMATE IT WITH THE LIFE
ANIMATE	418 – 5	MAN SUPERINTENDETH THE ANIMATE
ANIMATED	179 – 1	ANIMATED BY DIVINE LIFE LOVE AND LAW
ANIMATED	231 – 2	ANIMATED BY THE LIGHT OF LOVE
ANIMATED	241 – 4	ANIMATED BY PERFECT SPIRIT
ANIMATED	477 – 4	PURPOSES ARE ANIMATED AND INSPIRED
ANIMATES	056 – 4	SPIRIT ANIMATES EVERYTHING
ANIMATES	112 – 4	SPIRIT WHICH ANIMATES US
ANIMATES	167 – 4	ANIMATES EVERYTHING
ANIMATES	243 – 3	BREATH OF GOD ANIMATES CREATION
ANIMATES	477 – 2	VITALIZES THE BODY AND ANIMATES
ANIMOSITY	430 – 3	ANIMOSITY TOWARD OTHERS
ANIMOSITY	431 – 3	ANIMOSITY AND VINDICTIVENESS
ANNIHILATION	344 – 1	DID NOT TEACH THE ANNIHILATION
ANNOUNCE	052 – 1	MORE THAN ANNOUNCE A PRINCIPLE
ANNOUNCE	159 – 5	TRUTH WHICH WE ANNOUNCE
ANNOUNCE	252 – 2	ANNOUNCE THAT THEY ARE
ANNOUNCE	399 – 3	WE DO NOT PRAY WE ANNOUNCE
ANNOUNCED	074 – 3	THEN A PRINCIPLE IS ANNOUNCED
ANNOUNCED	127 – 1	ANNOUNCED THE UNIVERSALITY OF THE LAW
ANNOUNCED	157 – 4	ANNOUNCED THE LAW OF MIND
ANNOUNCED	161 – 4	ANNOUNCED THE LAW OF LIBERTY
ANNOUNCEMENT	188 – 2	AN ANNOUNCEMENT OF REALITY
ANNOUNCEMENT	219 – 2	ANNOUNCEMENT FROM SCIENTISTS

ANNOUNCER	188 – 3	ACTOR AND YOU ARE THE ANNOUNCER
ANNOUNCES	074 – 3	PRINCIPLES WHICH SCIENCE ANNOUNCES
ANNOUNCES	103 – 3	ANNOUNCES THAT ALL ARE GODS
ANNOUNCES	372 – 4	LIFE ANNOUNCES ITSELF
ANNOUNCES	503 – 3	ANNOUNCES THE EVER PRESENT
ANNOYED	381 – 2	ANNOYED BY THEIR PSYCHIC POWERS
ANOTHER	184 – 3	JUST AS QUICKLY AS FOR ANOTHER
ANOTHER	281 – 1	ANOTHER HAS MOVED HIMSELF
ANOTHER	369 – 1	ANOTHER WHO WALKS WITH HIM
ANSWER	044 – 2	ANSWER TO ALL OUR PROBLEMS
ANSWER	053 – 2	THE RIGHT ANSWER TO HIS PROBLEM
ANSWER	126 – 1	ANSWER TO WHAT WE SHALL BE
ANSWER	148 – 4	CALL UPON ME I WILL ANSWER
ANSWER	149 – 3	WHO MIGHT ANSWER SOME PRAYERS
ANSWER	153 – 2	PRAYER THEN IS ITS OWN ANSWER
ANSWER	153 – 2	BEFORE THEY CALL WILL I ANSWER
ANSWER	153 – 4	PRAYER IS ITS OWN ANSWER
ANSWER	164 – 4	ANSWER TO ALL PROBLEMS WILL BE FOUND IN
ANSWER	172 – 4	ANSWER TO THIS HE STATES
ANSWER	174 – 2	BEFORE THEY CALL WILL I ANSWER
ANSWER	178 – 2	PRAYER IS ITS OWN ANSWER
ANSWER	178 – 2	ITS ANSWER ALREADY EXISTS
ANSWER	190 – 2	THE ANSWER TO PRAYER IS
ANSWER	224 – 4	GIVE THANKS FOR THE ANSWER
ANSWER	272 – 4	WHICH ANSWER EVERY PERSON
ANSWER	273 – 3	KNOWS THE RIGHT ANSWER
ANSWER	273 – 3	ANSWER TO THAT PROBLEM
ANSWER	274 – 4	DEGREE AS THE ANSWER AND THE RESULT
ANSWER	281 – 1	TO ANSWER ONE MAN AND NOT ANOTHER
ANSWER	289 – 4	ONLY THE COMPLETION THE ANSWER
ANSWER	289 – 4	'BEFORE THEY CALL I WILL ANSWER'
ANSWER	363 – 2	RECEIVING A DIRECT ANSWER FROM IT
ANSWER	365 – 2	ANSWER TO EVERY QUESTION IS WITHIN MAN
ANSWER	420 – 2	THE ANSWER TO EVERY PROBLEM
ANSWER	422 – 3	ANSWER TO EVERY QUESTION
ANSWER	436 – 1	ANSWER TO PRAYER IS IN
ANSWER	436 – 1	ANSWER WHEN WE PRAY ARIGHT
ANSWER	456 – 2	THE ANSWER IS SELF-EVIDENT
ANSWER	458 – 3	AN ANSWER TO OUR PRAYERS
ANSWER	458 – 4	ANSWER AS AN IMAGE IN MIND
ANSWER	464 – 4	ONE ANSWER TO ALL QUESTIONS
ANSWER	465 – 1	ANSWER FROM THAT GREAT WITHIN
ANSWER	498 – 3	WE ALREADY HAVE THE ANSWER
ANSWERED	150 – 3	IF GOD EVER ANSWERED PRAYER
ANSWERED	156 – 2	ONE MAN'S PRAYERS ARE ANSWERED
ANSWERED	158 – 1	PRAYER MUST BE ANSWERED
ANSWERED	174 – 2	IT IS PRAYER ANSWERED
ANSWERED	280 – 2	ANSWERED ACCORDING TO OUR BELIEF
ANSWERED	481 – 4	ANSWERED ACCORDING TO LAW
ANSWERING	151 – 1	THE ANSWERING OF PRAYER
ANSWERING	273 – 4	AND GOD ANSWERING
ANSWERS	128 – 4	IT ANSWERS EVERY QUESTION
ANSWERS	188 – 3	IT ANSWERS EVERY QUESTION
ANSWERS	273 – 2	ANSWERS ITS OWN DEMAND
ANSWERS	277 – 3	ANSWERS TO OUR PROBLEMS WILL BE FOUND

ANSWERS	287 – 3	PRAYER ANSWERS THE BIG AND THE LITTLE
ANTAGONISTIC	412 – 4	BECOME ANTAGONISTIC TOWARD US
ANTHROPOMORPHIC	383 – 1	ANTHROPOMORPHIC DUALISM
ANTICHRIST	120 – 3	ANTICHRIST MEANS THE SPIRIT OF
ANTICHRIST	127 – 3	ANTICHRIST IS THE DESTRUCTIVE USE OF
ANTICIPATE	262 – 1	ANTICIPATE SUCH PLEASURE
ANTICIPATION	101 – 2	RECOLLECTION, ATTENTION AND ANTICIPATION
ANTICIPATION	246 – 2	ANTICIPATION KNOWING IT WILL
ANTIQUITY	068 – 2	THINKERS OF ANTIQUITY
ANXIETY	058 – 5	WORK NOT WITH ANXIETY
ANXIETY	243 – 3	SENSE OF ANXIETY OR STRAIN
ANXIETY	247 – 2	ANXIETY ABOUT ANY OUTCOME
ANXIETY	253 – 3	KIDNEY TROUBLE ARE WORRY, ANXIETY, FEAR
ANXIETY	256 – 3	OF WORRY, DISTRUST AND ANXIETY
ANXIOUS	225 – 2	ANXIOUS TENSE THOUGHTS CAN PRODUCE
ANYONE	452 – 4	ANYONE WHO WILLS TO KNOW TRUTH
ANYTHING	267 – 5	CAN HAVE ANYTHING YOU LIKE
ANYTHING	280 – 1	DOES NOT DO ANYTHING TO GOD
ANYTHING	288 – 2	ANYTHING YOU CAN DREAM
ANYTHING	299 – 1	ANYTHING AGAINST ANY LIVING SOUL
ANYTHING	397 – 4	ANYTHING THAT WE MAY WISH IT
APART	124 – 1	NOT SOMETHING APART FROM MATTER
APART	240 – 3	APART FROM GOD GOOD
APART	293 – 4	I CANNOT BE APART FROM THAT
APARTNESS	082 – 1	NO APARTNESS, NO SEPARATION FROM ITSELF
APARTNESS	179 – 1	THERE IS NO APARTNESS
APARTNESS	462 – 4	APARTNESS FROM THE ETERNAL GOOD
APOSTLES	329 – 3	APOSTLES SAID, IN SUBSTANCE
APPARENT	054 – 3	APPARENT LIMITED CONDITION
APPARENT	059 – 3	REMOVES THE APPARENT OBSTRUCTION
APPARENT	071 – 1	NOTHING IS MORE APPARENT
APPARENT	160 – 2	APPARENT MANIFESTATION OF
APPARENT	392 – 1	LAW OF THE APPARENT PART
APPARENT	445 – 1	APPARENT SEPARATION BETWEEN GOD
APPEAL	067 – 3	MADE SUCH AN APPEAL
APPEAR	057 – 2	THINGS WHICH DO APPEAR
APPEAR	109 – 2	APPEAR ON THE SCENE OF EXPERIENCE
APPEAR	133 – 5	ALL CONDITIONS WHICH APPEAR
APPEAR	187 – 3	THAT APPEAR TO BE DESTRUCTIVE
APPEAR	338 – 3	WHEN HE SHALL APPEAR
APPEAR	403 – 4	APPEAR TO BE A THING OF ITSELF
APPEAR	450 – 1	WE APPEAR TO HAVE LITTLE ENOUGH
APPEARANCE	059 – 3	DISSOLVES THE NEGATIVE APPEARANCE
APPEARANCE	113 – 2	EXTERNAL PERCEPTION IS BY APPEARANCE
APPEARANCE	152 – 3	TO JUDGE ACCORDING TO APPEARANCE
APPEARANCE	162 – 5	NO MATTER WHAT THE OUTSIDE APPEARANCE
APPEARANCE	179 – 2	WHAT THE APPEARANCE MAY BE
APPEARANCE	187 – 3	JUDGE NOT ACCORDING TO APPEARANCE
APPEARANCE	189 – 2	MUST SEE BEYOND THE APPEARANCE
APPEARANCE	189 – 3	THAT THE OUTWARD APPEARANCE
APPEARANCE	204 – 4	APPEARANCE AND THE DISAPPEARANCE
APPEARANCE	213 – 2	APPEARANCE IS THE REALITY
APPEARANCE	213 – 3	TRANSCEND THE APPEARANCE
APPEARANCE	214 – 1	APPEARANCE PERFECTION
APPEARANCE	217 – 1	PERSISTS IN MAKING ITS APPEARANCE

APPEARANCE	222 - 1	BACK OF ALL APPEARANCE
APPEARANCE	228 - 2	AN APPEARANCE OF DISEASE
APPEARANCE	320 - 2	NO MATTER WHAT THE APPEARANCE
APPEARANCE	337 - 1	RECOGNIZE THE APPEARANCE OF EVIL
APPEARANCE	342 - 2	CONSCIOUS APPEARANCE IN MAN
APPEARANCES	113 - 2	APPEARANCES WOULD LIMIT THE FUTURE
APPEARANCES	152 - 3	BE INFLUENCED BY APPEARANCES
APPEARANCES	170 - 1	DISSOLVE ALL FALSE APPEARANCES
APPEARANCES	406 - 4	NOT ACCORDING TO APPEARANCES
APPEARANCES	417 - 2	NOT ACCORDING TO APPEARANCES
APPEARED	073 - 1	APPEARED TO BE AN AUTOMATIC THING
APPEARING	052 - 5	WORKS BY APPEARING TO NOT WORK
APPEARS	108 - 3	EXPRESSION APPEARS TO LIMIT HIM
APPEARS	159 - 5	WHAT APPEARS TO CONTRADICT THIS
APPEARS	169 - 6	APPEARS TO BE WRONG
APPEARS	267 - 4	MAN APPEARS TO BE FINITE
APPEARS	302 - 4	IF ONE APPEARS TO HAVE FAILED
APPEARS	313 - 3	IT APPEARS LIMITED AND UNHAPPY
APPEASE	476 - 5	APPEASE AN APPETITE FOR LEARNING
APPETITE	253 - 2	APPETITE AND THE ASSIMILATION
APPETITE	262 - 2	APPETITE FROM WHICH HE IS
APPETITE	428 - 5	UNSATISFIED AND APPETITE UNAPPEASED
APPLICATION	026 - 3	RATHER A PRACTICAL APPLICATION
APPLICATION	051 - 2	BEYOND ITS APPLICATION
APPLICATION	051 - 2	PRACTICAL APPLICATION IS NECESSARY
APPLICATION	053 - 5	GAINED BY THE APPLICATION
APPLICATION	316 - 1	NOTHING WEIRD ABOUT THE APPLICATION
APPLICATION	318 - 2	MAKE PRACTICAL APPLICATION OF IT
APPLICATION	336 - 3	FOR A PRACTICAL APPLICATION
APPLICATION	475 - 3	APPLICATION OF THE SCIENCE OF MIND
APPLIED	085 - 2	PHILOSOPHY OF APPLIED METAPHYSICS
APPLY	137 - 1	KNOW A PRINCIPLE ANOTHER TO APPLY IT
APPLYING	271 - 4	CONSTANTLY APPLYING OURSELVES
APPLYING	271 - 4	APPLYING IT IN OUR ACTIONS
APPRAISE	085 - 2	WE CANNOT APPRAISE THEM
APPRECIATION	049 - 2	PRAYER, HOPE AND APPRECIATION
APPRECIATION	176 - 1	APPRECIATION OF WHAT THE IMAGE MEANS
APPRECIATION	452 - 3	THOSE OF APPRECIATION AND THANKSGIVING
APPROACH	038 - 4	THE APPROACH SHOULD BE DIRECT
APPROACH	042 - 3	HIS PARTICULAR APPROACH
APPROACH	042 - 4	APPROACH THE THING SIMPLY
APPROACH	075 - I	APPROACH THE SCIENCE OF MIND
APPROACH	139 - 4	APPROACH THE SUBJECT OF SPIRITUAL MIND
APPROACH	149 - 3	APPROACH WITH DOUBT IN HIS THOUGHT
APPROACH	153 - 3	APPROACH TO SPIRIT IS DIRECT
APPROACH	156 - 2	APPROACH TO REALITY, RECEIVE RESULTS
APPROACH	159 - 4	PRINCIPLE WHICH WE APPROACH
APPROACH	173 - 4	APPROACH THIS PRESENCE SIMPLY, DIRECTLY
APPROACH	259 - 3	INDIVIDUAL APPROACH TO REALITY
APPROACH	272 - 4	INTEGRITY APPROACH THE LAW
APPROACH	272 - 4	BEFORE WE CAN MAKE A DIRECT APPROACH
APPROACH	281 - 2	A NEW APPROACH TO AN OLD TRUTH
APPROACH	308 - 1	APPROACH REALITY AS NORMALLY
APPROACH	412 - I	IN THE WAY WE APPROACH IT
APPROACH	456 - 4	APPROACH OUR PROBLEMS

APPROACH	479 - 5	APPROACH REALITY THROUGH
APPROACHED	436 - 3	APPROACHED BY THE PURE IN HEART
APPROACHING	254 - 4	A CERTAIN WAY OF APPROACHING
APPROPRIATE	229 - 2	WE APPROPRIATE SOMETHING OF GOD
ARBITRARILY	129 - 3	BRINGS HIM ARBITRARILY TO A PLACE
ARBITRARY	334 - 4	LAW AS AN ARBITRARY FORCE
ARBITRARY	342 - 4	ALL ARBITRARY CONTROL OF MAN
ARBITRARY	365 - 3	ARBITRARY GOD SENDING SOME TO HEAVEN
ARGUE	092 - 2	DOES NOT ARGUE BUT AT ONCE BEGINS TO
ARGUE	116 - 1	I DO NOT ARGUE
ARGUE	199 - 2	AND DOES NOT ARGUE
ARGUE	264 - 5	ARGUE WITH NONE
ARGUE	330 - 1	MYSTICS DID NOT CONTEND OR ARGUE
ARGUE	416 - 2	CANNOT ARGUE BACK OR DENY ANY USE
ARGUES	461 - 4	GOD NEVER ARGUES
ARGUING	049 - 6	WASTE MUCH TIME IN ARGUING
ARGUING	219 - 4	ARGUING IS OFTEN A WASTE OF TIME
ARGUING	246 - 3	NO TIME ARGUING WITH ANYONE
ARGUING	319 - 3	ARGUING THAT HE CANNOT GIVE
ARGUMENT	068 - 3	ARGUMENT HAS BEEN SOMETHING
ARGUMENT	170 - 4	ARGUMENT IS NEVER WITH ANOTHER PERSON
ARGUMENT	170 - 4	PRESENTING A LOGICAL ARGUMENT
ARGUMENT	172 - 4	ARGUMENT WHICH PRODUCES
ARGUMENT	201 - 4	BASIS OF OUR ARGUMENT
ARGUMENT	233 - 2	ARRAY MENTAL ARGUMENT AGAINST IT
ARGUMENT	473 - 6	ARGUMENT WE EXPERIENCE BOTH
ARGUMENTATIVE	170 - 3	ARGUMENTATIVE AND THE OTHER REALIZATION
ARGUMENTATIVE	170 - 4	ARGUMENTATIVE METHOD IS JUST WHAT THE
ARGUMENTATIVE	172 - 3	DIFFERENCE BETWEEN THE ARGUMENTATIVE
ARGUMENTATIVE	172 - 4	ARGUMENTATIVE METHOD OF TREATING
ARGUMENTATIVE	172 - 4	ARGUMENTATIVE STATEMENTS MERELY CONDUCT
ARGUMENTATIVE	173 - 4	ARGUMENTATIVE METHOD OF TREATMENT IS A
ARGUMENTATIVE	459 - 6	BUT NEVER ARGUMENTATIVE
ARGUMENTS	218 - 2	CONFORM OUR ARGUMENTS
ARGUMENTS	304 - 1	ARGUMENTS WILL RISE AGAINST IT
ARGUMENTS	304 - 1	MEET THOSE ARGUMENTS
ARGUMENTS	474 - 4	ARGUMENTS THAT GO ON IN OUR
ARIGHT	158 - 1	TOUCHES REALITY PRAYS ARIGHT
ARIGHT	281 - 2	ANSWERED WHEN WE PRAY ARIGHT
ARISE	076 - 5	ARISE FROM WITHOUT
ARISE	156 - 3	ALL ARISE FROM THE BELIEF
ARISE	465 - 3	ARISE AND GO TO MY FATHER
ARISTOTLE	137 - 1	WHAT WE EXPECT, SAID ARISTOTLE, THAT WE FIND
ARISTOTLE	342 - 1	JESUS, PLATO, SOCRATES, ARISTOTLE
ARMIES	104 - 2	TREAD OF ARMIES WILL CEASE
ARMOR	494 - 6	ARMOR OF GOD IS FAITH
ARMS	110 - 3	THE WORLD ARMS FOR
ARMS	234 - 2	THE ARMS AND HANDS
ARMS	495 - 1	UNDERNEATH ARE THE EVERLASTING ARMS
AROUND	093 - 4	AROUND US THERE IS A FIELD
AROUND	423 - 3	PERFECTION WITHIN AND AROUND ABOUT
ARRANGEMENT	117 - 1	A DIFFERENCE IN THE ARRANGEMENT
ARRANGEMENT	313 - 2	FROM ANOTHER BECAUSE OF ARRANGEMENT
ARRAY	233 - 2	ARRAY MENTAL ARGUMENT AGAINST IT
ARRIVE	121 - 3	ARRIVE AT A CONSCIOUSNESS OF THE UNITY

ARRIVE	124 - 2	ARRIVE AT A CONSCIOUSNESS
ARRIVE	314 - 2	ARRIVE AT HEAVEN INSTEAD OF HELL
ARRIVE	479 - 5	BE THERE WHEN WE ARRIVE
ARRIVED	120 - 3	ARRIVED AT AN INTELLECTUAL CONCEPT
ARROW	344 - I	AS AN ARROW IS LOST IN ITS MARK
ART	198 - 4	ART AND SCIENCE
ART	199 - 3	UNDERTAKEN IN THE CURATIVE ART
ART	269 - 3	AN ARTIST FOR HIS ART
ART	423 - 3	I AM THAT WHICH THOU ART
ARTERIES	239 - 3	HARDENING OF THE ARTERIES
ARTERIES	248 - 2	ARTERIES CONVEY THIS BLOOD STREAM
ARTERIES	249 - 2	ARTERIES SHOULD BE TREATED
ARTIST	045 - 1	ARTIST EMBODIES THE SPIRIT
ARTIST	047 - 3	ARTIST CAN PAINT A PICTURE
ARTIST	072 - 2	THE ARTIST FEELS BEAUTY
ARTISTS	428 - 2	ARTISTS TURNED FOR INSPIRATION
AS	037 - 1	AS SYMBOLIZE HEAVEN AND HELL
ASCEND	493 - 7	ASCEND INTO A GREATER EXPRESSION
ASCENDED	472 - 3	ASCENDED UP TO HEAVEN
ASCENDING	336 - 2	IN EVER ASCENDING CYCLES
ASCENDING	439 - 2	ASCENDING HIGHER AND HIGHER
ASCENDING	490 - 5	DIVINE SCALE IS EVER ASCENDING
ASCERTAIN	316 - 2	ASCERTAIN IF THE WORK HAS BEEN DONE
ASHAMED	497 - 3	WE ARE NOT TO BE ASHAMED
ASHES	369 - 3	CHRIST RISES FROM THE ASHES
ASK	092 - 1	AS MANY FOR US AS WE ASK
ASK	157 - 3	ASK AND IT SHALL BE GIVEN UNTO YOU
ASK	198 - 3	HE DOES NOT ASK
ASK	300 - 4	ASK FOR WHAT WE WISH AND TAKE IT
ASK	307 - 3	'ASK AND IT SHALL BE GIVEN UNTO YOU'
ASK	333 - 3	WE ASK OR HOPE FOR MORE
ASK	435 - 3	THAT FOR WHICH WE ASK
ASK	436 - 1	ASK DIRECTLY FOR WHAT WE
ASK	458 - 3	WE ARE TO ASK FOR
ASK	458 - 6	ASK FOR ONE BELONGING TO ANOTHER
ASK	498 - 5	ASK FOR THAT WHICH IS
ASK FOR	398 - 3	ASK FOR OR MENTALLY ACCEPT
ASKING	277 - 2	ASKING GOD TO DO ANYTHING
ASKS	175 - I	EVERYONE WHO ASKS RECEIVES
ASPECT	347 - 2	WE DO HAVE A DUAL ASPECT
ASPECTS	090 - 3	THEY ARE REALLY TWO PARTS OR ASPECTS
ASPIRING	060 - 3	LONGED FOR BY ALL ASPIRING SOULS
ASSERT	417 - 2	TO ASSERT OUR INDIVIDUALITY
ASSERTION	283 - 5	FAITH IS MENTAL ASSERTION ELEVATED
ASSIMILATED	226 - 2	ALL IDEAS ARE ASSIMILATED
ASSIMILATED	226 - 2	SPIRITUAL SIGNIFICANCE IS ASSIMILATED
ASSIMILATED	259 - 4	IS PERFECTLY ASSIMILATED
ASSIMILATION	232 - 4	ASSIMILATION, ELIMINATION AND CIRCULATION
ASSIMILATION	239 - 3	ASSIMILATION, ELIMINATION AND CIRCULATION
ASSIMILATION	256 - 3	A PERFECT AID TO ASSIMILATION
ASSISTANCE	299 - 4	WITHOUT ANY HELP OR ASSISTANCE
ASSUME	048 - 1	ASSUME NO PARTICULAR FORM
ASSUME	343 - 4	OUTSIDE HIMSELF IS TO ASSUME
ASSUMPTION	499 - 5	ASSUMPTION AND AS SUCH NEVER
ASSURANCE	137 - 1	BIBLE WE HAVE THE ASSURANCE

ASSURANCE	161 - 2	ARRIVE AT THIS SAME ASSURANCE
ASSURANCE	201 - 3	GROW INTO DEEPER ASSURANCE
ASSURANCE	219 - 1	SILENT ASSURANCE THAT MAN
ASSURANCE	260 - 3	FULL ASSURANCE THAT HE IS DEALING
ASSURANCE	272 - 1	ASSURANCE THAT ON THE INNER SIDE
ASSURANCE	290 - 2	ACT WITH PERFECT ASSURANCE
ASSURED	293 - 4	GOOD IS ASSURED ME BY GOD
ASTHMA	243 - 1	OF ASTHMA AND HAY FEVER
ASTONISHED	352 - 3	ASTONISHED WHEN A PSYCHIC GIVES US
AT	124 - 2	LOOKING WITH AND LOOKING AT
AT HAND	366 - 2	HE IS EVER NEAR AT HAND
ATHIRST	027 - 3	HIM THAT IS ATHIRST
ATMOSPHERE	047 - 3	PROMOTE A SALUTARY ATMOSPHERE
ATMOSPHERE	087 - 6	IT IS OUR MENTAL ATMOSPHERE
ATMOSPHERE	120 - 1	ATMOSPHERE IN UNIVERSAL SUBJECTIVITY
ATMOSPHERE	124 - 4	ATMOSPHERE OR MENTAL CENTER
ATMOSPHERE	142 - 2	IMMERSED IN THE ATMOSPHERE OF OUR OWN
ATMOSPHERE	206 - 2	ATMOSPHERE IN THE ONE MIND
ATMOSPHERE	218 - 1	ATMOSPHERE OF PURE THOUGHT
ATMOSPHERE	234 - 4	THOUGHT AS OUR ATMOSPHERE
ATMOSPHERE	258 - 5	WITH DRYNESS OF ATMOSPHERE
ATMOSPHERE	294 - 2	SURROUNDED BY A THOUGHT ATMOSPHERE
ATMOSPHERE	294 - 2	THIS MENTAL ATMOSPHERE
ATMOSPHERE	294 - 2	EMBODYING THE ATMOSPHERE OF OUR DESIRE
ATMOSPHERE	296 - 2	MENTAL ATMOSPHERE OF ITS OWN
ATMOSPHERE	303 - 1	HIS OWN SUBJECTIVE ATMOSPHERE
ATMOSPHERE	309 - 3	SPIRITUAL ATMOSPHERE COMES INTO
ATMOSPHERE	328 - 4	SENSES THE ATMOSPHERE OF GOD
ATMOSPHERE	348 - 3	HAS A SUBJECTIVE ATMOSPHERE
ATMOSPHERE	348 - 3	JUST AS A CITY HAS ITS ATMOSPHERE
ATMOSPHERES	380 - 2	IN OUR MENTAL ATMOSPHERES
ATOM	066 - 3	INTELLIGENCE IN THE ATOM
ATOM	095 - 2	PHOTOGRAPHED THE ATOM
ATOM	103 - 2	IN THE ATOM
ATOM	229 - 4	EVERY TISSUE, ATOM AND FUNCTION
ATOM	235 - 3	ATOM IN MY BODY
ATOM	245 - 2	EVERY CELL, ATOM AND ORGAN
ATOM	245 - 2	ATOM OF MY BODY
ATOM	259 - 1	EVERY ATOM OF MY BODY RESPONDS
ATOM	261 - 2	PERMEATE EVERY ATOM OF MY BEING
ATOM	372 - 1	EVERY ATOM OF HIS PHYSICAL BEING
ATOMIC	123 - 4	OBSERVE IN CREATION AN ATOMIC INTELLIGENCE
AT ONCE	170 - 5	AT ONCE PRODUCE A HEALING
AT-ONE-MENT	331 - 4	JOYFUL UNION IN COMPLETE AT-ONE-MENT
AT-ONE-MENT	446 - 2	AT-ONE-MENT WITH REALITY
ATROCIOUS	467 - 1	ANY OF THESE ATROCIOUS THINGS
ATTACK	202 - 5	ATTACK THE THOUGHT THAT BINDS
ATTACK	260 - 3	TO MENTALLY ATTACK ANY PHYSICAL
ATTACKS	180 - 2	HE ATTACKS THE FALSE CLAIM
ATTACKS	253 - 3	ACUTE ATTACKS OF NEPHRITIS
ATTAIN	130 - 1	HE WISHES TO ATTAIN SELF-MASTERY
ATTAIN	450 - 4	IMAGE OF HIS INABILITY TO ATTAIN
ATTAINED	427 - 1	ATTAINED A CONSCIOUSNESS EQUAL TO HIS
ATTAIN IMMORTALITY	377 - 2	GOING TO ATTAIN IMMORTALITY
ATTAINMENT	072 - 3	FIRST DAY OF PERSONAL ATTAINMENT

ATTAINMENT	267 - 4	ATTAINMENT WILL INCREASE
ATTEMPT	399 - 5	ATTEMPT AT AN IMPOSSIBLE COERCION
ATTEMPTING	200 - 4	ATTEMPTING TO OPERATE
ATTEMPTS	167 - 3	ATTEMPTS TO HEAL HIMSELF
ATTEMPTS	170 - 1	HERE HE ATTEMPTS TO DISSOLVE
ATTEMPTS	206 - 4	ATTEMPTS TO KNOW THE TRUTH
ATTENTION	072 - 4	LITTLE ATTENTION HAS BEEN GIVEN
ATTENTION	101 - 2	RECOLLECTION, ATTENTION AND ANTICIPATION
ATTENTION	187 - 2	PAY NO ATTENTION TO THE OBJECTIVE
ATTENTION	192 - 2	ATTENTION TO CORRECT KNOWING
ATTENTION	193 - 3	THE WILL HOLDS ATTENTION
ATTENTION	194 - 1	FOCUSING THE MENTAL ATTENTION
ATTENTION	194 - 3	CONCENTRATE OUR ATTENTION
ATTENTION	195 - 4	CONCENTRATE THEN IS ATTENTION
ATTENTION	198 - 4	PAYS ESPECIAL ATTENTION
ATTENTION	254 - 4	PAY PARTICULAR ATTENTION
ATTENTION	274 - 2	THERE IS A MENTAL ATTENTION
ATTENTION	320 - 1	ENTIRE ATTENTION TO REALIZING
ATTENTION	352 - 3	THE ATTENTION OF OUR ANCESTORS
ATTENTION	380 - 2	CAN COMPEL THE ATTENTION
ATTENTION	397 - 5	MIND IS SPECIFIC MENTAL ATTENTION
ATTENTION	406 - 1	WHEREVER WE CENTER OUR ATTENTION
ATTENTION	411 - 4	GIVING OUR COMPLETE ATTENTION
ATTENTION	412 - 1	BY CONSTANT ATTENTION TO IT
ATTENTION	412 - 2	CREATED FROM THE VERY ATTENTION
ATTENTION	415 - 2	THE ATTENTION IS WINGED WITH LOVE
ATTENTION	447 - 3	ATTENTION TO THE SPIRITUAL UNIT
ATTITUDE	048 - 3	FAITH BEING A MENTAL ATTITUDE
ATTITUDE	048 - 3	FAITH IS A NECESSARY ATTITUDE
ATTITUDE	049 - 1	THE OPPOSITE MENTAL ATTITUDE
ATTITUDE	053 - 4	AFFIRMATIVE ATTITUDE OF MIND
ATTITUDE	060 - 2	MENTAL ATTITUDE OF THE PRACTITIONER
ATTITUDE	155 - 3	IN THE RELIGIOUS ATTITUDE
ATTITUDE	161 - 2	MENTAL ATTITUDE OF PEOPLE
ATTITUDE	190 - I	BEING A CERTAIN MENTAL ATTITUDE
ATTITUDE	217 - 2	AFFIRMATIVE ATTITUDE OF MIND
ATTITUDE	220 - 6	ATTITUDE FOR THAT IMPLIES THAT
ATTITUDE	222 - 3	SOME MENTAL ATTITUDE
ATTITUDE	222 - 3	THE MENTAL ATTITUDE IS AND REMOVE IT
ATTITUDE	225 - 1	THIS MENTAL ATTITUDE MUST
ATTITUDE	258 - 1	LISTENING ATTITUDE
ATTITUDE	258 - 1	ATTITUDE OF QUIETNESS AND CONFIDENCE
ATTITUDE	261 - 3	THE MENTAL ATTITUDE YOU HAVE
ATTITUDE	276 - 3	NO OTHER ATTITUDE COULD PRODUCE
ATTITUDE	277 - 4	THE ATTITUDE WE SHOULD HAVE
ATTITUDE	279 - I	AGGRESSIVE MENTAL ATTITUDE IN THE TRUTH
ATTITUDE	282 - 4	CAN EQUAL THIS ATTITUDE
ATTITUDE	283 - 3	IT IS A MENTAL ATTITUDE
ATTITUDE	283 - 4	ATTITUDE IS IN RELATIONSHIP TO GOD
ATTITUDE	283 - 4	FAITH IS A MENTAL ATTITUDE
ATTITUDE	283 - 4	ATTITUDE CAN BE CREATED
ATTITUDE	289 - 3	UNDERSTAND THIS ATTITUDE
ATTITUDE	297 - 4	CULTIVATE AN ATTITUDE OF FRIENDSHIP
ATTITUDE	298 - 1	A RELIGIOUS ATTITUDE OF MIND
ATTITUDE	306 - 3	DOMINANT ATTITUDE OF OUR MIND

ATTITUDE	398 - 4	TO ANY OTHER MENTAL ATTITUDE
ATTITUDE	404 - 2	REVERSE MENTAL ATTITUDE TO FAITH
ATTITUDE	404 - 3	FROM THAT MENTAL ATTITUDE
ATTITUDE	430 - 3	ATTITUDE THEN ARE WE TO ASSUME
ATTITUDE	469 - 1	REAL ATTITUDE WAS THAT GOD
ATTITUDE	487 - 1	MENTAL ATTITUDE TOWARD THE TRUTH
ATTITUDES	087 - 6	RESULT OF OUR MENTAL ATTITUDES
ATTITUDES	159 - 1	ONE OF THESE ATTITUDES
ATTITUDES	237 - 4	ATTITUDES PRODUCE CERTAIN PHYSICAL
ATTITUDES	302 - 2	HOPEFUL ATTITUDES OF MIND
ATTITUDES	322 - 2	HIS INNER MENTAL ATTITUDES
ATTITUDES	322 - 2	INNER MENTAL ATTITUDES MAY BE
ATTITUDES	400 - 1	TWO ATTITUDES OF MIND
ATTRACT	267 - 5	BUT WE DO ATTRACT TO OURSELVES
ATTRACT	294 - 1	WHAT WE SHALL ATTRACT
ATTRACT	294 - 2	THOUGHT CAN ATTRACT TO US
ATTRACT	298 - 1	WE ATTRACT TO US WHAT WE FIRST BECOME
ATTRACT	402 - 2	WE ATTRACT TO OURSELVES
ATTRACT	411 - 4	WE ATTRACT TO OURSELVES
ATTRACTED	287 - 2	EACH ATTRACTED TO HIMSELF
ATTRACTED	294 - 2	ATTRACTED TO SOMETHING WHICH IS GREATER
ATTRACTED	296 - 3	WE ARE MOST STRONGLY ATTRACTED
ATTRACTING	294 - 2	WE ARE EITHER ATTRACTING OR REPELLING
ATTRACTING	475 - 4	IF ONE IS NOT ATTRACTING
ATTRACTION	094 - 2	LAWS OF ATTRACTION AND REPULSION
ATTRACTION	119 - 1	LAWS OF ATTRACTION AND REPULSION
ATTRACTION	124 - 2	INVARIABLE LAW OF ATTRACTION
ATTRACTION	296 - 4	DRAWING POWER OF ATTRACTION
ATTRACTION	297 - 2	LAW OF ATTRACTION PRODUCES
ATTRACTION	322 - 2	ATTRACTION AND REPULSION ARE MENTAL
ATTRACTION	350 - 3	POWER OF PERSONAL ATTRACTION
ATTRACTS	142 - 2	THOUGHT ATTRACTS WHAT IS LIKE ITSELF
ATTRACTS	294 - 2	LIKE ATTRACTS LIKE
ATTRACTS	295 - 2	AUTOMATICALLY ATTRACTS TO HIMSELF
ATTRACTS	322 - 2	ATTRACTS TO HIMSELF A CORRESPONDENCE
ATTRACTS	450 - 3	LIKE ATTRACTS LIKE
ATTRIBUTE	050 - 1	LAW IS AN ATTRIBUTE OF GOD
ATTRIBUTE	196 - 3	ATTRIBUTE OF MAN
ATTRIBUTES	059 - 4	MANIFESTING THE ATTRIBUTES
ATTRIBUTES	071 - 2	ATTRIBUTES OF SELF-CHOICE
ATTRIBUTES	078 - 1	ONE OF THE MANY ATTRIBUTES OF GOD
ATTRIBUTES	081 - 3	ATTRIBUTES SPIRIT SOUL AND BODY
ATTRIBUTES	106 - 3	THE SAME INHERENT ATTRIBUTES
ATTRIBUTES	112 - 2	REPRODUCES ALL OF THE ATTRIBUTES
ATTRIBUTES	121 - 4	ATTRIBUTES OF THE LIMITLESS DEEP
ATTRIBUTES	157 - 2	ATTRIBUTES WHICH ARE CO-ETERNAL
ATTRIBUTES	363 - 2	THE IMPERSONAL ATTRIBUTES OF BEING
ATTRIBUTES	386 - 2	THOSE QUALITIES AND ATTRIBUTES
ATTRIBUTES	491 - 5	GOD'S IDEAS AND ATTRIBUTES
ATTUNED	057 - 3	ATTUNED TO THE TRUTH OF BEING
AUDIBLE	351 - 1	WITHOUT AUDIBLE WORDS BEING SPOKEN
AUDIENCE	380 - 1	THINK A LECTURE TO AN AUDIENCE
AUGHT	430 - 3	AUGHT BETWEEN US AND OUR FELLOWMEN
AUTHENTIC	341 - 5	AUTHENTIC RECORDS OF PEOPLE
AUTHORITY	161 - 1	AUTHORITY ON THE INVISIBLE PLANE

AUTHORITY	203 - 3	AUTHORITY AND NOT AS THE SCRIBES
AUTHORITY	277 - 2	HE EXERCISED AN AUTHORITY
AUTHORITY	332 - 1	AS ONE HAVING AUTHORITY
AUTHORITY	410 - 3	EXERCISE AN AUTHORITY OVER
AUTHORITY	437 - 3	AUTHORITY ON THE PHYSICAL PLANE
AUTHORITY	475 - 2	WITH IT GREAT AUTHORITY
AUTOCRATIC	365 - 3	AUTOCRATIC GOVERNMENT
AUTOMATIC	053 - 1	AUTOMATIC RESULT OF FAILING
AUTOMATIC	073 - 1	TO BE AN AUTOMATIC THING
AUTOMATIC	078 - 1	MENTAL MEDIUM IS AUTOMATIC
AUTOMATIC	108 - 1	AN AUTOMATIC INDIVIDUALITY
AUTOMATIC	131 - 3	AUTOMATIC AND OBEYS THE WILL
AUTOMATIC	132 - 5	AUTOMATIC REACTIONS TO SPIRIT
AUTOMATIC	176 - 1	OPPOSITE REACTION IS AUTOMATIC
AUTOMATIC	394 - S	THE AUTOMATIC PROCESSES OF NATURE
AUTOMATIC	395 - 1	AUTOMATIC FUNCTIONING BOTH
AUTOMATIC	395 - 2	AUTOMATIC AND NECESSARY FUNCTIONS
AUTOMATIC	416 - 4	AUTOMATIC ACTIONS OF THE PHYSICAL
AUTOMATICALLY	046 - 4	AUTOMATICALLY BECOMES THE LAW
AUTOMATICALLY	049 - 5	IT WILL AUTOMATICALLY DEMONSTRATE
AUTOMATICALLY	130 - 3	ALL IT CAN AUTOMATICALLY DO FOR MAN
AUTOMATICALLY	133 - 4	THIS LAW WORKS AUTOMATICALLY
AUTOMATICALLY	154 - 1	WE ARE AUTOMATICALLY BLESSED
AUTOMATICALLY	157 - 4	HIS PRAYER WILL AUTOMATICALLY
AUTOMATICALLY	186 - 4	AUTOMATICALLY WIPES OUT ANY PICTURE
AUTOMATICALLY	195 - 5	LAW WHICH AUTOMATICALLY PRODUCES
AUTOMATICALLY	218 - 3	WILL AUTOMATICALLY TAKE PLACE
AUTOMATICALLY	295 - 2	AUTOMATICALLY ATTRACTS TO HIMSELF
AUTOMATICALLY	358 - 2	LAW WILL BE WORKING AUTOMATICALLY
AUTOMATICALLY	411 - 4	WE AUTOMATICALLY EMBODY IT
AUTOMATICALLY	449 - 4	AUTOMATICALLY BECOMES THE BROTHER
AUTOMATICALLY	494 - 1	AUTOMATICALLY RENEWS THE OUTER MAN
AUTOMOBILE	340 - 3	ON TO THE AUTOMOBILE AND THE AIRPLANE
AUTO-SUGGESTION	118 - 4	AUTO-SUGGESTION THEN IT BECOMES
AVAILABILITY	052 - 2	THE AVAILABILITY OF THE LAW
AVAILABILITY	150 - 4	AVAILABILITY OF THE DIVINE SPIRIT
AVAILABILITY	167 - 3	AVAILABILITY OF GOOD
AVIALABLE	087 - 3	IN PART BUT WHICH IS EVER AVAILABLE
AVAILABLE	495 - 7	AVAILABLE TO ALL AND MAY BE USED
AVARICE	460 - 2	SWORD IN HATE, AVARICE OR LUST
AVENGE	487 - 4	GOD DOES NOT AVENGE
AVENUE	044 - 2	FIND AN AVENUE OF OUTLET
AVENUE	047 - 4	SUPPLY THE AVENUE
AVENUE	078 - 1	AVENUE THROUGH WHICH GOD OPERATES
AVENUE	113 - 2	AVENUE LEADING TO SELF-KNOWINGNESS
AVENUE	164 - 4	OURSELVES AN AVENUE THROUGH
AVENUE	269 - 2	A MENTAL AVENUE MUST BE PROVIDED
AVENUE	274 - 2	AVENUE THROUGH WHICH THEY MAY HAPPEN
AVENUE	301 - 4	PROVIDE A RECEPTIVE AVENUE FOR IT
AVENUE	355 - 2	MUST ALSO CONTAIN THE AVENUE
AVENUE	421 - 4	THROUGH THIS AVENUE
AVENUES	125 - 3	AVENUES OF HIS OWN THOUGHT
AVENUES	164 - 4	OPENS UP THE AVENUES OF THOUGHT
AVENUES	274 - 3	OPENS UP THE AVENUES OF THOUGHT
AVENUES	278 - 3	AVENUES OF MIND-ACTIVITY

AVENUES	339 - 1	HAVING MANY AVENUES OF EXPRESSION
AVERAGE	093 - 3	AVERAGE PERSON COMPREHENDS IT
AVERAGE	166 - 3	TO THE AVERAGE PERSON
AVERAGE	355 - 3	AVERAGE SPIRIT OF PROPHECY
AVERAGE	387 - 2	AVERAGE MEN DESIRES TO LIVE
AVERAGE	417 - 1	AVERAGE PERSON WHO HAS NO KNOWLEDGE
AVERAGE	427 - 1	AVERAGE MAN HAS ANY UNDERSTANDING
AVERAGE	452 - 4	AVERAGE MAN CANNOT CONCEIVE OF
AVOID	043 - 1	AVOID TWO GRAVE MISTAKES
AVOID	090 - 3	AVOID THE IMPRESSION
AVOID	303 - 2	THE ONLY WAY TO AVOID IT
AVOIRDUPOIS	253 - 2	FREE YOURSELF FROM AVOIRDUPOIS
AWAKE	145 - 4	AWAKE TO THE FACT THAT WE ARE ONE
AWAKE	307 - 3	AWAKE THOU THAT SLEEPEST
AWAKE	335 - 3	BUT AWAKE TO THE FACT
AWAKE	411 - 3	BUT WE MUST AWAKE TO IT
AWAKE	415 - 2	AWAKE TO THE REALIZATION
AWAKEN	339 - 1	WE SHOULD AWAKEN TO THE RECOGNITION
AWAKEN	413 - 2	PRESENCE OF GOD IS TO AWAKEN
AWAKENED	146 - 3	AWAKENED THOUGHT TO SPRING FORTH
AWAKENED	174 - 4	OUR OWN AWAKENED THOUGHT
AWAKENED	364 - 1	AWAKENED BY THE STILL SMALL VOICE
AWAKENED	373 - 3	WHEN MAN FIRST AWAKENED
AWAKENING	146 - 3	AWAKENING MUST BE WITHIN OUR THOUGHT
AWAKENING	219 - 4	GREAT SPIRITUAL AWAKENING
AWAKENING	336 - 1	AN AWAKENING OF THE DIVINITY
AWAKENING	337 - 2	EVOLUTION IS THE AWAKENING OF THE SOUL
AWAKENING	413 - 2	THE AWAKENING MUST BE
AWAKENING	465 - 1	THIS IS THE GREAT AWAKENING
AWAKENING	465 - 1	IN THIS DIVINE AWAKENING
AWAKENING	465 - 2	STILL IN THE AWAKENING
AWAKENING	487 - 7	AWAKENING IS A PROCESS
AWAKENS	075 - 4	IT AWAKENS AN INTUITIVE
AWAKES	130 - 4	MAN AWAKES TO SELF-CONSCIOUSNESS
AWARE	067 - 2	AWARE AND ACTIVE
AWARE	077 - 2	NOT AWARE OF THE FACT
AWARE	235 - 2	AWARE ONLY OF PERFECTION
AWARE	251 - 2	I AM AWARE OF MY IMMEDIATE ONENESS
AWARE	315 - 2	SOMETHING THE MIND BECOMES AWARE
AWARE	341 - 2	IMMEDIATELY IS AWARE
AWARE	347 - 2	ARE AWARE THAT WE ARE LIVING
AWARE	353 - 1	AWARE OF A DISTURBED INNER FEELING
AWARE	386 - 3	UNLESS I AM AWARE OF IT
AWARE	407 - 4	AWAKE AND AWARE
AWARENESS	079 - 3	SELF-CONSCIOUS AWARENESS
AWARENESS	183 - 3	INDUCING AN INTERIOR AWARENESS
AWARENESS	190 - 1	REACH A STATE OF SPIRITUAL AWARENESS
AWARENESS	341 - 2	INTERIOR AWARENESS A SPIRITUAL SENSE
AWAY	041 - 3	WE LOOK TOO FAR AWAY FOR REALITY
AWAY	266 - 3	LOOKING AWAY FROM THE CONDITIONS
AWAY	452 - 2	GOING AWAY BY THEMSELVES
AWE	027 - 2	IN AWE OF LIFE ITSELF
AWE	075 - 1	AWE BUT NOT WITH FEAR
AWFUL	302 - 3	COMING WITHOUT THAT AWFUL EFFORT

B

BACK	086 – 4	UNLESS BACK OF THE WORD
BACK	124 – 2	WHICH WE SEE COMES BACK
BACK	214 – 1	BACK OF THE APPEARANCE
BACK	222 – 1	BACK OF ALL APPEARANCE
BACK	491 – 3	STAND BACK OF ALL HUMAN THOUGHT
BACKGROUND	342 – 3	INTUITION REMAINS IN THE BACKGROUND
BACK UP	332 – 5	POWER TO BACK UP
BAD	092 – 2	KNOWS NEITHER GOOD NOR BAD
BAD	207 – 1	PEOPLE GO FROM BAD TO WORSE
BAD	298 – 3	MORE GOOD THAN BAD IN PEOPLE
BADE	432 – 3	JESUS BADE US TO COMPLETELY
BAD MATTERS	453 – 6	FALSE IDEAS MAKE BAD MATTERS WORSE
BALANCE	176 – 1	THE TWO WILL EXACTLY BALANCE
BALANCE	194 – 4	BALANCE IS STRUCK WHEN THE WILL
BALANCE	255 – 4	THE ORDERLY BALANCE OF THE BODY
BALANCE	304 – 5	BALANCE OF CONSCIOUSNESS IS
BALANCE	321 – 2	LAW OF PERFECT BALANCE
BALANCE	328 – 3	BALANCE OF OUR KNOWLEDGE OF GOD
BALANCE	363 – 2	ABLE TO BALANCE THE PERSONAL
BALANCE	433 – 2	THE LAW OF PERFECT BALANCE
BALANCE	501 – 6	AUTOMATICALLY BALANCE OUR MENTALITIES
BALANCED	337 – 3	COMPLETELY POISED AND PERFECTLY BALANCED
BALANCED	455 – 2	WLL FIND THEM BALANCED RIGHTLY
BALANCES	141 – 3	PERFECTLY BALANCES IT
BALANCES	321 – 2	THE OBJECTIVE WORLD PERFECTLY BALANCES
BALANCES	340 – 2	LIKENESS WHICH EXACTLY BALANCES
BALANCES	340 – 2	INVOLVED PERFECTLY BALANCES
BALANCES	433 – 2	EFFECT WHICH BALANCES
BALL	355 – 4	THE BALL IS HALFWAY TO IT
BAMBOO	123 – 3	OBSERVE THE BAMBOO
BAPTISM	260 – 3	BAPTISM OF SPIRIT AS THIS
BAPTISM	493 – 5	BAPTISM WHICH IS THE REALIZATION
BARE	501 – 6	BARE OUR SOULS TO ITS GREAT LIGHT
BARNS	432 – 3	WHO DO NOT GATHER INTO BARNS
BARREN	481 – 7	BARREN TREE DOES NOT EXPRESS
BARREN	482 – 1	A LIFE BARREN OF GOOD
BARRIER	199 – 4	BARRIER TO HEALING
BASED	183 – 1	BASED UPON THE CONCEPTION
BASED	298 – 3	WHOLE UNIVERSE IS BASED UPON IT
BASICALLY	189 – 2	WHICH IS BASICALLY PERFECT
BASIS	147 – 5	BASIS OUR ENTIRE SUPERSTRUCTURE RESTS
BATHING	128 – 4	BATHING ALL LIFE IN A CELESTIAL GLORY
BATHING	188 – 3	BATHING ALL LIFE IN GLORY
BATTLE HYMN	495 – 5	IS NOT A BATTLE HYMN OF RIGHTEOUSNESS
BE	044 – 1	UNFOLDMENT OF THE MORE YET TO BE
BE	188 – 1	BE WHAT YOU WISH TO BE
BE	269 – 1	LIFE HAS ONLY TO BE LIFE
BE	290 – 2	SEE IT, FEEL IT AND BE IT
BE	338 – 1	BE TO US WHAT WE BELIEVE
BE	364 – 2	WE COULD NOT BE ANYTHING ELSE
BE	438 – 4	INFINITE MIND KNOWS MUST BE
BEAMING	300 – 4	SEE THEM CHEERFUL BEAMING

BEAR	292 - 1	IT WILL COME UP AND BEAR FRUIT
BEARS WITNESS	478 - 5	BEARS WITNESS TO THE DIVINE FACT
BEAUTIFUL	041 - 3	BEAUTIFUL AND TRUE THOUGHT
BEAUTIFUL	428 - 3	BEAUTIFUL STORY ABOUT HELL
BEAUTIFUL	466 - 3	MORE BEAUTIFUL THOUGHT COULD NOT BE
BEAUTY	040 - 3	ESSENCE OF BEAUTY
BEAUTY	053 - 3	IT IS BEAUTY AND TRUTH
BEAUTY	072 - 2	WE DO NOT SEE BEAUTY
BEAUTY	072 - 2	THE ARTIST FEELS BEAUTY
BEAUTY	231 - 1	THE BEAUTY OF THE OMNIPRESENT GOD
BEAUTY	233 - 4	ITS EXPRESSIONS OF BEAUTY
BEAUTY	242 - 2	THIS BEAUTY, THIS PERFECT ACTION
BEAUTY	245 - 3	IN TRUTH AND IN BEAUTY
BEAUTY	258 - 1	MELODY, RHYTHM AND BEAUTY
BEAUTY	264 - 4	POISED IN PEACE AND BEAUTY
BEAUTY	412 - 1	WITH LOVE AND BEAUTY
BECAUSE	126 - 4	BECAUSE OF THE UNITY OF ALL MIND
BECAUSE	408 - 1	BECAUSE GOD IS CONSCIOUS OF HIM
BECOME	267 - 5	MAN MUST BECOME MORE
BECOME	298 - 1	WHAT WE FIRST BECOME
BECOME	402 - 3	BECOME TO US WHAT WE ARE TO IT
BECOME	412 - 4	CANNOT BE OR BECOME ANTAGONISTIC
BECOMES	045 - 2	BECOMES TO US THE PARTICULAR
BECOMES	197 - 1	BECOMES DEFINITE FORM
BECOMES	343 - 5	INTO US AND BECOMES US AND IS US
BECOMING	084 - 5	BECOMING THE THINGS IT MAKES
BECOMING	102 - 2	ETERNALLY BECOMING
BECOMING	132 - 1	BECOMING THE THING IT MAKES
BECOMING	146 - 4	BECOMING THE THING IT MAKES
BECOMING	164 - 1	BECOMING CONSCIOUS OF THIS ETERNAL TRUTH
BECOMING	292 - 4	WE ARE NOT BECOMING THIS LIFE
BECOMING	292 - 4	GOD IS NOT BECOMING GOD IS
BECOMING	304 - 5	BECOMING THE THINGS WHICH HE CREATES
BECOMING	312 - 2	ITS BEING PASSES INTO BECOMING
BECOMINGNESS	102 - 2	INFINITE BECOMINGNESS
BED	438 - 1	ARISE TAKE UP THY BED
BEELZEBUB	076 - 4	CAST OUT DEVILS BY BEELZEBUB
BEFORE	147 - 5	BEFORE WE ATTEMPT TO IMPROVE
BEFORE	176 - I	BEFORE THE IMAGE CAN REFLECT
BEFORE	222 - 3	BEFORE DISEASE DESTROYS
BEFORE	387 - 3	THEY HAVE ONLY GONE BEFORE
BEGAN	390 - 5	IT NEVER BEGAN NOR
BEGET	431 - 4	LOVE ALONE CAN BEGET LOVE
BEGETTING	357 - 2	THE ETERNAL IS FOREVER BEGETTING
BEGGING	150 - 5	BEGGING AS THOUGH HE WERE WITHHOLDING
BEGIN	049 - 3	CORRECTLY BEGIN THEIR TREATMENT
BEGIN	143 - 2	BEGIN RIGHT WHERE WE ARE
BEGIN	218 - 2	BEGIN BY THE REMOVAL OF DOUBT
BEGIN	271 - 4	BEGIN RIGHT WHERE WE ARE
BEGIN	282 - 3	BEGIN RIGHT WHERE WE ARE
BEGIN	319 - 4	BEGIN EACH TREATMENT AS IF
BEGIN	402 - 1	HAPPY TO BEGIN RIGHT WHERE WE ARE
BEGIN	403 - 2	BEGIN AT ONCE TO CONTROL
BEGINNING	060 - 1	PERFECT BELIEF IS THE BEGINNING
BEGINNING	067 - 1	HAS A BEGINNING AND AN END

BEGINNING	070 – 2	BEGINNING BUT NEVER ENDING
BEGINNING	117 – I	THEORETICAL BEGINNING OF CREATION
BEGINNING	310 – 3	IN THE BEGINNING WAS THE WORD
BEGINNINGS	373 – 4	IT MAY HAVE BEGINNINGS AND ENDS
BEGINS	171 – 3	BEGINS AND ENDS IN THE THOUGHT
BEGINS	178 – 6	TREATMENT BEGINS AND ENDS WITHIN
BEGINS	207 – 2	BEGINS AND ENDS WITHIN
BEGOT	357 – 2	GOD NEVER BEGOT BUT ONE SON
BEGOTTEN	368 – 1	THE SON BEGOTTEN OF THE ONLY FATHER
BEGUILES	473 – 6	BEGUILES US IN THIS WAY
BEHIND	099 – 1	BEHIND THE OBJECTIVE FORM
BEHIND	339 – 1	BEHIND EACH ONE STANDS
BEHIND	422 – 2	LEFT BEHIND A MENTAL PICTURE
BEHOLD	087 – 5	WE BEHOLD NOTHING VISIBLE
BEHOLD	109 – 2	BEHOLD I STAND AT THE DOOR
BEHOLD	147 – 3	BEHOLD A NEW HEAVEN
BEHOLD	217 – 2	BEHOLD THE KINGDOM OF HEAVEN
BEHOLD	489 – 6	BEHOLD THE IMAGE OF ETERNITY
BEHOLDING	114 – 2	BEHOLDING THE REAL UNIVERSE
BEING	025 – 2	IN THE INNERMOST BEING OF MAN
BEING	026 – 2	ONE WITH THE GREAT LAW OF ITS OWN BEING
BEING	029 – 2	MENTAL LAW OF OUR BEING
BEING	032 – 3	LIVES AND MOVES AND HAS HIS BEING
BEING	033 – 3	HIDDEN IN THE INNER BEING
BEING	034 – 1	THE DIVINE BEING
BEING	035 – 3	HAVE OUR BEING
BEING	046 – 4	AS IT PASSES INTO OUR BEING
BEING	050 – 1	THE NATURE OF BEING
BEING	050 – 2	THE NATURE OF BEING
BEING	068 – 2	NATURE OF THE DIVINE BEING
BEING	069 – 3	BEING WHOM WE CALL GOD
BEING	070 – 2	SUPPOSE THAT IT COULD STOP BEING
BEING	076 – 3	MOVE AND HAVE OUR BEING
BEING	080 – I	THE DIVINE BEING WHOM
BEING	080 – 3	A TRINITY OF BEING
BEING	081 – 4	IT IS CONSCIOUS BEING
BEING	085 – 3	UNCREATED CHANGELESS BEING
BEING	085 – 3	NOT A BEING WITH PARTS
BEING	085 – 3	BEING WITH POTENTIALITIES
BEING	085 – 4	BEING IS PURE SPIRIT
BEING	087 – 4	MOVE AND HAVE OUR BEING
BEING	094 – 1	AT THE CENTER OF OUR BEING
BEING	094 – 1	IN OUR BEING FOR HIM
BEING	100 – 2	SPIRIT IS THE ABSOLUTE BEING
BEING	102 – 2	ALL IS INFINITE BEING
BEING	106 – 2	NATURE OF THE DIVINE BEING
BEING	166 – 2	PERSON IS A DIVINE BEING
BEING	168 – 5	PERFECT MAN PERFECT BEING
BEING	180 – 2	REALIZES HIS OWN BEING AS SPIRITUAL
BEING	180 – 2	STATE OF HIS PATIENT'S BEING
BEING	186 – 1	PERFECT MAN AND PERFECT BEING
BEING	195 – 3	ONE OF SPONTANEOUS BEING
BEING	201 – 2	BEING NO LONGER SUBJECT
BEING	201 – 4	PERFECT MAN, PERFECT BEING
BEING	203 – 3	PATIENT IS A DIVINE BEING

BEING	218 - 2	PERFECT MAN AND PERFECT BEING
BEING	218 - 4	MAN'S ENTIRE BEING AS SPIRITUAL
BEING	225 - 1	COMPLETE STATEMENT OF THE REALITY OF BEING
BEING	228 - 3	PERFECT BEING PERFECT GOD
BEING	238 - 3	AT THE CENTER OF MAN'S BEING
BEING	249 - 1	THE CENTER OF MY BEING IS
BEING	261 - 3	PERFECT MAN AND PERFECT BEING
BEING	280 - 1	THE DIVINE BEING BY HIS PERSONAL EMBODIMENT
BEING	281 - 1	THE PRINCIPLE OF BEING
BEING	298 - 3	THE VERY REASON FOR OUR BEING
BEING	312 - 1	CONTRADICTORY TO THE DIVINE BEING
BEING	332 - 2	MOVE AND HAVE OUR BEING
BEING	333 - 6	HARD TO UNDERSTAND HOW A BEING
BEING	338 - 3	OUR PERFECT BEING
BEING	342 - 2	THE REALITIES OF BEING
BEING	353 - 3	A CONTINUATION OF BEING
BEING	363 - 3	WHERE THE BEING OF GOD BEGAN
BEING	369 - 3	HE IS AN ETERNAL BEING
BEING	391 - 3	AT THE CENTER OF MAN'S BEING
BEING	405 - 3	MAKE OUR OWN BEING
BEING	405 - 3	THE BEING WHICH WE ARE
BEING	418 - 3	REVEAL THE TRUTH OF BEING
BEING	420 - 4	WHOSE BEING IS EVER PRESENT
BEING	476 - 5	BEING NEEDS TO BE FED
BEINGS	068 - 3	TWO INFINITE BEINGS
BEINGS	077 - 1	TO RECOGNIZE OTHER BEINGS
BEINGS	137 - 2	THOUSANDS OF UNHAPPY BEINGS
BEINGS	138 - 4	WE ARE SPIRITUAL BEINGS
BEINGS	294 - 1	WE ARE THINKING BEINGS
BEINGS	313 - 3	SPIRITUAL BEINGS BUT WE DO NOT KNOW IT
BEINGS	451 - 3	WE ARE SPIRITUAL BEINGS
BELIEF	037 - 3	BECAUSE OF OUR BELIEF
BELIEF	037 - 4	OUR BELIEF SETS THE LIMIT
BELIEF	038 - 4	THOUGHT AND BELIEF
BELIEF	052 - 4	THE IMPULSE OF OUR CREATIVE BELIEF
BELIEF	052 - 5	IT DOES ACCORDING TO OUR BELIEF
BELIEF	060 - 1	PERFECT BELIEF IS THE BEGINNING
BELIEF	063 - 1	SUCH A BELIEF IS REASONABLE
BELIEF	086 - 3	OUR BELIEF
BELIEF	097 - 2	THE BELIEF FROM THE BELIEVER
BELIEF	128 - 1	IT IS A BELIEF IN SEPARATION
BELIEF	128 - 1	WE ARE BOUND BY NOTHING BUT BELIEF
BELIEF	155 - I	PRAYER, FAITH AND BELIEF ARE CLOSELY
BELIEF	156 - 2	BECAUSE OF THEIR BELIEF
BELIEF	175 - I	SOLELY UPON OUR BELIEF
BELIEF	189 - 3	BELIEF THAT THE OUTWARD APPEARANCE
BELIEF	190 - 1	A BELIEF IN GOD
BELIEF	190 - 2	BELIEF OF THE ONE PRAYING
BELIEF	224 - 3	BELIEF IN THE NECESSITY
BELIEF	235 - 1	ERASE THE BELIEF
BELIEF	241 - 2	FURTHER POWER IS GIVEN TO THE BELIEF
BELIEF	266 - 3	THROUGH RIGHT THOUGHT AND BELIEF
BELIEF	280 - 2	OUR BELIEF MEASURES THE EXTENT
BELIEF	280 - 2	ACCORDING TO OUR BELIEF
BELIEF	283 - 2	ON THE BELIEF IN SPIRIT

BELIEF	286 - 2	HEALS THE BELIEF IN INACTIVITY
BELIEF	288 - 1	OUR BELIEF IN THE POWER OF GOD
BELIEF	289 - 1	BELIEF IN BOTH GOOD AND EVIL
BELIEF	317 - 3	BELIEF IS LAW
BELIEF	404 - 4	FEAR IS A BELIEF IN LIMITATION
BELIEF	409 - 2	BELIEF IN THE NECESSITY OF SICKNESS
BELIEF	409 - 2	HE REPUDIATES THIS BELIEF
BELIEF	416 - 3	IMAGES OF HIS OWN BELIEF ABOUT HIMSELF
BELIEF	417 - 1	AFTER THE MOLD OF RACIAL BELIEF
BELIEF	418 - 3	WE SEPARATE THE BELIEF
BELIEF	427 - 1	BEARS WITNESS TO OUR OWN BELIEF
BELIEF	434 - 3	AT THE LEVEL OF THAT BELIEF
BELIEF	453 - 6	BELIEF IN DUALITY SUPPOSES
BELIEF	470 - 1	BELIEF IS ABSOLUTELY NECESSARY
BELIEF	475 - 5	OUTWARD SIGN OF THE INNER BELIEF
BELIEFS	032 - 1	REBUILDS ACCORDING TO OUR BELIEFS AND FAITH
BELIEFS	150 - 5	BELIEFS IN EVIL, SIN, SICKNESS, LIMITATION
BELIEFS	302 - 3	ONE BY ONE ALL FALSE BELIEFS
BELIEVE	034 - 1	EACH ONE OF US AS WE BELIEVE
BELIEVE	037 - 1	AS YOU BELIEVE
BELIEVE	038 - 1	HOW MUCH CAN WE BELIEVE
BELIEVE	038 - 1	BELIEVE WILL BE DONE UNTO US
BELIEVE	039 - 2	JUST WHAT ONE CAN BELIEVE
BELIEVE	052 - 5	BELIEVE THAT IT WILL NOT WORK
BELIEVE	058 - 3	AS MUCH AS WE BELIEVE
BELIEVE	058 - 5	WE MUST ACCEPT AND BELIEVE
BELIEVE	063 - 1	TO DISCOVER WHAT TO BELIEVE
BELIEVE	066 - 4	BELIEVE IN AN ABSOLUTE INTELLIGENCE
BELIEVE	140 - 2	DONE UNTO YOU AS YOU BELIEVE
BELIEVE	169 - 3	BELIEVE IF HE IS GOING TO BE A SUCCESSFUL
BELIEVE	191 - 4	CERTAINLY BELIEVE IN GOD
BELIEVE	261 - 3	BELIEVE AND YOU WILL BE
BELIEVE	280 - 1	AS YE BELIEVE IT SHALL BE DONE
BELIEVE	301 - 3	UNTO YOU AS YOU BELIEVE
BELIEVE	302 - 3	ALL WE HAVE TO DO IS TO BELIEVE
BELIEVE	317 - 3	MUST FIRST OF ALL BELIEVE
BELIEVE	318 - 1	BELIEVE BECAUSE GOD IS BELIEF
BELIEVE	338 - 1	UNTIL WE BELIEVE THAT IT IS
BELIEVE	402 - 1	TREAT OURSELVES UNTIL WE DO BELIEVE
BELIEVE	407 - 2	IS TO BELIEVE IN THE INVISIBLE
BELIEVE	446 - 4	I BELIEVE ABOUT THE CAUSE
BELIEVE	454 - 1	BELIEVE IN THE GOOD ALONE
BELIEVE	458 - 3	BELIEVE THAT WE RECEIVE THEM
BELIEVE	478 - 6	BELIEVE ALSO IN ME
BELIEVE	479 - 3	HE TOLD THEM TO BELIEVE IN GOD
BELIEVED	396 - 2	BELIEVED THAT WHICH IS NOT TRUE
BELIEVED	437 - 3	BELIEVED SO BE IT DONE UNTO THEE
BELIEVED	437 - 4	BELIEVED WHAT HE TAUGHT
BELIEVED	439 - 6	BELIEVED THAT HE WAS ABLE
BELIEVER	097 - 1	SEPARATE THE BELIEF FROM THE BELIEVER
BELIEVER	201 - 2	THE BELIEF FROM THE BELIEVER
BELIEVER	418 - 3	THE BELIEF FROM THE BELIEVER
BELIEVES	160 - 3	NO ONE WHO BELIEVES MORE IN FAITH
BELIEVES	169 - 3	BELIEVES WHEN HE SAYS IT THAT COUNTS
BELIEVES	280 - 2	WHICH DOES UNTO EACH AS HE BELIEVES

BELIEVES	315 - 2	IT HAS WHAT IT BELIEVES
BELIEVES	494 - 2	MIND HOLDS TO AND FIRMLY BELIEVES
BELIEVING	037 - 3	BELIEVING THAT IT IS NOT
BELIEVING	190 - 1	A CERTAIN WAY OF BELIEVING
BELIEVING	338 - 1	WE ARE BELIEVING IT IS NOT
BELIEVING	435 - 3	WE MUST ASK BELIEVING
BELITTLE	219 - 3	BELITTLE YOUR EFFORTS
BELONG	295 - 2	WE ARE JUST WHERE WE BELONG
BELONGS	490 - 6	BELONGS TO US AND IS OURS
BELOVED	335 - 3	BELOVED NOW ARE WE THE SONS OF GOD
BELOVED	338 - 3	BELOVED NOW ARE WE THE SONS OF GOD
BELOVED SON	361 - 2	THIS IS MY BELOVED SON
BELOVED SON	367 - 1	THIS IS MY BELOVED SON
BENEFICENCE	156 - 4	BENEFICENCE OF GOD AND
BENEFICIAL	401 - 3	BENEFICIAL BY DENYING ANY POWER
BENEFIT	137 - 2	KNOWLEDGE FOR THEIR BENEFIT
BENEFIT	268 - 2	WE SHALL RECEIVE NO GREAT BENEFIT
BENEFIT	316 - 1	TAKE IT IF IT WILL BENEFIT
BENEFITS	234 - 2	PARTAKER OF THE DIVINE BENEFITS
BESANT	078 - 2	ANNA BESANT STATED IT
BESET	158 - 5	BESET WITH OBSTACLES
BESPEAKS	497 - 2	BESPEAKS THE REALIZATION THAT WE ARE
BEST	198 - 1	WILL BE THE BEST HEALER
BEST	276 - 3	TAKE THE HIGHEST AND BEST
BEST	300 - 3	SO LIVE THAT THE BEST MAY BECOME
BEST	383 - 3	WE DO THE BEST THAT WE CAN
BEST	397 - 5	NECESSARY IN THE BEST USE OF MIND
BEST	414 - 3	BEST INTO OUR SPIRITUAL WORK
BE STILL	264 - 4	BE STILL AND KNOW THAT I AM
BE STILL	273 - 1	WE MUST BE STILL
BE STILL	369 - 2	BE STILL O SOUL AND KNOW
BETRAY	168 - 3	NO MORE BETRAY THIS TRUST
BETRAYAL	479 - 1	ON THE EVE OF HIS BETRAYAL
BETTER	036 - 3	WE SHALL FIND A BETTER GOD
BETTER	220 - 5	NO GOOD BETTER OR BEST
BETTER	276 - 2	PROVIDE A BETTER CONCEPT OF LIFE
BETTER	288 - 2	BETTER BECAUSE OF YOUR MISERY
BETTER	313 - 1	NOT NECESSARILY BETTER OR WORSE
BETTER	410 - 1	BETTER STATES OF CONSCIOUS BEING
BETWEEN	171 - 3	BETWEEN JOHN AND MARY
BETWEEN	171 - 3	BETWEEN THEM BUT IN THEM
BETWEEN	404 - 1	HAPPENS BETWEEN CAUSE AND EFFECT
BEWARE	315 - 1	BEWARE OF HOLDING TOO MUCH GOOD
BEWARE	440 - 2	BEWARE OF HOLDING TOO MUCH GOOD
BEYOND	051 - 2	PRINCIPLE GOES BEYOND
BEYOND	379 - 2	SEEN INTO THE BEYOND
BEYOND	465 - 2	BEYOND WHAT WE HAVE SO FAR
BHAGAVAD-GITA	286 - 1	THE BHAGAVAD-GITA SAYS
BIBLE	038 - 2	THE BIBLE CALLS THE WORD
BIBLE	064 - 3	CREATION AS GIVEN IN THE BIBLE
BIBLE	067 - 3	BIBLE IS THE GREATEST BOOK
BIBLE	075 - 3	THE BIBLE SAYS NO MAN HATH
BIBLE	076 - 3	THE BIBLE SAYS IN HIM WE LIVE
BIBLE	080 - 3	WHAT THE BIBLE CALLS THE WORD
BIBLE	082 - 3	PHILOSOPHY OF THE BIBLE

BIBLE	137 - 1	BIBLE WE HAVE THE ASSURANCE
BIBLE	145 - 4	BIBLE POINTS OUT THAT MAN HAS
BIBLE	153 - 2	THE BIBLE TELLS US
BIBLE	166 - 4	THE BIBLE TEACHES THE LAW
BIBLE	167 - 2	BIBLE DOES NOT TELL US HOW
BIBLE	167 - 2	TREATMENT IS IMPLIED IN THE BIBLE
BIBLE	272 - 4	THE BIBLE SAYS THERE IS NO
BIBLE	310 - 3	BIBLE CLEARLY SPEAKS OF THE PHYSICAL
BIBLE	310 - 4	BIBLE FURTHER EXPLAINS TO US
BIBLE	311 - 1	BIBLE SAYS THE FIRST MAN
BIBLE	311 - 1	BIBLE CLEARLY STATES
BIBLE	315 - 3	BIBLE TELLS US NOT TO COUNT
BIBLE	338 - 3	BIBLE WE READ BELOVED
BIBLE	359 - 4	BIBLE MAKES IT MORE THAN PLAIN
BIBLE	483 - 4	WHOLE TEACHING OF THE BIBLE
BIBLE	501 - 6	BIBLE TELLS US THAT GOD WILL
BIBLICAL	158 - 2	FAMILIAR WITH BIBLICAL HISTORY
BIDDING	130 - 4	NATURE DOES HIS BIDDING
BIER	385 - 3	STANDING AT THE BIER OF A LOVED ONE
BIG	086 - 4	KNOWING NO BIG AND NO LITTLE
BIG AND LITTLE	133 - 5	BIG AND LITTLE HAPPINESS AND MISERY
BIG AND LITTLE	312 - 1	ANYTHING ABOUT BIG AND LITTLE
BIGGEST	458 - I	BIGGEST LIFE IS THE ONE WHICH
BIND	037 - 1	WHICH APPEARS TO BIND US
BIND	237 - 1	MENTALLY TEAR OR BIND
BIND	402 - 4	BY THAT FREEDOM WE BIND
BIND	457 - 1	BIND ON EARTH SHALL BE BOUND
BINDS	321 - 1	WHICH BINDS HIM WILL FREE HIM
BINDS	322 - 1	BINDS HIMSELF THROUGH WRONG
BINDS	445 - 7	PRESENCE WHICH BINDS ALL TOGETHER
BIOGRAPHY	359 - 4	BIOGRAPHY OF HUNDREDS OF OTHER MEN
BIRDS	432 - 3	GOD CARES FOR THE BIRDS
BIRTH	161 - 4	PRIVILEGE OF GIVING BIRTH TO IT
BIRTH	305 - 4	WHICH THE MIND GIVES BIRTH
BIRTH	406 - 2	EVER GIVING BIRTH TO FORM
BIRTH	422 - 3	BIRTH TO ALL THE DIVINE IDEAS
BIRTH	471 - 5	REFERRING TO THE HEAVENLY BIRTH
BIRTHLESS	239 - 3	MAN IS BIRTHLESS DEATHLESS
BIRTHLESS	284 - 3	BIRTHLESS AND THE DEATHLESS REALITY
BIRTH OF THE SOUL	503 - 1	BIRTH OF THE SOUL INTO THE LIGHT
BIRTHRIGHT	025 - 3	FREEDOM IS THE BIRTHRIGHT
BIRTHRIGHT	183 - 2	CONCEPT OF OUR SPIRITUAL BIRTHRIGHT
BIRTHRIGHT	454 - 4	DIVINE BIRTHRIGHT OF THE SOUL
BIRTHRIGHT	486 - 1	KEEP HIMSELF FROM HIS BIRTHRIGHT
BIRTHRIGHT	486 - 3	ROB US OF OUR BIRTHRIGHT
BIT	278 - 4	BIT OF INFORMATION THAT WAS NEEDED
BITTERNESS	479 - 2	CUP OF BITTERNESS WERE BEING HELD
BLACK	172 - 2	I AM TREATING HENRY BLACK
BLACKBOARD	412 - 2	LIFE IS A BLACKBOARD
BLADDER	254 - 4	IN TREATING BLADDER TROUBLE
BLASPHEMED	437 - 5	BLASPHEMED GOD IN ATTEMPTING TO
BLESS	239 - 2	BLESS ETERNALLY NOT ONLY
BLESS	257 - 3	I BLESS MY BODY
BLESS	431 - 3	BLESS US ABUNDANTLY
BLESS	434 - 7	PRAISE AND CREATIVELY BLESS

BLESS	487 – 3	BLESS AND CURSE NOT
BLESSED	154 – 1	WE ARE AUTOMATICALLY BLESSED
BLESSED	223 – 2	BLESSED ARE THEY WHO DO HUNGER
BLESSED	334 – 2	BLESSED THE WORLD WITH THEIR PRESENCE
BLESSED	419 – 5	MYSTICS WHO HAVE BLESSED
BLESSED	429 – 1	BLESSED ARE THE MERCIFUL
BLESSED	451 – 2	BLESSED ARE YOUR EYES
BLESSING	435 – 1	BLESSING EVEN THOSE WHO SEEK TO INJURE
BLESSING	461 – 2	BLESSING AND A CURSE BEFORE
BLESSING	280 – 2	DEGREE OF OUR BLESSING
BLESSING	383 – 1	LIFE IS A BLESSING OR A CURSE
BLESSING	485 – 5	IT CARRIES A BLESSING WITH IT
BLIND	055 – 4	BLIND LEAD THE BLIND
BLIND	228 – 1	BLIND LEADING THE BLIND
BLIND	230 – 5	HAVE BEEN OUTWARDLY BLIND
BLIND	276 – 1	LAW IS A BLIND FORCE
BLIND	319 – 2	WHEREAS I WAS BLIND, NOW I SEE'
BLIND	415 – 2	BUT THE BLIND CANNOT LEAD THE BLIND
BLIND	428 – 4	AS BLIND MEN YEARN FOR LIGHT
BLIND	439 – 6	HEALING THE BLIND MEN
BLIND	453 – 5	BLIND LEAD THE BLIND
BLINDED	345 – 4	HAVE BEEN BLINDED BY THE LIGHT
BLIND FAITH	165 – 1	BE WORKING MUCH OF THE TIME ON BLIND FAITH
BLINDNESS	319 – 2	MAN HEALED OF BLINDNESS
BLINDNESS	456 – 5	REFLECTION OF HIS BLINDNESS BEFORE
BLITHELY	176 – 1	NOT BLITHELY REPEAT WORDS
BLOATED	041 – 2	BLOATED NOTHINGNESS OUT OF THE WAY
BLOCKED	497 – 3	WHEN THIS EMOTION IS BLOCKED
BLOCKS	404 – 3	BLOCKS THE MORE COMPLETE GIVINGNESS
BLOOD	116 – 2	WHO HAS FLESH AND BLOOD
BLOOD	249 – 3	BLOOD PRESSURE IS FOUND NORMAL
BLOOD	439 – 4	BLOOD TWELVE YEARS
BLOOD	467 – 1	BLOOD OF MY MOST PRECIOUS SON
BLOOD PRESSURE	175 – 4	BLOOD PRESSURE IS HIGH MIGHT SAY
BLOOD PRESSURE	250 – 2	THE BLOOD PRESSURE IS NORMAL
BLOOD PRESSURE	316 – 2	HIGH BLOOD PRESSURE OR LOW
BLOOD STREAM	247 – 3	BLOOD STREAM REPRESENTS THE CIRCULATION
BLOOD STREAM	248 – 1	BLOOD STREAM IS CONTINUOUSLY RENEWED
BLOOD STREAM	253 – 4	WHATEVER MY BLOOD STREAM NEEDS
BLOT	302 – 3	BEGIN TO BLOT OUT
BLOT	412 – 2	BLOT OUT THEIR TRANSGRESSIONS
BLOT	501 – 6	BLOT OUT THESE MISTAKES AND REMEMBER
BOAST	499 – 6	DECEIVE OURSELVES WHEN WE BOAST
BOAT	219 – 2	WE TAKE A BOAT
BODIES	098 – 1	INCLUDED ALL LESSER BODIES
BODIES	102 – 4	OUR HUMAN BODIES ARE MADE
BODIES	104 – 3	MIGHT BE INNUMERABLE BODIES
BODIES	117 – 1	BODIES ARE ONE WITH THE WHOLE BODY
BODIES	207 – 2	NEITHER BODIES NOR CONDITIONS
BODIES	374 – 1	OUR BODIES ARE LIKE A RIVER
BODIES	374 – 5	SHALL WE HAVE TANGIBLE BODIES
BODY	042 – 5	NATURE HERSELF IS THE BODY OF GOD
BODY	073 – 4	MY BODY IS OPERATED UPON
BODY	080 – 1	GOD IS RESULT OR BODY
BODY	081 – 3	SPIRIT, SOUL AND BODY

BODY	088 - 3	BODY OF THE UNIVERSE
BODY	098 - 1	BODY IS THE RESULT OF SPIRIT WORKING
BODY	098 - 1	THERE IS ONE BODY
BODY	098 - 1	THE BODY BEING THE RESULT
BODY	098 - 2	BODY MEANS THE ENTIRE
BODY	098 - 3	THE WORD BODY AS USED IN THE SCIENCE
BODY	099 - 1	BODY OF THE UNSEEN MAN
BODY	099 - 2	BODY IS ALWAYS AN EFFECT
BODY	099 - 2	BODY EXPRESSES INTELLIGENCE
BODY	099 - 2	BODY IS IN CONSCIOUSNESS
BODY	099 - 3	BODY IS NECESSARY TO THIS PLANE
BODY	099 - 4	THE REALITY OF THE BODY
BODY	099 - 4	NOT ONLY THE BODY BUT THE MIND
BODY	100 - 2	BODY OF THE UNIVERSE CANNOT HELP CHANGING
BODY	100 - 2	BODY THE MANIFESTATION
BODY	100 - 3	OUR PHYSICAL BODY IS LIKE
BODY	104 - 3	ONES BODY NOW OCCUPIES
BODY	104 - 4	A BODY WITHIN A BODY TO INFINITY
BODY	111 - 4	BODY OF GOD
BODY	115 - 3	BODY EFFECT AFFAIRS, CONDITIONS, HEALTH
BODY	116 - 2	THE OBJECTIVE MAN IS BODY
BODY	117 - 3	OUR BODY IS REALLY ONE WITH THE BODY OF GOD
BODY	117 - 3	BODY DOES NOT KNOW IT IS BODY
BODY	130 - 5	BODY IS AFFECTED BY HIS THINKING
BODY	177 - 3	BODY DEVOID OF MENTALITY
BODY	183 - 3	OR THE BODY OF ONE'S AFFAIRS
BODY	197 - 1	BODY WHICH IS UNCONSCIOUS FORM
BODY	197 - 1	THE BODY NEITHER THINKS SEES HEARS FEELS
BODY	212 - 5	WHAT WE CALL THE HUMAN BODY
BODY	222 - 3	DESTROYS THE PHYSICAL BODY
BODY	228 - 3	BODY OF MY PATIENT RIGHT NOW
BODY	228 - 3	THERE IS A PERFECT BODY
BODY	231 - 4	THE BODY IS AN EFFECT AND NOT A CURSE
BODY	231 - 4	NOT TREAT THE BODY
BODY	240 - 3	BODY IS PURE SPIRIT SUBSTANCE
BODY	242 - 1	PART OF THE BODY OF GOD
BODY	242 - 3	BODY REFLECTS THE PERFECT MOTION
BODY	243 - 4	BODY IS NOW A RECEPTIVE CHANNEL
BODY	247 - 1	BODY IS PURE SPIRITUAL SUBSTANCE
BODY	249 - 2	BODY IS CONTROLLED
BODY	373 - 4	BODY IS A CONCRETE MANIFESTATION
BODY	373 - 4	IS THE BODY OF GOD
BODY	374 - 2	THE BODY LIES COLD INERT
BODY	374 - 4	SOUL NEEDS A PHYSICAL BODY
BODY	375 - 1	CREATE AND SUSTAIN A BODY HERE
BODY	375 - 1	SOUL CREATES A NEW BODY
BODY	375 - 2	BODY WITHIN THE PHYSICAL ONE
BODY	375 - 2	BODY WITHIN A BODY TO INFINITY
BODY	376 - 1	THERE IS A NATURAL BODY
BODY	376 - 1	THERE IS A SPIRITUAL BODY
BODY	376 - 1	BODY WITHIN A BODY TO INFINITY
BODY	376 - 2	FUTURE BODY WILL RESEMBLE THIS ONE
BODY	476 - 5	MEAT FOR THE BODY
BODY	477 - 1	BODY HE PROVES THAT HE IS A REAL
BODY	491 - 6	IS NOT THE ETERNAL BODY

BODY	493 - 4	BODY IS SOME MANIFESTATION
BODY OF GOD	098 - 1	VISIBLE AND INVISIBLE IS THE BODY OF GOD
BOEHME	329 - 2	PEOPLE LIKE JACOB BOEHME A COBBLER
BOILS	248 - 3	BOILS, ECZEMA AND OTHER SKIN
BONDAGE	025 - 2	CREATE MAN IN BONDAGE AND LEAVE HIM BOUND
BONDAGE	025 - 3	BONDAGE IS NOT GOD ORDAINED
BONDAGE	033 - 2	THE BONDAGE OF HUMANITY
BONDAGE	107 - 2	BONDAGE CANNOT BE REAL FROM THE
BONDAGE	108 - 2	BONDAGE IS AN EXPERIENCE
BONDAGE	110 - 3	BONDAGE IS AN INVENTION OF IGNORANCE
BONDAGE	260 - 2	NO BONDAGE IN THE SPIRIT
BONDAGE	260 - 2	SPIRIT FREES US FROM EVERY TYPE OF BONDAGE
BONDAGE	392 - 1	EITHER FREEDOM OR BONDAGE
BONDAGE	395 - 1	SELF-IMPOSED BONDAGE
BONDAGE	417 - 2	FREEDOM RATHER THAN BONDAGE
BONDAGE	434 - 4	BONDAGE OF THESE FALSE IMPRESSIONS
BONDAGE	484 - 5	BONDAGE BUT ONE OF ADOPTION
BONDAGE	488 - 2	NOT ONE OF BONDAGE
BONDAGE	500 - 4	BONDAGE TO THOSE WHO MISUSE
BONDS	288 - 2	BREAK THE BONDS
BONE	402 - 2	INTO FLESH AND BONE
BONES	219 - 2	TO MENTALLY SET BONES
BORDERLAND	060 - 3	BORDERLAND OF A NEW EXPERIENCE
BOREDOM	384 - 4	WOULD BE ETERNAL BOREDOM
BORN	169 - 4	MAN IS BORN OF SPIRIT
BORN	239 - 3	LEAVES NOTHING TO BE BORN
BORN	281 - 4	BORN OUT OF A MENTAL CONCEPT
BORN	388 - 1	WE ARE BORN OF ETERNAL DAY
BORN	471 - 5	BORN INTO THE KNOWLEDGE OF TRUTH
BORN	471 - 5	BORN OF WATER AND SPIRIT
BORN	471 - 6	BORN OF THE SPIRIT IS SPIRIT
BORN	471 - 7	BEING BORN OF THE SPIRIT
BORN	471 - 7	BORN OF THE SPIRIT UNLESS WE
BORN	503 - 7	IS BORN OF LOVE IS BORN OF GOD
BORN AGAIN	471 - 5	MAN BE BORN AGAIN
BORNE	329 - 1	BORNE WITNESS TO THE SAME TRUTH
BORROW	446 - 2	BORROW ITS LIGHT FROM ANOTHER
BORROWED	415 - 1	LIGHT CANNOT BE BORROWED FROM
BOSOM	443 - 3	THE BOSOM OF THE FATHER
BOSOM	368 - 3	CHRIST COMES FROM THE BOSOM
BOSOM	369 - 3	LIVING FOREVER IN THE BOSOM OF THE FATHER
BOSOM	503 - 3	BOSOM OF THE UNIVERSE
BOTH	410 - 2	THAT BOTH THE LETTER AND THE SPIRIT
BOTHERS	381 - 2	SUBJECTIVITY AND IT BOTHERS THEM
BOTTLE	205 - 1	BOTTLE COULD NOT BE TURNED UPSIDE
BOUND	025 - 2	LEAVE HIM BOUND
BOUND	034 - 1	IT CANNOT BE BOUND
BOUND	037 - 1	BOUND BECAUSE WE ARE FIRST FREE
BOUND	096 - 3	BOUND BY ITS OWN NATURE
BOUND	120 - 1	BOUND TO BE PRODUCED IN OUR EXTERNAL
BOUND	128 - 1	BOUND BY NOTHING EXCEPT BELIEF
BOUND	133 - 6	BOUND BECAUSE WE ARE FIRST FREE
BOUND	184 - 2	SPIRIT IS NEVER BOUND
BOUND	223 - 2	BOUND BY ANY SENSE OF INFERIORITY
BOUND	226 - 4	BOUND BY MENTAL CONFUSION

BOUND	289 - 2	THEY ARE BOUND TOGETHER IN ONE
BOUND	416 - 1	BOUND IN ITS OBJECTIVE FORM
BOUNDLESS	450 - 5	BOUNDLESS SEA OF LIVINGNESS
BOUNDS	039 - 4	GOOD IS WITHOUT BOUNDS
BOUNTY	432 - 2	DIRECTLY UPON THE DIVINE BOUNTY
BRAIN	066 - 3	BRAIN OF A SOCRATES
BRAIN	073 - 1	BRAIN SEEMED TO BE
BRAIN	073 - 2	SOMETHING BEHIND THE BRAIN
BRAIN	226 - 2	BRAIN CENTERS IS ALWAYS UNRETARDED
BRAIN	374 - 3	THE BRAIN DOES NOT THINK
BRAIN	374 - 3	THINKER USING THE BRAIN
BRAIN	376 - 4	NOT THE BRAIN THAT THINKS
BRANCHES	313 - 4	YE ARE THE BRANCHES
BREAD	427 - 3	BREAD ALONE BUT BY EVERY WORD
BREAD	428 - 5	WHEN THEY ASKED FOR BREAD
BREAD AND BUTTER	451 - 3	AS IT NEEDS BREAD AND BUTTER
BREAK	288 - 2	BREAK THE BONDS OF APPARENT NECESSITY
BREAK	303 - 1	BREAK DOWN EVERYTHING EXCEPT
BREAK	452 - 5	ATTEMPT TO BREAK THROUGH THE VEIL
BREAKING	131 - 2	WITHOUT BREAKING UP THE UNITY
BREAKS	387 - 1	NO BREAKS IN ITS CONTINUITY
BREASTPLATE	495 - 2	BREASTPLATE OF RIGHTEOUSNESS COVERS
BREATH	229 - 2	WITH EVERY INDRAWN BREATH
BREATH	243 - 3	BREATH OF GOD ANIMATES CREATION
BREATH	252 - 3	EVERY BREATH YOU BREATHE
BREATH	398 - 5	VERY BREATH OF OUR BREATH
BREATHING	244 - 1	BREATHING IS NOT OBSTRUCTED
BREEDS	450 - 3	SO SUCCESS BREEDS GREATER SUCCESS
BRETHREN	449 - 4	WHO ARE MY BRETHREN
BRICK	116 - 2	STUFF FROM WHICH A BRICK IS MADE
BRIDGE	093 - 3	BRIDGE THAT PSYCHOLOGY MUST CROSS
BRIGHT	246 - 2	FUTURE IS BRIGHT WITH PROMISE
BRING	123 - 1	BRING INTO HIS EXPERIENCE
BRING	179 - 1	BRING OUT IN HIS OWN MIND
BRING	267 - 4	CAN BRING INTO HIS EXPERIENCE
BRING	466 - 1	EXPERIENCE WAS NECESSARY TO BRING
BRINGING	119 - 3	BRINGING SUCH CONDITIONS TO PASS
BRINGING	299 - 4	BRINGING INTO OUR EXPERIENCE
BROADCAST	214 - 1	HAVE BROADCAST IN ANY AGE
BROADENS	418 - 4	VISION TOWARD THE SPIRIT BROADENS
BROADER	113 - 2	GROWING INTO A BROADER DIVINITY
BROKEN LAW	202 - S	EVERY SO-CALLED BROKEN LAW
BROTHER	459 - 3	TO LOVE GOD AND OUR BROTHER
BROTHERHOOD	332 - 3	BROTHERHOOD OF MAN
BROTHERHOOD	449 - 5	LESSON IN THE BROTHERHOOD
BROTHERLY	104 - 2	SOFT NOTES OF BROTHERLY LOVE
BROTHERS	368 - 1	THAT ALL MEN ARE BROTHERS
BROTHERS	449 - 5	WITH THE TRUTH ARE BROTHERS IN IT
BROWNING	130 - 2	MUSED ROBERT BROWNING
BROWNING	169 - 1	BROWNING CALLED THIS
BROWNING	276 - 1	BROWNING THAT ALL'S LOVE YET ALL'S LAW
BROWNING	339 - 1	BROWNING SAID HE MAY DESECRATE
BRUTE	476 - 6	PHYSICAL PLANE IS TO BECOME A BRUTE
BUCKE	341 - 2	BUCKE DEFINES COSMIC CONSCIOUSNESS
BUCKE	345 - 2	BUCKE POINTS OUT THAT THE ILLUMINATION

BUCKETS	469 - 2	LET DOWN OUR OWN BUCKETS
BUDDHA	076 - 4	PERCEPTION THAT BUDDHA
BUDDHA	078 - 2	KARMIC LAW OF BUDDHA
BUDDHA	329 - 4	BUDDHA, PLATO, SOCRATES, EMERSON
BUDDHA	342 - 1	WE MAY READ BUDDHA
BUDDHA	344 - 1	THE MYSTICISM OF BUDDHA
BUDDHA	428 - 2	STORY OF JESUS OR BUDDHA
BUDDHIST	275 - 4	A METHODIST OR CATHOLIC OR BUDDHIST
BUDDHISTS	272 - 3	WHERE PEOPLE ARE BUDDHISTS
BUDDING	387 - 3	EVERYONE A BUDDING GENIUS
BUDGED	046 - 1	REFUSES TO BE BUDGED
BUGLE	104 - 2	THE BUGLE CALL WILL ECHO
BUILD	173 - 4	BUILD UP A FAITH
BUILD	255 - 3	BUILD UP NOT ONLY THE KIDNEYS
BUILDING	077 - 3	BUILDING INTO OUR MENTALITIES
BUILT	159 - 1	BUILT UP FROM BELIEF ACCEPTANCE
BUILT	318 - 1	UNIVERSE IS BUILT OUT OF BELIEF
BURDEN	127 - 4	A GREAT BURDEN IS REMOVED
BURDEN	199 - 4	SENSE OF DOUBT AND BURDEN
BURDEN	438 - 2	BURDEN OF PAST MISTAKES
BURDENS	335 - 4	BURDENS ON THE ALTAR OF LOVE
BURDENS	335 - 4	MAN WOULD HAVE NO BURDENS
BURIED	451 - 4	BURIED IN THE SUBJECTIVE MIND
BURN	311 - 2	BURN ARE PASSING BACK
BURNING	329 - 2	LAW FROM A BURNING BUSH
BURNISHED	495 - 1	BURNISHED WITH CLEAR VISION
BURNS	414 - 3	SPARK WHICH BURNS AT THE CENTER
BURNS	415 - 1	BURNS FROM THE OIL
BUSINESS	200 - 1	OUR BUSINESS TO GIVE THE TREATMENT
BUSINESS	200 - 1	BUSINESS OF THE LAW TO EXECUTE IT
BUSINESS	272 - 1	GO ABOUT HIS BUSINESS
BUSINESS	291 - 3	BUSINESS IS BAD THERE IS NO ACTIVITY
BUSINESS	300 - 4	MORE ACTIVITY IN HIS BUSINESS
BUSINESS	382 - 3	OUR BUSINESS TO EXPLAIN ALL MENTAL

C

CABBAGE	402 - 2	HOW CORNED BEEF AND CABBAGE
CABBAGE	455 - 6	KNEELING BESIDE HIS CABBAGE
CABBAGES	117 - 1	CABBAGES AND KINGS ARE ALL
CABBAGES	174 - 1	CABBAGES INTO BEING
CABBAGES	235 - 5	CABBAGES AND KINGS
CABBAGES	354 - 3	CABBAGE SEED WE GET CABBAGES
CAESAR	276 - 3	RENDER THEREFORE UNTO CAESAR
CAESAR	428 - 2	CAESAR AND A NAPOLEON
CALAMITY	295 - 2	NO MISFORTUNE NO CALAMITY
CALF	466 - 6	BRING HITHER THE FATTED CALF
CALF	467 - 3	CALF REPRESENTS THE ABUNDANCE OF GOD'S
CALL	038 - 3	CALL IT WHAT YOU WILL
CALL	148 - 4	DAY THEY THAT CALL UPON ME
CALL	174 - 2	BEFORE THEY CALL WILL I ANSWER
CALL	364 - 2	CALL IT UNIVERSAL SUBJECTIVITY
CALL	394 - 1	CALL TEMPORARY FORMS INTO BEING

CALLS	392 - 3	MAN CALLS IT FORTH INTO EXPRESSION
CALM	184 - 3	IN PERFECT PEACE AND CALM
CALM	218 - 3	A CALM SERENITY OF THOUGHT
CALM	246 - 4	CALM TO GIVE POISE
CALM	246 - 4	AND POISED IN AN ETERNAL CALM
CALM	247 - 1	IN TRUTH AND IN COMPLETE CALM
CALM	249 - 1	I AM CALM, POISED AND AT PEACE
CALM	255 - 1	SUSTAINED IN A DEEP INNER CALM
CALM	272 - 1	CALM PEACEFUL SENSE
CALM	283 - 2	BE CALM AND DISPASSIONATE
CALM	456 - 1	CALM WORDS OF JESUS
CAME	064 - 3	CREATION CAME INTO BEING
CAME	465 - 1	CAME TO HIMSELF
CAN	481 - 5	POWER WHICH CAN AND WILL WORK
CANCELS	188 - 3	CANCELS AND ERASES EVERYTHING
CANCER	175 - 2	REMOVAL OF A CANCER
CANCER	236 - 2	BE CANCER FIBROID TUMOR
CANCERS	235 - 2	IN TREATING CANCERS AND TUMORS
CANDLE	430 - 2	MAN IS THE CANDLE
CAN DO	170 - 2	CAN DO ALL THINGS
CAN DO	315 - 3	CAN DO JUST THIS
CAN DO	364 - 3	WITHIN THAT WE CAN DO IT
CAN DO	400 - 1	IT CAN DO NOTHING ELSE
CANNOT	051 - 1	THAT WHICH WE CANNOT
CANNOT	052 - 5	IT CANNOT AND WILL NOT
CANNOT	055 - 2	CANNOT OPERATE THROUGH HIM
CANNOT	107 - 2	CANNOT CHANGE ITS INHERENT REALITY
CANNOT	166 - 2	CANNOT SUGGEST ANYTHING TO HIM
CANNOT	199 - 2	CANNOT AND DOES NOT ARGUE
CANNOT	203 - 2	CANNOT HEAL SUCCESSFULLY
CANNOT	317 - 1	CANNOT ATTACH ITSELF TO THIS SPIRITUAL
CANNOT	336 - 5	CANNOT BE A LAW IN THE UNIVERSE
CANNOT	338 - 4	CANNOT CONCEIVE IMPERFECT IDEAS
CANNOT	481 - 4	WE CANNOT ASK AMISS
CAPABLE	242 - 5	CAPABLE OF EXPRESSING
CAPACITIES	113 - 2	REPRESENT SPIRITUAL CAPACITIES
CAPACITIES	371 - 1	CAPACITIES GO WITH US BEYOND THE GRAVE
CAPACITY	033 - 2	CAPACITY TO UNDERSTAND
CAPACITY	095 - 2	ENLARGING OUR CAPACITY TO KNOW
CAPACITY	118 - 2	CAPACITY TO UNDERSTAND IT
CAPACITY	122 - 2	CAPACITY TO CONSCIOUSLY KNOW
CAPACITY	187 - 1	CAPACITY TO IMAGINE WHAT LIFE IS
CAPACITY	287 - 1	MENTAL CAPACITY TO COMPREHEND
CAPACITY	390 - 4	INFINITE AS IS MAN'S CAPACITY
CAPRICE	078 - 2	BE CONFRONTED WITH CAPRICE
CARE	216 - 3	NOT SENSITIVE TO CARE
CARE	216 - 3	IT IS SENSITIVE TO CARE
CARED FOR	216 - 3	DEFINITION OF CURED IS CARED FOR
CAREFUL	047 - 2	CAREFUL WHAT HE THINKS
CAREFUL	048 - 2	CAREFUL NOT TO THINK
CAREFUL	276 - 1	CAREFUL TO FOLLOW A CONSTRUCTIVE
CAREFUL	400 - 1	CAREFUL TO DIFFERENTIATE
CAREFULLY	195 - 2	WE SHOULD CAREFULLY CONSIDER
CAREFULLY	434 - 4	CAREFULLY CHOOSE WHAT WE ARE TO THINK
CARES	048 - 1	NEITHER KNOWS NOR CARES

CARES	149 - 4	A GOD WHO CARES MORE FOR ONE PERSON
CARES	269 - 2	NEITHER KNOWS NOR CARES WHO USES IT
CARING	127 - 2	CANNOT IMAGINE GOD NOT CARING
CARING	403 - 3	WITHOUT CARING WHAT IT RECEIVES
CARING	403 - 3	WITHOUT CARING WHAT IT CREATES
CARNAL	484 - 3	CARNAL MIND IS NOT SUBJECT TO
CARNAL	484 - 3	CARNAL MIND SYMBOLIZES ANYTHING
CARPENTER	345 - 1	WHETHER IT WAS EDWARD CARPENTER
CARRIES	348 - 2	CARRIES AROUND WITH HIM
CARRIES	445 - 5	IT CARRIES A BLESSING WITH IT
CARRY	225 - 1	DO NOT CARRY THE THOUGHT
CARRY	371 - 2	MAN MUST CARRY WITH HIM
CARRY	409 - 5	WORDS CARRY THE MIND FORWARD
CART	340 - 3	IN A CART
CASE	126 - 2	BUT SUCH IS NOT THE CASE
CASE	175 - 5	HAVE TO WORK ON A CASE
CASE	200 - 3	EACH CASE IS SPECIFIC
CASE	228 - 3	UNTO THE CASE
CASES	414 - 1	CASES REPRESENT BUT DIFFERENT
CAST	140 - 2	WHATEVER IS CAST INTO IT
CAST OUT	054 - 2	CAST OUT THAT
CAST OUT	448 - 3	CAST OUT EVIL BY THE POWER OF EVIL
CASTS	396 - 1	FORM AND CASTS THEM BACK
CASTS	418 - 4	CASTS OUT THE IMAGE
CASTS	474 - 5	IT CASTS US FROM A PERFECT STATE
CASUAL	429 - 1	FROM CASUAL OBSERVATION
CASUALLY	200 - 2	IF SOMEONE SAYS TO YOU CASUALLY
CATEGORY	363 - 4	JESUS IN A DIFFERENT CATGEGORY
CATHOLIC	275 - 4	CATHOLIC OR BUDDHIST
CAUGHT	217 - 2	CAUGHT IN THE NEGATIVE STREAM
CAUGHT	317 - 1	CAUGHT IN ITS MENTAL VIBRATION
CAULIFLOWER	092 - 2	YOU MUST PLANT CAULIFLOWER
CAUSATION	053 - 3	WE ARE DEALING WITH CAUSATION
CAUSATION	072 - 2	NO ONE HAS EVER SEEN CAUSATION
CAUSATION	072 - 2	CAUSATION IS INVISIBLE
CAUSATION	102 - 5	UNDERSTAND ABSOLUTE CAUSATION
CAUSATION	145 - 3	THOUGHT LAYS HOLD OF CAUSATION
CAUSATION	205 - 3	CAUSATION IN MOTION
CAUSATION	235 - 3	GOD IS THE ONE CAUSATION
CAUSATION	237 - 3	MEANING OF CAUSATION
CAUSATION	321 - 1	CURRENTS OF CAUSATION
CAUSATION	354 - 1	IS MOVEMENT OF CAUSATION
CAUSATION	354 - 2	NOT SPIRITUAL CAUSATION
CAUSATION	407 - 3	MIND OF GOD IS ALL CAUSATION
CAUSATION	413 - 5	CAUSATION IS INDEPENDENT OF GOOD
CAUSATION	441 - 3	DEPTHS OF CREATIVE CAUSATION
CAUSE	031 - 1	NOT FATE BUT CAUSE AND EFFECT
CAUSE	035 - 3	IT IS FIRST CAUSE IT IS GOD
CAUSE	036 - 1	THE CAUSE OF EVERYTHING
CAUSE	036 - 2	THIS INVISIBLE CAUSE
CAUSE	036 - 2	ONE ORIGINAL CAUSE
CAUSE	052 - 5	THE LAW OF CAUSE AND EFFECT
CAUSE	053 - 3	WITH ORIGINAL CAUSE
CAUSE	058 - 2	THE LAW OF CAUSE AND EFFECT
CAUSE	060 - 4	STUDY OF FIRST CAUSE

CAUSE	063 - 1	NATURE OF THE INVISIBLE CAUSE
CAUSE	068 - 3	THE ULTIMATE CAUSE
CAUSE	068 - 4	ONLY CAUSE OF ALL THAT IS
CAUSE	069 - 1	IS ITS INITIAL CAUSE
CAUSE	071 - 1	EVOLVED FROM AN INTELLIGENT CAUSE
CAUSE	075 - 3	NO ONE HAS SEEN CAUSE
CAUSE	076 - 1	CAUSE OF THE OBJECT PERCEIVED
CAUSE	088 - 2	CAUSE MEDIUM AND EFFECT
CAUSE	101 - 3	IS SUBJECT TO ITS CAUSE
CAUSE	101 - 5	BOTH CAUSE AND EFFECT ARE SPIRITUAL
CAUSE	138 - 4	CAUSE OF EVERYTHING THAT HAS BEEN
CAUSE	153 - 2	CAUSE AND EFFECT ARE BUT TWO SIDES OF
CAUSE	153 - 2	IS BOTH CAUSE AND EFFECT
CAUSE	184 - 5	PERFECT CAUSE MUST PRODUCE
CAUSE	186 - 4	LAW OF CAUSE AND EFFECT
CAUSE	187 - 2	OF THE NATURE OF ITS CAUSE
CAUSE	189 - 2	BY CHANGING THE MENTAL CAUSE
CAUSE	194 - 1	ITS ESSENCE LAW AND CAUSE
CAUSE	194 - 5	CAUSE WE HAVE SET IN MOTION
CAUSE	201 - 5	FIRST HAVE A SUBJECTIVE CAUSE
CAUSE	217 - 1	CAUSE MEDIUM NOR EFFECT
CAUSE	222 - 3	GETTING AT ITS CAUSE
CAUSE	222 - 3	MEAN GETTING AT THE MENTAL CAUSE
CAUSE	231 - 4	NOT A CAUSE
CAUSE	233 - 2	PERCEIVE A DIFFERENT CAUSE
CAUSE	233 - 2	A PERFECT CAUSE BACK OF WHAT APPEARS
CAUSE	236 - 6	ONLY ONE FIRST CAUSE
CAUSE	264 - 3	SPIRIT IS THE ONLY CAUSE
CAUSE	296 - 1	THAT CAUSE AND EFFECT ARE THE SAME
CAUSE	305 - 5	THE LAW OF CAUSE AND EFFECT
CAUSE	354 - 1	PASSING FROM CAUSE TO EFFECT
CAUSE	362 - 1	FOUND ITS SPIRITUAL CAUSE
CAUSE	391 - 5	USE OF THE LAW OF CAUSE AND EFFECT
CAUSE	395 - 1	PERFECT CAUSE MUST PRODUCE
CAUSE	395 - 1	LAW OF CAUSE AND EFFECT IN OUR INDIVIDUAL
CAUSE	399 - 2	CAUSE BEING THAT WHATEVER
CAUSE	401 - 2	CAUSE AND EFFECT OF ITSELF
CAUSE	404 - 1	CIRCUMSTANCE CAUSE AND EFFECT
CAUSE	406 - 4	FINDS A NEW CAUSE AT WORK
CAUSE	431 - 4	CAUSE AND EFFECT
CAUSE	448 - 1	CAUSE OF THE MATERIAL
CAUSE	494 - 4	CAUSE IS FROM WITHIN
CAUSE AND EFFECT	110 - 3	LAWS OF CAUSE AND EFFECT IN THE UNIVERSE
CAUSE AND EFFECT	144 - 2	CAUSE AND EFFECT ARE REALLY ONE
CAUSE AND EFFECT	212 - 3	THE LAW OF CAUSE AND EFFECT
CAUSE AND EFFECT	303 - 2	ACCORDING TO THE LAW OF CAUSE AND EFFECT
CAUSE AND EFFECT	321 - 2	CAUSE AND EFFECT ARE BUT TWO SIDES
CAUSE AND EFFECT	401 - 2	THE LAW OF CAUSE AND EFFECT
CAUSE AND EFFECT	450 - 2	STATING THE LAW OF CAUSE AND EFFECT
CAUSED	378 - 1	ARE NOT CAUSED BY SPIRITS
CAUSELESS	069 - 3	IT MUST BE CAUSELESS
CAUSELESS	477 - 6	CAUSELESS OR SELF-EXISTENT ONE
CAUSE OF ALL	306 - 1	CAUSE OF ALL THAT IS OR IS TO BE
CAUSES	235 - 4	CAUSES ARE REMOVED BY
CAUSES	393 - 3	HIS DEMAND CAUSES ORIGINAL MIND

CAUSES	406 – 4	MIND IS THE REALM OF CAUSES
CAUSES	414 – 1	LEVEL OF THOSE SECONDARY CAUSES
CAUSES	444 – 4	SCIENCE SEEKS TO JOIN CAUSES
CAUSES	492 – 3	WE NEVER SEE CAUSES
CAUSING	130 – 6	CAUSING A CORRESPONDING ACTION
CEASE	070 – 2	THEY CANNOT CEASE
CEASE	109 – 3	WE SHALL CEASE TO SUFFER
CEASE	111 – 3	CEASE DOING EVIL AND DO GOOD
CEASE	161 – 2	CEASE CONTEMPLATING THE UNIVERSE
CEASE	390 – 5	NOR WILL IT EVER CEASE TO BE
CEASE	418 – 4	WE MAY CEASE EXPERIENCING
CEASING	497 – 1	PRAY WITHOUT CEASING
CELESTIAL	128 – 4	ALL LIFE IN A CELESTIAL GLORY
CELESTIAL	376 – 1	THERE ARE CELESTIAL BODIES
CEMENT	094 – 2	THE CEMENT OF MATTER
CENSURE	438 – 5	CENSURE WHEN WE MIGHT PRAISE
CENTER	082 – 1	THE CENTER AND CIRCUMFERENCE
CENTER	094 – 1	AT THE CENTER OF OUR BEING
CENTER	106 – 1	SELF-CONSCIOUS THINKING CENTER
CENTER	112 – 4	ABSOLUTE STANDS OPEN AT THE CENTER
CENTER	122 – 2	CENTER OF GOD-CONSCIOUSNESS
CENTER	130 – 6	THINKING CENTER IN A UNIVERSAL MIND
CENTER	170 – I	CENTER OF THE PRACTITIONER'S OWN
CENTER	239 – 2	KNOWN AS THE CENTER OF LOVE
CENTER	239 – 2	OUR HEART IS A LIVING CENTER
CENTER	249 – 1	THE CENTER OF MY BEING IS
CENTER	307 – 2	THE CENTER AND CIRCUMFERENCE
CENTER	323 – 2	CENTER OF GOD-CONSCIOUSNESS
CENTER	323 – 3	YOU ARE A CENTER IN THIS ONE
CENTER	330 – 2	WHOSE CENTER IS EVERYWHERE
CENTER	346 – 1	INTO THE VERY CENTER OF REALITY
CENTER	363 – 4	AT THE CENTER OF HIS OWN BEING
CENTER	366 – 3	THOU ART THE CENTER AND CIRCUMFERENCE
CENTER	391 – 3	AT THE CENTER OF MAN'S BEING
CENTER	404 – 4	THE DIVINE IS THE CENTER
CENTER	406 – 1	WE CENTER OUR ATTENTION
CENTER	406 – 2	AT THE CENTER OF ALL FORM
CENTER	406 – 2	SPIRIT IS AT THE CENTER OF EVERYTHING
CENTER	409 – 4	CENTER OF EVERYMAN'S LIFE
CENTER	414 – 4	AT THE CENTER OF THE UNIVERSE
CENTER	415 – 2	CENTER OF GOD CONSCIOUSNESS
CENTER	445 – 3	FLOWING FROM A DIVINE CENTER
CENTER	486 – 2	EXACTLY AT THE CENTER OF ITSELF
CENTERED	162 – 2	FAITH IS CENTERED IN
CENTERED	195 – 4	HOLD THOUGHT CENTERED
CENTERED	489 – 4	POWER OF YOUR MEDITATION IS CENTERED
CENTERS	035 – 2	CENTERS OF EXPRESSION THROUGH US
CENTERS	038 – 3	CONSCIOUS CENTERS OF LIFE
CENTERS	331 – 3	CENTERS OF GOD CONSCIOUSNESS
CENTERS	419 – 3	INDIVIDUALIZED CENTERS OF GOD
CENTURION	161 – 1	CENTURION CAME TO JESUS AND ASKED HIM
CENTURION	437 – 1	CENTURION WOULD NOT ALLOW JESUS
CERTAIN	147 – 5	BE CERTAIN IN OUR OWN MINDS
CERTAIN	153 – 5	WE CAN BE CERTAIN THAT THERE IS
CERTAIN	190 – 1	BEING A CERTAIN MENTAL ATTITUDE

CERTAIN	318 - 3	SHOULD BE CERTAIN TO DO SO
CERTAIN	342 - 4	CERTAIN EVIDENCE THAT THEY
CERTAIN	363 - 4	CERTAIN THAT HE IS BELOVED
CERTAIN	377 - 3	ONE THING IS CERTAIN
CERTAIN	419 - 1	CERTAIN THAT WE NOW HAVE THIS DESIRE
CERTAIN	441 - 1	BUT CERTAIN OF THEMSELVES
CERTAIN	450 - 3	CERTAIN OF THE OUTCOME
CERTAINTY	096 - 4	MATHEMATICAL CERTAINTY AND PRECISION
CERTAINTY	180 - 3	ABSOLUTE CERTAINTY OF HIMSELF
CERTAINTY	289 - 3	CONFIDENCE, PEACE AND CERTAINTY
CERTAINTY	445 - 2	CERTAINTY BEHIND HIM
CHAFF	429 - 2	GRIND THE CHAFF OF UNREALITY
CHAGRIN	440 - 7	DISCOVER TO THEIR GREAT CHAGRIN
CHAGRINED	059 - 1	DISAPPOINTED NOR CHAGRINED
CHAGRINS	491 - 2	TEMPORARY CHAGRINS OF LIFE
CHAIN	246 - 2	THE ONE UNBROKEN CHAIN OF LIFE
CHAINS	314 - 1	THE CHAINS HAD NO REALITY
CHAIR	200 - 1	DROP A CHAIR OVER THE SIDE
CHALICE	246 - 4	CHALICE OF THE HEART
CHALK	279 - 1	RUB A CHALK MARK OFF A BOARD
CHALK	412 - 2	WE HOLD THE CHALK
CHAMPION	422 - 3	NEEDS NO CHAMPION
CHANCE	103 - 1	NOTHING HAPPENS BY CHANCE
CHANCE	233 - 2	BY REASON OR BY CHANCE
CHANCE	305 - 5	UPON CHANCE BUT UPON THE LAW
CHANGE	052 - 4	THIS LAW WE CANNOT CHANGE
CHANGE	053 - 3	IS SUBJECT TO CHANGE
CHANGE	054 - 2	CHANGE THE CONSCIOUSNESS
CHANGE	066 - 5	CHANGE INTO BUT ITSELF
CHANGE	066 - 5	ALL CHANGE OR MANIFESTATION
CHANGE	068 - 3	CHANGE INTO ANYTHING BUT ITSELF
CHANGE	068 - 4	ALL SEEMING CHANGE IS MERELY
CHANGE	083 - 3	SPIRIT CANNOT CHANGE
CHANGE	119 - 3	CONSCIOUS STATE CAN CHANGE IT
CHANGE	126 - 1	WE CAN CHANGE OUR THINKING
CHANGE	128 - 2	WE MAY CHANGE THE TREND OF CAUSATION
CHANGE	131 - 5	CHANGE IS ALWAYS TAKING PLACE WITHIN THAT
CHANGE	195 - 2	CHANGE THE DESIRE
CHANGE	216 - 3	IT HAS TO CHANGE
CHANGE	226 - 3	HAS FOUND HIMSELF UNABLE TO CHANGE
CHANGE	227 - 2	WE COULD NOT CHANGE IT
CHANGE	227 - 2	CAN CONSCIOUSLY CHANGE
CHANGE	272 - 2	CHANGE OUR MODE OF LIVING
CHANGE	285 - 4	WILL EVER CHANGE ITS OWN NATURE
CHANGE	385 - 1	NATURE DEMANDS THE CHANGE
CHANGE	385 - 1	WHEN THE CHANGE COMES
CHANGE	490 - 4	THIS CHANGE IN THE OUTER
CHANGEABLE	491 - 3	BEHIND THE VISIBLE AND CHANGEABLE
CHANGED	115 - 2	TENDENCY CAN BE CHANGED
CHANGED	322 - 2	MAY BE CONSCIOUSLY CHANGED
CHANGED	490 - 5	CHANGED FROM GLORY TO GLORY
CHANGELESS	066 - 5	IT IS THE CHANGELESS
CHANGELESS	068 - 3	ONE MUST BE CHANGELESS
CHANGELESS	101 - 2	POWER BACK OF THEM IS CHANGELESS
CHANGELESS	131 - 5	WHICH IS CHANGELESS

CHANGELESS	184 - 2	SPIRIT IS CHANGELESS REALITY
CHANGELESS	204 - 2	CHANGELESS AND IT IS MY LIFE NOW
CHANGELESS	228 - 3	ETERNAL CHANGELESS AND PERFECT
CHANGELESS	491 - 5	IN CHANGE IS THE CHANGELESS
CHANGES	131 - 6	ONLY THING THAT CHANGES IS FROM
CHANGES	150 - 2	OUR IDEA OF PRAYER CHANGES
CHANGING	100 - 2	THE UNIVERSE CANNOT HELP CHANGING
CHANGING	216 - 3	CHANGING FOREVER TAKING ON NEW
CHANNEL	040 - 3	CHANNEL OF OUR OWN MINDS
CHANNEL	232 - 2	CHANNEL FOR GOOD TO FLOW
CHANNEL	243 - 3	THIS CHANNEL MUST BE PERFECT
CHANNEL	243 - 4	BODY IS NOW A RECEPTIVE CHANNEL
CHANNELS	045 - 3	FLOW INTO PARTICULAR CHANNELS
CHANNELS	113 - 2	CHANNELS REPRESENT SPIRITUAL CAPACITIES
CHANNELS	243 - 3	CHANNELS OF PURE RECEPTIVITY
CHANNELS	486 - 5	CHANNELS OF CREATIVE ENERGY
CHAOS	043 - 2	COSMOS AND NOT CHAOS
CHAOS	053 - 5	FROM CHAOS AND OLD NIGHT
CHAOS	146 - 4	WE ARE CREATING CHAOS
CHAOS	187 - 3	OUT OF ANY CHAOS WE CAN
CHARACTER	185 - 3	SOME WEAKNESS OF CHARACTER
CHARACTER	222 - 4	CHARACTER OF ONE'S THOUGHTS
CHARACTER	384 - 3	ANYTHING WITH US BUT OUR CHARACTER
CHARACTER	442 - 4	SOME FLAW IN HUMAN CHARACTER
CHARACTERISTIC	416 - 2	CHARACTERISTIC OF THE SUBJECTIVE LAW
CHARACTERISTICS	043 - 2	TWO FUNDAMENTAL CHARACTERISTICS
CHARACTERISTICS	412 - 1	TAKE ON ALL ITS CHARACTERISTICS
CHARGED	396 - 1	LAW IS CHARGED WITH THE POWER
CHARITY	301 - 3	CHARITY HAS EVER GIVEN TO IT
CHASED	310 - 2	PHYSICS HAS CHASED THIS FORM
CHEAT	153 - 2	WE CANNOT CHEAT PRINCIPLE
CHEER	231 - 2	WITH FRIENDLINESS AND GOOD CHEER
CHEER	438 - 5	WORDS OF CHEER AND FORGIVENESS
CHEERFULLY	232 - 2	FREELY, GENEROUSLY, CHEERFULLY
CHEERFULNESS	302 - 2	CHEERFULNESS INSTEAD OF DEPRESSION
CHEMICAL	254 - 3	CHEMICAL REQUIREMENT
CHEMICAL	414 - 3	A LAW AS IS CHEMICAL AFFINITY
CHEMICALIZE	451 - 5	CHEMICALIZE OPPOSING IDEAS
CHEMISTRY	086 - 2	LAWS OF CHEMISTRY AND PHYSICS
CHIEF	453 - 6	CHIEF AMONG THESE ERRORS
CHILD	041 - 3	CHILD HAS FROLICKED WITH
CHILD	210 - 4	CHILD ELSE ONE MIGHT HEAL
CHILD	361 - 3	I AM THE CHILD OF JOY
CHILD	456 - 3	CHILD IS LIVED IN NATURAL GOODNESS
CHILD-BIRTH	251 - 3	TREATMENT FOR CHILD-BIRTH
CHILD-LIKE	443 - 1	CHILD-LIKE MIND IS MORE RECEPTIVE
CHILDREN	211 - 2	CHILDREN ARE HAPPY FREE SPONTANEOUS
CHILDREN	364 - 2	CHILDREN OF THE MOST HIGH
CHILDREN	438 - 5	IN THE TRAINING OF CHILDREN
CHILDREN	456 - 3	BECOME AS LITTLE CHILDREN
CHOICE	042 - 6	SPONTANEOUS CHOICE VOLITION
CHOICE	043 - 3	PERSONAL VOLITION OF CHOICE
CHOICE	058 - 3	A POWER OF CHOICE
CHOICE	092 - 2	NO CHOICE AS TO WHAT IT IS TO PRODUCE
CHOICE	100 - 2	VOLITION, CHOICE OR WILL

CHOICE	143 - 3	EVERY SECOND THERE IS CHOICE
CHOICE	196 - 2	HIS OWN CHOICE
CHOICE	220 - 5	BY YOUR OWN CHOICE YOU DECIDE
CHOICE	272 - 2	OUR CORRECT CHOICE WILL BE
CHOICE	272 - 3	HOW TO MAKE A CHOICE
CHOICE	273 - 1	MAKE A CHOICE
CHOICE	301 - 3	MIND HAS NO CHOICE BUT
CHOICE	390 - 2	IT HAS VOLITION WILL CHOICE
CHOICE	398 - 1	IT HAS NO OTHER CHOICE
CHOICELESS	143 - 3	WE CANNOT LIVE A CHOICELESS LIFE
CHOOSE	092 - 2	IF IT COULD CHOOSE IT COULD REJECT
CHOOSE	195 - 5	MAN HAS THE ABILITY TO CHOOSE
CHOOSE	412 - 1	WE SHOULD CHOOSE
CHOOSE	412 - 1	LET US CHOOSE TO BE IDENTIFIED
CHOOSE	461 - 2	CHOOSE WHOM THEY WOULD SERVE
CHOOSES	081 - 5	IT IS WILL BECAUSE IT CHOOSES
CHOOSES	281 - 4	AS HE CHOOSES TO SEE THEM
CHOOSING	110 - 2	POSSIBILITY OF CHOOSING
CHOOSING	459 - 1	CHOOSING OF HOW WHERE WHY
CHOSEN	144 - 1	EXPERIENCING THAT WHICH IS CHOSEN
CHRIST	034 - 1	MEANING OF THE WORD CHRIST
CHRIST	127 - 3	CHRIST IS THE SPIRIT WHICH CONSTRUCTIVELY
CHRIST	127 - 3	ONLY THE SPIRIT OF CHRIST CAN SUCCEED
CHRIST	359 - 2	CHRIST IS THE EMBODIMENT
CHRIST	359 - 3	CHRIST COMES ALIKE TO EACH
CHRIST	265 - 1	I AM THE CHRIST
CHRIST	268 - 2	IDEA OF CHRIST TO HUMANITY
CHRIST	272 - 4	BETWEEN GOD AND MAN EXCEPT CHRIST
CHRIST	272 - 4	CHRIST MEANS THE TRUTH
CHRIST	273 - 5	WE HAVE THE MIND OF CHRIST
CHRIST	307 - 3	CHRIST SHALL GIVE THEE LIGHT
CHRIST	310 - 4	IN CHRIST ALL ARE MADE ALIVE
CHRIST	337 - 3	THE MAN JESUS BECAME THE CHRIST
CHRIST	357 - 1	WHO IS CHRIST
CHRIST	357 - 3	CHRIST MEANS THE UNIVERSAL IDEA
CHRIST	357 - 3	CHRIST IS REVEALED THROUGH HIM
CHRIST	359 - 2	CHRIST IS A UNIVERSAL PRESENCE
CHRIST	359 - 3	CHRIST IS NOT A PERSON BUT A PRINCIPLE
CHRIST	359 - 3	THEY BECOME THE CHRIST
CHRIST	361 - 5	CHRIST THE IDEA OF UNIVERSAL
CHRIST	363 - 4	CHRIST IS THE IMAGE OF GOD
CHRIST	363 - 4	CHRIST IS NOT LIMITED TO ANY PERSON
CHRIST	364 - 3	WHICH WAS ALSO IN CHRIST
CHRIST	366 - 2	LOOK AFAR TO SEE THE CHRIST
CHRIST	422 - 3	THE MYSTICAL CONCEPTION OF CHRIST
CHRIST	422 - 3	A PERSON HE BECOMES THE CHRIST
CHRIST	422 - 3	IDEAS CONSTITUTES THE MYSTIC CHRIST
CHRIST	484 - 2	WE ARE THE CHRIST
CHRIST	492 - 5	CHRIST DWELLS IN US IN LOVE
CHRIST	496 - 2	WE HAVE THE MIND OF CHRIST
CHRIST	503 - 2	CHRIST IN US IS OUR HOPE AND ASSURANCE
CHRIST	503 - 5	CHRIST INDWELLING EVERY SOUL
CHRISTIAN	056 - 2	THAT IT IS CHRISTIAN
CHRISTIAN	067 - 3	CHRISTIAN RELIGION GIVES MORE
CHRISTIAN	386 - 2	MILLIONS OF THE CHRISTIAN RELIGION

CHRISTIANITY	272 - 3	BEFORE THE ADVENT OF CHRISTIANITY
CHRISTIANITY	367 - 3	THE HISTORY OF CHRISTIANITY
CHRISTIANITY	386 - 2	THE PHILOSOPHY OF CHRISTIANITY
CHRISTIAN RELIGION	386 - 2	CHRISTIAN RELIGION ITSELF RESTS
CHRISTIANS	162 - 4	CHRISTIANS WERE TEACHING
CHRISTIANS	272 - 3	WHERE PEOPLE ARE CHRISTIANS
CHRIST JESUS	357 - 3	WHICH WAS ALSO IN CHRIST JESUS
CHRIST JESUS	495 - 6	MIND WHICH WAS IN CHRIST IESUS
CHRISTLIKE	186 - 4	THE MORE GODLIKE OR CHRISTLIKE
CHRIST SPIRIT	367 - 3	HUMAN TOOK ON THE CHRIST SPIRIT
CHURCH	191 - 4	WE BELIEVE IN EVERY CHURCH
CIRCLE	087 - 2	LITTLE CIRCLE WITHIN THE BIG CIRCLE
CIRCLE	331 - 2	GOD AS THE BIG CIRCLE
CIRCLES	434 - 4	EVERYTHING MOVES IN CIRCLES
CIRCULATION	213 - 1	FLOW AND CIRCULATION OF LIFE
CIRCULATION	232 - 4	ELIMINATION AND CIRCULATION
CIRCULATION	238 - 3	PERFECT CIRCULATION
CIRCULATION	239 - 3	ELIMINATION AND CIRCULATION
CIRCULATION	247 - 3	CIRCULATION OF PURE THOUGHT
CIRCULATION	249 - 4	THERE IS A DIVINE CIRCULATION
CIRCULATION	249 - 4	ALWAYS PERFECT CIRCULATION
CIRCULATION	249 - 5	CIRCULATION IS EQUALIZED
CIRCULATION	250 - 1	THERE IS ONE CIRCULATION
CIRCULATION	250 - 2	DIVINE AND UNINHIBITED CIRCULATION
CIRCULATION	250 - 3	SPIRIT OF PERFECT CIRCULATION
CIRCULATION	251 - 4	BREATHING THE CIRCULATION
CIRCULATION	440 - 2	CIRCULATION IS RETARDED, STAGNATION RESULTS
CIRCULATORY	249 - S	CIRCULATORY SYSTEM SEEMS INADEQUATE
CIRCUMFERENCE	082 - 1	CIRCUMFERENCE OF EVERYTHING THAT EXISTS
CIRCUMFERENCE	307 - 2	THE CENTER AND CIRCUMFERENCE
CIRCUMFERENCE	330 - 2	WHOSE CIRCUMFERENCE IS NOWHERE
CIRCUMFERENCE	366 - 3	CENTER AND CIRCUMFERENCE OF MY LIFE
CIRCUMFERENCE	484 - 3	IS THE CENTER AND CIRCUMFERENCE
CIRCUMSCRIBE	113 - 2	CIRCUMSCRIBE THE INFINITE
CIRCUMSCRIBED	406 - 3	NOT CIRCUMSCRIBED BY ANY FORM
CIRCUMSTANCE	414 - 1	OF ANY EXISTING CIRCUMSTANCE
CIRCUMSTANCES	400 - 3	FORM OBJECTIVE CIRCUMSTANCES
CIRCUMSTANCES	411 - 4	THAT CIRCUMSTANCES ARE FORMED
CIRCUMSTANCES	417 - 2	OF ANY EXISTING CIRCUMSTANCES
CITIES	072 - 4	CONQUERED THE AIR BUILT CITIES
CITIZEN	463 - 4	CITIZEN REFERRED TO MEANS THE ATTEMPT
CITY	348 - 3	AS A CITY HAS ITS ATMOSPHERE
CIVIL	433 - 4	CIVIL LAWS BE ENFORCED
CIVILIZATION	072 - 4	BUILT UP A GREAT CIVILIZATION
CIVILIZATION	328 - 3	BUILT UP A WONDERFUL CIVILIZATION
CIVILIZATION	367 - 3	ENLIGHTENMENT OF MODERN CIVILIZATION
CIVILIZED	417 - 1	MORE CIVILIZED THINKS
CIVIL LAWS	433 - 4	CIVIL LAWS BE ENFORCED
CLAIM	107 - 3	MAKES A TREMENDOUS CLAIM
CLAIM	175 - 4	TO CLAIM THAT HE IS PERFECTLY NORMAL
CLAIM	204 - 2	CLAIM THAT NO FORM
CLAIM	230 - 3	DO NOT FEAR TO CLAIM THIS
CLAIM	433 - 1	CLAIM UPON GOD
CLAIM	454 - 5	CLAIM A REAL UNITY WITH GOD
CLAIMING	480 - 1	JESUS WAS CLAIMING TO BE GOD

CLAIMING	500 - 1	CLAIMING A FRONT SEAT IN HEAVEN
CLAIMS	145 - 4	THAT IT CLAIMS FOR GOD
CLAIMS	409 - 2	CLAIMS HELD TO BE TRUE ABOUT
CLAIRVOYANCE	382 - 2	POWERS OF CLAIRVOYANCE TELEPATHY
CLAIRVOYANT	354 - 1	IN WHICH CLAIRVOYANT VISION OPERATES
CLAIRVOYANTLY	353 - 4	PREVIOUS INCIDENT CLAIRVOYANTLY
CLARIFIED	220 - 4	THINKING BECOMES CLARIFIED
CLARIFIED	241 - 4	CLARIFIED THOUGHT MAKES EASY
CLARIFIED	475 - 5	THIS INNER THOUGHT IS CLARIFIED
CLARIFIES	164 - 4	CLARIFIES THE MENTALITY
CLARIFIES	270 - 5	IT CLARIFIES IT
CLARIFIES	274 - 3	IT CLARIFIES THE MENTALITY
CLARIFY	435 - 2	CLARIFY OUR OWN VISION
CLASPS	370 - 2	HIS HAND CLASPS MINE
CLASS	115 - 3	WE CLASS AS A PART OF THIS BODY
CLASS	283 - 2	NO CLASS OF PEOPLE ON EARTH
CLAY	389 - 1	GRIEVE NOT OVER ITS FORM OF CLAY
CLEAN	453 - 1	THEN IS HE CLEAN INDEED
CLEANSES	235 - 3	CLEANSES HEALS AND RENEWS EVERY ORGAN
CLEANSING	261 - 2	CLEANSING POWER OF MY WORD
CLEAR	110 - 4	WE WISH TO MAKE CLEAR
CLEAR	128 - 2	CLEAR THAT THE INFINITE AND LIMITLESS
CLEAR	204 - 3	CLEAR YOUR CONSCIOUSNESS
CLEAR	336 - 3	A CLEAR IDEA OF LIVINGNESS
CLEAR	351 - 1	CLEAR MESSAGE MAY BE RECEIVED
CLEAR	421 - 4	RECEIVES A CLEAR IMPRESSION
CLEARER	493 - 6	TO MAKE A CLEARER STATEMENT OF TRUTH
CLEAREST	170 - 2	CLEAREST WHO HAS
CLEARLY	133 - 2	PROVIDED HE CAN CLEARLY CONCEIVE
CLEARLY	399 - 4	THINK CLEARLY AND ALLOW
CLEARLY	410 - 2	WE STATE CLEARLY IN WORDS
CLEARNESS	230 - 5	CLEARNESS OF SPIRITUAL VISION
CLEAR THINKING	405 - 4	PEACE, CLEAR THINKING AND HAPPINESS
CLEAR UP	166 - 2	CLEAR UP IN HIS OWN THOUGHT
CLEAR UP	303 - 1	CLEAR UP HIS OWN SUBJECTIVE
CLEAVAGE	312 - 3	IF YOUR MIND HAD A SHARP CLEAVAGE
CLEAVE	432 - 2	WE MUST CLEAVE TO THE GOOD
CLIMATE	259 - 1	HARMONIOUS IN EVERY CLIMATE
CLING	162 - 5	CLING STEADFASTLY TO THE KNOWLEDGE
CLING	267 - 2	AND CLING TO UNHAPPINESS
CLINGING	302 - 3	CLINGING TO ANYBODY OR ANYTHING
CLINIC	168 - 4	DOCTORS MIGHT IN A CLINIC
CLOAK	177 - 2	AN APPARENTLY IMPERFECT CLOAK
CLOAK	234 - 1	PERFECT OUTWARD CLOAK
CLOD	340 - 3	MAN FROM THE CLOD
CLOD	389 - 1	FREED NOW FROM CLOD
CLOSELY	155 - 1	PRAYER, FAITH AND BELIEF ARE CLOSELY
CLOSET	431 - 3	WE MUST ENTER THE CLOSET
CLOTH	439 - 2	NEW CLOTH ON AN OLD GARMENT
CLOTHE	375 - 1	CLOTHE ITSELF IN FORM
CLOTHE	492 - 2	CLOTHE ITSELF IN A BODY
CLOTHED	065 - 4	CLOTHED THIS SUBTLE ESSENCE
CLOTHED	373 - 3	CLOTHED ITSELF WITH THE FORM
CLOTHED	491 - 6	CLOTHED UPON FROM HEAVEN
CLOTHES	491 - 7	IT IMPLIES THAT IMMORTALITY CLOTHES

CLOUDS	258 - 5	LOVE THE CLOUDS
CLUTTER	232 - 4	CLUTTER UP OUR LIVES
CO-CREATOR	157 - 2	MAN BECOMES A CO-CREATOR WITH GOD
COERCE	140 - 3	WE NEED NOT COERCE
COERCE	264 - 1	STRAIN, WILL OR COERCE
COERCION	058 - 5	NOT BY COERCION BUT WITH CONVICTION
COERCION	274 - 2	TREATMENT IS NOT MENTAL COERCION
COERCION	399 - 5	AN IMPOSSIBLE COERCION
CO-ETERNAL	070 - 1	LAW IS CO-ETERNAL WITH GOD
CO-ETERNAL	084 - 2	CO-ETERNAL WITH SPIRIT
CO-ETERNAL	090 - 3	CO-ETERNAL WITH THE OTHER
CO-ETERNAL	157 - 2	ATTRIBUTES WHICH ARE CO-ETERNAL
CO-EXISTENT	070 - 1	CO-EXISTENT AND CO-ETERNAL WITH GOD
CO-EXISTENT	084 - 2	LAW MUST BE CO-EXISTENT
CO-EXISTENT	131 - 6	LAW AND UNITY ARE ALL CO-EXISTENT
CO-EXISTENT	157 - 2	CO-EXISTENT WITH GOD
CO-EXISTENT	488 - 2	FREEDOM ARE CO-EXISTENT
CO-EXISTS	050 - 1	IT CO-EXISTS WITH THE ETERNAL
COGNIZANT	366 - 2	COGNIZANT OF HIS RELATIONSHIP
COGNIZE	307 - 1	COMPEL THE MENTALITY TO COGNIZE
COGNIZES	121 - 4	COGNIZES OR REALIZES TRUTH
COHERENT	076 - 5	NATURE MAY BE COHERENT
COHERENT	380 - 1	TO RECEIVE A COHERENT MESSAGE
COIN	268 - 2	PAID IN MENTAL AND SPIRITUAL COIN
COLD	500 - 2	LAW IS A COLD HARD FACT
COLD-BLOODED	074 - 2	A COLD-BLOODED PROPOSITION
COLD-BLOODED	213 - 3	NOT SO COLD-BLOODED AS TO SAY
COLDNESS	252 - 5	COLDNESS OF HEART
COLDS	252 - 2	NOT THEY EXPERIENCE COLDS
COLDS	252 - 3	COLDS HAVE NO PART IN YOUR LIFE
COLDS	252 - 5	COLDS RESULT FROM DAMP SPIRIT
COLLECTIVE	115 - 2	COLLECTIVE UNCONSCIOUS CONTAINS
COLOR	088 - 4	LOSE ALL WARMTH AND COLOR
COLOR	089 - 2	NECESSITY FOR WARMTH AND COLOR
COLOR	105 - 3	DIFFERENT SHAPE AND COLOR
COLOR	148 - 3	CONSCIOUSNESS TAKING ITS COLOR
COLOR	388 - 3	GIVES LIGHT AND COLOR
COLOR	398 - 4	WARMTH, COLOR AND IMAGINATION
COLOR	411 - 4	TAKES ON FORM COLOR
COLORED	328 - 5	COLORED BY THE VIBRATION
COLORS	026 - 6	IF WE MIX CERTAIN COLORS
COLORS	026 - 6	BLENDS THESE PARTICULAR COLORS
COMBATING	183 - 2	NOT BY COMBATING DARKNESS
COMBINATION	334 - 4	COMBINATION OF THE TWO
COMBINATION	476 - 2	THERE MUST BE A COMBINATION OF THE TWO
COMBINATIONS	202 - 1	COMBINATIONS OF THINKING
COMBINATIONS	320 - 3	COMBINATIONS OF THOUGHT UNITE
COMBINATIONS	476 - 3	FROM COMBINATIONS OF THESE TWO
COMBINE	283 - 2	COMBINE THE LETTER AND THE SPIRIT
COMBINED	334 - 4	COMBINED THE PERSONAL
COME	321 - 2	TREATMENT WILL COME OUT OF IT
COME	335 - 4	COME UNTO ME ALL YE THAT LABOR
COME	422 - 3	CANNOT COME UNTO THE FATHER
COMEDY	195 - 1	COMEDY OR A TRAGEDY
COMEDY	237 - 2	LIFE IS A COMEDY

COME FORTH	359 - 4	DEAD MAN AND TELL HIM TO COME FORTH
COMETH	312 - 1	AND IT COMETH EVERYWHERE
COMETH	358 - 4	NO MAN COMETH UNTO THE FATHER
COMETH	479 - 5	NO MAN COMETH UNTO THE FATHER
COMFORT	479 - 2	SPOKE WORDS OF COMFORT TO THOSE
COMFORTABLE	259 - 1	I FEEL COMFORTABLE IN ALL
COMMAND	277 - 2	THEN COMMAND THE LAW TO WORK
COMMAND	331 - 5	COME FORTH THIS WAS COMMAND
COMMAND	396 - 3	IT IS HIS TO COMMAND HIS SERVANT
COMMANDMENTS	459 - 3	COMMANDMENTS ARE TO LOVE GOD AND
COMMERCE	348 - 3	WITH A SPIRIT OF COMMERCE
COMMERCIAL	137 - 2	MODERN COMMERCIAL WORLD
COMMINGLING	152 - 4	CONSCIOUS COMMINGLING OF OUR THOUGHT
COMMON	076 - 1	COMMON TO ALL INDIVIDUAL MEN
COMMON	113 - 3	HAVE ONE COMMON CENTER
COMMON	206 - 3	INTO ONE COMMON MIND
COMMON	273 - 5	COMMON WAY OF BITTER EXPERIENCE
COMMON	330 - 4	COMMON LAW OF LOVE
COMMON	413 - 1	ONE COMMON CREATIVE MIND
COMMON	434 - 3	COMMON TO ALL PEOPLE
COMMON	490 - 6	THE GLORY IN COMMON AFFAIRS
COMMON SENSE	484 - 2	IT IS COMMON SENSE
COMMUNED	276 - 1	A THING TO BE COMMUNED
COMMUNICATE	121 - 3	TO COMMUNICATE WITH EACH OTHER
COMMUNICATE	139 - 1	WE COMMUNICATE WITH EACH OTHER
COMMUNICATE	312 - 3	CAN COMMUNICATE WITH EACH OTHER
COMMUNICATE	371 - 1	TO COMMUNICATE AND TO RECEIVE
COMMUNICATE	378 - 2	COMMUNICATE WITHOUT THE TONGUE
COMMUNICATE	379 - 3	CAN COMMUNICATE WITH MENTALITY
COMMUNICATION	077 - 3	A SILENT COMMUNICATION
COMMUNICATION	077 - 3	COMMUNICATION WITH OTHERS
COMMUNICATION	160 - 3	CONSCIOUS AND SUBJECTIVE COMMUNICATION
COMMUNICATION	349 - 2	THROUGH UNCONSCIOUS COMMUNICATION
COMMUNICATION	379 - 2	POSSIBILITY OF SPIRIT COMMUNICATION
COMMUNICATION	379 - 3	SPIRIT COMMUNICATION MUST BE POSSIBLE
COMMUNICATION	421 - 4	COMMUNICATION TAKES PLACE AT ALL TIMES
COMMUNING	366 - 4	COMMUNING WITH HIS OWN SOUL
COMMUNION	152 - 4	COMMUNION WITH THE INFINITE
COMMUNION	277 - 2	RESULT OF HIS COMMUNION WITH THE SPIRIT
COMMUNION	343 - 3	COMMUNION WITH THE UNIVERSAL SPIRIT
COMMUNION	362 - 3	COME TO US A SENSE OF COMMUNION
COMMUNION	497 - 1	COMMUNION IS ESSENTIAL TO THE SOUL
COMPANIONS	143 - 4	CHOOSE THE KIND OF COMPANIONS
COMPANIONSHIP	276 - 3	PROVIDE A SENSE OF DIVINE COMPANIONSHIP
COMPANIONSHIP	452 - 2	DIVINE COMPANIONSHIP HAS EVER ATTENDED
COMPARATIVE	312 - 1	SUPERLATIVE CANNOT BE THE COMPARATIVE
COMPARED	133 - 4	INFINITE AS COMPARED
COMPASSION	238 - 2	SPIRIT OF DIVINE COMPASSION
COMPASSION	437 - 2	COMPASSION AND LOVE FOR HUMANITY
COMPASSION	466 - 2	HAD COMPASSION AND RAN
COMPASSIONATE	368 - 1	COMPASSIONATE IN HIS TENDERNESS
COMPEL	049 - 5	COMPEL THE MIND TO PERCEIVE
COMPEL	163 - 1	COMPEL THE FORCE TO WORK
COMPEL	194 - 2	NOT AN EFFORT TO COMPEL
COMPEL	274 - 2	TREAT TO COMPEL SOMETHING

COMPEL	278 - 1	NEED NOT COMPEL THINGS TO HAPPEN
COMPEL	278 - 4	EARTH HAD TO CHANGE TO COMPEL
COMPEL	307 - 1	COMPEL THE MENTALITY TO COGNIZE
COMPEL	322 - 1	COMPEL US TO ACT IN CORRECT MANNER
COMPEL	489 - 3	DO NOT WILL OR TRY TO COMPEL
COMPELLED	040 - 1	OUTLET WE SHALL BE COMPELLED
COMPELLED	056 - 4	COMPELLED TO DO THE RIGHT
COMPELLED	105 - 3	NOT COMPELLED TO ACCEPT
COMPELLED	109 - 2	COMPELLED MAN TO SUDDENLY APPEAR
COMPELLED	114 - 3	COMPELLED BY REASON OF ITS SUBJECTIVITY
COMPELLED	118 - 1	COMPELLED BY ITS VERY NATURE
COMPELLED	131 - 3	IT IS COMPELLED TO ACT
COMPELLED	198 - 2	COMPELLED BY REASON OF ITS NATURE
COMPELLED	253 - 4	I CANNOT BE COMPELLED TO SUFFER
COMPELLED	263 - 3	I AM COMPELLED TO MOVE
COMPELLED	269 - 2	IT IS COMPELLED BY ITS
COMPELLED	373 - 1	STILL BE COMPELLED TO MAKE
COMPELLED	398 - 1	COMPELLED TO RECEIVE THE IMAGES
COMPELLED	416 - 2	IT IS COMPELLED TO RECIEVE
COMPELLED	416 - 2	IT IS COMPELLED TO ACT UPON
COMPELLED	443 - 1	COMPELLED TO ACCEPT THE FACT
COMPELLING	300 - 1	COMPELLING THROUGH THE LAW
COMPELLING	340 - 3	COMPELLING MORE BETTER HIGHER
COMPELS	222 - 4	COMPELS THE INDIVIDUAL TO DO
COMPELS	241 - 2	COMPELS HIM TO ACT OUT
COMPENSATED	263 - 4	COMPENSATED FOR ALL MY EFFORTS
COMPENSATED	286 - 2	ACTIVE, OCCUPIED AND COMPENSATED
COMPENSATION	264 - 2	COMPENSATION IS ALWAYS OPEN
COMPENSATION	287 - 3	RECEIVE THE SAME COMPENSATION
COMPENSATION	429 - 2	COMPENSATION FOR ALL OUR WORK
COMPETE	263 - 6	COMPETE WITH ANYONE
COMPETITION	304 - 2	THE THOUGHT OF COMPETITION
COMPLEMENT	031 - 4	A COMPLEMENT OF THE OTHER
COMPLEMENT	167 - 1	AS A COMPLEMENT TO THIS
COMPLEMENT	196 - 2	COMPLEMENT OF THE OTHER
COMPLEMENT	310 - 3	MAN IS A COMPLEMENT OF THE UNIVERSE
COMPLEMENT	417 - 3	INDIVIDUAL I IS A COMPLEMENT
COMPLETE	036 - 5	SO COMPLETE IS OUR FREEDOM IN IT
COMPLETE	049 - 3	COMPLETE IT WITH THE THOUGHT
COMPLETE	053 - 4	SPIRIT THAT IS COMPLETE AND PERFECT
COMPLETE	184 - 5	GOD IS COMPLETE AND PERFECT
COMPLETE	192 - 2	UNDERSTANDING IS NOT YET COMPLETE
COMPLETE	218 - 2	IS COMPLETE AND PERFECT
COMPLETE	223 - 2	TRUTH WITHIN HIM IS COMPLETE
COMPLETE	245 - 2	I AM COMPLETE AND PERFECT NOW
COMPLETE	285 - 4	COMPLETE CONVICTION THAT THE SPIRIT
COMPLETE	292 - 4	COMPLETE THIS STATEMENT BY SAYING
COMPLETE	397 - 5	COMPLETE MENTAL ACCEPTANCE
COMPLETE	398 - 3	GAINING A COMPLETE MENTAL
COMPLETE	399 - 2	COMPLETE MENTAL PICTURE OF HIMSELF
COMPLETE	410 - 2	NOT COMPLETE WITHOUT THE OTHER
COMPLETE	411 - 4	GIVING OUR COMPLETE ATTENTION
COMPLETE	447 - 3	LIFE ITSELF IS COMPLETE
COMPLETED	354 - 3	EXIST AS A COMPLETED THING
COMPLETELY	047 - 2	MORE COMPLETELY HE BELIEVES

COMPLETELY	337 - 3	COMPLETELY MANIFEST THE WHOLE IDEA
COMPLETENESS	128 - 3	NOTHING BUT COMPLETENESS
COMPLETING	336 - 2	YET FOREVER COMPLETING ITSELF
COMPLETION	289 - 4	IT KNOWS ONLY THE COMPLETION
COMPLETION	334 - 4	A SENSE OF REAL COMPLETION
COMPLETION	482 - 3	JOY OF A SENSE OF COMPLETION
COMPLEX	225 - 3	SUBJECTIVE COMPLEX OR MENTAL KNOT
COMPLEX	236 - 3	REMOVE THIS COMPLEX
COMPLEX	236 - 5	PROBE DEEPLY INTO THE COMPLEX
COMPLIANCE	096 - 4	COMPLIANCE WITH THE LAW
COMPLIANCE	157 - 3	WORK IN COMPLIANCE WITH OUR DEMAND
COMPLIANCE	437 - 4	COMPLIANCE WITH THE LAW OF TRUTH
COMPLY	109 - 3	AS WE MORE AND MORE COMPLY
COMPLY	174 - 1	COMPLY WITH THE LAW OF NATURE
COMPLY	175 - 1	TO COMPLY WITH THE LAW
COMPLY	266 - 1	COMPLY WITH ITS TEACHINGS
COMPLY	267 - 2	IF WE COMPLY WITH THE LAW
COMPLY	268 - 2	UNLESS WE ARE WILLING TO COMPLY
COMPLYING	268 - 1	NECESSITY OF COMPLYING WITH LAW
COMPOSED	373 - 5	BODY IS COMPOSED OF MATTER
COMPOSITION	116 - 2	DIFFERENT IN ITS COMPOSITION
COMPREHEND	082 - 2	COMPREHEND SUCH A COMPLETE LIFE
COMPREHEND	138 - 4	COMPREHEND THE MEANING
COMPREHEND	232 - 5	COMPREHEND THE FULL SIGNIFICANCE
COMPREHEND	287 - 1	MENTAL CAPACITY TO COMPREHEND
COMPREHEND	358 - 4	WE COMPREHEND THE INFINITE
COMPREHEND	390 - 4	COMPREHEND ITS OWN POWER
COMPREHEND	422 - 3	COMPREHEND THE INFINITY ONLY
COMPREHEND	468 - 2	COMPREHEND SUCH AN INFINITE POSSIBILITY
COMPREHENDING	414 - 2	EXTERNAL TO SOME COMPREHENDING MIND
COMPREHENSION	033 - 2	OUR COMPREHENSION OF HER
COMPREHENSION	165 - 1	COMPREHENSION OF HOW LAW OPERATES
COMPREHENSION	173 - 4	INTERIOR IN OUR COMPREHENSION
COMPREHENSION	191 - 4	COMPLETE COMPREHENSION OF GOD
COMPREHENSIVE	186 - 3	UNIVERSAL AND COMPREHENSIVE
COMPREHENSIVE	451 - 4	COMPREHENSIVE WAY TO ILLUSTRATE
COMPROMISE	049 - 4	AN UNCONSCIOUS COMPROMISE
COMPROMISE	049 - 4	NO COMPROMISE WITH THE CONSCIOUSNESS
COMPROMISES	189 - 2	GOOD NEVER COMPROMISES
COMPULSION	058 - 5	NOT THROUGH COMPULSION
COMPULSION	109 - 2	A FREEDOM UNDER COMPULSION
COMPULSION	272 - 1	NO IDEA OF COMPULSION
COMPULSORY	072 - 3	NO COMPULSORY EVOLUTION
COMPUTING	356 - 1	COMPUTING THE TIME IT WILL TAKE
CONCEAL	449 - 2	IMPOSSIBLE FOR A MAN TO CONCEAL
CONCEIT	307 - 3	NOT CONCEIT IT IS THE TRUTH
CONCEIT	444 - 2	NOT PRODUCE AN UNDUE CONCEIT
CONCEIT	469 - 1	RIGHTEOUSNESS AND PERSONAL CONCEIT
CONCEIVE	044 - 5	POSSIBLE AS WE CAN CONCEIVE
CONCEIVE	133 - 2	CLEARLY CONCEIVE OF SUCH CONDITIONS BEING
CONCEIVE	147 - 1	POSSIBLE FOR US TO CONCEIVE
CONCEIVE	168 - 1	ABLE TO CONCEIVE SHOULD BE AFFIRMED
CONCEIVE	267 - 4	ONLY THAT WHICH HE CAN CONCEIVE
CONCEIVE	289 - 2	CONCEIVE OF THE ULTIMATE OF THE IDEA
CONCEIVE	301 - 2	OUR ABILITY TO CONCEIVE

CONCEIVE	321 - 2	CANNOT CONCEIVE FAILURE
CONCEIVE	338 - 4	CANNOT CONCEIVE IMPERFECT IDEAS
CONCEIVE	407 - 1	CONCEIVE OF SOME DEFINITE IDEA
CONCEIVE	454 - 2	CONCEIVE OF MAN ONLY AS PART OF HIMSELF
CONCEIVED	037 - 3	BECAUSE WE HAVE CONCEIVED IT
CONCEIVED	254 - 2	CONCEIVED IS NOW PERFECT
CONCEIVES	363 - 4	THE MAN THAT SPIRIT CONCEIVES
CONCEIVES	441 - 4	NO LONGER CONCEIVES EVIL
CONCEIVES	450 - 2	CONCEIVES OF HIMSELF AS POSSESSING
CONCENTRATE	174 - 1	LESS IT TRIES TO CONCENTRATE
CONCENTRATE	194 - 1	TO CONCENTRATE MEANS TO BRING
CONCENTRATE	194 - 3	CONCENTRATE OUR ATTENTION
CONCENTRATE	195 - 4	WE CONCENTRATE THEN IS ATTENTION
CONCENTRATE	274 - 2	CONCENTRATE FOR ANY LENGTH OF TIME
CONCENTRATE	406 - 1	CONCENTRATE SUBSTANCE INTO THE FORM
CONCENTRATION	193 - 5	THE TRUE MEANING OF CONCENTRATION
CONCENTRATION	194 - 2	CONCENTRATION OF THOUGHT
CONCENTRATION	194 - 2	TO FORCE THROUGH CONCENTRATION
CONCENTRATION	194 - 3	WILL AND CONCENTRATION
CONCENTRATION	195 - 4	ANY METHODS OF CONCENTRATION
CONCENTRATION	274 - 2	IT IS NOT CONCENTRATION
CONCENTRATION	309 - 1	IDEA OF MENTAL CONCENTRATION
CONCENTRATION	345 - 3	NOT A TRICK OF CONCENTRATION
CONCENTRATION	397 - 5	THE ONLY CONCENTRATION NECESSARY
CONCENTRATION	470 - 5	COMPLETE CONCENTRATION OF PURPOSE
CONCEPT	035 - 2	LEVEL OF MAN'S CONCEPT OF IT
CONCEPT	047 - 2	DEMONSTRATING HIS CONCEPT OF LIFE
CONCEPT	055 - 3	MENTAL AND SPIRITUAL CONCEPT
CONCEPT	069 - 1	THE WORD IS THE CONCEPT IDEA
CONCEPT	070 - 2	A WONDERFUL CONCEPT
CONCEPT	141 - 5	CONCEPT THEN THE MOVEMENT
CONCEPT	153 - 2	OF OUR MOST SUBTLE CONCEPT
CONCEPT	163 - 3	A NEW CONCEPT OF GOD
CONCEPT	175 - 6	HAVE A TRUE SUBJECTIVE CONCEPT
CONCEPT	196 - 2	A PERFECT CONCEPT OF MAN
CONCEPT	204 - 3	A CLEAR CONCEPT OF REALITY
CONCEPT	219 - 2	AT THE LEVEL OF OUR CONCEPT
CONCEPT	220 - 4	CONCEPT OF AN ALREADY ESTABLISHED TRUTH
CONCEPT	282 - 1	MANIFEST ACCORDING TO THE CONCEPT
CONCEPT	321 - 2	JUDGE THE SUBJECTIVE CONCEPT
CONCEPT	363 - 3	FUNDAMENTAL TO HIS CONCEPT OF LIFE
CONCEPT	363 - 4	CONCEPT OF GOD AND MAN
CONCEPT	383 - 1	CONCEPT OF GOD WOULD CREATE
CONCEPT	406 - 1	FUNDAMENTAL TO OUR CONCEPT
CONCEPT	433 - 3	CONCEPT SUPPOSES THAT WE ARE
CONCEPT	436 - 4	THE POPULAR CONCEPT OF HELL
CONCEPT	475 - 2	CONCEPT OF UNITY TAKES PLACE
CONCEPT	490 - 6	NO LIMITED CONCEPT
CONCEPTION	121 - 3	ONLY THROUGH THIS CONCEPTION
CONCEPTION	148 - 4	A PERFECT CONCEPTION
CONCEPTION	268 - 3	CONCEPTION OF THE RELATIONSHIP OF JESUS
CONCEPTION	407 - 1	TO THE CONCEPTION OF ANOTHER
CONCEPTION	422 - 3	THE MYSTICAL CONCEPTION OF CHRIST
CONCEPTS	032 - 1	OUR SPIRITUAL AND MATERIAL CONCEPTS
CONCEPTS	048 - 2	CONCEPTS DECIDE THE SHAPE

CONCEPTS	178 - 6	ACT OF INDUCING RIGHT CONCEPTS
CONCEPTS	490 - 3	HIS CONCEPTS BECOME ENLARGED
CONCERNED	179 - 1	CONCERNED ONLY WITH HIS OWN THOUGHT
CONCLUSION	069 - 3	ARRIVE AT THE CONCLUSION
CONCLUSION	077 - 4	LEADS TO THE CONCLUSION
CONCLUSION	101 - 1	REPRESENTS A FALSE CONCLUSION
CONCLUSION	224 - 4	CONCLUSION WHEN GIVING A TREATMENT
CONCLUSION	355 - 4	DRAWING A LOGICAL CONCLUSION
CONCLUSION	407 - 3	ARRIVED AT THE CONCLUSION
CONCLUSION	423 - 1	IN CONCLUSION WHAT THE WORLD
CONCLUSION	461 - 4	ALREADY THE CORRECT CONCLUSION
CONCLUSIONS	068 - 2	ARRIVED AT SIMILAR CONCLUSIONS
CONCLUSIONS	074 - 1	MOST IMPORTANT CONCLUSIONS
CONCLUSIONS	159 - 2	CONCLUSIONS MUST BE BUILT ON
CONCLUSIONS	170 - 1	ALL ERRONEOUS CONCLUSIONS
CONCLUSIONS	346 - 1	THESE HAVE BEEN THEIR CONCLUSIONS
CONCLUSIONS	400 - 4	DECISIONS ARE MERELY CONCLUSIONS
CONCLUSIVE	378 - 1	TO HIM CONCLUSIVE ARGUMENT
CONCLUSIVELY	376 - 1	IT HAS BEEN SHOWN CONCLUSIVELY
CONCORD	344 - 3	ACROSS THE COMMON IN CONCORD
CONCRETE	046 - 5	CONSCIOUS CONCRETE AND EXPLICIT
CONCRETE	076 - 3	INDIVIDUAL AND CONCRETE
CONCRETE	144 - 2	CONCRETE MANIFESTATION EQUAL TO ITSELF
CONCRETE	278 - 4	CONCRETE ACCEPTANCE OF HIS DESIRE
CONCRETE	393 - 1	BECOME THINGS IN THE CONCRETE
CONCRETE	405 - 2	RECEIVE IN THE CONCRETE
CONCRETE	444 - 4	ABSTRACT WITH THE CONCRETE
CONDEMN	259 - 1	I DO NOT CONDEMN
CONDEMN	434 - 3	PRAISE AND NOT CONDEMN
CONDEMN	438 - 5	CONDEMN WHEN WE SHOULD FORGIVE
CONDEMN	469 - 1	CONDEMN EVERYTHING THAT HE
CONDEMN	503 - 6	EVEN IF OUR HEARTS CONDEMN US
CONDEMNATION	233 - 4	WORRY, CONDEMNATION AND FEAR
CONDEMNATION	237 - 2	A COMPLEX OF CONDEMNATION
CONDEMNATION	237 - 2	CONDEMNATION WHICH THE RACE HOLDS
CONDEMNATION	254 - 2	NO DISCOURAGEMENT AND NO CONDEMNATION
CONDEMNATION	254 - 5	ANY SENSE OF CONDEMNATION
CONDEMNATION	259 - 4	THERE IS NO CONDEMNATION
CONDEMNATION	291 - 2	THERE IS NO CONDEMNATION
CONDEMNATION	291 - 2	UNLESS WE BELIEVE IN CONDEMNATION
CONDEMNATION	307 - 3	RECEIVE ANYONE'S CONDEMNATION
CONDEMNATION	433 - 4	CONDEMNATION CAN BE ENTIRELY ELIMINATED
CONDEMNATION	433 - 4	JUDGMENT, CRITICISM AND CONDEMNATION
CONDEMNATION	434 - 2	LAW RESPONDING TO CONDEMNATION
CONDEMNATION	434 - 3	CONTINUOUS STATE OF CONDEMNATION
CONDEMNATION	438 - 2	CONDEMNATION IS GREAT ENOUGH
CONDEMNATION	439 - 1	BURDEN OF OUR OWN CONDEMNATION
CONDEMNATION	484 - 1	THEREFORE NOW NO CONDEMNATION
CONDEMNED	501 - 6	CONDEMNED FOR OUR MISTAKES
CONDEMNING	259 - 3	IF WE ARE CONSTANTLY CONDEMNING IT
CONDEMNING	502 - 4	CONDEMNING OR DAMNING ANYONE
CONDEMNS	383 - 1	CONDEMNS US BUT OURSELVES
CONDEMNS	449 - 3	CONDEMNS OR JUSTIFIES HIMSELF
CONDEMNS	457 - 6	CONDEMNS UNDERSTANDS NOT THE TRUTH
CONDENSATION	403 - 2	CONDENSATION OF THE IDEA OF WANT

CONDITION	054 - 2	FALSE CONDITION WILL DISAPPEAR
CONDITION	054 - 3	APPARENT LIMITED CONDITION
CONDITION	060 - 2	TOWARD EVERY FALSE CONDITION
CONDITION	126 - 2	RETURN AGAIN AS SOME CONDITION
CONDITION	133 - 2	MAY CHANGE ANY CONDITION
CONDITION	159 - 5	CONDITION WE ARE TO CHANGE
CONDITION	164 - 3	AWAY FROM THE CONDITION
CONDITION	174 - 5	ENVIRONMENT, CONDITION, LOCATION
CONDITION	184 - 2	ANY APPARENT CAUSE OR CONDITION
CONDITION	186 - 1	TURN ENTIRELY AWAY FROM THE CONDITION
CONDITION	186 - 1	TURN ENTIRELY FROM THE CONDITION
CONDITION	228 - 4	CAUSE OF THE FALSE CONDITION
CONDITION	231 - 3	RECOGNIZING THE CONDITION
CONDITION	234 - 4	SOME BODILY CONDITION
CONDITION	256 - 2	DISTURBED MENTAL CONDITION
CONDITION	278 - 3	RETURNS TO ME AS SOME CONDITION
CONDITION	316 - 3	COMPLETELY FROM THE CONDITION
CONDITION	320 - 2	IN BETTER CONDITION THAN BEFORE
CONDITION	322 - 1	HE REVERSES THE CONDITION ATTENDANT
CONDITION	410 - 4	MERELY A CONDITION
CONDITIONED	300 - 2	LIMITLESS AND THE CONDITIONED
CONDITIONS	037 - 1	CONDITIONS FROM WHICH WE SUFFER
CONDITIONS	054 - 2	THAT WRONG CONDITIONS EXIST
CONDITIONS	054 - 2	CONDITIONS ARE NOT ENTITIES
CONDITIONS	074 - 1	BRING NEW CONDITIONS INTO HIS LIFE
CONDITIONS	086 - 3	PRODUCED UNPLEASANT CONDITIONS
CONDITIONS	107 - 3	CONDITIONS UNDER WHICH FREEDOM
CONDITIONS	174 - 1	PROVIDES THE CONDITIONS WHICH
CONDITIONS	183 - 3	WITH UNPLEASANT CONDITIONS
CONDITIONS	185 - 1	MAY BE INFLUENCED BY CONDITIONS
CONDITIONS	188 - 4	IN DEMONSTRATING OVER CONDITIONS
CONDITIONS	231 - 4	BODIES AND CONDITIONS NEVER MOVE
CONDITIONS	266 - 1	MENTAL CONTROL OF CONDITIONS
CONDITIONS	266 - 3	THE CONDITIONS WE CONTACT
CONDITIONS	266 - 3	A CONTROL OF CONDITIONS
CONDITIONS	266 - 3	CONDITIONS WHICH NOW EXIST
CONDITIONS	291 - 2	CONDITIONS ARE THE REFLECTIONS
CONDITIONS	390 - 2	THINK INDEPENDENTLY OF CONDITIONS
CONDITIONS	394 - 3	THE CONTROL OF CONDITIONS AROUND US
CONDITIONS	402 - 3	CONDITIONS NECESSARY TO PRODUCE LACK
CONDITIONS	403 - 4	ALL CONDITIONS AND EVERY CIRCUMSTANCE
CONDITIONS	404 - 1	LAW CAN KNOW NO CONDITIONS
CONDITIONS	406 - 4	CONDITIONS ARE IN THE REALM OF EFFECTS
CONDITIONS	414 - 1	CONTEMPLATION OF CONDITIONS
CONDITIONS	490 - 4	EVENTS AND RE-MOLDS CONDITIONS
CONDUCT	160 - 2	CONDUCT OUR MINDS THROUGH
CONDUCT	172 - 4	CONDUCT THE MIND OF THE PRACTITIONER
CONFESS	501 - 5	CONFESS OUR FAULTS
CONFESSION	501 - 7	CONFESSION OF SINS OR MISTAKES HELPS US
CONFIDENCE	156 - 1	CONFIDENCE IN HIMSELF
CONFIDENCE	159 - 4	CONFIDENCE IN OUR APPROACH TO IT
CONFIDENCE	159 - 4	WE HAVE ABOUNDING CONFIDENCE
CONFIDENCE	168 - 3	THE SACREDNESS OF THE CONFIDENCE
CONFIDENCE	179 - 1	IN FULL CONFIDENCE THAT THE LAW WILL
CONFIDENCE	189 - 3	AND IN CALM CONFIDENCE

CONFIDENCE	245 - 3	CONFIDENCE IN GOOD
CONFIDENCE	245 - 3	I HAVE COMPLETE CONFIDENCE
CONFIDENCE	246 - 4	GIVE POISE AND CONFIDENCE
CONFIDENCE	258 - 1	QUIETNESS AND CONFIDENCE
CONFIDENCE	265 - 2	I AM THE SPIRIT OF CONFIDENCE
CONFIDENCE	272 - 1	CONFIDENCE WE SHOULD WAIT UPON
CONFIDENCE	272 - 2	FAITH AND CONFIDENCE
CONFIDENCE	289 - 3	CONFIDENCE PEACE AND CERTAINTY
CONFIDENCE	296 - 2	WITH AN ATMOSPHERE OF CONFIDENCE
CONFIDENCE	305 - 5	PEACE, CONFIDENCE AND JOY
CONFIDENCE	384 - 1	PEACE AND IN QUIET CONFIDENCE
CONFIDENCE	404 - 4	CONFIDENCE OVERCOMES THE DEPRESSION
CONFIDENCE	432 - 3	CONFIDENCE WILL BE MISPLACED
CONFIDENCE	447 - 1	COME IN QUIET CONFIDENCE
CONFIDENTLY	229 - 4	TRUSTINGLY, CONFIDENTLY
CONFINE	218 - 3	CONFINE OUR STATEMENTS TO A REALIZATION
CONFINES	302 - 3	NO BOUNDS AND HAS NO CONFINES
CONFINES	448 - 1	CONFINES OF HIS OWN CONSCIOUSNESS
CONFLICT	224 - 1	NO SENSE OF CONFLICT
CONFLICT	237 - 1	BY SOME INNER CONFLICT
CONFLICT	237 - 1	OPPOSING DESIRES WHICH CONFLICT
CONFLICT	256 - 4	CONFLICT IN THE EMOTIONAL NATURE
CONFLICT	366 - 4	BACK OF THE CONFLICT OF IDEAS
CONFLICTS	226 - 4	CONFLICTS HAD ENTERED INTO HIS LIFE
CONFORM	218 - 2	MUST CONFORM OUR ARGUMENTS
CONFORM	261 - 3	CONFORM ALL STATEMENTS TO THIS
CONFORM	309 - 2	IN TREATMENT CONFORM YOUR THOUGHT
CONFORMITY	162 - 5	CONFORMITY WITH THE PRINCIPLES
CONFORMS	382 - 1	CONFORMS TO THE ONE
CONFRONTED	429 - 1	CONFRONTED WITH AN APPARENT
CONFRONTING	388 - 2	THESE FACTS CONFRONTING US
CONFRONTS	444 - 4	SAME PROBLEM CONFRONTS RELIGION
CONFUSED	053 - 4	CONFUSED OVER ANY GIVEN FORM
CONFUSED	065 - 2	DIVINE MIND IS NEVER CONFUSED
CONFUSED	168 - 5	GOD IS NEVER CONFUSED
CONFUSED	308 - 2	CONFUSED WITH MENTAL CONCENTRATION
CONFUSED	321 - 2	THE SPIRIT IS NOT CONFUSED
CONFUSION	120 - 3	CONFUSION WHICH TOOK PLACE IN THE PSYCHIC
CONFUSION	160 - 2	FILLED WITH FEAR AND CONFUSION
CONFUSION	187 - 2	CONFUSION IN THE THOUGHT BACK
CONFUSION	226 - 2	NOR CONFUSION IN SPIRIT
CONFUSION	252 - 2	MENTAL CONFLICTS ALSO CAUSE CONFUSION
CONFUSION	252 - 2	CONFUSION MAY CAUSE COLDS
CONFUSION	283 - 2	NO CONFUSION IN THE APPROACH
CONFUSION	285 - 4	IN A STATE OF CONFUSION
CONFUSION	291 - 2	IT NEVER THINKS CONFUSION
CONFUSION	295 - 2	NO TROUBLE NO CONFUSION
CONFUSION	329 - 3	THAN TEN THOUSAND WITH CONFUSION
CONFUSION	329 - 3	GOD IS NOT THE AUTHOR OF CONFUSION
CONFUSION	342 - 1	PSYCHICS WE ENTER CONFUSION
CONFUSION	453 - 6	CONFUSION OF THE WORLD ARISES FROM
CONFUSION	453 - 6	THE DITCH OF OUR OWN CONFUSION
CONFUSION	493 - 2	OTHER THAN PEACE SUGGESTS CONFUSION
CONFUSION	497 - 4	PRODUCING MENTAL AND PHYSICAL CONFUSION
CONGEALED	033 - 1	CONGEALED BY PRIDE

CONGEST	497 – 4	CONGEST THE SOUL AND HINDER
CONGESTED	497 – 3	CONGESTED EMOTIONS ARE DISASTROUS
CONGESTION	225 – 2	CONGESTION IN THE HEAD
CONNECT	152 – 5	CONNECT OUR MINDS
CONNECTED	169 – 4	DISEASE AS BEING CONNECTED
CONNECTION	406 – 3	CONNECTION BETWEEN THE ABSOLUTE
CONNECTS	399 – 4	CONNECTS US WITH LIMITLESS POWER
CONQUERS	130 – 4	CONQUERS HIS ENVIRONMENT THROUGH
CONSCIENCE	367 – 1	CALL IT CONSCIENCE
CONSCIENTIOUSLY	060 – 2	DO OUR WORK CONSCIENTIOUSLY
CONSCIENTIOUSLY	222 – 1	CLEARLY FULLY AND CONSCIENTIOUSLY
CONSCIOUS	026 – 4	THROUGH THE CONSCIOUS USE
CONSCIOUS	030 – 2	AT THE POINT OF CONSCIOUS PERCEPTION
CONSCIOUS	030 – 4	MOTION BY THE CONSCIOUS THOUGHT
CONSCIOUS	035 – 2	FINDING CONSCIOUS AND INDIVIDUALIZED
CONSCIOUS	038 – 3	CONSCIOUS CENTERS OF LIFE
CONSCIOUS	040 – 3	CONSCIOUS CONNECTION MUST BE MADE
CONSCIOUS	042 – 6	CHOICE, VOLITION, CONSCIOUS ACTION
CONSCIOUS	044 – 4	FIRST THROUGH OUR CONSCIOUS
CONSCIOUS	045 – 3	CONSCIOUS RECEPTIVITY DIFFERENTIATE
CONSCIOUS	046 – 4	MORE FULLY CONSCIOUS
CONSCIOUS	046 – 4	CONSCIOUS THAT IT IS DOING SO
CONSCIOUS	046 – 5	CONSCIOUS OF THIS PARTICULAR GOOD
CONSCIOUS	046 – S	CONSCIOUS, CONCRETE AND EXPLICIT
CONSCIOUS	047 – 2	CONSCIOUS POWER TO HIS THOUGHT
CONSCIOUS	048 – 2	CONSCIOUS AND SPECIFIC THOUGHT
CONSCIOUS	050 – 1	IN-WORKING OF THE CONSCIOUS
CONSCIOUS	052 – 3	CONSCIOUS MENTAL USE
CONSCIOUS	052 – 3	BY CONSCIOUS THINKING
CONSCIOUS	052 – 3	GIVE CONSCIOUS DIRECTION TO IT
CONSCIOUS	052 – 3	OUR CONSCIOUS OR SUBJECTIVE DIRECTION
CONSCIOUS	054 – 1	WITH THE CONSCIOUS KNOWLEDGE
CONSCIOUS	054 – 2	CONSCIOUS CAST OUT THAT
CONSCIOUS	058 – 5	STATE OF CONSCIOUS RECOGNITION
CONSCIOUS	067 – 2	UNLESS IT WERE CONSCIOUS
CONSCIOUS	067 – 2	SPIRIT TO BE CONSCIOUS INTELLIGENCE
CONSCIOUS	067 – 2	SPIRIT IS CONSCIOUS
CONSCIOUS	072 – 3	CONSCIOUS UNION WITH LIFE
CONSCIOUS	074 – 1	RESULT OF CONSCIOUS THOUGHT
CONSCIOUS	079 – 2	CONSCIOUS VOLITION IN THE UNIVERSE
CONSCIOUS	090 – 1	CONSCIOUS INTELLIGENCE SUBJECTIVE LAW
CONSCIOUS	092 – 2	HAVING NO CONSCIOUS MIND OF ITS OWN
CONSCIOUS	093 – 5	POINT OF CONSCIOUS PERCEPTION
CONSCIOUS	097 – 3	SUBJECT TO THE CONSCIOUS THOUGHT
CONSCIOUS	100 – 2	IN ORDER TO BE CONSCIOUS
CONSCIOUS	119 – 1	CONSCIOUS TO START WITH
CONSCIOUS	129 – 3	CONSCIOUS CO-OPERATION WITH REALITY
CONSCIOUS	145 – 3	THOUGHT IS THE CONSCIOUS ACTIVITY
CONSCIOUS	152 – 4	CONSCIOUS WELL-BEING OF THE SOUL
CONSCIOUS	164 – 1	CONSCIOUS OF THIS ETERNAL TRUTH
CONSCIOUS	164 – 2	CONSCIOUS RECOGNITION THAT HEALTH
CONSCIOUS	166 – 2	CONSCIOUS OF HIS OWN SPIRITUAL BEING
CONSCIOUS	166 – 3	A DEFINITE CONSCIOUS IDEA
CONSCIOUS	171 – 2	MAKE CONSCIOUS USE OF THIS LAW
CONSCIOUS	178 – 2	CONSCIOUS WELL-BEING OF THE SOUL

CONSCIOUS	196 - 3	MAN IS CONSCIOUS MIND
CONSCIOUS	196 - 3	LIFE IN A CONSCIOUS STATE
CONSCIOUS	198 - 2	CONSCIOUS MIND IS THE ONLY ACTOR
CONSCIOUS	202 - 1	NOT CONSCIOUS IN THE THOUGHT
CONSCIOUS	208 - 5	GOD IS NOT CONSCIOUS OF MATTER
CONSCIOUS	209 - 2	CONSCIOUS MIND BUT IS NEVERTHELESS
CONSCIOUS	210 - 4	CONSCIOUS THOUGHT OF THE PEOPLE
CONSCIOUS	228 - 3	CONSCIOUS THAT THE WORD HE SPEAKS
CONSCIOUS	230 - 6	CONSCIOUS OF THE IDEA OF WHOLENESS
CONSCIOUS	250 - 5	FULLY INTO CONSCIOUS SONSHIP
CONSCIOUS	252 - 2	ERASE FROM THE CONSCIOUS MIND
CONSCIOUS	253 - 3	CONSCIOUS KNOWLEDGE
CONSCIOUS	261 - 4	I AM CONSCIOUS OF MY ABILITY
CONSCIOUS	271 - 4	MAKE CONSCIOUS USE OF THE LAW
CONSCIOUS	277 - 2	CONSCIOUS AGGRESSIVE MENTAL MOVEMENT
CONSCIOUS	294 - 2	RESULT OF HIS CONSCIOUS AND UNCONSCIOUS
CONSCIOUS	299 - 4	RESULT OF CONSCIOUS THOUGHT
CONSCIOUS	318 - 2	CREATIVE ACT IS ALWAYS CONSCIOUS
CONSCIOUS	320 - 3	HELD IN THE CONSCIOUS MIND
CONSCIOUS	321 - 2	TREATMENT IS A DEFINITE CONSCIOUS
CONSCIOUS	322 - 2	CONSCIOUS THOUGHT CONTROLS THE
CONSCIOUS	329 - 3	CONSCIOUS COURTING OF THE DIVINE PRESENCE
CONSCIOUS	334 - 4	RESPONSIVE CONSCIOUS LIVING REALITY
CONSCIOUS	338 - 1	THROUGH CONSCIOUS ENDEAVOR
CONSCIOUS	343 - 2	IS MAN'S CONSCIOUS MENTALITY
CONSCIOUS	365 - 4	THE LIMITLESS CONSCIOUS LIFE
CONSCIOUS	390 - 2	THE CONSCIOUS MIND OF MAN
CONSCIOUS	390 - 5	THE ONLY CONSCIOUS INTELLIGENCE
CONSCIOUS	392 - 3	MIND IN A CONSCIOUS STATE
CONSCIOUS	393 - 2	CONSCIOUS USE OF THE LAW
CONSCIOUS	394 - 2	OUR CONSCIOUS MIND IS LIMITED
CONSCIOUS	397 - 1	WITH CONSCIOUS KNOWLEDGE THAT IT
CONSCIOUS	397 - 2	GOD AS CONSCIOUS MIND IS SPIRIT
CONSCIOUS	397 - 3	HAVE AT OUR CONSCIOUS DISPOSAL
CONSCIOUS	400 - 1	CONSCIOUS THOUGHT IS THE STARTING POINT
CONSCIOUS	400 - 4	THE CONSCIOUS MIND MAY CHANGE
CONSCIOUS	401 - 2	MIND IN ITS CONSCIOUS STATE IS SPIRIT
CONSCIOUS	401 - 1	CONSCIOUS PART OF MIND, THE SPIRIT OF MAN
CONSCIOUS	401 - 3	A CONSCIOUS CONVICTION OF OUR ABILITY
CONSCIOUS	403 - 3	CONSCIOUS MIND CONTROLS THE LAW
CONSCIOUS	407 - 4	ALIVE CONSCIOUS AWAKE AND AWARE
CONSCIOUS	407 - 5	CONSCIOUS OF ITSELF AND OF WHAT IT DOES
CONSCIOUS	408 - 1	GOD MUST BE CONSCIOUS OF ALL
CONSCIOUS	408 - 2	SPIRIT IS CONSCIOUS OF LOVE
CONSCIOUS	409 - 1	TO BECOME CONSCIOUS OF PERFECTION ALONE
CONSCIOUS	410 - 1	BETTER STATES OF CONSCIOUS BEING
CONSCIOUS	415 - 3	WE COULD NOT BE CONSCIOUS OF LIVING
CONSCIOUS	417 - 3	HIS CONSCIOUS CO-OPERATION
CONSCIOUS	419 - 2	WITHOUT CONSCIOUS MENTAL PROCESS
CONSCIOUS	420 - 2	NO SALVATION OUTSIDE OF CONSCIOUS
CONSCIOUS	421 - 3	CONSCIOUS OF GOD, EVIL DISAPPEARS
CONSCIOUS	435 - 4	CONSCIOUS ACT OF THE MIND
CONSCIOUS	442 - 3	CONSCIOUS ONLY OF HERSELF
CONSCIOUS	445 - 3	CONSCIOUS UNITY OF THE PERSONAL MAN
CONSCIOUS	447 - 3	CONSCIOUS UNITY MAKES OUR MIND

CONSCIOUS	462 – 3	CONSCIOUS SEPARATION FROM GOD
CONSCIOUS	472 – 1	CONSCIOUS UNION WITH GOD
CONSCIOUS	478 – 2	CONSCIOUS OF WHAT IT KNOWS
CONSCIOUS	481 – 4	THROUGH THE CONSCIOUS REALIZATION
CONSCIOUS	487 – 2	CONSCIOUS ONE AND MAY BE PRACTICED
CONSCIOUS	488 – 3	CONSCIOUS OF PERFECT LIFE
CONSCIOUS	503 – 4	RETURN IS A CONSCIOUS ACT ON OUR PART
CONSCIOUS ACTOR	129 – 2	CONSCIOUS ACTOR
CONSCIOUSLY	030 – 4	MAY CONSCIOUSLY USE IT
CONSCIOUSLY	031 – 2	CREATIVE FORCE MAY CONSCIOUSLY BE DIRECTED
CONSCIOUSLY	046 – 4	WE CONSCIOUSLY ALLOW IT TO DO SO
CONSCIOUSLY	059 – 3	PRACTITIONER CONSCIOUSLY REMOVES
CONSCIOUSLY	073 – 2	CONSCIOUSLY THINK AND DECIDE
CONSCIOUSLY	126 – 1	EITHER CONSCIOUSLY OR UNCONSCIOUSLY
CONSCIOUSLY	130 – 5	CONSCIOUSLY AND MENTAL LAW ACTS
CONSCIOUSLY	145 – 3	CONSCIOUSLY SET IN MOTION
CONSCIOUSLY	150 – 2	CAN BE CONSCIOUSLY USED
CONSCIOUSLY	169 – 5	CONCRETELY AND CONSCIOUSLY
CONSCIOUSLY	177 – 5	NOT CONSCIOUSLY THINK NEGATION
CONSCIOUSLY	186 – 1	WHICH STATEMENT CONSCIOUSLY REMOVES
CONSCIOUSLY	191 – 2	CONSCIOUSLY USED FOR DEFINITE
CONSCIOUSLY	221 – 3	DYNAMIC AND IS CONSCIOUSLY DONE
CONSCIOUSLY	224 – 2	BY THINKING CONSCIOUSLY
CONSCIOUSLY	235 – 2	EITHER CONSCIOUSLY OR UNCONSCIOUSLY
CONSCIOUSLY	251 – 2	CONTACTS AND CONSCIOUSLY BECOMES ONE
CONSCIOUSLY	252 – 4	CONSCIOUSLY HARMONIZE OURSELVES
CONSCIOUSLY	258 – 2	CO-OPERATES CONSCIOUSLY AND SUBJECTIVELY
CONSCIOUSLY	290 – 2	CONSCIOUSLY DIRECTING OUR DESTINY
CONSCIOUSLY	306 – 1	SPEAK THE WORD CONSCIOUSLY
CONSCIOUSLY	320 – 4	WE MAY CONSCIOUSLY USE IT
CONSCIOUSLY	322 – 2	CONSCIOUSLY AND UNCONSCIOUSLY HELD
CONSCIOUSLY	322 – 2	MAY BE CONSCIOUSLY CHANGED
CONSCIOUSLY	333 – 3	TO THE DEGREE THAT WE CONSCIOUSLY
CONSCIOUSLY	333 – 6	MYSTICS HAVE CONSCIOUSLY WALKED WITH GOD
CONSCIOUSLY	363 – 3	TO WHICH HE CONSCIOUSLY TALKED
CONSCIOUSLY	371 – 1	ABLE TO THINK CONSCIOUSLY
CONSCIOUSLY	379 – 4	IF IT IS CONSCIOUSLY PRESENT
CONSCIOUSLY	381 – 3	CONSCIOUSLY AND OBJECTIVELY EXERCISE
CONSCIOUSLY	390 – 4	CONSCIOUSLY CO-OPERATE WITH
CONSCIOUSLY	400 – 4	MAY CONSCIOUSLY DECIDE
CONSCIOUSLY	401 – 3	WE MUST CONSCIOUSLY KNOW
CONSCIOUSLY	421 – 2	CONSCIOUSLY ENTER INTO THE ONE
CONSCIOUSLY	450 – 5	DO SO CONSCIOUSLY TO CONCEIVE
CONSCIOUSLY	470 – S	CONSCIOUSLY AND DEFINITELY
CONSCIOUSLY	503 – 4	CONSCIOUSLY COME INTO OUR BIRTHRIGHT
CONSCIOUS MIND	030 – 4	THE CONSCIOUS MIND IS SUPERIOR
CONSCIOUS MIND	112 – 3	CONSCIOUS MIND COMES WHAT WE KNOW
CONSCIOUS MIND	132 – 2	CONSCIOUS MIND AND SPIRIT HAVE THE SAME
CONSCIOUSNESS	028 – 3	WE MEAN CONSCIOUSNESS
CONSCIOUSNESS	028 – 3	VEHICLE FOR CONSCIOUSNESS
CONSCIOUSNESS	029 – 1	DESCRIBING STATES OF CONSCIOUSNESS
CONSCIOUSNESS	032 – 3	EVOLUTION OF MAN'S CONSCIOUSNESS
CONSCIOUSNESS	038 – 2	WHEN THE CONSCIOUSNESS SPEAKS
CONSCIOUSNESS	039 – 2	WE FIND IN OUR CONSCIOUSNESS
CONSCIOUSNESS	045 – 1	CONSCIOUSNESS TAPS THE SAME SOURCE

CONSCIOUSNESS	045 – 3	ONE STATE OF CONSCIOUSNESS
CONSCIOUSNESS	046 – 4	PASS THROUGH OUR CONSCIOUSNESS
CONSCIOUSNESS	049 – 4	NO COMPROMISE WITH THE CONSCIOUSNESS
CONSCIOUSNESS	054 – 2	EXPERIENCE MUST BE IN CONSCIOUSNESS
CONSCIOUSNESS	054 – 2	CHANGE THE CONSCIOUSNESS
CONSCIOUSNESS	054 – 2	WHICH HAS NO CONSCIOUSNESS
CONSCIOUSNESS	054 – 3	AN EXPERIENCE OF CONSCIOUSNESS
CONSCIOUSNESS	058 – 1	AT THE LEVEL OF HIS CONSCIOUSNESS
CONSCIOUSNESS	064 – 2	IT IS SELF-EXISTENT CONSCIOUSNESS
CONSCIOUSNESS	064 – 2	BE AN ACT OF CONSCIOUSNESS
CONSCIOUSNESS	066 – 4	AN ABSOLUTE CONSCIOUSNESS
CONSCIOUSNESS	066 – 4	BELIEVE THAT CONSCIOUSNESS
CONSCIOUSNESS	069 – 2	AN INNER PROCESS OF CONSCIOUSNESS
CONSCIOUSNESS	087 – 5	A LIMITLESS IMAGINATION A CONSCIOUSNESS
CONSCIOUSNESS	087 – 5	ACTION OF THIS CONSCIOUSNESS BEING IDEA
CONSCIOUSNESS	096 – 1	CONSCIOUSNESS IS ALWAYS A UNITY
CONSCIOUSNESS	096 – 1	ACTIVITIES OF CONSCIOUSNESS
CONSCIOUSNESS	096 – 4	WITHOUT CONSCIOUS CONSCIOUSNESS
CONSCIOUSNESS	099 – 2	CONSCIOUSNESS WHICH PERMEATES IT
CONSCIOUSNESS	099 – 2	BODY IS IN CONSCIOUSNESS
CONSCIOUSNESS	099 – 2	PAIN AND FEAR ARE IN CONSCIOUSNESS
CONSCIOUSNESS	102 – 3	OPERATING AS CONSCIOUSNESS AND LAW
CONSCIOUSNESS	104 – 5	SPIRITUALIZATION OF HIS CONSCIOUSNESS
CONSCIOUSNESS	104 – 5	ARE STATES OF CONSCIOUSNESS
CONSCIOUSNESS	105 – 1	CONSCIOUSNESS OF THE SPIRIT
CONSCIOUSNESS	143 – 2	CONSCIOUSNESS IN THIS SENSE MEANS AN INNER
CONSCIOUSNESS	151 – 1	NO CONSCIOUSNESS SEPARATE FROM
CONSCIOUSNESS	151 – 2	A CONSCIOUSNESS OF ONE'S UNION
CONSCIOUSNESS	152 – 5	A FLOOD OF ITS CONSCIOUSNESS
CONSCIOUSNESS	153 – 3	THIS INNER CHAMBER OF CONSCIOUSNESS
CONSCIOUSNESS	158 – 3	IN THEIR CONSCIOUSNESS
CONSCIOUSNESS	163 – 1	BY A CONSCIOUSNESS OF LOVE
CONSCIOUSNESS	163 – 3	HEALING POWER IS A CONSCIOUSNESS
CONSCIOUSNESS	165 – 1	AS ACTIVE CONSCIOUSNESS
CONSCIOUSNESS	165 – 2	PEACE IN HIS CONSCIOUSNESS
CONSCIOUSNESS	166 – 4	CONTEMPLATION OF ITS CONSCIOUSNESS
CONSCIOUSNESS	167 – 3	THOUGHTS TO CONTROL HIS CONSCIOUSNESS
CONSCIOUSNESS	170 – 2	WHOSE CONSCIOUSNESS IS THE CLEAREST
CONSCIOUSNESS	175 – 2	THERE IS A STATE OF CONSCIOUSNESS
CONSCIOUSNESS	183 – 1	DEFINITE STATES OF CONSCIOUSNESS
CONSCIOUSNESS	184 – 3	IN CONSCIOUSNESS WITH THE INFINITE
CONSCIOUSNESS	184 – 3	HAVE A CONSCIOUSNESS OF LOVE
CONSCIOUSNESS	186 – 3	CONSCIOUSNESS BACK OF THE WORD
CONSCIOUSNESS	186 – 3	CONSCIOUSNESS MEANS THE INNER EMBODIMENT
CONSCIOUSNESS	188 – 2	WHERE THE INNER CONSCIOUSNESS BELIEVES
CONSCIOUSNESS	191 – 4	IN THE CONSCIOUSNESS OF MAN
CONSCIOUSNESS	192 – 2	CONSCIOUSNESS OF TRUTH ALONE
CONSCIOUSNESS	197 – 2	SUBJECTIVE TO THE RACE CONSCIOUSNESS
CONSCIOUSNESS	198 – 1	RACE CONSCIOUSNESS UNFOLDS
CONSCIOUSNESS	198 – 3	IN HIS OWN CONSCIOUSNESS
CONSCIOUSNESS	201 – 5	INNER STATE OF CONSCIOUSNESS
CONSCIOUSNESS	203 – 4	PRESENTS ITSELF TO CONSCIOUSNESS
CONSCIOUSNESS	204 – 1	GET A CLEAR CONSCIOUSNESS
CONSCIOUSNESS	204 – 3	CLEAR YOUR CONSCIOUSNESS
CONSCIOUSNESS	204 – 5	CONSTANTLY POURED INTO CONSCIOUSNESS

CONSCIOUSNESS	205 - 2	SUPPLY A SPIRITUAL CONSCIOUSNESS
CONSCIOUSNESS	207 - 2	WITHIN HIS OWN CONSCIOUSNESS
CONSCIOUSNESS	209 - 3	OUR SUBJECTIVE CONSCIOUSNESS
CONSCIOUSNESS	210 - 2	EXERCISING UPON THE RACE CONSCIOUSNESS
CONSCIOUSNESS	213 - 3	CONSCIOUSNESS THAT IT IS THERE
CONSCIOUSNESS	217 - 2	NEGATIVE STREAM OF CONSCIOUSNESS
CONSCIOUSNESS	217 - 2	WITHIN OUR OWN CONSCIOUSNESS
CONSCIOUSNESS	218 - 1	HEAVENLY CONSCIOUSNESS
CONSCIOUSNESS	220 - 3	CONSCIOUSNESS WHERE THE SOUL
CONSCIOUSNESS	220 - 4	INDUCE WITHIN CONSCIOUSNESS
CONSCIOUSNESS	222 - 4	AT THE LEVEL OF HIS CONSCIOUSNESS
CONSCIOUSNESS	224 - 1	COMES TO YOUR CONSCIOUSNESS A DEEP
CONSCIOUSNESS	226 - 2	IN THE CONSCIOUSNESS
CONSCIOUSNESS	226 - 3	COME UP THROUGH HIS CONSCIOUSNESS
CONSCIOUSNESS	227 - 3	ENTER OUR INNER CONSCIOUSNESS
CONSCIOUSNESS	228 - 1	CONSCIOUSNESS OF THE PRACTITIONER
CONSCIOUSNESS	229 - 4	ERASE FROM MY CONSCIOUSNESS
CONSCIOUSNESS	230 - 5	POINT IN OUR CONSCIOUSNESS
CONSCIOUSNESS	233 - 2	PREVENT THE CONSCIOUSNESS
CONSCIOUSNESS	235 - 2	HARMONIZING OF THE CONSCIOUSNESS
CONSCIOUSNESS	235 - 2	FROM MY CONSCIOUSNESS
CONSCIOUSNESS	236 - 4	CONSCIOUSNESS BY CLEAR THINKING
CONSCIOUSNESS	236 - 4	INNER CONSCIOUSNESS AGREES WITH THE TRUTH
CONSCIOUSNESS	239 - 3	CONSCIOUSNESS OF OUR WORK
CONSCIOUSNESS	240 - 3	LODGE IN CONSCIOUSNESS
CONSCIOUSNESS	241 - 3	MADE HIM WHOLE IN CONSCIOUSNESS
CONSCIOUSNESS	241 - 3	CONSCIOUSNESS OF THE ONE INDWELLING
CONSCIOUSNESS	241 - 3	PATIENT MUST ACCEPT THIS CONSCIOUSNESS
CONSCIOUSNESS	243 - 2	HIGHER ALTITUDES OF CONSCIOUSNESS
CONSCIOUSNESS	243 - 3	LIFTED YOUR CONSCIOUSNESS
CONSCIOUSNESS	247 - 3	CONSCIOUSNESS OF LOVE
CONSCIOUSNESS	248 - 4	TO HIS OUTER CONSCIOUSNESS
CONSCIOUSNESS	252 - 2	HAVE NOT FREED THEIR CONSCIOUSNESS
CONSCIOUSNESS	252 - 5	BE A CONSCIOUSNESS OF POISE
CONSCIOUSNESS	263 - 4	CONSCIOUSNESS OF RIGHT ACTION
CONSCIOUSNESS	273 - 1	CONSCIOUSNESS AND KNOW THAT
CONSCIOUSNESS	274 - 3	EXPANDS THE CONSCIOUSNESS
CONSCIOUSNESS	278 - 1	A SUBJECTIVE CREATIVE CONSCIOUSNESS
CONSCIOUSNESS	278 - 3	I AM KNOWN IN CONSCIOUSNESS
CONSCIOUSNESS	278 - 4	ACTUALLY INDUCE WITHIN CONSCIOUSNESS
CONSCIOUSNESS	279 - 1	ERASE FROM OUR CONSCIOUSNESS
CONSCIOUSNESS	279 - 1	ERASE THOUGHT FROM CONSCIOUSNESS
CONSCIOUSNESS	282 - 2	WE CAN UNFOLD OUR CONSCIOUSNESS
CONSCIOUSNESS	285 - 1	A CONSCIOUSNESS OF THE DIVINE PRESENCE
CONSCIOUSNESS	287 - 1	CONTINUOUSLY INCREASE HIS CONSCIOUSNESS
CONSCIOUSNESS	287 - 3	ENLARGED CONSCIOUSNESS EACH MIGHT RECEIVE
CONSCIOUSNESS	287 - 3	THE MAN WHOSE CONSCIOUSNESS
CONSCIOUSNESS	290 - 3	STAYS IN THE CONSCIOUSNESS
CONSCIOUSNESS	292 - 2	ACQUAINT THE CONSCIOUSNESS WITH THIS IDEA
CONSCIOUSNESS	295 - 2	HIS STATEMENTS INTO CONSCIOUSNESS
CONSCIOUSNESS	297 - 2	DAWNS UPON THE CONSCIOUSNESS
CONSCIOUSNESS	304 - 5	THE BALANCE OF CONSCIOUSNESS
CONSCIOUSNESS	306 - 2	THROUGH THE UNFOLDING OF CONSCIOUSNESS
CONSCIOUSNESS	307 - 1	COMPEL THE CONSCIOUSNESS
CONSCIOUSNESS	309 - 5	CONSCIOUSNESS OF A STATE OF UNITY

CONSCIOUSNESS	311 - 1	ACTION OF CONSCIOUSNESS AS LAW
CONSCIOUSNESS	311 - 3	GAVE US THIS SPIRITUAL CONSCIOUSNESS
CONSCIOUSNESS	318 - 3	THE PERSON IN CONSCIOUSNESS
CONSCIOUSNESS	318 - 4	THE CONSCIOUSNESS OF HIS PATIENT
CONSCIOUSNESS	319 - 1	CONSCIOUSNESS WILL EXTERNALIZE AT ITS OWN
CONSCIOUSNESS	321 - 2	CONSCIOUSNESS WILL EXTERNALIZE
CONSCIOUSNESS	331 - 1	THAT ONE HAS A CONSCIOUSNESS OF POWER
CONSCIOUSNESS	331 - 2	THIS CONSCIOUSNESS IN OUR WORD
CONSCIOUSNESS	331 - 3	UNIVERSAL CONSCIOUSNESS WHICH IS GOD
CONSCIOUSNESS	337 - 1	ARE STATES OF CONSCIOUSNESS
CONSCIOUSNESS	339 - 3	A MOVEMENT OF CONSCIOUSNESS
CONSCIOUSNESS	343 - 2	THE GREATER THE CONSCIOUSNESS OF GOD
CONSCIOUSNESS	344 - 2	THE GREATER A MAN'S CONSCIOUSNESS
CONSCIOUSNESS	345 - 3	WITH AN EXPANSION OF CONSCIOUSNESS
CONSCIOUSNESS	347 - 2	SUBJECTIVE STATES OF CONSCIOUSNESS
CONSCIOUSNESS	348 - 3	CREATES A NATIONAL CONSCIOUSNESS
CONSCIOUSNESS	352 - 2	IN HIS STREAM OF CONSCIOUSNESS
CONSCIOUSNESS	352 - 5	INTO OUR STREAM OF CONSCIOUSNESS
CONSCIOUSNESS	358 - 2	POINT OF OUR OWN CONSCIOUSNESS
CONSCIOUSNESS	363 - 1	CONSCIOUSNESS COMES TO THIS TRUTH
CONSCIOUSNESS	371 - 1	STREAM OF THE SAME CONSCIOUSNESS
CONSCIOUSNESS	372 - 3	INTELLIGENCE AND CONSCIOUSNESS
CONSCIOUSNESS	373 - 3	IF CONSCIOUSNESS IS TO REMAIN TRUE
CONSCIOUSNESS	374 - 2	INDIVIDUALIZED STREAM OF CONSCIOUSNESS
CONSCIOUSNESS	374 - 5	NO CONSCIOUSNESS WITHOUT SOMETHING
CONSCIOUSNESS	375 - 1	CONSCIOUSNESS TO CLOTHE ITSELF IN FORM
CONSCIOUSNESS	376 - 2	CONTINUOUS STREAM OF CONSCIOUSNESS
CONSCIOUSNESS	378 - 2	A CERTAIN STATE OF CONSCIOUSNESS
CONSCIOUSNESS	382 - 1	CONSCIOUSNESS OF THE ONE
CONSCIOUSNESS	384 - 2	STREAM OF CONSCIOUSNESS
CONSCIOUSNESS	385 - 2	STREAM OF CONSCIOUSNESS
CONSCIOUSNESS	386 - 2	PERSONAL STREAM OF CONSCIOUSNESS
OCNSCIOUSNESS	387 - 1	AN UNFOLDING CONSCIOUSNESS OF THAT WHICH
CONSCIOUSNESS	388 - 4	SLIP FROM OUR CONSCIOUSNESS
CONSCIOUSNESS	396 - 2	CONSCIOUSNESS OF GOD IN HIM
CONSCIOUSNESS	396 - 3	HE IS THE CONSCIOUSNESS OF SPIRIT
CONSCIOUSNESS	407 - 5	CONSCIOUSNESS IS ITS LAW
CONSCIOUSNESS	407 - 5	ITS CONSCIOUSNESS IS PERFECT
CONSCIOUSNESS	408 - 1	GOD'S CONSCIOUSNESS OF MAN
CONSCIOUSNESS	408 - 3	MAN'S CONSCIOUSNESS OF GOD
CONSCIOUSNESS	408 - 4	CONSCIOUSNESS OF GOD IS OUR REAL SELF
CONSCIOUSNESS	410 - 2	THESE ESSENTIAL STATES OF CONSCIOUSNESS
CONSCIOUSNESS	411 - 4	EXPERIENCE OUR STATES OF CONSCIOUSNESS
CONSCIOUSNESS	413 - 2	WITHIN US THE CHRIST CONSCIOUSNESS
CONSCIOUSNESS	415 - 2	GOD CONSCIOUSNESS WHICH WE ARE
CONSCIOUSNESS	415 - 4	OUR CONSCIOUSNESS OF THE PRESENCE
CONSCIOUSNESS	419 - 3	A POINT IN UNIVERSAL CONSCIOUSNESS
CONSCIOUSNESS	420 - 5	ONE'S CONSCIOUSNESS OF HIS UNITY
CONSCIOUSNESS	422 - 2	A STREAM OF CONSCIOUSNESS
CONSCIOUSNESS	422 - 2	CONSCIOUSNESS IS ALWAYS OMNIPRESENT
CONSCIOUSNESS	431 - 4	INTO THE HEAVENLY CONSCIOUSNESS
CONSCIOUSNESS	446 - 4	MY OWN CONSCIOUSNESS
CONSCIOUSNESS	446 - 5	CONSCIOUSNESS DOES NOT COME BY SIMPLY
CONSCIOUSNESS	453 - 3	LIFE IS WHAT CONSCIOUSNESS MAKES IT
CONSCIOUSNESS	461 - 2	CONSCIOUSNESS NECESSARY TO REAL INDIVIDUALITY

CONSCIOUSNESS	476 - 5	CONSCIOUSNESS FOR THE SPIRIT
CONSCIOUS SPIRIT	132 - 6	CONSCIOUS SPIRIT PERMEATE ALL THINGS
CONSCIOUS STATE	353 - 2	WHILE ONE IS IN A CONSCIOUS STATE
CONSCIOUS UNION	153 - 1	WE LONG FOR AND NEED A CONSCIOUS UNION
CONSCIOUS WORLD	333 - 2	SPIRIT OF GOD IN THE CONSCIOUS WORLD
CONSENSUS	417 - 1	REFLECTION OF WHAT THE CONSENSUS
CONSEQUENCE	383 - 1	PUNISHMENT A CONSEQUENCE
CONSEQUENCE	500 - 3	NO PUNISHMENT BUT A CONSEQUENCE
CONSEQUENCES	383 - 2	WE SUFFER THE CONSEQUENCES
CONSIDERED	454 - 2	CONSIDERED BEFORE ACCEPTING IT
CONSISTENT	382 - 2	IN A CONSISTENT PHILOSOPHY
CONSISTENTLY	109 - 4	KNOW DEFINITELY AND CONSISTENTLY
CONSPIRES	268 - 3	ALL NATURE CONSPIRES TO PRODUCE
CONSTANT	126 - 2	CONSTANT ACTION ON THE SUBJECTIVE
CONSTANT	276 - 3	CONSTANT REALIZATION OF THE PRESENCE
CONSTANT	497 - 1	CONSTANT RECOGNITION OF OUR RELATIONSHIP
CONSTANTLY	204 - 5	CONSTANTLY POURED INTO CONSCIOUSNESS
CONSTANTLY	343 - 2	CONSTANTLY ENDEAVORS TO LET THE TRUTH
CONSTERNATION	092 - 2	CONSTERNATION WOULD PREVAIL
CONSTIPATION	231 - 5	CONSTIPATION IS OFTEN DUE TO
CONSTIPATION	233 - 3	IN THE CASE OF CONSTIPATION
CONSTIPATION	240 - 4	AS IN CONSTIPATION
CONSTITUTES	035 - 1	CONSTITUTES THE SCIENCE OF MIND
CONSTITUTES	041 - 4	CONSTITUTES OUR RECEPTIVITY TO IT
CONSTITUTES	100 - 2	CONSTITUTES THE ETERNAL ACTIVITY
CONSTITUTES	184 - 3	CONSTITUTES A COMPLETE MAJORITY
CONSTITUTES	452 - 2	CONSTITUTES SOME OF THE MOST
CONSTITUTES	475 - 4	CONSTITUTES THE SUM TOTAL
CONSTRUCTIVE	045 - 5	TOWARD A CONSTRUCTIVE PROGRAM
CONSTRUCTIVE	120 - 3	FOR CONSTRUCTIVE PURPOSES ONLY
CONSTRUCTIVE	142 - 3	CONSTRUCTIVE WORD IS INVINCIBLE
CONSTRUCTIVE	143 - 1	BECOME ACTIVELY CONSTRUCTIVE AND HAPPY
CONSTRUCTIVE	178 - 1	CONSTRUCTIVE BASIS FOR OUR THINKING
CONSTRUCTIVE	263 - 1	THINGS WHICH ARE CONSTRUCTIVE
CONSTRUCTIVE	294 - 1	THE CONSTRUCTIVE USE OF A MENTAL LAW
CONSTRUCTIVE	423 - 2	STEADFASTLY TO THE CONSTRUCTIVE
CONSTRUCTIVELY	053 - 1	RESULT OF FAILING CONSTRUCTIVELY
CONSTRUCTIVELY	146 - 3	WE MUST KNOW CONSTRUCTIVELY
CONSTRUCTIVELY	223 - 1	EXPRESS THEMSELVES CONSTRUCTIVELY
CONSTRUCTIVELY	314 - 2	BETTER USE IT CONSTRUCTIVELY
CONSTRUCTIVELY	394 - 2	POWER IF WE USE IT CONSTRUCTIVELY
CONSUMED	335 - 4	MAY BE CONSUMED BY THE FIRE
CONSUMES	448 - 5	CONSUMES ITSELF IN THE FLAME
CONSUMMATION	103 - 2	TO ITS CONSUMMATION POINT HERE
CONTACT	112 - 4	CONTACT THE LARGER SPIRIT
CONTACT	153 - 1	TO MAKE CONTACT WITH HIM
CONTACT	272 - 4	CONTACT UNIVERSAL LAWS
CONTACT	309 - 3	CONTACT WHAT APPEARS TO BE IMPERFECT
CONTACT	350 - 2	DIRECT CONTACT WITH THE SPIRIT
CONTACT	356 - 1	CONTACT WITH THE CONDITION
CONTACT	383 - 2	THE WAY THEY CONTACT LIFE
CONTACT	394 - 2	CONTACT THE LAW OF THE UNIVERSE
CONTACT	399 - 1	ONLY PLACE WE CAN CONTACT IT
CONTACT	404 - 5	CONTACT A LARGER FIELD OF FAITH
CONTACTING	349 - 4	CONTACTING THE SUBJECTIVE SIDE

CONTACTS	312 - 3	CONTACTS AND COMMUNICATES WITH ITSELF
CONTACTS	352 - 2	ANY INDIVIDUAL CONTACTS ANOTHER
CONTAIN	107 - 1	IT DOES CONTAIN WITHIN ITSELF
CONTAINED	126 - 1	WHAT WE SHALL BE IS CONTAINED
CONTAINED	392 - 4	IN UNIVERSAL MIND IS CONTAINED
CONTAMINATE	234 - 1	TO CONGEST OR CONTAMINATE
CONTEMPLATE	116 - 1	AS I CONTEMPLATE I LET FALL
CONTEMPLATE	161 - 2	WONDERFUL TO CONTEMPLATE
CONTEMPLATE	245 - 2	TO CONTEMPLATE THE GOOD
CONTEMPLATE	316 - 3	MUST CONTEMPLATE IT
CONTEMPLATE	336 - 1	WHEN WE NO LONGER CONTEMPLATE IT
CONTEMPLATE	405 - 5	LEARN TO CONTEMPLATE THOSE THINGS
CONTEMPLATE	409 - 4	TO CONTEMPLATE THAT DIVINE LIFE
CONTEMPLATING	170 - 5	CONTEMPLATING THE PERFECT MAN
CONTEMPLATING	488 - 4	CONTEMPLATING PLENTY, ABUNDANCE, SUCCESS
CONTEMPLATING	492 - 1	BUT BY CONTEMPLATING ETERNAL LIFE
CONTEMPLATION	068 - 5	SELF-CONTEMPLATION OF SPIRIT
CONTEMPLATION	068 - 5	SELF-CONTEMPLATION OF GOD
CONTEMPLATION	085 - 1	SPIRIT CREATES BY CONTEMPLATION
CONTEMPLATION	086 - 1	THE CONTEMPLATION OF SPIRIT
CONTEMPLATION	101 - 5	THE CONTEMPLATION OF SPIRIT
CONTEMPLATION	102 - 2	RESULT OF THIS CONTEMPLATION
CONTEMPLATION	116 - 1	AS A RESULT OF ITS CONTEMPLATION
CONTEMPLATION	119 - 3	PROVIDE A HIGHER CONTEMPLATION
CONTEMPLATION	166 - 4	CONTEMPLATION OF ITS CONSCIOUSNESS
CONTEMPLATION	193 - 3	INTO A STATE OF NEUTRAL CONTEMPLATION
CONTEMPLATION	196 - 4	RESULT OF THE CONTEMPLATION
CONTEMPLATION	241 - 4	RESTS IN CONTEMPLATION
CONTEMPLATION	267 - 2	IN THE CONTEMPLATION OF LIMITATION
CONTEMPLATION	367 - 1	SILENT CONTEMPLATION
CONTEMPLATION	414 - 1	THE CONTEMPLATION OF CONDITIONS
CONTEMPLATION	461 - 4	CONTEMPLATION CREATES A FORM
CONTEMPLATION	470 - 2	SIT IN QUIET CONTEMPLATION OF GOOD
CONTEMPLATION	477 - 2	CONTEMPLATION OF ACCOMPLISHMENT
CONTEMPLATOR	196 - 3	MIND OF MAN IS THE CONTEMPLATOR
CONTEND	264 - 5	CONTEND WITH NONE
CONTEND	330 - 1	MYSTICS DID NOT CONTEND OR ARGUE
CONTENT	475 - 4	THIS INNER THOUGHT CONTENT IS
CONTENTION	377 - 2	OUR CONTENTION IS NOT
CONTINGENT	274 - 4	CONTINGENT UPON ANY EXISTING CIRCUMSTANCES
CONTINGENT	303 - 1	NOT CONTINGENT UPON ANY PLACE PERSON
CONTINUALLY	167 - 4	CONTINUALLY IMPRESSED WITH THE IMAGES
CONTINUALLY	189 - 3	CONTINUALLY REMIND OURSELVES
CONTINUALLY	382 - 3	CONTINUALLY HAPPENING IN MORE AND MORE
CONTINUANCE	384 - 2	LOGICAL CONTINUANCE OF YESTERDAY
CONTINUATION	353 - 3	CONTINUATION OF BEING
CONTINUATION	354 - 1	CONTINUATION OF THE PAST
CONTINUATION	385 - 2	CONTINUATION OF THE PERSONAL LIFE
CONTINUATION	386 - 3	IMMORTALITY OF THE CONTINUATION
CONTINUATIONS	246 - 2	CONTINUATIONS OF THE ONE
CONTINUE	384 - 3	CONTINUE TO LIVE THAT WAY
CONTINUE	448 - 4	GOOD WHILE WE CONTINUE TO DO EVIL
CONTINUE	457 - 3	CONTINUE UNTIL THE LESSON IS LEARNED
CONTINUITY	368 - 1	CONTINUITY OF THE INDIVIDUAL SOUL
CONTINUITY	378 - 3	THE CONTINUITY OF LIFE

CONTINUITY	384 - 2	A CONTINUITY OF EXPERIENCES
CONTINUITY	385 - 2	IN THE CONTINUITY
CONTINUITY	387 - 1	NO BREAKS IN ITS CONTINUITY
CONTINUITY	387 - 3	CONTINUITY OF THE INDIVIDUAL SOUL
CONTINUITY	387 - 3	AS A CONTINUITY OF TIME
CONTINUOUS	212 - 1	KNOW THAT IT IS CONTINUOUS
CONTINUOUS	282 - 2	THERE IS A CONTINUOUS GROWTH
CONTINUOUS	288 - 2	LIFE AS ONE CONTINUOUS EXPRESSION
CONTINUOUSLY	271 - 3	CONTINUOUSLY GROWING
CONTRACT	287 - 1	WE CANNOT CONTRACT THE INFINITE
CONTRACT	405 - 3	CANNOT CONTRACT THE ABSOLUTE
CONTRACT	464 - 5	CONTRACT THE INFINITE
CONTRACTS	200 - 3	DISHONEST IF HE CONTRACTS
CONTRADICT	032 - 1	CONTRADICT THE INEVITABLE
CONTRADICT	095 - 2	CONTRADICT THEIR EXISTENCE
CONTRADICT	102 - 4	THE MANY NEVER CONTRADICT
CONTRADICT	140 - 2	CANNOT CONTRADICT ANY THOUGHT
CONTRADICT	159 - 5	APPEARS TO CONTRADICT THIS
CONTRADICT	161 - 3	DOES NOT CONTRADICT THE GENERAL GOOD
CONTRADICT	260 - 3	CONTRADICT HUMAN EXPERIENCE
CONTRADICT	268 - 3	CONTRADICT THE NATURE OF THE UNIVERSE
CONTRADICT	328 - 4	MORE OR LESS CONTRADICT EACH OTHER
CONTRADICT	354 - 3	NEVER DOES IT CONTRADICT
CONTRADICT	413 - 5	CONTRADICT WHAT APPEARS TO BE SO
CONTRADICT	415 - 5	WOULD CONTRADICT ITS OWN NATURE
CONTRADICT	432 - 3	POSITION TO CONTRADICT THIS THEORY
CONTRADICT	454 - 2	CONTRADICT THE DIVINE NATURE
CONTRADICT	496 - 2	CONTRADICT THE FUNDAMENTAL GOODNESS
CONTRADICTION	055 - 1	CONTRADICTION OF HIS STATEMENTS
CONTRADICTION	283 - 3	NO LONGER ANY CONTRADICTION
CONTRADICTION	283 - 4	ANY CONTRADICTION IS
CONTRADICTION	285 - 4	ANY SUBJECTIVE CONTRADICTION
CONTRADICTION	429 - 1	WITH AN APPARENT CONTRADICTION
CONTRADICTIONS	057 - 4	WHAT THE APPARENT CONTRADICTIONS
CONTRADICTORY	312 - 1	CONTRADICTORY TO THE DIVINE BEING
CONTRADICTS	055 - 2	EVERYTHING THAT CONTRADICTS
CONTRADICTS	171 - 1	HE CONTRADICTS WHAT APPEARS
CONTRADICTS	192 - 5	CONTRADICTS THE MAIN FOUNDATION
CONTRADICTS	283 - 4	CONTRADICTS OUR OBJECTIVE AFFIRMATION
CONTRARY	161 - 2	CONTRARY TO THE UNIVERSAL GOOD
CONTRARY	167 - 4	EVIDENCE CONTRARY TO GOOD
CONTRARY	266 - 3	CONTRARY TO THE NATURE OF
CONTROL	053 - 4	CONTROL OUR THOUGHT PROCESSES
CONTROL	125 - 3	CONSCIOUSLY CONTROL THE STREAM OF THOUGHT
CONTROL	126 - 2	WE AND WE ALONE CONTROL OUR DESTINY
CONTROL	137 - 1	POWER TO CONTROL ITS OWN DESTINY
CONTROL	139 - 4	CONTROL OUR ENVIRONMENT
CONTROL	147 - 2	CONTROL ALL THOUGHT THAT DENIES THE REAL
CONTROL	210 - 1	FROM ANY THOUGHT OF CONTROL
CONTROL	223 - 1	UNLESS WE CONTROL THOUGHT
CONTROL	266 - 3	A CONTROL OF CONDITIONS
CONTROL	338 - 2	SPIRIT DOES NOT SEEK TO CONTROL US
CONTROL	338 - 2	CONTROL THIS INDIVIDUALITY
CONTROL	381 - 4	SHOULD CONTROL THE SUBJECTIVE
CONTROL	394 - 3	CONTROL OF CONDITIONS AROUND US

CONTROL	396 - 2	CONSCIOUS CONTROL OF THE SPIRIT
CONTROL	399 - 2	CONTROL OF AFFAIRS
CONTROL	403 - 2	CONTROL OUR THOUGHT PATTERNS
CONTROLLED	100 - 1	CONTROLLED BY THE SOUL LIFE
CONTROLLED	167 - 4	LIFE IS CONTROLLED BY LOVE
CONTROLLED	209 - 2	NEVERTHELESS CONTROLLED BY IT
CONTROLLED	295 - 1	OUTSIDE THINGS CONTROLLED US
CONTROLS	099 - 4	MIND COMPLETELY CONTROLS
CONTROLS	232 - 2	CONTROLS AND DIRECTS ALL
CONTROLS	244 - 4	AS IT CONTROLS THE HUMAN BODY
CONTROLS	256 - 2	THOUGHT CONTROLS THE BODY
CONTROLS	402 - 3	THE SPIRIT CONTROLS THE LAW
CONTROLS	403 - 3	CONTROLS THE LAW OF MIND
CONTROVERSIES	120 - 4	CONTROVERSIES ABOUT THE USE AND MISUSE
CONTROVERSY	056 - 2	WRITTEN IN A SPIRIT OF CONTROVERSY
CONTROVERSY	199 - 3	WITHOUT CONTROVERSY WE WORK
CONTROVERSY	440 - 6	NO CONTROVERSY, NO ARGUMENT
CONVERSATION	055 - 3	REFUSE TO HOLD CONVERSATION
CONVERSATION	055 - 4	CONVERSATION BE IN HEAVEN
CONVERSATION	077 - 3	UNCONSCIOUS MENTAL CONVERSATION
CONVERSATION	445 - 5	CONVERSATION WE ASSUME GREAT KNOWLEDGE
CONVERSE	312 - 3	WE COULD NOT CONVERSE
CONVERT	255 - 4	CONVERT CERTAIN SUBSTANCES
CONVERT	439 - 2	CONVERT IT INTO A GREATER GOOD
CONVERTING	159 - 2	CONVERTING THOUGHT TO A BELIEF
CONVERTING	502 - 5	CONVERTING THEM INTO GREAT LESSONS
CONVERTS	255 - 4	CONVERTS THEM INTO NEW SUBSTANCES
CONVICTION	030 - 3	CONVICTION BEHIND THE THOUGHT
CONVICTION	056 - 2	IT IS ONE OF CONVICTION
CONVICTION	058 - 5	BUT WITH CONVICTION
CONVICTION	094 - 1	CONVICTION BEHIND THE THOUGHT
CONVICTION	159 - 1	WE MUST HAVE A CONVICTION
CONVICTION	159 - 1	WILL WEAKEN THIS CONVICTION
CONVICTION	159 - 2	BE STEADY IN ITS CONVICTION
CONVICTION	162 - 5	ABLE TO SAY WITH CONVICTION
CONVICTION	163 - 2	WITH A DEEP INNER CONVICTION
CONVICTION	173 - 4	CONVICTION HE MUST ACQUIRE
CONVICTION	178 - 4	STEADY IN ITS CONVICTION
CONVICTION	200 - 4	CONVICTION IN THE MIND
CONVICTION	208 - 1	RESULT OF A CONVICTION
CONVICTION	219 - 4	CONVICTION THAT WE ARE ONE
CONVICTION	252 - 4	A CONVICTION THAT THE GOD WITHIN
CONVICTION	262 - 2	PRACTITIONER'S MIND A CONVICTION
CONVICTION	280 - 2	NECESSITY OF FAITH CONVICTION
CONVICTION	284 - 5	UNDERSTANDING WITH GREATER CONVICTION
CONVICTION	285 - 3	EQUAL ITS INWARD CONVICTION
CONVICTION	285 - 4	COMPLETE CONVICTION THAT THE SPIRIT
CONVICTION	285 - 4	CONVICTION IS IN LINE WITH REALITY
CONVICTION	309 - 3	CONVICTION DAWNS THAT GOD IS ALL THERE IS
CONVICTION	318 - 1	FAITH, BELIEF, ACCEPTANCE, CONVICTION
CONVICTION	318 - 2	OUR CONVICTION IN CONCRETE FORM
CONVICTION	398 - 4	FILLED WITH CONVICTION
CONVICTION	399 - 4	POWER AND WITH CONVICTION
CONVICTION	400 - 2	HOLDS TO IT WITH CONVICTION
CONVICTION	410 - 2	WORDS WILL BRING CONVICTION

CONVICTION	410 - 2	CONVICTION IS THE MOLTEN SUBSTANCE
CONVICTION	413 - 4	AS MUCH CONVICTION AS WE HAVE
CONVICTION	413 - 5	THE CONVICTION THAT HEALS
CONVICTION	414 - 3	WITHOUT MENTAL CONVICTION
CONVICTION	415 - 1	SPEAK THE CONVICTION THAT IS WITHIN US
CONVICTION	423 - 1	WORLD NEEDS IS SPIRITUAL CONVICTION
CONVICTION	441 - 4	REMAINS FOR INDIVIDUAL CONVICTION
CONVICTION	450 - 3	CONVICTION IS ATTENDED BY CERTAINTY
CONVICTION	450 - 3	CONVICTION OF THE INNER POWER
CONVICTION	476 - 2	WITHOUT CONVICTION HAVE NO POWER
CONVICTION	476 - 2	CONVICTION WITHOUT WORDS
CONVICTION	499 - 6	CONVICTION IS WORTH MORE THAN
CONVICTION	499 - 6	CONVICTION IS WORTH MANY POUNDS
CONVICTIONS	451 - 3	WITH SPIRITUAL CONVICTIONS COME ALL ELSE
CONVINCE	086 - 4	CONVINCE OURSELVES OF THE REALITY
CONVINCE	206 - 4	TRIES TO CONVINCE HIMSELF
CONVINCE	212 - 4	CONVINCE HIMSELF OF THE PERFECTNESS
CONVINCE	220 - 4	CONVINCE HIMSELF OF THE TRUTH
CONVINCED	056 - 2	A MAN CONVINCED AGAINST
CONVINCED	157 - 4	ONE PRAYING BECOMES CONVINCED
CONVINCED	170 - 2	CONVINCED OF THE POWER
CONVINCED	174 - 3	ARE CONVINCED IS THE TRUTH
CONVINCED	250 - 2	MORE CONVINCED A PRACTITIONER IS
CONVINCED	379 - 2	ENTIRELY CONVINCED OF THE REALITY
CONVINCED	398 - 4	CONVINCED THAT SPIRIT RESPONDS
CONVINCED	421 - 3	CONVINCED OF IMMORTALITY NOW
CONVINCED	500 - 2	CONVINCED WE ARE TRANSGRESSORS
CONVINCES	198 - 3	CONVINCES HIS OWN MIND
CONVINCING	058 - 3	CONVINCING OURSELVES OF THE TRUTH
CONVOLUTIONS	066 - 3	CONVOLUTIONS OF THOUGHT
CO-OPERATE	154 - 1	CO-OPERATE WITH THESE ETERNAL REALITIES
CO-OPERATE	239 - 3	CO-OPERATE MENTALLY WITH THIS LAW OF LIFE
CO-OPERATE	305 - 1	CO-OPERATE WITH IT
CO-OPERATE	333 - 3	WE CONSCIOUSLY CO-OPERATE
CO-OPERATES	162 - 2	CO-OPERATES WITH DIVINE MIND
CO-OPERATES	258 - 2	CO-OPERATES CONSCIOUSLY AND SUBJECTIVELY
CO-OPERATES	482 - 2	CONSCIOUSLY CO-OPERATES WITH IT
CO-OPERATION	130 - 1	CO-OPERATION WITH HER PURPOSE
CO-OPERATION	316 - 2	CO-OPERATION WILL BE BROUGHT ABOUT
CO-OPERATION	342 - 4	HIS RECOGNITION AND CO-OPERATION
CO-OPERATION	417 - 3	UPON HIS CONSCIOUS CO-OPERATION
CO-ORDINATES	415 - 4	CO-ORDINATES EVERYTHING INTO ONE
CO-ORDINATION	242 - 2	PERFECT CO-ORDINATION AND FUNCTIONING
CORD	454 - 3	CORD THAT BINDS
CORNERSTONES	496 - 5	GRACE AND TRUTH ARE THE CORNERSTONES
CORPSE	197 - 1	BODY AND IT BECOMES A CORPSE
CORPSE	432 - 4	CORPSE OF A MISTAKEN YESTERDAY
CORRECT	150 - 2	PRAYING IS THE CORRECT WAY
CORRECT	179 - 5	CORRECT MENTAL PRACTICE
CORRECT	254 - 4	CORRECT METHOD FOR PRACTICE
CORRECT	272 - 2	CORRECT CHOICE WILL BE
CORRECT	277 - 2	THE CORRECT MANNER OF APPROACH
CORRECT	282 - 3	PLACE A CORRECT CONCEPT OF LIFE
CORRECT	289 - 4	CORRECT PRACTICE SHOULD KNOW THAT
CORRECT	304 - 4	IT IS CORRECT TO SAY

CORRECT	322 - 1	ACT IN A CORRECT MANNER
CORRECT	393 - 2	CORRECT UNDERSTANDING THAT MIND
CORRECT	461 - 4	GOD IS ALREADY THE CORRECT
CORRECT KNOWING	487 - 1	ACCOMPLISHED BY CORRECT KNOWING
CORRECTLY	049 - 3	CORRECTLY BEGIN THEIR TREATMENT
CORRECTLY	052 - 3	PROVED THAT BY THINKING CORRECTLY
CORRECTLY	056 - 2	WHEN WE VIEW IT CORRECTLY
CORRECTLY	483 - 2	BY CORRECTLY VIEWING THE SEEN
CORRESPONDENCE	120 - 3	CORRESPONDENCE IN THE FORM OF A DELUGE
CORRESPONDENCE	285 - 3	CORRESPONDENCE IN THE OBJECTIVE
CORRESPONDENCE	306 - 2	THE LAW OF CORRESPONDENCE WORKS
CORRESPONDENCE	322 - 2	ATTRACTS TO HIMSELF A CORRESPONDENCE
CORRESPONDENCE	396 - 1	RESPONDS BY CORRESPONDENCE
CORRESPONDENT	177 - 5	THE PHYSICAL CORRESPONDENT
CORRESPONDENTS	483 - 1	GREAT LAW OF CORRESPONDENTS
CORRESPONDING	028 - 2	RESPONDED BY CORRESPONDING
CORRESPONDING	139 - 2	IT CAN RESPOND ONLY BY CORRESPONDING
CORRESPONDING	383 - 1	FIND THEIR CORRESPONDING EFFECTS
CORRESPONDS	319 - 1	CORRESPONDS TO OUR MENTAL STATES
CORRIDORS	348 - 4	CORRIDORS AND READ THE WRITINGS
COSMIC	123 - 4	THEN A COSMIC CONSCIOUSNESS
COSMIC	201 - 2	NOT A COSMIC PROBLEM
COSMIC	273 - 4	IN A COSMIC CUPBOARD SOMEWHERE
COSMIC	289 - 4	COSMIC CREATION IS FROM IDEA
COSMIC	336 - 1	A PERSONAL AND NOT A COSMIC PROBLEM
COSMIC	341 - 2	DR. BUCKE DEFINES COSMIC CONSCIOUSNESS
COSMIC	341 - 4	PLOTINUS HAD SEVEN DISTINCT PERIODS OF COSMIC
COSMIC	341 - 5	COSMIC CONSCIOUSNESS
COSMIC	341 - 5	HAD DEFINITE COSMIC EXPERIENCES
COSMIC	343 - 2	COSMIC CONSCIOUSNESS IS NOT A MYSTERY
COSMIC	363 - 1	THE MORE COSMIC SWEEP IT HAS
COSMIC	395 - 2	THE COSMIC ENGINE IS STARTED
COSMIC	420 - 5	COSMIC CONSCIOUSNESS WE MEAN
COSMIC ENTITY	337 - 1	EVIL AS A COSMIC ENTITY
COSMIC LESSON	473 - 3	TRYING TO TEACH A COSMIC LESSON
COSMIC LIFE	127 - 3	IN LINE WITH THE COSMIC LIFE
COSMIC LIGHT	344 - 3	ALL MYSTICS HAVE SEEN THIS COSMIC LIGHT
COSMIC ORDER	313 - 3	THE COSMIC ORDER IS THE DIVINE MIND
COSMIC SOUL	449 - 5	JESUS WAS A CONSCIOUSLY COSMIC SOUL
COSMIC STUFF	098 - 1	PRIMORDIAL OR COSMIC STUFF
COSMIC STUFF	311 - 2	ETERNALITY OF ENERGY AND COSMIC STUFF
COSMOS	043 - 2	COSMOS AND NOT CHAOS
COSMOS	314 - 1	COSMOS IN OUR INDIVIDUAL WORLD
COSMOS	329 - 2	THE REFLECTION OF THE COSMOS
COSMOS	337 - 2	THAT THE ENTIRE COSMOS IS
COSMOS	407 - 4	IT IS A COSMOS
COUNCIL	369 - 2	TAKE COUNCIL FROM HIM
COUNTED	301 - 3	COUNTED OUT OF OUR LIVES
COUNSELLED	440 - 5	HE COUNSELLED HIS FOLLOWERS AGAINST
COUNTERFEIT	459 - 6	COUNTERFEIT FOR THE REAL
COUNTERPART	099 - 3	COUNTERPART OF AN INVISIBLE BODY
COUNTERPART	483 - 1	THE PHYSICAL IS COUNTERPART
COUNTLESS	144 - 2	COUNTLESS NUMBERS OF FORMS
COUPLED	202 - 6	COUPLED WITH A REALIZATION THAT
COUPLED	276 - 2	COUPLED WITH THE DEFINITE KNOWLEDGE

COURSE	056 – 4	FOLLOW THE RIGHT COURSE
COURTED	045 – 1	COURTED THE PARTICULAR PRESENCE
COURTING	329 – 3	CONSCIOUS COURTING OF THE DIVINE PRESENCE
COVERED	441 – 2	COVERED THAT SHALL NOT BE REVEALED
CRADLE	429 – 1	CRADLE AND ENDS WITH
CRAVING	339 – 4	THERE IS AN EMOTIONAL CRAVING
CREATE	031 – 6	WE DO NOT CREATE LAWS AND PRINCIPLES
CREATE	064 – 5	IT IS HIS NATURE TO CREATE
CREATE	067 – 2	MUST ALWAYS CREATE
CREATE	067 – 2	SPIRITUAL IS TO CREATE
CREATE	095 – 2	DO NOT CREATE LAWS AND PRINCIPLES
CREATE	197 – 2	TO CREATE NEW SUBJECTIVE THOUGHT
CREATE	274 – 4	WE DO NOT CREATE
CREATE	285 – 1	THOSE WHICH CREATE DISEASE
CREATE	302 – 1	WE SHALL CREATE A NEW PATTERN
CREATE	302 – 3	CREATE FOR US ALL THAT WE NEED
CREATE	375 – 1	CREATE AND SUSTAIN ONE HEREAFTER
CREATE	397 – 1	WE FIRST CREATE THE THOUGHT MOLD
CREATE	400 – 2	LIFE WILL CREATE SUCCESS
CREATE	400 – 3	CREATE MENTAL IMAGES THAT ARE DEFINITE
CREATE	406 – 3	AS EASILY CREATE A NEW FORM
CREATE	406 – 4	NEW THOUGHTS CREATE
CREATE	411 – 2	COULD AS EASILY CREATE FREEDOM
CREATE	416 – 4	AS EASILY AND AS WILLINGLY CREATE ABUNDANCE
CREATED	076 – 5	SAME INTELLIGENCE THAT CREATED IT
CREATED	085 – 3	SPIRIT WAS NOT CREATED
CREATED	194 – 5	ALWAYS CAUSING SOMETHING TO BE CREATED
CREATED	339 – 3	CREATED OUT OF THIS ONE
CREATES	038 – 3	BELIEF CREATES A TENDENCY
CREATES	078 – 2	WITHOUT KNOWING WHAT IT CREATES
CREATES	085 – 1	SPIRIT CREATES BY CONTEMPLATION
CREATES	108 – 1	HE CREATES HIS OWN EXPERIENCE
CREATES	116 – 1	NATURE CREATES—IT CONTEMPLATES
CREATES	140 – 1	POWER OF THE ONE MIND WHICH CREATES FOR US
CREATES	148 – 1	CREATES BY CONTEMPLATION
CREATES	166 – 4	CREATES BY THE POWER OF ITS WORD
CREATES	194 – 3	LAW CREATES THE FORM
CREATES	224 – 2	THE LAW WHICH CREATES
CREATES	281 – 4	CREATES UNLOVELY REACTIONS
CREATES	296 – 4	ONE POWER THAT CREATES ALL
CREATES	410 – 2	WHILE THE SPIRIT CREATES
CREATES	416 – 3	CREATES A FORM AROUND THESE IMAGES
CREATES	483 – 4	CREATES BY THE POWER OF HIS WORD
CREATING	064 – 5	HE IS ALWAYS CREATING
CREATING	212 – 4	CREATING A PERFECT IDEA
CREATING	294 – 1	CANNOT STOP CREATING
CREATING	294 – 1	CREATING SOMETHING FOR US
CREATING	416 – 4	CREATING THEM AND CAUSING THEM
CREATION	060 – 4	THE POWER BACK OF CREATION
CREATION	064 – 3	ACCOUNT OF CREATION
CREATION	065 – 1	THE RESULT IS CREATION
CREATION	065 – 8	STORY OF CREATION
CREATION	066 – 2	ANY ACCOUNT OF CREATION
CREATION	066 – 5	CREATION MEANS THE GIVING
CREATION	067 – 2	THE ACCOUNT OF CREATION

CREATION	069 - 1	STARTING POINT OF ALL CREATION
CREATION	070 - 2	CREATION IS ALWAYS BEGINNING
CREATION	070 - 2	CREATION GOES ON FOREVER
CREATION	083 - 3	CREATION DOES NOT MEAN
CREATION	083 - 3	CREATION IS THE PASSING OF SPIRIT
CREATION	084 - 4	CREATION THE ACTIVITY OF GOD
CREATION	100 - 2	CREATION ETERNALLY GOING ON
CREATION	103 - 2	CARRYING CREATION FORWARD
CREATION	123 - 3	ALL CREATION IS AN EFFECT
CREATION	131 - 5	CREATION IS ETERNALLY GOING ON
CREATION	131 - 6	CREATION IS THE PLAY OF LIFE UPON ITSELF
CREATION	273 - 3	IT IS A NEW CREATION
CREATION	273 - 4	ITSELF INTO CREATION
CREATION	298 - 3	SOLE IMPULSE FOR CREATION
CREATION	310 - 3	SPIRIT UPON ITSELF PRODUCES CREATION
CREATION	339 - 4	THE STARTING POINT OF CREATION
CREATION	357 - 2	CREATION GOES ON FOREVER
CREATION	393 - 3	A NEW CREATION PRODUCED
CREATION	400 - 1	NEW CREATION
CREATION	407 - 4	ALL CREATION IS SPIRITUAL
CREATION	420 - 4	CREATION IS THE LOGICAL RESULT
CREATION	461 - 4	MEANING AND PROCESS OF CREATION
CREATION	465 - 1	CREATION IS THE PLAY OF LIFE
CREATION	493 - 3	CREATION IS THIS BODY
CREATIVE	025 - 2	CREATIVE INTELLIGENCE OF THE UNIVERSE
CREATIVE	025 - 2	DISHONOR THE CREATIVE POWER
CREATIVE	029 - 1	SET IN MOTION AS A CREATIVE THING
CREATIVE	029 - 2	THE CREATIVE FACTOR WITHIN US
CREATIVE	030 - 2	THERE IS A CREATIVE FIELD
CREATIVE	030 - 2	WE ALL USE THE CREATIVE POWER
CREATIVE	030 - 3	ALL THOUGHT IS CREATIVE
CREATIVE	031 - 2	LAW OF CREATIVE FORCE MAY CONSCIOUSLY BE
CREATIVE	032 - 3	IS GOOD AS WELL AS CREATIVE
CREATIVE	036 - 1	THIS ORIGINAL CREATIVE THING
CREATIVE	079 - 3	INTELLIGENT AND CREATIVE ONE
CREATIVE	082 - 4	SPIRIT, IT IS CREATIVE
CREATIVE	082 - 4	CREATIVE LIFE EXPRESSING ITSELF
CREATIVE	090 - 2	SOUL OF THE UNIVERSE IS THE CREATIVE
CREATIVE	092 - 2	GREATER CREATIVE MEDIUM OF THE SPIRIT
CREATIVE	094 - 1	THOUGHT IS CREATIVE
CREATIVE	094 - 1	ALL THOUGHT IS CREATIVE
CREATIVE	118 - 1	A CREATIVE INTELLIGENCE AT OUR DISPOSAL
CREATIVE	132 - 8	CREATIVE THROUGH HIS SUBCONSCIOUS
CREATIVE	155 - 2	CREATIVE OF THE DESIRED RESULTS
CREATIVE	163 - 1	NATURE OF THE CREATIVE POWER
CREATIVE	179 - 3	ALL LIVE IN ONE CREATIVE MIND
CREATIVE	183 - 1	OPERATE THROUGH A CREATIVE FIELD
CREATIVE	192 - 3	THAT WILL POWER IS CREATIVE
CREATIVE	192 - 3	WILL IS DIRECTIVE BUT NOT CREATIVE
CREATIVE	192 - 3	IN THE CREATIVE ORDER
CREATIVE	193 - 2	THE IMAGINATION IS CREATIVE
CREATIVE	193 - 3	THE WILL BECOME CREATIVE
CREATIVE	193 - 4	CREATIVE CURRENTS
CREATIVE	194 - 2	STREAM OF CREATIVE ENERGY
CREATIVE	194 - 5	CREATIVE PROCESS WILL GO ON

CREATIVE	207 – 4	CREATIVE SOIL WILL
CREATIVE	208 – 1	THE TREATMENT IS CREATIVE
CREATIVE	208 – 4	INTO THE CREATIVE MEDIUM
CREATIVE	222 – 4	CREATIVE MIND LOOSES ENERGY
CREATIVE	228 – 2	CREATIVE MEDIUM OF HIS THOUGHT
CREATIVE	244 – 2	OUR THOUGHT IS CREATIVE
CREATIVE	251 – 4	THE CREATIVE LAW WITHIN YOU KNOWS
CREATIVE	255 – 3	CREATIVE, ENERGIZING, VITALIZING, ONES
CREATIVE	267 – 3	LAW IN MOTION WHICH IS CREATIVE
CREATIVE	278 – 1	CREATIVE CONSCIOUSNESS WHICH IS RECEPTIVE
CREATIVE	283 – 2	FEELING AND EMOTION ARE CREATIVE
CREATIVE	294 – 3	HE USES THE SAME CREATIVE PROCESS
CREATIVE	298 – 3	THE REAL CREATIVE INSTINCT
CREATIVE	310 – 3	HIS WORD IS CREATIVE
CREATIVE	313 – 5	THOUGHT IS CREATIVE IN OUR WORLD
CREATIVE	390 – 4	THE CREATIVE ORDER OF THE UNIVERSE
CREATIVE	392 – 2	A CREATIVE UNIVERSAL ENERGY
CREATIVE	403 – 3	IT IS CREATIVE WITHOUT CARING WHAT IT
CREATIVE	403 – 4	STARTING POINT FOR A CREATIVE PATTERN
CREATIVE	416 – 2	IT IS SENSITIVE, CREATIVE
CREATIVE	418 – 4	THE CREATIVE GENIUS OF THE INNER LIFE
CREATIVE ACT	318 – 2	CREATIVE ACT IS ALWAYS CONSCIOUS
CREATIVE AGENCY	105 – 3	INTELLIGENCE IS THE ULTIMATE CREATIVE AGENCY
CREATIVE AGENCY	392 – 4	SOLE AND ONLY CREATIVE AGENCY
CREATIVE ENERGY	047 – 4	CREATIVE ENERGY CAN PRODUCE
CREATIVE ENERGY	050 – 1	OF THE CREATIVE ENERGY
CREATIVE FACTOR	494 – 1	CREATIVE FACTOR WITHIN US
CREATIVENESS	284 – 2	ESSENCE OF CREATIVENESS
CREATIVENESS	391 – 2	HENCE ITS CREATIVENESS
CREATIVENESS	392 – 2	SUBSTANCE AND CREATIVENESS
CREATIVENESS	393 – 2	SUCH A CREATIVENESS IS NOT ENOUGH
CREATIVENESS	403 – 3	CREATIVENESS IS THE OFFICE OF THE INNER
CREATIVENESS	406 – 3	CONNECTS US WITH THE CREATIVENESS
CREATIVENESS	411 – 2	THE USE OF OUR CREATIVENESS IN
CREATIVE ORDER	038 – 2	FIRST STEP OF THE CREATIVE ORDER
CREATIVE ORDER	194 – 3	RIGHTLY BELONG IN THE CREATIVE ORDER
CREATIVE POWER	146 – 3	CREATIVE POWER OF MIND IS
CREATIVE POWER	192 – 5	WE USE A CREATIVE POWER
CREATIVE POWER	193 – 3	THE CREATIVE POWER OF MIND
CREATIVE POWER	401 – 2	CREATIVE POWER OF THE UNIVERSE
CREATIVE POWER	500 – 4	CREATIVE POWER OF OUR THOUGHT
CREATIVE SOIL	123 – 3	CREATIVE SOIL THAT WHICH IS UNIQUE
CREATIVE SPIRIT	163 – 1	CREATIVE SPIRIT IS ALWAYS AT WORK
CREATOR	101 – 4	THE CREATOR IS GREATER
CREATOR	185 – 2	BELIEVE IN ANOTHER CREATOR
CREATURE	484 – 4	EFFECT A CREATURE OF TIME
CREATURE	485 – 4	CREATURE SHALL BE DELIVERED FROM
CREDULITY	027 – 1	TO STRETCH OUR CREDULITY
CREED	383 – 3	HAVE SUBSCRIBED TO SOME CREED
CRIME	338 – 2	CRIME AGAINST HIS REAL SELF
CRIME	381 – 4	IT IS A CRIME AGAINST INDIVIDUALITY
CRITERION	269 – 1	SANE AND INTELLIGENT CRITERION
CRITERION	270 – 2	THE CRITERION FOR ANY MAN
CRITERION	270 – 2	THE CRITERION IS: DOES THE THING I WISH
CRITICISM	137 – 2	CRITICISM OF THE POWER OF THOUGHT

CRITICISM	248 - 4	CRITICISM AND INABILITY TO LIVE
CRITICISM	253 - 3	ANXIETY, FEAR AND CRITICISM
CRITICISM	433 - 4	THOUGHT OF JUDGMENT, CRITICISM
CRITICIZE	260 - 3	CRITICIZE HIM FOR SUCH
CROSS	428 - 2	CROSS IS MIGHTIER THAN THE CROWN
CROSS	472 - 6	CROSS REPRESENTS THE TREE OF LIFE
CROSS	474 - 6	EACH MUST LIFT HIMSELF TO THE CROSS
CROSS CURRENTS	288 - 2	WE HAVE CROSS CURRENTS OF THOUGHT
CROWD	399 - 4	WE DO NOT CROWD
CROWN	428 - 2	CROSS IS MIGHTIER THAN THE CROWN
CROWNED	391 - 4	CROWNED HIM WITH GLORY
CRUEL	149 - 4	ONE DAY AND CRUEL THE NEXT
CRUEL	232 - 3	HE THAT IS CRUEL TROUBLETH
CRUEL	232 - 3	EVERY ADVERSE THOUGHT IS CRUEL
CRUELTY	232 - 3	CRUELTY IS DISTURBING TO THE ENTIRE BODY
CRUMBLE	427 - 5	RISEN ONLY TO CRUMBLE IN DUST
CRUX	052 - 2	CRUX OF THE WHOLE MATTER
CUBE	175 - 2	EXTRACT THE CUBE ROOT
CUBIT	194 - 3	ADD ONE CUBIT TO HIS STATURE
CUBIT	489 - 3	YOU DO NOT ADD ONE CUBIT
CULMINATE	309 - 3	CULMINATE IN THE MENTAL EVIDENCE
CULMINATES	489 - 3	CULMINATES IN THE DESIRED RESULT
CULMINATION	035 - 1	CULMINATION OF ALL REVELATIONS
CULTIVATE	157 - 2	CULTIVATE A FAITH IN THESE
CULTIVATE	297 - 4	CULTIVATE AN ATTITUDE OF FRIENDSHIP
CULTURE	348 - 3	WITH A SPIRIT OF CULTURE
CULTURE	446 - 4	ONLY THROUGH SOIL CULTURE
CUP	246 - 4	THE CUP OF ACCEPTANCE
CUP	277 - 2	LET THIS CUP PASS FROM ME
CUPBOARD	273 - 4	A COSMIC CUPBOARD SOMEWHERE
CURABLE	216 - 1	OPPOSED TO A CURABLE
CURATIVE	199 - 3	UNDERTAKEN IN THE CURATIVE ART
CURE	190 - 3	NO FORM OF CURE WILL BE PERMANENT
CURED	216 - 3	SUSCEPTIBLE OF BEING CURED
CURED	216 - 3	NOT BEING CURED
CURRENT	440 - 2	ALLOW THE DIVINE CURRENT
CURRENTS	219 - 1	THE HEALING CURRENTS OF LIFE
CURRENTS	321 - 1	CHANGES THE CURRENTS OF CAUSATION
CURRENTS	463 - 2	CURRENTS OF DIVINITY RAN THROUGH
CURSE	383 - 1	A BLESSING OR A CURSE
CURSE	487 - 3	BLESS AND CURSE NOT
CUT	148 - 4	CUT RIGHT THROUGH ALL THAT APPEARS
CUT OFF	117 - 3	CUT OFF AND STILL BE ABLE TO RUN DOWN
CUT OFF	372 - 1	CUT OFF HIS ENTIRE PAST
CUTTING	173 - 2	CUTTING THROUGH OF ALL APPEARANCES
CUTTING OFF	386 - 1	CUTTING OFF OF ALL CONSCIOUS LIFE
CYCLES	336 - 2	IN EVER ASCENDING CYCLES
CYCLES	404 - 4	PSYCHOLOGY OF ECONOMIC CYCLES PROVES
CYST	236 - 2	A CYST OR GALLSTONES

D

| DAILY | 056 - 4 | IDEAS COME TO ME DAILY |

DAILY	057 - 4	DAILY TAKE THE TIME TO MEDITATE
DAILY	147 - 2	DAILY WE MUST CONTROL
DAILY	148 - 4	DAILY FEEL A DEEPER UNION WITH LIFE
DAILY	160 - 3	HE WHO PRACTICES DAILY
DAILY	168 - 1	FROM SUCH DAILY MEDITATION
DAILY	179 - 5	DAILY SEE THE PERFECT MAN
DAILY	185 - 2	DAILY MEDITATE ON THE PERFECT LIFE
DAILY	187 - 2	DAILY IN THOUGHT TO CONCEIVE
DAILY	225 - 1	DAILY UNTIL A HEALING TAKES
DAILY	247 - 3	LIFE IS RENEWED DAILY
DAILY	271 - 4	IF DAILY WE ARE REALIZING
DAILY	295 - 2	HE SHOULD DEFINITELY DAILY
DAILY	358 - 4	DAILY PRACTICE IN OUR MEDITATIONS
DAILY	419 - 1	DAILY PRACTICE CORRECT THINKING
DAILY	502 - 1	DAILY TO THE SPIRIT OF GOODNESS
DAMASCUS	344 - 3	SAUL ON HIS RETURN TO DAMASCUS
DAMNATION	335 - 3	DAMNATION HAS BEEN AS FOREIGN
DAMNATION	420 - 2	NO DAMNATION OUTSIDE OF ONE'S STATE
DAMNATION	486 - 1	NO SUCH THING AS ETERNAL DAMNATION
DAMNS	383 - 3	UNIVERSE WHICH DAMNS US
DAMP	252 - 5	COLDS RESULT FROM DAMP SPIRITS
DAMPNESS	259 - 1	THE DAMPNESS OF THE OCEAN
DANGEROUS	266 - 1	DANGEROUS BECAUSE OF THE MISUNDERSTANDING
DANGEROUS	381 - 3	SUBJECTIVITY IS VERY DANGEROUS
DARE	184 - 3	DARE TO SPEAK AND TO KNOW
DARES	142 - 3	DARES TO FLING HIS THOUGHT OUT
DARKENED	410 - 4	INTO A DARKENED ROOM
DARKER	158 - 4	DARKER BECAUSE WE HAVE LOST FAITH
DARKNESS	158 - 5	DARKNESS ONLY WHEN WE ARE WITHOUT
DARKNESS	183 - 2	POWER TO OVERCOME DARKNESS
DARKNESS	183 - 2	THE DARKNESS COMPREHENDED IT NOT
DARKNESS	200 - 4	ANY MORE THAN DARKNESS
DARKNESS	343 - 1	DARKNESS OF HIS OWN SUBJECTIVE
DARKNESS	345 - 3	THE LIGHT SHINES IN THE DARKNESS
DARKNESS	410 - 4	WHERE DOES THE DARKNESS GO
DARKNESS	410 - 4	DARKNESS NEITHER CAME NOR DID IT GO
DARKNESS	411 - 1	LIGHT IS GREATER THAN THE DARKNESS
DARKNESS	457 - 3	GOD TO REMAIN IN DARKNESS
DARKNESS	487 - 3	DARKNESS HAS NO POWER OVER LIGHT
DARKNESS	487 - 6	CAST OFF THE WORKS OF DARKNESS
DARKNESS	494 - 4	DARKNESS IS THE POWER OF FALSE
DAVID	328 - 2	DAVID, SOLOMON, JESUS, PLOTINUS
DAWN	369 - 3	DAWN OF ETERNAL EXPANSION
DAWNS	288 - 2	DAWNS UPON THE INNER THOUGHT
DAWNS	309 - 3	CONVICTION DAWNS THAT GOD IS ALL
DAWNS	484 - 4	DAWNS UPON THE SUBJECTIVE STATE
DAWNS	485 - 4	AS THE INNER LIGHT DAWNS
DAY	204 - 3	IF CARRIED OUT EVERY DAY
DAY	233 - 4	ONCE A DAY AT LEAST
DAY	271 - 5	TAKE TIME EVERY DAY
DAY	290 - 2	EVERY DAY FOR A FEW MINUTES
DAY	306 - 3	EVERY DAY THINGS ARE A LITTLE BETTER
DAY	329 - 4	DAY IN WHICH THEY ARE GIVEN
DAY	432 - 4	GOOD OF THE PRESENT DAY
DAY AFTER DAY	228 - 4	DAY AFTER DAY THE PATIENT WILL BE RELIEVED

DAY BY DAY	271 - 4	IF DAY BY DAY WE HAVE A GREATER
DEAD	311 - 1	GOD IS NOT A GOD OF THE DEAD
DEAD	315 - 2	SPIRITUAL POWER TO RAISE THE DEAD
DEAD	335 - 3	NOT THE GOD OF THE DEAD
DEAD	365 - 2	THE RAISING OF THE DEAD
DEAD	377 - 2	NOT THAT DEAD MEN LIVE AGAIN
DEAD	377 - 3	WHO ARE SUPPOSED TO BE DEAD
DEAD	379 - 1	THE LIVING OR THE SO-CALLED DEAD
DEAD	488 - 1	LIVING AND NOT OF THE DEAD
DEAFNESS	236 - 5	BLINDNESS, DEAFNESS, MUTISM
DEAL	046 - 5	DEAL WITH IT INTELLIGENTLY
DEAL	072 - 2	WE DEAL WITH ITS EFFECTS
DEAL	317 - 1	DOES NOT DEAL WITH THE MATERIAL MAN
DEAL	401 - 2	DEAL WITH THE FORMLESS
DEALING	046 - 5	DEALING WITH INTELLIGENCE
DEALING	048 - 2	DEALING WITH THE SUBTLE ENERGY
DEALING	053 - 3	DEALING WITH CAUSATION
DEALING	118 - 1	WE ARE DEALING WITH SELF-CONSCIOUS MIND
DEALING	125 - 5	DEALING WITH A NEUTRAL CREATIVE
DEALING	143 - 2	WE ARE DEALING WITH LAW
DEALING	215 - 1	IF WE WERE DEALING ONLY
DEALING	249 - 4	DEALING WITH OBJECTIVE SYMPTOMS
DEALING	297 - 2	WE ARE DEALING WITH CAUSATION
DEALING	301 - 1	WE ARE DEALING WITH INTELLIGENCE
DEALING	309 - 5	HE IS DEALING NOT WITH MENTAL SUGGESTION
DEALING	408 - 5	NOT DEALING WITH A SICK BODY
DEAR ONES	387 - 3	OVER THE LOSS OF DEAR ONES
DEATH	108 - 2	DEATH OR ANY HUMAN SUFFERING
DEATH	211 - 2	PEOPLE TALK ABOUT DEATH
DEATH	240 - 2	GRIEF OFTEN CAUSES INSTANT DEATH
DEATH	268 - 5	WILL OF GOD CANNOT BE DEATH
DEATH	269 - 1	CANNOT PRODUCE DEATH
DEATH	310 - 4	DEATH AND RESURRECTION ARE INVENTIONS
DEATH	313 - 3	BY MAN CAME DEATH
DEATH	352 - 5	SHALL HAVE SUFFERED PHYSICAL DEATH
DEATH	369 - 3	CHRIST TRIUMPHS OVER DEATH
DEATH	371 - 1	EXPERIENCE OF PHYSICAL DEATH
DEATH	372 - 2	DEATH CANNOT ROB HIM
DEATH	376 - 4	SOME THINK THAT DEATH ROBS US
DEATH	385 - 2	THE EXPERIENCE OF PHYSICAL DEATH
DEATH	413 - 2	FOR DEATH IS TO THE ILLUSION ALONE
DEATH	457 - 2	DEATH CANNOT CHANGE ALL
DEATH	457 - 2	HE WILL CONTINUE TO LIVE AFTER DEATH
DEATH	473 - 1	ONLY AS MATTER IS DEATH
DEATH	478 - 2	DEATH HAS NOTHING TO DO WITH LIFE
DEATH	491 - 8	DEATH IS OVERCOME
DEATH	492 - 1	COMPLETELY UNCONSCIOUS OF DEATH
DEATH	492 - 1	DEATH WOULD BE SWALLOWED UP
DEATH	504 - 1	HEAVEN IS LIFE AND NOT DEATH
DEATHLESS	239 - 3	MAN IS BIRTHLESS, DEATHLESS
DEATHLESS	250 - 5	MY LIFE IN GOD IS AGELESS, DEATHLESS
DEATHLESS	368 - 1	PROCLAIMING THE DEATHLESS REALITY
DEBATE	386 - 3	FOR THE PURPOSE OF DEBATE
DEBT	452 - 3	DEBT THAT CANNOT BE PAID
DECEIT	459 - 6	LOVES SINCERITY AND ABHORS DECEIT

DECEIVE	176 - 1	LET US NOT DECEIVE OURSELVES ABOUT OUR
DECEIVE	499 - 6	DECEIVE OURSELVES WHEN WE BOAST
DECEIVED	479 - 4	NO FALSE PROMISES NEVER DECEIVED
DECEPTION	379 - 2	A LARGE FIELD FOR DECEPTION
DECIDE	073 - 2	CONSCIOUSLY THINK AND DECIDE
DECIDE	193 - 1	DECIDE WHAT FORM THE ENERGY
DECIDE	195-1	THE WILL TO DECIDE THE ISSUE
DECIDE	288 - 1	ABLE TO DECIDE AND DEMONSTRATE
DECIDE	400 - 4	MAY CONSCIOUSLY DECIDE
DECIDE	419 - 1	DECIDE WHAT WE WISH TO HAVE HAPPEN
DECIDES	118 - 4	DECIDES HOW THE LAW OF ATTRACTION
DECIDES	126 - 2	DECIDES WHAT IS GOING TO HAPPEN
DECIDES	142 - 2	DECIDES WHAT IS TO TAKE PLACE
DECIDES	296 - 2	ATMOSPHERE DECIDES WHAT IS TO BE
DECIDES	300 - 2	DECIDES WHAT IS GOING
DECIDES	476 - 1	MOLD WHICH DECIDES WHAT FORM
DECIDING	210 - 1	DECIDING WHAT WE SHALL THINK
DECISION	113 - 1	EQUIPPED WITH DECISION
DECISION	194 - 4	INTELLECT HAS MADE THIS DECISION
DECISION	245 - 2	POWER AND DECISION OF SPIRIT
DECISIONS	400 - 4	ALL SUBJECTIVE DECISIONS ARE
DECLARATION	220 - 2	DECLARATION THAT THERE IS ONE
DECLARATIONS	171 - 1	DECLARATIONS ABOUT THIS NAME
DECLARE	055 - 2	STOP AND DECLARE
DECLARE	068 - 5	SPIRIT TO DECLARE
DECLARE	167 - 4	DECLARE THAT THE SPIRIT WITHIN
DECLARE	179 - 5	DECLARE FOR HIS OBJECTIVE APPEARANCE
DECLARE	198 - 4	DECLARE THE BODY TO BE
DECLARE	230 - 6	DECLARE DAILY
DECLARE	252 - 3	DECLARE OUR DISBELIEF IN COLDS
DECLARE	253 - 2	DECLARE THAT YOU ARE AN OFFSPRING
DECLARE	290 - 2	DECLARE EVERY DAY
DECLARE	290 - 2	DECLARE THERE IS ONE SUPREME
DECLARE	290 - 2	DECLARE FURTHER EVERYTHING NECESSARY
DECLARE	292 - 3	DECLARE THERE WERE NO MISTAKES
DECLARE	295 - 2	DECLARE THE TRUTH ABOUT HIMSELF
DECLARE	297 - 3	DECLARE THAT THEIR PRESENCE IS NOW
DECLARE	302 - 2	DECLARE YOUR FREEDOM
DECLARE	357 - 3	DECLARE OUR WORD TO BE
DECLARES	166 - 2	DECLARES THE TRUTH ABOUT THE PERSON
DECLARES	171 - 1	DECLARES THE TRUTH ABOUT HER
DECLARES	206 - 3	DECLARES THE TRUTH ABOUT
DECLARES	310 - 4	DECLARES THAT DEATH AND RESURRECTION
DECLARING	303 - 3	HE IS DECLARING THE TRUTH
DECREE	109 - 3	DIVINE DECREE ORDAINS SUFFERING
DECREE	311 - 1	NOT A DECREE OF THE ALMIGHTY
DECREES	395 - 3	POWER HE DECREES IT TO HAVE
DEDICATED	168 - 2	PRACTITIONER IS ONE WHO HAS DEDICATED
DEDUCE	079 - 4	DEDUCE WHAT THE NATURE OF GOD
DEDUCE	209 - 2	CAN DEDUCE ONLY
DEDUCE	354 - 3	SUBJECTIVE MIND CAN DEDUCE ONLY
DEDUCE	355 - 3	SUBJECTIVE MIND CAN DEDUCE
DEDUCTIONS	123 - 2	SPIRITUAL DEDUCTIONS OF THE AGES
DEDUCTIONS	197 - 2	CERTAIN CONCLUSIONS AND DEDUCTIONS
DEDUCTIONS	312 - 3	SPIRITUAL DEDUCTIONS OF THE AGES

DEDUCTIVE	208 - 3	DEDUCTIVE, RECEPTIVE, PLASTIC
DEDUCTIVE	209 - 4	DEDUCTIVE ONLY CANNOT REFUSE
DEDUCTIVE	356 - 1	LOGICAL DEDUCTIVE CONCLUSIVE POWER
DEDUCTIVE	416 - 2	FROM A DEDUCTIVE VIEWPOINT
DEDUCTIVE	416 - 2	AND BEING DEDUCTIVE
DEDUCTIVELY	096 - 3	GOD CAN ONLY REASON DEDUCTIVELY
DEDUCTIVELY	097 - 1	SOUL CAN ONLY REASON DEDUCTIVELY
DEDUCTIVELY	208 - 4	THINKS ONLY DEDUCTIVELY
DEDUCTIVELY	397 - 4	TO REASON OTHER THAN DEDUCTIVELY
DEDUCTIVE REASONING	096 - 2	DEDUCTIVE REASONING FOLLOWS
DEEDS	229 - 2	EXPRESSED IN FAITH AND GOOD DEEDS
DEEP	163 - 2	WITH A DEEP INNER CONVICTION
DEEPER	141 - 2	DEEPER REALIZATION OF LIFE
DEEPER SEAT	350 - 2	MUCH DEEPER SEAT OF KNOWLEDGE
DEEPEST	032 - 2	DEEPEST THINKERS OF EVERY AGE
DEFACE	323 - 2	HE CANNOT DEFACE HIS REAL BEING
DEFACED	454 - 6	FATHER CANNOT BE DEFACED
DEFEAT	175 - 2	WE SHOULD NEVER ADMIT DEFEAT
DEFEAT	479 - 2	DEFEAT INTO GLORIOUS VICTORY
DEFEATED	422 - 3	IS NEVER DEFEATED
DEFEATING	460 - 2	DEFEATING ITS OWN PURPOSE
DEFEND	441 - 1	CALLED UPON TO DEFEND THEIR FAITH
DEFENSE	236 - 5	OBSESSION OR THE DEFENSE MECHANISM
DEFIES	478 - 4	DEFIES ANALYSIS AS DOES LIFE
DEFILES	453 - 1	WHAT WE THINK DEFILES
DEFINED	194 - 2	WELL KNOWN AND DEFINED MENTAL LAW
DEFINED	284 - 5	PRINCIPLE THAT HAS BEEN DEFINED
DEFINED	446 - 2	SPIRITUALITY MAY BE DEFINED
DEFINITE	045 - 4	MENTAL WORK IS DEFINITE
DEFINITE	049 - 2	ANYTHING AT ALL, THEY ARE DEFINITE
DEFINITE	105 - 1	DEFINITE MENTAL IMAGE CONCEPT
DEFINITE	044 - 4	DEFINITE KNOWLEDGE OF SOME PARTICULAR
DEFINITE	148 - 4	POWER FOR DEFINITE PURPOSES
DEFINITE	183 - 1	DEFINITE STATES OF CONSCIOUSNESS
DEFINITE	191 - 2	CONSCIOUSLY USED FOR DEFINITE PURPOSES
DEFINITE	194 - 1	DEFINITE AND DESIRED THOUGHT
DEFINITE	195 - 2	DEFINITE PURPOSE IN OUR IMAGINATION
DEFINITE	198 - 3	DEFINITE PIECE OF MENTAL WORK
DEFINITE	201 - 1	POWER YOU ARE USING IS DEFINITE
DEFINITE	211 - 3	DEFINITE IN YOUR MENTAL WORK
DEFINITE	221 - 3	THE WORK IS DEFINITE
DEFINITE	237 - 3	CONCRETE, DEFINITE AND REAL
DEFINITE	396 - 1	UNIVERSE INTO DEFINITE CREATION
DEFINITE	407 - 1	CONCEIVE OF SOME DEFINITE IDEA
DEFINITE	440 - 2	GIVING AND RECEIVING IS DEFINITE
DEFINITELY	054 - 2	DEFINITELY AND FOR SPECIFIC PURPOSES
DEFINITELY	054 - 2	THE MORE DEFINITELY HE USES THE LAW
DEFINITELY	201 - 2	DEFINITELY, SPECIFICALLY AND CONSCIOUSLY
DEFINITELY	204 - 4	ERASES JUST AS DEFINITELY
DEFINITELY	207 - 2	GRADUALLY, DEFINITELY AND INTELLIGENTLY
DEFINITELY	207 - 4	DOING JUST AS DEFINITELY
DEFINITELY	318 - 2	DEFINITELY SPEAK OUR CONVICTION
DEFINITELY	397 - 1	IT SHOULD BE USED DEFINITELY
DEFINITENESS	435 - 3	DEFINITENESS OF SPIRITUAL AND MENTAL WORK
DEFINITION	081 - 1	DEFINITION OF SPIRIT IS

DEFINITION	081 – 2	DEFINITION OF GOD AS SPIRIT
DEGENERATIVE	250 – 1	NO DEGENERATIVE PROCESSES
DEGENERATIVE	255 – 3	DEGENERATIVE THOUGHTS CAN
DEGRADATION	187 – 1	POVERTY, DEGRADATION AND MISERY
DEGREE	041 – 1	DEGREE AS WE EMBODY
DEGREE	087 – 2	DEGREE APPARENTLY DIFFERENT
DEGREE	154 – 1	DEGREE AS WE CO-OPERATE
DEGREE	206 – 3	DEGREE THAT THE PRACTITIONER
DEGREE	224 – 2	HEALING TAKES PLACE TO THE DEGREE
DEGREE	271 – 2	DEGREE THAT WE UNDERSTAND
DEGREE	276 – 2	DEGREE AS OUR KNOWLEDGE PARTAKES
DEGREE	309 – 3	GREATER DEGREE OF ACCEPTANCE
DEGREE	357 – 3	DEGREE THAT THE CHRIST IS REVEALED
DEGREE	393 – 3	ANY APPARENT DIFFERENCE IS IN DEGREE ONLY
DEGREE	422 – 3	DEGREE THAT IT EXPRESSES ITSELF
DEGREE	451 – 1	DEGREE OF REAL CONVICTION
DEGREES	139 – 3	SUCCESSIVE DEGREES OF INCARNATION
DEGREES	468 – 2	DEMONSTRATE THIS ONLY IN DEGREES
DEITY	081 – 2	TERM USED IN DESCRIBING DEITY
DEITY	131 – 2	MAN'S IDEA OF DEITY EVOLVES
DEITY	307 – 3	THE DEITY WILL ONLOOK THEE
DEITY	420 – 3	A FOREVER MANIFESTING DEITY
DEITY	487 – 3	VERY NATURE OF DEITY
DELIGHTED	300 – 4	SEE THEM DELIGHTED
DELIVER	191 – 2	DELIVER HIMSELF FROM SICKNESS
DELIVERANCE	414 – 3	NO DELIVERANCE OF THE REAL SELF
DELIVERED	312 – 4	DELIVERED EVERYTHING TO HIM
DELIVERED	430 – 4	BE DELIVERED TO THE JUDGMENT
DELIVERS	485 – 4	DELIVERS THE OUTER LIFE FROM
DELUSION	149 – 3	DELUSION THAT GOD IS A BEING OF MOODS
DELUSION	176 – 2	PROLIFIC FIELD FOR DELUSION
DELUSION	188 – 4	CREATE NO DELUSION
DELUSION	209 – 2	LABOR UNDER THE DELUSION
DELUSION	223 – 2	DELUSION OR FEAR OF DELUSION
DELUSION	227 – 4	LABOR UNDER A DELUSION
DELUSION	268 – 1	NEED NOT LABOR UNDER THE DELUSION
DELUSION	296 – 2	HAS BEEN LABORING UNDER A DELUSION
DELUSION	299 – 4	A MISTAKE AND A DELUSION
DEMAND	157 – 3	COMPLIANCE WITH OUR DEMAND
DEMAND	157 – 3	IS AWAITING OUR DEMAND
DEMAND	174 – 2	MAKES HIS DEMAND
DEMAND	273 – 2	INTELLIGENCE MAKES A DEMAND
DEMAND	273 – 2	ANSWERS ITS OWN DEMAND OUT
DEMAND	273 – 2	MAKES A DEMAND UPON ITSELF
DEMAND	273 – 2	OUT OF THAT VERY DEMAND IS CREATED
DEMAND	273 – 2	DEMAND IS IN THE NATURE
DEMAND	393 – 3	MAN MAKES A DEMAND UPON
DEMANDED	433 – 1	HE DEMANDED A COMPLETE
DEMONSTRATE	039 – 2	HOW MUCH CAN ONE DEMONSTRATE
DEMONSTRATE	046 – 5	DEMONSTRATE SOME PARTICULAR GOOD
DEMONSTRATE	118 – 2	CANNOT DEMONSTRATE BEYOND OUR ABILITY
DEMONSTRATE	119 – 3	THE REASON THAT WE DO NOT DEMONSTRATE
DEMONSTRATE	124 – 3	DEMONSTRATE THE HEALING OF THE BODY
DEMONSTRATE	143 – 2	WISHES TO DEMONSTRATE PROSPERITY
DEMONSTRATE	155 – 2	DEMONSTRATE AN INVISIBLE LAW

DEMONSTRATE	159 - 4	DEMONSTRATE THAT SPIRITUAL THOUGHT FORCE
DEMONSTRATE	167 - 4	SEEKING TO DEMONSTRATE THE POWER
DEMONSTRATE	174 - 4	DEMONSTRATE IN SPITE OF OURSELVES
DEMONSTRATE	266 - 3	EXPECT TO DEMONSTRATE
DEMONSTRATE	267 - 2	NO MAN CAN DEMONSTRATE PEACE
DEMONSTRATE	271 - 3	WE DEMONSTRATE AT THE LEVEL OF OUR
DEMONSTRATE	282 - 2	DEMONSTRATE MORE IN OUR EXPERIENCE
DEMONSTRATE	300 - 5	EXPECT THAT THE STORE WOULD DEMONSTRATE
DEMONSTRATE	306 - 2	DEMONSTRATE DEPENDS UPON OUR
DEMONSTRATE	314 - 3	TO DEMONSTRATE MEANS TO PROVE
DEMONSTRATE	362 - 3	WE WOULD DEMONSTRATE INSTANTANEOUSLY
DEMONSTRATE	399 - 2	WOULD SOON DEMONSTRATE
DEMONSTRATE	437 - 4	HE WAS ABLE TO DEMONSTRATE
DEMONSTRATE	468 - 2	DEMONSTRATE THIS ONLY IN DEGREES
DEMONSTRATE	488 - 6	DEMONSTRATE LIBERTY, DROP ALL NEGATIVE
DEMONSTRATED	051 - 2	UNTIL DEMONSTRATED THEY ARE SUPPOSITIONAL
DEMONSTRATED	086 - 4	TRUTH KNOWN IS DEMONSTRATED
DEMONSTRATED	364 - 2	LAW AND DEMONSTRATED IT
DEMONSTRATED	464 - 1	DEMONSTRATED THAT HIS STATE OF BEING
DEMONSTRATED	468 - 1	KNOWN IS INSTANTLY DEMONSTRATED
DEMONSTRATING	038 - 5	DEMONSTRATING THAT HE CANNOT
DEMONSTRATING	174 - 5	DEMONSTRATING DOES NOT DEPEND UPON
DEMONSTRATING	188 - 4	IN DEMONSTRATING OVER CONDITIONS
DEMONSTRATING	266 - 3	DEMONSTRATING A CONTROL OF CONDITIONS
DEMONSTRATING	304 - 5	HINDER IT FROM DEMONSTRATING
DEMONSTRATING	483 - 3	DEMONSTRATING THE LAW OF GOOD
DEMONSTRATION	037 - 4	DEMONSTRATION OF A PRINCIPLE
DEMONSTRATION	047 - 3	PRODUCE AN ACTIVE DEMONSTRATION
DEMONSTRATION	051 - 1	PROVE BY ACTUAL DEMONSTRATION
DEMONSTRATION	057 - 2	INSTANTANEOUS IN ITS DEMONSTRATION
DEMONSTRATION	057 - 3	DEMONSTRATION TAKE PLACE
DEMONSTRATION	060 - 1	HINDER THE DEMONSTRATION
DEMONSTRATION	086 - 4	DEMONSTRATION RESTS NOT IN
DEMONSTRATION	173 - 5	TO FIGURE OUT HOW THE DEMONSTRATION
DEMONSTRATION	174 - 2	DEMONSTRATION IS MADE WHEN
DEMONSTRATION	174 - 2	DEMONSTRATION IS A MANIFESTATION
DEMONSTRATION	174 - 2	THIS IS A DEMONSTRATION
DEMONSTRATION	174 - 2	THIS IS DEMONSTRATION
DEMONSTRATION	175 - 3	DEMONSTRATION WE BELIEVE IN
DEMONSTRATION	187 - 2	MAKING A DEMONSTRATION WE PAY NO
DEMONSTRATION	236 - 4	DEMONSTRATION TAKES PLACE
DEMONSTRATION	246 - 3	PROVEN BY DEMONSTRATION
DEMONSTRATION	262 - 3	DEMONSTRATION OF SUCCESS IN FINANCIAL
DEMONSTRATION	278 - 4	A GOOD DEMONSTRATION IS MADE
DEMONSTRATION	278 - 4	KNOW WHEN HE HAS MADE A DEMONSTRATION
DEMONSTRATION	282 - 1	THIS IS HIS DEMONSTRATION
DEMONSTRATION	297 - 2	THE OTHER IS THE DEMONSTRATION
DEMONSTRATION	299 - 4	WE MEAN BY DEMONSTRATION
DEMONSTRATION	303 - 1	A DEMONSTRATION IS MADE WHEN IT COMES
DEMONSTRATION	303 - 1	WHO WISHES TO MAKE A DEMONSTRATION
DEMONSTRATION	305 - 5	WHEN WE MAKE A DEMONSTRATION
DEMONSTRATION	314 - 3	WHAT IS MEANT BY A DEMONSTRATION
DEMONSTRATION	322 - 3	DEMONSTRATION TAKES PLACE THROUGH
DEMONSTRATION	440 - 1	DEMONSTRATION OF SPIRITUAL POWER
DEMONSTRATION	470 - 1	NECESSARY TO RIGHT DEMONSTRATION

DEMONSTRATION	500 - 1	DEMONSTRATION OF A BELIEF IN GOD
DEMOSTHENES	137 - 1	WHAT WE WISH, SAID DEMONTHENES, THAT WE
DENIAL	060 - 2	DENIAL TOWARD EVERY FALSE
DENIAL	186 - 2	DENIAL IS BASED UPON THE RECOGNITION
DENIAL	275 - 2	ANY DENIAL WE MAKE IN TREATMENT
DENIAL	372 - 4	DENIAL OF OUR EXISTENCE
DENIAL	404 - 4	DENIAL THAT THE DIVINE IS
DENIAL	411 - 1	GREAT DENIAL OF THE LIGHT
DENIALS	039 - 2	BY OUR OWN DENIALS
DENIALS	159 - 2	DENIALS ARE FOR THE PURPOSE
DENIALS	173 - 4	AFFIRMATIONS AND DENIALS
DENIED	167 - 4	DENIED AND IN ITS PLACE
DENIED	284 - 2	CANNOT BE DENIED TO THE MIND
DENIED	332 - 4	CANNOT BE DENIED
DENIED	419 - 4	MYSTICS HAVE NOT DENIED THE REALITY
DENIES	055 - 2	HE DENIES ANYTHING
DENIES	151 - 1	DENIES THE POWER AND PRESENCE
DENIES	161 - 3	DENIES THE INDIVIDUAL'S GOOD
DENIES	186 - 1	DENIES SUCH MANIFESTATION
DENIES	278 - 2	ANYTHING IN US WHICH DENIES IT
DENIES	284 - 4	FAITH AFFIRMS THIS AND DENIES
DENY	066 - 3	DENY SUCH INTELLIGENCE
DENY	092 - 3	CANNOT ANALYZE, DISSECT, OR DENY
DENY	102 - 3	DENY THE THEORY OF EVOLUTION
DENY	172 - 2	WHAT THOUGHT TO DENY
DENY	175 - 1	UNIVERSE WILL NEVER DENY
DENY	189 - 1	DENY US THE RIGHT
DENY	217 - 1	TO DENY THE PRESENCE OF EVIL
DENY	221 - 2	THAT CAN DENY GOD IS YOURSELF
DENY	244 - 4	DENY THAT PEOPLE SUFFER
DENY	382 - 3	NOT TO DENY WHAT HAPPENS
DENY	386 - 3	SHOULD HE DENY THE EVIDENCE
DENY	394 - 4	NEVER DENY ITS OWN NATURE
DENY	401 - 3	WHO DENY US OR THEMSELVES
DENY	412 - 3	WILL NEVER DENY US ANYTHING
DENY	416 - 2	CANNOT ARGUE BACK OR DENY ANY USE
DENYING	034 - 1	DENYING OF IT WLL NEVER CHANGE
DENYING	311 - 4	NOT DENYING THE PHYSICAL UNIVERSE
DEPART	375 - 3	DO NOT DEPART FROM REASON
DEPARTED	379 - 3	TO COMMUNICATE WITH THE DEPARTED
DEPARTED	380 - 1	IF THE DEPARTED WERE TRYING
DEPARTED	380 - 3	OF THOSE WHO ARE DEPARTED
DEPEND	128 - 2	DEPEND IN MAN'S EXPRESSION
DEPEND	146 - 4	DEPEND UPON ANY CONDITION
DEPEND	174 - 5	DEMONSTRATING DOES NOT DEPEND
DEPEND	432 - 2	LEARN TO DEPEND MORE AND MORE
DEPENDS	140 - 4	DEPENDS UPON WHAT WE ARE THINKING
DEPENDS	301 - 2	DEPENDS UPON OUR ABILITY
DEPENDS	306 - 2	DEPENDS UPON OUR ABILITY
DEPENDS	404 - 1	DEPENDS ON ANYTHING BUT IDEAS
DEPENDS	416 - 1	DEPENDS UPON A REALIZATION
DEPICT	349 - 3	COULD CONSCIOUSLY DEPICT IT
DEPICT	428 - 2	ENABLES THEM TO DEPICT THE IDEAL
DEPICTED	112 - 2	FIND ALL OF THEM DEPICTED
DEPICTS	463 - 4	DEPICTS THE STATE OF HUMANITY

DEPLETED	228 - 3	IT IS NEVER DEPLETED
DEPLETED	293 - 3	MY GOOD CAN NEVER BE DEPLETED
DEPOSIT	144 - 3	DEPOSIT AROUND THE JOINTS
DEPRESS	244 - 3	DEPRESS WHILE OTHERS
DEPRESSED	440 - 4	LET THE ONE WHO IS SAD, DEPRESSED
DEPRESSED	478 - 6	HIS DISCIPLES WERE DEPRESSED
DEPRESSION	235 - 3	THE DEPRESSION
DEPRESSION	239 - 3	DEPRESSION, FEAR OR SUGGESTION
DEPRESSION	245 - 2	INDECISION, ANXIETY, DEPRESSION
DEPRESSION	302 - 2	CHEERFULNESS INSTEAD OF DEPRESSION
DEPRESSION	404 - 4	CONFIDENCE OVERCOMES THE DEPRESSION
DEPRESSION	404 - 4	PHYSICAL AND FINANCIAL DEPRESSION
DEPRESSION	450 - 5	DEPRESSION MUST BE ERASED
DEPTHS	030 - 2	PLUMB THE DEPTHS OF
DEPTHS	031 - 5	PLUMBED THE DEPTHS OF EITHER
DERANGED	227 - 4	MIND APPEARS TO BE DERANGED
DERANGED	227 - 4	CEASE TO BE DERANGED
DESCEND	341 - 3	DOES DESCEND INTO OUR MINDS
DESCENT	462 - 3	IT SYMBOLIZES THE DESCENT OF THE SOUL
DESCRIBE	066 - 2	DESCRIBE IT AS GOD
DESCRIPTION	452 - 2	DESCRIPTION OF THE THINGS
DESECRATE	169 - 1	DESECRATE BUT NEVER QUITE LOSE
DESECRATE	339 - 1	MAY DESECRATE BUT HE CAN NEVER LOSE
DESERT	072 - 4	MADE THE DESERT TO BLOOM
DESERT	259 - 1	LOVE THE HEAT OF THE DESERT
DESERT	282 - 4	TO DESERT THE TRUTH
DESERT	476 - 6	DESERT ANY ONE OF THESE
DESERTED	491 - 1	APPEAR TO BE DESERTED
DESERTING	053 - 3	FOREVER DESERTING THE FORM
DESIGNATE	206 - 2	DESIGNATE IT AS HIS SUBJECTIVE
DESIGNATE	297 - 3	SPECIFICALLY DESIGNATE THE KIND
DESIGNS	476 - 1	DESIGNS AS ARE DESIRABLE
DESIRABLE	264 - 1	WORTHWHILE AND DESIRABLE
DESIRABLE	405 - 5	THINGS WHICH ARE DESIRABLE
DESIRE	083 - 4	ITS DESIRE IS SATISFIED
DESIRE	091 - 3	INTELLIGENCE TO EXECUTE THE DESIRE
DESIRE	146 - 2	WHATEVER PURPOSE WE DESIRE
DESIRE	174 - 2	DESIRE IS GIVEN A SUBJECTIVE MOLD
DESIRE	180 - 2	DESIRE IS ALREADY AN ACCOMPLISHED
DESIRE	194 - 2	THE DESIRE TO PERMIT
DESIRE	195 - 2	FORM OF SOME DESIRE IN OUR LIVES
DESIRE	195 - 2	IF WE CHANGE THE DESIRE
DESIRE	195 - 3	WORD FOLLOWS THE DESIRE
DESIRE	195 - 3	DESIRE ARISES FROM THE NECESSITY
DESIRE	198 - 3	NOT SIMPLY DESIRE
DESIRE	222 - 4	THE DESIRE TO EXPRESS LIFE
DESIRE	222 - 4	DESIRE FOR SOMETHING
DESIRE	222 - 4	A HABIT IS DESIRE OBJECTIFIED
DESIRE	278 - 4	CONCRETE ACCEPTANCE OF HIS DESIRE
DESIRE	289 - 3	SEE THE DESIRE AS AN ALREADY
DESIRE	387 - 2	WHERE THIS DESIRE IS LACKING
DESIRE	395 - 3	SUBJECTIVE TO THE DESIRE OF MAN
DESIRE	399 - 2	ALL THE DETAILS OF HIS DESIRE
DESIRE	500 - 5	DESIRE OF SPIRIT TO HEAR AND ANSWER
DESIRES	030 - 1	WHATSOEVER HE DESIRES

DESIRES	039 – 5	HARVEST OF FULFILLED DESIRES
DESIRES	047 – 1	CONCRETE IDEA OF OUR DESIRES
DESIRES	088 – 5	DESIRES TO THINK OF GOD AS PERSON
DESIRES	157 – 1	BRINGS OUR DESIRES TO PASS
DESIRES	237 – 1	OPPOSING DESIRES WHICH CONFLICT
DESIRES	237 – 1	MAY BE ANY SUPPRESSED DESIRES
DESIRES	272 – 1	MAKE KNOWN OUR DESIRES
DESIRES	278 – 2	DENIES THAT WHICH HE DESIRES
DESIRES	291 – 2	IT IS WHAT IT DESIRES
DESIRES	387 – 2	DESIRES TO LIVE BEYOND THE GRAVE
DESIRES	393 – 2	POTENTIAL OF ALL OUR DESIRES
DESIRES	398 – 3	ACCEPTANCE OF OUR DESIRES
DESPAIR	049 – 4	BETTER THAN DESPAIR
DESPISE	175 – 2	LET US NOT DESPISE OUR SUMS
DESPISE	491 – 2	NOT DESPISE APPARENT FAILURES
DESTINIES	103 – 1	IN HUMAN DESTINIES
DESTINY	115 – 3	DESTINY, RICHES, POVERTY, BUSINESS
DESTINY	126 – 2	WE AND WE ALONE CONTROL OUR DESTINY
DESTINY	137 – 1	TO CONTROL ITS OWN DESTINY
DESTINY	181 – 1	DETERMINING DESTINY
DESTINY	290 – 2	CONSCIOUSLY DIRECTING OUR DESTINY
DESTINY	333 – 5	MAN'S DESTINY IS DIVINE AND SURE
DESTINY	387 – 3	AN ETERNAL DESTINY
DESTINY	388 – 3	MAN IS AN ETERNAL DESTINY
DESTINY	391 – 4	WORK OUT HIS OWN DESTINY
DESTINY	409 – 4	WE ARE FULFILLING OUR DESTINY
DESTINY	415 – 2	HOPE OF DESTINY IS LATENT
DESTITUTE	456 – 3	DESTITUTE OF DIVINE GUIDANCE
DESTROY	078 – 3	WE CANNOT DESTROY THE LAW
DESTROY	083 – 1	IT WOULD DESTROY ITSELF
DESTROY	127 – 3	ULTIMATELY DESTROY HIM
DESTROY	130 – 3	ALL HE CAN DESTROY IS SOME
DESTROY	180 – 2	COMPLETELY DESTROY THE FALSE CLAIM
DESTROY	192 – 1	HAS HELPED TO DESTROY MAN
DESTROY	196 – 1	DESTROY THE IDEA OF HIMSELF
DESTROY	228 – 3	ENTIRELY DESTROY THE FALSE THOUGHT
DESTROY	291 – 2	DESTROY THE THOUGHT
DESTROY	313 – 3	CANNOT DESTROY IT NOR BREAK ITS LAWS
DESTROYED	211 – 3	DESTROYED BY ANY OPPOSING FORCE
DESTROYED	491 – 1	WE ARE NOT DESTROYED
DESTROYS	159 – 1	DESTROYS IN ANY DEGREE
DESTROYS	202 – 5	YOUR WORD DESTROYS IT
DESTRUCTION	120 – 2	DESTRUCTION IT WOULD DESTROY
DESTRUCTION	428 – 1	STREWN THE EARTH WITH DESTRUCTION
DESTRUCTIVE	234 – 4	DESTRUCTIVE EMOTIONS, DESIRES
DESTRUCTIVE	381 – 2	IS LIKELY TO BE DESTRUCTIVE
DESTRUCTIVE	394 – 2	USE IT FOR DESTRUCTIVE PURPOSES
DESTRUCTIVE	412 – 3	DESTRUCTIVE WE SHALL SUFFER
DESTRUCTIVELY	120 – 3	THEY USED THE LAW DESTRUCTIVELY
DESTRUCTIVELY	223 – 1	AND SOME DESTRUCTIVELY
DESTRUCTIVELY	483 – 4	POWER OF HIS THOUGHT DESTRUCTIVELY
DETACHED	463 – 1	DETACHED FROM SPIRITUAL WHOLENESS
DETAIL	289 – 2	DETAIL SHOULD BE THE ALPHA AND OMEGA
DETAIL	398 – 3	DETAIL INTO OUR MENTAL WORK
DETERMINATION	168 – 1	DETERMINATION TO BE AND A JOY

DETERMINATION	176 - 3	DETERMINATION TO CONTINUE
DETERMINATION	239 - 1	A DETERMINATION TO THINK
DETERMINATION	455 - 5	DETERMINATION TO ATTAIN SOME PURPOSE
DETERMINE	122 - 3	SUBCONSCIOUS MIND OF MAN DETERMINE
DETERMINE	391 - 4	DETERMINE WHAT MANNER OF LIFE
DETERMINED	079 - 1	WE HAVE SIMPLY DETERMINED
DETERMINED	148 - 3	DETERMINED THAT CREATION
DETERMINES	126 - 2	DETERMINES THE ATTRACTION AND REPULSION
DEVELOP	289 - 2	CAUSE IT TO DEVELOP, UNFOLD
DEVELOP	401 - 3	DEVELOP A CONSCIOUS CONVICTION
DEVELOPED	112 - 3	IT IS NOT FULLY DEVLOPED
DEVELOPMENT	198 - 1	GREATER DEVELOPMENT OF LIFE
DEVELOPMENT	439 - 2	LESSON IN RELIGIOUS DEVELOPMENT
DEVIATE	282 - 4	NEVER DEVIATE FROM IT
DEVIATE	347 - 3	DEVIATE FROM THAT WHICH PSYCHOLOGY
DEVIL	217 - 1	DEVIL IS A MYTH
DEVIL	337 - 1	NO DEVIL, NO HELL, NO TORMENT
DEVIL	383 - 2	EITHER GOD OR THE DEVIL
DEVIL	383 - 2	THERE IS NO DEVIL
DEVIL	420 - 2	NO DEVIL, NO DAMNATION
DEVIL	442 - 2	THEY SAY HE HATH A DEVIL
DEVIL	453 - 6	THAT A SUPPOSITIONAL DEVIL DIVIDES
DEVIL	456 - 1	AND JESUS REBUKED THE DEVIL
DEVIL	473 - 6	DEVIL HAS EQUAL POWER
DEVILS	076 - 4	THE PRINCE OF DEVILS
DEVILS	448 - 3	IF I CAST OUT DEVILS BY THE SPIRIT
DEVITALIZES	438 - 2	HE DEVITALIZES HIS BODY
DEVITALIZING	343 - 3	GREATER THAN THE DEVITALIZING ONES
DEVOID	111 - 5	DEVOID OF MIND OR INTELLIGENCE
DEVOID	177 - 3	BODY DEVOID OF MENTALITY
DEVOID	197 - 1	DEVOID OF MENTALITY
DEVOUTLY	385 - 2	DEVOUTLY LONGED FOR AND SOUGHT
DIABETES	253 - 4	DIABETES: SINCE THE LIFE OF GOD IS PURE
DIABETES	253 - 4	DIABETES IS NEITHER PERSON, PLACE
DIABETES	254 - 1	FREE FROM ALL CLAIM TO DIABETES
DIAGNOSE	316 - 3	PHYSICIAN WHO MUST DIAGNOSE
DIAGNOSES	237 - 4	DIAGNOSES HIS THOUGHT
DICTATES	339 - 1	LAW OBEYING THE DICTATES
DICTATOR	152 - 5	GOD AS A HEAVENLY DICTATOR
DID NOT	069 - 4	GOD DID NOT MAKE GOD
DID NOT	467 - 2	GOD DID NOT ANSWER HIS SON
DIE	239 - 3	MATURE, DECAY AND DIE
DIE	313 - 3	AND EVEN APPEARS TO DIE
DIE	376 - 3	NEED NOT DIE TO RECEIVE ONE
DIE	376 - 3	DIE FROM ONE PLANE TO ANOTHER
DIE	376 - 4	OBJECTIVE FACULTIES DIE WITH THE BRAIN
DIE	384 - 2	WE GO WHEN WE DIE
DIE	388 - 4	PREPARE NOT TO DIE BUT TO LIVE
DIE	413 - 2	GOD DID NOT DIE
DIED	145 - 2	DIED OF GREAT GRIEF
DIED	492 - 1	NEVER KNOW THAT HE DIED
DIES	377 - 2	THAT A LIVING MAN NEVER DIES
DIET	259 - 3	GUIDE US INTO A PROPER DIET
DIFFERENCE	123 - 1	DIFFERENCE WHICH TOO FEW REALIZE
DIFFERENCE	173 - 2	IT MAKES NO DIFFERENCE

DIFFERENCE	178 - 7	NO DIFFERENCE BETWEEN AN ABSENT
DIFFERENCE	186 - 2	INFINITE KNOWS NO DIFFERENCE
DIFFERENCE	208 - 6	GREAT DIFFERENCE BETWEEN CONSCIOUS
DIFFERENCE	336 - 4	DIFFERENCE IN OUR REACTION
DIFFERENCE	393 - 3	APPARENT DIFFERENCE IS IN DEGREE ONLY
DIFFERENCE	399 - 5	VAST DIFFERENCE BETWEEN HOLDING
DIFFERENCE	416 - 4	ALL THE DIFFERENCE IN THE WORLD
DIFFERENCE	427 - 2	NOR DOES IT MAKE ANY DIFFERENCE
DIFFERENCE	474 - 5	DIFFERENCE IS NOT IN THE THING ITSELF
DIFFERENCE	500 - 1	DIFFERENCE BETWEEN SAINT AND SINNER
DIFFERENT	124 - 2	DIFFERENT MENTAL DEPTHS AND HEIGHTS
DIFFERENT	296 - 1	DIFFERENT WAY OF SAYING KNOW THE TRUTH
DIFFERENT	321 - 2	BUT NOT A DIFFERENT TYPE
DIFFERENT	367 - 3	WAS DIFFERENT FROM OTHER MEN
DIFFERENT	396 - 3	MAKES MAN DISTINCT AND DIFFERENT
DIFFERENT	400 - 4	CAUSE A DIFFERENT FLOW OF ENERGY
DIFFERENT	403 - 1	DIFFERENT USE OF THE ONE LAW
DIFFERENTIATE	045 - 3	DIFFERENTIATE ONE KIND OF A RESULT
DIFFERENTIATE	078 - 2	DIFFERENTIATE BETWEEN UNIVERSAL MIND
DIFFERENTIATE	275 - 3	DIFFERENTIATE BETWEEN THE SPIRIT
DIFFERENTIATE	276 - 1	DIFFERENTIATE BETWEEN THE DIVINE
DIFFERENTIATE	400 - 1	CAREFUL TO DIFFERENTIATE BETWEEN
DIFFERENTIATING	045 - 1	OF DIFFERENTIATING IS LIMITLESS
DIFFERENTIATIONS	052 - 2	DIFFERENTIATIONS OF ITSELF
DIFFERENTLY	313 - 1	IT THINKS DIFFERENTLY
DIFFICULT	034 - 3	TO FIND SOMETHING DIFFICULT
DIFFICULT	315 - 3	THING IS DIFFICULT AND ANOTHER EASY
DIFFICULT	344 - 3	IT IS AS DIFFICULT TO BELIEVE
DIFFICULT	379 - 3	DIFFICULT TO COMMUNICATE
DIFFICULT	406 - 3	IF IT IS DIFFICULT TO SEE THIS
DIFFICULT	456 - 6	A PASSAGE DIFFICULT TO UNDERSTAND
DIFFICULTIES	051 - 1	ONE OF THE GREAT DIFFICULTIES
DIFFICULTY	107 - 5	NO INTELLECTUAL DIFFICULTY
DIFFICULTY	185 - 3	DIFFICULTY IN THROWING OFF
DIGESTANT	256 - 3	A WONDERFUL DIGESTANT
DIGESTION	259 - 4	DIGESTION IS ALSO A SPIRITUAL IDEA
DILIGENCE	238 - 4	THY HEART WITH ALL DILIGENCE
DIN	366 - 4	BACK OF THE DIN OF EXTERNAL LIFE
DIPPER	287 - 1	WILL A PINT DIPPER EVER HOLD MORE
DIPPER	287 - 1	RIM OF THE DIPPER
DIRE	502 - 1	TO PERPETUATE THEIR DIRE RESULTS
DIRECT	038 - 4	THE APPROACH SHOULD BE DIRECT
DIRECT	042 - 3	DIRECT APPROACH IS ALWAYS
DIRECT	119 - 3	MOST DIRECT METHOD IMAGINABLE
DIRECT	146 - 3	DIRECT THEIR ACTIVITIES
DIRECT	202 - 6	DIRECT STATEMENT OF BELIEF
DIRECT	290 - 3	THIS IS A DIRECT BELIEF THAT
DIRECT	294 - 2	DIRECT REASON FOR AND CAUSE OF
DIRECT	304 - 5	THROUGH THE DIRECT
DIRECT	363 - 2	RECEIVING A DIRECT ANSWER FROM IT
DIRECT	366 - 4	DIRECT REVELATION OF HIS SONSHIP
DIRECT	410 - 3	ABLE TO CONSCIOUSLY DIRECT
DIRECT	431 - 4	THIS IS A DIRECT STATEMENT
DIRECT	445 - 2	HIS DIRECT RELATIONSHIP TO THE UNIVERSE
DIRECT	477 - 4	IMMUTABLE LAW TO DIRECT

DIRECTED	031 - 2	DIRECTED AND DEFINITELY USED
DIRECTED	056 - 4	I AM CONTINUOUSLY DIRECTED
DIRECTED	057 - 4	NOW CONSCIOUSLY DIRECTED
DIRECTED	179 - 1	DIRECTED BY POSITIVE INTELLIGENCE
DIRECTED	242 - 5	INSPIRED AND DIRECTED BY INFINITE MIND
DIRECTED	309 - 5	MAY BE DIRECTED BY CONSCIOUSNESS
DIRECTED	315 - 3	IT IS USED PROPERLY DIRECTED
DIRECT INTUITION	160 - 2	REACHED BY DIRECT INTUITION
DIRECTION	048 - 2	PURPOSE AND DIRECTION
DIRECTION	052 - 3	GIVE CONSCIOUS DIRECTION TO IT
DIRECTION	052 - 3	CONSCIOUS OR SUBJECTIVE DIRECTION
DIRECTION	054 - 3	RESULT IN THE OPPOSITE DIRECTION
DIRECTION	169 - 5	GIVES DIRECTION TO A LAW
DIRECTION	263 - 3	IN THE RIGHT DIRECTION
DIRECTION	306 - 3	ARE GOING IN THE RIGHT DIRECTION
DIRECTION	395 - 1	NO OTHER DIRECTION FOR US
DIRECTION	396 - 3	LAW IS HELPLESS WITHOUT DIRECTION
DIRECTION	418 - 4	VISION IN AN OPPOSITE DIRECTION
DIRECTIVE	192 - 3	WILL IS DIRECTIVE BUT NOT CREATIVE
DIRECTIVE	192 - 3	CONSCIOUS DIRECTIVE POWER OF THE INTELLECT
DIRECTIVE	193 - 2	THE WILL IS DIRECTIVE
DIRECTIVE	390 - 5	THE ONLY DIRECTIVE INTELLIGENCE
DIRECTIVE	391 - 1	IS CONSCIOUS AND DIRECTIVE
DIRECTLY	054 - 2	DIRECTLY WILL IT RESPOND
DIRECTLY	329 - 5	WE DIRECTLY EXPERIENCE OURSELVES
DIRECTLY	428 - 5	DIRECTLY BY THE HAND OF GOD
DIRECTLY	432 - 2	DIRECTLY UPON THE DIVINE BOUNTY
DIRECTLY	436 - 1	ASK DIRECTLY FOR WHAT WE WANT
DIRECTLY	444 - 2	DIRECTLY THROUGH THE SON
DIRECT RESULT	142 - 2	DIRECT RESULT OF ALL WE HAVE EVER SAID
DIRECTS	179 - 2	DIRECTS THE POWER AND LETS IT WORK
DIRECTS	232 - 2	DIRECTS ALL OF THE ORGANS
DISAGREEMENT	239 - 2	DISAGREEMENT WITH A LOVED ONE
DISAPPEAR	131 - 5	DISAPPEAR IN A MEDIUM
DISAPPEAR	150 - 5	DEATH TEND TO DISAPPEAR
DISAPPEAR	335 - 2	DISAPPEAR WHEN WE STOP LOOKING
DISAPPEARANCE	104 - 5	PHYSICAL DISAPPEARANCE OF JESUS
DISAPPOINTED	059 - 1	SHALL NOT BE DISAPPOINTED
DISAPPOINTMENT	239 - 2	DISAPPOINTMENT OR DISAGREEMENT
DISAPPOINTMENT	256 - 4	DISAPPOINTMENT WILL OBJECTIFY
DISAPPOINTMENTS	387 - 2	DISAPPOINTMENTS AND DISILLUSIONMENTS
DISASTROUS	211 - 2	WILL PROVE DISASTROUS
DISASTROUS	266 - 2	IT MIGHT BE DISASTROUS
DISASTROUS	497 - 3	CONGESTED EMOTIONS ARE DISASTROUS
DISBELIEF	498 - 4	ALL TROUBLE COMES FROM DISBELIEF
DISBELIEVES	484 - 3	DISBELIEVES IN THE SUPREMACY
DISCARD	116 - 3	WE DISCARD MANY OF THEM IN OUR PATH
DISCARD	320 - 1	DISCARD THESE THOUGHTS AND GIVE
DISCARDED	418 - 3	REAL MAN MUST BE DISCARDED
DISCERN	381 - 3	ABLE TO DISCERN MENTAL CAUSES
DISCERNED	060 - 2	MUST BE SPIRITUALLY DISCERNED
DISCERNED	427 - 1	MUST BE SPIRITUALLY DISCERNED
DISCERNED	427 - 2	JESUS DISCERNED SPIRITUAL TRUTH
DISCERNED	483 - 3	SPIRITUAL IDEA BE DISCERNED
DISCERNING	254 - 6	DISCERNING INTELLIGENCE

DISCERNMENT	146 - 2	THROUGH SPIRITUAL DISCERNMENT
DISCIPLES	054 - 1	STROVE TO TEACH HIS DISCIPLES
DISCIPLES	162 - 4	JESUS REMAINED WITH THE DISCIPLES
DISCLAIM	282 - 3	DISCLAIM WHAT HE APPEARS TO BE
DISCLAIM	453 - 2	APPEAR TO DISCLAIM THIS FACT
DISCLOSURES	329 - 4	DISCLOSURES OF MOST PSYCHICS
DISCOMFORT	221 - 1	KNOWS DEGREES OF DISCOMFORT
DISCONNECTED	152 - 5	BELIEVE OURSELVES DISCONNECTED
DISCORD	110 - 3	IF WE TALK ABOUT DISCORD
DISCORD	201 - 1	DISCORD FLEEING BEFORE HARMONY
DISCORD	204 - 5	DISCORD MIGHT BE LIKENED
DISCORD	225 - 3	NEARLY EVERY DISCORD OR DISORDER
DISCORD	395 - 1	DISCORD INTO TEMPORARY BEING
DISCORD	409 - 2	NECESSITY OF SICKNESS OR DISCORD
DISCORD	430 - 3	NOT BE APPROACHED THROUGH DISCORD
DISCORD	464 - 5	HARMONY CAN NEVER BECOME DISCORD
DISCORD	471 - 2	DISCORD, MISERY, AND UNHAPPINESS
DISCORDANT	053 - 5	LOOK A DISCORDANT FACT
DISCORDANT	145 - 2	DISCORDANT MENTAL STATE IS CERTAIN TO
DISCORDANT	413 - 4	ABOUT A DISCORDANT CONDITION
DISCORDANT	418 - 3	WHATEVER IS OF A DISCORDANT NATURE
DISCORDANT	446 - 5	EXPERIENCE IS DISCORDANT
DISCOURAGED	291 - 4	CANNOT BECOME EITHER DISCOURAGED
DISCOURAGEMENT	149 - 3	BRING GREATER DISCOURAGEMENT
DISCOURAGEMENT	254 - 2	THERE IS NO DISCOURAGEMENT
DISCOURAGEMENT	256 - 4	SENSE OF DISCOURAGEMENT
DISCOURAGEMENT	291 - 4	REAL MAN KNOWS NO DISCOURAGEMENT
DISCOURAGING	443 - 4	DISCOURAGING IN OUR PRESENT STATE
DISCOVER	032 - 1	DISCOVER AND MAKE USE OF THEM
DISCOVER	034 - 3	MIND WHICH WE DISCOVER WITHIN US
DISCOVER	063 - 1	DISCOVER WHAT TO BELIEVE IN
DISCOVER	063 - 1	TO DISCOVER HOW THIS CAUSE WORKS
DISCOVER	071 - 2	BE LEFT ALONE TO DISCOVER HIS TRUE
DISCOVER	095 - 2	DISCOVER AND MAKE USE OF THEM
DISCOVER	109 - 3	LET ALONE TO DISCOVER HIMSELF
DISCOVER	130 - 3	DISCOVER THE SECRETS OF LIFE FOR HIMSELF
DISCOVER	338 - 2	ALONE TO DISCOVER OURSELVES
DISCOVER	363 - 2	DISCOVER A FEW SIMPLE IDEAS
DISCOVER	415 - 4	WHICH WE MAY DISCOVER
DISCOVER	416 - 3	ALONE TO DISCOVER HIMSELF
DISCOVERED	333 - 2	NOW DISCOVERED A UNITY
DISCOVERED	363 - 4	JESUS DISCOVERED AND TAUGHT
DISCOVERIES	415 - 4	ONE OF THE FIRST DISCOVERIES WE MAKE
DISCOVERS	043 - 3	MAN'S MIND DISCOVERS THE LAW
DISCOVERS	043 - 4	DISCOVERS AND MAKES USE OF
DISCOVERS	130 - 2	HE DISCOVERS AND USES
DISCOVERS	130 - 5	DISCOVERS HIS ABILITY TO THINK
DISCOVERY	031 - 2	THIS IS THE GREATEST DISCOVERY OF ALL TIME
DISCOVERY	043 - 3	OBSERVE ANY SCIENTIFIC DISCOVERY
DISCOVERY	071 - 2	MAKE THIS GREAT DISCOVERY
DISCOVERY	072 - 1	HIS DISCOVERY OF HIMSELF
DISCOVERY	072 - 3	THE FIRST GREAT DISCOVERY
DISCOVERY	073 - 1	MAN'S FIRST DISCOVERY
DISCOVERY	073 - 2	GREATEST DISCOVERY OF ALL TIME
DISCOVERY	107 - 2	DISCOVERY OF OUR TRUE NATURE

DISCOVERY	191 - 2	TO HIS DISCOVERY OF HIMSELF
DISCOVERY	362 - 2	GREAT DISCOVERY FOR HIMSELF
DISCOVERY	391 - 3	THE DISCOVERY OF THIS, THE GREATEST
DISCOVERY	391 - 3	GREATEST DISCOVERY OF THE AGES
DISCOVERY	416 - 3	IN THIS DISCOVERY OF THE SELF
DISCREDIT	137 - 2	DISCREDIT ALL HUMAN TESTIMONY
DISCRIMINATION	242 - 5	DISCRIMINATION AND JUDGMENT
DISCUSS	427 - 1	DISCUSS ALL THE SAYINGS OF
DISEASE	027 - 6	HEALED OF PHYSICAL DISEASE
DISEASE	097 - 2	DISEASE, POVERTY, UNHAPPINESS
DISEASE	101 - 1	IT IS THE FORM OF DISEASE
DISEASE	169 - 4	DISEASE AS BEING CONNECTED
DISEASE	179 - 6	DISSOLVES ALL DISEASE INTO THOUGHT
DISEASE	186 - 1	DISEASE AND LIMITATION
DISEASE	200 - 4	DISEASE MEANS LACK OF EASE
DISEASE	200 - 4	DISEASE IS AN IMPERSONAL THING
DISEASE	200 - 5	DISEASE IS AN EXPERIENCE
DISEASE	202 - 3	THE FACT THAT EVERY DISEASE
DISEASE	202 - 4	DISEASE AS BELONGING TO HIM
DISEASE	209 - 5	OPPOSED TO A LAW OF DISEASE
DISEASE	216 - 1	THERE IS NO INCURABLE DISEASE
DISEASE	216 - 1	THE LAW KNOWS NOTHING ABOUT DISEASE
DISEASE	216 - 3	NO INCURABLE DISEASE
DISEASE	221 - 1	DISEASE IS HARD TO HEAL
DISEASE	221 - 3	DISEASE AS AN ENTITY
DISEASE	231 - 4	DISEASE IS NOT IN THE BODY
DISEASE	231 - 6	DISEASE OF ALL KINDS
DISEASE	234 - 4	DISEASE WITHOUT THOUGHT
DISEASE	315 - 3	THERE IS NO DISEASE
DISEASE	316 - 3	ENTIRELY AWAY FROM THE DISEASE
DISEASE	316 - 3	THIS IS WHAT DISEASE IS. LACK OF EASE
DISEASE	365 - 2	THE HEALING OF ALL DISEASE
DISEASE	374 - 4	BY REASON OF DISEASE, DECAY
DISEASE	409 - 1	DISEASE IS NEITHER PERSON, PLACE
DISEASE	413 - 5	NOT A PATIENT NOR A DISEASE
DISEASED	169 - 4	NOT AS A DISEASED CONDITION
DISEASED	172 - 4	SPIRIT CANNOT BE DISEASED
DISEASES	237 - 1	SEVENTY PER CENT OF ALL DISEASES
DISEASES	501 - 4	IF WE COULD GIVE UP OUR DISEASES
DISENTANGLE	317 - 1	DISENTANGLE OUR IMAGINATION
DISHONEST	200 - 3	DISHONEST IF HE CONTRACTS
DISHONESTY	231 - 2	THOUGHTS OF DISHONESTY AND SUSPICION
DISHONOR	253 - 1	DISHONOR GOD WHEN WE FEAR IT
DISHONOR	253 - 1	TO DISHONOR THE SPIRITUAL MAN
DISILLUSIONED	296 - 2	HE NEEDS TO BE DISILLUSIONED
DISINTEGRATE	192 - 4	DISINTEGRATE AS SOON AS THE UNNATURAL
DISINTEGRATE	197 - 1	DISINTEGRATE AND TO RESOLVE INTO
DISLIKES	225 - 3	THE LIKES AND DISLIKES
DISLODGE	465 - 2	NOTHING CAN DISLODGE THIS INNER
DISLODGE	498 - 5	LET US DISLODGE DOUBT
DISORDER	198 - 4	APPEARS AS THE PHYSICAL DISORDER
DISORDERS	033 - 1	CAUSE PHYSICAL DISORDERS
DISPASSIONATE	283 - 2	DISPASSIONATE BUT FILLED WITH FEELING
DISPELLED	056 - 4	WRONG ACTION IS DISPELLED
DISPELS	235 - 5	DISPELS EVERY DISCORDANT

DISPLEASE	430 - 3	PLEASE OR WHETHER WE DISPLEASE
DISPOSAL	118 - 1	CREATIVE INTELLIGENCE AT OUR DISPOSAL
DISPOSAL	122 - 4	MAN HAS AT HIS DISPOSAL
DISPOSAL	133 - 2	MAN HAS AT HIS DISPOSAL
DISPOSAL	349 - 4	DISPOSAL AN EMOTIONAL KNOWLEDGE
DISPOSED	149 - 4	KINDLY DISPOSED ONE DAY
DISSECT	092 - 3	CANNOT ANALYZE, DISSECT OR DENY
DISSECT	193 - 4	DISSECT AND THEN DECIDE
DISSECT	372 - 1	DISSECT EVERY ATOM OF HIS
DISSECTING	434 - 5	DISSECTING THE NATURE OF EVIL
DISSIPATES	235 - 5	LIGHT OF SPIRIT DISSIPATES
DISSOLVE	170 - 1	DISSOLVE ALL FALSE APPEARANCES
DISSOLVE	209 - 5	UNCREATE OR DISSOLVE THEM
DISSOLVE	234 - 5	DISSOLVE THE IDEA OF FALSE GROWTHS
DISSOLVED	444 - 1	DISSOLVED IN HIS DIVINE INDIVIDUALITY
DISSOLVES	059 - 3	DISSOLVES THE NEGATIVE APPEARANCE
DISSOLVES	179 - 6	DISSOLVES ALL DISEASE INTO THOUGHT
DISSUADE	461 - 4	DID NOT TRY TO DISSUADE HIM
DISTANCE	206 - 2	BE AT A PHYSICAL DISTANCE
DISTANCE	208 - 2	THAT A PERSON AT A DISTANCE
DISTANT	089 - 2	INFINITE NOT MORE DISTANT
DISTASTEFUL	321 - 1	FROM ALL DISTASTEFUL CONDITIONS
DISTINCT	065 - 1	THERE ARE MANY FORMS, EACH DISTINCT
DISTINCT	352 - 2	OBJECTIVE STATE IS A DISTINCT
DISTINCT	396 - 3	MAKES MAN DISTINCT AND DIFFERENT
DISTINCT	419 - 3	A SEPARATE AND DISTINCT ENTITY
DISTINCT	422 - 1	MAN IS SEPARATE AND DISTINCT
DISTINGUISH	078 - 2	DISTINGUISH BETWEEN THE LAW OF MIND
DISTINGUISH	079 - 3	DISTINGUISH BETWEEN CONSCIOUS
DISTINGUISH	399 - 3	DISTINGUISH DAY DREAMING
DISTINGUISHING	313 - 2	DISTINGUISHING OBJECTS ONE
DISTINGUISHING	341 - 5	DISTINGUISHING BETWEEN PSYCHIC
DISTRAUGHT	176 - 1	DISTRAUGHT CANNOT GIVE A GOOD
DISTRESS	203 - 2	USING TO RELIEVE DISTRESS
DISTRESS	464 - 3	GREAT NEED AND DIRE DISTRESS
DISTRIBUTE	193 - 1	WE DISTRIBUTE IT
DISTRIBUTED	100 - 3	EQUALLY DISTRIBUTED IN THE UNIVERSE
DISTRIBUTES	430 - 1	DISTRIBUTES HIS GIFTS TO THOSE
DISTRIBUTES	476 - 3	ONE GENERATES, THE OTHER DISTRIBUTES
DISTRUST	233 - 4	LET GO OF DOUBT, DISTRUST, WORRY
DISTRUST	256 - 3	OF WORRY, DISTRUST AND ANXIETY
DISTRUST	465 - 4	SELF-CONDEMNATION AND PERSONAL DISTRUST
DISTURB	438 - 4	WHY SHOULD IT DISTURB ANYONE
DISTURBANCE	165 - 2	THERE IS A MENTAL DISTURBANCE
DISTURBANCE	177 - 5	PRODUCE PHYSICAL DISTURBANCE
DISTURBED	055 - 3	NOT BE DISTURBED
DISTURBED	144 - 2	NOR SHOULD WE BE DISTURBED
DISTURBED	187 - 3	DISTURBED BY THINGS
DISTURBED	236 - 3	PRACTITIONER MUST NOT BE DISTURBED BY
DISTURBED	256 - 2	DISTURBED MENTAL CONDITION
DISTURBING	232 - 3	DISTURBING TO THE ENTIRE BODY
DITCH	055 - 4	SHALL FALL INTO THE DITCH
DITCH	453 - 5	BOTH SHALL FALL INTO THE DITCH
DITCH	453 - 6	DITCH OF OUR OWN CONFUSION
DIVIDE	095 - 3	IMPOSSIBLE TO DIVIDE MIND

DIVIDE	161 - 4	DIVIDE OUR MENTAL HOUSE
DIVIDE	477 - 3	MUST UNIFY AND NOT DIVIDE
DIVIDED	053 - 3	UNIVERSE IS NOT DIVIDED
DIVIDED	068 - 3	DIVIDED AGAINST ITSELF
DIVIDED	076 - 4	HOUSE DIVIDED AGAINST ITSELF
DIVIDED	286 - 1	NO LONGER BE DIVIDED AGAINST ITSELF
DIVIDED	330 - 2	INFINITE CANNOT BE DIVIDED
DIVIDED	448 - 3	HOUSE DIVIDED AGAINST ITSELF CANNOT STAND
DIVIDED	470 - 2	UNIVERSE WILL NOT BE DIVIDED
DIVIDED	499 - 3	DIVIDED AGAINST ITSELF CANNOT STAND
DIVINE	025 - 3	THE DIVINE PLAN IS ONE OF FREEDOM
DIVINE	034 - 1	WE ARE DIVINE
DIVINE	142 - 3	REALIZES HIS DIVINE NATURE
DIVINE	183 - 2	REALIZATION OF THE DIVINE PRESENCE
DIVINE	186 - 3	DIRECT RELATIONSHIP TO THE DIVINE
DIVINE	198 - 4	PATIENT IS A DIVINE SPIRITUAL
DIVINE	232 - 4	SOMETHING RESEMBLING THE DIVINE
DIVINE	250 - 2	SENSE THIS PERSON AS BEING DIVINE
DIVINE	370 - 3	OF ETERNAL STUFF FASHIONED AFTER A DIVINE
DIVINE	410 - 1	THE HUMAN IS REALLY DIVINE
DIVINE	420 - 4	AN IMPULSE PLANTED BY THE DIVINE
DIVINE	420 - 4	THE DIVINE IS LIMITLESS AND PERFECT
DIVINE	422 - 3	GIVES WAY TO THE DIVINE
DIVINE BEING	336 - 1	EVERYONE AS A DIVINE BEING
DIVINE BODY	212 - 5	MUST BE A DIVINE BODY
DIVINE CALLING	466 - 1	FALLEN SHORT OF THE DIVINE CALLING
DIVINE CALLING	471 - 3	SHORT OF THE DIVINE CALLING
DIVINE EAR	430 - 3	DIVINE EAR IS ATTUNED TO HARMONY
DIVINE GLORY	490 - 2	REFLECT THE DIVINE GLORY
DIVINE GOODNESS	428 - 3	BELIEF IN THE DIVINE GOODNESS
DIVINE HARMONY	112 - 4	DIVINE HARMONY BE REFLECTED THROUGH US
DIVINE HOST	430 - 1	DIVINE HOST SERVES NOT HIS BOUNTY
DIVINE IDEAS	131 - 1	DIVINE IDEAS ARE PERFECT
DIVINE IDEAS	491 - 3	DIVINE IDEAS STAND BACK OF ALL
DIVINE INFLUX	113 - 3	OUR MINDS AS OPEN TO THE DIVINE INFLUX
DIVINE INFLUX	113 - 3	MAN IS OPEN TO THE DIVINE INFLUX
DIVINE LAW	339 - 1	DIVINE LAW OBEYING THE DICTATES
DIVINELY	286 - 2	EACH ONE OF THESE MEN IS DIVINELY ACTIVE
DIVINE MIND	437 - 4	IN ACCORD WITH THE DIVINE MIND
DIVINE MIND	495 - 6	DIVINE MIND OF THE CREATOR
DIVINE ORDER	254 - 6	DIVINE ORDER IN EVERY ORGAN
DIVINE REALITY	421 - 2	MAN AS A DIVINE REALITY
DIVINE SCALE	490 - 5	DIVINE SCALE IS EVER ASCENDING
DIVINE SPARK	130 - 3	DIVINE SPARK IS ALWAYS INTACT IN POTENTIAL
DIVINE URGE	157 - 3	DIVINE URGE WITHIN US IS GOD'S WAY
DIVINE URGE	469 - 3	DIVINE URGE WITHIN, EVER PUSHING
DIVINE WILL	160 - 3	NECESSITY OF THE DIVINE WILL
DIVINITY	042 - 5	THAT ALL IS DIVINITY
DIVINITY	142 - 3	SOUL THAT KNOWS ITS OWN DIVINITY
DIVINITY	161 - 5	DOES NOT DENY THE DIVINITY OF JESUS
DIVINITY	161 - 5	AFFIRM THE DIVINITY OF ALL PEOPLE
DIVINITY	167 - 3	GREET THE DIVINITY IN EVERY MAN
DIVINITY	223 - 2	TO EXPRESS HIS OWN DIVINITY
DIVINITY	238 - 2	GUARANTEE OF OUR DIVINITY
DIVINITY	251 - 2	I KNOW MY DIVINITY

DIVINITY	336 - 1	DIVINITY WHICH IS LATENT IN ALL
DIVISION	208 - 5	NOT AS DIVISION
DIVISION	321 - 2	MULTIPLICITY BUT NEVER DIVISION
DIVISION	359 - 3	DIVISION GAVE WAY TO THE WILL
DIVORCE	198 - 1	CANNOT DIVORCE TRUE MENTAL HEALING
DIVORCE	441 - 4	DIVORCE OUR LIVES FROM THE THOUGHT
DIVORCED	191 - 5	FOR THE TWO CANNOT BE DIVORCED
DIVORCED	262 - 1	DIVORCED FROM MY IMAGINATION
DIVORCED	336 - 1	DIVORCED FROM THE MENTAL ACT
DO	108 - 3	DO, SAY AND THINK AS ONE WISHES
DO	339 - 1	MAY DO AS HE WILLS
DO	404 - 4	MUST DO ALL IN OUR POWER
DO	499 - 5	WHAT WE KNOW WE CAN DO
DO	499 - 5	DO THE WILL OF TRUTH ENTER IN
DOCTOR	199 - 3	ANY DOCTOR THE PATIENT MAY DESIRE
DOCTOR	316 - 2	DOCTOR WHO CAN WEIGH AND MEASURE
DOCTRINE	441 - 4	PROOF OF THIS DOCTRINE REMAINS
DOER	073 - 2	THE THINKER AND THE DOER
DOER	079 - 2	DOER BUT NOT A KNOWER
DOER	091 - 1	IT IS A DOER OR EXECUTOR OF THE WILL
DOER	392 - 3	SUBJECTIVE MIND IS A DOER
DOER	500 - 2	DOER AND NOT A KNOWER
DOERS	499 - 5	DOERS OF THE WORD
DOES	299 - 4	WHAT IT DOES FOR US IT MUST DO THROUGH
DOES NOT	058 - 3	DOES NOT BELIEVE
DOES NOT	106 - 2	DOES NOT MEAN THAT MAN IS GOD
DOES NOT	111 - 2	DOES NOT MEAN THAT WE CAN
DOES NOT	318 - 2	DOES NOT BECOME SUBJECTIVE
DOES NOT	343 - 4	DOES NOT MEAN THAT MAN IS GOD
DOES NOT MATTER	169 - 3	IT DOES NOT MATTER SO MUCH
DOGMATIC	218 - 4	NOT TO BE CONSIDERED DOGMATIC
DOING	273 - 4	GOD IS FOREVER DOING
DOING	278 - 2	PROVE HIS KNOWING BY DOING
DOLLARS	186 - 2	A MILLION DOLLARS AND A PENNY
DOLLARS	286 - 1	THAT FIFTEEN DOLLARS IS MATERIAL
DOMINANT	144 - 3	DOMINANT MENTAL AND SPIRITUAL STATES
DOMINION	065 - 5	DOMINION OVER EVERYTHING
DOMINION	065 - 6	POWER TO HAVE DOMINION
DOMINION	250 - 6	CLAIM OUR POWER AND DOMINION
DOMINION	252 - 5	WE SHOULD CLAIM OUR DOMINION
DOMINION	460 - 3	THE ETERNITY OF HER DOMINION
DONE	034 - 1	IT IS DONE UNTO EACH ONE
DONE	037 - 1	IT IS DONE UNTO YOU AS YOU BELIEVE
DONE	068 - 5	SPAKE AND IT WAS DONE
DONE	069 - 3	GOD SPEAKS AND IT IS DONE
DONE	084 - 1	SPEAKS AND IT IS DONE
DONE	161 - 1	SO BE IT DONE UNTO THEE
DONE	301 - 3	IT IS DONE UNTO YOU
DONE	355 - 2	THE THING AS ALREADY DONE
DONE	404 - 5	THIS IS DONE BY UNDERSTANDING
DONE UNTO US	152 - 1	IT IS DONE UNTO US AS WE
DO NOT	386 - 4	I DO NOT BELIEVE IN THE RETURN
DON'T	272 - 3	DON'T KNOW HOW TO MAKE
DOORKEEPER	243 - 2	DOORKEEPER TO THE TEMPLE
DOORMAT	459 - 5	FOR ONE TO MAKE A DOORMAT OF HIMSELF

DOORWAY	112 - 4	DOORWAY TO THE ABSOLUTE
DOORWAY	450 - 3	DOORWAY OF HIS CONSCIOUSNESS
DOORWAY	491 - 3	THROUGH THE DOORWAY OF THE MIND
DOUBLE-MINDED	498 - 3	DOUBLE-MINDED MAN GETS NOWHERE
DOUBT	049 - 4	NEUTRALIZES ALL DOUBT
DOUBT	057 - 1	NO UNBELIEF, NO DOUBT, NO UNCERTAINTY
DOUBT	057 - 1	DOUBT VANISH FROM MY MIND
DOUBT	058 - 4	TO REMOVE THIS DOUBT
DOUBT	104 - 1	CAN WE DOUBT
DOUBT	188 - 3	WITHOUT A SHADOW OF DOUBT
DOUBT	218 - 2	THE REMOVAL OF DOUBT AND FEAR
DOUBT	220 - 4	DOUBT IN A TREATMENT
DOUBT	225 - 1	TO DO SO IS TO DOUBT
DOUBT	227 - 4	NO DOUBT OR CONFUSION
DOUBT	233 - 4	LET GO OF DOUBT, DISTRUST, WORRY
DOUBT	245 - 3	THOUGHTS OF DOUBT AND WORRY THAT
DOUBT	250 - 5	SURRENDER EVERY PERSONAL DOUBT
DOUBT	272 - 2	DOUBT AND FEAR MUST GO
DOUBT	277 - 3	TREATMENT REMOVES DOUBT
DOUBT	289 - 3	DOUBT YOUR ABILITY TO DEMONSTRATE
DOUBT	319 - 3	DOUBT MY ABILITY TO HEAL
DOUBT	374 - 2	DOUBT THAT SOMETHING TANGIBLE
DOUBT	401 - 4	DOUBT OUR ABILITY TO USE THE LAW
DOUBT	408 - 4	SUCH A POWER ALL DOUBT
DOUBTS	048 - 3	OVERCOME HIS DOUBTS
DOUBTS	053 - 1	BECAUSE OF OUR DOUBTS AND FEARS
DOUBTS	058 - 4	DOUBTS HIS ABILITY TO GIVE
DOUBTS	220 - 4	WERE NO SUBJECTIVE DOUBTS
DOUBTS	456 - 3	IN THEIR MINDS THERE ARE NO DOUBTS
DOWN AND OUT	207 - 1	GET DOWN AND OUT MENTALLY
DRAIN	205 - 1	DRAIN OUT ALL THE IMPURITIES
DRAIN	209 - 6	DRAIN ON ONE TO TREAT
DRAW	040 - 3	MAY DRAW FROM
DRAW	040 - 3	WE MUST DRAW THROUGH
DRAW	056 - 1	DRAW ALL MEN UNTO ME
DRAW	264 - 1	DRAW ALL TOWARD ME
DRAW	298 - 2	WILL DRAW TO YOU SO MANY FRIENDS
DRAWING	123 - 1	DRAWING FROM LIFE WHAT HE THINKS
DRAWN	128 - 2	DRAWN FROM THIS ONE MIND
DRAWN	142 - 2	DRAWN TOWARD THOSE THINGS
DRAWN	142 - 2	DRAWN SILENTLY TOWARD IT
DRAWN	298 - 2	TWO WILL BE DRAWN TOGETHER
DRAWS	133 - 3	DRAWS FROM IT ALL OF HIS EXPERIENCES
DRAWS	197 - 2	DRAWS CERTAIN CONCLUSIONS
DRAWS	349 - 3	SUBJECTIVE DRAWS TO ITSELF
DRAWS FORTH	045 - 4	DRAWS FORTH A DIFFERENT RESULT
DREAM	083 - 5	CONSTRUCT ONLY A DREAM
DREAM	108 - 3	THINK AND DREAM OF FREEDOM
DREAM	288 - 2	ANYTHING YOU CAN DREAM
DREAM	297 - 3	NOT AS A DREAM BUT AS AN EXPERIENCE
DREAM	386 - 3	AS A VAGUE DREAM
DREAM	399 - 3	DO NOT DREAM WE STATE
DREAM	477 - 4	DREAM COME TRUE IN HUMAN EXPERIENCE
DREAM	487 - 5	DREAM FROM WHICH WE MUST AWAKE
DREAM	487 - 6	THE DREAM OF A LIVING DEATH

DREAMER	476 - 6	DREAMER WITHOUT ANY PRACTICAL
DREAMING	399 - 3	DISTINGUISH DAY DREAMING
DREAMS	026 - 1	BEYOND OUR FONDEST DREAMS
DREAMS	103 - 3	THAN THIS WORLD DREAMS
DREAMS	287 - 5	ALL OUR BEAUTIFUL DREAMS
DREAMS	477 - 4	DREAMS TO COME TO FULL FRUITION
DREAM WORLD	108 - 3	REMAIN IN A DREAM WORLD
DRESS	442 - 3	SHE MAY DRESS IN MANY GARMENTS
DRINK	246 - 4	MAY FREELY DRINK
DRINKING	246 - 4	WE MUST DO THE DRINKING
DRIVE	058 - 5	NOT HAVE TO DRIVE OR PUSH
DROP	107 - 1	DROP OF WATER IS NOT THE WHOLE OCEAN
DROP	204 - 5	A DROP AT A TIME
DROP	205 - 1	A DROP AT A TIME
DROPPING	227 - 1	DROPPING OPPOSING THOUGHTS
DRY	267 - 2	INTO THE WATER AND REMAIN DRY
DUAL	042 - 6	WE HAVE A DUAL UNITY
DUAL	347 - 2	WE DO HAVE A DUAL ASPECT
DUAL	473 - 4	MEANS THE POSSIBILITY OF DUAL
DUAL	473 - 5	DUAL NATURE OF MAN
DUAL	474 - 4	TASTING OF DUAL EXPERIENCE
DUAL	477 - 6	I AM HAS A DUAL MEANING
DUALISM	383 - 1	AN ANTHROPOMORPHIC DUALISM
DUALITY	039 - 4	DUALITY RATHER THAN UNITY
DUALITY	124 - 4	THIS WOULD BE DUALITY
DUALITY	160 - 1	RISES ABOVE A BELIEF IN DUALITY
DUALITY	191 - 5	THAT A BELIEF IN DUALITY
DUALITY	209 - 4	DUALITY IN THE UNIVERSE
DUALITY	279 - 2	APPEAR IN HIS EXPERIENCE AS DUALITY
DUALITY	279 - 2	HE HAS BELIEVED IN DUALITY
DUALITY	289 - 1	FROM A BELIEF IN DUALITY
DUALITY	453 - 6	BELIEF IN DUALITY
DUALITY	461 - 2	POSSIBILITY OF AN APPARENT DUALITY
DUAL NATURE	473 - 5	DUAL NATURE OF MAN
DUE	433 - 2	EVERYONE RECEIVES HIS JUST DUE
DUE	487 - 4	EXACTLY WHAT IS HIS DUE
DUPLICATE	378 - 3	ENDOWED US WITH DUPLICATE SENSES
DUPLICATED	378 - 2	DUPLICATED IN THE MIND ALONE
DURATION	312 - 2	EXPERIENCE BUT NOT DURATION
DUST	410 - 4	DUST IF THOU SEEST DUST
DUST	438 - 4	THOUGHT WEIGHS HIM TO THE DUST
DUTY	270 - 5	DOES NOT LESSEN OUR DUTY
DWELL	169 - 3	DWELL IN THE SECRET PLACE
DWELL	216 - 5	DWELL TOO MUCH ON THE NEGATIVE
DWELL	243 - 3	DWELL NOT ON BREATH
DWELL	245 - 2	I DWELL IN THE REALM OF PEACE
DWELL	488 - 6	DO NOT DWELL UPON ADVERSITY
DWELLETH	150 - 5	THE FATHER WHO DWELLETH IN ME
DWELLETH	330 - 4	THE FATHER THAT DWELLETH IN ME
DWELLING	220 - 4	DWELLING ON ITS MEANING
DWELLS	484 - 4	RAISED JESUS DWELLS IN ALL
DWELT	306 - 5	ALWAYS DWELT ON LIMITED THOUGHTS
DYNAMIC	138 - 1	DYNAMIC FORCES OF THE MENTAL REALM
DYNAMIC	201 - 1	DYNAMIC SPIRITUAL ABSOLUTE
DYNAMIC	221 - 3	WORK IS DEFINITE AND DYNAMIC

DYNAMIC	285 - 2	IT IS A DYNAMIC FACT
DYNAMIC	363 - 4	WITH THIS DYNAMIC REALIZATION
DYNAMIC	367 - 4	HIS METHOD WAS DIRECT DYNAMIC

E

EACH	067 - 3	EACH POINTS TO ONE CENTRAL
EACH	278 - 2	EACH ONE SHOULD REALIZE THAT
EACH	408 - 3	EACH IS IN DIRECT RELATIONSHIP
EACH	482 - 2	EACH IS A CENTER OF THE ALL
EACH TIME	319 - 4	TRYING TO REALIZE EACH TIME
EAGLE	388 - 4	AS THE EAGLE FREED FROM ITS CAGE
EAR	179 - 3	EAR LISTENING TO AND HEARING EVERYTHING
EAR	257 - 6	JEHOVAH HATH OPENED THINE EAR
EAR	441 - 2	COSMIC EAR HEARS EVERYTHING
EARS	258 - 1	TRAIN OUR EARS TO LISTEN
EARS	334 - 1	HE WHO MADE THE EARS CAN HEAR
EARTH	025 - 3	THE EARTH CONTAINS UNTOLD RICHES
EARTH	072 - 4	SEEMED TO POSSESS THE EARTH
EARTH	092 - 1	THE CREATIVE SOIL OF THE EARTH
EARTH	385 - 2	MY LIFE HAPPY WHILE ON EARTH
EARTHY	311 - 1	IS OF THE EARTH EARTHY
EASE	300 - 3	NATURALLY AND WITH A SENSE OF EASE
EASIER	423 - 1	EASIER TO TEACH THE TRUTH
EASY	218 - 3	EASY TO BELIEVE THAT GOD IS PERFECT
EASY	263 - 1	KNOWS NO HARD AND NO EASY
EASY	319 - 2	NOT ALWAYS EASY TO TURN
EASY	403 - 2	NOT ALWAYS EASY TO SEE THIS NOR
EASY	414 - I	NO EASY CASE TO HANDLE
EAT	260 - 2	WHAT WE SHOULD EAT
EATING	442 - 2	THE SON OF MAN CAME EATING
ECHO	032 - 1	ECHO OF THE ETERNAL THING
ECHO	104 - 2	WILL ECHO THE SOFT NOTES
ECKHART	357 - 2	ECKHART ONE OF THE GREAT MYSTICS
ECSTASY	127 - 2	KNEELS IN ECSTASY OR LIES DRUNK
ECSTASY	366 - 2	ECSTASY OF SELF-REALIZATION HE PROCLAIMED
ECZEMA	248 - 3	ECZEMA AND OTHER SKIN IRRITATIONS
EDEN	310 - 4	EDEN AND THE FALL
EDEN	410 - 3	ALLEGORY OF EDEN
EDIFICE	437 - 1	EDIFICE FALLS ABOUT HIM IN RUINS
EDUCATION	460 - 4	HISTORY OF RELIGIOUS EDUCATION
EFFECT	075 - 3	BECAUSE WE SEE AN EFFECT
EFFECT	086 - 2	VIBRATION AND ARE IN EFFECT
EFFECT	086 - 3	PRODUCE AN ENTIRELY DIFFERENT EFFECT
EFFECT	099 - 2	BODY IS ALWAYS AN EFFECT
EFFECT	101 - 3	EFFECT IS SUBJECT TO ITS CAUSE
EFFECT	101 - 5	CAUSE AND EFFECT ARE SPIRITUAL
EFFECT	114 - 4	AN EFFECT AND NOT A CAUSE
EFFECT	117 - 3	PHYSICAL UNIVERSE IS AN EFFECT
EFFECT	123 - 3	ALL CREATION IS AN EFFECT
EFFECT	131 - 1	VISIBLE WORLD IS AN EFFECT
EFFECT	184 - 5	MUST PRODUCE A PERFECT EFFECT
EFFECT	194 - 5	SOME KIND OF AN EFFECT

EFFECT	198 - 2	THE BODY IS AN EFFECT
EFFECT	217 - 1	NEITHER CAUSE, MEDIUM, NOR EFFECT
EFFECT	231 - 4	BODY IS AN EFFECT
EFFECT	233 - 2	AWAY FROM THE EFFECT
EFFECT	305 - 4	EFFECT EXACTLY LIKE ITS CAUSE
EFFECT	321 - 1	THE PHYSICAL UNIVERSE IS AN EFFECT
EFFECT	321 - 2	BY ITS OBJECTIVE EFFECT
EFFECT	322 - 3	THE LAW PRODUCES THE EFFECT
EFFECT	401 - 2	PARTICULAR EFFECT MAY BE CHANGED
EFFECT	407 - 3	MIND IS ALSO ALL EFFECT
EFFECT	420 - 3	AN EFFECT OF INTELLIGENCE
EFFECT	483 - 2	EFFECT MUST PARTAKE OF ITS INWARD
EFFECT	492 - 3	EFFECT LOUDLY AFFIRMS THE NATURE
EFFECT	494 - 4	EFFECT IS FOREVER WITHOUT
EFEECTIVE	042 - 3	BEST AND THE MOST EFFECTIVE
EFFECTIVE	150 - 2	PRAYERS WHICH ARE EFFECTIVE
EFFECTIVE	155 - 2	MAKES PRAYER EFFECTIVE
EFFECTIVE	163 - 2	EFFECTIVE BECAUSE THE LAW
EFFECTIVE	221 - 4	WORK WILL BE EFFECTIVE
EFFECTIVE	249 - 3	RECOGNIZED AS EFFECTIVE
EFFECTIVE	284 - 5	ESSENTIAL TO EFFECTIVE MENTAL TREATMENT
EFFECTIVE	285 - 2	KNOWS IT WILL BE EFFECTIVE
EFFECTIVE	334 - 3	METHOD IS BY FAR THE MOST EFFECTIVE
EFFECTIVE	414 - 1	EFFECTIVE TREATMENT MUST BE INDEPENDENT
EFFECTIVELY	459 - 1	WE PRAY EFFECTIVELY
EFFECTS	030 - 3	EXCUSES NO ONE FROM ITS EFFECTS
EFFECTS	102 - 5	PRODUCING EFFECTS WHICH LIVE
EFFECTS	189 - 2	ALL MANIFESTATIONS ARE EFFECTS
EFFECTS	406 - 4	EFFECTS FLOW FROM CAUSES
EFFFCTS	407 - 4	COMPLETE AND PERFECT EFFECTS
EFFECTS	447 - 2	EFFECTS OF RIGHT RELATIONSHIPS
EFFECTS	463 - 4	EFFECTS MUST FOLLOW CAUSES
EFFECTS	473 - 2	EFFECTS APART FROM TRUE CAUSE
EFFECTUAL	501 - 4	EFFECTUAL AND FERVENT PRAYER
EFFORT	056 - 4	SUSTAIN ME WITHOUT EFFORT
EFFORT	083 - 4	NOT CONSCIOUS OF ANY EFFORT
EFFORT	132 - 1	THERE IS NO EFFORT IN THE PROCESS
EFFORT	174 - 1	EFFORT WHICH ATTEMPTS TO
EFFORT	195 - 3	NO EFFORT IN THE PROCESS
EFFORT	287 - 2	WITHOUT EFFORT
EFFORT	302 - 3	EFFORT WHICH DESTROYS THE PEACE OF MIND
EFFORT	322 - 1	NEITHER EFFORT NOR STRAIN
EFFORTLESS	330 - 5	A SILENT EFFORTLESS PROCESS
EFFULGENCE	474 - 3	MIND WITH ITS CLEAR EFFULGENCE
EGYPT	071 - 2	OUT OF THE LAND OF EGYPT
EINSTEIN	066 - 3	BRAIN OF A SOCRATES OR EINSTEIN
ELABORATE	378 - 1	ELABORATE PROCESS OF REASONING
ELATES	256 - 5	ELATES MY ENTIRE BEING
ELATION	207 - 5	PEACE OR ELATION A VIBRATION
ELDER	469 - 1	ELDER SON HAD MISSED THE MARK
ELECTRICIAN	275 - 4	ELECTRICIAN MAY BE A METHODIST
ELECTRICITY	071 - 2	ELECTRICITY WAS A REALITY
ELECTRICITY	072 - 4	HE HAS HARNESSED ELECTRICITY
ELECTRICITY	078 - 1	WE COULD CALL ELECTRICITY GOD
ELECTRICITY	079 - 3	ELECTRICITY WHICH WILL EITHER LIGHT

ELECTRICITY	080 - 2	THERE IS ELECTRICITY, THE WAY IT WORKS
ELECTRICITY	125 - 5	ELECTRICITY OR ANY OTHER NATURAL FORCE
ELECTRICITY	127 - 2	ELECTRICITY CARE WHETHER IT COOKS
ELECTRICITY	275 - 4	ELECTRICITY BEING A NATURAL LAW
ELECTRICITY	328 - 3	HE HAS HARNESSED ELECTRICITY
ELECTROCUTE	079 - 3	WILL ELECTROCUTE US IF
ELECTROCUTES	127 - 2	ELECTROCUTES A CRIMINAL OR WARMS
ELECTRONS	094 - 2	NO TWO ELECTRONS
ELEMENT	043 - 3	THIS IS THE SPONTANEOUS ELEMENT
ELEMENT	281 - 4	A STRONG ELEMENT IN HIMSELF
ELEMENTS	343 - 3	ELEMENTS IN IT HAVE BEEN GREATER
ELEMENTS	374 - 2	BACK TO THE NATIVE ELEMENTS
ELEVATE	228 - 3	ELEVATE HIS OWN THOUGHT
ELEVATED	473 - 1	MOSES ELEVATED THE LIFE PRINCIPLE
ELIMINATION	186 - 4	LAW OF ELIMINATION AND OBLITERATION
ELIMINATION	232 - 3	PERFECT ELIMINATION IN THE BODY
ELIMINATION	232 - 4	SUCH PERFECT ASSIMILATION, ELIMINATION
ELUSIVE	478 - 5	ESSENCE OF LOVE WHILE ELUSIVE
EMANATE	217 - 1	EMANATE FROM GOD
EMANATED	422 - 2	ONE FROM WHOM IT EMANATED
EMANATES	352 - 4	VIBRATION WHICH HE EMANATES
EMANATION	296 - 3	SUBTLE EMANATION THAT SOMETHING
EMANATION	347 - 3	IS OUR MENTAL EMANATION
EMANCIPATES	264 - 1	EMANCIPATES ME FROM
EMANCIPATION	163 - 3	EMANCIPATION OF THE MIND
EMBODIED	158 - 3	EMBODIED THIS LIVING FAITH
EMBODIED	357 - 1	EMBODIED IN ANY INDIVIDUAL
EMBODIED	399 - 2	REALLY BELIEVED IN AND EMBODIED
EMBODIED	422 - 3	SONSHIP EMBODIED IN ANY INDIVIDUAL
EMBODIES	045 - 1	EMBODIES THE SPIRIT OF HIS ART
EMBODIES	151 - 3	HE EMBODIES LOVE, HE IS LOVE
EMBODIES	361 - 5	THE HUMAN EMBODIES THE DIVINE
EMBODIES	440 - 3	EMBODIES ALL OTHER LIVES
EMBODIMENT	030 - 1	LIVING EMBODIMENT OF HIS THOUGHTS
EMBODIMENT	081 - 1	APART FROM PHYSICAL EMBODIMENT
EMBODIMENT	086 - 4	EMBODIMENT IN IT
EMBODIMENT	086 - 4	EMBODIMENT OF THE IDEA
EMBODIMENT	118 - 2	OUR INWARD EMBODIMENT
EMBODIMENT	141 - 3	EQUAL TO THE EMBODIMENT OF THE THOUGHT
EMBODIMENT	159 - 5	THE EMBODIMENT OF AN IDEA
EMBODIMENT	166 - 1	EMBODIMENT OF THE THOUGHT
EMBODIMENT	169 - 4	EMBODIMENT OF PERFECTION
EMBODIMENT	170 - 5	EMBODIMENT OF THE IDEA
EMBODIMENT	176 - 1	EMBODIMENT OF THE IMAGE
EMBODIMENT	176 - 1	WORD AND NOT AN EMBODIMENT
EMBODIMENT	186 - 3	CONSCIOUSNESS MEANS THE INNER EMBODIMENT
EMBODIMENT	201 - 2	EMBODIMENT OF PERFECTION
EMBODIMENT	218 - 3	EMBODIMENT THE OBJECTIVE HEALING
EMBODIMENT	267 - 1	BECOME A SUBJECTIVE EMBODIMENT
EMBODIMENT	279 - 1	IF WE HAVE A REAL EMBODIMENT
EMBODIMENT	280 - 1	EMBODIMENT OF THE DIVINE NATURE
EMBODIMENT	280 - 2	INCREASE OUR EMBODIMENT
EMBODIMENT	280 - 2	THE EMBODIMENT OF THAT BELIEF
EMBODIMENT	319 - 1	WE MAY CALL IT EMBODIMENT
EMBODIMENT	359 - 2	CHRIST IS THE EMBODIMENT OF DIVINE SONSHIP

EMBODIMENT	359 - 3	LIVING EMBODIMENT OF THE CHRIST
EMBODIMENT	363 - 2	EMBODIMENT OF WHICH ENABLED HIM
EMBODIMENT	398 - 3	ACCEPTANCE AND EMBODIMENT OF OUR DESIRES
EMBODIMENT	400 - 2	ITSELF INTO A SUBJECTIVE EMBODIMENT
EMBODIMENTS	402 - 2	FORM OF OUR SUBJECTIVE EMBODIMENTS
EMBODY	041 - 1	AS WE EMBODY ITS INTELLIGENCE
EMBODY	044 - 3	OF THIS LIFE AS WE EMBODY
EMBODY	044 - 3	AS WE UNDERSTAND AND EMBODY
EMBODY	045 - 1	HIS ABILITY TO EMBODY
EMBODY	050 - 2	AS MUCH OF IT AS WE CAN EMBODY
EMBODY	118 - 2	UNDERSTAND IT TO EMBODY IT
EMBODY	133 - 2	MAN'S INABILITY TO EMBODY THE TRUTH
EMBODY	142 - 2	EMBODY WHAT WE WISH
EMBODY	146 - 3	POWER TO USE AS WE BELIEVE IN AND EMBODY
EMBODY	150 - 2	EMBODY CERTAIN UNIVERSAL PRINCIPLES
EMBODY	174 - 3	MENTALLY EMBODY AN IDEA
EMBODY	176 - 1	HE TRIES TO EMBODY THE IMAGE
EMBODY	184 - 4	WOULD EMBODY THE GREATEST GOOD
EMBODY	185 - 2	DAILY EMBODY THE GREAT IDEAL
EMBODY	275 - 2	AS MUCH POWER AS I EMBODY
EMBODY	280 - 2	AS MUCH AS HE CAN EMBODY
EMBODY	293 - 1	ALL THE GOOD I CAN EMBODY
EMBODY	294 - 2	WE FIRST MENTALLY EMBODY
EMBODY	411 - 4	WE AUTOMATICALLY EMBODY IT
EMBODY	412 - 1	WHICH WE WISH TO EMBODY
EMBODY	445 - 6	PEACE UNTIL WE EMBODY
EMBODY	447 - 3	EMBODY GOD OR TRUTH
EMBODY	447 - 3	EMBODY THE INFINITE IN DEGREE
EMBODY	447 - 3	EMBODY REALITY WE BECOME
EMBODY	455 - 4	IF ONE WISHES TO EMBODY AN IDEAL
EMBODYING	047 - 1	EMBODYING THE CONCRETE IDEA
EMBODYING	294 - 2	FIRST EMBODYING THE ATMOSPHERE
EMBRACE	502 - 6	EMBRACE AND MAKE HIM WHOLE AGAIN
EMBRACES	143 - 2	EMBRACES A MORE VITAL CONCEPT
EMERGE	420 - 4	ALL EMERGE FROM THAT ONE
EMERGENCE	104 - 1	UNIVERSE IS A SPONTANEOUS EMERGENCE
EMERGENCIES	378 - 3	PROVIDES FOR ALL EMERGENCIES
EMERGENT	273 - 2	CALLED EMERGENT EVOLUTION
EMERGES	332 - 5	EMERGES FROM THE UNIVERSAL
EMERSON	037 - 3	IF WE SAY, WITH EMERSON
EMERSON	041 - 2	EMERSON ADVISES THAT
EMERSON	045 - 4	THIS IS WHAT EMERSON MEANT
EMERSON	076 - 1	EMERSON WOULD HAVE US UNDERSTAND
EMERSON	103 - 3	EMERSON TELLS US THAT NATURE IS SPIRIT
EMERSON	112 - 4	EMERSON SAID THAT WE ANIMATE WHAT WE
EMERSON	152 - 2	EMERSON SAID, IS NOT PRAYER A STUDY OF
EMERSON	297 - 2	EMERSON SAID, IF YOU WANT A FRIEND
EMERSON	310 - 2	WHAT EMERSON HAD IN MIND
EMERSON	311 - 4	EMERSON SAID, THERE IS NO GREAT AND NO
EMERSON	315 - 1	EMERSON SAYS TO CAST THEM
EMERSON	336 - 2	EMERSON SAID HE WAS OFTEN CONSCIOUS
EMERSON	342 - 1	EMERSON, WHITMAN, BROWNING
EMERSON	344 - 3	EMERSON WALKING ACROSS THE COMMON
EMERSON	345 - 2	EMERSON WALKED ON THE VERGE OF THIS
EMERSON	388 - 1	EMERSON TELLS US LIES STRETCHED IN

EMERSON	433 - 2	EMERSON CALLED THE HIGH CHANCELLOR
EMERSON	440 - 2	EMERSON TELLS US TO BEWARE OF
EMERSON	474 - 2	EMERSON TELLS US THAT VIRTUE
EMERSON	486 - 1	EMERSON TELLS US THAT
EMERSON	489 - 7	EMERSON TELLS US THAT WE ARE
EMERSON	500 - 3	EMERSON TELLS US THERE IS NO SIN
EMMANUEL	034 - 1	MEANING OF THE WORD, EMMANUEL
EMMANUEL	113 - 1	EMMANUEL OR GOD WITH US
EMOTION	030 - 3	EMOTION OR CONVICTION BEHIND THE THOUGHT
EMOTION	033 - 1	EMOTION CONGESTED BY FEAR
EMOTION	035 - 4	OUR THOUGHT AND EMOTION
EMOTION	204 - 4	EMOTION AND SENSE OF LOSS
EMOTION	225 - 3	SOME SUPPRESSED EMOTION
EMOTION	228 - 2	PASSION, AN UNEXPRESSED EMOTION
EMOTION	283 - 2	FEELING AND EMOTION ARE CREATIVE
EMOTION	497 - 3	SPIRITUAL EMOTION IS COMMON
EMOTIONAL	143 - 1	EMOTIONAL REACTION ESTABLISHED
EMOTIONAL	144 - 3	EMOTIONAL CONDITIONS ARE MENTAL
EMOTIONAL	208 - 1	INTO AN EMOTIONAL STATE
EMOTIONAL	241 - 1	EMOTIONAL NATURE TO DEAL
EMOTIONAL	339 - 4	EMOTIONAL CRAVING OR DESIRE
EMOTIONS	053 - 3	WITH THOUGHTS, IMPULSES, EMOTIONS
EMOTIONS	122 - 2	UNEXPRESSED EMOTIONS WE FEEL
EMOTIONS	144 - 4	EMOTIONS WE HAVE
EMOTIONS	194 - 4	THE EMOTIONS ARE RIGHTLY POISED
EMOTIONS	194 - 4	EMOTIONS ARE TO RESPOND TO
EMOTIONS	211 - 2	EMOTIONS BECOME MORE COMPLEX
EMOTIONS	211 - 2	REACT TO THESE EMOTIONS SUBJECTIVELY
EMOTIONS	234 - 4	EMOTIONS, DESIRES, OR IDEAS
EMOTIONS	237 - 1	RESULT OF SUPPRESSED EMOTIONS
EMOTIONS	237 - 1	NOT NECESSARILY SEX EMOTIONS
EMOTIONS	238 - 4	EMOTIONS SHOULD BE EXPRESSED
EMOTIONS	240 - 2	EMOTIONS DO AFFECT THE HEART
EMOTIONS	253 - 3	EMOTIONAL REACTION TO CIRCUMSTANCES
EMOTIONS	349 - 3	EMOTIONS WHICH THEY HAVE CONTACTED
EMOTIONS	478 - 5	STIMULATES THE EMOTIONS
EMOTIONS	497 - 3	EMOTIONS WHICH ARE ALTOGETHER SPIRITUAL
EMPHASIZE	350 - 4	EMPHASIZE IS THAT MENTAL TELEPATHY
EMPHASIZING	439 - 5	JESUS EMPHASIZING THE TEACHING
EMPHATIC	270 - 2	WE MAY BE QUITE EMPHATIC IN SAYING
EMPHATICALLY	293 - 2	EMPHATICALLY THE ANSWER TO MY PRAYER
EMPLOYMENT	286 - 1	TREATMENT TO OBTAIN EMPLOYMENT
EMULATE	438 - 5	WE SHOULD EMULATE THIS DIVINE
EMULATES	369 - 1	HIS PERSONALITY BUT POORLY EMULATES
ENABLED	332 - 2	PRAYER THAT ENABLED THOSE
ENABLES	155 - 1	ENABLES US TO KNOW
ENABLES	177 - 2	ENABLES HIM TO COVER A PERFECT IDEA
ENABLES	321 - 1	MAN'S INDIVIDUALITY ENABLES
ENABLES	391 - 3	ENABLES MAN TO BE AN INDIVIDUAL
ENACTED	351 - 3	WAS ENACTED TWO THOUSAND
ENCOMPASS	028 - 4	WE CAN NEVER ENCOMPASS IT
ENCOMPASS	028 - 4	WE SHALL NEVER ENCOMPASS GOD
ENCOMPASS	031 - 5	WE CANNOT ENCOMPASS INFINITY
ENCOMPASS	095 - 2	WE CANNOT ENCOMPASS INFINITY
ENCOMPASS	138 - 4	GREAT ENOUGH TO ENCOMPASS THE PAST

ENCOMPASS	493 - 7	CAN NEVER COMPLETELY ENCOMPASS IT
ENCOMPASSED	303 - 4	NOW ENCOMPASSED BY PERFECT LIFE
ENCOURAGING	119 - 3	THE ENCOURAGING MESSAGE
END	060 - 1	END OF ALL GOOD MENTAL WORK
END	157 - 4	PRAYER IS NOT AN END OF ITSELF
END	490 - 5	END TO THE DIVINE NATURE
END	493 - 1	THEN GOD WOULD END
ENDEAVOR	240 - 4	ENDEAVOR TO RECOGNIZE
ENDEAVOR	260 - 2	ENDEAVOR TO REALIZE THAT
ENDEAVOR	405 - 2	ENDEAVOR TO STOP LIMITING GOD
ENDEAVOR	462 - 4	ENDEAVOR OF MANKIND IS TO
ENDEAVOR	486 - 2	WHOLE ENDEAVOR IS TO BE
ENDEAVORS	309 - 5	PRACTITIONER ENDEAVORS TO ENTER INTO
ENDEAVORS	343 - 3	ENDEAVORS TO LET THE TRUTH
ENDEAVORS	421 - 1	ENDEAVORS TO LET THE TRUTH OPERATE
ENDING	070 - 2	BEGINNING BUT NEVER ENDING
ENDLESS	030 - 2	ETERNAL AND ENDLESS EXPANSION
ENDLESS	064 - 5	INTELLIGENCE AND ENDLESS BEING
ENDLESS	093 - 5	ENDLESS AND AN ETERNAL EXPANSION
ENDOWED	071 - 2	ENDOWED WITH THE ATTRIBUTES
ENDOWED	378 - 3	ENDOWED US WITH DUPLICATE SENSES
ENDOWED	437 - 4	ESPECIALLY ENDOWED WITH POWER
ENDS	178 - 6	BEGINS AND ENDS WITHIN THE THOUGHT
ENDS	185 - 3	ALL THE ENDS OF THE EARTH
ENDS	207 - 2	BEGINS AND ENDS WITHIN HIS OWN
ENDS	373 - 4	OF ITSELF NEITHER BEGINS NOR ENDS
ENDS	407 - 3	TWO ENDS OF ONE UNITY
ENDURE	155 - 2	ONLY HELP US TO ENDURE
ENDURE	453 - 4	TRUTH ALONE CAN ENDURE
ENDURES	423 - 2	TO THAT WHICH ENDURES
ENDURES	437 - 1	TRUTH ALONE ENDURES TO ETERNAL DAY
ENEMIES	082 - 1	IT HAS NO ENEMIES, NO DIFFERENCES
ENEMIES	315 - 3	NOT TO COUNT OUR ENEMIES
ENEMIES	430 - 5	TO LOVE OUR ENEMIES
ENEMIES	441 - 3	NO ENEMIES EXTERNAL TO OUR OWN MIND
ENEMY	404 - 2	FEAR IS THE GREAT ENEMY OF MAN
ENEMY	492 - 2	LAST ENEMY IS OVERCOME
ENERGIES	193 - 2	NATURAL ENERGIES ALREADY EXISTS
ENERGIES	458 - 4	DIVINE ENERGIES CAN PLAY UPON IT
ENERGIZE	489 - 3	ENERGIZE THE ESSENCE OF BEING
ENERGIZED	035 - 3	THROUGH ALL THAT IS ENERGIZED
ENERGIZED	035 - 3	BACK OF ALL THAT IS ENERGIZED
ENERGIZING	242 - 1	ENERGIZING EVERY PART
ENERGIZING	255 - 3	INTO CREATIVE, ENERGIZING, VITALIZING ONES
ENERGY	035 - 2	AS BEING UNIVERSAL ENERGY
ENERGY	035 - 3	ENERGY IS IN EVERYTHING
ENERGY	048 - 2	SUBTLE ENERGY OF SPIRIT
ENERGY	048 - 2	PART OF THE UNIVERSAL ENERGY
ENERGY	085 - 3	AND ORIGINAL CREATIVE ENERGY
ENERGY	123 - 2	PHYSICAL UNIVERSE INTO ENERGY
ENERGY	174 - 1	CONCENTRATE THE ENERGY OF GOD
ENERGY	193 - 1	WE DO NOT CREATE ENERGY
ENERGY	193 - 1	TRANSFORM ENERGY FROM ONE TYPE TO
ENERGY	193 - 1	NEED TO CREATE THE ENERGY
ENERGY	194 - 2	STREAM OF CREATIVE ENERGY

ENERGY	195 - 2	THIS ENERGY WHICH IS ALSO INTELLIGENCE
ENERGY	261 - 2	ENERGY OF THE PURE
ENERGY	268 - 3	UNLOOSE ITS OWN ENERGY
ENERGY	288 - 2	THE ENERGY WHICH HOLDS THE UNIVERSE
ENERGY	311 - 2	PASSING BACK INTO ENERGY
ENERGY	311 - 2	HAPPENED TO THE ENERGY
ENERGY	315 - 3	ENERGY UNCONNECTED DOES NOTHING
ENERGY	392 - 2	A POTENTIAL ENERGY AND A LATENT POWER
ENERGY	393 - 3	ORIGINAL MIND AND ORIGINAL ENERGY
ENERGY	393 - 3	IT IS ENERGY PLUS INTELLIGENCE
ENERGY	393 - 3	IS CONSCIOUS ENERGY WORKING
ENERGY	397 - 4	POWER AND ENERGY
ENERGY	398 - 5	ENERGY THAT EXECUTES THAT THOUGHT
ENERGY	480 - 1	ENERGY RUNNING THROUGH ALL
ENERGY	480 - 3	ENERGY RETURN AGAIN INTO THEIR SOURCE
ENERGY OF GOD	174 - 1	ENERGY OF GOD IS ALREADY CONCENTRATED
ENERGY OF MIND	193 - 2	ENERGY OF MIND
ENGINE	395 - 2	THE COSMIC ENGINE IS STARTED
ENGINE	395 - 3	ENGINE OF THE SUBJECTIVE MIND
ENIGMAS	396 - 1	GREAT ENIGMAS OF THE UNIVERSE
ENJOY	046 - 3	TO LIVE AND TO ENJOY LIVING
ENJOY	065 - 5	ALL THINGS TO ENJOY
ENJOY	258 - 5	AND I ENJOY ALL
ENJOY	297 - 3	TO ENJOY THEM IN OUR MENTALITIES
ENJOY	300 - 4	ENJOY THE ATMOSPHERE OF HIS PLACE
ENJOY	432 - 4	ENJOY TODAY
ENJOYMENT	114 - 2	NO REAL ENJOYMENT OF LIFE UNTIL
ENJOYS	114 - 1	SPIRIT ENJOYS ITSELF ONLY IN ITS OWN
ENJOYS	390 - 3	HE NEEDS OR ENJOYS ON THE PATHWAY
ENLARGE	142 - 3	ENLARGE OUR THOUGHT PROCESSES
ENLARGE	143 - 2	ATTEMPT TO ENLARGE ON THIS CONSCIOUSNESS
ENLARGED	331 - 1	TO THE DEITY BECOMES ENLARGED
ENLARGEMENT	479 - 5	AN ENLARGEMENT OF THE EXPERIENCE
ENLARGING	031 - 5	ENLARGING OUR CAPACITY TO KNOW
ENLARGING	095 - 2	ALWAYS ENLARGING OUR CAPACITY
ENLIGHTENED	238 - 2	ENLIGHTENED SOUL UNDERSTAND
ENLIGHTENED	313 - 2	THAT THE ENLIGHTENED SHOULD SEE BACK
ENLIGHTENED	365 - 3	NOW WE ARE MORE ENLIGHTENED
ENLIGHTENMENT	364 - 3	THE ENLIGHTENMENT OF THE SOUL
ENLIGHTENMENT	367 - 3	ENLIGHTENMENT OF MODERN CIVILIZATION
ENLIGHTENMENT	383 - 2	BY REASON OF ENLIGHTENMENT
ENLIGHTENMENT	418 - 4	UNTIL THE DAY OF ENLIGHTENMENT
ENMITIES	431 - 4	ENMITIES AGAINST THE WORLD
ENOUGH	319 - 4	TREATED A PATIENT LONG ENOUGH
ENRICH	209 - 4	MAKES US POOR CAN ENRICH US
ENTER	037 - 3	CANNOT ENTER WHILE THERE IS UNBELIEF
ENTER	053 - 1	WE DO NOT ENTER IN BECAUSE
ENTER	056 - 2	HINDER THOSE WHO WOULD ENTER
ENTER	112 - 4	ENTER THE ABSOLUTE
ENTER	114 - 1	ENTER INTO THE SPIRIT OF LIFE
ENTER	243 - 2	WHAT SHALL ENTER THERE
ENTER	405 - 2	ENTER IN BECAUSE OF THEIR UNBELIEF
ENTER	421 - 2	ENTER INTO THE ONE
ENTERING	417 - 2	MEANT BY ENTERING THE ABSOLUTE
ENTERS	343 - 5	THE ONE ENTERS INTO US

ENTERTAIN	178 - 1	ENTERTAIN RIGHT THOUGHTS
ENTERTAIN	244 - 1	NOT ENTERTAIN A DISAGREEABLE SENTIMENT
ENTERTAIN	368 - 4	WOULD ENTERTAIN THE CHRIST
ENTERTAINING	210 - 4	ENTERTAINING FEARS FOR THE HEALTH
ENTHUSIASM	184 - 3	HAVE ENTHUSIASM
ENTHUSIASM	226 - 3	WITH THE SAME ENTHUSIASM
ENTHUSIASM	440 - 4	ENTHUSIASM TO ANY LEGITIMATE PURPOSE
ENTIRE	195 - 3	THE ENTIRE ORDER IS ONE
ENTIRE	313 - 1	ONE WITH THE ENTIRE PHYSICAL UNIVERSE
ENTIRELY	350 - 3	ALMOST ENTIRELY SUBJECTIVE
ENTIRELY	440 - 3	NO MAN LIVES ENTIRELY UNTO HIMSELF
ENTIRETY	406 - 1	SPIRIT IS PRESENT IN ITS ENTIRETY
ENTITIES	054 - 2	CONDITIONS ARE NOT ENTITIES
ENTITIES	054 - 2	WE ARE ENTITIES
ENTITIES	331 - 3	WE ARE SEPARATE ENTITIES IN IT
ENTITIES	419 - 3	WE ARE SEPARATE ENTITIES IN IT
ENTITY	057 - 4	IT IS A SPIRITUAL ENTITY
ENTITY	058 - 2	SPIRITUAL ENTITY IN THE MENTAL WORLD
ENTITY	086 - 5	IS TO BE A SPIRITUAL ENTITY
ENTITY	097 - 2	IS NEVER AN ENTITY
ENTITY	097 - 3	IS A SPIRITUAL ENTITY
ENTITY	099 - 4	AN EFFECT NOT AN ENTITY
ENTITY	200 - 4	DISEASE IS NOT AN ENTITY
ENTITY	217 - 2	ENTITY LIVING IN A PERFECT UNIVERSE
ENTITY	231 - 3	NOT ACKNOWLEDGING IT AS AN ENTITY
ENTITY	304 - 3	IT IS AN ENTITY OF INFINITE
ENTITY	331 - 3	SEPARATED BUT AS A SEPARATE ENTITY
ENTITY	352 - 4	INDIVIDUAL ENTITY IN MIND
ENTITY	401 - 2	OF ITSELF IS NOT AN ENTITY
ENTITY	419 - 3	SEPARATE AND DISTINCT ENTITY
ENTRANCE	301 - 2	GAVE IT ENTRANCE TO YOUR MIND
ENVIRONMENT	138 - 3	CHANGING ENVIRONMENT
ENVIRONMENT	177 - 1	CHANGING ENVIRONMENT CONTROLLING
ENVIRONMENT	204 - 2	ENVIRONMENT GOVERNS YOU
ENVIRONMENT	266 - 3	INFLUENCE OUR ENVIRONMENT
ENVIRONMENT	270 - 4	IMPRESSION UPON HIS ENVIRONMENT
ENVIRONMENT	274 - 3	ONE DOES TO AN ENVIRONMENT
ENVIRONMENT	284 - 3	ENVIRONMENT IS ALSO A PART OF THIS
ENVIRONMENT	410 - 3	HIS WHOLE PHYSICAL ENVIRONMENT
ENVY	240 - 3	NO THOUGHT OF ENVY
EQUAL	118 - 2	IT CAN ONLY EQUAL OUR INDIVIDUAL CAPACITY
EQUAL	176 - 1	ABSOLUTE AND EQUAL OBJECTIVE FACT
EQUAL	217 - 2	EQUAL TO THE DEMANDS MADE UPON IT
EQUILIBRIUM	160 - 2	A STATE OF EQUILIBRIUM
EQUIPMENT	414 - 2	OUR ENTIRE EQUIPMENT IS THOUGHT
EQUIPPED	058 - 2	EQUIPPED WITH POWER AND VOLITION
EQUIPPED	065 - 2	EQUIPPED TO PERPETUATE ITSELF
EQUIPPED	113 - 1	SPIRIT OF MAN IS EQUIPPED WITH DECISION
EQUIPPED	130 - 4	EQUIPPED WITH A MENTALITY, A BODY
EQUIPPED	211 - 3	EQUIPPED WITH THE POWER TO EXECUTE
EQUIVALENT	281 - 3	EQUIVALENT OF ITS RESPONSE
EQUIVALENT	281 - 4	IN HIS MIND A MENTAL EQUIVALENT
EQUIVALENT	285 - 4	MENTAL EQUIVALENT OF HATE
EQUIVALENT	288 - 1	HAVE THE MENTAL EQUIVALENT
EQUIVALENT	306 - 2	A MENTAL EQUIVALENT OF OUR DESIRES

EQUIVALENTS	269 - 2	LAW OF MENTAL EQUIVALENTS
EQUIVALENTS	280 - 2	LAW OF MENTAL EQUIVALENTS
EQUIVALENTS	280 - 3	LAW OF MENTAL EQUIVALENTS
EQUIVALENTS	282 - 2	STILL GREATER MENTAL EQUIVALENTS
EQUIVALENTS	285 - 1	PROVIDE DIFFERENT MENTAL EQUIVALENTS
EQUIVALENTS	304 - 3	ADEQUATE MENTAL EQUIVALENTS
EQUIVALENTS	358 - 3	THE MENTAL EQUIVALENTS OF LIFE
ERADICATED	235 - 3	IS NOW ERADICATED
ERASE	089 - 1	ERASE FROM THE HUMAN MIND
ERASE	153 - 2	THING THAT CAN ERASE IT
ERASE	183 - 2	TO ERASE IT JUST AS LIGHT HAS THE POWER
ERASE	224 - 2	ERASE THE THOUGHT OF PAIN
ERASE	229 - 4	ERASE FROM MY CONSCIOUSNESS
ERASE	245 - 3	ERASE THE THOUGHTS OF DOUBT
ERASE	245 - 4	ERASE THE THOUGHTS OF YESTERDAY
ERASE	246 - 3	ERASE ANY NEGATIVE STREAM
ERASE	246 - 4	ERASE ALL THOUGHT OF FEAR
ERASE	255 - 5	ERASE EVERY UNPLEASANT EXPERIENCE
ERASE	279 - 1	WE SHOULD BE SURE TO ERASE
ERASE	279 - 1	ERASE THOUGHT FROM CONSCIOUSNESS
ERASE	303 - 3	SO WE ERASE ANY IDEA OF FAILURE
ERASE	501 - 3	ERASE FALSE IDEAS FROM OUR INNER THOUGHT
ERASED	118 - 4	IF THE THOUGHT IS NOT ERASED
ERASED	451 - 1	ERASED FROM THE MENTALITY
ERASER	412 - 2	CHALK AND THE ERASER IN OUR HAND
ERASER	412 - 2	THE CHALK AND THE ERASER
ERASES	128 - 4	ERASES EVERYTHING UNLIKE ITSELF
ERASES	188 - 3	CANCELS AND ERASES EVERYTHING UNLIKE
ERASES	204 - 4	ERASES JUST AS DEFINITELY
ERASING	197 - 3	ERASING FALSE IMAGES OF THOUGHT
ERASURE	501 - 5	ERASURE OF FALSE BELIEFS
ERASURE	501 - 6	ERASURE OF ALL MISTAKES
ERNEST HOLMES	278 - 3	ERNEST HOLMES FOR THAT IS MY NAME
ERRATIC	349 - 3	THEM HAVE BEEN SO ERRATIC
ERRED	383 - 3	ERRED THROUGH HUMAN IGNORANCE
ERRONEOUS	115 - 2	SUM TOTAL OF ALL ERRONEOUS HUMAN BELIEF
ERRONEOUS	128 - 2	RESULT OF HIS OWN ERRONEOUS CONCLUSIONS
ERRONEOUS	170 - 1	AND ALL ERRONEOUS CONCLUSIONS
ERRONEOUS	236 - 2	ERRONEOUS CONCLUSION IS WIPED OUT
ERROR	365 - 4	GREAT AN ERROR AS IN THE OLD THOUGHT
ERROR	417 - 4	ERROR THAT IT IS HUMAN WILL
ERROR	474 - 3	ERROR IS EVER A COWARD
ERRORS	453 - 6	CHIEF AMONG THESE ERRORS
ERUPT	234 - 1	BREAK THROUGH AND ERUPT
ESCAPE	244 - 2	ESCAPE FROM ITS EFFECTS
ESCAPE	462 - 3	CANNOT ESCAPE THE DIVINE PRESENCE
ESCAPE	483 - 4	FROM THIS HE CANNOT ESCAPE
ESCAPE	500 - 4	ESCAPE FROM THE CREATIVE POWER
ESSENCE	026 - 3	THAT INVISIBLE ESSENCE
ESSENCE	035 - 2	ESSENCE OF THE WHOLE TEACHING
ESSENCE	036 - 4	THE ESSENCE OF PURITY
ESSENCE	040 - 3	ABSTRACT ESSENCE OF BEAUTY
ESSENCE	045 - 2	THE ESSENCE OF SIMPLICITY
ESSENCE	045 - 2	THE ESSENCE OF ALL THINGS
ESSENCE	052 - 4	THE ULTIMATE ESSENCE

ESSENCE	060 - 4	THAT INVISIBLE ESSENCE
ESSENCE	065 - 4	ESSENCE OF HIMSELF
ESSENCE	081 - 1	ESSENCE, FORCE, ENERGY
ESSENCE	081 - 4	THE ABSOLUTE ESSENCE OF ALL THAT IS
ESSENCE	085 - 4	ESSENCE OF CONCRETE PERSONALITY
ESSENCE	087 - 2	THE SAME ESSENCE
ESSENCE	088 - 4	NOT TO FORGET THE ESSENCE
ESSENCE	139 - 1	ESSENCE WHEREVER WE FIND IT
ESSENCE	148 - 1	MUST BE OF THE SAME ESSENCE
ESSENCE	160 - 1	RECOGNIZE THE PURE ESSENCE
ESSENCE	162 - 4	WAS OF THE SAME ESSENCE AS HIS
ESSENCE	164 - 2	THE VERY ESSENCE AND TRUTH
ESSENCE	194 - 1	ITS ESSENCE, LAW AND CAUSE
ESSENCE	233 - 4	ESSENCE IN AND THROUGH YOU
ESSENCE	244 - 1	BREATHE IN THE ETERNAL LIFE ESSENCE
ESSENCE	256 - 1	DIVINE, POWERFUL, VITAL, ESSENCE
ESSENCE	280 - 3	ESSENCE OF THE SPIRIT EMBODIED IN IT
ESSENCE	284 - 2	THE ESSENCE OF CREATIVENESS
ESSENCE	293 - 4	THE INDWELLING ESSENCE OF MY LIFE
ESSENCE	294 - 3	THE ESSENCE OF MAN'S LIFE IS GOD
ESSENCE	343 - 3	THIS ESSENCE HAS RUN THROUGH ALL
ESSENCE	392 - 4	THE ESSENCE OF EVERYTHING THAT EVER WAS
ESSENCE	393 - 3	ESSENCE OF MIND IS SUBSTANCE
ESSENCE	393 - 3	ARE ONE IN ESSENCE
ESSENCE	409 - 4	VERY ESSENCE OF MENTAL HEALING
ESSENCE	416 - 2	VERY ESSENCE OF SENSITIVENESS
ESSENCE	423 - 3	THE ESSENCE OF SPIRITUAL MIND HEALING
ESSENCE	473 - 3	LIFE IN ITS PURE ESSENCE
ESSENCE OF LIFE	499 - 2	WILL REMAIN THE ESSENCE OF LIFE
ESSENTIAL	142 - 3	ESSENTIAL DIVINITY OF OUR OWN NATURE
ESSENTIAL	143 - 4	ESSENTIAL ELEMENTS OF SPONTANEITY
ESSENTIAL	152 - 4	THOUGHT WITH SPIRIT IS ESSENTIAL
ESSENTIAL	245 - 1	ESSENTIAL TO AN ESTABLISHMENT
ESSENTIAL	410 - 2	ESSENTIAL STATES OF CONSCIOUSNESS
ESSENTIAL	497 - 1	ESSENTIAL TO THE SOUL
ESTABLISH	139 - 1	WE ESTABLISH THE FACT
ESTABLISH	152 - 3	ESTABLISH CLOSER CONTACT
ESTABLISHED	048 - 3	ESTABLISHED BY EXPLAINING
ESTABLISHED	400 - 2	ESTABLISHED IN THE CONSCIOUS MIND
ESTABLISHES	312 - 3	ESTABLISHES THE UNITY OF MIND
ESTABLISHING	303 - 4	WORD IS NOW ESTABLISHING IT FOREVER
ESTIMATE	454 - 6	ESTIMATE OF HIMSELF THE ISOLATED PERSON
ETERNAL	030 - 2	POSSIBILITY OF ETERNAL
ETERNAL	032 - 1	THE ETERNAL THING ITSELF
ETERNAL	033 - 3	THING WHICH CAUSES THE ETERNAL QUEST
ETERNAL	067 - 2	AN ETERNAL CREATIVE PRINCIPLE
ETERNAL	093 - 2	EACH IS ETERNAL
ETERNAL	101 - 2	MIND IS ETERNAL
ETERNAL	108 - 4	THEREFORE WE ARE ETERNAL
ETERNAL	132 - 9	ETERNAL STATE OF COMPLETE UNITY
ETERNAL	139 - 1	POSSIBILITY OF AN ETERNAL EXPANSION
ETERNAL	156 - 3	THE PROMISES OF ETERNAL LIFE
ETERNAL	188 - 3	THE SUNLIGHT OF ETERNAL TRUTH
ETERNAL	229 - 3	ETERNAL CAN NEVER BE NON-EXISTENT
ETERNAL	357 - 2	ETERNAL IS FOREVER BEGETTING

ETERNAL	387 - 2	AVERAGE MAN DESIRES AN ETERNAL
ETERNAL	387 - 3	UNFOLDING SOUL AN ETERNAL DESTINY
ETERNAL	388 - 1	WE ARE BORN OF ETERNAL DAY
ETERNAL	409 - 4	ITS ETERNAL PERFECTION
ETERNAL	429 - 2	BUILDING ON AN ETERNAL FOUNDATION
ETERNAL	467 - 2	EVIL WOULD BE AN ETERNAL REALITY
ETERNAL	478 - 2	TRUTH IS ETERNAL
ETERNAL	491 - 5	ATTRIBUTES ARE ETERNAL
ETERNALITY	344 - 1	ETERNALITY OF AN EVER-EXPANDING
ETERNALITY	386 - 2	ETERNALITY OF THE SOUL
ETERNALLY	100 - 2	ETERNALLY GOING ON
ETERNAL PRESENT	471 - 4	ETERNAL PRESENT OF GOD'S HAPPY SMILE
ETERNAL THING	032 - 1	ECHO OF THE ETERNAL THING
ETERNITY	038 - 5	THING THAT OVER-SHADOWS ETERNITY
ETERNITY	065 - 4	OUT OF THE STUFF OF ETERNITY
ETERNITY	160 - 3	SUFFER THROUGH ALL ETERNITY
ETERNITY	384 - 2	DOWN THE VISTA OF ETERNITY
ETERNITY	384 - 5	THIS UNDERSTANDING OF ETERNITY
ETERNITY	385 - 1	THE ETERNITY OF OUR OWN BEING
ETERNITY	387 - 3	THE CURRENTS OF ETERNITY
ETERNITY	387 - 3	SO WE SHALL VIEW ETERNITY
ETERNITY	388 - 1	TIME ENOUGH IN ETERNITY TO PROVE
ETERNITY	388 - 1	AN INCARNATION OF ETERNITY
ETERNITY	436 - 4	ETERNITY MUST BE MADE UP OF
ETERNITY	471 - 4	BRIGHT ETERNITIES OF AN ENDLESS FUTURE
ETERNITY	478 - 2	ETERNITY IS TIMELESS
ETERNITY	489 - 6	IMAGE OF ETERNITY WITHIN OURSELVES
ETHER	091 - 2	ETHER OF SCIENCE
ETHER	094 - 2	ETHER THE CEMENT OF MATTER
ETHER	094 - 2	OPERATE THROUGH THE ETHER
ETHER	094 - 2	PERHAPS THE ETHER IS MIND
ETHER	095 - 1	THINK OF THE ETHER OF MIND
ETHER	095 - 1	THE ETHER OF SPACE
ETHER	100 - 3	ETHER OF SPACE
ETHER	104 - 3	ETHER IS MORE SOLID THAN MATTER
ETHER	116 - 4	MATTER RESOLVES IT INTO A UNIVERSAL ETHER
ETHER	375 - 1	THE NEW IDEA OF ETHER
ETHER	375 - 2	ETHER IS MORE SOLID THAN MATTER
ETHERIC	116 - 3	AN ETHERIC WHIRL OF ENERGY
ETHERIC	378 - 3	ETHERIC AND SUBTLE QUALITIES OF THE SOUL
ETHERIC	407 - 2	ETHERIC MOVEMENT AT THE CENTER
ETHICS	056 - 2	SIMPLE ETHICS OF JESUS
EVE	473 - 5	EVE, THE WOMAN IN THE CASE,
EVE	479 - 1	EVE OF HIS BETRAYAL
EVE	482 - 3	EVE OF HIS GREATEST LESSON
EVENT	388 - 4	EVENT OF THE SOUL
EVENTS	372 - 1	CAN ANTICIPATE FUTURE EVENTS
EVENTS	479 - 3	EVENTS CANNOT HINDER THE ONWARD MARCH
EVENTUATE	145 - 2	CERTAIN TO EVENTUATE IN SOME FORM
EVER-EXPANDING	439 - 2	EVER-EXPANDING EXPERIENCE
EVERLASTING	473 - 1	IT BECOMES LIFE EVERLASTING
EVERLASTING	478 - 2	WITH LIFE EVERLASTING
EVER MORE	384 - 2	NOT LESS BUT EVER MORE
EVER-PRESENT	052 - 2	EVER-PRESENT AND AVAILABLE
EVER-PRESENT	142 - 3	EVER-PRESENT AND EVER-AVAILABLE

EVER-PRESENT	421 - 5	VIBRATIONS ARE EVER-PRESENT
EVERY	033 - 4	THAT WITHIN EVERY INDIVIDUAL
EVERY	146 - 1	EVERY WORD WHICH WE HEAR
EVERYDAY	114 - 2	PART OF THE EVERYDAY LIFE
EVERYDAY	140 - 1	PROBLEMS OF EVERYDAY LIVING
EVERYDAY	283 - 2	TO SAY IN EVERYDAY LANGUAGE
EVERYDAY	387 - 1	A FACT OF EVERYDAY LIFE
EVERYDAY	419 - 1	PART OF OUR EVERYDAY PRACTICE
EVERYDAY	490 - 6	COMMON AFFAIRS OF EVERYDAY LIFE
EVERYONE	052 - 4	WILL RESPOND TO EVERYONE
EVERYONE	175 - 1	EVERYONE WHO ASKS RECEIVES
EVERYONE	422 - 2	EVERYONE WHO HAS EVER LIVED
EVERYONE	434 - 6	EVERYONE IS A LAW UNTO HIMSELF
EVERYONE	435 - 1	EVERYONE IS AN EVOLVING CHRIST
EVERYTHING	070 - 2	EVERYTHING THAT SPIRIT THINKS
EVERYTHING	077 - 1	GOD EXISTS IN EVERYTHING
EVERYTHING	082 - 2	LOVE THROUGH EVERYTHING
EVERYTHING	128 - 3	EVERYTHING COMES FROM INTELLIGENCE
EVERYTHING	132 - 6	EVERYTHING RESPONDS TO THIS
EVERYTHING	179 - 6	EVERYTHING IS MENTAL
EVERYTHING	197 - 4	EVERYTHING IS MIND
EVERYTHING	252 - 4	HARMONIZE OURSELVES WITH EVERYTHING
EVERYTHING	362 - 4	GOD IS IN EVERYTHING
EVERYTHING	485 - 4	EVERYTHING IS FROM WITHIN OUT
EVERY TIME	093 - 5	MIND EVERY TIME WE THINK
EVERY TIME	323 - 3	EVERY TIME MAN THINKS HE USES IT
EVERYWHERE	241 - 3	EVERYWHERE PRESENT IN MIND
EVERYWHERE	352 - 5	THOUGHT IS EVERYWHERE PRESENT
EVIDENCE	073 - 2	REALITY IS THE EVIDENCE
EVIDENCE	156 - 5	THE EVIDENCE OF THINGS NOT SEEN
EVIDENCE	170 - 4	EVIDENCE IN FAVOR OF HIS PATIENT
EVIDENCE	176 - 1	EVIDENCE THAT OUR WORD HAS ACCOMPLISHED
EVIDENCE	178 - 4	THE EVIDENCE OF THINGS NOT SEEN
EVIDENCE	180 - 2	EVIDENCE OF TRUTH TO BEAR
EVIDENCE	301 - 4	EVIDENCE OF THINGS NOT SEEN
EVIDENT	337 - 4	EVIDENT IF THIS REALIZATION
EVIDENT	418 - 1	EVIDENT THAT WE MUST NOT ALLOW
EVIDENT	478 - 4	EVIDENT IN THE RESPONSE OF PLANTS
EVIL	032 - 3	PROBLEM OF LIMITATION, EVIL, SUFFERING
EVIL	039 - 4	POWER OF EVIL
EVIL	039 - 4	WE EXPERIENCE GOOD AND EVIL
EVIL	039 - 5	APPARENT EVIL BEHIND
EVIL	045 - 5	GOOD AND EVIL FROM THE ONE SOURCE
EVIL	103 - 1	IN WHAT IS CALLED EVIL
EVIL	110 - 1	EVIL IS NEITHER PERSON, PLACE NOR THING
EVIL	111 - 2	AN EVIL POWER
EVIL	111 - 3	EVIL IS NOT A THING OF ITSELF
EVIL	111 - 3	EVIL WILL DISAPPEAR WHEN WE NO LONGER
EVIL	123 - 2	EVIL IS APPARENT LIMITATION
EVIL	142 - 3	NO EVIL CAN LIVE IN THIS PRESENCE
EVIL	151 - 2	UPON EVIL OR ADVERSITY
EVIL	189 - 3	TAKE AWAY THE BELIEF IN EVIL
EVIL	189 - 3	THE INNER REALITY EVIL FLEES
EVIL	191 - 5	POWER OF EVIL
EVIL	201 - 2	EVIL IS NOT A PROBLEM

EVIL	217 - 1	DENY THE PRESENCE OF EVIL
EVIL	230 - 1	THINE EYE BE EVIL
EVIL	264 - 3	EVIL HAS NO HISTORY
EVIL	268 - 4	INEVITABILITY OF EVIL
EVIL	303 - 2	NON-RECOGNITION OF EVIL
EVIL	335 - 2	EVIL IS NOT AN ULTIMATE REALITY
EVIL	335 - 2	EVIL IS NOT AN ENTITY
EVIL	335 - 2	TO TURN FROM EVIL AND DO GOOD
EVIL	335 - 3	ANY CONCEPT OF EVIL MUST BE
EVIL	336 - 1	THE PROBLEM OF EVIL
EVIL	337 - 1	EVIL HAS ONLY THE POWER TO DESTROY ITSELF
EVIL	337 - 1	RECOGNIZE THE APPEARANCE OF EVIL
EVIL	346 - 1	OVERCOMING OF ALL EVIL BY GOOD
EVIL	346 - 2	GOD IS SUFFICIENT, EVIL DISAPPEARS
EVIL	394 - 1	HANGS THE TALE OF GOOD AND EVIL
EVIL	410 - 4	SEE GOOD WHERE EVIL APPEARS TO BE
EVIL	420 - 2	THERE IS NO ULTIMATE REALITY TO EVIL
EVIL	421 - 3	OVERCOMING OF ALL EVIL BY GOOD
EVIL	421 - 3	CONSCIOUS OF GOD, EVIL DISAPPEARS
EVIL	432 - 2	IF OUR EYE BE FILLED WITH EVIL
EVIL	434 - 5	EVIL EXPERIENCE
EVIL	434 - 5	EVIL IS NOT AN ENTITY
EVIL	438 - 3	TOO PURE TO BEHOLD EVIL
EVIL	438 - 5	HOLDS NO EVIL TOWARD MAN
EVIL	441 - 3	EVIL WHICH CAME UPON ME
EVIL	441 - 3	PARTICULAR EVIL BE REAL TO ONE
EVIL	441 - 4	FROM THE THOUGHT OF EVIL
EVIL	441 - 4	EVIL CANNOT EXIST FOR US
EVIL	448 - 4	EVIL IS CAST OUT
EVIL	456 - 2	EVIL IS BUT AN OBSESSION
EVIL	456 - 2	IF EVIL WERE A REAL ENTITY
EVIL	456 - 2	EVIL FLEES BEFORE REALITY
EVIL	467 - 2	GOD DOES NOT KNOW EVIL
EVIL	467 - 2	EVIL WOULD BE AN ETERNAL REALITY
EVIL	485 - 5	EVIL IS SALUTARY, LEADING US
EVIL	499 - 1	EVIL IS MAN CREATED
EVIL	499 - 1	EVIL IS THE DIRECT AND SUPPOSITIONAL
EVIL ONE	448 - 2	WAS OF THE EVIL ONE
EVILS	156 - 4	CORRECT ALL THE EVILS OF THE WORLD
EVOLUTION	032 - 3	EVOLUTION OF MAN'S CONSCIOUSNESS
EVOLUTION	038 - 2	EVOLUTION IS THE EFFECT
EVOLUTION	038 - 2	WHICH FOLLOWS IS EVOLUTION
EVOLUTION	044 - 1	EVOLUTION IS AN ETERNAL UNFOLDMENT
EVOLUTION	050 - 1	EVOLUTION IS THE OUT-WORKING
EVOLUTION	051 - 2	EVOLUTION OF ITS ACCOMPLISHMENTS
EVOLUTION	057 - 2	LOGICAL AND SEQUENTIAL EVOLUTION
EVOLUTION	060 - 3	EVOLUTION OF THE GREAT PRESENCE
EVOLUTION	071 - 1	THE RESULT OF EVOLUTION
EVOLUTION	071 - 2	ORDER OF MAN'S EVOLUTION
EVOLUTION	072 - 3	NO COMPULSORY EVOLUTION
EVOLUTION	087 - 3	EVOLUTION IS THE UNFOLDING
EVOLUTION	089 - 2	EVOLUTION SHOULD MAKE THE INFINITE
EVOLUTION	102 - 1	EVOLUTION IS THE PASSING OF THOUGHT INTO
EVOLUTION	102 - 2	THIS IS EVOLUTION
EVOLUTION	102 - 3	EVOLUTION IS THE PROCESS, THE WAY

EVOLUTION	102 - 3	EVOLUTION IS AN EFFECT OF INTELLIGENCE
EVOLUTION	102 - 3	THE THEORY OF EVOLUTION
EVOLUTION	104 - 1	EMERGENCE THROUGH EVOLUTION
EVOLUTION	104 - 2	EVOLUTION DEPENDS UPON OUR ABILITY TO
EVOLUTION	151 - 4	EVOLUTION WORK THROUGH MAN'S IMAGINATION
EVOLUTION	273 - 2	EMERGENT EVOLUTION
EVOLUTION	290 - 1	LAW OF EVOLUTION AND GROWTH
EVOLUTION	292 - 4	EVOLUTION IS NOT THE EXPRESSION
EVOLUTION	297 - 2	EVOLUTION, THE THOUGHT INVOLVED
EVOLUTION	317 - 2	NATURAL PROCESSES OF EVOLUTION
EVOLUTION	317 - 3	LINE OF OUR SPIRITUAL EVOLUTION
EVOLUTION	337 - 2	EVOLUTION IS THE AWAKENING OF THE SOUL
EVOLUTION	337 - 2	MATERIAL EVOLUTION IS AN EFFECT
EVOLUTION	337 - 2	EVOLUTION IS THE RESULT OF INTELLIGENCE
EVOLUTION	337 - 3	THE AIM OF EVOLUTION IS TO PRODUCE A MAN
EVOLUTION	338 - 3	THIS PROCESS OF EVOLUTION
EVOLUTION	339 - 2	EVOLUTION IS A PRINCIPLE
EVOLUTION	339 - 2	EVOLUTION IS AN EFFECT OF INTELLIGENCE
EVOLUTION	339 - 2	EVOLUTION CAN ONLY FOLLOW INVOLUTION
EVOLUTION	339 - 2	EVOLUTION FOLLOWS WITH MECHANICAL
EVOLUTION	364 - 3	THE EVOLUTION OF THE INDIVIDUAL
EVOLUTION	380 - 3	IN OUR PRESENT STATE OF EVOLUTION
EVOLUTION	387 - 1	EVOLUTION CARRIES US FORWARD
EVOLUTION	387 - 1	OUR EVOLUTION IS THE RESULT
EVOLUTION	410 - 3	THE STORY OF HUMAN EVOLUTION
EVOLUTION	417 - 3	THE WHOLE AIM OF EVOLUTION
EVOLUTION	420 - 3	EVOLUTION IS THE TIME AND THE PROCESS
EVOLUTION	420 - 3	EVOLUTION WILL GO ON FOREVER
EVOLUTION	420 - 3	EVOLUTION IS AN EFFECT OF INTELLIGENCE
EVOLUTION	443 - 4	OUR PRESENT STATE OF EVOLUTION
EVOLUTION	482 - 2	EVOLUTION HAS BROUGHT MAN
EVOLUTION	485 - 3	EVOLUTION WILL BRING THIS ABOUT
EVOLUTION	487 - 7	AWAKENING IS A PROCESS OF EVOLUTION
EVOLUTIONIST	103 - 2	THE EVOLUTIONIST READS
EVOLUTION OF MAN	129 - 3	EVOLUTION OF MAN BRINGS HIM
EVOLVE	071 - 1	IN ORDER TO EVOLVE
EVOLVE	101 - 5	THE SPIRIT INVOLVES MUST EVOLVE
EVOLVE	109 - 2	EVOLVE A SPONTANEOUS INDIVIDUAL
EVOLVE	300 - 2	WHATEVER IS INVOLVED IN IT, WILL EVOLVE
EVOLVE	301 - 1	TO EVOLVE OUR CONCEPT EXACTLY
EVOLVE	410 - 1	WILL EVER EVOLVE INTO NEWER
EVOLVE	439 - 2	ONLY BY EXPANSION CAN IT EVOLVE
EVOLVE	488 - 3	EVOLVE A MORE PERFECT BODY
EVOLVED	071 - 1	EVOLVED FROM AN INTELLIGENT CAUSE
EVOLVED	099 - 3	THE PHYSICAL BODY IS EVOLVED
EVOLVED	106 - 1	EVOLVED FROM THE UNIVERSE
EVOLVED	112 - 4	EVOLVED TO A REALIZATION
EVOLVED	267 - 4	EVOLVED TO A COMPLETE UNDERSTANDING
EVOLVED	297 - 2	AND THE RESULT EVOLVED
EVOLVED	362 - 4	AN EVOLVED SOUL IS ALWAYS
EVOLVED	372 - 3	WE MUST HAVE EVOLVED FROM
EVOLVED	434 - 1	EVOLVED SOUL JUDGES NO ONE
EVOLVES	131 - 2	MAN'S IDEA OF DEITY EVOLVES WITH HIS OTHER
EVOLVES	198 - 1	UNFOLDS AND EVOLVES
EVOLVES	340 - 1	THAT WHICH IS INVOLVED EVOLVES

EVOLVES	340 - 1	THE LAW EVOLVES
EVOLVING	072 - 4	MAN IS EVOLVING
EVOLVING	435 - 1	EVERYONE IS AN EVOLVING CHRIST
EXACT	487 - 1	SUBJECT TO THE EXACT LAWS OF MIND
EXACTING	268 - 2	IT IS EXACT AND EXACTING
EXACTLY	241 - 3	EXACTLY THE SAME POWER
EXACTLY	288 - 1	LAW WHICH GIVES US EXACTLY
EXACTLY	380 - 1	EXACTLY WHAT WOULD HAPPEN
EXALT	244 - 3	WHILE OTHERS WOULD EXALT
EXALTATION	243 - 2	VITALIZATION AND EXALTATION
EXALTED	147 - 2	RADIANCE OF OUR EXALTED THOUGHT
EXALTED	186 - 4	THE MORE EXALTED
EXAMINE	067 - 3	EXAMINE THE BASIC PRINCIPLES
EXAMINE	450 - 1	EXAMINE THIS SAYING IN THE LIGHT
EXAMPLE	241 - 3	EXAMPLE FOR US TO FOLLOW
EXAMPLE	359 - 4	HIS LIFE AS A LIVING EXAMPLE
EXCUSES	033 - 2	EXCUSES NO MAN FROM THEIR EFFECTS
EXCUSES	038 - 4	EXCUSES NO ONE
EXECUTE	096 - 4	IT PROCEEDS TO EXECUTE
EXECUTE	100 - 2	TO EXECUTE THE PURPOSE GIVEN IT
EXECUTE	200 - 1	OF THE LAW TO EXECUTE IT
EXECUTES	038 - 2	LAW RECEIVES AND EXECUTES
EXECUTES	050 - 1	THIS LAW EXECUTES THE WORD
EXECUTES	323 - 2	LAW EXECUTES THE WILL OF LOVE
EXECUTES	398 - 5	ENERGY THAT EXECUTES THAT THOUGHT
EXECUTES	406 - 1	THE LAW EXECUTES
EXECUTION	340 - 2	THE PURPOSE AND THE EXECUTION
EXECUTOR	091 - 1	EXECUTOR OF THE WILL OF THE SPIRIT
EXECUTOR	196 - 2	EXECUTOR OF ALL FEELING
EXEMPT	219 - 1	IS EXEMPT FROM NEGATION
EXERCISE	410 - 3	EXERCISE AN AUTHORITY OVER ALL
EXERCISED	277 - 2	HE EXERCISED AN AUTHORITY
EXERCISES	210 - 1	EXERCISES A PERSONAL THOUGHT FORCE
EXERCISING	210 - 2	EXERCISING UPON THE RACE CONSCIOUSNESS
EXHAUST	493 - 7	NO MAN CAN EXHAUST
EXHAUSTED	210 - 1	WILL-POWER WOULD BECOME EXHAUSTED
EXHAUSTED	293 - 3	I CAN NEVER BE EXHAUSTED
EXHAUSTED	408 - 3	FIVE WOULD BECOME EXHAUSTED
EXHAUSTED	480 - 4	REALITY WAS NOT EXHAUSTED
EXHAUSTING	193 - 4	THE WILL WITHOUT EXHAUSTING THE MIND
EXHILARATION	243 - 2	EXHILARATION, VITALIZATION
EXIST	077 - 1	EXIST IN A STATE OF INNER UNITY
EXIST	122 - 2	NOT EXIST AS AN EXPRESSED BEING
EXIST	270 - 4	DOES EXIST TO EXPRESS HIMSELF
EXIST	355 - 1	EXIST SOMEWHERE IN THE SEED
EXIST	386 - 3	EXIST TO ME UNLESS I AM AWARE
EXIST	393 - 1	EXIST IN THE UNIVERSAL MIND AS IDEAS
EXISTED	071 - 2	HAVE EXISTED ALWAYS
EXISTED	071 - 2	THEY HAVE ALWAYS EXISTED
EXISTENCE	095 - 2	MAY CONTRADICT THEIR EXISTENCE
EXISTENCE	172 - 2	IN DENYING ITS EXISTENCE
EXISTENCE	250 - 5	EXISTENCE IS A HARMONIOUS PROGRESSION
EXISTENCE	266 - 3	THE NATURE OF OUR OWN EXISTENCE
EXISTENCE	284 - 4	THE SUPREME FACT OF EXISTENCE
EXISTS	066 - 4	THAT CONSCIOUSNESS EXISTS

EXISTS	125 - 5	UNIVERSE WHICH EXISTS BY VIRTUE
EXISTS	270 - 3	EXISTS FOR THE EXPRESSION OF SPIRIT
EXISTS	276 - 1	THEREFORE LAW NO LONGER EXISTS
EXISTS	406 - 2	SPIRIT EXISTS AT THE CENTER OF ALL FORM
EXPAND	148 - 3	EXPAND INTO A GREATER LIVINGNESS
EXPAND	148 - 4	SHOULD EXPAND OUR THOUGHT
EXPAND	150 - 5	EXPAND SPIRITUALLY AND INTELLECTUALLY
EXPAND	246 - 2	EXPAND MY OPPORTUNITY
EXPAND	271 - 3	CONSTANTLY EXPAND AND INCREASE
EXPAND	287 - 1	WE CAN EXPAND THE FINITE
EXPAND	333 - 3	FROM NOW ON WE SHALL EXPAND
EXPAND	405 - 3	HAVE TO EXPAND THE RELATIVE
EXPANDING	031 - 5	WE SHALL ALWAYS BE EXPANDING
EXPANDING	095 - 2	SHALL ALWAYS BE EXPANDING
EXPANDING	344 - 1	EVER EXPANDING PRINCIPLE OF THE SOUL
EXPANDING	354 - 2	FOREVER AND EVER EXPANDING
EXPANDING	387 - 3	FOREVER AND EVER EXPANDING
EXPANDING	387 - 4	SATISFIES THE EXPANDING SOUL
EXPANDING	388 - 3	FOREVER EXPANDING PRINCIPLE
EXPANDING	405 - 2	FOREVER EXPANDING THE FINITE
EXPANDING	439 - 2	ENDLESS AND EVER-EXPANDING EXPERIENCE
EXPANDS	074 - 4	THE SCIENCE EXPANDS
EXPANDS	164 - 4	EXPANDS THE CONSCIOUSNESS
EXPANDS	274 - 3	EXPANDS THE CONSCIOUSNESS
EXPANSION	030 - 2	ENDLESS EXPANSION
EXPANSION	093 - 5	AN ENDLESS AND AN ETERNAL EXPANSION
EXPANSION	250 - 5	A DAILY EXPANSION INTO REALMS OF LIFE
EXPANSION	269 - 1	SHOULD TEND TO EXPANSION
EXPANSION	345 - 3	WITH AN EXPANSION OF CONSCIOUSNESS
EXPANSION	387 - 1	PROGRESSIVE EXPANSION IS ITS LAW
EXPANSION	387 - 2	PROGRESS AN EVERLASTING EXPANSION
EXPANSION	390 - 1	POSSIBILITY OF EXPANSION
EXPECT	184 - 3	ALWAYS EXPECT THE GOOD
EXPECT	215 - 1	SHOULD NOT EXPECT TO HEAL ANYTHING
EXPECT	259 - 2	EXPECT TO HAVE OUR FOOD AGREE
EXPECT	360 - 3	WE SHOULD EXPECT THE BEST
EXPECT	384 - 4	EXPECT TO MEET FRIENDS
EXPECTANCY	055 - 2	EXPECTANCY OF GOOD
EXPECTANCY	058 - 5	BUT WITH EXPECTANCY
EXPECTANCY	189 - 3	DONE IN QUIET EXPECTANCY
EXPECTANCY	302 - 2	WITH FAITH, HOPE AND EXPECTANCY
EXPECTANT	046 - 3	THE MOST EXPECTANT
EXPECTANT	163 - 2	A CALM, EXPECTANT MANNER
EXPECTATION	435 - 1	EXPECTATION AND A CLEARER JOY
EXPECTATION	485 - 3	EXPECTATION LOOKS FOR A MORE COMPLETE
EXPECTATIONS	044 - 3	OUR HOPES AND FEARS, OUR EXPECTATIONS
EXPENSE	269 - 4	AT THE EXPENSE OF SOCIETY OR OTHER
EXPENSE	270 - 2	DONE AT THE EXPENSE OF ANYONE
EXPERIENCE	031 - 2	EXPERIENCE HAS TAUGHT US
EXPERIENCE	031 - 5	CAPACITY TO KNOW AND TO EXPERIENCE
EXPERIENCE	041 - 2	PATHWAY OF OUR OWN EXPERIENCE
EXPERIENCE	049 - 5	EXPERIENCE HAS PROVED THIS TO BE
EXPERIENCE	052 - 1	TO BE FACTS IN OUR EXPERIENCE
EXPERIENCE	054 - 2	EXPERIENCE MUST BE IN CONSCIOUSNESS
EXPERIENCE	059 - 2	INTO OUR OBJECTIVE EXPERIENCE

EXPERIENCE	060 - 3	THE BORDERLAND OF A NEW EXPERIENCE
EXPERIENCE	095 - 2	TO KNOW AND TO EXPERIENCE
EXPERIENCE	102 - 3	THE EXPERIENCE THAT TRANSPIRES
EXPERIENCE	110 - 1	EXPERIENCE WHICH WE ARE ALLOWED
EXPERIENCE	157 - 2	BUT A THRILLING EXPERIENCE
EXPERIENCE	174 - 3	IS BETWEEN OUR EXPERIENCE
EXPERIENCE	186 - 2	YOU DO NOT WISH TO EXPERIENCE
EXPERIENCE	194 - 5	SHOULD LIKE TO EXPERIENCE
EXPERIENCE	200 - 4	EXPERIENCE TO THE ONE
EXPERIENCE	203 - 2	ACTUALITY OF ITS EXPERIENCE
EXPERIENCE	213 - 2	EXPERIENCE BUT NOT A SPIRITUAL REALITY
EXPERIENCE	256 - 2	EXPERIENCE HAS UPSET MY STOMACH
EXPERIENCE	267 - 4	EXPERIENCE ONLY THAT WHICH HE CAN CONCEIVE
EXPERIENCE	273 - 5	COMMON WAY OF BITTER EXPERIENCE
EXPERIENCE	299 - 1	WILL SOMEDAY EXPERIENCE IN THE OUTER
EXPERIENCE	300 - 2	IN HIS OBJECTIVE EXPERIENCE
EXPERIENCE	316 - 1	EXPERIENCE WHICH DENIES GOD
EXPERIENCE	329 - 5	WE DIRECTLY EXPERIENCE OURSELVES
EXPERIENCE	335 - 2	EXPERIENCE OF THE SOUL
EXPERIENCE	410 - 2	SOME NEEDED EXPERIENCE
EXPERIENCE	412 - 2	NEED NOT CONTINUE TO EXPERIENCE
EXPERIENCE	423 - 1	FOLLOWED BY SPIRITUAL EXPERIENCE
EXPERIENCE	429 - 2	CANNOT ALTER NOR EXPERIENCE DESTROY
EXPERIENCE	437 - 1	STORMS OF EXPERIENCE TEAR THE WALLS
EXPERIENCE	445 - 4	WE NEED SPIRITUAL EXPERIENCE
EXPERIENCE	445 - 4	UNTIL IT BECOMES AN EXPERIENCE
EXPERIENCE	445 - 5	KNOW ONLY THAT WHICH WE EXPERIENCE
EXPERIENCE	460 - 5	EXPERIENCE IN AWAKENING TO THIS
EXPERIENCE	462 - 1	EXPERIENCE ALONE WILL TEACH US
EXPERIENCE	469 - 2	DOWN TO OUR OWN EXPERIENCE
EXPERIENCE	469 - 3	EXPERIENCE IN ORDER TO COME
EXPERIENCED	274 - 3	SPIRITUALLY EXPERIENCED
EXPERIENCES	133 - 3	ONE ARE MANY EXPERIENCES
EXPERIENCES	284 - 2	REAL TO THE ONE WHO EXPERIENCES IT
EXPERIENCES	386 - 3	HIS REASON AND HIS PERSONAL EXPERIENCES
EXPERIMENT	027 - 4	GLAD TO EXPERIMENT
EXPERIMENT	075 - 1	GLAD TO EXPERIMENT WITH IT
EXPERIMENT	271 - 4	A WONDERFUL EXPERIMENT
EXPERIMENT	334 - 3	A WONDERFUL EXPERIMENT
EXPERIMENTS	074 - 3	AFTER MANY EXPERIMENTS
EXPERIMENTS	074 - 4	EXPERIMENTS ARE MADE
EXPLAIN	382 - 3	TO EXPLAIN ALL MENTAL ACTION
EXPLAINABLE	382 - 3	AT PRESENT IT IS EXPLAINABLE
EXPLAINED	444 - 2	EXPLAINED THAT GOD INDWELLS
EXPLAINED	478 - 4	IS AND CANNOT BE EXPLAINED
EXPLAINING	449 - 4	EXPLAINING THAT ANYONE WHO LIVES
EXPLAINS	058 - 1	WHICH EXPLAINS CREATION
EXPLAINS	108 - 1	EXPLAINS WHY MAN SUFFERS
EXPLAINS	237 - 4	EXPLAINS TO HIM THE LAW
EXPLAINS	409 - 2	EXPLAINS TO HIMSELF
EXPLAINS	452 - 2	EXPLAINS THE WAY OF THE ILLUMINED
EXPLANATION	067 - 3	ONLY ONE EXPLANATION
EXPLANATION	382 - 3	LOGICAL AND SCIENTIFIC EXPLANATION OF IT
EXPLANATION	409 - 2	CONSCIOUS AS HIS EXPLANATION GOES
EXPLANATION	427 - 1	PERFECT EXPLANATION OF OUR OWN PHILOSOPHY

EXPLANATION	437 - 4	EXPLANATION OF THE POWER OF JESUS
EXPLANATION	443 - 3	EXPLANATION CAN WE FIND TO THIS PASSAGE
EXPLICITLY	436 - 1	EXPLICITLY TELLS US TO ASK DIRECTLY
EXPRESS	025 - 3	SEEKING TO EXPRESS ITSELF
EXPRESS	042 - 3	EXPRESS IN OUR OWN LIVES
EXPRESS	046 - 4	EXPRESS THROUGH US
EXPRESS	188 - 4	EXPRESS A GREATER DEGREE OF LIVINGNESS
EXPRESS	188 - 4	EXPRESS A MORE ABUNDANT LIFE
EXPRESS	222 - 4	DESIRE TO EXPRESS LIFE
EXPRESS	222 - 4	AN URGE TO EXPRESS
EXPRESS	222 - 4	IMPULSE OF SPIRIT TO EXPRESS
EXPRESS	223 - 1	EXPRESS THEMSELVES CONSTRUCTIVELY
EXPRESS	223 - 1	THE DESIRE TO EXPRESS LIFE
EXPRESS	223 - 2	LONGING TO EXPRESS HIS OWN DIVINITY
EXPRESS	229 - 3	EXPRESS THROUGH A SPIRITUAL BODY
EXPRESS	240 - 3	EXPRESS AND MANIFEST GOD
EXPRESS	263 - 5	TO EXPRESS THE FULLEST LIFE
EXPRESS	269 - 1	ENABLE US TO EXPRESS GREATER LIFE
EXPRESS	269 - 3	INDIVIDUAL MAY EXPRESS HIMSELF
EXPRESS	270 - 2	WISH TO DO EXPRESS MORE LIFE
EXPRESS	270 - 4	EXIST TO EXPRESS HIMSELF
EXPRESS	272 - 1	EXPRESS ITSELF IN THE EXPERIENCE
EXPRESS	279 - 2	HIM TO MORE COMPLETELY EXPRESS
EXPRESS	344 - 2	EXPRESS THROUGH THEIR MENTALITIES
EXPRESS	355 - 2	POWER TO DEVELOP AND TO EXPRESS
EXPRESS	367 - 1	PERFECTLY EXPRESS THROUGH HIM
EXPRESSED	238 - 4	EMOTIONS SHOULD BE EXPRESSED
EXPRESSED	262 - 3	SPIRIT IS NOT EXPRESSED
EXPRESSED	391 - 3	WOULD NOT BE COMPLETELY EXPRESSED
EXPRESSED	404 - 3	EXPRESSED THROUGH THE MAN
EXPRESSES	269 - 1	EXPRESSES LIFE WITHOUT HURT
EXPRESSES	358 - 4	IT EXPRESSES ITSELF THROUGH US
EXPRESSES	422 - 3	IT EXPRESSES ITSELF THROUGH US
EXPRESSING	035 - 4	LIFE EXPRESSING THROUGH US
EXPRESSING	046 - 4	EXPRESSING ITSELF THROUGH US
EXPRESSING	223 - 2	EXPRESSING ALL THE ATTRIBUTES OF GOD
EXPRESSING	223 - 2	EXPRESSING LIFE AND HAPPINESS
EXPRESSING	229 - 2	WE ARE EXPRESSING GOD
EXPRESSING	306 - 3	WE ARE EXPRESSING MORE LIFE
EXPRESSING	339 - 4	GOD EXPRESSING HIMSELF
EXPRESSION	035 - 3	BACK OF ALL EXPRESSION
EXPRESSION	046 - 2	AMPLE LATITUDE FOR PERSONAL EXPRESSION
EXPRESSION	102 - 3	INTO CONCRETE EXPRESSION
EXPRESSION	106 - 2	WORLD OF INDIVIDUAL EXPRESSION
EXPRESSION	107 - 4	A PERFECT EXPRESSION OF LIFE
EXPRESSION	148 - 1	EXPRESSION OF THE DIVINE MIND
EXPRESSION	151 - 3	EXPRESSION OF ITS DIVINE NATURE
EXPRESSION	155 - 3	FINDS ITS HIGHEST EXPRESSION
EXPRESSION	185 - 2	COME FORTH INTO EXPRESSION THROUGH ME
EXPRESSION	187 - 2	TO THE OBJECTIVE EXPRESSION
EXPRESSION	189 - 1	GREATEST POSSIBLE EXPRESSION OF LIFE
EXPRESSION	216 - 3	NEW WAYS OF EXPRESSION
EXPRESSION	223 - 2	EXPRESSION OF TRUTH
EXPRESSION	228 - 3	PERFECT MAN, PERFECT EXPRESSION
EXPRESSION	230 - 6	ON ANY PLANE OF EXPRESSION

EXPRESSION	238 – 2	EXPRESSION THROUGH OUR HUMANITY
EXPRESSION	256 – 4	AN EXPRESSION OF SELFISHNESS
EXPRESSION	270 – 3	EXISTS FOR THE EXPRESSION OF SPIRIT
EXPRESSION	270 – 3	HE IS THE EXPRESSION OF SPIRIT
EXPRESSION	288 – 2	LIFE AS ONE CONTINUOUS EXPRESSION
EXPRESSION	291 – 1	SEEKING EXPRESSION THROUGH US
EXPRESSION	292 – 3	EVIDENCE OF ITS FULL EXPRESSION
EXPRESSION	301 – 4	THE OUTER EXPRESSION OF OUR AFFAIRS
EXPRESSION	332 – 4	PERSONIFIED EXPRESSION
EXPRESSION	333 – 2	FROM ALL THREE MODES OF EXPRESSION
EXPRESSION	339 – 4	CRAVING OR DESIRE FOR EXPRESSION
EXPRESSION	371 – 2	SELF-CONSCIOUS EXPRESSION
EXPRESSION	392 – 2	CALLED INTO FORM OR EXPRESSION
EXPRESSION	394 – 1	AN EXPRESSION OF ORIGINAL MIND
EXPRESSION	405 – 1	SUBSTANCE OF HUMAN LIFE AND EXPRESSION
EXPRESSION	448 – 1	EXPRESSION WILL LACK PROPER HARMONY
EXPRESSION	493 – 1	NECESSARY TO THE EXPRESSION OF SPIRIT
EXTEND	282 – 2	DOES NOT EXTEND FAR BEYOND
EXTENSIVE	378 – 1	GOES THROUGH AN EXTENSIVE
EXTENT	139 – 4	EXTENT THAT WE LEARN TO CONTROL
EXTERNAL	113 – 2	EXTERNAL AND AN INTERNAL PERCEPTION
EXTERNAL	414 – 2	EXTERNAL TO SOME COMPREHENDING MIND
EXTERNAL	441 – 3	NO ENEMIES EXTERNAL TO OUR OWN MIND
EXTERNALIZATION	115 – 3	EXTERNALIZATION OF MAN'S THOUGHT
EXTERNALIZATION	143 – 1	MORE WHOLESOME EXTERNALIZATION
EXTERNALIZE	166 – 1	EXTERNALIZE FOR HIM AT THE LEVEL
EXTERNALIZE	321 – 2	CONSCIOUSNESS WILL EXTERNALIZE
EXTERNALIZED	292 – 2	IS EXTERNALIZED IN YOUR LIFE
EXTREMITY	464 – 3	IN OUR GREATEST EXTREMITY
EYE	229 – 5	LIGHT OF THE BODY IS THE EYE
EYE	229 – 5	THINE EYE BE SINGLE
EYE	230 – 1	IF THINE EYE BE EVIL
EYE	349 – 2	RETAINS ALL THAT THE EYE HAS SEEN
EYE	366 – 1	INNER EYE THAT SEES SO CLEARLY
EYE	375 – 2	SEE WITH THE NAKED EYE
EYE	429 – 1	EYE VIEWS THE WORLD AS ONE
EYE	432 – 2	EYE BE FILLED WITH EVIL
EYES	026 – 5	HIDDEN FROM OUR EYES
EYES	036 – 3	THROUGH OUR OWN EYES
EYES	041 – 3	IN THE EYES OF HIS BELOVED
EYES	230 – 2	EYES OF THEMSELVES CANNOT SEE
EYES	230 – 4	EYES ARE THE ORGANS OF THE SOUL
EYES	231 – 2	SUSPICION MAKE THE EYES SHIFTY
EYES	231 – 2	HOPELESSNESS MAKE THE EYES LUSTERLESS
EYES	231 – 3	LIFT UP MY EYES UNTO GOD
EYESIGHT	230 – 2	STRONG CLEAR EYESIGHT

F

FACE	131 – 1	BEHOLD THOU MY FACE FOREVERMORE
FACE	185 – 3	THOU MY FACE FOREVERMORE
FACE	344 – 3	HIS FACE WAS SO BRIGHT
FACE	387 – 2	IN THE FACE OF ALL DIFFICULTIES

FACT	187 - 2	AN ACCOMPLISHED FACT IN EXPERIENCE
FACT	189 - 2	LOOK A FACT IN THE FACE
FACT	196 - 2	AS AN ALREADY ACCOMPLISHED FACT
FACT	202 - 3	THIS DOES NOT ALTER THE FACT
FACT	203 - I	ALREADY AN ACCOMPLISHED FACT
FACT	213 - 2	DISEASE IS A FACT
FACT	213 - 3	WE ADMIT IT AS A FACT
FACT	213 - 4	FACT BUT NOT A TRUTH
FACT	275 - 2	NOT OF THE OLD FACT
FACT	285 - 2	IT IS A DYNAMIC FACT
FACT	312 - 3	VERY FACT THAT WE ARE HERE
FACT	350 - 4	MAIN FACT TO EMPHASIZE
FACT	387 - 1	A FACT OF EVERYDAY LIFE
FACT	443 - 1	THE SELF-EVIDENT FACT OF LIVING
FACT	446 - 2	SPIRITUAL EXPERIENCE IS A FACT
FACT	470 - 2	FACT OF OUR TRUE BEING
FACTOR	069 - 4	BUT ONE VOLITIONAL FACTOR
FACTOR	122 - 4	CREATIVE FACTOR WITHIN HIM
FACTS	074 - 2	FACTS BASED UPON
FACTS	074 - 2	FACTS OF SCIENCE ARE DEMONSTRABLE
FACTS	074 - 4	FACTS ARE PROVEN TO BE TRUE
FACTS	074 - 4	NUMBER OF KNOWN FACTS ABOUT ITS INVISIBLE
FACTS	275 - 2	MUST NOT CONSIDER THE FACTS
FACTS	275 - 2	THE FACTS ARE RELATIVE
FACTS	372 - 4	FACTS ADMIT OF PROOF
FACTS	379 - 1	VERY FACTS IN THE CASE PROVE
FACTS	384 - 3	UP TO THE FACTS OF BEING
FACULTIES	337 - 3	HIS PHYSICAL AND SPIRITUAL FACULTIES
FACULTIES	376 - 4	THE OBJECTIVE FACULTIES
FACULTY	155 - 3	FACULTY OF THE MIND
FACULTY	372 - 1	WHERE IS THIS FACULTY
FACULTY	372 - 1	NON-PHYSICAL FACULTY OF PERCEPTION
FAIL	162 - 3	BECAUSE WE FAIL TO REALIZE
FAIL	303 - 1	LIKELY TO FAIL AGAIN THIS YEAR
FAILED	302 - 4	IF ONE APPEARS TO HAVE FAILED
FAILED	317 - 3	DISCIPLES THAT THEY HAD FAILED
FAILING	187 - 1	FAILING OR SUCCEEDING
FAILS	165 - 2	FAILS TO SLEEP BECAUSE THERE IS
FAILURE	150 - 3	FAILURE IT IS IN MAN'S IGNORANCE
FAILURE	276 - 3	TO MAKE A COMPLETE FAILURE
FAILURE	282 - 1	MENTAL EQUIVALENT OF FAILURE
FAILURE	296 - 2	WITH AN ATMOSPHERE OF FAILURE
FAILURE	301 - 2	THOUGHT FAILURE OR WANTED TO FAIL
FAILURE	301 - 3	THOUGHTS OF FAILURE, LIMITATION
FAILURE	302 - 3	NO FAILURE IN GOD'S MIND
FAILURE	302 - 4	ERASE THE IDEA OF FAILURE
FAILURE	303 - 3	THERE IS NO FAILURE
FAILURE	315 - 4	GOD IS NOT A FAILURE
FAILURE	316 - 1	EXPERIENCE WHICH HAS BEEN A FAILURE
FAILURE	321 - 2	TURNS OUT TO BE A FAILURE
FAILURE	403 - 4	FAILURE AND SUCCESS ARE BUT TWO ENDS
FAILURE	450 - 4	WHO BELIEVE ONLY IN FAILURE
FAILURE	456 - 1	NO SENSE OF APPROACHING FAILURE
FAILURES	302 - 4	THERE ARE NO FAILURES IN THE UNIVERSE
FAILURES	491 - 2	NOT DESPISE APPARENT FAILURES

FAIRLY	204 - 4	THOUGHT HITS FAIRLY AND SQUARELY
FAITH	025 - 1	SCIENCE MUST JUSTIFY FAITH IN THE INVISIBLE
FAITH	032 - 1	ACCORDING TO OUR BELIEFS AND FAITH
FAITH	032 - 3	HONORS OUR FAITH
FAITH	039 - 6	KNOWLEDGE AND PERFECT FAITH
FAITH	041 - 3	SIMPLICITY OF FAITH
FAITH	046 - 4	WE SHOULD HAVE FAITH IN IT
FAITH	047 - 1	FAITH THAT THE LAW WORKS FOR US
FAITH	048 - 3	HAS FAITH IN HIS POWER
FAITH	048 - 3	FAITH BEING A MENTAL ATTITUDE
FAITH	048 - 3	CREATE THE DESIRED FAITH
FAITH	048 - 3	FAITH IS A NECESSARY ATTITUDE
FAITH	048 - 4	FAITH IN A CERTAIN SPECIFIC
FAITH	049 - 2	IF THOUGHT AND FAITH, PRAYER
FAITH	054 - 2	OUR FAITH IS WEAK
FAITH	057 - 4	AN OUTLET THROUGH HIS FAITH IN IT
FAITH	143 - 2	THIS IS MORE THAN FAITH
FAITH	155 - 3	FAITH HAS BEEN RECOGNIZED AS A POWER
FAITH	155 - 3	FAITH IS A FACULTY OF THE MIND THAT FINDS
FAITH	156 - 1	THOSE WHO HAVE GREAT FAITH
FAITH	156 - 2	FAITH IS AN AFFIRMATIVE MENTAL APPROACH
FAITH	156 - 4	THE NEGATIVE USE OF FAITH
FAITH	156 - 5	FAITH BASED ON THE KNOWLEDGE
FAITH	158 - 2	NEED A LESSON ABOUT FAITH
FAITH	158 - 2	FAITH SUBDUED KINGDOMS
FAITH	158 - 4	FAITH IS A QUALITY UNCONFINED TO AGE
FAITH	158 - 4	BECAUSE WE HAVE LOST FAITH
FAITH	158 - 5	ONE WILL HAVE FAITH IN HIMSELF
FAITH	158 - 5	FAITH WILL LIGHT THE PLACE IN WHICH HE
FAITH	159 - 1	IN ORDER TO KEEP FAITH
FAITH	159 - 5	FAITH IS A SPIRITUAL CONVICTION
FAITH	161 - 2	PERFECT FAITH
FAITH	162 - 2	FAITH IS CENTERED IN
FAITH	178 - 3	FAITH IS BASED ON IMMUTABLE PRINCIPLE
FAITH	178 - 4	FAITH IN HIMSELF
FAITH	178 - 4	FAITH IS THE SUBSTANCE OF THINGS HOPED FOR
FAITH	185 - 3	FAITH THAT HE IS GOING TO OVERCOME
FAITH	190 - 1	HEALED THROUGH PRAYER AND FAITH
FAITH	217 - 2	FAITH IS EQUAL TO THE DEMANDS
FAITH	229 - 2	EXPRESSED IN FAITH AND GOOD DEEDS
FAITH	230 - 5	YOUR FAITH IN SPIRITUAL SUBSTANCE
FAITH	230 - 5	FAITH TOUCHES A CERTAIN POINT
FAITH	235 - 4	AFFIRMATIVE OUTLOOK OF FAITH AND TRUST
FAITH	245 - 3	FAITH MUST OVERCOME FEAR
FAITH	245 - 3	STRONG STATEMENTS OF FAITH
FAITH	245 - 3	I ABIDE IN FAITH
FAITH	245 - 3	I CAN REMAIN IN FAITH
FAITH	247 - 2	FAITH IN GOD AS THE LIGHT
FAITH	256 - 5	MY FAITH FILLS ME
FAITH	280 - 2	NECESSITY OF FAITH, CONVICTION
FAITH	280 - 3	THE POWER OF PRAYER IS FAITH
FAITH	280 - 3	LAW OF FAITH AND ACCEPTANCE
FAITH	281 - 2	FAITH THEN TOUCHES A PRINCIPLE
FAITH	281 -2	NOR IS IT FOOLISH TO CULTIVATE FAITH
FAITH	281 - 2	CONSCIOUSLY ARRIVING AT FAITH

FAITH	283 - 2	AS FAR AS ANYONE CAN GO IN FAITH
FAITH	283 - 3	FAITH IS THE POWER OF PRAYER
FAITH	283 - 3	NOW WHAT IS FAITH
FAITH	283 - 3	WHEN YOU ANALYZE FAITH
FAITH	283 - 3	GREAT FAITH IN FEAR
FAITH	283 - 3	FAITH IN THE FEAR
FAITH	283 - 4	THAT IS FAITH IN GOD
FAITH	283 - 4	FAITH IN ONE'S CREATIVE ABILITY
FAITH	283 - 5	FAITH IS MENTAL ASSERTION ELEVATED
FAITH	284 - 2	FAITH IS REAL TO THE ONE WHO EXPERIENCES IT
FAITH	284 - 2	THIS FAITH WE SHOULD HAVE
FAITH	284 - 2	FAITH THAT THERE IS BUT ONE MIND
FAITH	284 - 4	FAITH LOOKS TO THE INVISIBLE
FAITH	284 - 4	FAITH IS NOT HOPE
FAITH	284 - 5	FAITH IS ESSENTIAL TO EFFECTIVE
FAITH	284 - 5	FAITH MAY BE SAID TO BE SCIENTIFIC
FAITH	285 - 2	THE TRUE MEANING OF FAITH
FAITH	301 - 4	POSITIVE FAITH IN THE EVIDENCE OF THINGS
FAITH	302 - 2	WITH FAITH, HOPE, AND EXPECTANCY
FAITH	317 - 3	BECAUSE OF LACK OF FAITH
FAITH	317 - 3	HAVE THE FAITH OF GOD
FAITH	335 - 4	FIRE OF FAITH IN THE LIVING SPIRIT
FAITH	401 - 4	ROAD OF FAITH AND UNDERSTANDING
FAITH	404 - 2	REVERSE MENTAL ATTITUDE TO FAITH
FAITH	405 - 5	FEAR THROUGH FAITH
FAITH	407 - 2	WITHOUT HAVING FAITH
FAITH	415 - 1	OF FAITH IN ONESELF AND IN OTHERS
FAITH	439 - 5	THY FAITH HATH MADE THEE WHOLE
FAITH	443 - 1	CHILD-LIKE FAITH IN THE UNIVERSE
FAITH	450 - 3	ABSOLUTE FAITH IN OUR WORK
FAITH	498 - 3	IN FAITH BELIEVING
FAITH	498 - 4	FAITH IN GOD AND IN OURSELVES
FAITHFUL	218 - 3	FAITHFUL TO THIS VISION
FAITH IN GOD	317 - 3	THEY DID HAVE FAITH IN GOD
FAITH OF GOD	162 - 5	FAITH OF GOD INSTEAD OF MERELY A FAITH IN
FAITH PRINCIPLES	159 - 3	SCIENCES ARE BUILT UPON FAITH PRINCIPLES
FAITHS	045 - 3	RECEPTIVITY OF OUR DIFFERENT FAITHS
FALL	115 - 4	FALL THE FORMS OF HIS THOUGHT
FALL	310 - 4	THE FALL TO SHOW THE WRONG USE
FALL	314 - 4	WE FALL DOWN AND WORSHIP THEM
FALL	365 - 4	FALL INTO AS GREAT AN ERROR
FALL	459 - 6	WILL FALL BY ITS OWN WEIGHT
FALL	473 - 3	THE FALL TAKEN LITERALLY
FALLACIOUS	454 - 1	MAY SEEM FALLACIOUS TO MANY
FALLEN	055 - 4	LIFT UP THE FALLEN
FALLEN	414 - 1	FALLEN TO THE LEVEL OF
FALLEN	457 - 4	FALLEN SHORT OF THE DIVINE CALLING
FALLING	418 - 2	ARE FALLING UNDER THE ILLUSION
FALSE	180 - 1	FALSE THOUGHT AND RECOGNIZES
FALSE	221 - 3	THE FALSE FROM THE TRUE
FALSE	234 - 5	DISSOLVE THE IDEA OF FALSE GROWTHS
FALSE	254 - 6	SEPARATES THE FALSE FROM THE TRUE
FALSE	262 - 2	FALSE DESIRE IS EXACTLY
FALSE	303 - 3	FALSE THOUGHT AND HAS NO TRUTH
FALSE	376 - 4	THIS IS PROVED TO BE FALSE

FALSE	409 - 2	KNOWING THAT THEY ARE FALSE
FALSE	430 - 4	FALSE BY OUR ACCEPTANCE OF IT
FALSE	453 - 6	FALSE IDEAS MAKE BAD MATTERS WORSE
FALSE	457 - 3	FALSE EXPERIENCE WILL CONTINUE
FALSE	469 - 1	EVIL FOR BOTH ARE FALSE
FALSE	479 - 4	NO FALSE PROMISES NEVER DECEIVED
FALSE	502 - 6	FALSE IDEAS DO NOT PAY
FALSE ACTION	238 - 3	THERE IS NO FALSE ACTION
FALSE BELIEF	494 - 4	POWER OF FALSE BELIEF AND SUPERSTITION
FALSE GROWTH	236 - 2	FALSE GROWTH IS NEITHER PERSON
FALSE GROWTHS	234 - 4	THOUGHT OF FALSE GROWTHS
FALSE GROWTHS	234 - 5	DISSOLVE THE IDEA OF FALSE GROWTHS
FALSEHOOD	049 - 5	REPUDIATE THE FALSEHOOD
FAMILIAR	310 - 2	FAMILIAR WITH THE IDEA OF UNITY
FAMILIAR	381 - 4	AGAINST HAVING FAMILIAR SPIRITS
FAMILY	348 - 1	FAMILY AND RACE CHARACTERISTICS
FAMINE	033 - 3	A COSMIC FAMINE
FAMINE	462 - 5	MIGHTY FAMINE IN THAT LAND
FANCY	030 - 3	NOT WITH WHIMSICAL FANCY
FANNING	361 - 1	FANNING THE HUMAN INTO A BLAZE DIVINE
FANTASY	144 - 1	WOULD BE MERELY A FANTASY
FAR COUNTRY	462 - 3	ALL IN THIS FAR COUNTRY
FAR COUNTRY	462 - 4	FAR COUNTRY HAS AS REAL A MEANING TODAY
FARMER	038 - 2	FARMER PLANTS A SEED
FARMER	455 - 6	FARMER KNEELING BESIDE HIS CABBAGE
FAR OFF	147 - 3	FAR OFF PLACE BUT HERE AND NOW
FAR OFF	149 - 3	GOD IS SOME FAR OFF
FAR-REACHING	041 - 1	FAR-REACHING THOUGHT
FAR-REACHING	351 - 2	FAR-REACHING THIS BOOK MAY BE
FAR-REACHING	375 - 2	IDEA IS VERY FAR-REACHING
FARTHING	487 - 4	EXACTS THE UTTERMOST FARTHING
FARTHING	502 - 3	FARTHING IS PAID WHEN WE
FASHIONED	157 - 1	WHICH WAS FASHIONED IN THE MIND
FASHIONING	281 - 4	MIND IS THE FASHIONING FACTOR
FAST	432 - 1	FAST WITHOUT OUTWARD SIGN
FAST	442 - 3	DESIRE TO FAST AND BE WISE
FASTING	253 - 1	THAT EITHER FASTING OR FEASTING
FASTING	274 - 2	NEITHER FASTING NOR FEASTING
FASTING	455 - 3	PHYSICAL ACT OF FASTING
FASTING AND PRAYING	455 - 7	LIVE IN A FASTING AND PRAYING WORLD
FAT	471 - 2	WITH THE FAT OF THE LAND
FATALISTIC	128 - 2	NOT IN ANY SENSE FATALISTIC
FATALISTIC	280 - 2	THERE IS NOTHING FATALISTIC
FATALISTIC	354 - 2	THERE IS NOTHING FATALISTIC ABOUT THIS
FATE	031 - 1	NOT FATE BUT CAUSE AND EFFECT
FATE	078 - 2	CONFUSED WITH KISMET, WHICH IS FATE
FATHER	076 - 4	HATH SEEN THE FATHER
FATHER	088 - 2	THE FATHER, SON AND HOLY GHOST
FATHER	088 - 3	THE FATHER IS ABSOLUTE
FATHER	106 - 3	FATHER HATH LIFE WITHIN HIMSELF
FATHER	217 - 2	ALL THE FATHER HATH IS THINE
FATHER	275 - 3	FATHER IS A DIVINE PRESENCE
FATHER	296 - 4	I AND MY FATHER ARE ONE
FATHER	306 - 4	FATHER INCARNATE IN MAN
FATHER	330 - 4	I AND THE FATHER ARE ONE

FATHER	330 – 4	FATHER THAT DWELLETH IN ME
FATHER	344 – 2	THE FATHER THAT DWELLETH IN ME
FATHER	401 – 4	FATHER IN ME WHO DOETH THE WORK
FATHER	422 – 3	FATHER CONCEIVING WITHIN HIMSELF
FATHER	431 – 5	FATHER WHO SEEST IN SECRET
FATHER	453 – 6	FATHER TO A GREATER PART
FATHER	461 – 1	THOUGHT IS EVER FATHER TO THE ACT
FATHER	467 – 2	FATHER TALKED ABOUT SOMETHING ELSE
FATHER	475 – 6	FATHER HAS LIFE SO THE SON HAS LIFE
FATHER	480 – 4	FATHER IS GLORIFIED IN THE SON
FATHER	480 – 6	FATHER BEGETS THE ETERNAL
FATHER	483 – 3	IDEA IS FATHER TO THE FACT
FATHER	493 – 6	ONE GOD AND FATHER
FATHER AND MOTHER	449 – 5	THE FATHER AND MOTHER OF ALL
FATHERHOOD	332 – 3	THE FATHERHOOD OF GOD
FATHER-MOTHER	082 – 1	SPIRIT IS THE FATHER-MOTHER GOD
FATHER'S	404 – 2	YOUR FATHER'S GOOD PLEASURE
FATHER'S HOUSE	464 – 3	CAN RETURN TO THE FATHER'S HOUSE
FATHER'S HOUSE	464 – 4	FATHER'S HOUSE IS ALWAYS OPEN
FATHOM	043 – 4	FATHOM THE INFINITE MIND
FATHOM	372 – 3	FATHOM THAT WHICH IS SELF-EXISTENT
FATHOMED	450 – 1	FATHOMED THE DEPTHS OF ITS MEANING
FATIGUE	226 – 3	COMPLAIN OF HABITUAL FATIGUE
FATIGUE	227 – 3	FEELING OF APPROACHING FATIGUE
FATIGUED	226 – 3	FORTY YEARS OF AGE IS EASILY FATIGUED
FAULT	299 – 1	CANNOT AFFORD TO FIND FAULT
FAVOR	309 – 3	IN FAVOR OF PERFECT GOD
FAVORITES	027 – 3	UNIVERSE HAS NO FAVORITES
FAVORITES	455 – 3	GOD PLAYS NO FAVORITES
FAVORITES	492 – 5	UNIVERSE PLAYS NO FAVORITES
FEAR	027 – 4	WITH AWE BUT NOT WITH FEAR
FEAR	099 – 2	FEAR ARE IN CONSCIOUSNESS
FEAR	144 – 3	FEAR HAS BEEN KNOWN TO CAUSE
FEAR	153 – 1	FEAR THAT WE SHOULD NEVER
FEAR	156 – 3	THE FEAR THAT GOD WILL NOT
FEAR	156 – 4	FEAR NOTHING MORE NOR LESS THAN
FEAR	180 – 4	SECURITY WHICH KNOWS NO FEAR
FEAR	188 – 3	FEAR BE QUIET
FEAR	188 – 3	VAGUE, SUBTLE, UNCONSCIOUS FEAR
FEAR	201 – 1	FEAR COME INTO YOUR THOUGHT
FEAR	203 – 3	FEAR FROM YOUR OWN THOUGHT
FEAR	218 – 2	THE REMOVAL OF DOUBT AND FEAR
FEAR	231 – 2	THOUGHTS OF FEAR, DESOLATION
FEAR	231 – 6	FEAR OF LACK OF TROUBLE
FEAR	232 – 1	FEAR THOUGHT RETARDS
FEAR	238 – 4	FEAR ALL KINDS OF FEAR
FEAR	238 – 4	LOVE CASTETH OUT FEAR
FEAR	245 – 3	FAITH MUST OVERCOME FEAR
FEAR	246 – 2	NOT HAVE FEAR FOR THE FUTURE
FEAR	246 – 4	ERASE ALL THOUGHT OF FEAR
FEAR	249 – 4	NO THOUGHT OF FEAR OR CONGESTION
FEAR	253 – 3	TROUBLE ARE WORRY, ANXIETY, FEAR
FEAR	264 – 5	NO FEAR AS A RESULT OF MY PAST
FEAR	272 – 2	FEAR MUST GO
FEAR	277 – 3	TREATMENT REMOVES DOUBT AND FEAR

FEAR	283 - 3	GREAT FAITH IN FEAR
FEAR	383 - 2	NOT FEAR EITHER GOD OR THE DEVIL
FEAR	383 - 3	FEAR NOTHING IN THE UNIVERSE
FEAR	404 - 2	FEAR IS THE GREAT ENEMY OF MAN
FEAR	404 - 2	FEAR IS A MENTAL ATTITUDE
FEAR	404 - 3	FEAR ARISES FROM THAT MENTAL ATTITUDE
FEAR	404 - 4	PERFECT LOVE CASTS OUT FEAR
FEAR	404 - 4	OVERCOME FEAR IS THE GREATEST ADVENTURE
FEAR	405 - 3	FEAR IS OF LACK PAIN, SICKNESS
FEAR	485 - 1	NO FEAR IN THE SPIRIT
FEAR	492 - 1	DEATH AND ALL FEAR
FEAR	495 - 3	FEAR AND DOUBT CANNOT FIND ENTRANCE
FEARED	301 - 2	YOU EVEN FEARED IT WOULD COME
FEARLESSNESS	232 - 4	INTELLIGENCE AND FEARLESSNESS
FEARLESSNESS	238 - 4	A DIVINE FEARLESSNESS
FEAR NOT	108 - 4	FEAR NOT LITTLE FLOCK IT IS YOUR FATHER'S
F'EAR OF LACK	156 - 3	FEAR OF LACK IS NOTHING MORE
FEAR OF DEATH	156 - 3	FEAR OF DEATH IS THE BELIEF
FEARS	053 - 1	BECAUSE OF OUR DOUBTS AND FEARS
FEAST	442 - 3	FEAST AND STILL BE WISE
FEASTING	274 - 2	FEASTING, WAILING, NOR PRAISING
FEASTING	442 - 4	FEASTING MAY APPEAR TO BE A GREATER VIRTUE
FEATS	353 - 2	WONDERFUL FEATS OF THE MIND
FED	476 - 5	WHOLE BEING NEEDS TO BE FED
FED	496 - 5	FED FROM THE TABLE OF THE UNIVERSE
FEEL	153 - 3	COMMUNE WITH SPIRIT TO SENSE AND FEEL IT
FEEL	167 - 4	SHOULD FEEL A UNITY OF SPIRIT
FEEL	188 - 1	FEEL WHAT YOU WISH TO
FEEL	207 - 3	SHOULD FEEL ANYTHING UNUSUAL
FEEL	207 - 3	FEEL ANYTHING OTHER THAN
FEEL	224 - 4	ALWAYS FEEL THAT IT IS DONE
FEEL	307 - 3	FEEL THAT YOU ARE WONDERFUL
FEEL	385 - 2	FEEL THAT I SHALL AGAIN MEET
FEEL	385 - 3	FEEL THAT THEY STILL LIVE
FEEL	387 - 2	EVEN THE BEST MEN FEEL
FEEL	398 - 4	FEEL THE REALITY OF WHAT WE ARE
FEELING	044 - 4	BY STATING AND FEELING THAT OUR MIND
FEELING	079 - 4	PLUS THAT INTUITIVE FEELING
FEELING	184 - 3	A RADIANT FEELING FLOWING THROUGH
FEELING	196 - 2	LOVE PULSATING WITH FEELING
FEELING	196 - 2	EXECUTOR OF ALL FEELING
FEELING	208 - 1	FEELING THERE IS
FEELING	224 - 2	WITH DEEP FEELING
FEELING	237 - 2	FEELING THAT HURTS
FEELING	248 - 5	OUR HABITUAL FEELING TOWARD PERSONS
FEELING	248 - 5	CLAIMING THE SAME FEELING FOR OURSELVES
FEELING	283 - 2	WITH FEELING, BECAUSE FEELING
FEELING	398 - 4	CREATIVE POWER RESPONDS TO FEELING MORE
FEELING	409 - 5	IT IS AN INWARD FEELING
FEELING	414 - 4	FEELING IS AT THE CENTER OF THE UNIVERSE
FEELINGS	256 - 4	BECAUSE OF HURT FEELINGS
FEELS	180 - 2	MIND ACTUALLY FEELS THAT THE OBJECT OF ITS
FEELS	197 - 1	BODY NEITHER THINKS, SEES, HEARS, FEELS
FEELS	237 - 2	TRAGEDY TO HIM WHO FEELS
FEET	234 - 3	FEET AND LEGS REPRESENT MAN'S ABILITY

FEET	435 - 2	FEET STILL WALK IN DARKNESS
FELL	410 - 3	LIMITATION FELL UPON HUMANITY
FELLOWMAN	178 - 4	FAITH IN HIS FELLOWMAN
FELLOWMAN	459 - 3	FELLOWMAN ALONE IS NOT SUFFICIENT
FELLOWMEN	155 - 3	FAITH IN ONE'S FELLOWMEN
FELLOWMEN	158 - 5	FAITH IN HIS FELLOWMEN
FELT	342 - 4	MYSTICS HAVE FELT THIS
FELT	343 - 3	HAVE FELT THE POSSIBILITY
FEMININE	082 - 1	FEMININE PRINCIPLES
FEMININE	096 - 3	THE UNIVERSAL FEMININE
FERVENT	501 - 4	BY EFFECTUAL AND FERVENT PRAYER
FEVER	250 - 6	TREATMENT FOR FEVER
FEVER	251 - 1	EFFECTIVE ALLAYING FEVER
FIELD	030 - 2	THERE IS A CREATIVE FIELD
FIELD	050 - 2	FIELD THROUGH WHICH THOUGHT
FIELD	086 - 4	MECHANICAL FIELD AND MUST OPERATE
FIELD	093 - 4	THERE IS A CREATIVE FIELD
FIELD	095 - 1	INTO THE FIELD OF MIND
FIELD	141 - 3	FIELD OF MECHANICAL
FIELD	199 - 3	IN THE FIELD OF MIND
FIELD	260 - 3	FIELD OF SPIRITUAL THOUGHT
FIELD	316 - 1	DEAL WITH HIS FIELD ALONE
FIELD	316 - 1	SHOULD REMAIN IN HIS OWN FIELD
FIELD	414 - 1	ENTER THAT FIELD OF CAUSATION
FIELD	421 - 5	FIELD OF SUBJECTIVITY IS UNIVERSAL
FIELD OF MIND	179 - 1	FIELD OF MIND AND SPIRIT
FIELD OF MIND	199 - 3	FIELD OF MIND
FIELD OF MIND	316 - 2	WORKS IN THE FIELD OF MIND ALONE
FIELD OF THOUGHT	316 - 1	IS ALWAYS THE FIELD OF THOUGHT
FIELDS	455 - 3	FIELDS OF RECEPTIVITY IN OUR MINDS
FIGHT	046 - 1	WE CANNOT FIGHT THE UNIVERSE
FIGHT	471 - 4	NO LONGER FIGHT THE OLD
FIGURATIVE	481 - 3	FIGURATIVE MEANING IN THESE WORDS
FIGURATIVELY	041 - 1	IT IS TO BE TAKEN FIGURATIVELY
FIGURE OUT	173 - 5	STOPS TRYING TO FIGURE OUT HOW
FILL	055 - 2	FILL HIS THOUGHT
FILL	287 - 1	EACH COULD RECEIVE ONLY HIS FILL
FILLED	048 - 2	FILLED BY THE SUBSTANCE NECESSARY
FILLED	146 - 3	FILLED WITH INFINITE GOOD
FILLED	246 - 1	FILLED WITH LOVE AND PROTECTION
FILLED	264 - 5	FILLED WITH WONDERFUL PEACE
FILLS	161 - 4	INFINITE FILLS ALL MOLDS AND FOREVER
FINAL	091 - 3	FINAL ANALYSIS OF MATTER
FINAL	383 - 3	ALL WILL ARRIVE AT THE FINAL GOAL
FINALITY	287 - 3	NOTHING IN THE NATURE OF FINALITY
FINALLY	166 - 2	FINALLY HE COMES TO A PLACE
FINANCIAL	239 - 2	LOSS FROM FINANCIAL REVERSES
FINANCIAL	262 - 3	SUCCESS IN FINANCIAL MATTERS
FIND	116 - 1	IT IS EXACTLY WHAT WE DO FIND
FIND	334 - 2	SHOULD TURN WITHIN AND FIND GOD
FIND	419 - 5	TURN WITHIN AND FIND GOD
FINDETH	440 - 3	FINDETH HIS LIFE SHALL LOSE IT
FINER	376 - 1	STILL FINER THAN THE ETHER
FINISHED	126 - 2	HE IS FINISHED WITH THEM
FINITE	033 - 3	FINITE ALONE HAS WROUGHT

FINITE	082 - 2	FINITE MIND TO COMPREHEND
FINITE	087 - 2	FINITE MUST COME FROM THE INFINITE
FINITE	112 - 4	FINITE MUST BE DRAWN FROM THE INFINITE
FINITE	139 - 1	FINITE INTELLIGENCE RESPONDING TO FINITE
FINITE	267 - 4	MAN APPEARS TO BE FINITE
FINITE	269 - 1	INFINITE CAN NEVER BE FINITE
FINITE	312 - 1	TO KNOW THAT WHICH IS FINITE
FINITE	388 - 1	A MANIFESTATION IN THE FINITE
FINITE	405 - 2	FOREVER EXPANDING THE FINITE
FINITE	429 - 1	FINITE OUTLOOK FROM A LIMITED CONCEPT
FINITE	444 - 4	INFINITE WITH THE FINITE
FIRE	335 - 4	CONSUMED BY THE FIRE OF FAITH
FIRE	463 - 1	FROM THE DIVINE FIRE
FIRE	478 - 3	THE VERY FIRE ITSELF
FIRES	368 - 3	FIRES OF THE UNIVERSAL FLAME
FIRES	477 - 2	FIRES THE SOUL WITH ENERGY
FIRM	307 - 3	BE FIRM AND YE SHALL BE MADE FIRM
FIRMLY	376 - 3	AS WE FIRMLY BELIEVE
FIRST	038 - 2	FIRST STEP OF THE CREATIVE ORDER
FIRST	044 - 2	MIND WHICH MUST FIRST
FIRST	054 - 3	FIRST HE REALIZES
FIRST	076 - 2	FIRST A SUBJECTIVE WORLD
FIRST	141 - 5	FIRST IS INTELLIGENCE
FIRST	168 - 3	FIRST REQUISITE FOR THE MENTAL
FIRST	180 - 2	PRACTITIONER FIRST REALIZES HIS OWN
FIRST	193 - 4	THE WILL HAS FIRST ADMITTED
FIRST	201 - 2	FIRST THING A PRACTITIONER DOES
FIRST	201 - 5	FIRST HAVE A SUBJECTIVE CAUSE
FIRST	202 - 5	FIRST RECOGNIZE YOUR OWN PERFECTION
FIRST	203 - 3	FIRST ELIMINATE DOUBT AND FEAR
FIRST	223 - 2	FIRST RECOGNIZE WHO AND WHAT
FIRST	248 - 5	FIRST STEP TOWARD HEALING IS
FIRST	281 - 2	THE FIRST NECESSITY IS FAITH
FIRST	318 - 3	FIRST RECOGNITION, SECOND UNIFICATION
FIRST	332 - 1	FIRST REALIZE THAT DIVINE POWER
FIRST	396 - 2	HE FIRST SAYS FOR HIMSELF
FIRST	400 - 2	MUST FIRST BECOME ESTABLISHED
FIRST	402 - 3	AS WE FIRST KNOW OURSELVES
FIRST	458 - 4	THERE IS FIRST AN IMAGE
FIRST	476 - 3	FIRST A REALIZATION OF POWER
FIRST	490 - 1	SEEK THE KINGDOM OF GOD FIRST
FIRST CAUSE	026 - 3	SCIENCE OF MIND IS A STUDY OF FIRST CAUSE
FIRST CAUSE	060 - 4	DEALS DIRECTLY WITH FIRST CAUSE
FIRST CAUSE	069 - 3	FIRST CAUSE MUST BE SELF-EXISTENT
FIRST CAUSE	084 - 1	FIRST CAUSE SPEAKS AND IT IS DONE
FIRST-HAND	445 - 4	A FIRST-HAND KNOWLEDGE OF LIFE
FIRST MAN	311 - 1	THE FIRST MAN IS OF THE EARTH, EARTHY
FIRST PERSON	056 - 3	TREATMENT IN THE FIRST PERSON
FISH	306 - 5	HOW MANY FISH
FISHES	341 - 1	MULTIPLY THE LOAVES AND FISHES
FIT	439 - 2	DO NOT FIT NICELY TOGETHER
FITTED	468 - 2	NOT YET FITTED TO PERCEIVE
FIVE	408 - 3	FIVE WOULD BECOME EXHAUSTED
FLAME	368 - 3	FIRES OF THE UNIVERSAL FLAME
FLAME	414 - 3	ETERNAL FLAME OF THE SPIRIT

FLAME	478 - 3	LOVE IS THE CENTRAL FLAME
FLAMES	345 - 1	NEW YORK CITY WAS IN FLAMES
FAASH	344 - 3	SEES REALITY IN A FLASH
FLASHES	346 - 1	IN FLASHES OF ILLUMINATION
FLASHES	421 - 3	IN FLASHES OF ILLUMINATION
FLASH-LIKE	370 - 2	FLASH-LIKE VISIONS OF MYSTIC
FLAT DENIAL	372 - 4	FLAT DENIAL OF OUR EXISTENCE
FLAW	442 - 3	WORLD EVER FINDS SOME FLAW
FLEES	456 - 2	EVIL FLEES BEFORE REALITY
FLESH	144 - 3	TO WHICH THE FLESH IS HEIR
FLESH	244 - 4	RUNNING THROUGH THE FLESH
FLESH	314 - 2	THE WORD BECOMES FLESH
FLESH	330 - 4	IN MY FLESH SHALL I SEE GOD
FLESH	353 - 1	IN THE FLESH OR OUT OF IT
FLESH	359 - 3	FLESH GAVE WAY TO SPIRIT
FLESH	380 - 2	PEOPLE OUT OF THE FLESH
FLESH	382 - 1	NO POWER IN THE FLESH OR OUT
FLESH	388 - 4	HOME OF HEAVY FLESH WILL RISE
FLESH	422 - 2	IN THE FLESH OR OUT OF IT
FLESH	491 - 8	KNOW NO MAN AFTER THE FLESH
FLESH	492 - 2	KNOW NO MAN AFTER THE FLESH
FLEXIBILITY	243 - 3	FLEXIBILITY FREE YOUR THOUGHT
FLING	142 - 3	FLING HIS THOUGHT OUT
FLOCK	404 - 2	FEAR NOT LITTLE FLOCK
FLOOD	120 - 3	THE MEANING OF THE FLOOD
FLOOD	344 - 3	A GREAT FLOOD OF LIGHT
FLOURISH	235 - 2	FLOURISH UNLESS THERE IS SOMETHING
FLOURISH	495 - 4	FLOURISH IN THE HOME OF THE SOUL
FLOW	041 - 4	DECIDES ITS FLOW THROUGH US
FLOW	045 - 3	FLOW INTO PARTICULAR CHANNELS
FLOW	052 - 2	IT MUST FLOW THROUGH US
FLOW	219 - 1	FLOW THROUGH HIM
FLOW	226 - 2	FLOW OF LIFE-FORCE TO THE BRAIN
FLOW	233 - 4	STATE OF ETERNAL FLOW
FLOW	358 - 2	PERFECT LIFE FLOW THROUGH US
FLOW	376 - 2	MORE COMPLETE FLOW OF THE SPIRIT
FLOW	400 - 4	CAUSE A DIFFERENT FLOW OF ENERGY
FLOW	440 - 2	DIVINE CURRENT TO FLOW
FLOW	489 - 3	FLOW THROUGH THE THING
FLOWER	463 - 4	FLOWER IS ALREADY IN THE SEED
FLOWING	038 - 3	FLOWING THROUGH US
FLOWING	052 - 4	BY FLOWING THROUGH US
FLOWING	054 - 3	LIBERTY IS FLOWING THROUGH HIM
FLOWING	117 - 1	FLOWING INTO FORM AND FOREVER FLOWING
FLOWING	184 - 3	A RADIANT FEELING FLOWING
FLOWING	374 - 1	LIKE A RIVER FOREVER FLOWING
FLOWING	412 - 4	IS ALWAYS FLOWING INTO US
FLOWING	445 - 3	FLOWING FROM A DIVINE CENTER
FLOWS	052 - 2	THE LAW ALSO FLOWS THROUGH US
FLOWS	052 - 2	IT FLOWS THROUGH EVERYTHING
FLOWS	226 - 2	FLOWS THROUGH MAN
FLOWS	252 - 3	LIFE OF GOD FLOWS FREELY
FLOWS	387 - 3	THEIR LIFE STILL FLOWS ON
FLOWS	388 - 3	FLOWS THROUGH ALL THINGS
FLOWS	393 - 3	FLOWS THROUGH THE SELF

FLUENT	053 - 3	DEALING WITH A FLUENT FORCE
FLUENT	394 - 3	BODY AND AFFAIRS ARE FLUENT
FLUID	310 - 2	THAT EVERY FACT IS FLUID
FLYING	273 - 4	FLYING MACHINES UNTIL MAN
FOCUSED	112 - 4	WHOLE OF SPIRIT IS POTENTIALLY FOCUSED
FOCUSING	194 - 1	FOCUSING THE MENTAL ATTENTION
FOE	431 - 1	FOE ALIKE MAY FALL AWAY
FOES	441 - 3	FOES SHALL BE THEY OF HIS OWN HOUSEHOLD
FOLDED	470 - 5	FOLDED IN THE ARMS OF LOVE
FOLLOW	039 - 4	FOLLOW ME ALL THE DAYS OF MY LIFE
FOLLOW	414 - 3	FOLLOW THIS FAITH THROUGH
FOLLOWERS	162 - 4	YEARS PASSED AND HIS FOLLOWERS
FOLLOWS	195 - 3	LAW FOLLOWS THE WORD
FOOD	253 - 1	FOOD IS A SYMBOL OF GOD'S
FOOD	253 - 1	FOOD DOES NOT HARM MAN
FOOD	259 - 3	FOOD MUST BE A SPIRITUAL IDEA
FOOD	259 - 4	FOOD AGREES WITH ME
FOOD	259 - 4	FOOD IS A SPIRITUAL IDEA
FOOL	153 - 2	A FORCE WE CANNOT FOOL
FOOL	175 - 2	NOT FOOL OURSELVES ABOUT ANY
FOOLED	474 - 2	PART OF US WHICH CAN BE FOOLED
FOOLISH	281 - 2	NOR IS IT FOOLISH TO CULTIVATE FAITH
FOOLISH	285 - 2	FAITH IS NOT A FOOLISH FANCY
FOOLISH	378 - 3	NATURE IS NOT FOOLISH
FOOLISH	437 - 1	FOOLISH MAN LIVING ONLY IN SENSE
FOOL PROOF	110 - 1	UNIVERSE IS FOOL PROOF
FOOL PROOF	394 - 2	THE UNIVERSE IS FOOL PROOF
FOOL PROOF	412 - 3	IT IS FOOL PROOF
FORCE	031 - 2	LAW OF CREATIVE FORCE
FORCE	053 - 3	DEALING WITH A FLUENT FORCE
FORCE	057 - 4	FORCE NOW CONSCIOUSLY DIRECTED
FORCE	079 - 2	CALLED IT A BLIND FORCE
FORCE	079 - 3	A FORCE OF NATURE
FORCE	083 - 2	BLIND FORCE NOT KNOWING
FORCE	084 - 1	SOME FORM OF UNIVERSAL FORCE
FORCE	092 - 2	BLIND FORCE NOT KNOWING, ONLY DOING
FORCE	129 - 2	SOUL AS A BLIND FORCE
FORCE	153 - 2	WE ARE DEALING WITH A FORCE
FORCE	192 - 3	FORCE THINGS TO HAPPEN
FORCE	194 - 2	FORCE THROUGH CONCENTRATION
FORCE	209 - 4	FORCE WHICH MAKES US SICK
FORCE	210 - 1	A PERSONAL THOUGHT FORCE
FORCE	237 - 3	ACTING THROUGH A THOUGHT FORCE
FORCE	254 - 3	GIVING FORCE OF PURE SPIRIT
FORCE	275 - 3	LAW IS A MECHANICAL FORCE
FORCE	276 - 1	IS SIMPLY A BLIND FORCE
FORCE	309 - 5	HE DOES NOT SEEK TO FORCE
FORCE	323 - 2	LOVE IS THE IMPELLING FORCE
FORCE	334 - 4	LAW AS AN ARBITRARY FORCE
FORCE	369 - 1	FORCE ITSELF UPON ANY
FORCE	395 - 2	NOT BY FORCE BUT BY AGREEMENT
FORCE	396 - 2	LAW IS A FORCE IN NATURE
FORCED	137 - 2	FORCED TO THE CONCLUSION
FORCES	031 - 2	NATURE'S FORCES AND LAWS
FORCES	104 - 1	FORCES WHICH CANNOT BE EXPLAINED

FORCES	104 - 2	A UNITY WITH NATURE AND HER FORCES
FORCES	278 - 3	THOUGHT SETS DEFINITE FORCES IN MOTION
FORCES	282 - 3	FORCES SWEEPING EVERYTHING BEFORE THEM
FOREKNEW	378 - 3	SHE FOREKNEW OUR NEED
FOREKNEW	479 - 2	FOREKNEW THAT HE WOULD TURN
FOREKNOWN	48b - 1	FOREKNOWN AND PREDETERMINED
FOREKNOWS	485 - 6	FOREKNOWS HIS OWN PERFECTION
FOREVER	070 - 2	CREATION GOES ON FOREVER
FOREVER	262 - 1	FOREVER FREE FROM THIS THOUGHT
FOREVER	291 - 1	FOREVER SEEKING EXPRESSION
FOREVER	303 - 4	WORD IS NOW ESTABLISHING IT FOREVER
FOREVER	311 - 1	FOREVER PRODUCING FORM
FOREVER	407 - 5	MIND IS FOREVER CONSCIOUS
FORGET	172 - 2	FORGET ALL ABOUT HENRY BLACK
FORGET	308 - 1	FORGET THAT PHILOSOPHY IS PROFOUND
FORGET	358 - 2	FORGET ALL ABOUT THE LAW
FORGET	358 - 2	WE MUST FORGET EVERYTHING ELSE
FORGET	371 - 2	TO SUPPOSE THAT MAN CAN FORGET
FORGET	396 - 4	NOT FORGET THAT IT HAS INFINITE
FORGET	405 - 5	DESIRABLE AND TO FORGET THE REST
FORGET	441 - 1	NEVER FORGET THAT THERE IS AN
FORGETTING	459 - 5	LOVE THIS GOD FORGETTING ALL ELSE
FORGIVE	261 - 2	FORGIVE ALL AND AM FORGIVEN
FORGIVE	431 - 4	GOD WILL FORGIVE US AFTER
FORGIVE	438 - 1	EASIER TO FORGIVE OR TO HEAL
FORGIVE	438 - 5	WE SHOULD FORGIVE
FORGIVE	457 - 4	FORGIVE UNTIL SEVENTY TIMES SEVEN
FORGIVEN	261 - 2	AM FORGIVEN OF ALL AND BY ALL
FORGIVEN	298 - 4	LOVED MUCH, MUCH IS FORGIVEN
FORGIVEN	298 - 4	MUCH WILL BE FORGIVEN HIM
FORGIVEN	458 - 2	LOVES MUCH IS FORGIVEN
FORGIVENESS	365 - 2	FORGIVENESS OF ALL SIN IS WITHIN MAN
FORGIVENESS	457 - 4	MEANING OF DIVINE FORGIVENESS
FORGIVENESS	457 - 4	FORGIVENESS IS ETERNAL AND EVER AVAILABLE
FORM	052 - 2	EVERY FORM WITH DIFFERENTIATIONS
FORM	052 - 4	READY AND WILLING TO TAKE FORM
FORM	053 - 3	IT IS FOREVER TAKING FORM
FORM	053 - 3	FOREVER DESERTING THE FORM
FORM	063 - 2	NO VISIBLE FORM
FORM	066 - 5	GIVING OF FORM TO THE SUBSTANCE
FORM	068 - 5	ITSELF INTO MANIFESTATION INTO FORM
FORM	070 - 2	PROJECTING THE FORM
FORM	083 - 3	FORM AND IS ETERNALLY
FORM	086 - 5	MIND IN ITS SELF-CONSCIOUS FORM
FORM	087 - 5	THINGS ARE IDEAS IN FORM
FORM	090 - 1	SUBJECTIVE LAW AND FORM
FORM	091 - 2	FORM FINALLY BECOMES SOUL-STUFF AGAIN
FORM	095 - 2	ITSELF CREATE A NEW FORM
FORM	100 - 2	SPIRIT PASSING INTO FORM
FORM	100 - 3	FORM IS A MATERIALIZATION FROM THE
FORM	100 - 3	FORM IS ENTIRELY IN THE REALM OF EFFECT
FORM	101 - 2	WE HAVE FORM AND TIME
FORM	101 - 2	FORM IS REAL AS FORM
FORM	101 - 5	BRING THIS IDEA INTO FORM
FORM	104 - 3	FORM WITHIN THE VERY FORM

FORM	105 - 2	SPIRIT LETS FALL THE FORM
FORM	117 - 2	FORM TO A FORMLESS STUFF
FORM	129 - 2	LAW TO PRODUCE FORM
FORM	131 - 6	ONLY THING THAT CHANGES IS FORM
FORM	165 - 1	WE CALL FORM OR CREATION
FORM	183 - 1	REPRODUCE THEMSELVES IN FORM
FORM	184 - 2	NEVER BOUND BY THE FORM IT TAKES
FORM	190 - 3	NO FORM OF CURE WILL BE PERMANENT
FORM	191 - 3	NO OBJECTION TO ANY FORM OF HEALING
FORM	195 - 2	FORM OF SOME DESIRE IN OUR LIVES
FORM	197 - 1	BECOMES DEFINITE FORM
FORM	208 - 5	GOD IS CONSCIOUS OF FORM
FORM	268 - 3	BUT WILL TAKE FORM
FORM	277 - 2	IT WILL TAKE FORM
FORM	285 - 2	FORM OF THE THOUGHT OF SPIRIT
FORM	296 - 1	REFLECTS INTO MIND TENDS TO TAKE FORM
FORM	310 - 2	ALL PHYSICAL FORM IS MADE OF ONE
FORM	311 - 4	PHYSICAL FORM IS REAL
FORM	312 - 2	GOD KNOWS FORM BUT NOT SIZE
FORM	317 - 2	FROM ANY FORM OF LIMITATION
FORM	373 - 3	BODY OF FORM IS THE NECESSARY OUTCOME
FORM	374 - 5	FORM IS NECESSARY TO SELF-EXPRESSION
FORM	375 - 1	SOUL CLOTHES ITSELF IN FORM
FORM	375 - 2	THE OUTER BODY IN FORM
FORM	376 - 1	FORM CAN LIE WITHIN FORM
FORM	381 - 4	THE FORM FOR REAL SUBSTANCE
FORM	392 - 2	WAITS TO BE CALLED INTO FORM
FORM	404 - 1	IT KNOWS FORM BUT NOT SIZE
FORM	404 - 1	IDEAS ARE FORM
FORM	407 - 2	ALL FORM IS TEMPORARY
FORM	411 - 4	TAKES ON FORM, COLOR
FORM	412 - 2	FORM TO WHICH WE GIVE OUR ATTENTION
FORM	461 - 4	CONTEMPLATION CREATES A FORM
FORMED	166 - 2	THIS IS A FORMED TREATMENT
FORMED	415 - 2	FORMED BETWEEN THE SEEN
FORMING	180 - 3	FORMING WITHIN HIM
FORMLESS	066 - 5	ITSELF IS FORMLESS
FORMLESS	096 - 3	IT IS FORMLESS
FORMLESS	100 - 3	FORM IS WITHIN THE FORMLESS
FORMLESS	116 - 3	CONSTANTLY FLOWING FORMLESS SUBSTANCE
FORMLESS	311 - 1	CHANGES BUT THE FORMLESS NEVER
FORMLESS	317 - 2	HE TURNS TO THE FORMLESS
FORMLESS	392 - 2	AN ABSTRACT AND FORMLESS STATE
FORMLESS	392 - 2	FORMLESS BUT READY TO TAKE FORM
FORMLESS	393 - 4	ALL FORMS RETURN INTO THE FORMLESS
FORMLESS	401 - 2	WE DEAL WITH THE FORMLESS
FORMLESS	483 - 2	THE FORMLESS CREATES FORM
FORMS	045 - 2	FORMS ARE BUT DIFFERENT MANIFESTATIONS
FORMS	052 - 4	OBJECTIVE FORMS AND CONDITIONS
FORMS	070 - 1	FROM ETERNITY TO ETERNITY FORMS
FORMS	070 - 1	AND NUMBERLESS FORMS
FORMS	100 - 3	SUBSTANCE OF ALL FORMS
FORMS	184 - 2	NOT ONLY FILLS ALL FORMS
FORMS	191 - 4	IN ALL FORMS OF WORSHIP
FORMS	197 - 2	FORMS OF THOUGHT WHICH HE IMAGES

FORMS	406 - 2	FORMS COME AND GO BUT
FORMS	493 - 4	FORMS COME FROM ONE ULTIMATE
FORMULATED	239 - 3	FORMULATED AS TO RECOGNIZE
FORTH	334 - 4	FORTH AGAIN INTO CREATION
FORTH	388 - 1	COMING FORTH OF GOD
FORTHCOMING	193 - 4	FORTHCOMING IN THE EXPERIENCE
FORTUNE	187 - 3	GOOD FORTUNE AND BAD
FORTY	226 - 3	FORTY DARE TO UNDERTAKE
FORTY YEARS	226 - 3	FORTY YEARS OF AGE IS EASILY FATIGUED
FOR US	141 - 2	SPIRIT CAN DO FOR US ONLY
FORWARD	192 - 2	LOOK FORWARD TO THE DAY
FORWARD	387 - 1	EVOLUTION CARRIES US FORWARD
FORWARD	439 - 2	PRESS BOLDLY FORWARD
FOUND	364 - 2	WE HAVE FOUND IT
FOUND	364 - 2	WE HAVE FOUND THE LAW
FOUNDATION	060 - 3	FOUNDATION OF THE HUMAN RACE
FOUNDATION	159 - 2	FOUNDATION FOR CORRECT MENTAL TREATMENT
FOUNDATION	438 - 3	FOUNDATION OF THE UNIVERSE
FOUNDATIONS	471 - 1	FOUNDATIONS OF THE UNIVERSE
FOUNDRY	047 - 5	IN AN IRON FOUNDRY
FOUNTAIN	100 - 3	FOUNTAIN OF ALL IDEAS
FOUNTAIN	152 - 3	CONTACT WITH THE FOUNTAIN OF WISDOM
FOUNTAIN	446 - 2	NEVER-FAILING FOUNTAIN OF LIFE
FOUNTS	066 - 3	FOUNTS FROM WHICH WE GATHER
FOUR	114 - 3	HAVING THREE OR FOUR MINDS
FOUR MEN	286 - 1	FOUR MEN, A, B, C, AND D
FRACTIONAL	104 - 3	A FRACTIONAL PART
FRAGMENTS	447 - 2	WE SEEK FRAGMENTS
FRAILTIES	458 - 2	FRAILTIES OF HUMAN NATURE
FRAMED	153 - 2	OUR PRAYER IS FRAMED IN WORDS
FRAMED	178 - 2	BEFORE OUR PRAYER IS FRAMED
FRAUGHT	398 - 2	FRAUGHT WITH THE GREATEST MEANING
FRAUGHT	470 - 5	BE FRAUGHT WITH HAPPINESS
FREE	032 - 1	BE MADE FREE AND HAPPY
FREE	033 - 2	TRUTH WILL AUTOMATICALLY FREE HIM
FREE	037 - 1	WE ARE FIRST FREE
FREE	057 - 1	TRUTH MAY MAKE ME FREE
FREE	107 - 3	FREE FROM THE BONDAGE OF SICKNESS
FREE	160 - 3	FREE US FROM THIS IGNORANCE
FREE	184 - 2	CONDITION BUT IS FOREVER FREE
FREE	223 - 2	FREE FROM ANY SENSE
FREE	232 - 5	TRUTH SHALL MAKE YOU FREE
FREE	248 - 3	TRUTH SHALL MAKE YOU FREE
FREE	250 - 5	FREE AND UNAFRAID
FREE	264 - 1	TRUTH MAKES ME FREE
FREE	295 - 2	BUT OURSELVES THAT CAN FREE US
FREE	296 - 1	THE TRUTH SHALL MAKE YOU FREE
FREE	321 - 1	WHICH BINDS HIM WILL FREE HIM
FREE	395 - 2	MAN IS FREE TO DO AS HE WILLS
FREE	439 - 1	THAT OUR HEARTS MAY BE FREE
FREE	488 - 3	PURE SPIRIT WE ARE MADE FREE
FREED	244 - 1	I AM FREED FROM THE BELIEF
FREED	491 - 1	FATHER'S HOUSE AS FREED SOULS
FREEDOM	025 - 2	THE SEED OF FREEDOM MUST BE PLANTED
FREEDOM	025 - 3	THE DIVINE PLAN IS ONE OF FREEDOM

FREEDOM	025 – 3	FREEDOM IS THE BIRTHRIGHT OF EVERY LIVING
FREEDOM	025 – 3	EXPRESS ITSELF IN TERMS OF FREEDOM
FREEDOM	026 – 1	OF A FREEDOM WHICH THE SOUL CRAVES
FREEDOM	030 – 4	LIES THE PATH TO FREEDOM
FREEDOM	031 – 2	THE ROAD TO FREEDOM LIES
FREEDOM	046 – 3	TO EXPRESS FREEDOM
FREEDOM	055 – 1	HIS STATEMENTS OF FREEDOM
FREEDOM	108 – 1	POWER TO BACK UP THAT FREEDOM
FREEDOM	108 – 3	FREEDOM OF WILL MEANS THE ABILITY TO DO
FREEDOM	109 – 2	FREEDOM UNDER COMPULSION
FREEDOM	110 – 2	FREEDOM IMPLIES THE POSSIBILITY OF
FREEDOM	128 – 3	NOTHING BUT FREEDOM
FREEDOM	134 – 1	WITHIN HIMSELF THE KEY TO FREEDOM
FREEDOM	185 – 2	ROYAL ROAD TO FREEDOM
FREEDOM	189 – 3	BECAUSE TRUTH IS FREEDOM
FREEDOM	209 – 5	BY OUR VERY FREEDOM
FREEDOM	241 – 1	THERE IS PERFECT FREEDOM
FREEDOM	241 – 1	IN THIS FREEDOM NOTHING CAN BIND
FREEDOM	241 – 2	GOD IS HIS FREEDOM
FREEDOM	243 – 3	FREEDOM OF THIS GOD-LIFE
FREEDOM	259 – 2	FEEL MY FREEDOM
FREEDOM	259 – 2	THIS FREEDOM I REJOICE
FREEDOM	267 – 2	FREEDOM FROM SUCH LIMITATION
FREEDOM	268 – 3	MANIFEST THE FREEDOM
FREEDOM	276 – 1	IS THE LAW OF FREEDOM
FREEDOM	295 – 1	GIVEN US FREEDOM FROM BONDAGE
FREEDOM	302 – 2	DECLARE YOUR FREEDOM
FREEDOM	392 – 1	PRODUCE EITHER FREEDOM OR BONDAGE
FREEDOM	402 – 4	IS ONE OF FREEDOM
FREEDOM	411 – 2	COULD AS EASILY CREATE FREEDOM
FREEDOM	411 – 3	THE REAL FREEDOM EXISTS
FREEDOM	416 – 1	MAY NOT BE REFLECTING FREEDOM
FREEDOM	417 – 2	FREEDOM RATHER THAN BONDAGE
FREEDOM	488 – 2	FREEDOM AND LIBERTY ARE ALSO
FREEDOM	502 – 7	FREEDOM AND NOT OF BONDAGE
FREE-FLOWING	242 – 1	FREE-FLOWING LIFE OF SPIRIT
FREELY	440 – 2	FREELY YE HAVE RECEIVED, FREELY GIVE
FREES	078 – 2	FREES THE WISE
FREES	260 – 2	SPIRIT FREES US FROM EVERY TYPE OF BONDAGE
FREE SPIRIT	081 – 5	IT IS FREE SPIRIT
FREE WILL	071 – 2	SELF-CHOICE AND FREE WILL
FREE WILL	130 – 3	FREE WILL AND SELF-CHOICE CAUSE
FREE WILL	209 – 5	FREE WILL CREATES THE CONDITIONS
FREE WILL	210 – 1	FREE WILL MEANS MERELY
FREQUENTLY	149 – 1	QUESTIONS MOST FREQUENTLY ASKED
FRESH	403 – 4	A FRESH STARTING POINT
FRESHNESS	235 – 4	REMOVED BY A FRESHNESS OF THOUGHT
FRICTION	227 – 1	FRICTION TOOK PLACE
FRIEND	297 – 2	WANT A FRIEND, BE A FRIEND
FRIEND	298 – 2	WHOLE WORLD AS YOUR FRIEND
FRIEND	299 – 1	WORLD AS HIS FRIEND AND LOVES IT
FRIENDS	077 – 3	BETWEEN FRIENDS THERE IS
FRIENDS	147 – 2	A WORLD PEOPLED WITH FRIENDS
FRIENDS	231 – 6	FEAR OF LOSS OF FRIENDS
FRIENDS	279 – 1	IF WE ARE WITHOUT FRIENDS

FRIENDS	298 - 2	FIND WE ARE WITHOUT FRIENDS
FRIENDS	300 - 3	LAW AND THE SPIRIT AS FRIENDS
FRIENDS	380 - 2	FRIENDS ARE ALWAYS IN OUR MENTAL
FRIENDS	384 - 4	FRIENDS WHO ARE ON THE OTHER SIDE
FRIENDS	384 - 4	MET BY LOVING FRIENDS
FRIENDS	385 - 2	AGAIN MEET THOSE FRIENDS
FRIENDS	387 - 3	FRIENDS HAVE MET THEM
FRIENDS	421 - 4	BETWEEN FRIENDS ON THE SUBJECTIVE SIDE
FRIENDSHIP	298 - 4	FOR GENUINE FRIENDSHIP
FRIENDSHIP	318 - 4	NEED FOR LOVE AND FRIENDSHIP
FRIENDSHIP	388 - 2	JOY OF FRIENDSHIP AND LOVE
FROLICKED	041 - 3	HAS FROLICKED WITH HIM AT PLAY
FROWARD	402 - 3	WILT SHOW THYSELF FROWARD
FRUIT	313 - 4	IT SHALL NOT BEAR FRUIT
FRUIT	474 - 2	FRUIT OF DUAL EXPERIENCE
FRUIT	481 - 7	THAT YE BEAR MUCH FRUIT
FRUITION	270 - 6	ITS OWN FRUITION
FRUITION	477 - 4	DREAMS TO COME TO FULL FRUITION
FRUITS	436 - 2	TRUTH BY ITS FRUITS
FRUSTRATION	235 - 3	THE FRUSTRATION WHICH
FULFILL	084 - 1	SPIRIT OPERATES TO FULFILL
FULFILL	459 - 2	WE FULFILL GOD'S LAW
FULFILL	477 - 7	FULFILL IT EXCEPT BY TEACHING
FULFILLING	408 - 2	LOVE IS THE FULFILLING
FULFILLING	409 - 4	WE ARE FULFILLING OUR DESTINY
FULFILLMENT	057 - 1	BROUGHT TO ITS FULFILLMENT
FULFILLMENT	273 - 2	DEMAND IS CREATED, ITS FULFILLMENT
FULFILLMENT	355 - 2	FULFILLMENT OF ITS DESIRE IN MOTION
FULFILLS	233 - 3	LOVE FULFILLS ALL THE LAWS OF LIFE
FULL	168 - 3	FULL SENSE OF THE SACREDNESS
FULL	377 - 2	IN FULL AND COMPLETE RETENTION
FULLEST	289 - 2	WORD FOR THE FULLEST EXPRESSION
FULLNESS	492 - 6	FULLNESS OF GOD IS TO MANIFEST
FULL-ORBED	109 - 2	FULL-ORBED WITH ALL HIS FREEDOM
FULL-ORBED	162 - 5	SPRING FULL-ORBED INTO BEING
FULL-ORBED	391 - 4	APPEARS FULL-ORBED IN MAN ALONE
FULL-ORBED	468 - 1	SPRING FORTH FULL-ORBED
FULL-ORBED	473 - 6	COME FULL-ORBED INTO INDIVIDUALITY
FUMING	469 - 1	FUMING WITH ANGER OVER HIS
FUNCTION	058 - 1	CREATIVE FUNCTION IN HIS LIFE
FUNCTION	092 - 2	FUNCTION ACCORDING TO THE LAW
FUNCTION	254 - 2	PERFORM THEIR NATURAL FUNCTION
FUNCTION	391 - 3	MAN MAY FUNCTION INDIVIDUALLY
FUNCTION	435 - 4	SPIRITUAL FUNCTION OF INTELLIGENCE
FUNCTION	500 - 3	WAY THE UNIVERSE COULD FUNCTION
FUNCTIONING	124 - 1	FUNCTIONING AT DIFFERENT LEVELS
FUNCTIONING	394 - 4	MIND OF GOD FUNCTIONING
FUNCTIONS	232 - 1	INTERFERING WITH THE FUNCTIONS
FUNCTIONS	347 - 2	MENTALITY WHICH FUNCTIONS CONSCIOUSLY
FUNCTIONS	395 - 2	FUNCTIONS OF UNIVERSAL MIND
FUNDAMENTAL	036 - 1	TO A FUNDAMENTAL UNIT
FUNDAMENTAL	082 - 3	THE FUNDAMENTAL PREMISE UPON
FUNDAMENTAL	086 - 4	FUNDAMENTAL TO OUR PRACTICE
FUNDAMENTAL	363 - 3	FUNDAMENTAL TO HIS CONCEPT OF LIFE
FUNDAMENTAL	406 - 1	FUNDAMENTAL TO OUR CONCEPT

FUNDAMENTAL LAWS	340 - 3	FUNDAMENTAL LAWS OF NECESSITY
FUNDAMENTALLY	201 - 4	MAN IS FUNDAMENTALLY PERFECT
FUNDAMENTALLY	313 - 2	DIFFERENT YET FUNDAMENTALLY ALIKE
FURNISHES	313 - 2	FURNISHES THE BACKGROUND
FURNISHING	373 - 3	FURNISHING A VEHICLE
FURTHER	129 - 3	FURTHER EVOLUTION MUST BE
FUTILE	372 - 3	ATTEMPT TO DO SO IS FUTILE
FUTURE	044 - 2	FUTURE POSSIBILITY FOR THE RACE
FUTURE	095 - 1	NO PAST, PRESENT OR FUTURE
FUTURE	138 - 4	FATHER OF THE FUTURE
FUTURE	246 - 2	NOT HAVE FEAR FOR THE FUTURE
FUTURE	246 - 2	FUTURE IS BRIGHT WITH PROMISE
FUTURE	246 - 2	NO FUTURE TO BE AFRAID OF
FUTURE	264 - 3	NO PAST, PRESENT, AND FUTURE TO IT
FUTURE	384 - 4	JUDGING THE FUTURE BY THE PAST
FUTURE	471 - 4	FUTURE WILL ALL BE GOOD
FUTURE DATE	346 - 1	ACHIEVED AT SOME FUTURE DATE
FUTURITY	289 - 4	IN A STATE OF FUTURITY

G

GAINED	053 - 5	GAINED BY THE APPLICATION OF
GAINED	502 - 2	NOTHING IS GAINED BY HOLDING
GALILEE	462 - 4	GALILEE NEARLY TWO THOUSAND YEARS AGO
GALLERY	348 - 1	COMPARED TO A PICTURE GALLERY
GAME	194 - 4	GAME OF LIVING COMMENCES
GAME	194 - 5	PART OF THE GAME SHE IS PLAYING
GAPS	378 - 3	LEAVES NO GAPS AND PROVIDES
GARDENER	039 - 3	GARDENER GOES FORTH IN FAITH
GARDENER	103 - 2	THE GARDENER FINDS
GARDENER	289 - 4	GARDENER HOLDS HIS SEED IN HIS HAND
GARDEN OF EDEN	473 -3	GARDEN OF EDEN TYPIFIES LIFE
GARMENTS	447 -1	CLAD IN GARMENTS OF RIGHTEOUSNESS
GARNER	485 -5	GARNER KNOWLEDGE FROM EXPERIENCE
GATES	430 -1	GATES WITH PEACE IN THEIR MINDS
GATEWAY	358 -5	OUR OWN NATURE IS THE GATEWAY
GATEWAY	504 -2	THROUGH THE GATEWAY OF LOVE
GATHER	113 -2	WHICH WE GATHER KNOWLEDGE
GATHER	385 - 1	GATHER THE EXPERIENCE NECESSARY
GAVE	334 - 4	GAVE HE THE POWER
GAVE	464 - 2	NO MAN GAVE UNTO HIM
GAZE	284 - 4	FASTENS ITS GAZE UPON A SOLID REALITY
GAZE	491 - 4	IF WE GAZE LONGINGLY AT JOY
GENERATE	301 - 2	ACTIVITY WHICH WE GENERATE
GENERATE	346 - 2	CAN GENERATE AT THAT TIME
GENERATED	398 - 2	MAY BE CONSCIOUSLY GENERATED
GENERATED	498 - 4	SHOULD BE CONSCIOUSLY GENERATED
GENERATES	476 - 3	ONE GENERATES, THE OTHER DISTRIBUTES
GENERIC	408 - 1	GENERIC MAN MUST BE HELD
GENERIC	473 - 3	MAN IN GENERAL, GENERIC MAN
GENERIC	477 - 5	PRINCIPLE INHERENT IN GENERIC MAN
GENERIC	480 - 6	THIS SON IS GENERIC
GENERIC	493 - 5	GENERIC MAN OR THE UNIVERSAL SON

GENIUS	103 - 2	THE SPIRITUAL GENIUS DISCLOSES
GENIUS	186 - 4	SPIRITUAL GENIUS WOULD HAVE TO BE
GENIUS	315 - 1	SPIRITUAL GENIUS HAS TAUGHT
GENIUS	387 - 3	EVERYONE A BUDDING GENIUS
GENIUS	394 - 5	ACCESS TO THE ORIGINAL CREATIVE GENIUS
GENIUS	415 - 2	GENIUS LIES BURIED UNTIL
GEOLOGIST	103 - 2	GEOLOGIST FINDS THE IMPRINT
GERANIUM	329 - 2	GERANIUM PLANT THE REFLECTION
GESTURE	478 - 2	IMPATIENT GESTURE OF THE SOUL
GET	266 - 2	CAN GET WHAT YOU WANT
GETHSEMANE	277 - 2	IN THE GARDEN OF GETHSEMANE
GET RICH QUICK	266 - 1	GET RICH QUICK SCHEME
GETTING	044 - 4	WITH ALL OUR GETTING
GHOST	314 - 3	THAT PERTAINS TO GHOST WALKING
GIFT	036 - 3	NO GIFT THAT WE DO NOT ACCEPT
GIFT	042 - 4	NOT YET ACCEPTED THE GREATER GIFT
GIFT	151 - 4	THE SPIRIT BRINGS ITS GIFT
GIFT	280 - 3	CAN BE NO GIFT WITHOUT A RECEIVER
GIFT	280 - 1	ETERNAL GIFT IS ALWAYS MADE
GIFT	280 - 1	THE GIFT OF GOD IS THE NATURE
GIFT	280 - 1	CANNOT HELP MAKING THE GIFT
GIFT	280 - 1	GOD IS THE GIFT
GIFT	280 - 3	THE GIFT WITHOUT THE GIVER IS BARE
GIFT	285 - 4	THE SPIRIT WILL MAKE THE GIFT
GIFT	285 - 4	GIFT TO THE ALTAR
GIFT	405 - 1	OUR PRIVILEGE TO ACCEPT THE GIFT
GIFT	405 - 2	GIFT OF HEAVEN IS FOREVER MADE
GIFT	499 - 3	GIFT COMETH FROM THE FATHER
GIFT	504 - 1	GIFT OF HEAVEN IS LIFE
GIFTS	270 - 6	MULTIPLY OUR GIFTS
GIFTS	423 - 2	GIFTS OF HEAVEN COME ALIKE TO ALL
GIFTS	423 - 2	USE THESE GIFTS IS ALL THAT MATTERS
GIFTS	430 - 3	GIFTS BROUGHT TO THE ALTAR OF LIFE
GIFTS	436 - 1	HOW MUCH MORE WILL GOD GIVE GOOD GIFTS
GIFTS	459 - 2	GOD'S GIFTS ARE GIVEN AS FREELY
GIGANTIC	187 - 1	ASSUMED GIGANTIC PROPORTIONS
GIVE	060 - 1	GIVE UP ANYTHING AND EVERYTHING
GIVE	151 - 4	IT CAN GIVE TO US ONLY WHAT WE TAKE
GIVE	192 - 2	GIVE HIS WHOLE TIME
GIVE	267 - 2	MUST BE WILLING TO GIVE
GIVE	361 - 3	TO ALL WHO WILL I GIVE LIFE
GIVE	361 - 4	ALL THAT I HAVE I GIVE
GIVE	368 - 4	GIVE ONLY WHAT WE HAVE
GIVE	435 - 2	GIVE THAT WHICH WE DO NOT POSSESS
GIVE	461 - 3	GIVE ME THE PORTION OF GOODS
GIVE	464 - 3	GIVE UNTO US BUT OURSELVES
GIVE	498 - 3	GIVE US ONLY WHAT WE TAKE
GIVEN	058 - 2	GIVEN TO IT BY THE MIND
GIVEN	395 - 1	WE ARE GIVEN THE POWER
GIVEN	397 - 2	IS GIVEN US TO BE USED
GIVEN	405 - 2	ALL THINGS ARE GIVEN UNTO US
GIVEN	406 - 1	THAT WHICH WE CAN TAKE IS GIVEN US
GIVEN	423 - 2	IS GIVEN WHAT HE NEEDS
GIVEN	449 - 6	TO HIM SHALL BE GIVEN
GIVER	150 - 1	DIVINE AND IMPARTIAL GIVER

GIVER	404 - 5	THAT GOD IS THE GIVER
GIVES	383 - 2	NO ONE GIVES TO US BUT OURSELVES
GIVES	396 - 2	HE GIVES IT POWER
GIVES	405 - 2	GOD GIVES IN THE ABSTRACT
GIVES	462 - 1	GIVES US WHAT WE ASK
GIVES WAY	359 - 5	HUMAN GIVES WAY TO THE DIVINE
GIVE UP	455 - 4	GIVE UP ALL ELSE TO ATTAIN IT
GIVING	204 - 4	GIVING A TREATMENT YOU ARE THINKING
GIVING	267 - 2	GIVING LIFE IS SELF-EXPRESSED
GIVING	308 - 2	HAVE IN GIVING A TREATMENT
GIVING	440 - 2	LAW OF GIVING AND RECEIVING
GIVING	445 - 6	THE SPIRIT IS EVER GIVING
GIVINGNESS	041 - 3	A DIVINE GIVINGNESS
GIVINGNESS	043 - 1	LOVE IS THE DIVINE GIVINGNESS
GIVINGNESS	404 - 3	COMPLETE GIVINGNESS OF THE SPIRIT
GIVINGNESS	460 - 6	GOD IS THE DIVINE GIVINGNESS
GLAD	254 - 2	HEALED AND MADE GLAD
GLADNESS	272 - 1	GLADNESS THEN WE SHOULD MAKE KNOWN
GLANCE	418 - 5	WITH RIGHT GLANCE
GLASS	489 - 5	BEHOLDING AS IN A GLASS
GLASSES	220 - 2	TAKE OFF MY GLASSES
GLASSES	220 - 2	WILL NO LONGER NEED GLASSES
GLASSES	231 - 3	IF WE FIND GLASSES HELPFUL
GLEAM	042 - 3	SOME GLEAM OF THE ETERNAL GLORY
GLIMPSE	327 - 3	GLIMPSE OF ULTIMATE REALITY
GLOBE	072 - 4	COMMERCE AROUND THE GLOBE
GLOBE	328 - 3	HE HAS BELTED THE GLOBE
GLOBE	348 - 4	MENTAL ATMOSPHERE OF THE GLOBE
GLORIFIED	313 - 4	FATHER GLORIFIED IN THE SON
GLORIFIED	480 - 4	FATHER IS GLORIFIED
GLORIFIED	481 - 7	HEREIN IS MY FATHER GLORIFIED
GLORIFY	230 - 5	WE GLORIFY THE GOOD
GLORIFY	430 - 2	GLORIFY THAT INDWELLING GOD
GLORIOUS	067 - 2	WHAT A GLORIOUS CONCEPT
GLORY	042 - 3	GLEAM OF THE ETERNAL GLORY
GLORY	188 - 3	BATHING ALL LIFE IN GLORY
GLORY	251 - 2	GLORY OF MY THOUGHT
GLORY	256 - 5	THE GLORY OF MY THOUGHT MAKES ME
GLORY	338 - 3	TRANSFORMED FROM GLORY TO GLORY
GLORY	365 - 3	HELL AND ALL FOR HIS GLORY
GLORY	388 - 1	THE GLORY OF THE SOUL
GLORY	391 - 4	WITH GLORY AND HONOR
GLORY	490 - 2	LIMITATION TO THE GREATER GLORY
GLOW	414 - 4	GLOW WHEREVER THE THOUGHT TRAVELS
GLUTTON	253 - 1	IF ONE IS A GLUTTON, IT IS BECAUSE
GLUTTONOUS	253 - 1	BY BECOMING GLUTTONOUS
GNATS	442 - 4	STRAINING AT GNATS
GO	437 - 3	GO THY WAY
GOAL	383 - 3	ALL WILL ARRIVE AT THE FINAL GOAL
GOAL	434 - 1	SEEKING THE SAME GOAL
GOAL	469 - 3	US FORWARD TO THE GOAL
GO BACK	204 - 1	GO BACK TO YOUR ANALYSIS OF ULTIMATE
GOD	027 - 5	GOD IS IN, THROUGH, AROUND
GOD	028 - 4	WE SHALL ALWAYS BE IN GOD AND OF GOD
GOD	033 - 3	GOD IS ALWAYS GOD

GOD	036 - 1	NOT ROBBING GOD
GOD	041 - 1	WE CAN KNOW GOD ONLY
GOD	041 - 1	AS WE CAN BECOME GOD
GOD	041 - 3	PURE IN HEART SEE GOD
GOD	042 - 3	HE HAS PROCLAIMED GOD
GOD	063 - 2	IN THE BEGINNING, GOD
GOD	064 - 4	GOD IS NOT ONLY PURE SPIRIT
GOD	066 - 2	WE CALL THIS INTELLIGENCE GOD
GOD	069 - 4	GOD DID NOT MAKE GOD
GOD	075 - 2	GOD IS IN, THROUGH, AROUND
GOD	075 - 3	NO MAN HATH SEEN GOD
GOD	077 - 1	GOD EXISTS IN EVERYTHING
GOD	077 - 1	GOD EXISTS IN ME
GOD	078 - 1	GOD OPERATES AS LAW
GOD	082 - 1	GOD AND SOMETHING ELSE
GOD	103 - 2	THAT IS, GOD IS
GOD	141 - 2	GOD WHO IS PERSONAL TO US BY VIRTUE OF
GOD	149 - 4	NO GOD WHO CREATES US
GOD	188 - 3	ALL THERE REALLY IS IS GOD
GOD	190 - 1	A BELIEF IN GOD
GOD	203 - 5	GOD IS ALL THERE IS
GOD	208 - 5	GOD IS NOT CONSCIOUS OF MATTER
GOD	228 - 3	THIS BODY IS THE BODY OF GOD
GOD	247 - 2	THE WAY GOD GOES WITH US
GOD	273 - 4	THIS IS GOD IN MAN
GOD	275 - 3	THE SPIRIT OF GOD
GOD	292 - 4	GOD IS NOT GROWING
GOD	292 - 4	GOD IS NOT TRYING TO FIND
GOD	294 - 3	MAN'S LIFE IS GOD
GOD	301 - 4	GOD IS THE SILENT POWER
GOD	312 - 2	GOD KNOWS FORM BUT NOT SIZE
GOD	315 - 4	GOD IS NOT A FAILURE
GOD	317 - 3	HAVE THE FAITH OF GOD
GOD	317 - 3	DIFFERENT FROM A FAITH IN GOD
GOD	339 - 3	GOD MUST MOVE WITHIN GOD
GOD	339 - 4	GOD MOVES UPON GOD
GOD	339 - 4	IT IS GOD EXPRESSING HIMSELF
GOD	343 - 4	GOD OF HIS OWN INNER LIFE
GOD	362 - 4	ALL THAT WE ARE IS GOD
GOD	363 - 2	GOD IS PERSONAL TO ALL
GOD	373 - 1	GOD COULD NOT TELL WHY GOD
GOD	383 - 1	GOD NEITHER PUNISHES NOR REWARDS
GOD	388 - 3	GOD AS MAN, IN MAN, IS MAN
GOD	391 - 3	GOD WOULD NOT BE COMPLETELY
GOD	407 - 3	MIND OF GOD IS ALL CAUSATION
GOD	410 - 4	GOD IF THOU SEEST GOD
GOD	416 - 3	INTENTION GOD COULD HAVE
GOD	435 - 3	GOD IS INTELLIGENT MIND
GOD	438 - 4	GOD KNOWS NOTHING OF HIS SIN
GOD	443 - 3	GOD ALONE KNOWS THE REAL SON
GOD	446 - 4	GOD IS FREE, HAPPY, PEACEFUL
GOD	454 - 2	GOD CAN CONCEIVE OF MAN ONLY
GOD	455 - 6	PRAYS TO HIS GOD OF ART
GOD	459 - 3	GOD ALONE IS NOT ENOUGH
GOD	459 - 4	GOD AS THE LIFE PRINCIPLE IN ALL

GOD	461 – 4	GOD DID NOT ARGUE
GOD	464 – 4	GOD ALLOW SUCH A THING
GOD	464 – 4	GOD IS ALWAYS GOD
GOD	464 – 5	GOD CANNOT ENTER THE PIG PEN
GOD	466 – 7	GOD NEVER REPROACHES
GOD	477 – 3	GOD MUST FLOW THROUGH MAN
GOD	478 – 5	GOD IS LOVE
GOD	482 – 2	GOD GOES FORTH ANEW
GOD	482 – 3	GOD AS MAN, IN MAN, IS MAN
GOD	488 – 1	GOD OF THE LIVING
GOD	500 – 2	GOD IS NATURAL GOODNESS
GOD	501 – 2	GOD CANNOT HEAL THE SICK
GOD	501 – 6	GOD IS OF PURE EYE AND PERFECT MIND
GOD	502 – 4	GOD IS NATURAL GOODNESS
GOD	503 – 6	GOD IS NATURAL GOODNESS AND ETERNAL
GOD	503 – 7	GOD IS LOVE
GODHEAD	454 – 3	IN THE INFINITE GODHEAD
GODHEAD	454 – 3	GODHEAD ONE WITH THE PERFECT WHOLE
GOD HIMSELF	160 – 1	GOD HIMSELF GOES FORTH ANEW
GOD-INTENDED	338 – 3	ETERNAL GOD-INTENDED MAN
GOD-INTENDED	339 – 1	GOD-INTENDED MAN ALREADY KNOWS
GOD-KNOWING	139 – 1	SELF-KNOWING WHICH IS GOD-KNOWING
GOD-LIFE	239 – 3	GOD-LIFE ALL ABOUT
GOD-LIKE	198 – 1	GOD-LIKE THAT IS THE TRUEST
GODLIKE	178 – 5	GODLIKE THE MENTALITY
GODLIKE	186 – 3	THE MORE GODLIKE IT MUST BECOME
GODLIKE	186 – 4	GODLIKE OR CHRISTLIKE THE THOUGHT IS
GOD-ORDAINED	032 – 3	IS NOT GOD-ORDAINED
GOD-ORDAINED	337 – 1	THAT IT IS NOT GOD-ORDAINED
GOD SPEAKING	273 – 4	GOD SPEAKING AND GOD ANSWERING
GOD WILL NOT	151 – 4	GOD WILL NOT ANSWER MY PRAYER
GOD WILLS	459 – 2	GOD WILLS US TO HAVE EVERYTHING
GODS	088 – 2	NOT THREE GODS
GODS	131 – 2	BELIEF IN MANY GODS
GODS	333 – 5	YE ARE GODS
GOD'S LOVE	502 – 7	GOD'S LOVE IS COMPLETE IN US
GOD'S WORD	117 – 1	GOD'S WORD IN THE GREAT CREATION
GOING	399 – 3	EXPECT SOMETHING IS GOING TO HAPPEN
GOOD	032 – 3	BEHIND EVERYTHING IS GOOD
GOOD	033 – 2	NATURE MAY BE FILLED WITH GOOD
GOOD	033 – 2	REALLY GOOD AND SATISFYING
GOOD	035 – 1	WE TAKE THE GOOD WHEREVER
GOOD	035 – 1	GOOD IS UNIVERSAL
GOOD	036 – 4	IT IS GOOD
GOOD	037 – 3	EXPERIENCE A LITTLE GOOD
GOOD	037 – 3	EXPERIENCE A GREATER GOOD
GOOD	038 – 5	HAVE OR ACCOMPLISH GOOD
GOOD	039 – 1	KNOW THAT GOOD IS NOW MINE
GOOD	039 – 3	CONCEIVE ONLY A LITTLE GOOD
GOOD	039 – 4	GOOD IS WITHOUT BOUNDS
GOOD	039 – 4	POWER OF GOOD
GOOD	039 – 4	WE EXPERIENCE GOOD AND EVIL
GOOD	039 – 5	ACCEPT TODAY MORE GOOD
GOOD	044 – 4	KNOWLEDGE OF SOME PARTICULAR GOOD
GOOD	045 – 5	BOTH GOOD AND EVIL

GOOD	046 - 5	CONSCIOUS OF THIS PARTICULAR GOOD
GOOD	048 - 2	IF WE WISH A CERTAIN GOOD
GOOD	048 - 2	REALIZATION OF THIS SPECIFIC GOOD
GOOD	048 - 2	OF THIS GOOD IN OUR LIVES
GOOD	049 - 3	SOME GOOD WILL COME ALONG
GOOD	049 - 4	HOPE IS GOOD
GOOD	050 - 2	INFINITE GOOD IS OURS
GOOD	055 - 2	EXPECTANCY OF GOOD
GOOD	055 - 2	LAW OF GOOD
GOOD	065 - 7	SAW THAT IT WAS GOOD
GOOD	075 - 1	DERIVE THIS GREAT GOOD
GOOD	092 - 2	KNOWS NEITHER GOOD NOR BAD
GOOD	103 - 1	THROUGH GOOD
GOOD	103 - 3	GOOD IN EVERYTHING
GOOD	137 - 1	NOTHING EITHER GOOD OR BAD
GOOD	151 - 2	THAN THE GOOD OF ALL MEN
GOOD	152 - 4	PRODUCTIVE OF THE HIGHEST GOOD
GOOD	156 - 2	MORE GOOD FOR ONE PERSON THAN ANOTHER
GOOD	157 - 3	GOOD WERE NOT ALREADY OURS
GOOD	161 - 3	INTERFERE WITH THE GENERAL GOOD
GOOD	162 - 5	KNOWLEDGE THAT GOD IS GOOD
GOOD	174 - 4	LAW IS NEITHER GOOD NOR BAD
GOOD	180 - 3	GREATEST GOOD THAT CAN COME TO ANYONE
GOOD	184 - 3	ALWAYS EXPECT THE GOOD
GOOD	185 - 2	LET US SEEK THE GOOD
GOOD	186 - 4	GOOD TREATMENT IS ALWAYS FILLED
GOOD	189 - 2	GOOD NEVER COMPROMISES
GOOD	189 - 3	IN THE ETERNAL LAW OF GOOD
GOOD	210 - 2	NEVER SAY I AM NOT GOOD
GOOD	217 - 2	DEVOTED TO HIS GOOD
GOOD	220 - 5	NOT GOOD ENOUGH TO TREAT
GOOD	229 - 5	KEPT SINGLE TO THE GOOD
GOOD	230 - 2	HIS ONENESS WITH ALL GOOD
GOOD	230 - 5	WE GLORIFY THE GOOD
GOOD	232 - 2	GOOD TO FLOW IN AND THROUGH ME
GOOD	235 - 2	EVERY THOUGHT UNLIKE GOD (GOOD)
GOOD	238 - 2	ELSE HE WILL DO BUT LITTLE GOOD
GOOD	243 - 1	THAT YOU ARE BUSY EXPRESSING GOOD
GOOD	243 - 2	INFLOW AND THE OUTFLOW OF GOOD
GOOD	243 - 2	YOU ARE SENSITIVE ONLY TO GOOD
GOOD	245 - 1	GOOD ALONE IS REAL AND TRUE
GOOD	245 - 1	INFINITE POWER FOR GOOD
GOOD	245 - 2	MIND TO CONTEMPLATE THE GOOD
GOOD	245 - 3	GAIN CONFIDENCE IN GOOD
GOOD	245 - 4	ONE UNBROKEN STREAM OF GOOD
GOOD	250 - 6	TO GIVE PEACE TO THE MIND IS GOOD
GOOD	256 - 5	GOD AS MY EVERPRESENT GOOD
GOOD	257 - 4	MY GOOD IS AROUND AND WITH ME
GOOD	265 - 1	THAT IT IS GOOD
GOOD	265 - 1	IT IS ALSO GOOD AND VERY GOOD
GOOD	268 - 1	DRAW A GREATER GOOD INTO HIS LIFE
GOOD	268 - 4	WILL OF GOD IS ALWAYS GOOD
GOOD	272 - 2	LED BY THE SPIRIT INTO ALL GOOD
GOOD	276 - 1	GOD IS GOOD
GOOD	278 - 2	OUR UNITY WITH GOOD

GOOD	288 – 2	GOOD INTO YOUR LIFE
GOOD	293 – 1	ALL THE GOOD I CAN EMBODY
GOOD	293 – 3	IN THIS MOMENT MY GOOD COMES TO ME
GOOD	298 – 3	MORE GOOD THAN BAD IN PEOPLE
GOOD	298 – 3	SEEING THE GOOD TENDS TO BRING IT FORTH
GOOD	300 – 3	FROM GOOD TO MORE GOOD
GOOD	315 – 1	TOO MUCH GOOD IN YOUR HAND
GOOD	321 – 1	SENSE OF SEPARATION FROM GOOD
GOOD	335 – 2	TO TURN FROM EVIL AND DO GOOD
GOOD	346 – 1	OF ALL EVIL BY GOOD
GOOD	383 – 2	PROBLEM OF GOOD AND EVIL
GOOD	405 – 2	NOT WITHHELD GOOD FROM US
GOOD	410 – 2	TO SOME DESIRED GOOD
GOOD	410 – 4	CAN WE SEE GOOD
GOOD	413 – 5	IS INDEPENDENT OF GOOD
GOOD	415 – 2	NO GOOD CAN COME TO US UNLESS
GOOD	430 – 5	GOOD TO THEM WHO WOULD
GOOD	430 – 6	GOOD FOR THE PURE LOVE OF GOOD
GOOD	439 – 2	GOOD THE OLD HAS TO OFFER
GOOD	446 – 3	EVERYTHING MUST BE GOOD
GOOD	458 – 6	GOOD TO HAVE A HOME
GOOD	459 – 2	GOOD ENOUGH TO GO AROUND
GOOD	470 – 2	GOOD WHICH HE CONTEMPLATES
GOOD	485 – 5	ALL THINGS WORK FOR OUR GOOD
GOOD	487 – 7	GOOD IS THE ONLY POWER
GOODNESS	045 – 5	FIRST PRINCIPLE IS GOODNESS
GOODNESS	046 – 4	IT IS GOODNESS, LIFE, LAW
GOODNESS	065 – 7	GOD BEING GOODNESS
GOODNESS	159 – 3	SEEN GOODNESS, TRUTH, OR BEAUTY
GOODNESS	160 – 2	GOODNESS MUST BE GREATER THAN ANY
GOODNESS	161 – 3	CONTRADICT GOODNESS ITSELF
GOODNESS	264 – 5	GOODNESS AND BEAUTY FOLLOW ME
GOODNESS	284 – 2	THE ESSENCE OF GOODNESS
GOODNESS	308 – 1	SPIRITUALITY IS NATURAL GOODNESS
GOODNESS	428 – 3	DIVINE GOODNESS BEEN THE THEME OF OUR
GOODNESS	472 – 1	SPIRIT IS GOODNESS
GOODNESS	482 – 3	ETERNAL GOODNESS GIVES ITSELF TO ALL
GOOD PRACTICE	306 – 5	GOOD PRACTICE IS TO DWELL
GOOD REPORT	226 – 1	WHATSOEVER THINGS ARE OF GOOD REPORT
GOOD REPORT	496 – 4	THINGS WHICH ARE OF GOOD REPORT
GOVERN	065 – 6	POWER TO GOVERN THE UNIVERSE
GOVERN	412 – 2	MESSAGES WHICH GOVERN US
GOVERNED	142 – 1	UNIVERSE COULD BE GOVERNED
GOVERNED	258 – 4	GOVERNED BY ANY WEATHER
GOVERNING	284 – 5	HOW TO USE THE LAW GOVERNING
GOVERNING	315 – 4	GOD AS GOVERNING, CONTROLLING
GOVERNING	321 – 1	THE LAW GOVERNING THIS POWER
GOVERNING	434 – 6	CAUSE AND EFFECT GOVERNING ALL THINGS
GOVERNMENT	103 – 1	GOVERNMENT OF LAW
GOVERNMENT	408 – 2	ITS GOVERNMENT IS ONE OF LOVE
GOVERNS	034 – 3	THE MIND THAT GOVERNS EVERYTHING
GOVERNS	290 – 2	WHICH GOVERNS, GUIDES AND GUARDS
GRACE	256 – 3	SAY GRACE BEFORE MEALS
GRACE	280 – 2	WE GROW IN GRACE AS IT WERE
GRACE	455 – 3	GRACE TO A KINDNESS

GRACE	496 - 5	GRACE AND TRUTH ARE THE CORNERSTONES
GRADUAL	446 - 5	ONE OF A GRADUAL UNFOLDMENT
GRADUALLY	172 - 4	GRADUALLY BECOMES CONVINCED
GRADUALLY	271 - 4	SEE IT GRADUALLY TAKE FORM
GRADUALLY	294 - 1	WORLD IS GRADUALLY BEGINNING
GRADUALLY	300 - 3	GRADUALLY GO FROM GOOD TO MORE
GRADUALLY	490 - 3	GRADUALLY AS THIS PROCESS TAKES PLACE
GRANDEUR	307 - 1	THE GRANDEUR OF EVERYTHING
GRANDFATHER	128 - 2	THOSE OF HIS GRANDFATHER
GRAND MAN	408 - 3	IN THIS ONE OR GRAND MAN
GRASP	034 - 3	SOMETHING DIFFICULT TO GRASP
GRASP	124 - 3	WE SHOULD GRASP THE IDEA
GRASP	234 - 2	ABILITY TO GRASP IDEAS
GRATEFUL	231 - 3	GRATEFUL FOR THE HELP
GRATITUDE	497 - 2	GRATITUDE IS MOST SALUTORY
GRATITUDE	497 - 2	GRATITUDE IS ONE OF THE CHIEF GRACES
GRAVE	369 - 3	OVER DEATH AND THE GRAVE
GRAVE	371 - 1	GO WITH US BEYOND THE GRAVE
GRAVE	372 - 2	HE NOW IS BEYOND THE GRAVE
GRAVE	385 - 1	THE GRAVE ITS VICTORY
GRAVE	385 - 2	TO LIVE BEYOND THE GRAVE
GRAVE	387 - 2	DESIRES TO LIVE BEYOND THE GRAVE
GRAVE	429 - 1	AND ENDS WITH THE GRAVE
GRAVITATE	142 - 3	ALL ELSE MUST GRAVITATE
GRAVITATION	094 - 2	ATTRACTION AND REPULSION, GRAVITATION
GREAT	037 - 3	NO GREAT AND NO SMALL
GREAT	305 - 4	HOW GREAT A RESPONSIBILITY
GREAT	311 - 4	NO GREAT AND NO SMALL
GREATER	132 - 8	IS GREATER THAN THE SON
GREATER	314 - 1	FATHER IS GREATER THAN THE SON
GREATEST	073 - 2	GREATEST DISCOVERY OF ALL TIME
GREATEST	391 - 3	THE GREATEST DISCOVERY OF THE AGES
GREATEST	482 - 3	GREATEST OBJECT LESSON EVER TAUGHT
GREATEST POWER	483 - 5	THE GREATEST POWER KNOWN
GREATEST TRUTH	146 - 4	THIS GREATEST TRUTH ABOUT LIFE
GREAT LIGHT	502 - 6	ALL THAT HURTS TO THE GREAT LIGHT
GREAT SPIRIT	368 - 1	GREAT SPIRIT SPEAK THROUGH HIM
GREAT WHOLE	395 - 1	IN THE GREAT WHOLE
GREAT WORLD	393 - 2	GOD IN THE GREAT WORLD
GREED	232 - 5	GREED, UNDUE ACQUISITIVENESS
GREED	255 - 3	GREED, SELFISHNESS AND JEALOUSY
GREEK	137 - 1	GREEK PHILOSOPHERS UNDERSTOOD
GREEK	386 - 2	GREEK THOUGHT AND IDEALS
GREET	167 - 3	GREET THE DIVINITY IN EVERY MAN
GREETED	147 - 3	GREETED WITH OUTSTRETCHED HANDS
GRIEF	240 - 2	GRIEF OFTEN CAUSES INSTANT DEATH
GRIEF	253 - 3	CAUSED BY SUDDEN SHOCK AND GRIEF
GRIEF	387 - 3	OUR GRIEF OF HOPELESSNESS
GRIEF	417 - 2	JOY IN THE PLACE OF GRIEF
GRIEF	438 - 5	GRIEF OF HEART MIGHT BE RELIEVED
GRIEVE	387 - 3	GRIEVE OVER THE LOSS OF DEAR ONES
GRIEVE	389 - 1	GRIEVE NOT O'ER ITS FORM
GRIMM	380 - 3	THE RETURN OF PETER GRIMM
GROPING	381 - 1	SHE FELT A BLIND GROPING
GROUNDWORK	201 - 2	GROUNDWORK OF ALL MOVEMENT

GROW	201 - 3	GROW INTO DEEPER ASSURANCE
GROW	280 - 2	WE GROW IN POWER
GROW	398 - 5	GROW INTO THE UNDERSTANDING
GROW	402 - 1	BEGIN RIGHT WHERE WE ARE AND GROW
GROW	451 - 4	GROW INTO A REAL CONDITION
GROWING	271 - 3	GROWING IN OUR ABILITY
GROW OLD	249 - 2	NEED NOT GROW OLD
GROWS	162 - 5	GROWS BY KNOWLEDGE AND EXPERIENCE
GROWS	309 - 3	CONVICTION GROWS THE WORK IS DONE
GROWS OLD	239 - 3	AS ONE GROWS OLD
GROWTH	290 - 1	NATURAL LAW OF EVOLUTION AND GROWTH
GUARANTEE	122 - 2	AN ABSOLUTE GUARANTEE THAT HE
GUARANTEE	122 - 2	THE ONLY GUARANTEE OF HIS DIVINITY
GUARANTEE	238 - 2	GUARANTEE OF OUR DIVINITY
GUARANTEED	423 - 2	MAKES THE ATTEMPT, MUCH IS GUARANTEED
GUARD	453 - 5	BE ON GUARD AGAINST ACCEPTING
GUARDS	290 - 2	GOVERNS, GUIDES AND GUARDS
GUEST	041 - 3	SOFT TREAD OF THE UNSEEN GUEST
GUIDANCE	167 - 4	BELIEVE IN DIVINE GUIDANCE
GUIDANCE	272 - 3	GUIDANCE IS JUST AS TRUE IN INDIA
GUIDANCE	303 - 4	BY ALL POWER, BY ALL GUIDANCE
GUIDANCE	400 - 3	FOR GUIDANCE INTO THE KNOWLEDGE OF
GUIDE	054 - 1	WILLINGNESS TO LET THIS INNER SPIRIT GUIDE
GUIDE	153 - 5	THAT WILL GUIDE AND INSPIRE US
GUIDE	259 - 3	WILL GUIDE US INTO A PROPER DIET
GUIDE	259 - 3	GUIDE US INTO A PROPER DIET
GUIDE	273 - 1	WILL GUIDE US
GUIDE	435 - 2	GUIDE OUR BROTHER ARIGHT
GUIDE	477 - 4	INVISIBLE INTELLIGENCE TO GUIDE
GUIDED	056 - 4	MY AFFAIRS ARE DIVINELY GUIDED
GUIDED	234 - 3	GUIDED INTO ALL TRUTH
GUIDED	263 - 3	LED, GUIDED AND INSPIRED BY
GUIDED	272 - 2	GUIDED INTO TRUTH AND LIBERTY
GUIDED	331 - 4	WE ARE GUIDED DAILY
GUIDED	395 - 3	SUBJECTIVE MIND MUST BE GUIDED
GUIDES	395 - 2	MAN GUIDES IT IN HIS OWN LIFE
GUIDES	406 - 1	THE SPIRIT GUIDES
GUIDING	168 - 1	FOREVER GUIDING AND SUSTAINING
GUISES	402 - 3	PRESENTING ITSELF IN VARYING GUISES
GUTTER	127 - 2	LIES DRUNK IN THE GUTTER

H

HABIT	222 - 4	HABIT IS DESIRE OBJECTIFIED
HABIT	222 - 4	AT THE ROOT OF ALL HABIT
HABIT	223 - 1	NOT TREAT THAT HABIT
HABIT	223 - 1	FOR THE HABIT APPEARS TO HAVE
HABIT	223 - 2	HABIT IS COMPLETELY DESTROYED
HABIT	230 - 2	A HABIT OF SAYING I SEE
HABIT	262 - 1	FREE FROM THIS HABIT
HABITS	142 - 4	HABITS OF WRONG THINKING CAN BE
HABITS	232 - 4	MAN IN HIS ACQUISITIVE HABITS
HABITUAL	248 - 5	HABITUAL FEELING TOWARD PERSONS

HABITUAL	400 - 2	SUCCESS WILL BECOME HABITUAL
HABITUAL	450 - 4	THE HABITUAL FAILURE BEARS
HABITUAL	475 - 4	HABITUAL ATTITUDE TOWARD LIFE
HALF	119 - 3	THIS IS ONLY HALF THE TREATMENT
HALF	277 - 3	HALF USING THE LAW
HALF	468 - 1	IS TO GO HALF WAY
HALLUCINATION	108 - 2	AN ILLUSION OR HALLUCINATION
HALLUCINATIONS	328 - 5	HE IS SUBJECT TO HALLUCINATIONS
HALO	345 - 1	HALO AROUND THE HEADS OF SAINTS
HAND	153 - 2	THE HAND WRITES AND PASSES ON
HAND	212 - 3	SAW A PERFECT HAND
HAND	428 - 5	DIRECTLY BY THE HAND OF GOD HIMSELF
HAND	434 - 2	BY THE HAND OF THE ALMIGHTY
HAND IN HAND	408 - 2	LOVE AND LAW GO HAND IN HAND
HANDLE	304 - 2	HANDLE THE THOUGHT OF COMPETITION
HANDMAID	444 - 4	HANDMAID OF RELIGION AND PHILOSOPHY
HANDS	207 - 2	HANDS ON HIS PATIENT
HANDS	234 - 2	HANDS REPRESENT MAN'S ABILITY TO GRASP
HANDS	235 - 5	HANDS AND HOUSES
HANDS	384 - 4	LOVING HANDS TO GREET US
HANG	459 - 3	HANG ALL THE LAW AND THE PROPHETS
HANG-OVER	059 - 4	HANG-OVER OF BELIEF FROM PAST
HANGS	394 - 1	HANGS THE TALE OF GOOD AND EVIL
HAPPEN	128 - 2	HAPPEN TO HIM THAT DOES NOT HAPPEN
HAPPEN	274 - 2	MAKING THINGS HAPPEN
HAPPEN	274 - 2	WHICH THEY MAY HAPPEN
HAPPEN	300 - 2	HAPPEN TO HIM IN HIS OBJECTIVE
HAPPEN	399 - 5	LETTING SOMETHING HAPPEN
HAPPENING	309 - 4	ANYTHING IS REALLY HAPPENING
HAPPENINGS	413 - 5	BY OBSERVING OUTSIDE HAPPENINGS
HAPPENS	318 - 1	AS THIS HAPPENS A DEMONSTRATION
HAPPENS	441 - 3	HAPPENS THROUGH US
HAPPIER	266 - 1	HAPPIER CONDITIONS
HAPPILY	027 - 4	HAPPILY, WILLING TO ACCEPT
HAPPINESS	047 - 1	KEY TO HAPPINESS
HAPPINESS	163 - 3	THE HEALTH AND HAPPINESS
HAPPINESS	164 - 2	HAPPINESS AND PEACE
HAPPINESS	164 - 3	HEALTH, HAPPINESS AND SUCCESS
HAPPINESS	178 - 2	PRAYER IS ESSENTIAL TO HAPPINESS
HAPPINESS	223 - 2	EXPRESSING LIFE AND HAPPINESS
HAPPINESS	245 - 4	ROB US OF TODAY'S HAPPINESS
HAPPINESS	264 - 5	HAPPINESS AND WHOLENESS FILL
HAPPINESS	269 - 1	GREATER HAPPINESS, GREATER POWER
HAPPINESS	299 - 3	ALL HEALTH, ALL HAPPINESS, ALL SUCCESS
HAPPINESS	302 - 2	HIS MIND ON THOUGHTS OF HAPPINESS
HAPPINESS	314 - 2	IN HAPPINESS RATHER THAN IN MISERY
HAPPINESS	412 - 1	WITH PEACE AND HAPPINESS
HAPPINESS	498 - 5	UNITY INCLUDES HEALTH, HAPPINESS
HAPPY	032 - 1	SHALL BE MADE FREE AND HAPPY
HAPPY	044 - 3	A COMPLETE, NORMAL, HAPPY
HAPPY	046 - 3	TO BE WELL, HAPPY
HAPPY	060 - 3	HAPPY ARE WE IF
HAPPY	099 - 5	THE MIND, PEACEFUL AND HAPPY
HAPPY	161 - 3	THE RIGHT TO BE HAPPY
HAPPY	209 - 4	CAN MAKE US HAPPY

HAPPY	211 - 2	ARE HAPPY, FREE, SPONTANEOUS
HAPPY	246 - 2	TOMORROWS WILL BE HAPPY
HAPPY	250 - 5	A JOYOUS HAPPY EXPRESSION
HAPPY	263 - 5	MAKE LIFE HAPPY AND OPULENT
HAPPY	314 - 4	MORE OF WHAT IT TAKES TO BE HAPPY
HAPPY	383 - 2	SOME ARE HAPPY, SOME UNHAPPY
HAPPY	390 - 5	COMPLETE AND PERFECT, HAPPY AND WHOLE
HAPPY	402 - 1	HAPPY TO BEGIN RIGHT WHERE WE ARE
HAPPY	412 - 2	HAPPY IS THE ONE
HAPPY	434 - 1	HAPPY OUTLOOK ON LIFE IS ALWAYS
HAPPY	440 - 4	BECOMES NORMAL AND HAPPY
HARD	202 - 6	NOT BE THOUGHT OF AS HARD
HARD	209 - 5	WORK HARD ON THIS CASE
HARD	221 - 1	DISEASE IS HARD TO HEAL
HARD	263 - 1	TO DO WILL BE HARD OR EASY
HARD	414 - 1	THERE IS NO HARD
HARD	450 - 1	SOUNDS LIKE A VERY HARD SAYING
HARDEN	248 - 2	NEITHER HARDEN NOR SOFTEN
HARDENING	249 - 2	HARDENING OF THE ARTERIES
HARD SAYING	430 - 3	HERE IS A HARD SAYING
HARD SAYING	450 - 1	SOUNDS LIKE A VERY HARD SAYING
HARD SAYINGS	441 - 3	ONE OF THOSE HARD SAYINGS
HARKING	433 - 1	HARKING DOWN THE AGES
HARM	269 - 1	AS IT DOES NOT HARM ANYONE
HARM	270 - 2	AT THE SAME TIME HARM NO ONE
HARM	353 - 2	NO HARM CAN COME FROM IT
HARMLESS	353 - 2	NORMAL STATE OF MIND IS HARMLESS
HARMONIOUS	044 - 3	HARMONIOUS AND PEACEFUL EXISTENCE
HARMONIOUS	082 - 5	IT IS HARMONIOUS
HARMONIOUS	099 - 4	MUST BE PEACEFUL AND HARMONIOUS
HARMONIOUS	198 - 4	BODY TO BE HARMONIOUS
HARMONIOUS	198 - 4	IT IS HARMONIOUS
HARMONIOUS	218 - 2	PERFECT, HARMONIOUS AND WHOLE
HARMONIOUS	218 - 3	DENIAL OF AN HARMONIOUS
HARMONIOUS	231 - 5	ALL ACTION IS NORMAL, HARMONIOUS
HARMONIOUS	237 - 4	HARMONIOUS IN HIS THINKING
HARMONIOUS	238 -3	ITS ACTION IS HARMONIOUS
HARMONIOUS	250 -5	I AM HARMONIOUS, PEACEFUL
HARMONIOUS	254 -2	PERFECT AND HARMONIOUS RIGHT NOW
HARMONIOUS	259 - 1	HARMONIOUS IN EVERY CLIMATE
HARMONIOUS	306 - 3	A LITTLE MORE HARMONIOUS
HARMONIOUSLY	245 - 2	PEACEFULLY AND HARMONIOUSLY
HARMONIZE	252 - 4	CONSCIOUSLY HARMONIZE OURSELVES
HARMONIZE	493 - 2	WE HARMONIZE WITH THIS UNITY
HARMONIZES	219 - 1	HARMONIZES MAN'S ENTIRE BEING
HARMONY	053 - 3	WHICH IS NOT OF THE ORIGINAL HARMONY
HARMONY	053 - 3	ORIGINAL SPIRIT IS HARMONY
HARMONY	167 - 4	BY LOVE, HARMONY, AND PEACE
HARMONY	187 - 1	LOOK AT HARMONY, HAPPINESS
HARMONY	187 - 3	WE CAN PRODUCE HARMONY
HARMONY	211 - 3	THE LAW OF HARMONY
HARMONY	217 - 1	LACK OF AN IDEA OF HARMONY
HARMONY	219 - 1	IDEA OF DIVINE HARMONY
HARMONY	232 - 3	WILL PRODUCE HARMONY
HARMONY	233 - 4	IN THE RHYTHM AND HARMONY

HARMONY	239 – 3	HARMONY WITHIN US
HARMONY	242 – 2	IN PERFECT RHYTHM AND HARMONY
HARMONY	245 – 1	A STATEMENT OF HARMONY
HARMONY	245 – 2	MANIFESTS AS PERFECT HARMONY
HARMONY	247 – 1	I AM POISED IN HARMONY
HARMONY	247 – 1	MY PHYSICAL BODY WITH HARMONY
HARMONY	248 – 1	LOVE, HARMONY, AND PEACE REIGN
HARMONY	248 – 3	THE RHYTHMIC HARMONY OF LIFE
HARMONY	258 – 3	VIBRATION OF PERFECT HARMONY
HARMONY	269 – 1	BEAUTY, TRUTH AND HARMONY
HARMONY	363 – 4	THIS WILL WAS IN HARMONY
HARMONY	367 – 2	I HAVE HEARD THAT GREAT HARMONY
HARMONY	384 – 3	WITH THE LAW OF HARMONY
HARMONY	384 – 4	HARMONY WITH THE DIVINE LAW
HARMONY	409 – 3	TRUTH, GOODNESS AND HARMONY
HARMONY	430 – 3	DIVINE EAR IS ATTUNED TO HARMONY
HARMONY	432 – 1	HARMONY AND PERFECT LOVE
HARMONY	436 – 1	FUNDAMENTAL HARMONY
HARMONY	436 – 3	ENTERS THE KINGDOM OF HARMONY
HARMONY	446 – 3	MUST BE LOVE AND HARMONY
HARMONY	446 – 3	HARMONY WITH SOME SPECIAL GOOD
HARMONY	464 – 5	HARMONY CAN NEVER BECOME DISCORD
HARMONY	481 – 4	HARMONY ONLY THROUGH TRUE UNITY
HARMONY	484 – 2	WE LIVE IN HARMONY WITH IT
HARNESSED	362 – 2	HAS HARNESSED SUBTLE FORCES
HARVEST	448 – 5	BEAR A HARVEST OF GOOD DEEDS
HASTE	148 – 4	WE NEED NOT MAKE HASTE
HATE	285 – 4	MENTAL EQUIVALENT OF HATE
HATE	460 – 3	HATE BEGETS HATE
HATE	467 – 1	KNOWS NOTHING ABOUT HATE
HAVE-NOT	315 – 2	PROJECTS THE FORM OF HAVE-NOT
HAVE-NOT	315 – 2	IN TAKING THE FORM OF HAVE-NOT
HAY FEVER	242 – 2	HAY FEVER ATTACKS ONLY THOSE
HAY FEVER	242 – 5	HAY FEVER HAS NO POWER
HE	420 – 3	HE IS GRADUALLY BECOMING CONSCIOUS
HE	477 – 1	HE IS SPIRIT, SOUL AND BODY
HE	501 – 6	HE IS PERFECT SPIRIT
HE	503 – 2	THIS HE MEANS OURSELVES
HEADACHE	225 – 4	ONE IS SUFFERING FROM HEADACHE
HEADACHE	225 – 4	HEADACHE IS THINKING CORRECTLY
HEADACHE	320 – 2	PROCESS GIVES YOU A HEADACHE
HEAL	167 – 3	ATTEMPTS TO HEAL HIMSELF OR ANOTHER
HEAL	175 – 2	WHICH CAN HEAL INSTANTLY
HEAL	192 – 1	UNITY ALONE WILL HEAL HIM
HEAL	197 – 5	NO LIMIT TO THE POWER TO HEAL
HEAL	203 – 1	THAT YOU MUST HEAL ANYONE
HEAL	215 – 1	NOT EXPECT TO HEAL
HEAL	222 – 3	YOU CANNOT HEAL ANYONE OF HIS TROUBLE
HEAL	252 – 5	THE THOUGHT TO HEAL IS CONFUSION
HEAL	256 – 1	HEAL, CLEANSE AND UPLIFT
HEAL	260 – 4	TO KNOW THAT YOU CAN HEAL
HEAL	315 – 3	ONE WHO CAN DO JUST THIS CAN HEAL
HEAL	319 – 3	HE LACKS THE POWER TO HEAL
HEAL	448 – 4	HEAL EVIL EXCEPT BY THE POWER OF GOOD
HEALED	027 – 6	MANY HAVE BEEN HEALED OF PHYSICAL DISEASE

HEALED	028 - 1	HEALED THROUGH PRAYER WHILE OTHERS NOT
HEALED	190 - 1	HEALED THROUGH PRAYER AND FAITH
HEALED	254 - 2	I AM NOW HEALED
HEALED	320 - 1	HEALED WHEN HE NO LONGER NEEDS
HEALED	408 - 5	NO ONE TO BE HEALED IN THE TRUTH
HEALED	409 - 1	HEALED IS THE PRACTITIONER
HEALED	487 - 2	HEALED AS THE INNER MIND
HEALED	488 - 1	TO BE HEALED, MADE PROSPEROUS
HEALED	502 - 5	HEALED WHEN WE COME TO THE SPIRIT
HEALER	170 - 2	WILL BE THE BEST HEALER
HEALER	198 - 1	WILL BE THE BEST HEALER
HEALER	418 - 3	THE HEALER DOES IS TO MENTALLY UNCOVER
HEALING	057 - 3	HEALING AND DEMONSTRATION
HEALING	057 - 3	NO PROCESS OF HEALING
HEALING	124 - 3	HEALING OF THE BODY OR OF CONDITIONS
HEALING	138 - 3	HEALING PHYSICAL DISEASE
HEALING	157 - 4	MANY INSTANCES OF HEALING THROUGH FAITH
HEALING	163 - 3	HEALING INCLUDES THE EMANCIPATION
HEALING	176 - 2	ON THE RESPONSIBILITY OF HEALING
HEALING	178 - 5	HEALING IS ACCOMPLISHED
HEALING	179 - 4	HEALING IS NOT A PROCESS
HEALING	183 - 1	HEALING IS BASED UPON THE CONCEPTION
HEALING	190 - 1	CONTACTED A HEALING LAW
HEALING	191 - 1	BE HEALING THEIR BODIES
HEALING	191 - 1	THIS IS SPIRITUAL MIND HEALING
HEALING	191 - 3	TO ANY FORM OF HEALING
HEALING	191 - 5	HEALING MUST ALSO BE SPIRITUAL
HEALING	197 - 3	HEALING THEN IS ACCOMPLISHED
HEALING	199 - 2	REAL METAPHYSICAL HEALING
HEALING	199 - 4	IS A BARRIER TO HEALING
HEALING	205 - 1	AND PRODUCE A HEALING
HEALING	212 - 4	HEALING IS NOT A PROCESS
HEALING	220 - 4	WHY MENTAL HEALING IS SCIENTIFIC
HEALING	220 - 6	YOU THINK YOU ARE DOING THE HEALING
HEALING	225 - 1	HEALING TAKES PLACE
HEALING	225 - 1	UNTIL A HEALING IS ACCOMPLISHED
HEALING	227 - 2	HEALING WOULD BE IMPOSSIBLE
HEALING	233 - 2	THE WORD OF HEALING IS SPOKEN
HEALING	233 - 3	LOVE IS ALWAYS HEALING
HEALING	239 - 2	HEALING BALM FOR EVERY INHARMONIOUS
HEALING	298 - 3	LOVE IS THE GRANDEST HEALING
HEALING	320 - 2	HEALING IS NOT ACCOMPLISHED
HEALING	358 - 2	WE COULD NOT HELP HEALING PEOPLE
HEALING	358 - 2	THE HIGHEST FORM OF HEALING
HEALING	365 - 2	HEALING OF ALL DISEASE IS WITHIN MAN
HEALING	394 - 3	HEALING OF THE PHYSICAL BODY
HEALING	409 - 3	HEALING IS REALLY THE ACTION
HEALING	418 - 3	SPIRITUAL MAN NEEDS NO HEALING
HEALING	437 - 2	HEALING OF THE CENTURION'S SERVANT
HEALING	439 - 5	LESSON IN IMPERSONAL HEALING
HEALING	447 - 1	HEALING OF OUR WOUNDS
HEALING	447 - 2	SOME FORM OF HEALING
HEALING	447 - 2	HEALING CAN TAKE PLACE ONLY WHEN ONE IS
HEALING AGENCY	145 - 3	MOST POWERFUL HEALING AGENCY
HEALING POWER	115 - 1	HEALING POWER OF THE SPOKEN WORD

HEALING PROCESS	164 - 1	HEALING PROCESS IS IN BECOMING CONSCIOUS
HEALS	235 - 3	CLEANSES, HEALS AND RENEWS EVERY ORGAN
HEALS	413 - 3	DIVINE PRESENCE WHICH HEALS
HEALS	418 - 2	REALLY HEALS IS THE KNOWLEDGE
HEALS	500 - 5	HEALS THE SICK THROUGH THE LAW
HEALTH	143 - 2	EMBODY THE IDEA OF HEALTH
HEALTH	156 - 3	FEAR OF LOSS OF HEALTH
HEALTH	164 - 2	HEALTH HAS ALWAYS BEEN OURS
HEALTH	190 - 3	HEALTH IS A MENTAL AS WELL AS A PHYSICAL
HEALTH	201 - 2	WILL SEE HEALTH MANIFESTED
HEALTH	203 - 1	HEALTH IS AN OMNIPRESENT REALITY
HEALTH	203 - 1	HEALTH WAS THERE ALL THE TIME
HEALTH	209 - 5	HEALTH AS OPPOSED TO
HEALTH	251 - 4	LAWS OF HEALTH AND ACTION
HEALTHY	099 - 5	THE BODY WILL BE NORMAL AND HEALTHY
HEALTHY	144 - 3	HEALTHY MIND REFLECTS ITSELF
HEAR	334 - 1	HE WHO MADE THE EARS CAN HEAR
HEAR	378 - 2	HEAR WITHOUT THE AGENCY
HEAR	451 - 2	LOOKING SEE OR LISTENING HEAR
HEAR	451 - 3	HEAR THAT INNER VOICE OF TRUTH
HEARERS	499 - 5	NOT HEARERS ONLY
HEARETH	258 - 1	THY SERVANT HEARETH
HEARING	258 - 2	HEARING IS A DIVINE IDEA
HEARING	258 - 3	YOUR HEARING IS PERFECT
HEART	041 - 3	PURE IN HEART SEE GOD
HEART	137 - 1	AS A MAN THINKETH IN HIS HEART SO IS HE
HEART	163 - 3	CAUSES THE HEART TO BEAT
HEART	232 - 4	IF THE HEART KEPT
HEART	238 - 3	THE HEART IS THE CENTER
HEART	238 - 3	YOUR HEART BE TROUBLED
HEART	238 - 4	HEART WITH ALL DILIGENCE
HEART	240 - 2	HEART IS CONTROLLED
HEART	306 - 4	THE MAN OF THE HEART
HEART	367 - 2	ONLY THE HEART KNOWS THE SONGS
HEART	438 - 3	ETERNAL HEART IS ONE OF LOVE
HEART	444 - 3	POWER AT THE HEART OF GOD
HEART	449 - 2	MOUTH SPEAKS FROM THE HEART
HEART TROUBLE	239 - 2	HEART TROUBLE CAN BE TRACED
HEAT	252 - 5	SPIRIT IS NOT SUBJECT TO HEAT OR COLD
HEAT	258 - 5	I AM ONE WITH HEAT
HEAT	259 - 1	LOVE THE HEAT OF THE DESERT
HEAVEN	037 - 1	SYMBOLIZE HEAVEN AND HELL
HEAVEN	054 - 1	HEAVEN AND EARTH SHALL PASS AWAY
HEAVEN	055 - 4	CONVERSATION BE IN HEAVEN
HEAVEN	103 - 3	HEAVEN IS THE NATIVE HOME
HEAVEN	124 - 2	HEAVEN AND HELL ARE STATES OF CONSCIOUSNESS
HEAVEN	147 - 3	NEW HEAVEN AND A NEW EARTH
HEAVEN	180 - 3	HEAVEN AS BEING OUTSIDE HIMSELF
HEAVEN	185 - 2	WHICH IS IN HEAVEN IS PERFECT
HEAVEN	212 - 2	HEAVEN AND EARTH SHALL
HEAVEN	217 - 1	HEAVEN IS LOST MERELY
HEAVEN	217 - 2	THE KINGDOM OF HEAVEN IS
HEAVEN	218 - 3	FIRE CAUGHT FROM HEAVEN
HEAVEN	314 - 2	WE THINK OF HEAVEN
HEAVEN	337 - 1	HEAVEN AND HELL ARE STATES OF CONSCIOUSNESS

HEAVEN	365 - 2	HEAVEN IS WITHIN MAN
HEAVEN	383 - 3	PURCHASED A SEAT IN HEAVEN
HEAVEN	395 - 2	HEAVEN AND HELL ARE TIED UP IN MAN'S BELIEFS
HEAVEN	405 - 3	PEACE, SUCCESS AND HEAVEN FROM US
HEAVEN	422 - 3	FATHER WHICH ART IN HEAVEN
HEAVEN	423 - 2	GIFTS OF HEAVEN COME ALIKE TO ALL
HEAVEN	423 - 3	IT IS THE HOPE OF HEAVEN
HEAVEN	434 - 1	FIND HIS HOME IN HEAVEN
HEAVEN	451 - 5	HEAVEN IS LIKE LEAVEN
HEAVEN	452 - 3	NEWS WE HAVE OF HEAVEN
HEAVEN	457 - 1	EARTH SHALL BE BOUND IN HEAVEN
HEAVEN	472 - 3	ASCENDED UP TO HEAVEN
HEAVEN	472 - 3	HEAVEN, UNLESS HE IS ALREADY THERE
HEAVEN	472 - 4	HEAVEN IS NOT A PLACE
HEAVEN	496 - 5	HEAVEN ALONE IS GIVEN AWAY
HEAVEN	504 - 1	HEAVEN IS LIFE AND NOT DEATH
HEAVEN AND HELL	037 - 1	AS SYMBOLIZE HEAVEN AND HELL
HEAVEN AND HELL	133 - 5	HEAVEN AND HELL, GOOD AND BAD
HEAVENLY	041 - 3	HEAVENLY HOST IN HIS FIELDS
HEAVENLY	186 - 4	THE MORE HEAVENLY
HEAVENLY	246 - 4	THE HEAVENLY FLOW MAY FILL IT
HEAVENLY	452 - 1	BRING ABOUT A HEAVENLY STATE
HEAVENLY	465 - 1	WE CAME FROM A HEAVENLY STATE
HEAVENS	067 - 2	GOD CREATED THE HEAVENS
HEBREWS	158 - 2	ELEVENTH CHAPTER OF HEBREWS
HEEDLESS	464 - 4	HEEDLESS ABOUT HIS SON'S WELFARE
HEIGHTS	327 - 3	THE HEIGHTS OF SPIRITUAL VISION
HEIGHTS	358 - 3	HEIGHTS OF ITS GREATEST REALIZATIONS
HEIRS	485 - 2	HEIRS TO THE HEAVEN OF REALITY
HELD	119 - 3	HELD IN CONSCIOUSNESS
HELD	411 - 4	FORMED AND HELD IN PLACE
HELL	037 - 1	SYMBOLIZE HEAVEN AND HELL
HELL	124 - 2	HELL IS THE PHANTOM ABODE OF OUR MORBID
HELL	204 - 2	HELL, HOROSCOPE OR ANY OTHER FALSE BELIEF
HELL	314 - 2	HELL COOLS OFF WHEN
HELL	337 - 1	NO DEVIL, NO HELL, NO TORMENT
HELL	428 - 3	STORY ABOUT HELL
HELL	436 - 4	THEOLOGICAL HELL
HELL	436 - 4	POPULAR CONCEPT OF HELL
HELP	165 - 3	WHO ASKED FOR HELP
HELP	315 - 2	HELP OURSELVES AND EACH OTHER
HELP	440 - 5	ATTEMPTING TO HELP PEOPLE
HELP	440 - 5	THEY WISHED NO HELP
HELPFULNESS	434 - 1	HELPFULNESS TOWARD ALL
HELPING	168 - 2	HELPING OTHERS THROUGH MENTAL
HELPLESS	055 - 4	TO HELP THE HELPLESS
HELPLESS	396 - 3	LAW IS HELPLESS WITHOUT DIRECTION
HEM	439 - 4	TOUCHED THE HEM OF HIS GARMENT
HEMORRHAGE	256 - 4	HEMORRHAGE OR STOMACH ULCER
HENCE	052 - 5	HENCE IT FOLLOWS
HER	130 - 1	OPERATION WITH HER LAWS
HERE	146 - 3	POWER OF MIND IS RIGHT HERE
HERE	175 - 5	THE EVER-PRESENT HERE
HEREAFTER	375 - 1	CREATE AND SUSTAIN ONE HEREAFTER
HEREAFTER	383 - 2	EITHER HERE OR HEREAFTER

HEREAFTER	383 - 3	SOULS BOTH HERE AND HEREAFTER
HEREAFTER	384 - 3	OUR PLACE HEREAFTER WILL BE
HEREAFTER	384 - 4	A HEREAFTER WITHOUT ACTIVITY
HEREAFTER	503 - 1	NOT IN THE HEREAFTER BUT IN THE NOW
HERITAGE	328 - 3	SPIRITUAL HERITAGE OF THE AGES
HERITAGE	419 - 2	INTELLECTUAL AND SPIRITUAL HERITAGE
HERSELF	384 - 4	NATURE PROVIDES FOR HERSELF
HESITATE	364 - 3	SHOULD NEVER HESITATE TO SAY
HID	441 - 2	HID THAT SHALL NOT BE KNOWN
HIDDEN	075 - 3	PRINCIPLE IS FOREVER HIDDEN
HIDDEN	362 - 2	THE HIDDEN MEANING OF THINGS
HIDDEN	443 - 3	HIDDEN MEANING BEHIND THESE WORDS
HIDDEN	449 - 2	NOTHING IS OR CAN BE HIDDEN
HIDDEN	472 - 3	HIDDEN MEANINGS WHICH PLACES JESUS
HIDDEN	503 - 3	HIDDEN IN THE INNERMOST RECESSES
HIGH	039 - 6	AS HIGH AS WE SHALL MAKE OUR MARK
HIGH CHANCELLOR	433 - 2	HIGH CHANCELLOR OF GOD
HIGHER	036 - 3	ARRIVED AT A HIGHER STANDARD
HIGHER	178 - 3	HIGHER THAN THAT OF THE INTELLECT
HIGHER PRINCIPLE	306 - 4	CONTACT THIS HIGHER PRINCIPLE
HIGHEST	143 - 2	TAKE THE HIGHEST THOUGHT WE HAVE
HIGHEST	276 - 2	HIGHEST REALIZATION WE CAN HAVE
HIGHEST	344 - 2	THE HIGHEST MENTAL PRACTICE
HIGHEST	359 - 1	HIGHEST FACULTY IN MAN IS INTUITION
HIGHEST	404 - 3	HIGHEST FORM OF MANIFESTATION
HIGHEST	411 - 3	MOLDED FROM THE HIGHEST SENSE
HIGHEST GOD	394 - 4	THE HIGHEST GOD
HIGH INVOCATION	295 - 3	IN MYSTICISM, HIGH INVOCATION
HIGH PLACES	494 - 5	WICKEDNESS IN HIGH PLACES MEANS
HIGHROAD	147 - 3	HIGHROAD TO THE FULFILLMENT OF OUR LIVES
HIGH TIME	487 - 5	HIGH TIME TO AWAKE OUT OF SLEEP
HIGH WATCH	335 - 4	HIGH WATCH TOWARD THE ONE
HIM	503 - 3	SEE HIM WITH THE SPIRITUAL EYE
HIMSELF	128 - 3	DO THIS FOR HIMSELF
HIMSELF	200 - 1	PRACTITIONER MUST TREAT HIMSELF
HIMSELF	212 - 3	HIMSELF EXPERIENCE THE RESULT OF SUCH
HIMSELF	291 - 3	THE PRACTITIONER TREATS HIMSELF
HIMSELF	367 - 4	COMPELLED TO BELIEVE IN HIMSELF
HINDER	054 - 1	NOTHING CAN HINDER IT
HINDER	296 - 5	NOTHING CAN HINDER
HINDER	331 - 4	CONFUSION WHICH CAN HINDER
HINDER	358 - 3	NOTHING TO HINDER THE WHOLE FROM COMING
HINDER	479 - 3	CANNOT HINDER THE ONWARD MARCH
HINDERED	082 - 1	IT CANNOT BE HINDERED
HINDERED	233 - 2	HINDERED BY SOME OBSTRUCTION
HINDERS	146 - 3	HINDERS ITS OPERATION BUT OURSELVES
HIRE	445 - 3	HIRE OTHERS TO WORK FOR US
HIS	166 - 2	HIS BELIEF ABOUT THE PERSON
HIS ETERNITY	478 - 1	AN INDIVIDUALIZATION OF HIS ETERNITY
HISTORY	095 - 1	HISTORY OF MAN EXISTS TODAY
HISTORY	103 - 2	HISTORY OF COSMIC ACTIVITIES
HISTORY	157 - 4	HISTORY HAS RECORDED MANY INSTANCES
HISTORY	264 - 3	EVIL HAS NO HISTORY
HISTORY	349 - 1	READING THE RACE HISTORY
HISTORY	352 - 3	COMPLETE HISTORY OF OUR FAMILY

HISTORY	427 - 2	UNIQUE PLACE IN THE HISTORY
HISTORY	460 - 1	OVER THE PAGES OF HISTORY
HISTORY	460 - 1	HISTORY HAS PROVEN THAT STRIFE
HIT	233 - 2	YOU HIT UPON THE THING
HOARDED	232 - 4	HOARDED THE AIR THEY TAKE IN
HOCUS-POCUS	046 - 5	NO HOCUS-POCUS IN A MENTAL TREATMENT
HOLD	171 - 3	HOLD A THOUGHT
HOLD	199 - 2	HOLD A THOUGHT
HOLD	200 - 2	HOLD A GOOD THOUGHT
HOLD	206 - 4	HOLD A THOUGHT
HOLD	309 - 1	HOLD THE MIND TO ONE THOUGHT
HOLD	318 - 3	HOLD THIS CONSCIOUSNESS A WHILE
HOLD	409 - 4	DIVINE MUST HOLD US
HOLD	446 - 5	HOLD THE MENTAL ATTENTION TO AN IDEAL
HOLD A THOUGHT	171 - 1	HE DOES NOT TRY TO HOLD A THOUGHT
HOLD GOOD	352 - 5	LAW MUST STILL HOLD GOOD
HOLDING	030 - 1	BY HOLDING THOUGHTS
HOLDING	123 - 1	NOT DONE BY HOLDING THOUGHTS
HOLDING	200 - 2	HOLDING A GOOD THOUGHT
HOLDING	282 - 1	HOLDING TO THAT EQUIVALENT
HOLDING	320 - 2	HOLDING THOUGHTS HAS NOTHING TO DO
HOLDING	399 - 5	DIFFERENCE BETWEEN HOLDING THOUGHTS
HOLDS	120 - 1	MIND HOLDS LONG ENOUGH
HOLDS	193 - 3	HOLDS TO THE IDEA
HOLDS	400 - 2	HOLDS TO IT WITH CONVICTION
HOLDS	494 - 2	HOLDS TO AND FIRMLY BELIEVES
HOLD THOUGHT	179 - 2	DOES NOT HOLD THOUGHT IN MENTAL HEALING
HOLD THOUGHT	195 - 4	TO HOLD THOUGHT CENTERED
HOLD THOUGHTS	399 - 5	HOLD THOUGHTS
HOLINESS	494 - 1	CREATED IN TRUE HOLINESS
HOLINESS	494 - 1	AFTER TRUE HOLINESS OR WHOLENESS
HOLY	365 - 5	HOLY INNER PRESENCE, GREAT AND MIGHTY
HOLY	443 - 3	DIVINE HOLY AND INDESTRUCTIBLE
HOLY COMFORTER	480 - 5	HOLY COMFORTER THE SPIRIT OF TRUTH
HOLY COMFORTER	480 - 6	AS THE HOLY COMFORTER COMES
HOLY GHOST	088 - 2	FATHER, SON AND HOLY GHOST
HOLY GHOST	088 - 3	HOLY GHOST IS THE SERVANT
HOLY GHOST	090 - 2	HOLY GHOST OR THIRD PERSON
HOLY ONE	304 - 3	LIMITED THE HOLY ONE OF ISRAEL
HOLY ONE	405 - 2	THE HOLY ONE OF ISRAEL
HOLY SPIRIT	196 - 4	HOLY SPIRIT WHICH IS GOD
HOLY WOMB	088 - 2	SOUL OF THE UNIVERSE IS THE HOLY WOMB
HOME	288 - 1	EQUIVALENT OF A COMMODIOUS HOME
HOME	288 - 1	THE KIND OF HOME WE DESIRE
HOME	398 - 3	MENTALLY ACCEPT A HOME
HOMES	458 - 6	GOOD FOR ALL PEOPLE TO HAVE HOMES
HONOR	486 - 4	HONOR GOD MORE
HONORABLE	226 - 1	WHATSOEVER THINGS ARE HONORABLE
HONORS	032 - 3	HONORS OUR FAITH IN IT
HOOKED	315 - 2	BE HOOKED UP WITH OUR THOUGHT
HOPE	049 - 3	HOPE IT DOES
HOPE	049 - 4	HOPE IS GOOD
HOPE	198 - 3	HE DOES NOT JUST HOPE
HOPE	274 - 1	THE DIVINE HOPE IN US
HOPE	284 - 4	FAITH IS NOT HOPE

HOPE	386 - 2	RESTS ITS GREATEST HOPE
HOPE	399 - 3	WE DO NOT HOPE, WE ACCEPT
HOPE	423 - 3	IT IS THE HOPE OF HEAVEN
HOPELESSNESS	387 - 3	OUR GRIEF OF HOPELESSNESS
HOPES	386 - 3	MY HOPES OF IMMORTALITY
HOPES	429 - 1	ALL OUR HOPES, NOT ONLY FORLORN
HOPING	047 - 3	HOPING THAT SOMETHING MAY HAPPEN
HORIZON	448 - 1	HORIZON IS LIMITED TO THE CONFINES
HORN	462 - 1	THE UNIVERSAL HORN OF PLENTY
HOROSCOPE	204 - 2	HELL, HOROSCOPE OR ANY OTHER FALSE BELIEF
HORSE	340 - 3	RIDING UPON A HORSE
HORSE	463 - 4	THE CART BEFORE THE HORSE
HOST	041 - 3	HEAVENLY HOST IN HIS FIELDS
HOST	471 - 1	GOD HIMSELF SHALL BE OUR HOST
HOUR	154 - 1	HOUR WE ARE MEETING THE ETERNAL
HOUR	282 - 4	HOUR OF NEED IS TO PROVE
HOUR	388 - 2	AND EACH HOUR IN THE DAY
HOUR	407 - 4	THIS VERY HOUR
HOUSE	037 - 3	A HOUSE DIVIDED AGAINST ITSELF
HOUSE	143 - 4	HOUSE WE WOULD LIKE TO LIVE
HOUSE	333 - 4	BACK TO ITS FATHER'S HOUSE
HOUSE	383 - 1	SUCH A HOUSE CANNOT STAND
HOUSE	388 - 4	RETURN INTO ITS FATHER'S HOUSE
HOUSE	419 - 4	ITS FATHER'S HOUSE
HOUSE	448 - 3	HOUSE DIVIDED AGAINST ITSELF
HOUSE	453 - 1	KEEP THE MENTAL HOUSE FREE
HOUSE	468 - 1	EVERYTHING IN THE FATHER'S HOUSE
HOUSEHOLD	441 - 3	SHALL BE THEY OF HIS OWN HOUSEHOLD
HOW	301 - 1	OUTLINING HOW IT SHALL BE DONE
HOW	340 - 2	WE MUST LEARN HOW IT WORKS
HOW	392 - 3	IT KNOWS HOW TO DO BUT
HOW	402 - 2	LAW KNOWS HOW TO MAKE THINGS
HUDSON	378 - 1	HUDSON IN HIS LAW OF PSYCHIC PHENOMENA
HUMAN	052 - 2	POSSIBILITY OF ALL HUMAN PROBABILITY
HUMAN	160 - 1	LET GO OF ALL HUMAN WILL
HUMAN	211 - 1	FROM THE HUMAN STANDPOINT
HUMAN	224 - 2	INTELLIGENCE OF THE HUMAN RACE
HUMAN	229 - 2	HUMAN LIFE IS THE INCARNATION
HUMAN	274 - 1	THAN THE HUMAN MIND COULD DIGEST
HUMAN	298 - 4	DYING FOR REAL HUMAN INTEREST
HUMAN	310 - 4	INVENTIONS OF THE HUMAN MIND
HUMAN	328 - 4	DOES NOT READ HUMAN THOUGHT
HUMAN	359 - 3	HUMAN GAVE WAY TO THE DIVINE
HUMAN	402 - 4	A LAW OF HUMAN THOUGHT
HUMAN	410 - 1	THE HUMAN IS REALLY DIVINE
HUMAN	410 - 3	STORY OF HUMAN EVOLUTION
HUMAN	422 - 3	HUMAN GIVES WAY TO THE DIVINE
HUMAN	422 - 3	HUMAN TOOK ON THE CHRIST
HUMAN	427 - 4	PHYSICAL BENEFITS OF THE HUMAN
HUMAN	430 - 3	HUMAN EXPERIENCE HAS TAUGHT
HUMAN	436 - 1	HUMAN AND CONSEQUENTLY LIMITED
HUMAN	479 - 3	HUMAN CANNOT DIM
HUMAN BODY	313 - 1	HUMAN BODY IS ONE WITH THE ENTIRE
HUMANITARIAN	042 - 3	THE HUMANITARIAN AND THE EMPIRE BUILDER
HUMANITY	137 - 1	HUMANITY THOUSANDS OF YEARS

HUMANITY	192 - 2	HELP TROUBLED HUMANITY
HUMANITY	238 - 2	EXPRESSION THROUGH OUR HUMANITY
HUMANITY	268 - 3	IDEA OF CHRIST TO HUMANITY
HUMANITY	299 - 2	ALL HUMANITY SPEAKS TO ME
HUMANITY	360 - 1	THROUGH HIS OWN LOVE OF HUMANITY
HUMANITY	368 - 1	HIS DIVINITY THROUGH HIS HUMANITY
HUMANITY	368 - 3	HIS OWN LOVE OF HUMANITY
HUMANITY	410 - 3	LIMITATION FELL UPON HUMANITY
HUMAN MIND	121 - 1	THERE IS NO HUMAN MIND TO DESTROY
HUMAN MIND	163 - 2	THAT THE HUMAN MIND
HUMAN MISERY	160 - 3	HUMAN MISERY IS A RESULT OF IGNORANCE
HUMAN RACE	118 - 1	INTELLIGENCE OF THE HUMAN RACE
HUMAN RACE	139 - 3	PROGRESS OF THE HUMAN RACE
HUMAN SOUL	368 - 1	HUMAN SOUL MORE THAN JESUS
HUMBLE	027 - 4	WITH TRULY A HUMBLE THOUGHT
HUMBLE	368 - 1	HUMBLE BEFORE THE GREATNESS OF THE WHOLE
HUNGER	223 - 2	BLESSED ARE THEY WHO DO HUNGER
HUNGER	253 - 1	YOUR HUNGER AND YOUR APPETITE
HUNGER	427 - 4	WILL CONTINUALLY HUNGER
HUNGER	428 - 4	HUNGER AND THIRST AFTER RIGHTEOUSNESS
HUNGER	428 - 5	HUNGER HAS BEEN BLESSED
HUNGER	464 - 6	PERISH WITH HUNGER
HURRY	272 - 1	ANY SENSE OF HURRY
HURT	195 - 2	BE ANY HURT IN THEM
HURT	195 - 2	HURT FOR OTHERS
HURT	269 - 1	EXPRESSES LIFE WITHOUT HURT
HURTS	288 - 2	HURTS NO MAN AND BRINGS HAPPINESS
HURTS	502 - 6	FROM ALL THAT HURTS TO THE GREAT
HYMN	495 - 5	NOT A BATTLE HYMN
HYPNOTIC	204 - 2	HYPNOTIC CONDITION INTO WHICH
HYPNOTIC	297 - 3	FOR THIS WOULD BE HYPNOTIC
HYPNOTISM	210 - 1	SOME FORM OF HYPNOTISM
HYPNOTIZE	179 - 2	HYPNOTIZE OR MENTALLY INFLUENCE
HYPNOTIZE	206 - 3	NOT TRY TO HYPNOTIZE HIM
HYPNOTIZED	226 - 3	HYPNOTIZED INTO THIS BELIEF
HYPNOTIZED	226 - 3	RACE SUGGESTION HAS HYPNOTIZED
HYPOCRISY	435 - 2	TO SUPPOSE SO IS HYPOCRISY
HYPOCRISY	435 - 2	FROM THE SHOULDERS OF HYPOCRISY
HYPOTHESIS	104 - 3	PRESENT HYPOTHESIS OF SCIENCE

I

I	385 - 2	I BELIEVE IN THE CONTINUATION
I	385 - 2	THAT WHICH I REALLY AM
I	401 - 4	IT IS NOT I BUT THE SPIRIT
I	417 - 3	INDIVIDUAL "I" IS A COMPLEMENT
I AM	069 - 3	THE TEACHING OF THE I AM
I AM	072 - 3	WHEN HE FIRST SAID I AM
I AM	157 - 4	IT ONLY KNOWS I AM
I AM	217 - 1	THE UNIVERSAL I AM
I AM	265 - 1	I AM THE CHRIST
I AM	295 - 3	ACT AS THOUGH I AM AND I WILL BE
I AM	313 - 4	I AM THE VINE

I AM	323 - 3	EVERY TIME MAN SAYS "I AM"
I AM	332 - 4	"I AM THE LIGHT OF THE WORLD"
I AM	336 - 2	WHEN A MAN SAYS I AM
I AM	344 - 2	THIS INDWELLING I AM
I AM	368 - 2	BECAUSE THOU ART I AM
I AM	374 - 2	THIS I AM APPEARS NO LONGER
I AM	413 - 1	THE I AM IS BOTH INDIVIDUAL
I AM	413 - 3	"I AM IS IN THE MIDST OF THEE"
I AM	417 - 3	COMPLEMENT TO THE UNIVERSAL I AM
I AM	423 - 3	I AM THAT WHICH THOU ART
I AM	477 - 5	I AM THE LIGHT OF THE WORLD
I AM	477 - 6	"I AM" HAS A DUAL MEANING
I AM	477 - 6	I AM THE UNIVERSAL CAUSE
I AM	478 - 1	UNTO THE PERFECT I AM
I AM	479 - 5	I AM THE WAY, THE TRUTH AND THE LIFE
I AM	479 - 5	SON OF THE ETERNAL I AM
I-AM-NESS	196 - 4	HIS OWN I-AM-NESS
I-AM-NESS	220 - 3	ITS OWN I-AM-NESS
I-AM-NESS	336 - 3	RECOGNIZING THE I-AM-NESS
I-AM-NESS	367 - 5	SELF REALIZATION AND I-AM-NESS
I AM THE WAY	358 - 4	I AM THE WAY, THE TRUTH AND THE LIFE
ICE	141 - 4	ICE WOULD STILL BE WATER
ICE	184 - 2	ICE IS FORMED FROM WATER
IDEA	030 - 3	IDEA IS ACCEPTED AND POURED
IDEA	055 - 2	WITH THE IDEA OF FAITH
IDEA	064 - 3	IN EXPOUNDING HIS IDEA
IDEA	069 - 1	THE WORD IS THE CONCEPT, IDEA, IMAGE
IDEA	072 - 2	AS IS OUR IDEA OF SPIRIT
IDEA	087 - 5	ACTION OF THIS CONSCIOUSNESS BEING IDEA
IDEA	098 - 3	DISTINGUISHED FROM THE IDEA
IDEA	098 - 3	THE IDEA IS INVISIBLE
IDEA	100 - 3	IDEA OF BODY
IDEA	103 - 2	THIS IDEA PRODUCES A PLANT
IDEA	105 - 1	IMAGE, CONCEPT OR IDEA
IDEA	155 - 2	BUT THE IDEA SYMBOLIZED
IDEA	166 - 3	IDEA HAS BEEN SET IN MOTION
IDEA	177 - 2	ENABLES HIM TO COVER A PERFECT IDEA
IDEA	194 - 1	DEALING WITH THE IDEA
IDEA	196 - 1	DESTROY THE IDEA OF HIMSELF
IDEA	197 - 2	MAN IS INHERENTLY A PERFECT IDEA
IDEA	198 - 4	PERFECT IDEA
IDEA	212 - 3	DEALS ONLY WITH THE IDEA
IDEA	213 - 2	A PERFECT IDEA OF HEART
IDEA	219 - 1	THE IDEA OF DIVINE HARMONY
IDEA	221 - 4	CAN IMPRESS A DEFINITE IDEA
IDEA	224 - 2	MIND REPRODUCES THIS IDEA
IDEA	241 - 3	AN IDEA EVERYWHERE PRESENT
IDEA	254 - 4	THE SPECIFIC IDEA WHICH CAUSES
IDEA	259 - 3	FOOD MUST BE A SPIRITUAL IDEA
IDEA	268 - 3	THE IDEA OF CHRIST TO HUMANITY
IDEA	305 - 4	EVERY IDEA IS BOUND TO PRODUCE
IDEA	338 - 4	MUST BE A PERFECT IDEA
IDEA	339 - 4	EVERY TIME ONE CONCEIVES AN IDEA
IDEA	354 - 3	THE FULL AND PERFECT IDEA
IDEA	422 - 3	IDEA OF THE UNIVERSALITY OF SONSHIP

IDEA	451 - 4	IDEA PLANTED OR BURIED
IDEA	483 - 2	BEHIND FORM IS IDEA
IDEA	483 - 3	IDEA IS FATHER TO THE FACT
IDEAL	173 - 2	ATTAINED THE IDEAL METHOD
IDEAL	218 - 2	UP TO THIS HIGH IDEAL
IDEAL	271 - 5	A MENTAL PICTURE OF HIS IDEAL
IDEAL	455 - 4	WISHES TO EMBODY AN IDEAL
IDEAS	069 - 2	AN INFINITE VARIETY OF IDEAS
IDEAS	070 - 2	A MANIFESTATION OF DIVINE IDEAS
IDEAS	087 - 5	THINGS ARE IDEAS IN FORM
IDEAS	087 - 5	TO MAKE THINGS EXCEPT IDEAS
IDEAS	088 - 3	IMPREGNATING IT WITH THE DIVINE IDEAS
IDEAS	117 - 2	ONE LAW BUT MANY IDEAS
IDEAS	131 - 1	IDEAS WHICH ARE THE REAL CAUSE
IDEAS	207 - 2	DEALS SOLELY WITH IDEAS
IDEAS	218 - 4	SUPPLIES THESE SPIRITUAL IDEAS
IDEAS	234 - 2	ABILITY TO GRASP IDEAS
IDEAS	257 - 3	IDEAS CAN WAIT UNTIL LATER
IDEAS	338 - 4	CANNOT CONCEIVE IMPERFECT IDEAS
IDEAS	393 - 1	IDEAS TAKE FORM AND BECOME THINGS
IDEAS	393 - 3	IDEAS IS THE ORIGINAL MIND
IDEAS	402 - 2	MAKE THINGS OUT OF IDEAS
IDEAS	404 - 1	IDEAS ARE FORM
IDEAS	410 - 2	THESE IDEAS MEAN TO US
IDENTICAL	106 - 2	NATURE IS IDENTICAL WITH GODS
IDENTICAL	121 - 3	ROOTED IN THAT WHICH IS IDENTICAL
IDENTICAL	301 - 1	FIND THEM TO BE IDENTICAL
IDENTIFIED	412 - 1	BE IDENTIFIED WITH POWER
IDENTIFIES	284 - 1	IDENTIFIES ITSELF WITH REALITY
IDENTIFY	412 - 1	IDENTIFY OURSELVES WITH ABUNDANCE
IDENTITY	029 - 4	MAINTAINS HIS IDENTITY IN LAW
IDENTITY	087 - 6	IDENTITY IN INFINITE MIND
IDENTITY	132 - 10	MAN IS AN IDENTITY IN THE UNIVERSE
IDENTITY	371 - 2	IDENTITY OF COURSE POSTULATES MEMORY
IDENTITY	372 - 1	CONSCIOUS IDENTITY
IDENTITY	374 - 1	SPIRIT ALONE MAINTAINS THE IDENTITY
IDENTITY	377 - 2	MAINTAIN AN IDENTITY INDEPENDENT
IDENTITY	391 - 3	INDIVIDUAL UNIT, SEPARATE IN IDENTITY
IDLE	499 - 5	IDLE TALK ABOUT OUR UNDERSTANDING
IGNORANCE	030 - 3	IGNORANCE OF THIS EXCUSES NO ONE
IGNORANCE	032 - 3	IS THE RESULT OF IGNORANCE
IGNORANCE	033 - 2	IGNORANCE OF WHICH EXCUSES NO MAN
IGNORANCE	036 - 5	IN OUR IGNORANCE OF THE TRUTH
IGNORANCE	038 - 4	IGNORANCE OF THE LAW EXCUSES NO ONE
IGNORANCE	109 - 3	IN IGNORANCE HE VIOLATES THIS LAW
IGNORANCE	147 - 4	OUTSIDE OUR OWN IGNORANCE
IGNORANCE	150 - 3	IT IS IN MAN'S IGNORANCE
IGNORANCE	160 - 3	MISERY IS A RESULT OF IGNORANCE
IGNORANCE	180 - 4	UNHAPPINESS IS IGNORANCE
IGNORANCE	272 - 4	SUPERSTITION AND IGNORANCE
IGNORANCE	301 - 2	BUT IGNORANCE OF THE LAW DOES NOT
IGNORANCE	313 - 3	IN OUR IGNORANCE WE MISUSE OUR DIVINITY
IGNORANCE	314 - 1	IGNORANCE THAT WE APPEAR TO
IGNORANCE	354 - 2	HUMAN MIND IN ITS IGNORANCE
IGNORANCE	382 - 2	ADMIT HIS OWN IGNORANCE

IGNORANCE	383 - 3	ERRED THROUGH HUMAN IGNORANCE
IGNORANCE	395 - 1	WE INTERFERE WITH THESE IN OUR IGNORANCE
IGNORANCE	395 - 1	ON THE SCALE OF MAN'S IGNORANCE
IGNORANCE	405 - 2	IGNORANCE OF THE TRUE LAW OF SUPPLY
IGNORANCE	418 - 4	IGNORANCE STAYS WITH US UNTIL
IGNORANCE	420 - 2	SELF-INFLICTED THROUGH IGNORANCE
IGNORANCE	433 - 3	CONSCIOUSLY OR IN IGNORANCE
IGNORANCE	434 - 1	IGNORANCE OF HIS OWN TRUE NATURE
IGNORANCE	471 - 2	IGNORANCE OF THE LAW EXCUSES
IGNORANCE	486 - 1	NO SIN BUT IGNORANCE
IGNORANCE	498 - 4	IGNORANCE OF THE LAW OF GOOD
IGNORANCE	500 - 3	NO SIN BUT IGNORANCE
IGNORANT	037 - 1	IGNORANT OF OUR TRUE NATURE
IGNORANT	078 - 2	BINDS THE IGNORANT
IGNORANT	133 - 1	AT FIRST HE IS IGNORANT
IGNORANT	350 - 1	BETTER REMAIN IGNORANT
IGNORANT	402 - 4	IGNORANT USE OF THE LAW
IGNORANT	412 - 2	BUT ARE IGNORANT OF THIS FACT
I KNOW	057 - 1	I KNOW AND I KNOW THAT I KNOW
I KNOW	161 - 2	NOT AFRAID TO SAY I KNOW
ILL	388 - 2	WHICH WISHES ANYONE ILL
ILLEGITIMATE	499 - 3	ILLEGITIMATE CHILD OF SUPERSTITION
ILLUMINATES	468 - 1	LIGHT INSTANTLY ILLUMINATES IT
ILLUMINATING	335 - 2	ONE OF THE MOST ILLUMINATING THINGS
ILLUMINATING	420 - 2	ONE OF THE MOST ILLUMINATING
ILLUMINATION	359 - 1	PATH WHICH LEADS TO ILLUMINATION
ILLUMINATION	343 - 3	ILLUMINATION WILL COME AS MAN
ILLUMINATION	344 - 3	AFTER A PERIOD OF ILLUMINATION
ILLUMINATION	345 - 2	THE ILLUMINATION OF ALL MYSTICS
ILLUMINATION	350 - 2	WITH THE SPIRIT IS ILLUMINATION
ILLUMINATION	359 - 1	LEADS TO ILLUMINATION
ILLUMINATION	364 - 3	THE ILLUMINATION OF THE SPIRIT
ILLUMINATION	421 - 1	ILLUMINATION WILL COME AS MAN
ILLUMINATION	421 - 3	IN FLASHES OF ILLUMINATION
ILLUMINATION	497 - 5	WE CALL IT ILLUMINATION
ILLUMINED	185 - 2	THE SOUL WILL BECOME ILLUMINED
ILLUMINED	329 - 5	THE TEACHING OF THE ILLUMINED
ILLUMINED	335 - 1	THE GREAT MYSTICS HAVE BEEN ILLUMINED
ILLUMINED	343 - 2	ILLUMINED DO NOT BECOME LESS
ILLUMINED	367 - 5	TO THE ILLUMINED HAS EVER COME
ILLUMINED	444 - 2	TAUGHT BY THE ILLUMINED
ILLUMINED	452 - 2	EXPLAINS THE WAY OF THE ILLUMINED
ILLUMINED	452 - 4	ILLUMINED HAVE HAD EXPERIENCES
ILLUMINED	484 - 4	IS ILLUMINED BY THE SPIRIT
ILLUMINES	455 - 1	ILLUMINES THE PATHWAY
ILLUMINING	366 - 3	LIGHT OF THE SPIRIT ILLUMINING
ILLUSION	049 - 4	IT IS A SUBTLE ILLUSION
ILLUSION	053 - 5	IS BORROWED FROM ILLUSION
ILLUSION	054 - 2	ILLUSION SEEN AND UNDERSTOOD
ILLUSION	100 - 3	FORM IS NOT AN ILLUSION
ILLUSION	108 - 2	BONDAGE IS NOT EVEN AN ILLUSION
ILLUSION	180 - 4	AGE IS AN ILLUSION
ILLUSION	187 - 1	ILLUSION IS IN THE WAY WE LOOK
ILLUSION	327 - 1	OR MAY NOT BE AN ILLUSION
ILLUSION	337 - 1	IT IS AN ILLUSION

ILLUSION	344 - 2	WILL NEVER LEAD TO ILLUSION
ILLUSION	381 - 4	TEACHING OF THE ILLUSION OF MIND
ILLUSION	413 - 2	DEATH IS TO THE ILLUSION ALONE
ILLUSION	418 - 2	ILLUSION THAT WE ARE USING
ILLUSION	428 - 5	SEE IF IT BE AN ILLUSION
ILLUSION	435 - 2	LAST SHRED OF ILLUSION
ILLUSION	436 - 2	ILLUSION OF ACCEPTING THE FALSE
ILLUSIONS	093 - 2	TEACHINGS OF THE ILLUSIONS
ILLUSIONS	117 - 3	TO SAY THAT THEY ARE ILLUSIONS
ILLUSIONS	379 - 2	ALL ILLUSIONS IS TO THROW THE LIE
ILLUSIONS	486 - 1	NUMBERED WITH PAST ILLUSIONS
ILLUSTRATE	451 - 4	WAY TO ILLUSTRATE HIS POINT
ILLUSTRATION	141 - 4	ILLUSTRATION THAT THE UNIVERSE
ILLUSTRATION	165 - 2	ILLUSTRATION OF THE IMPORTANCE OF THIS
ILLUSTRATION	171 - 1	ILLUSTRATION LET US SUPPOSE
ILLUSTRATION	172 - 3	ILLUSTRATION OF THE DIFFERENCE BETWEEN
ILLUSTRATION	346 - 1	GOOD ILLUSTRATION WOULD BE
IMAGE	065 - 4	HIS OWN IMAGE AND LIKENESS
IMAGE	069 - 1	IMAGE OR THOUGHT OF GOD
IMAGE	100 - 3	IMAGE DERIVED FROM THE FOUNTAIN
IMAGE	105 - 1	IMAGE, CONCEPT OR IDEA
IMAGE	105 - 3	CONCRETE MENTAL IMAGE
IMAGE	108 - 1	IMAGE OF PERFECTION
IMAGE	142 - 2	WHICH WE MENTALLY IMAGE
IMAGE	176 - 1	TRIES TO EMBODY THE IMAGE
IMAGE	176 - 1	WHAT THE IMAGE MEANS
IMAGE	185 - 3	KEEPS THE IMAGE OF IT BEFORE HIM
IMAGE	196 - 1	CANNOT DESTROY THE DIVINE IMAGE
IMAGE	196 - 2	IS THE DIVINE IMAGE
IMAGE	208 - 3	IMAGE OF THOUGHT
IMAGE	224 - 3	KNOW THAT IT IS A FALSE IMAGE
IMAGE	268 - 3	AN ADEQUATE SUBJECTIVE IMAGE
IMAGE	297 - 3	TO IMAGE IDEAL RELATIONSHIPS
IMAGE	301 - 1	THE REFLECTION OF THAT IMAGE
IMAGE	332 - 5	CREATED IN THE IMAGE OF PERFECTION
IMAGE	363 - 4	CHRIST IS THE IMAGE OF GOD
IMAGE	399 - 4	THE IMAGE OF OUR THOUGHTS
IMAGE	406 - 1	IMAGE MUST CONCENTRATE SUBSTANCE
IMAGE	408 - 3	EACH IS AN IMAGE OF GOD
IMAGE	411 - 2	WHAT WE IMAGE OUR OURSELVES
IMAGE	450 - 4	IMAGE OF HIS INABILITY TO ATTAIN
IMAGE	458 - 4	IMAGE IT CANNOT MOVE
IMAGE	483 - 1	SPIRITUAL WORLD CONTAINS AN IMAGE
IMAGERY	187 - 1	POWER TO PRODUCE THIS IMAGERY
IMAGES	055 - 2	THESE IMAGES OF LIMITATION
IMAGES	076 - 5	IMAGES OF THOUGHT
IMAGES	077 - 1	OUR IMAGES OF THOUGHT
IMAGES	088 - 1	ARE RETAINED ALL OF THE IMAGES
IMAGES	091 - 1	REFLECT THE IMAGES THAT SPIRIT CASTS
IMAGES	167 - 4	THE IMAGES OF RIGHT ACTION
IMAGES	185 - 3	NECESSARY IMAGES IN MIND
IMAGES	193 - 1	UPON THE IMAGES OF THOUGHT
IMAGES	196 - 6	ACCEPTS THESE IMAGES OF THOUGHT
IMAGES	197 - 4	ERASING FALSE IMAGES OF THOUGHT
IMAGES	320 - 4	THE IMAGES OF OUR THINKING

IMAGES	321 – 2	IMAGES WITHIN THE SUBJECTIVE WORLD
IMAGES	367 – 1	IMAGES OF THE MOST HIGH
IMAGES	397 – 1	MENTAL IMAGES IMPRESSED UPON
IMAGES	398 – 1	RECEIVE THE IMAGES OF YOUR THOUGHT
IMAGES	400 – 3	MENTAL IMAGES THAT ARE DEFINITE
IMAGES	416 – 3	IMAGES OF HIS OWN BELIEF
IMAGES	416 – 3	CREATES A FORM AROUND THESE IMAGES
IMAGES	500 – 5	IMAGES OF THOUGHT ARE HELD
IMAGINATION	087 – 5	A LIMITLESS IMAGINATION
IMAGINATION	151 – 4	WORK THROUGH MAN'S IMAGINATION AND WILL
IMAGINATION	193 – 2	THE IMAGINATION IS CREATIVE
IMAGINATION	193 – 4	THE INNER IMAGINATION TO WORK ON
IMAGINATION	194 – 3	IMAGINATION, WILL AND CONCENTRATION
IMAGINATION	194 – 4	THE IMAGINATION IS CALLED INTO PLAY
IMAGINATION	194 – 4	THE IMAGINATION IS TO RESPOND
IMAGINATION	195 – 2	PURPOSE IN OUR IMAGINATION
IMAGINATION	217 – 1	IMAGINATION, IDEA NOR REFLECTION
IMAGINATION	218 – 3	IMAGINATION BY FIRE CAUGHT
IMAGINATION	246 – 4	THIS IN OUR IMAGINATION
IMAGINATION	262 – 1	DIVORCED FROM MY IMAGINATION
IMAGINATION	317 – 1	DISENTANGLE OUR IMAGINATION
IMAGINATION	398 – 4	WARMTH, COLOR AND IMAGINATION
IMAGINATION	398 – 5	THE IMAGINATION BACK OF OUR WORD
IMAGINATION	418 – 4	THE WILL AND THE IMAGINATION
IMAGINATION	418 – 4	THE OFFICE OF THE IMAGINATION
IMAGINE	084 – 3	IMAGINE THE LAW EVER FAILING
IMAGINE	108 – 1	CANNOT IMAGINE A MECHANICAL
IMAGINE	108 – 3	IMAGINE WITHOUT THE POWER TO MANIFEST
IMAGINE	187 – 1	CAPACITY TO IMAGINE WHAT LIFE IS
IMAGINED	066 – 1	WHICH CAN ONLY BE IMAGINED
IMBUED	107 – 4	IMBUED WITH GOODNESS
IMBUED	459 – 6	IMBUED WITH DIVINE GOODNESS
IMBUING	251 – 4	IMBUING IT WITH ITS OWN LAWS
IMITATE	263 – 6	DO NOT NEED TO IMITATE
IMMATERIAL	091 – 2	SOUL IS IMMATERIAL AS WE THINK OF MATTER
IMMATERIAL	098 – 1	SOUL IS THE IMMATERIAL
IMMATERIAL	197 – 1	MADE OF IMMATERIAL SUBSTANCE
IMMATURE	454 – 4	IMMATURE IDEAS WHICH DENY
IMMEDIATE	251 – 2	IMMEDIATE ONENESS WITH GOD
IMMEDIATE	283 – 2	ITS IMMEDIATE RESPONSE
IMMEDIATE	378 – 2	PERSONAL AND IMMEDIATE EXPERIENCE
IMMEDIATE	406 – 3	THE IMMEDIATE CONNECTION BETWEEN
IMMEDIATELY	272 – 4	IMMEDIATELY AND DIRECTLY
IMMEDIATELY	290 – 1	YOU WILL IMMEDIATELY HAVE
IMMERSED	038 – 3	SURROUNDED BY, IMMERSED IN
IMMERSED	040 – 1	IMMERSED IN AN INFINITE INTELLIGENCE
IMMERSED	042 – 3	IMMERSED IN AN INFINITE KNOWINGNESS
IMMERSED	044 – 3	IMMERSED IN A PERFECT LIFE
IMMERSED	050 – 2	IMMERSED IN AN INFINITE GOOD
IMMERSED	140 – 2	IMMERSED IN AN INFINITE CREATIVE MEDIUM
IMMERSED	142 – 2	IMMERSED IN THE ATMOSPHERE
IMMERSED	454 – 3	IMMERSED IN THE INFINITE GODHEAD
IMMERSED	471 – 6	IMMERSED IN AN EVERLASTING SPIRIT
IMMERSION	471 – 6	COMPLETE IMMERSION IN SPIRIT
IMMORTAL	377 – 2	WE ARE NOW IMMORTAL

IMMORTAL	386 - 2	MAN IS AN IMMORTAL BEING
IMMORTAL	408 - 3	HIS REAL AND IMMORTAL SELF
IMMORTAL	479 - 1	HE WAS AN IMMORTAL BEING
IMMORTALITY	104 - 4	FROM THE STANDPOINT OF IMMORTALITY
IMMORTALITY	335 - 3	THE IMMORTALITY OF EVERY SOUL
IMMORTALITY	335 - 3	IMMORTALITY IS HERE AND NOW
IMMORTALITY	346 - 1	FIRMLY CONVINCED OF IMMORTALITY
IMMORTALITY	346 - 1	IMMORTALITY NOW
IMMORTALITY	371 - 1	IMMORTALITY MEANS THAT WE SHALL PERSIST
IMMORTALITY	372 - 2	THE THOUGHT THAT IMMORTALITY
IMMORTALITY	372 - 2	IMMORTALITY WORTHY OF THE NAME
IMMORTALITY	376 - 3	NOT DIE TO TAKE ON IMMORTALITY
IMMORTALITY	385 - 3	SUBSTANTIATE THE CLAIM OF IMMORTALITY
IMMORTALITY	386 - 1	UNLESS IMMORTALITY MEANS THIS
IMMORTALITY	386 - 2	ON ITS TEACHINGS OF IMMORTALITY
IMMORTALITY	386 - 3	BASE MY HOPES OF IMMORTALITY
IMMORTALITY	386 - 3	I LOOK UPON THE BELIEF IN IMMORTALITY
IMMORTALITY	386 - 3	IMMORTALITY OR THE CONTINUATION OF
IMMORTALITY	387 - 3	TRUE REALIZATION OF THE IMMORTALITY
IMMORTALITY	421 - 3	CONVINCED OF IMMORTALITY NOW
IMMUNE	121 - 1	IS IMMUNE FROM MALPRACTICE
IMMUNE	251 - 2	IMMUNE TO NEGATIVE EXPERIENCES
IMMUNE	256 - 5	IMMUNE TO NEGATIVE EXPERIENCES
IMMUTABILITY	052 - 2	IMMUTABILITY AND THE AVAILABILITY OF
IMMUTABILITY	054 - 2	THE IMMUTABILITY OF THE LAW
IMMUTABLE	026 - 5	BUILT UPON IMMUTABLE INVISIBLE PRINCIPLES
IMMUTABLE	033 - 2	GOVERNED BY IMMUTABLE LAWS
IMMUTABLE	034 - 1	IT IS AN IMMUTABLE LAW
IMMUTABLE	042 - 5	LAWS OF NATURE ARE SET AND IMMUTABLE
IMMUTABLE	043 - 2	AN INFINITE AND IMMUTABLE LAW
IMMUTABLE	043 - 3	IMMUTABLE REACTIONS INHERENT
IMMUTABLE	044 - 3	WILL REACT AS IMMUTABLE LAW
IMMUTABLE	048 - 3	IMMUTABLE AND IMPERSONAL
IMMUTABLE	052 - 2	IMMUTABLE AS THE LAW IS
IMMUTABLE	111 - 2	IMMUTABLE LAW OF CAUSE AND EFFECT
IMMUTABLE	288 - 1	THE EXISTENCE OF THAT IMMUTABLE LAW
IMMUTABLE	339 - 2	PROPELLED BY AN IMMUTABLE LAW
IMMUTABLE	395 - 1	LAWS OF BEING ARE SET AND IMMUTABLE
IMMUTABLE	433 - 3	CAUSE AND EFFECT IS IMMUTABLE
IMMUTABLE	434 - 2	IMMUTABLE LAW OF CAUSE AND EFFECT
IMMUTABLE LAW	489 - 3	HAPPEN BY AN IMMUTABLE LAW
IMMUTABLE PRINCIPLE	178 - 3	IS BASED ON IMMUTABLE PRINCIPLE
IMPART	041 - 2	ITS NATURE IS TO IMPART
IMPARTATION	139 - 2	DIRECT IMPARTATION OF ITSELF THROUGH US
IMPARTATION	328 - 3	A DIRECT IMPARTATION FROM HIM
IMPARTATION	478 - 3	THE IMPARTATION OF THE DIVINE
IMPARTIAL	093 - 2	IMPARTIAL IMPERSONAL SOUL
IMPARTIAL	150 - 1	DIVINE AND IMPARTIAL GIVER
IMPARTIAL	433 - 3	IS ENTIRELY IMPARTIAL
IMPARTING	065 - 4	IMPARTING HIS OWN NATURE
IMPARTING	329 - 5	IMPARTING TO US WHAT WE KNOW
IMPARTING	360 - 2	IMPARTING TO IT HER OWN BEING
IMPARTS	040 - 4	IMPARTS OF ITSELF ONLY
IMPATIENT	478 - 2	IMPATIENT GESTURE OF THE SOUL
IMPELLING	366 - 3	THE INFINITE LOVE IMPELLING ME

IMPELS	127 - 2	URGE WHICH IMPELS PEOPLE
IMPELS	168 - 3	IMPELS HIM TO POUR OUT
IMPERATIVE	319 - 2	IMPERATIVE THAT WE TURN FROM
IMPERATIVE	380 - 2	IMPERATIVE THAT WE MAKE
IMPERFECT	130 - 3	CAUSE HIM TO APPEAR IMPERFECT
IMPERFECT	131 - 1	TO APPEAR IMPERFECT
IMPERFECT	185 - 1	THAT WHICH APPEARS IMPERFECT WILL
IMPERFECT	309 - 3	IMPERFECT MAN
IMPERFECTION	185 - 2	IMPERFECTION FOR A SINGLE SECOND
IMPERSONAL	041 - 2	THE UNIVERSE IS IMPERSONAL
IMPERSONAL	043 - 1	LAW IS IMPERSONAL
IMPERSONAL	048 - 3	IMMUTABLE AND IMPERSONAL LAWS
IMPERSONAL	050 - 1	PERSONAL AND IMPERSONAL PRINCIPLES
IMPERSONAL	078 - 2	AN ABSOLUTELY IMPERSONAL THING
IMPERSONAL	083 - 2	SUBJECTIVE IS ALWAYS IMPERSONAL
IMPERSONAL	093 - 2	IMPERSONAL SOUL IS THE MEDIUM
IMPERSONAL	096 - 3	IT IS IMPERSONAL
IMPERSONAL	184 - 3	WITH AN IMPERSONAL PRINCIPLE
IMPERSONAL	192 - 4	NATURAL LAWS ARE IMPERSONAL
IMPERSONAL	200 - 4	DISEASE IS AN IMPERSONAL
IMPERSONAL	208 - 3	IMPERSONAL AND CREATIVE
IMPERSONAL	221 - 3	IMPERSONAL THOUGHT-FORCE
IMPERSONAL	245 - 1	WHICH IS AN IMPERSONAL
IMPERSONAL	269 - 2	IT IS IMPERSONAL
IMPERSONAL	269 - 2	BECAUSE IT IS IMPERSONAL
IMPERSONAL	276 - 1	ITS IMPERSONAL ACTION IMPLICITLY
IMPERSONAL	278 - 1	IS RECEPTIVE, NEUTRAL, IMPERSONAL
IMPERSONAL	320 - 4	LAW IS ALWAYS IMPERSONAL, NEUTRAL
IMPERSONAL	334 - 4	THE IMPERSONAL ATTRIBUTES OF LIFE
IMPERSONAL	408 - 4	IT IS IMPERSONAL
IMPERSONAL	439 - 5	LESSON IN IMPERSONAL HEALING
IMPERSONALLY	042 - 6	IMPERSONALLY RESPONSIVE TO EACH
IMPERSONALNESS	039 - 3	IMPERSONALNESS OF THE LAW
IMPETUS	160 - 4	A GREAT IMPETUS TOWARD FAITH
IMPLANT	224 - 2	IMPLANT THE RIGHT IDEA
IMPLANTED	236 - 1	THINGS WHICH ARE NOT IMPLANTED
IMPLICIT	402 - 2	IMPLICIT FAITH THAT THEY WILL
IMPLIED	167 - 2	TREATMENT IS IMPLIED IN THE BIBLE
IMPLIES	110 - 2	IMPLIES THE POSSIBILITY OF SUFFERING
IMPLIES	415 - 4	PHYSICAL WORLD AROUND US IMPLIES
IMPLIES	419 - 1	IMPLIES NO HURT FOR ANYONE
IMPLY	297 - 3	THIS WOULD IMPLY DOUBT
IMPORT	205 - 3	REALLY IS OF SMALL IMPORT
IMPORTANT	074 - 1	MOST IMPORTANT CONCLUSIONS
IMPORTANT	192 - 3	IMPORTANT PLACE IN THE CREATIVE ORDER
IMPOSE	107 - 2	IMPOSE FREEDOM OR BONDAGE
IMPOSED	037 - 1	IMPOSED UPON US
IMPOSED	053 - 1	IMPOSED UPON US BY THE SPIRIT
IMPOSED	393 - 2	FORM MUST BE IMPOSED UPON IT
IMPOSSIBLE	069 - 3	IT IS IMPOSSIBLE TO CONCEIVE
IMPOSSIBLE	084 - 2	IMPOSSIBLE TO THINK OF A TIME
IMPOSSIBLE	084 - 2	IT IS IMPOSSIBLE TO CONCEIVE
IMPOSSIBLE	095 - 3	IT IS IMPOSSIBLE TO DIVIDE MIND
IMPOSSIBLE	312 - 1	IMPOSSIBLE FOR THE INFINITE TO KNOW
IMPOSSIBLE	344 - 3	IMPOSSIBLE TO PUT INTO WORDS

IMPOSSIBLE	359 - 3	IMPOSSIBLE FOR JESUS NOT TO
IMPOSSIBLE	399 - 1	OUTSIDE AND THIS IS IMPOSSIBLE
IMPOSSIBLE	449 - 2	IMPOSSIBLE FOR A MAN TO CONCEAL
IMPOVERISH	250 - 3	NOTHING CAN IMPOVERISH THAT FLOW
IMPOVERISHED	054 - 3	ONE FINDS HIMSELF IMPOVERISHED
IMPREGNATED	407 - 4	IMPREGNATED WITH DIVINE IDEAS
IMPREGNATING	088 - 2	IMPREGNATING IT WITH IDEAS
IMPREGNATING	088 - 3	IMPREGNATING IT WITH THE DIVINE IDEAS
IMPRESS	193 - 1	WE IMPRESS IT WITH
IMPRESS	199 - 2	IMPRESS OF OUR THOUGHT
IMPRESS	207 - 1	IMPRESS OF OUR THOUGHT
IMPRESS	208 - 3	IMPRESS UPON IT
IMPRESS	221 - 4	IMPRESS A DEFINITE IDEA
IMPRESS	234 - 4	WHICH RECEIVES THE IMPRESS
IMPRESS	278 - 1	RECEIVING THE IMPRESS OF OUR THOUGHT
IMPRESS	319 - 2	LIMITATION IS TO IMPRESS IT
IMPRESS	320 - 4	THE IMPRESS OF OUR THOUGHT
IMPRESS	380 - 1	TRYING TO IMPRESS OUR THOUGHT
IMPRESS	381 - 1	HE WAS TRYING TO IMPRESS HER
IMPRESS	400 - 1	WE IMPRESS IT
IMPRESSED	118 - 2	IDEA IMPRESSED UPON IT
IMPRESSES	416 - 3	MAN IMPRESSES THE LAW
IMPRESSING	126 - 4	IMPRESSING OUR THOUGHT UPON
IMPRESSING	126 - 4	IMPRESSING OUR THOUGHT UPON IT IS NOT
IMPRESSING	416 - 4	WHAT WE ARE IMPRESSING UPON THE LAW
IMPRESSING	417 - 4	WE ARE IMPRESSING THE LAW
IMPRESSING	458 - 5	IMPRESSING THEM UPON IT
IMPRESSION	252 - 2	THE MENTAL IMPRESSION
IMPRESSION	270 - 4	IMPRESSION UPON HIS ENVIRONMENT
IMPRESSION	270 - 4	THAT WE MAY LEAVE ANY IMPRESSION
IMPRESSION	380 - 2	ONLY A MENTAL IMPRESSION
IMPRESSION	416 - 2	SLIGHTEST IMPRESSION OF THOUGHT
IMPRESSION	421 - 4	CLEAR IMPRESSION OF THOUGHT
IMPRESSIONS	075 - 4	OUR MENTAL IMPRESSIONS
IMPRESSIONS	077 - 3	IMPRESSIONS ARE MORE OR LESS VAGUE
IMPRESSIONS	088 - 1	RETAINED ALL OF THE IMAGES, IMPRESSIONS
IMPRESSIONS	091 - 1	RECEIVES IMPRESSIONS FROM SPIRIT
IMPRESSIONS	097 - 3	THE IMPRESSIONS OF SPIRIT
IMPRESSIONS	209 - 3	RECEIVED FALSE IMPRESSIONS
IMPRESSIONS	211 - 2	NOT REPRODUCE FALSE IMPRESSIONS
IMPRESSIONS	328 - 5	IMPRESSIONS ARE MORE OR LESS COLORED
IMPRESSIONS	381 - 2	CONTINUALLY GETTING IMPRESSIONS
IMPRESSIONS	382 - 1	ANY MENTAL IMPRESSIONS OR IMAGES
IMPRINT	348 - 4	IMPRINT ON THE WALLS OF TIME
IMPRINT	450 - 3	IMPRINT OF SUCCESS WRITTEN IN BOLD LETTERS
IMPRINTED	490 - 2	IMAGE OF GOD IS IMPRINTED
IMPRISONED	311 - 2	IT WAS TEMPORARILY IMPRISONED
IMPROVEMENT	175 - 5	SOME SIGN OF IMPROVEMENT FROM THE FIRST
IMPULSE	030 - 3	ACCORDING TO THE NATURE, IMPULSE, EMOTION
IMPULSE	052 - 4	THE IMPULSE OF OUR CREATIVE BELIEF
IMPULSE	067 - 2	IMPULSE TO MOVE UNLESS
IMPULSE	094 - 1	ACCORDING TO THE IMPULSE
IMPULSE	222 - 4	IMPULSE MUST EXPRESS AT THE LEVEL
IMPULSE	420 - 4	AN IMPULSE PLANTED BY THE DIVINE
IMPULSES	031 - 3	MISTAKING SUBJECTIVE IMPULSES FOR

IMPULSES	053 - 3	WITH THOUGHTS, IMPULSES, EMOTIONS
IMPULSES	149 - 4	IMPULSES WE CAN SCARCELY COMPREHEND
IMPULSION	285 - 1	IMPULSION OF MENTAL TREATMENT
IMPURITIES	205 - 1	DRAIN OUT ALL THE IMPURITIES
IMPURITIES	205 - 1	IMPURITIES AND PRODUCE A HEALING
IMPURITIES	261 - 2	IMPURITIES OF THE FLESH
IMPURITY	453 - 3	THINKS IMPURITY,THEN HIS ACTS WILL BE IMPURE
IN	052 - 2	IT MUST BE IN AND THROUGH US
IN	267 - 3	IT IS IN MAN AS WELL AS OUTSIDE HIM
IN	285 - 1	IN THE ONE WE ARE SEEKING TO HELP
IN	322 - 3	ONE MUST BELIEVE IN IT
INABILITY	133 - 2	MAN'S INABILITY TO EMBODY
INABILITY	197 - 5	INABILITY TO SEE PERFECTION
INABILITY	257 - 1	INABILITY TO LET GO
INACTION	231 - 5	NO INACTION, NO LIMITED ACTION
INACTION	233 - 4	INACTION WILL QUICKLY DISAPPEAR
INACTION	241 - 5	NO INACTION OR PARALYSIS IN MIND
INACTION	247 - 3	NO STRAIN NO INACTION OR OVERACTION
INACTION	255 - 1	NO OVERACTION, NO INACTION
INACTION	258 - 3	NO BELIEF IN INACTION
INACTION	289 - 3	PERFECTLY PRACTICE INACTION
INACTION	295 - 4	INACTION ALL THINGS ARE POSSIBLE
INACTIVE	240 - 4	BECOME PARALYZED OR INACTIVE
INACTIVE	240 - 4	NEITHER INACTIVE NOR IS IT TOO ACTIVE
INACTIVITY	286 - 2	HEALS THE BELIEF IN INACTIVITY
INACTIVITY	291 - 4	THERE IS NO BELIEF IN INACTIVITY
IN ALL	265 - 1	GOD IS IN ALL
IN ALL	323 - 3	IN ALL, OVER ALL, AND THROUGH ALL
INANIMATE	418 - 5	ANIMATE AND THE INANIMATE
INCARNATE	150 - 5	SPIRIT AS BEING INCARNATE
INCARNATED	042 - 2	ONE GOD INCARNATED IN ALL PEOPLES
INCARNATED	042 - 5	INCARNATED IN ALL MEN
INCARNATED	159 - 2	SPIRIT IS INCARNATED
INCARNATED	159 - 5	SPIRIT INCARNATED IN US
INCARNATED	160 - 1	ETERNAL IS INCARNATED IN US
INCARNATED	178 - 4	SPIRIT IS INCARNATED IN US
INCARNATED	263 - 6	DIVINE HAS NOT INCARNATED
INCARNATED	284 - 2	ALREADY INCARNATED THROUGH ALL
INCARNATED	454 - 6	THE INCARNATED AND REAL EGO
INCARNATION	042 - 3	THE DIVINE INCARNATION IS INHERENT
INCARNATION	139 - 3	THROUGH THE ACT OF INCARNATION
INCARNATION	139 - 3	INCARNATION THROUGH EVOLUTION
INCARNATION	217 - 1	INCARNATION OF THE UNIVERSAL I AM
INCARNATION	229 - 2	INCARNATION OF GOD IN MAN
INCARNATION	341 - 3	DIRECT INCARNATION OF THE ORIGINAL
INCARNATION	360 - 1	INCARNATION OF THE DIVINE
INCARNATION	383 - 3	MAN IS AN INCARNATION OF GOD
INCENTIVE	298 - 3	GREATEST INCENTIVE IN HIS LIFE
INCIDENT	351 - 3	EVERY INCIDENT WHICH HAS EVER
INCIDENTS	348 - 1	ALL THE INCIDENTS WHICH HE
INCLUDED	166 - 4	THAT MAN IS INCLUDED
INCLUDES	032 - 2	INCLUDES THE MATERIAL
INCLUDES	454 - 5	GREATER ALWAYS INCLUDES THE LESSER
INCLUSIVE	430 - 5	ARMS WHICH ARE ALL INCLUSIVE
INCOMPLETENESS	387 - 2	HAVE BEEN MARRED BY INCOMPLETENESS

INCOMPLETION	338 - 3	IN THIS STATE OF INCOMPLETION
INCOMPLETION	464 - 4	NEVER CONSCIOUS OF INCOMPLETION
INCORPORATE	035 - 1	INCORPORATE IN HIS LIFE
INCORPORATE	164 - 2	TREATMENT SHOULD INCORPORATE
INCORPORATE	244 - 5	INCORPORATE THOUGHTS OF PEACE
INCORPORATE	331 - 2	WE INCORPORATE THIS CONSCIOUSNESS
INCORPORATED	143 - 1	ACCEPTED AND INCORPORATED
INCORPORATES	197 - 2	INCORPORATES THEM WITH HIS
INCREASE	271 - 4	GRADUALLY INCREASE IN WISDOM
INCREASED	268 - 1	THE MOLD WE PROVIDE IS INCREASED
INCREASES	482 - 2	INCREASES KNOWLEDGE ABOUT AN OLD ONE
INCREDIBLE	138 - 1	INCREDIBLE POSSIBILITIES OF DOMINION
INCREDULOUS	137 - 2	DAY FOR INCREDULOUS SKEPTICISM
INCURABLE	216 - 1	THERE IS NO INCURABLE
INCURABLE	216 - 3	INCURABLE DISEASE
INCURABLE	216 - 3	INCURABLE MEANS NOT SUSCEPTIBLE OF
INDECISION	245 - 2	ALL BELIEF IN INDECISION
INDEFINABLE	311 - 3	SUBSTANCE INDEFINABLE AND INDIVISIBLE
INDEPENDENCE	307 - 3	INDEPENDENCE OF YOUR OWN MENTALITY
INDEPENDENT	200 - 1	INDEPENDENT EVEN OF HIMSELF
INDEPENDENT	377 - 2	INDEPENDENT OF THE PHYSICAL BODY
INDEPENDENT	391 - 3	NO INDEPENDENT OFFSPRING
INDEPENDENT	406 - 3	INDEPENDENT OF ALL FORMS
INDEPENDENT	407 - 2	INDEPENDENT OF ANY FORM
INDEPENDENT	414 - 1	TREATMENT MUST BE INDEPENDENT
INDEPENDENT	414 - 2	HAVE NO INDEPENDENT EXISTENCE
INDEPENDENT	415 - 3	INDEPENDENT OF ANY INDIVIDUAL ACTION
INDEPENDENTLY	210 - 3	PRINCIPLE WORKS INDEPENDENTLY
INDEPENDENTLY	378 - 2	SOUL CAN OPERATE INDEPENDENTLY
INDEPENDENTLY	390 - 2	THINK INDEPENDENTLY OF CONDITIONS
INDEPENDENTLY	406 - 4	THINK INDEPENDENTLY OF ANY GIVEN
INDEPENDENTLY	417 - 2	LEARNING TO THINK INDEPENDENTLY
INDESTRUCTIBILITY	311 - 2	INDESTRUCTIBILITY AND ETERNALITY
INDESTRUCTIBLE	116 - 3	IT IS AS INDESTRUCTIBLE AS GOD
INDESTRUCTIBLE	230 - 6	PERFECT AND INDESTRUCTIBLE RIGHT NOW
INDESTRUCTIBLE	338 - 3	EACH ONE OF US IS AN INDESTRUCTIBLE
INDESTRUCTIBLE	369 - 3	INDIVIDUALITY IS INDESTRUCTIBLE
INDIA	272 - 3	JUST AS TRUE IN INDIA
INDIFFERENT	211 - 2	GOOD, BAD AND INDIFFERENT
INDISPENSABLE	302 - 2	ATTITUDES OF MIND ARE INDISPENSABLE
INDIVIDUAL	025 - 2	MAKE MAN AS AN INDIVIDUAL
INDIVIDUAL	029 - 2	OUR INDIVIDUAL USE OF THAT GREATER
INDIVIDUAL	029 - 4	EACH INDIVIDUAL MAINTAINS HIS IDENTITY
INDIVIDUAL	030 - 2	THE OTHER IS INDIVIDUAL
INDIVIDUAL	030 - 2	INDIVIDUAL ONLY AT THE POINT
INDIVIDUAL	071 - 2	MAKE A MECHANICAL INDIVIDUAL
INDIVIDUAL	087 - 1	MAN IS AN INDIVIDUAL
INDIVIDUAL	106 - 1	TRUE OF THE INDIVIDUAL
INDIVIDUAL	107 - 3	INDIVIDUAL SHOULD BE FREE FROM THE BONDAGE
INDIVIDUAL	196 - 1	MAN IS AN INDIVIDUAL
INDIVIDUAL	219 - 4	MUST COME TO EACH INDIVIDUAL
INDIVIDUAL	237 - 3	INDIVIDUAL IS SIMPLY A POINT
INDIVIDUAL	313 - 2	INDIVIDUAL ENTITIES IN A UNIVERSE
INDIVIDUAL	347 - 3	OUR INDIVIDUAL USE OF MENTAL LAW
INDIVIDUAL	364 - 2	INDIVIDUAL USE OF UNIVERSAL LAW

INDIVIDUAL	384 - 2	CONTINUE IN OUR OWN INDIVIDUAL
INDIVIDUAL	395 - 2	CAN KNOW ABOUT THE INDIVIDUAL
INDIVIDUAL	401 - 2	IT BE INDIVIDUAL OR UNIVERSAL
INDIVIDUAL	441 - 4	INDIVIDUAL CONVICTION THROUGH
INDIVIDUAL	448 - 1	INDIVIDUAL MUST MAKE THE TEST
INDIVIDUAL	461 - 2	INDIVIDUAL AND CAN DO AS HE CHOOSES
INDIVIDUAL	477 - 6	BOTH INDIVIDUAL AND UNIVERSAL
INDIVIDUALITIES	415 - 4	ARE STILL SPONTANEOUS INDIVIDUALITIES
INDIVIDUALITY	025 - 2	INDIVIDUALITY MUST BE SPONTANEOUS
INDIVIDUALITY	108 - 1	INDIVIDUALITY IS MEANT SELF-CHIOCE
INDIVIDUALITY	108 - 1	INDIVIDUALITY MUST BE CREATED IN THE IMAGE
INDIVIDUALITY	143 - 4	A MECHANISTIC INDIVIDUALITY
INDIVIDUALITY	165 - 1	WITH OUR OWN INDIVIDUALITY
INDIVIDUALITY	196 - 1	INDIVIDUALITY CANNOT BE AUTOMATICALLY
INDIVIDUALITY	223 - 2	HE IS A UNIQUE INDIVIDUALITY
INDIVIDUALITY	279 - 2	INDIVIDUALITY COMPELS INFINITY
INDIVIDUALITY	332 - 5	INDIVIDUALITY MEANS SELF-CHOICE, VOLITION
INDIVIDUALITY	334 - 2	WHAT ONE DOES WITH HIS INDIVIDUALITY
INDIVIDUALITY	338 - 2	OWN INDIVIDUALITY
INDIVIDUALITY	338 - 2	CONTROL THIS INDIVIDUALITY
INDIVIDUALITY	346 - 1	INDIVIDUALITY GOD AS PERSONAL
INDIVIDUALITY	350 - 1	HIS INDIVIDUALITY IN THE PROCESS
INDIVIDUALITY	354 - 3	MAINTAINS THE INDIVIDUALITY
INDIVIDUALITY	369 - 3	HIS INDIVIDUALITY IS INDESTRUCTIBLE
INDIVIDUALITY	372 - 1	INDIVIDUALITY MIGHT REMAIN WITHOUT
INDIVIDUALITY	381 - 3	ALONE CONSTITUTE INDIVIDUALITY
INDIVIDUALITY	381 - 4	IT IS A CRIME AGAINST INDIVIDUALITY
INDIVIDUALITY	413 - 1	ALL INDIVIDUALITY MERGES
INDIVIDUALITY	417 - 2	TO ASSERT OUR INDIVIDUALITY
INDIVIDUALITY	419 - 4	THE REALITY OF INDIVIDUALITY
INDIVIDUALITY	419 - 5	ONE DOES WITH HIS INDIVIDUALITY
INDIVIDUALITY	462 - 1	CLEARER STATEMENT OF INDIVIDUALITY
INDIVIDUALITY	469 - 3	OUR DIVINE INDIVIDUALITY
INDIVIDUALIZATION	313 - 1	THE INDIVIDUALIZATION OF THE UNIVERSAL
INDIVIDUALIZATION	344 - 1	SENSED THE INDIVIDUALIZATION OF BEING
INDIVIDUALIZATION	421 - 2	SENSED THE INDIVIDUALIZATION OF BEING
INDIVIDUALIZATION	477 - 1	HE IS A REAL INDIVIDUALIZATION
INDIVIDUALIZED	030 - 2	OUR LAW BECAUSE WE HAVE INDIVIDUALIZED IT
INDIVIDUALIZED	030 - 2	INDIVIDUAL BUT IS INDIVIDUALIZED
INDIVIDUALIZED	065 - 1	AN INDIVIDUALIZED IDEA OF GOD
INDIVIDUALIZED	093 - 4	BECAUSE WE HAVE INDIVIDUALIZED
INDIVIDUALIZED	093 - 4	NOT REALLY INDIVIDUAL BUT INDIVIDUALIZED
INDIVIDUALIZED	093 - 5	WITHIN THE INDIVIDUALIZED POINT
INDIVIDUALIZED	263 - 6	FOREVER INDIVIDUALIZED
INDIVIDUALIZED	331 - 3	INDIVIDUALIZED CENTERS OF GOD CONSCIOUSNESS
INDIVIDUALIZED	332 - 4	A POINT OF INDIVIDUALIZED
INDIVIDUALIZED	352 - 2	DISTINCT AND INDIVIDUALIZED CENTER
INDIVIDUALIZED	352 - 4	SEPARATE AND INDIVIDUALIZED PERSONALITY
INDIVIDUALIZED	391 - 3	IN AN INDIVIDUALIZED STATE, GOD
INDIVIDUALIZED	392 - 1	INDIVIDUALIZED AS A LAW
INDIVIDUALIZED	394 - 2	INDIVIDUALIZED SUBJECTIVE MIND
INDIVIDUALIZED	396 - 3	INDIVIDUALIZED THE PERSONALITY OF GOD
INDIVIDUALIZED	419 - 3	INDIVIDUALIZED CENTERS OF GOD CONSCIOUSNESS
INDIVIDUALIZED	481 - 3	INDIVIDUALIZED CENTER OF GOD CONSCIOUSNESS
INDIVIDUALIZES	391 - 5	MAN INDIVIDUALIZES HIMSELF

INDIVIDUALIZES	397 - 4	WHERE HE INDIVIDUALIZES
INDIVIDUALLY	313 - 1	IT IS THINKING INDIVIDUALLY
INDIVIDUAL SOUL	114 - 4	INDIVIDUAL SOUL IS AN EFFECT AND NOT A
INDIVISIBLE	184 - 5	THE TRUTH IS INDIVISIBLE
INDIVISIBLE	205 - 4	THIS MIND IS INDIVISIBLE
INDIVISIBLY	337 - 2	SO INDIVISIBLY UNITED WITH IT
INDUCE	144 - 2	WE SHALL INDUCE IN MIND
INDUCE	220 - 4	INDUCE WITHIN CONSCIOUSNESS
INDUCE	278 - 4	ANY INDIVIDUAL CAN ACTUALLY INDUCE
INDUCE	282 - 2	INDUCE A GREATER CONCEPT
INDUCED	185 - 3	NOT INDUCED THE NECESSARY IMAGES
INDUCED	338 - 1	INDUCED INTO A SUBJECTIVE STATE
INDUCES	204 - 3	INDUCES A CLEAR CONCEPT OF REALITY
INDUCING	164 - 3	TREATMENT IS THE SCIENCE OF INDUCING
INDUCING	170 - 5	INDUCING AN INNER REALIZATION
INDUCING	183 - 3	INDUCING AN INTERIOR AWARENESS
INDUCING	198 - 4	SCIENCE OF INDUCING THOUGHT
INDUCTIVE	123 - 2	BY THE ROUTE OF INDUCTIVE SCIENCE
INDUCTIVELY	208 - 4	BOTH INDUCTIVELY AND DEDUCTIVELY
INDUCTIVE REASONING	096 - 2	INDUCTIVE REASONING IS AN INQUIRY INTO
INDUCTIVE REASONING	096 - 3	NO INDUCTIVE REASONING EITHER IN THE SPIRIT
INDULGE	051 - 1	INDULGE IN TOO MUCH THEORY
INDULGE	335 - 2	AS LONG AS WE INDULGE IN IT
INDULGE	430 - 4	INDULGE IN EVIL DOING
INDULGED	465 - 4	NEVER BE INDULGED IN BY ANYONE
INDUSTRY	428 - 2	NOR EVEN THE CAPTAINS OF INDUSTRY
INDWELLING	217 - 1	ALWAYS AN INDWELLING PRESENCE
INDWELLING	217 - 2	IT IS INDWELLING
INDWELLING	251 - 2	WITH THE INDWELLING ALMIGHTY
INDWELLING	257 - 5	INDWELLING CHRIST WITHIN ME DISSOLVES
INDWELLING	293 - 4	THE INDWELLING ESSENCE OF MY LIFE
INDWELLING	306 - 4	THE INFINITE INDWELLING
INDWELLING	306 - 4	FEEL THIS INDWELLING GOOD
INDWELLING	306 - 4	MEDITATE UPON THIS INDWELLING GOD
INDWELLING	328 - 3	LIVING PRESENCE INDWELLING ALL
INDWELLING	330 - 3	THIS INDWELLING SPIRIT
INDWELLING	343 - 4	NOT EXTERNAL BUT IS INDWELLING
INDWELLING	358 - 4	INDWELLING SPIRIT WITHIN ME
INDWELLING	374 - 1	INDWELLING SPIRIT ALONE MAINTAINS
INDWELLING	418 - 3	THIS INDWELLING PRESENCE IS ALREADY
INDWELLING	430 - 2	INDWELLING GOD WHO IS THE HEAVENLY
INDWELLING	431 - 1	INDWELLING SPIRIT WHO LIVES IN
INDWELLING	441 - 1	SPIRIT INDWELLING THEIR LIVES
INDWELLING	503 - 5	CHRIST INDWELLING EVERY SOUL
INDWELLING CHRIST	245 - 2	INDWELLING CHRIST IN ME DISSOLVES
INDWELLS	250 - 2	THE SPIRIT INDWELLS HIM
INDWELLS	303 - 3	THE SPIRIT THAT INDWELLS HIM
INDWELLS	369 - 1	CHRIST INDWELLS OUR OWN LIVES
INDWELLS	444 - 2	GOD INDWELLS EVERY SOUL
INDWELT	368 - 1	GOD INDWELT HIS OWN SOUL
INEFFECTIVE	413 - 5	INEFFECTIVE WORKER IN THIS FIELD
INERT	374 - 2	BODY LIES COLD, INERT, LIFELESS
INEVITABLE	032 - 1	CONTRADICT THE INEVITABLE
INEVITABLE	032 - 2	SEEMS AN INEVITABLE CONCLUSION
INEVITABLE	111 - 1	AN INEVITABLE CONSEQUENCE

INEVITABLE	304 – 5	INEVITABLE FOR THIS IS THE WAY
INEVITABLE	316 – 2	INEVITABLE THAT THE DAY SHALL COME
INEVITABLE	340 – 4	INEVITABLE END OF LOCOMOTION
INEVITABLE	433 – 2	INEVITABLE CONSEQUENCE
INEVITABLY	140 – 4	CONVICTIONS INEVITABLY OUT-PICTURE
INEVITABLY	145 – 2	MIND ACTIVITY INEVITABLY TENDS
INEXCUSABLE	382 – 2	WOULD BE INEXCUSABLE
INEXHAUSTIBLE	302 – 3	THE UNIVERSE IS INEXHAUSTIBLE
INEXHAUSTIBLE	446 – 4	INEXHAUSTIBLE ONE
INEXORABLE	089 – 2	MORE THAN AN INEXORABLE LAW
INFANCY	138 – 2	MIND IS STILL IN ITS INFANCY
INFANT	210 – 4	IN THE CASE OF AN INFANT
INFER	378 – 3	INFER THAT IN PROVIDING
INFERIORITY	223 – 2	INFERIORITY WHICH HE NEEDS TO COVER UP
INFINITE	028 – 4	SINCE IT IS INFINITE
INFINITE	030 – 1	MEDIUM THAT IS INFINITE IN ITS ABILITY
INFINITE	036 – 4	ORIGINAL LIFE IS INFINITE
INFINITE	040 – 1	DIVINE MIND IS INFINITE
INFINITE	042 – 3	IMMERSED IN AN INFINITE KNOWLEDGE
INFINITE	050 – 2	THOUGHT OPERATES IS INFINITE
INFINITE	069 – 2	IN THE MIND OF THE INFINITE
INFINITE	087 – 2	INFINITE CANNOT COME FROM THE FINITE
INFINITE	091 – 4	INTELLIGENCE WHICH IS INFINITE
INFINITE	100 – 3	INANIMATE AND INFINITE STUFF
INFINITE	174 – 2	DEMAND ON THE INFINITE
INFINITE	215 – 2	LAW OF GOD IS INFINITE
INFINITE	267 – 4	MAN OPERATES IS INFINITE
INFINITE	269 – 1	INFINITE CAN NEVER BE FINITE
INFINITE	323 – 3	THERE IS ONE INFINITE MIND
INFINITE	330 – 2	INFINITE CANNOT BE DIVIDED
INFINITE	390 – 4	MIND OF GOD IS INFINITE
INFINITE	390 – 4	INFINITE AS IS MAN'S CAPACITY
INFINITE	396 – 4	INFINITE INTELLIGENCE WITHIN ITSELF
INFINITELY	400 – 3	MIND KNOWS INFINITELY MORE
INFINITE MIND	108 – 4	INFINITE MIND IS ALSO IN US
INFINITE PERSON	088 – 4	GOD AS INFINITE PERSON
INFINITY	031 – 5	WE REACH OUT TO INFINITY
INFINITY	095 – 2	IN BOTH DIRECTIONS WE REACH OUT TO INFINITY
INFINITY	104 – 4	WITHIN A BODY TO INFINITY
INFINITY	279 – 2	INDIVIDUALITY COMPELS INFINITY
INFINITY	37$ – 2	BODY WITHIN A BODY TO INFINITY
INFINITY	376 – 1	BODY WITHIN A BODY TO INFINITY
INFINITY	377 – 2	BODY WITHIN A BODY TO INFINITY
INFLAMMATION	247 – 1	INFLAMMATION OF THE NERVES
INFLAMMATION	247 – 1	IRRITATION, AGITATION NOR INFLAMMATION
INFLAMMATION	254 – 6	AGITATION OR INFLAMMATION IN SPIRIT
INFLEXIBLE	233 – 4	STATIC, FIXED, INFLEXIBLE OUTLOOK
INFLOW	440 – 4	FIND A NEW INFLOW OF LIFE
INFLUENCE	055 – 2	FREE FROM THEIR INFLUENCE
INFLUENCE	156 – 4	WHOSE INFLUENCE AND ABILITY
INFLUENCE	179 – 2	HYPNOTIZE OR MENTALLY INFLUENCE
INFLUENCE	192 – 3	TO INFLUENCE PEOPLE IS A MISTAKE
INFLUENCE	192 – 4	POWER OF WILL CAN INFLUENCE US
INFLUENCE	266 – 3	GREATLY INFLUENCE OUR ENVIRONMENT
INFLUENCE	310 – 3	THOUGHT CAN INFLUENCE

INFLUENCE	348 - 2	THE MEANING OF MENTAL INFLUENCE
INFLUENCE	350 - 2	IS THAT SUBTLE INFLUENCE
INFLUENCE	421 - 4	SILENT INFLUENCE IS ALWAYS GOING ON
INFLUENCE	451 - 5	INFLUENCE ALL THOUGHT AND ACTION
INFLUENCES	210 - 4	OF THE PARENTS INFLUENCES THE CHILD
INFLUENZA	252 - 5	CONGESTION, INFLUENZA AND GRIPPE
INFLUX	059 - 3	NEW INFLUX OF SPIRIT
INFORMATION	193 - 3	DRAW SOME INFORMATION TO OURSELVES
INFRINGEMENT	109 - 3	SOME INFRINGEMENT OF THESE LAWS
INGE	341 - 4	DEAN INGE PERHAPS THE BEST THINKER
INHABIT	479 - 4	WE SHALL INHABIT EACH IN TIME
INHABITING	480 - 5	ETERNAL REALITY INHABITING ETERNITY
INHARMOMOUS	239 - 2	EVERY INHARMONIOUS THOUGHT
INHARMONIOUS	256 - 1	CAN CHANGE INHARMONIOUS THOUGHTS
INHARMONY	083 - 1	INHARMONY DISCORD OR DECAY
INHARMONY	239 - 2	STRAIN AND INHARMONY
INHERENT	087 - 1	INHERENT LIFE IS REAL LIFE
INHERENT	106 - 3	INHERENT LIFE, REAL LIFE
INHERENT	130 - 4	LINES OF THEIR INHERENT BEING
INHERENT	439 - 3	POSSIBILITY INHERENT IN ALL MEN
INHERENT	485 - 3	INHERENT WITHIN OUR REAL NATURE
INHERIT	428 - 2	MEEK SHALL INHERIT THE EARTH
INHERITED	088 - 1	IMPRESSIONS, INHERITED TENDENCIES
INHERITED	114 - 3	IT CONTAINS OUR INHERITED TENDENCIES
INHERITED	119 - 3	NO INHERITED TENDENCY
INHIBIT	249 - 4	NOTHING TO INHIBIT IT
INHIBITED	213 - 1	IT IS NOT INHIBITED
INHIBITIONS	233 - 3	NO INHIBITIONS IN LOVE
IN HIS NAME	151 - 2	IN HIS NAME, MEANS LIKE HIS NATURE
INITIAL	407 - 2	THIS INITIAL MOVEMENT STARTS
INITIATE	209 - 2	CANNOT OF ITSELF INITIATE
INITIATIVE	354 - 3	POWER OF INITIATIVE OR SELF-CHOICE
INITIATIVE	392 - 2	READY BUT HAVING NO INITIATIVE
INJECT	486 - 5	INJECT THOSE OF LIBERTY
INLETS	489 - 7	EMERSON TELLS US THAT WE ARE INLETS
INNER	026 - 1	LISTEN TO THIS INNER VOICE
INNER	033 - 3	HIDDEN IN THE INNER BEING
INNER	054 - 1	WILLINGNESS TO LET THIS INNER SPIRIT GUIDE
INNER	064 - 2	SOME INNER ACT UPON ITSELF
INNER	068 - 4	THROUGH SOME INNER ACTION
INNER	068 - 4	POWER OF SOME INNER MOVEMENT
INNER	069 - 2	INNER PROCESS OF CONSCIOUSNESS
INNER	069 - 3	INNER MEANING OF THE TEACHING
INNER	080 - 1	INNER TEACHING OF THE TRINITY
INNER	125 - 4	THOUGHT IS AN INNER MOVEMENT
INNER	143 - 2	INNER EMBODIMENT OF IDEAS
INNER	184 - 3	AN INNER SENSE OF UNITY
INNER	186 - 3	INNER EMBODIMENT OF AN IDEA
INNER	191 - 2	AWAY IN THE INNER NATURE
INNER	201 - 5	INNER STATE OF CONSCIOUSNESS
INNER	227 - 3	TO ENTER OUR INNER CONSCIOUSNESS
INNER	230 - 4	ONE MUST USE THE INNER SIGHT
INNER	234 - 1	INNER CALM THAT PLACE WHERE LIFE
INNER	236 - 3	INNER EMOTIONS CREATE OUTER CONDITIONS
INNER	236 - 4	INNER CONSCIOUSNESS AGREES

INNER	237 - 1	CAUSED BY SOME INNER CONFLICT
INNER	249 - 1	INNER AGITATION IS NOW WIPED AWAY
INNER	251 - 2	SACRED REFUGE IS THIS INNER PLACE
INNER	254 - 4	REMOVE ANY SENSE OF INNER IRRITATION
INNER	258 - 1	SPEAK TO THE INNER EAR
INNER	258 - 3	LET THE INNER EAR LISTEN
INNER	260 - 1	CANNOT CREATE ANY INNER DISTURBANCE
INNER	263 - 6	INNER UNDERSTANDING OF MY PLACE
INNER	265 - 1	INNER MIND OF MINE IS NOW
INNER	272 - 1	THE INNER SIDE OF LIFE
INNER	288 - 2	DAWNS UPON THE INNER THOUGHT
INNER	294 - 2	OUR INNER UNDERSTANDING
INNER	295 - 4	PENETRATES ITS INNER MEANING
INNER	322 - 2	INNER MENTAL ATTITUDES
INNER	327 - 1	DEEP INNER SENSE OF LIFE
INNER	338 - 2	COMPLETELY MANIFEST THE INNER LIFE
INNER	366 - 4	INNER THOUGHT THAT WE CONTACT GOD
INNER	400 - 3	THE INNER MIND KNOWS INFINITELY MORE
INNER	411 - 4	FROM THIS INNER RECOGNITION
INNER	423 - 3	IS AN INNER REALIZATION
INNER	431 - 3	RELIANCE UPON THIS INNER
INNER	445 - 2	PEACE IS AN INNER CALM
INNER	445 - 3	INNER PRINCIPLE OF HIS LIFE
INNER	446 - 1	QUICKENING OF THE INNER MAN
INNER	446 - 5	UNFOLDMENT OF THE INNER SELF
INNER	497 - 3	INNER LIGHT THAT LIGHTS EVERY MAN'S
INNER LIGHT	447 - 3	ALWAYS AN INNER LIGHT
INNER MAN	492 - 3	INNER MAN IS CHRIST
INNER MENTALITY	343 - 2	POINT OF THE INNER MENTALITY
INNER MIND	432 - 1	INNER MIND OPEN AND RECEPTIVE
INNERMOST	366 - 4	BACK IN THE INNERMOST RECESSES
INNERMOST	388 - 3	HIGHEST GOD AND THE INNERMOST GOD IS ONE
INNERMOST	394 - 4	INNERMOST GOD IS ONE GOD
INNERMOST	475 - 2	INNERMOST PARTS OF OUR BEING
INNERMOST	481 - 1	INNERMOST RECESSES OF THE SPIRIT
INNER PROCESSES	142 - 2	INNER PROCESSES OF OUR THOUGHT
INNER QUICKENING	475 - 5	THIS IS THE INNER QUICKENING
INNER SUBSTANCE	476 - 4	INNER SUBSTANCE WHICH IS SPIRITUAL
INNER VOICE	344 - 2	LISTEN TO THIS INNER VOICE
INNOCENT	211 - 1	INNOCENT BECAUSE IT IS NOT
INNUMERABLE	375 - 3	ONE OF INNUMERABLE PLANES
INNUMERABLE	408 - 3	THERE ARE INNUMERABLE PERSONS
INNUMERABLE	417 - 3	TO PRODUCE INNUMERABLE SELVES
INQUIRE	372 - 3	TO INQUIRE WHY LIFE ITSELF IS
INQUIRY	096 - 2	INQUIRY INTO THE TRUTH
INQUIRY	096 - 3	AN INQUIRY INTO TRUTH
INQUIRY	362 - 2	INQUIRY INTO THE HIDDEN MEANING
INQUIRY	373 - 1	INQUIRY INTO TRUTH STARTS
INSEPARABILITY	331 - 2	ONENESS, INSEPARABILITY, INDIVISIBILITY
INSIDE	289 - 2	ONE IS THE INSIDE, THE OTHER THE OUTSIDE
INSIGHT	433 - 2	DEEP INSIGHT INTO THE UNIVERSAL LAW
INSISTENT	186 - 1	NOT TO BE TOO INSISTENT
INSISTENTLY	142 - 3	HEALING IS INSISTENTLY ON GOD
INSOMNIA	165 - 2	TREATMENT FOR INSOMNIA
INSOMNIA	257 - 1	INSOMNIA IS THE RESULT OF

INSOMNIA	257 - 1	TREATMENT FOR INSOMNIA
INSPIRATION	082 - 2	MOMENTS OF REAL INSPIRATION
INSPIRATION	087 - 3	SOURCE OF ALL LIFE AND INSPIRATION
INSPIRATION	167 - 2	TREMENDOUS SPIRITUAL INSPIRATION
INSPIRATION	229 - 2	NEW INSPIRATION OF THOUGHT
INSPIRATION	247 - 2	INSPIRATION OF OUR LIFE
INSPIRATION	273 - 5	INSPIRATION OR INTUITION
INSPIRATION	305 - 2	SUSTAINING THAT INSPIRATION
INSPIRATION	333 - 5	RECEIVE INSPIRATION FROM ON HIGH
INSPIRATION	339 - 1	COME TO IT FOR INSPIRATION AND REVELATION
INSPIRATION	359 - 1	REALIZATION TO INSPIRATION
INSPIRATION	418 - 1	THE INSPIRATION TO CONTINUE
INSPIRATION	477 - 1	FROM THE SPIRIT HE RECEIVES INSPIRATION
INSPIRATION	477 - 2	SWING FROM INSPIRATION TO ACTION
INSPIRATION	497 - 5	WE CALL IT INSPIRATION
INSPIRE	153 - 5	WILL GUIDE AND INSPIRE US
INSPIRE	201 - 3	INSPIRE YOU TO PERCEIVE
INSPIRED	045 - 4	INSPIRED BY THE SAME SPIRIT
INSPIRED	242 - 5	INSPIRED AND DIRECTED BY INFINITE MIND
INSPIRED	263 - 3	INSPIRED BY THE LIVING SPIRIT
INSPIRED	346 - 1	THE INSPIRED HAVE SEEN INTO THE VERY CENTER
INSPIRED	408 - 2	IT IS INSPIRED BY LOVE
INSPIRED	421 - 3	INSPIRED HAVE SEEN INTO
INSPIRED	428 - 3	INSPIRED THOUSANDS TO THE UPLIFTING
INSPIRING	359 - 4	INSPIRING THAN TO CONTEMPLATE
INSTABILITY	436 - 5	THE SHIFTING SANDS OF INSTABILITY
INSTANCE	318 - 3	INSTANCE SUPPOSE WE HAVE
INSTANCES	382 - 3	IN MORE AND MORE INSTANCES
INSTANT	173 - 2	INSTANT CUTTING THROUGH OF ALL APPEARANCES
INSTANT	338 - 2	ONE INSTANT TO ALLOW ANY OUTSIDE
INSTANTANEOUS	057 - 2	INSTANTANEOUS IN ITS DEMONSTRATION
INSTANTANEOUS	086 - 4	SIMULTANEOUS AND INSTANTANEOUS
INSTANTANEOUS	175 - 5	WITH THE INSTANTANEOUS
INSTANTANEOUS	468 - 2	INSTANTANEOUS RECONCILIATION WITH
INSTANTLY	094 - 1	KNOWN AT ALL POINTS INSTANTLY
INSTANTLY	174 - 2	INSTANTLY MANIFEST ON THE INVISIBLE
INSTANTLY	175 - 2	WHICH CAN HEAL INSTANTLY
INSTANTLY	359 - 1	HE INSTANTLY KNOWS
INSTANTLY	468 - 1	KNOWN IS INSTANTLY DEMONSTRATED
INSTILL	048 - 2	INSTILL INTO OUR OWN MINDS
INSTINCT	342 - 2	WE CALL INSTINCT
INSTINCT	342 - 2	INSTINCT GUIDES THE ANIMAL
INSTINCTIVE	158 - 3	INSTINCTIVE FAITH AND MARCHED BOLDLY
INSTINCTIVE	331 - 4	THAT INSTINCTIVE LIFE WITHIN
INSTINCTIVE	416 - 4	INSTINCTIVE AND AUTOMATIC ACTIONS
INSTINCTIVE	478 - 6	INSTINCTIVE SENSE THAT JESUS WAS
INSTINCTIVE LIFE	373 - 3	FORM SHOWING THAT INSTINCTIVE LIFE
INSTINCTIVELY	025 - 3	ALL INSTINCTIVELY FEEL THIS
INSTINCTIVELY	211 - 2	THEY LIVE INSTINCTIVELY
INSTINCTIVE MAN	375 - 2	INSTINCTIVE MAN HAS MOLDED
INSTITUTIONS	362 - 2	FILLED WITH INSTITUTIONS OF LEARNING
INSTRUCTIONS	113 - 3	RECEIVE INSTRUCTION DIRECTLY
INSTRUMENT	073 - 2	USED IT AS AN INSTRUMENT
INSTRUMENT	099 - 3	NO LONGER A FIT INSTRUMENT
INSTRUMENT	104 - 4	NO LONGER A FIT INSTRUMENT

INSTRUMENT	121 - 4	INSTRUMENT WHICH PERCEIVES REALITY
INSTRUMENT	197 - 4	INSTRUMENT OF MIND IS THOUGHT
INSTRUMENT	305 - 3	INSTRUMENT THROUGH WHICH LIFE FLOWS
INSTRUMENT	351 - 1	INSTRUMENT IS PROPERLY ADJUSTED
INSTRUMENT	374 - 4	NO LONGER AN ADEQUATE INSTRUMENT
INSTRUMENT	406 - 4	THOUGHT IS THE INSTRUMENT OF MIND
INSTRUMENTS	339 - 1	USING MANY INSTRUMENTS
INSUFFICIENT	317 - 3	THAT THIS WAS INSUFFICIENT
INTANGIBLE	051 - 2	PRINCIPLES ARE AS INTANGIBLE
INTANGIBLE VALUES	025 - 1	REFUSES TO ACCEPT INTANGIBLE VALUES
INTEGRITY	123 - 3	THE TYPE MAINTAINS ITS INTEGRITY ALWAYS
INTEGRITY	156 - 4	LAYS HOLD OF THE INTEGRITY
INTEGRITY	272 - 4	INTEGRITY APPROACH THE LAW
INTEGRITY	446 - 3	INTEGRITY OF THE UNIVERSE
INTEGRITY	479 - 3	ETERNAL INTEGRITY OF THE DIVINE
INTELLECT	178 - 3	HIGHER THAN THAT OF THE INTELLECT
INTELLECT	192 - 3	POWER OF THE INTELLECT
INTELLECT	194 - 4	INTELLECT HAS MADE THIS DECISION
INTELLECT	267 - 1	THE INTELLECT FURNISHES BUT A MENTAL
INTELLECT	273 - 3	THROUGH HIS INTELLECT
INTELLECT	400 - 3	INFINITELY MORE THAN THE INTELLECT
INTELLECT	492 - 4	SO FAR AS THE INTELLECT ALLOWS
INTELLECT	498 - 1	INTELLECT DECIDE TO WHAT
INTELLECTUAL	443 - 1	OVER-INTELLECTUAL WHO DEMAND
INTELLECTUAL	476 - 6	LIVE ON THE INTELLECTUAL
INTELLECTUALLY	150 - 5	SPIRITUALLY AND INTELLECTUALLY
INTELLECTUALLY	266 - 3	ACCEPT THIS INTELLECTUALLY
INTELLIGENCE	026 - 3	ULTIMATE STUFF AND INTELLIGENCE
INTELLIGENCE	031 - 3	WORD OF CONSCIOUS INTELLIGENCE
INTELLIGENCE	032 - 2	INTELLIGENCE AND PERFECT LIFE
INTELLIGENCE	032 - 3	CHANGELESS INTELLIGENCE
INTELLIGENCE	035 - 3	UNIVERSAL MIND, SPIRIT, INTELLIGENCE
INTELLIGENCE	036 - 4	ULTIMATE OF INTELLIGENCE
INTELLIGENCE	040 - 1	IMMERSED IN AN INFINITE INTELLIGENCE
INTELLIGENCE	059 - 4	THE FLOW OF DIVINE INTELLIGENCE
INTELLIGENCE	063 - 2	INTELLIGENCE ONLY
INTELLIGENCE	065 - 5	OF LESS INTELLIGENCE THAN HIMSELF
INTELLIGENCE	066 - 3	AN ABSOLUTE INTELLIGENCE
INTELLIGENCE	066 - 3	TO DENY SUCH INTELLIGENCE
INTELLIGENCE	076 - 5	SAME INTELLIGENCE THAT CREATED IT
INTELLIGENCE	077 - 3	THE CONSCIOUS INTELLIGENCE
INTELLIGENCE	085 - 1	INTELLIGENCE OF THE HUMAN
INTELLIGENCE	088 - 3	ABSOLUTE POSITIVE INTELLIGENCE
INTELLIGENCE	088 - 3	SOUL OF RECEPTIVE INTELLIGENCE
INTELLIGENCE	091 - 3	THE CONSCIOUS INTELLIGENCE TO CHOOSE
INTELLIGENCE	091 - 4	INTELLIGENCE OF THE RACE
INTELLIGENCE	102 - 4	WITH AN INFINITE INTELLIGENCE
INTELLIGENCE	105 - 3	ONLY IN REAL INTELLIGENCE
INTELLIGENCE	105 - 3	INTELLIGENCE IS THE ULTIMATE CREATIVE
INTELLIGENCE	111 - 5	DEVOID OF MIND OR INTELLIGENCE
INTELLIGENCE	124 - 4	WE THINK FROM CONSCIOUS INTELLIGENCE
INTELLIGENCE	138 - 4	INTELLIGENCE WHICH IS BEYOND HUMAN
INTELLIGENCE	139 - 1	INTELLIGENCE RESPONDS TO INTELLIGENCE
INTELLIGENCE	139 - 3	WHEREBY INTELLIGENCE PASSES
INTELLIGENCE	155 - 1	LAWS ARE THOSE OF INTELLIGENCE

INTELLIGENCE	183 - 1	IN A UNIVERSE OF INTELLIGENCE
INTELLIGENCE	195 - 2	INTELLIGENCE IS NOW TAKING THE FORM
INTELLIGENCE	197 - 1	HAVING NO CONSCIOUS INTELLIGENCE
INTELLIGENCE	198 - 2	NO INTELLIGENCE OF ITS OWN
INTELLIGENCE	211 - 3	ARE DEALING WITH INTELLIGENCE
INTELLIGENCE	216 - 2	THE INTELLIGENCE TO EXECUTE
INTELLIGENCE	224 - 2	UNITED INTELLIGENCE OF THE HUMAN RACE
INTELLIGENCE	228 - 1	ONE INTELLIGENCE IN THE UNIVERSE
INTELLIGENCE	234 - 4	IN IT AS INTELLIGENCE
INTELLIGENCE	237 - 3	INTELLIGENCE IS BACK OF ALL THINGS
INTELLIGENCE	259 - 3	INTELLIGENCE WILL GUIDE US
INTELLIGENCE	272 - 3	INTELLIGENCE WITHIN US THAT DOES
INTELLIGENCE	273 - 3	INTELLIGENCE THAT KNOWS THE RIGHT ANSWER
INTELLIGENCE	273 - 5	INTELLIGENCE OF THE UNIVERSE
INTELLIGENCE	300 - 4	DEALING WITH INTELLIGENCE
INTELLIGENCE	304 - 1	THE INTELLIGENCE WHICH WE ARE
INTELLIGENCE	304 - 1	BACKED BY THAT GREATER INTELLIGENCE
INTELLIGENCE	311 - 4	INTELLIGENCE WOULD NOT BE EXPRESSED
INTELLIGENCE	337 - 2	EVOLUTION IS THE RESULT OF INTELLIGENCE
INTELLIGENCE	363 - 3	FATHER WAS AN INTELLIGENCE
INTELLIGENCE	364 - 2	OUR CONSCIOUS INTELLIGENCE
INTELLIGENCE	388 - 3	CONSCIOUS INTELLIGENCE
INTELLIGENCE	390 - 5	THE ONLY DIRECTIVE INTELLIGENCE
INTELLIGENCE	393 - 3	IT IS ENERGY PLUS INTELLIGENCE
INTELLIGENCE	435 - 4	FUNCTION OF INTELLIGENCE
INTELLIGENT	043 - 1	INTELLIGENT STUDY OF THE TEACHINGS
INTELLIGENT	052 - 4	AN INTELLIGENT FORCE AND SUBSTANCE
INTELLIGENT	057 - 4	INTELLIGENT ENERGY IN THE INVISIBLE
INTELLIGENT	078 - 2	BOTH INTELLIGENT AND CONSCIOUS
INTELLIGENT	112 - 1	BUT IT IS NOT INTELLIGENT
INTELLIGENT	144 - 2	INTELLIGENT IDEA IN MIND
INTELLIGENT	209 - 2	INFINITELY MORE INTELLIGENT
INTELLIGENT ENERGY	480 - 1	INTELLIGENT ENERGY RUNNING THROUGH
INTELLIGENTLY	046 - 5	DEAL WITH IT INTELLIGENTLY
INTELLIGENTLY	211 - 3	DEAL WITH IT INTELLIGENTLY
INTEMPERANCE	261 - 4	NO PLEASURE IN INTEMPERANCE
INTENDED	433 - 4	WERE INTENDED FOR OURSELVES OR OTHERS
INTENDED	488 - 1	COMPLETE AS WE WERE INTENDED
INTENDS	411 - 2	DIVINE INTENDS FREEDOM FOR US
INTENT	470 - 5	INTENT AND A COMPLETE CONCENTRATION
INTENTION	195 - 4	THIS IS DONE THROUGH INTENTION
INTENTION	255 - 2	INTENTION IS THAT AS A RESULT
INTENTION	321 - 2	INTENTION IN A TREATMENT
INTENTION	393 - 2	NO INTENTION OF ITS OWN
INTENTION	394 - 5	THE INTENTION THAT WE GIVE
INTENTION	416 - 2	GOD HAS ANY INTENTION FOR HIM
INTERACT	094 - 2	MIND AND ETHER INTERACT
INTERCOMMUNICATION	120 - 1	INTERCOMMUNICATION TAKES PLACE ON EVERY
INTERFERE	161 - 3	INTERFERE WITH THE GENERAL GOOD
INTERFERE	266 - 2	INTERFERE WITH THE WELL BEING
INTERFERE	395 - 1	INTERFERE WITH THESE IN OUR IGNORANCE
INTERFERENCE	351 - 1	GREAT DEAL OF INTERFERENCE
INTERFERENCE	376 - 1	WITHIN FORM WITHOUT INTERFERENCE
INTERIOR	173 - 4	INTERIOR IN OUR COMPREHENSION
INTERIOR	219 - 4	INTERIOR CONVICTION THAT WE ARE ONE

INTERIOR	339 - 3	IS BY AN INTERIOR MOVEMENT
INTERNAL	113 - 2	EXTERNAL AND AN INTERNAL PERCEPTION
INTERNATIONAL	460 - 2	INTERNATIONAL STRIFE ALL NATIONS ARE BEATEN
INTERPRET	036 - 3	INTERPRET HIMSELF TO MAN
INTERPRET	036 - 3	INTERPRET HIMSELF THROUGH MAN
INTERPRET	187 - 2	INTERPRET CAUSES BY CONDITIONS
INTERPRET	269 - 1	INTERPRET THE WILL OF GOD
INTERPRETATION	085 - 4	INTERPRETATION OF THE UNIVERSE
INTERPRETED	122 - 2	INTERPRETED THEMSELVES THROUGH MAN'S
INTERPRETING	356 - 1	SIMPLY INTERPRETING WHAT COMES
INTER-RELATED	242 - 2	INTER-RELATED ACTION IS IN PERFECT
INTERSPHERE	088 - 2	INTERSPHERE EACH OTHER
INTERSPHERE	131 - 5	SUBSTANCE INTERSPHERE EACH OTHER
INTERVAL	225 - 1	INTERVAL BETWEEN TREATMENTS
INTIMATE	089 - 2	BUT MORE INTIMATE
INTIMATE	141 - 2	INTIMATE CONCEPT OF AN ALREADY
INTO	126 - 4	WE ARE THINKING INTO IT
INTOLERABLE	295 - 2	HOWEVER INTOLERABLE THE SITUATION
INTOLERANT	469 - 1	IN OUR INTOLERANT ATTITUDE
INTOXICATION	223 - 1	IN TERMS OF INTOXICATION
INTREATED	468 -5	FATHER OUT AND INTREATED HIM
INTRODUCING	382 - 2	INTRODUCING ANY DISCUSSION
INTROSPECTION	374 - 2	THROUGH INTROSPECTION I KNOW THAT I AM
INTROSPECTIVE	465 - 4	STATE OF INTROSPECTIVE MORBIDITY
INTROSPECTIVE	474 - 3	INTROSPECTIVE AND MEDITATIVE PART
INTUITION	025 - 1	INTUITION IS EVER SPREADING ITS WINGS
INTUITION	076 - 2	INDIVIDUAL THROUGH INTUITION
INTUITION	113 - 2	ITS INTERNAL THROUGH INTUITION
INTUITION	113 - 2	INTUITION IS SPIRIT KNOWING ITSELF
INTUITION	121 - 4	VISION INTUITION AND REVELATION
INTUITION	160 - 2	REACHED BY DIRECT INTUITION
INTUITION	162 - 3	THROUGH INTUITION FAITH FINDS
INTUITION	178 - 3	BORN OF INTUITION
INTUITION	273 - 5	PURE INSPIRATION OR INTUITION
INTUITION	342 - 2	INTUITION IS GOD IN MAN
INTUITION	342 - 2	SO WOULD INTUITION GUIDE MAN
INTUITION	342 - 3	INTUITION REMAINS IN THE BACKGROUND
INTUITION	342 - 4	INTUITION WHICH IS NOTHING LESS THAN GOD
INTUITION	359 - 1	HIGHEST FACULTY IN MAN IS INTUITION
INTUITION	367- 1	CALL IT CONSCIENCE INTUITION
INTUITION	465 - 2	WE KNOW BY INTUITION
INTUITION	480 - 6	INTUITION IS THE SPEECH OF THIS COMFORTER
INTUITIVE	075 - 4	AWAKENS AN INTUITIVE PERCEPTION
INTUITIVE	076 - 1	THE INTUITIVE PERCEPTION
INTUITIVE	079 - 4	PLUS THAT INTUITIVE FEELING
INTUITIVE	359 - 1	TO THE INTUITIVE PERCEPTION OF EVERYTHING
INTUITIVE	465 - 2	INTUITIVE PERCEPTION FROM OUR MENTALITY
INTUITIVE KNOWLEDGE	103 - 2	DISCLOSES AN INTUITIVE KNOWLEDGE
INTUITIVELY	032 - 3	INTUITIVELY WE SENSE THAT
INTUITIVELY	327 - 2	WHO INTUITIVELY PERCEIVES TRUTH
INTUITIVELY	419 - 2	WHO INTUITIVELY PERCEIVES TRUTH
INTUITIVE PERCEPTION	112 - 4	THE CENTER OF OUR INTUITIVE PERCEPTION
INVARIABLE	321 - 2	THE INVARIABLE RULE FOR KNOWING
INVENTION	040 - 2	INVENTION, ART, LITERATURE
INVENTION	110 - 3	AN INVENTION OF IGNORANCE

INVENTION	362 - 2	INVENTION HAS HARNESSED SUBTLE FORCES
INVENTIONS	196 - 1	SOUGHT OUT MANY INVENTIONS
INVENTIONS	310 - 4	MAN HAS SOUGHT OUT MANY INVENTIONS
INVENTIONS	310 - 4	INVENTIONS OF THE HUMAN MIND
INVERSION	164 - 2	INVERSION OF ETERNAL GOOD
INVERTED	494 - 5	INVERTED USE OF THE LAW OF RIGHTEOUSNESS
INVESTIGATE	498 - 2	INVESTIGATE UNTIL WE KNOW THE TRUTH
INVESTIGATION	074 - 2	THE SCIENTIFIC INVESTIGATION
INVESTIGATORS	123 - 4	ACCEPTED BY MOST INVESTIGATORS
INVIGORATING	248 - 2	LIFE FOREVER INVIGORATING
INVINCIBLE	142 - 3	CONSTRUCTIVE WORD IS INVINCIBLE
INVIOLATE	168 - 3	PRACTITIONER SHOULD KEEP SACRED, INVIOLATE
INVISIBLE	025 - 1	VISIBLE TO THE INVISIBLE
INVISIBLE	026 - 3	THAT INVISIBLE ESSENCE
INVISIBLE	057 - 2	WE MUST TRUST THE INVISIBLE
INVISIBLE	060 - 3	INVISIBLE PASSES INTO VISIBILITY
INVISIBLE	074 - 4	NUMBER OF KNOWN FACTS ABOUT ITS INVISIBLE
INVISIBLE	114 - 2	ESSENCE OF REALITY IS INVISIBLE
INVISIBLE	114 - 2	INVISIBLE IS SEEN AND HEARD AND IS A PART
INVISIBLE	159 - 3	ALL PRINCIPLES ARE INVISIBLE
INVISIBLE	161 - 1	AUTHORITY ON THE INVISIBLE PLANE
INVISIBLE	217 - 1	NEITHER VISIBLE NOR INVISIBLE
INVISIBLE	284 - 1	INVISIBLE BECOMES VISIBLE
INVISIBLE	330 - 5	IS FROM AN INVISIBLE TO VISIBLE
INVISIBLE	407 - 2	IS TO BELIEVE IN THE INVISIBLE
INVISIBLE	436 - 2	INVISIBLE THINGS OF GOD
INVISIBLE	477 - 4	INVISIBLE INTELLIGENCE TO GUIDE
INVISIBLE CAUSE	321 - 1	VIRTUE OF SOME INVISIBLE CAUSE
INVISIBLE SUPPLY	157 - 3	OURS IN THE INVISIBLE SUPPLY
INVITE	368 - 4	MUST INVITE HIM
INVITING	444 - 2	INVITING PEOPLE TO PENETRATE MORE DEEPLY
INVOKE	455 - 6	INVOKE THE SPIRIT OF POETRY
INVOKES	038 - 2	HE INVOKES THE LAW
INVOKING	295 - 3	INVOKING THE DIVINE MIND
INVOLUTION	038 - 2	INVOLUTION IS THE CAUSE
INVOLUTION	038 - 2	DEALING WITH INVOLUTION
INVOLUTION	050 - 1	INVOLUTION IS THE IN-WORKING
INVOLUTION	102 - 2	INVOLUTION THROUGH THE SELF-CONTEMPLATION
INVOLUTION	292 - 4	LOGICAL RESULT OF INVOLUTION
INVOLUTION	297 - 2	THE GREAT TEACHING OF INVOLUTION
INVOLUTION	339 - 2	EVOLUTION CAN ONLY FOLLOW INVOLUTION
INVOLUTION	339 - 2	INVOLUTION PRECEDES EVOLUTION
INVOLUTION	340 - 2	INVOLUTION AND EVOLUTION
INVOLUTION	420 - 3	EVOLUTION FOLLOWS INVOLUTION
INVOLVE	301 - 1	EXACTLY AS WE INVOLVE IT
INVOLVED	300 - 2	INVOLVED IN IT WILL EVOLVE
INVOLVES	101 - 5	THE SPIRIT INVOLVES
INVOLVES	224 - 2	PRACTITIONER INVOLVES AN IDEA IN MIND
INVOLVES	340 - 1	THE SPIRIT INVOLVES
INWARD	409 - 5	IT IS AN INWARD FEELING
INWARD	455 - 7	REALIZE ITS INWARD SIGNIFICANCE
INWARD	479 - 5	INWARD GAZE ALONE CAN REVEAL
INWARD	483 - 2	PARTAKE OF ITS INWARD NATURE
INWARDLY	407 - 3	MAY BE INWARDLY PERCEIVED
IRON	047 - 5	IN AN IRON FOUNDRY

IRON	048 - 1	IRON ITSELF NEITHER KNOWS
IRRATIONAL	189 - 2	THIS WILL NOT BE IRRATIONAL
IRRESISTIBLE	296 - 4	THAT IT WILL BECOME IRRESISTIBLE
IRRESISTIBLE	362 - 3	SENSE OF AN IRRESISTIBLE UNION
IRRESISTIBLE	386 - 3	AS IRRESISTIBLE AS THE RECURRING SEASONS
IRRESISTIBLY	264 - 1	IRRESISTIBLY DRAWN TOWARD ME
IRRESPECTIVE	043 - 1	IRRESPECTIVE OF LAW AND ORDER
IRRITATION	247 - 1	IRRITATION, AGITATION NOR INFLAMMATION
IRRITATION	249 - 1	THERE IS NO IRRITATION, FRUSTRATION
IS	064 - 2	WHAT GOD KNOWS IS
IS	103 - 2	GOD IS AND IS IN EVERYTHING
IS	291 - 2	IT IS WHAT IT DESIRES
IS	292 - 4	A GOD WHO ALREADY IS
IS	312 - 2	ANYTHING THAT SPIRIT KNOWS IS
IS	386 - 3	SOMETHING THAT KNOWS THAT IT IS
IS	408 - 1	IS BECAUSE GOD IS CONSCIOUS OF HIM
IS	475 - 6	WORD IS LIFE, POWER AND ACTION
IS	478 - 4	WHICH IS AND CANNOT BE EXPLAINED
ISAIAH	212 - 2	ISAIAH UNDERSTOOD SOMETHING OF THIS
ISAIAH	257 - 6	THE WORDS OF ISAIAH
I SEE	230 - 2	HABIT OF SAYING I SEE
IS MAN	482 - 3	GOD AS MAN IN MAN IS MAN
ISOLATE	374 - 3	ISOLATE IT AND IT WILL NOT THINK
ISOLATED	093 - 3	SUBJECTIVE MINDS WERE ISOLATED
ISOLATED	360 - 1	AN ISOLATED WILL
ISOLATED	417 - 4	AS ISOLATED PERSONALITIES WE ARE
ISOLATED	462 - 3	AN ISOLATED STATE
ISOLATION	454 - 5	LET GO OF THE THOUGHT OF ISOLATION
ISOLATION	462 - 4	NEARLY ALL FEEL THE ISOLATION
ISOLATION	484 - 3	A BELIEF IN ISOLATION
IS POISED	234 - 1	LIFE IS POISED IN ITSELF
ISRAEL	071 - 2	MOSES LED THE CHILDREN OF ISRAEL
ISRAEL	128 - 1	LIMITED THE HOLY ONE OF ISRAEL
ISRAEL	304 - 3	THE HOLY ONE OF ISRAEL
ISSUES	238 - 4	OUT OF IT ARE THE ISSUES
ISSUES	399 - 5	THOUGH WE WERE FORCING ISSUES
ISSUES	453 - 1	ISSUES OF LIFE ARE FROM WITHIN
IT	078 - 1	COULD NOT THINK OF IT AS
IT	080 - 3	WHAT IT DOES, IS THE RESULT
IT	083 - 4	IT IS CONSCIOUS THAT ITS DESIRE
IT	382 - 3	GOVERNING IT IS THE WHOLE ANSWER
IT	391 - 1	IT IS TO MAN WHAT GOD
IT	393 - 1	IT WORKING IN DIFFERENT WAYS
IT	404 - 1	IT IS WHAT WE KNOW IT TO BE
IT	415 - 3	WE ARE IN IT AND IT FLOWS
IT	415 - 3	IT IS ALWAYS MORE THAN WE ARE
ITSELF	068 - 3	CHANGE INTO ANYTHING BUT ITSELF
ITSELF	078 - 2	THE POWER THAT KNOWS ITSELF
ITSELF	082 - 1	KNOW NOTHING OUTSIDE ITSELF
ITSELF	086 - 5	THE POWER THAT KNOWS ITSELF
ITSELF	165 - 1	IS LIKE ITSELF ON A MINIATURE SCALE
ITSELF	267 - 2	THE LAW ITSELF MUST BE WILLING
ITSELF	273 - 2	A DEMAND UPON ITSELF
ITSELF	373 - 4	ITSELF NEITHER BEGINS NOR ENDS
ITSELF	390 - 3	NOT A THING OF ITSELF

J

JAMES	500 - 2	JAMES SPEAKS OF BEING CONVINCED
JAMES	501 - 5	JAMES TELLS US TO CONFESS
JEALOUS	454 - 4	NOT BECAUSE GOD IS JEALOUS
JEALOUSY	255 - 3	SELFISHNESS AND JEALOUSY
JEHOVAH	257 - 6	JEHOVAH HATH OPENED THINE EAR
JESUS	028 - 1	JESUS SAID THAT GOD
JESUS	037 - 1	JESUS SUMMED UP HIS WHOLE PHILOSOPHY
JESUS	054 - 1	JESUS AS HE STROVE TO TEACH
JESUS	054 - 2	AS EASILY AS JESUS DID
JESUS	069 - 2	TO THE TEACHING OF JESUS
JESUS	076 - 3	JESUS SAID REALITY IS NOT
JESUS	076 - 4	JESUS AND OTHER GREAT SPIRITUAL
JESUS	076 - 4	JESUS HAD ARRIVED
JESUS	076 - 4	JESUS SAW IT
JESUS	081 - 2	JESUS IN TALKING WITH THE WOMAN
JESUS	082 - 4	JESUS UNDOUBTEDLY MEANT JUST THIS
JESUS	087 - 1	THIS IS WHAT JESUS MEANT
JESUS	098 - 2	ARE MANY MANSIONS SAID JESUS
JESUS	103 - 3	JESUS PROCLAIMED THAT THE VERY WORDS
JESUS	104 - 5	PHYSICAL DISAPPEARANCE OF JESUS
JESUS	106 - 3	WHAT JESUS MEANT
JESUS	110 - 3	JESUS UNDERSTOOD THESE GREAT LAWS
JESUS	127 - 1	JESUS SAID "AS THOU HAST BELIEVED, SO BE
JESUS	139 - 2	WITH JESUS WE MAY SAY
JESUS	140 - 2	JESUS UNDERSTOOD THIS
JESUS	157 - 3	JESUS SAID "AND I SAY UNTO YOU ASK AND IT SHALL
JESUS	157 - 4	JESUS ANNOUNCED THE LAW OF MIND
JESUS	160 - 4	REMARKABLE CHARACTER OF JESUS
JESUS	161 - 1	THE CENTURION CAME TO JESUS
JESUS	161 - 1	ACCEPTED THE WORD OF JESUS
JESUS	161 - 1	JESUS SAID "I HAVE NOT FOUND SO GREAT FAITH
JESUS	162 - 1	JESUS WAS THE SON OF GOD
JESUS	162 - 2	JESUS SAID "IF YE HAVE FAITH
JESUS	162 - 4	PROVED THE DIVINITY OF JESUS
JESUS	173 - 4	JESUS SAID "HEAVEN AND EARTH SHALL PASS"
JESUS	187 - 3	AS JESUS SAID, WE "JUDGE NOT
JESUS	188 - 2	WORDS WHICH JESUS SPOKE
JESUS	194 - 3	OF THE TEACHING OF JESUS
JESUS	203 - 3	JESUS HIS POWER
JESUS	206 - 4	JESUS MEANT WHEN HE SAID
JESUS	212 - 3	IF JESUS SAW AN IMPERFECT HAND
JESUS	212 - 3	JESUS MUST HAVE SEEN ONLY
JESUS	217 - 2	JESUS COULD NOT HAVE
JESUS	237 - 2	JESUS FORGAVE THE MAN HIS SINS
JESUS	237 - 2	WHY JESUS SAID
JESUS	241 - 3	JESUS HEALED THE PARALYZED
JESUS	241 - 3	POWER BY WHICH JESUS RAISED HIS BODY
JESUS	260 - 3	COULD JESUS HAVE TOLD THE BLIND MAN
JESUS	268 - 3	THE RELATIONSHIP OF JESUS

JESUS	276 - 2	SECRET OF THE POWER OF JESUS
JESUS	277 - 2	NO RECORD OF JESUS ASKING GOD
JESUS	277 - 2	JESUS' METHOD OF APPROACH
JESUS	277 - 2	WHEN JESUS HEALED PEOPLE
JESUS	280 - 1	JESUS REVEALED THE NATURE
JESUS	280 - 2	TEACHING OF JESUS WAS BASED
JESUS	281 - 3	JESUS COULD SAY TO THE PARALYZED MAN
JESUS	285 - 4	REMEMBER WHAT JESUS SAID
JESUS	286 - 1	JESUS SAID "GIVE US THIS DAY
JESUS	290 - 1	JESUS SAID "WHEN YE PRAY BELIEVE
JESUS	310 - 4	STORY OF JESUS THE CHRIST
JESUS	311 - 1	DISCIPLES OF JESUS ASKED HIM
JESUS	311 - 3	MEN LIKE JESUS BASED THEIR WHOLE SYSTEM
JESUS	312 - 4	THE CONCEPT JESUS HAD WHEN HE SAID
JESUS	313 - 4	JESUS' WORDS WERE SYMBOLS
JESUS	317 - 3	WHEN JESUS EXPLAINED
JESUS	329 - 4	THE PHILOSOPHY OF JESUS
JESUS	329 - 6	JESUS TAUGHT A POWER TRANSCENDENT
JESUS	330 - 3	SPIRIT THAT JESUS PRAYED
JESUS	331 - 2	WHICH JESUS HAD
JESUS	331 - 5	POWER OF JESUS IS UNDERSTOOD
JESUS	332 - 2	JESUS PRAYED THAT ALL MIGHT
JESUS	334 - 4	THE POWER OF JESUS LAY
JESUS	335 - 4	AS JESUS KNEW THAT IT WOULD BE IMPOSSIBLE
JESUS	337 - 3	THE MAN JESUS BECAME THE CHRIST
JESUS	343 - 5	THE GREAT MYSTICS LIKE JESUS
JESUS	344 - 3	JESUS WAS THE GREATEST OF ALL
JESUS	344 - 3	JESUS AFTER THE RESURRECTION
JESUS	359 - 3	THE UNIQUE PERSONAGE OF JESUS
JESUS	359 - 3	JESUS MORE OF GOD WAS MANIFEST
JESUS	361 - 5	JESUS NEVER THOUGHT OF HIMSELF
JESUS	362 - 2	REALIZATION IS WHAT GAVE JESUS
JESUS	363 - 2	JESUS WAS ABLE TO DO
JESUS	363 - 2	JESUS THE MOST UNIQUE CHARACTER
JESUS	363 - 3	JESUS LOCATED GOD IN HIS OWN SOUL
JESUS	363 - 3	GOD BEGAN AND JESUS CEASED TO BE
JESUS	365 - 2	JESUS PRAYED TO THIS INDWELLING I AM
JESUS	366 - 2	JESUS STANDS ALONE
JESUS	366 - 4	JESUS SPENT MUCH OF HIS TIME
JESUS	367 - 3	AS THE EXTERNAL JESUS GAVE WAY
JESUS	368 - 1	JESUS SPOKE FROM THE HEIGHTS OF SPIRITUAL
JESUS	377 - 2	JESUS REVEALED HIMSELF
JESUS	381 - 3	JESUS WAS SUCH AN ONE
JESUS	386 - 2	JESUS ROSE FROM THE DEAD
JESUS	421 - 2	THE GREAT MYSTICS LIKE JESUS
JESUS	422 - 3	JESUS DISCOVERED AND TAUGHT
JESUS	422 - 3	JESUS STANDS ALONE AS A MAN
JESUS	422 - 3	JESUS GAVE WAY TO THE DIVINE
JESUS	427 - 1	ALL THE SAYINGS OF JESUS
JESUS	427 - 2	JESUS DISCERNED SPIRITUAL TRUTH
JESUS	428 - 3	JESUS WAS RIGHT WHEN HE SAID
JESUS	429 - 2	JESUS SAW BEYOND THE VEIL
JESUS	429 - 2	JESUS KNOW ANOTHER LIFE, WHICH TO HIM
JESUS	430 - 3	JESUS TELLS US THAT OUR GIFTS
JESUS	430 - 6	JESUS IS TEACHING THE LESSON

JESUS	431 - 1	CAUSE AND EFFECT ABOUT WHICH JESUS
JESUS	433 - 1	JESUS MADE THE GREATEST CLAIM
JESUS	435 - 2	JESUS TEARS THE MANTLE
JESUS	437 - 2	JESUS WHICH SHOWS HIS GREAT COMPASSION
JESUS	437 - 3	JESUS MARVELED AT THIS FAITH
JESUS	437 - 5	HEARD JESUS TELL THE SICK MAN
JESUS	438 - 1	JESUS READING THEIR THOUGHTS
JESUS	439 - 5	JESUS WAS AWARE OF HER PRESENCE
JESUS	440 - 5	JESUS WAS WISE
JESUS	441 - 2	JESUS WAS REFERRING TO THE MIND
JESUS	444 - 1	JESUS KNEW THAT HIS HUMAN PERSONALITY
JESUS	448 - 2	AND JESUS KNEW THEIR THOUGHTS
JESUS	449 - 3	JESUS PLAINLY TELLS US
JESUS	449 - 5	JESUS WAS A CONSCIOUSLY COSMIC SOUL
JESUS	456 - 1	CALM WORDS OF JESUS
JESUS	457 - 4	JESUS CLEARLY EXPLAINS
JESUS	460 - 1	JESUS STANDS SURE AND TRUE
JESUS	463 - 4	JESUS WAS A JEW
JESUS	467 - 1	JESUS IS SHOWING THAT GOD IS LOVE
JESUS	472 - 2	JESUS AMONG THE GREAT MYSTICS
JESUS	472 - 5	JESUS COULD NOT HAVE BEEN
JESUS	479 - 2	JESUS STANDING AT THE THRESHOLD
JESUS	480 - 1	JESUS WAS CLAIMING TO BE GOD
JESUS	480 - 5	NOT UNTO JESUS ALONE
JESUS	481 - 5	JESUS IMPLIES A POWER WHICH CAN
JESUS	482 - 3	JESUS REFERS TO HIS JOY
JESUS	490 - 1	JESUS TELLS US TO SEEK
JESUS	495 - 7	THE SAME MIND THAT JESUS USED
JESUS	496 - 3	NOT THE NAME OF JESUS BUT
JEW	463 - 4	JESUS WAS A JEW
JEWS	463 - 4	JEWS DID NOT CONSIDER THE MEAT
JOB	108 - 2	JOB "THOUGH I DIE YET SHALL I LIVE"
JOB	330 - 4	THIS CONCEPT ENABLED JOB
JOHN	171 - 2	JOHN USED A LAW
JOHN	442 - 2	HEARERS ABOUT JOHN THE BAPTIST
JOINT HEIRS	485 - 2	JOINT HEIRS WITH CHRIST
JOURNEY	499 - 2	RETURN JOURNEY INTO RIGHTEOUSNESS
JOVE	336 - 2	CONSCIOUS OF JOVE NODDING TO JOVE
JOY	163 - 3	WITH JOY AND GLADNESS
JOY	168 - 1	A JOY IN BECOMING
JOY	222 - 4	FOR THE JOY OF WORKING
JOY	226 - 2	PERFECT EXPRESSION IN JOY
JOY	231 - 2	JOY, FAITH OR NOBLE PURPOSE
JOY	243 - 2	THOUGHTS OF PEACE, LOVE AND JOY
JOY	256 - 5	IS LOVE AND JOY
JOY	261 - 2	THE JOY OF THE LORD GOD
JOY	264 - 5	PEACE AND JOY ACCOMPANY ME
JOY	290 - 2	EXPERIENCE OF JOY IS MINE NOW
JOY	292 - 3	I AM JOY, PEACE AND HAPPINESS
JOY	292 - 3	I AM THE SPIRIT OF JOY WITHIN ME
JOY	302 - 2	HE SHOULD RADIATE JOY
JOY	305 - 5	IN PEACE, CONFIDENCE AND JOY
JOY	388 - 2	IN THE JOY OF FRIENDSHIP AND LOVE
JOY	417 - 2	JOY IN THE PLACE OF GRIEF
JOY	435 - 1	LOVE, PEACE AND JOY

JOY	447 – I	WITH SPONTANEOUS JOY
JOY	482 – 3	JOY WHICH IS FULL AND COMPLETE
JOY	486 – 3	JOY TO KNOW THAT ALL IS WELL
JOY	491 – 4	GAZE LONGINGLY AT JOY
JOYFUL	331 – 4	MEETS IT IN JOYFUL UNION
JOYFULLY	229 – 4	JOYFULLY, PEACEFULLY
JOYOUS	247 – 3	SPIRIT IN JOYOUS SELF-RECOGNITION
JOYOUS	250 – 5	A JOYOUS, HAPPY EXPRESSION
JOYOUS	255 – 1	JOYOUS FREE FLOW OF LIFE
JOYOUSLY	251 – 2	RESOLUTELY AND JOYOUSLY TO FAITH
JOYOUSLY	270 – 5	IT ENABLES US TO DO JOYOUSLY
JUDGE	085 – 1	ABLE TO JUDGE
JUDGE	113 – 2	JUDGE RIGHTEOUSLY AND NOT BY APPEARANCES
JUDGE	187 – 3	JUDGE NOT ACCORDING TO APPEARANCE
JUDGE	187 – 3	JUDGE RIGHTEOUS JUDGMENT
JUDGE	406 – 4	JUDGE NOT ACCORDING TO APPEARANCES
JUDGE	417 – 2	JUDGE NOT ACCORDING TO APPEARANCES
JUDGE	433 – 2	JUDGE NOT THAT YE BE NOT JUDGED
JUDGED	413 – 5	WHO JUDGED THE POSSIBILITIES
JUDGES	383 – 1	NO ONE JUDGES US BUT OURSELVES
JUDGES	383 – 2	NO ONE JUDGES US BUT OURSELVES
JUDGES	434 – 2	NOTHING JUDGES US BUT THE IMMUTABLE
JUDGMENT	242 – 5	DISCRIMINATION AND JUDGMENT
JUST	226 – 1	WHATSOEVER THINGS ARE JUST
JUST	298 – 2	JUST AS YOU WISH THEM TO BE
JUSTICE	472 – 1	MERCY, JUSTICE AND TRUTH
JUSTIFICATION	442 – 3	OUTER FOR JUSTIFICATION
JUSTIFIED	433 – 1	HAVE BEEN JUSTIFIED IN THEIR FAITH
JUSTIFIES	449 – 3	THINKER CONDEMNS OR JUSTIFIES

K

KALAMAZOO	300 – 5	IN KALAMAZOO FOR THE MUMPS
KANT	075 – 4	KANT SAYS WE ARE ABLE TO PERCEIVE
KARMA	114 – 3	KARMA MEANS THE LAW OF CAUSE AND EFFECT
KARMA	204 – 2	KARMA, FATALISM, THEOLOGY
KARMA	392 – 1	KARMA IT IS THE LAW OF THE WHOLE
KARMIC	092 – 3	THE KARMIC LAW WHICH MEANS THE LAW
KARMIC LAW	030 – 4	KARMIC LAW IS NOT KISMET
KARMIC LAW	096 – 3	KARMIC LAW BECAUSE IT IS SUBJECTIVE TO
KARMIC LAW	114 – 3	KARMIC LAW BECAUSE IT IS THE USE
KEEP	160 – 2	HE MUST KEEP HIMSELF
KEEPING	387 – 3	THEY ARE IN GOD'S KEEPING
KEEPING ON	384 – 2	WE SHALL KEEP ON KEEPING ON
KEEP ON	336 – 1	THAT WE CAN KEEP ON DOING EVIL
KEPT	493 – 2	KEPT THROUGH THE BONDS OF PEACE
KEY	033 – 2	THE KEY TO THIS DOOR
KEY	047 – 1	KEY TO HAPPINESS
KEY	134 – 1	HAS WITHIN HIMSELF THE KEY
KEY	261 – 3	KEY THOUGHT
KEY	305 – 3	MY KEY TO LIFE OPENS ALL DOORS
KEY	342 – 1	KEY TO THEIR LANGUAGE
KEY	393 – 2	IS THE KEY TO ALL PROPER MENTAL

KEYNOTE	094 - 1	TUNED INTO THE KEYNOTE OF HIS BEING
KEYNOTE	262 - 3	KEYNOTE TO A REALIZATION
KIDNEY	253 - 3	KIDNEY TROUBLE ARE WORRY
KIDNEYS	254 - 2	KIDNEYS PERFORM THEIR NATURAL FUNCTION
KINDNESS	433 - 1	KINDNESS OF THE CREATOR
KINDS	254 - 5	KINDS OF THOUGHT GIVE RISE
KINGDOM	150 - 4	KINGDOM OF GOD IS WITHIN
KINGDOM	150 - 5	THE KINGDOM OF GOD IS WITHIN YOU
KINGDOM	162 - 1	KINGDOM OF GOD WAS REVEALED
KINGDOM	162 - 1	KINGDOM OF GOD IS ALSO REVEALED THROUGH
KINGDOM	217 - 2	KINGDOM OF HEAVEN IS AT HAND
KINGDOM	231 - 1	PERFECTION OF HIS KINGDOM
KINGDOM	250 - 6	KNOWLEDGE OF THE KINGDOM WITHIN
KINGDOM	335 - 1	THE KINGDOM OF GOD IS NOW PRESENT
KINGDOM	335 - 1	SENSED THAT THIS KINGDOM IS WITHIN
KINGDOM	343 - 4	THE KINGDOM OF HEAVEN IS WITHIN
KINGDOM	345 - 3	THE KINGDOM OF HEAVEN
KINGDOM	362 - 1	THE KINGDOM OF HEAVEN WITHIN
KINGDOM	365 - 2	KINGDOM OF HEAVEN IS WITHIN YOU
KINGDOM	404 - 2	GIVE YOU THE KINGDOM
KINGDOM	405 - 1	PLEASURE TO GIVE US THE KINGDOM
KINGDOM	432 - 3	BUT WE ARE TO SEEK THE KINGDOM FIRST
KISMET	030 - 4	KARMIC LAW IS NOT KISMET
KISMET	078 - 2	NOT TO BE CONFUSED WITH KISMET
KNEW	281 - 3	JESUS KNEW WHEN HE SAID THIS
KNEW	438 - 4	JESUS KNEW THIS
KNEW	438 - 4	KNEW JUST WHAT STEP TO TAKE
KNEW	479 - 1	KNEW THAT HE WAS AN IMMORTAL
KNOCK	342 - 3	I STAND AT THE DOOR AND KNOCK
KNOCK	435 - 3	KNOCK AND WE SHALL FIND
KNOCKS	369 - 1	STANDS AT THE DOOR AND KNOCKS
KNOT	225 - 3	KNOT THAT NEEDS TO BE UNTIED
KNOW	039 - 1	KNOW THAT GOOD IS NOW MINE
KNOW	046 - 2	WE ALREADY DO KNOW
KNOW	072 - 4	"MAN KNOW THYSELF"
KNOW	079 - 4	KNOW GOD EXCEPT BY STUDYING MAN
KNOW	082 - 1	KNOW NOTHING OUTSIDE ITSELF
KNOW	084 - 1	LAW DOES NOT KNOW ITSELF
KNOW	095 - 2	TO KNOW AND TO EXPERIENCE
KNOW	137 - 1	TO KNOW A PRINCIPLE
KNOW	159 - 4	WE MUST KNOW THAT WE KNOW
KNOW	162 - 5	I KNOW IN WHOM I HAVE BELIEVED
KNOW	179 - 2	KNOW THAT MAN IS NOW A SPIRITUAL BEING
KNOW	184 - 3	TO KNOW THAT WHAT YOU SPEAK
KNOW	188 - 1	KNOW YOUR OWN MIND
KNOW	188 - 2	YOU MUST KNOW THIS WITHIN
KNOW	188 - 3	KNOW WITHOUT A SHADOW OF DOUBT
KNOW	189 - 1	KNOW THAT ONLY PERFECTION STANDS
KNOW	206 - 4	KNOW THE TRUTH OF WHAT
KNOW	211 - 3	KNOW THAT IT BREAKS
KNOW	224 - 1	KNOW THIS UNTIL THERE COMES TO YOUR
KNOW	251 - 2	THAT I KNOW MY DIVINITY
KNOW	258 - 3	TREAT TO KNOW YOUR HEARING
KNOW	264 - 3	MUST COME TO KNOW
KNOW	264 - 4	BE STILL AND KNOW

KNOW	271 - 3	LEVEL OF OUR ABILITY TO KNOW
KNOW	278 - 2	HOW SHALL I KNOW WHEN I KNOW
KNOW	278 - 2	PROVES HE DOES NOT KNOW
KNOW	290 - 2	KNOW THIS, SEE IT, FEEL IT AND BE IT
KNOW	298 - 2	KNOW THAT THIS THOUGHT WILL MEET
KNOW	298 - 2	KNOW THAT EVERYONE WANTS YOU
KNOW	302 - 2	KNOW THAT NO MATTER
KNOW	303 - 4	SEE THIS, FEEL IT, KNOW IT
KNOW	312 - 1	DOES NOT KNOW ANYTHING ABOUT
KNOW	322 - 1	WHEN WE KNOW THE TRUTH
KNOW	364 - 3	SAY THAT WE KNOW THE TRUTH
KNOW	369 - 2	BE STILL O SOUL AND KNOW
KNOW	393 - 2	TO KNOW THAT WE ARE SURROUNDED BY
KNOW	396 - 1	IT DOES NOT KNOW THAT IT IS DOING
KNOW	399 - 3	WE DO NOT WISH TO KNOW
KNOW	301 - 2	KNOW THAT WE CAN USE CREATIVE POWER
KNOW	436 - 2	KNOW THE TRUTH BY ITS FRUITS
KNOW	445 - 2	KNOW THAT HE IS AN ETERNAL BEING
KNOW	445 - 5	KNOW ONLY THAT WHICH WE EXPERIENCE
KNOW	452 - 4	ANYONE WHO WILLS TO KNOW TRUTH
KNOW	478 - 2	TO KNOW THIS AND TO UNDERSTAND
KNOW	499 - 5	WHAT WE KNOW WE CAN DO
KNOW ENOUGH	341 - 1	KNOW ENOUGH WE SHALL BE ABLE
KNOWER	091 - 1	NOT A KNOWER
KNOWER	276 - 2	SPIRIT IS THE SUPREME KNOWER
KNOWER	372 - 1	THING THAT KNOWS THE KNOWER
KNOWER	392 - 3	NOT A SELF-CONSCIOUS KNOWER
KNOWING	030 - 1	BY KNOWING THE TRUTH
KNOWING	038 - 3	KNOWING CONSCIOUS CENTERS OF LIFE
KNOWING	039 - 5	KNOWING THAT THE THING CAN WORK
KNOWING	047 - 3	KNOWING SOME SPECIFIED GOOD
KNOWING	070 - 2	SINCE IT CANNOT STOP KNOWING
KNOWING	074 - 2	WE SPEAK ABOUT KNOWING
KNOWING	079 - 2	NOT KNOWING, ONLY DOING
KNOWING	083 - 2	A BLIND FORCE NOT KNOWING, ONLY DOING
KNOWING	086 - 4	KNOWING NO BIG AND NO LITTLE
KNOWING	092 - 2	BLIND FORCE, NOT KNOWING, DOING
KNOWING	093 - 2	BLIND FORCE NOT KNOWING
KNOWING	119 - 3	CONSCIOUSLY KNOWING THAT THERE IS NO
KNOWING	171 - 3	KNOWING WITHIN THE SAME MIND
KNOWING	190 - 3	KNOWING THAT TO THE DEGREE
KNOWING	192 - 2	ATTENTION TO CORRECT KNOWING
KNOWING	224 - 2	WITH DEEP FEELING, KNOWING
KNOWING	227 - 3	KNOWING THAT WE HAVE WITHIN US
KNOWING	227 - 4	KNOWING THERE IS JUST THE ONE MIND
KNOWING	251 - 4	OF THIS KNOWING INTELLIGENCE
KNOWING	260 - 3	KNOWING THAT IT IS DONE
KNOWING	278 - 2	PROVE HIS KNOWING BY DOING
KNOWING	284 - 6	SPIRITUAL KNOWING IS CORRECT
KNOWING	296 - 4	KNOWING MEANS USING THE LAW
KNOWING	320 - 2	BY KNOWING THE TRUTH
KNOWING	321 - 2	RULE FOR KNOWING HOW TO TREAT
KNOWING	322 - 1	COMPELLED THROUGH RIGHT KNOWING
KNOWING	322 - 2	RIGHT THINKING AND CORRECT KNOWING
KNOWING	339 - 4	KNOWING AND ETERNALLY KNOWN

KNOWING	435 - 4	KNOWING FACULTY
KNOWING	446 - 5	KNOWING THE TRUTH
KNOWING	465 - 2	GOD IN US KNOWING HIMSELF
KNOWINGNESS	041 - 1	KNOWINGNESS BECOMES OUR WISDOM
KNOWINGNESS	102 - 2	INFINITE KNOWINGNESS
KNOW IT	302 - 2	FEEL IT, KNOW IT
KNOWLEDGE	039 - 6	WORK WITH THIS SOUND KNOWLEDGE
KNOWLEDGE	040 - 1	CONTAINS ALL KNOWLEDGE AND WISDOM
KNOWLEDGE	044 - 5	MIND CONTAINS ALL KNOWLEDGE
KNOWLEDGE	054 - 1	WITH THE CONSCIOUS KNOWLEDGE
KNOWLEDGE	063 - 1	MAY USE THIS KNOWLEDGE
KNOWLEDGE	074 - 2	SCIENCE IS THE KNOWLEDGE OF FACTS
KNOWLEDGE	113 - 2	KNOWLEDGE THROUGH SCIENCE THROUGH OPINION
KNOWLEDGE	160 - 3	KNOWLEDGE CAN FREE US FROM THIS IGNORANCE
KNOWLEDGE	271 - 3	IN KNOWLEDGE AND UNDERSTANDING
KNOWLEDGE	276 - 2	KNOWLEDGE OR NATURE IT HAS POWER
KNOWLEDGE	276 - 2	KNOWLEDGE OF THE UNIVERSAL LAW
KNOWLEDGE	362 - 2	KNOWLEDGE OF SPIRITUAL LAW IN THE MENTAL
KNOWLEDGE	392 - 3	CONSCIOUS KNOWLEDGE THAT IT IS DOING
KNOWLEDGE	393 - 2	THIS KNOWLEDGE FOR DEFINITE PURPOSES
KNOWLEDGE	395 - 1	KNOWLEDGE ALONE CAN FREE MAN
KNOWLEDGE	400 - 3	GUIDANCE INTO THE KNOWLEDGE
KNOWLEDGE	414 - 2	A KNOWLEDGE OF THE POWER
KNOWLEDGE	419 - 1	KNOWLEDGE OF UNSEEN PRINCIPLE
KNOWLEDGE	445 - 2	WITHOUT KNOWLEDGE, THERE IS NO
KNOWLEDGE	445 - 5	KNOWLEDGE OF RELIGION AND PHILOSOPHY
KNOWLEDGE	471 - 2	KNOWLEDGE CLOTHES US IN THE SEAMLESS ROBE
KNOWN	086 - 4	TRUTH KNOWN IS DEMONSTRATED
KNOWN	172 - 1	KNOWN BY ANY PART OF UNIVERSAL MIND IS
KNOWN	172 - 1	KNOWN BY EVERY PART OF IT
KNOWN	373 - 3	SOMETHING TO BE KNOWN
KNOWN	384 - 4	TO KNOW AND BE KNOWN
KNOWN	385 - 2	TO MAKE ITSELF KNOWN
KNOWS	040 - 3	THAT KNOWS EVERYTHING
KNOWS	044 - 4	KNOWS THE TRUTH
KNOWS	070 - 2	KNOWS AND CANNOT STOP KNOWING
KNOWS	078 - 2	IT KNOWS HOW TO CREATE
KNOWS	082 - 1	KNOWS ITSELF
KNOWS	086 - 5	THAT KNOWS ITSELF
KNOWS	091 - 1	KNOWS ONLY TO DO
KNOWS	112 - 3	KNOWS THAT HE HAS LIFE
KNOWS	191 - 2	SPIRIT KNOWS AND THE LAW OBEYS
KNOWS	205 - 5	PRACTITIONER KNOWS WITHIN HIMSELF
KNOWS	207 - 4	KNOWS WHAT HE IS DOING
KNOWS	359 - 1	HE INSTANTLY KNOWS
KNOWS	273 - 3	KNOWS THE RIGHT ANSWER
KNOWS	277 - 3	BUT UNTIL HE KNOWS THIS
KNOWS	284 - 3	FAITH KNOWS THAT THE UNIVERSE IS
KNOWS	302 - 3	KNOWS NO BOUNDS
KNOWS	331 - 4	KNOWS IN US THE REASON
KNOWS	386 - 3	IS SOMETHING THAT KNOWS
KNOWS	395 - 2	ONLY WHAT HE KNOWS ABOUT HIMSELF
KNOWS	441 - 1	INDWELLING SPIRIT WHICH KNOWS
KNOWS	441 - 2	MIND THAT KNOWS
KNOWS	496 - 6	KNOWS NEITHER DEPRESSION NOR CONFUSION

L

LABOR	209 - 2	NOT TO LABOR UNDER THE DELUSION
LABORATORY	255 - 4	LEVER, THE GREAT LABORATORY OF THE BODY
LABORED	362 - 2	LABORED IN THE VINEYARD OF HUMAN
LABORING	038 - 5	SUPPOSE ONE IS LABORING
LABORING	296 - 2	LABORING UNDER A DELUSION
LABORING	342 - 4	NOT LABORING UNDER DELUSIONS
LABORIOUS	202 - 6	NOT BE DIFFICULT OR LABORIOUS
LABORS	438 - 4	MAN LABORS UNDER THE SENSE
LABOUR	444 - 1	LABOUR AND ARE HEAVY LADEN
LACK	124 - 2	LACK OF A PERCEPTION
LACK	173 - 5	TURNS AWAY FROM LACK
LACK	180 - 1	EXCEPT A LACK OF FAITH
LACK	247 - 3	LACK OF THE CONSCIOUSNESS
LACK	262 - 3	THE DIVINE CANNOT LACK
LACK	262 - 3	WE SHOULD NOT LACK FOR ANYTHING
LACK	279 - 1	IF WE LACK
LACK	303 - 3	IT IS A BELIEF IN LACK
LACK	336 - 5	DEMANDS EVIL, LACK, LIMITATION
LACK	402 - 4	LACK A LAW OF HUMAN THOUGHT
LACK	438 - 4	NOTHING OF HIS LACK
LACKS	448 - 1	LACKS A TRUE PERSPECTIVE
LADDER	443 - 4	LADDER WHICH EVER SPIRALS UPWARD
LADEN	335 - 4	HEAVY LADEN AND I WILL GIVE
LADEN	444 - 1	LABOUR AND ARE HEAVY LADEN
LAMP	410 - 4	WHEN WE BRING A LAMP
LANGUAGE	042 - 3	THAT LANGUAGE WHICH
LANGUAGE	066 - 1	PUTTING INTO HUMAN LANGUAGE
LAP	103 - 2	THE LAP OF AN INFINITE INTELLIGENCE
LARGELY	404 - 3	THROUGH THE MAN WHO LIVES LARGELY
LARGER	140 - 4	LARGER LIFE OF THE UNIVERSE
LATCH	464 - 4	LATCH STRING EVER HANGING OUT
LATENT	117 - 3	PHYSICAL BODY IS A LATENT MASS
LATENT	336 - 1	IS LATENT IN ALL PEOPLE
LATENT	392 - 2	ENERGY AND A LATENT POWER
LATENT	415 - 2	LATENT IN THE SLUMBERING THOUGHT
LATENT	476 - 2	STIR UP LATENT ENERGY
LATITUDE	046 - 2	LATITUDE FOR PERSONAL EXPRESSION
LAVISH	465 - 1	IT IS ABUNDANT LAVISH
LAW	025 - 1	GOVERNMENT OF LAW WHOSE PRINCIPLES
LAW	025 - 1	RELIGION WITH LAW
LAW	025 - 3	THE TRUTH POINTS TO FREEDOM UNDER LAW
LAW	026 - 2	THIS IS THE TEACHING LOVE AND LAW
LAW	026 - 2	SO THE LAW OF GOD IS ALSO PERFECT
LAW	029 - 2	WITHIN US IS A MENTAL LAW
LAW	029 - 2	SEAT OF ALL MENTAL LAW AND ACTION
LAW	029 - 3	AND BECOMES THE LAW OF HIS LIFE
LAW	029 - 3	THROUGH THE ONE GREAT LAW OF LIFE
LAW	029 - 4	HIS IDENTITY IN LAW
LAW	030 - 2	IT BECOMES OUR LAW BECAUSE WE HAVE

LAW	030 - 3	FOR WE ARE DEALING WITH LAW
LAW	031 - 2	TENDENCY OF THIS INTELLIGENT LAW
LAW	031 - 2	THE LAW OF MIND IS A NATURAL LAW
LAW	031 - 3	OF LAW AND MECHANICAL ORDER
LAW	031 - 4	THE SUBJECTIVE MIND IS LAW
LAW	032 - 1	THE UNIVERSE FILLED WITH LAW
LAW	032 - 1	WE ARE SPIRIT AND WE ARE LAW
LAW	032 - 1	THE LAW OF OUR LIFE
LAW	032 - 3	THERE IS A LAW IN THE UNIVERSE
LAW	034 - 1	IT IS AN IMMUTABLE LAW
LAW	034 - 2	GREAT LAW OF THE UNIVERSE
LAW	034 - 2	LAW OF THE WHOLE
LAW	036 - 4	IT IS LAW
LAW	038 - 1	LAW IS A FUNDAMENTAL TENET
LAW	038 - 2	LAW RECEIVES AND EXECUTES
LAW	038 - 2	HE INVOKES THE LAW
LAW	039 - 3	LAW WORKS FOR ALL ALIKE
LAW	039 - 3	IMPERSONALNESS OF THE LAW
LAW	039 - 3	AVAILABILITY OF THE LAW
LAW	039 - 3	MECHANICAL ACCURACY OF THE LAW
LAW	042 - 6	ANY LAW IS AVAILABLE
LAW	043 - 1	ALL IS LAW
LAW	043 - 1	LOVES RULES THROUGH LAW
LAW	043 - 1	LAW IS IMPERSONAL
LAW	043 - 1	OF LAW AND ORDER
LAW	043 - 2	LAW MAKES THE WAY POSSIBLE
LAW	043 - 3	MAN'S MIND DISCOVERS THE LAW
LAW	043 - 4	USE OF THE MECHANICAL LAW
LAW	044 - 4	AN UNDERSTANDING OF ANY LAW
LAW	047 - 1	THE LAW WORKS FOR US
LAW	050 - 1	THIS LAW EXECUTES THE WORD
LAW	050 - 1	GOD DID NOT MAKE LAW
LAW	052 - 2	THE AVAILABILITY OF THE LAW
LAW	052 - 2	THE LAW IS INFINITE
LAW	052 - 2	THE LAW ALSO FLOWS THROUGH US
LAW	052 - 4	LAW IS NO RESPECTER OF PERSONS
LAW	052 - 4	THIS LAW WE DID NOT CREATE
LAW	052 - 5	PUNISHMENT THROUGH THE LAW
LAW	053 - 1	TO USE THE LAW OF GOD
LAW	054 - 2	DEFINITELY HE USES THE LAW
LAW	054 - 3	NO REAL LAW TO SUPPORT IT
LAW	054 - 3	THE LAW OF LIFE IS
LAW	054 - 3	A LAW OF LIBERTY OF FREEDOM
LAW	055 - 2	NO REAL LAW TO SUPPORT THEM
LAW	058 - 2	LAW OF CAUSE AND EFFECT
LAW	058 - 5	LEAVE EVERYTHING TO THE LAW
LAW	059 - 1	LAW IS OUR FAITHFUL SERVANT
LAW	064 - 4	PERFECT AND IMMUTABLE LAW
LAW	069 - 3	GOD IS LAW
LAW	070 - 1	GOD DID NOT MAKE LAW
LAW	070 - 1	LAW IS CO-ETERNAL WITH GOD
LAW	078 - 1	LAW OF MENTAL ACTION
LAW	078 - 2	LAW MUST BE SUBJECTIVE
LAW	078 - 2	INFINITE LAW WHICH KNOWS HOW
LAW	078 - 2	KARMIC LAW OF BUDDHA

LAW	080 – 1	GOD IS LAW AND ACTION
LAW	084 – 1	HIS WORD IS LAW
LAW	084 – 1	GOD IS LAW
LAW	084 – 1	LAW SERVANT OF THE SPIRIT
LAW	084 – 1	LAW KNOWS ONLY TO DO
LAW	084 – 2	DID GOD MAKE LAW
LAW	084 – 2	LAW MUST BE CO-EXISTENT AND CO-ETERNAL
LAW	084 – 3	SPIRIT OPERATES THROUGH LAW
LAW	084 – 3	IMAGINE THE LAW EVER FAILING
LAW	084 – 4	INFINITE SPIRIT AND AN INFINITE LAW
LAW	084 – 4	GOD WORKING THROUGH LAW
LAW	084 – 5	ACCORDING TO LAW AND ORDER
LAW	086 – 3	LAW OF CAUSE AND EFFECT
LAW	092 – 3	UNIVERSAL LAW OF MIND
LAW	092 – 3	ALL LAW IS MIND IN ACTION
LAW	105 – 1	KNOWS UPON ITSELF AS LAW
LAW	105 – 2	LAW CAN NEVER SAY "I WILL NOT"
LAW	122 – 4	THOUGHT BECOMES THE LAW OF HIS LIFE
LAW	126 – 3	LAW IS MIND IN ACTION
LAW	131 – 3	LAW OF MIND IS AN IMPERSONAL FORCE
LAW	132 – 5	LAW AND MANIFESTATION ARE AUTOMATIC
LAW	133 – 4	LAW WORKS AUTOMATICALLY UNTIL IT IS
LAW	140 – 4	LAW IN OUR INDIVIDUAL LIVES
LAW	166 – 4	THE BIBLE TEACHES THE LAW OF CAUSE
LAW	174 – 4	LAW IS NEITHER GOOD NOR BAD
LAW	174 – 4	LAW IS AND RESPONDS
LAW	186 – 4	LAW OF CAUSE AND EFFECT
LAW	186 – 4	FOR GOD IS LAW
LAW	189 – 1	SPIRIT BACK OF THE LAW
LAW	190 – 1	HOW DID THEY CONTACT THIS LAW
LAW	190 – 2	SETS IN MOTION THE LAW OF LOVE
LAW	191 – 2	LAW IS LAW WHEREVER WE FIND IT
LAW	194 – 2	LAW IN THE SPIRITUAL WORLD
LAW	194 – 3	THE LAW CREATES THE FORM
LAW	195 – 3	THE LAW FOLLOWS THE WORD
LAW	200 – 1	NOT RESPONSIBLE FOR THE LAW
LAW	205 – 5	SETS THE LAW IN MOTION
LAW	220 – 5	OPERATIVE THROUGH THE LAW
LAW	221 – 1	THIS IS THE LAW OF GOD
LAW	221 – 5	LAW GOVERNING THIS PRINCIPLE
LAW	224 – 2	IT IS THE LAW WHICH CREATES
LAW	228 – 3	THE WORD HE SPEAKS IS LAW
LAW	228 – 3	IT IS THE LAW
LAW	236 – 1	HAVE NO LAW TO SUPPORT THEM
LAW	239 – 3	LIFE IS GOVERNED BY DIVINE LAW
LAW	239 – 3	CO-OPERATE MENTALLY WITH THIS LAW OF LIFE
LAW	262 – 2	THE LAW UNTO THAT THING
LAW	263 – 3	IT IS THE LAW UNTO THAT
LAW	267 – 2	THE LAW COMPLIES WITH US
LAW	268 – 2	NOT A LAW OF LICENSE
LAW	268 – 3	THIS LAW WE DID NOT MAKE
LAW	272 – 1	OVER TO THE LAW
LAW	272 – 1	LET THE LAW WORK THROUGH
LAW	272 – 2	PART OF THE WORKING OF THE LAW
LAW	275 – 3	LAW IS A MECHANICAL FORCE

LAW	276 - 2	UNIVERSAL LAW OF MIND
LAW	280 - 2	SURROUNDED BY AN INTELLIGENT LAW
LAW	280 - 3	LAW OF MENTAL EQUIVALENTS
LAW	286 - 2	SET A LAW IN MOTION
LAW	297 - 2	WE MAY LEAVE IT TO THE LAW
LAW	299 - 1	LAW THAT THE MAN WHO SEES
LAW	300 - 3	IT IS A NATURAL LAW
LAW	301 - 3	LAW WILL ALWAYS OBTAIN
LAW	304 - 1	A LAW UNTO THE THING FOR WHICH IT IS SPOKEN
LAW	305 - 5	SETTING THE LAW IN MOTION
LAW	323 - 2	YET ALL IS LAW
LAW	323 - 3	THERE IS ONE INFINITE LAW
LAW	358 - 2	FORGET ALL ABOUT THE LAW
LAW	390 - 3	THE LAW OF MIND IN ACTION
LAW	396 - 2	THIS LAW IS A FORCE IN NATURE
LAW	396 - 3	LAW IS UNCONSCIOUS INTELLIGENCE
LAW	397 - 2	LAW OF GOD'S MIND
LAW	397 - 3	THE LAW OF MIND OBEYS
LAW	397 - 4	BY THE LAW OF MIND
LAW	400 - 1	LAW KNOWS ONLY TO OBEY
LAW	418 - 4	INTO LIBERTY UNDER LAW
LAW	429 - 2	LAW OF CAUSE AND EFFECT TAKES CARE OF ALL
LAW	447 - 3	THE LAW OF ITS OWN NATURE
LAW	455 - 2	LAW OF COMPENSATION WHICH WEIGHS
LAW	459 - 3	LAW AND THE PROPHETS
LAW	460 - 6	LAW OF GOD IS OMNIPRESENT
LAW	460 - 6	LAW OF GOD IS THE LAW OF CAUSE AND EFFECT
LAW	477 - 7	LAW OF MOSES BUT TO FULFILL IT
LAW	482 - 2	LAW IS ONE OF GROWTH AND UNFOLDMENT
LAW	483 - 1	GREAT LAW OF CORRESPONDENTS
LAW	485 - 4	LAW WILL FREE THE BODY
LAW	500 - 2	LAW IS A COLD HARD FACT RETURNING TO EACH
LAW	500 - 2	LAW IS NEUTRAL
LAW	500 - 4	LAW OF FREEDOM TO THE RIGHTEOUS
LAW	501 - 2	LAW CANNOT AND WILL NOT DEPART
LAW OF ATTRACTION	118 - 4	DECIDES HOW THE LAW OF ATTRACTION
LAW OF AVERAGES	115 - 2	LIFTS HIMSELF ABOVE THE LAW OF AVERAGES
LAW OF AVERAGES	417 - 2	RISE ABOVE THE LAW OF AVERAGES
LAW OF BELIEF	127 - 1	HE CALLED IT A LAW OF BELIEF
LAW OF GOD	488 - 2	LAW OF GOD IS ONE OF LIBERTY
LAW OF MIND	115 - 1	LAW OF MIND IS ALWAYS SUBJECTIVE
LAW OF MIND	403 - 3	THE LAW OF MIND IS NOT SELECTIVE
LAW OF THOUGHT	141 - 2	LAW OF LIFE IS A LAW OF THOUGHT
LAWS	033 - 2	SUBTLE LAWS OF NATURE
LAWS	043 - 1	MADE UP ONLY OF MECHANICAL LAWS
LAWS	050 - 1	WE DISCOVER LAWS
LAWS	072 - 1	DISCOVERY OF NATURAL LAWS
LAWS	233 - 3	LOVE FULFILLS ALL THE LAWS OF LIFE
LAWS	280 - 3	THESE ARE THE TWO GREAT LAWS
LAWS	380 - 2	LAWS ARE THE SAME ON EVERY PLANE
LAWS	403 - 3	NATURAL LAWS ARE OF A LIKE CHARACTER
LAWYER	168 - 3	LAWYER WHO HANDLES THE BUSINESS
LAY	335 - 4	LAY OUR BURDENS ON THE ALTAR
LAY HANDS	207 - 2	LAY HANDS ON HIS PATIENT
LAY HOLD	233 - 4	LAY HOLD OF REALITY

LAY HOLD	233 - 4	LAY HOLD OF LIFE
LAZARUS	217 - 2	RAISED LAZARUS FROM AMONG THOSE
LAZARUS	331 - 5	CONSIDER HIS RAISING OF LAZARUS
LEAD	147 - 3	LEAD US INTO ALL GOOD
LEAD	185 - 2	LEAD ME EVER INTO THE PATHS
LEAD	220 - 3	TRY TO LEAD THE THOUGHT
LEADING	491 - 2	LEADING THE SOUL TO THE INNER CHRIST
LEAGUE	463 - 4	MAN SEEKS TO LEAGUE HIMSELF
LEARN	038 - 4	LEARN TO BELIEVE
LEARN	133 - 4	TO THINK IS TO LEARN HOW TO LIVE
LEARN	308 - 2	ONE THING WE SHOULD LEARN
LEARN	340 - 2	MUST LEARN HOW IT WORKS
LEARN	434 - 3	LEARN TO PRAISE AND NOT CONDEMN
LEARNED	107 - 4	LEARNED ALL IT SHOULD
LEARNED	208 - 3	LEARNED THE MEANING AND NATURE
LEARNING	407 - 2	LEARNING MUST FOLLOW THIS RULE
LEARNING	417 - 2	LEARNING TO THINK INDEPENDENTLY
LEAST	490 - 6	APPARENT LEAST TO THE APPARENT GREATEST
LEAVE	060 - 2	LEAVE THE RESULTS TO THAT LAW
LEAVE	431 - 3	LEAVE ALL ELSE BEHIND
LEAVE	459 - 1	LEAVE THE IDEA FREE
LEAVEN	451 - 5	LEAVEN THE WHOLE LUMP OF SUBJECTIVITY
LED	234 - 3	LED BY THE EVERPRESENT MIND
LED	272 - 2	LED BY THE SPIRIT
LEFT	374 - 2	REAL HAS LEFT THIS PLANE
LEGACY	158 - 3	LEGACY OF FAITH
LEGITIMATE	100 - 1	BODY AS A LEGITIMATE EFFECT
LEGITIMATE	114 - 4	A LEGITIMATE POINT OF VIEW
LEGITIMATE	138 - 1	APPROVED AS A LEGITIMATE
LEGITIMATE	192 - 2	LEGITIMATE TO USE ALL METHODS
LEGITIMATE	269 - 3	THIS IS LEGITIMATE SELF-EXPRESSION
LEGITIMATE	440 - 4	TO ANY LEGITIMATE PURPOSE
LEGITIMATE	477 - 4	PLACE IN ANY LEGITIMATE ACTIVITY
LEGS	234 - 3	LEGS REPRESENT MAN'S ABILITY
LEND	188 - 4	LEND THEMSELVES TO A CONSTRUCTIVE
LENGTH	212 - 4	LENGTH OF TIME IT TAKES
LESSER	401 - 2	RISE TO LESSER CAUSES AND EFFECTS
LESSER IDEAS	354 - 3	LESSER IDEAS WHICH ARE TO ACT
LESSON	412 - 3	UNTIL THE LESSON IS LEARNED
LESSON	435 - 2	LESSON WE HAVE NOT LEARNED
LESSON	439 - 5	LESSON IN IMPERSONAL HEALING
LESSON	444 - 2	LESSON TAUGHT BY THE ILLUMINED
LESSON	460 - 5	LESSON WE HAVE TO LEARN
LESSON	466 - 3	MOST PERFECT LESSON EVER TAUGHT
LESSON	469 - 2	A LESSON FOR EVERYONE FOR ALL TIME
LESSON	473 - 3	LESSON OF RIGHT AND WRONG
LESSON	474 - 1	THE LESSON OF RIGHT AND WRONG
LESSON	482 - 3	GREATEST OBJECT LESSON
LESSON	484 - 4	LESSON IN MENTAL AND SPIRITUAL HEALING
LESSONS	452 - 2	MOST VALUABLE LESSONS THE WORLD
LESSONS	467 - 2	MOST WONDERFUL LESSONS
LESSONS	502 - 5	LESSONS EVER POINTING THE WAY
LET	140 - 3	LET THIS GREAT POWER OPERATE THROUGH US
LET	304 - 4	LET THEM COME FROM WHERE THEY MAY
LET	416 - 3	LET THE INDIVIDUAL ALONE

LET	502 - 2	LET GO AND FORGET THEM ALTOGETHER
LET	502 - 3	CONSCIOUSLY LET GO ALL OUR TROUBLES
L-E-T	489 - 3	L-E-T IS A BIG WORD
LET GO	160 - 1	LET GO OF ALL HUMAN WILL
LET GO	233 - 4	LET GO OF ALL THAT IS NOT TRUE
LET GO	233 - 4	LET GO OF DOUBT
LET GO	381 - 3	TO LET GO
LET GO	454 - 5	LET GO OF THE THOUGHT OF ISOLATION
LET GO	502 - 2	LEARN TO LET GO OF OUR MISTAKES
LET GO	502 - 3	PAID WHEN WE LET GO AND TRUST
LETTER	283 - 2	THE LETTER AND THE SPIRIT OF THE LAW
LETTER	410 - 2	SPIRIT TO THE LETTER OF THE LAW
LETTER	414 - 4	LETTER WITHOUT THE SPIRIT
LETTING	399 - 5	LETTING SOMETHING HAPPEN
LETTING GO	455 - 5	LETTING GO OF ALL THAT OPPOSES
LEVEL	035 - 2	LEVEL OF MAN'S CONCEPT
LEVEL	124 - 2	FROM WHATEVER LEVEL WE WORK
LEVEL	139 - 1	LEVEL OF OUR SELF-COMPREHENSION
LEVEL	147 - 1	LIFE EXTERNALIZES AT THE LEVEL OF OUR
LEVEL	166 - 1	LEVEL OF THE EMBODIMENT
LEVEL	219 - 2	LEVEL OF OUR CONCEPT
LEVEL	220 - 1	LEVEL OF OUR RECOGNITION
LEVEL	287 - 2	REACH ITS OWN LEVEL BY ITS OWN WEIGHT
LEVEL	287 - 2	LEVEL OF THE SUBJECTIVE THOUGHT
LEVEL	287 - 5	NO HIGHER LEVEL IN OUR EXPERIENCE
LEVEL	394 - 4	GOD FUNCTIONING AT THE LEVEL
LEVEL	414 - 1	LEVEL OF THOSE SECONDARY CAUSES
LEVEL	434 - 3	LEVEL OF THAT BELIEF
LIABILITY	144 - 1	LIABILITY OF EXPERIENCING
LIABILITY	394 - 2	IS NO LIABILITY IN USING
LIBERTY	110 - 1	LAW IS A LAW OF LIBERTY
LIBERTY	161 - 4	ANNOUNCED THE LAW OF LIBERTY
LIBERTY	268 - 2	THE LAW IS A LAW OF LIBERTY
LIBERTY	269 - 2	OPERATE AS A LAW OF LIBERTY
LIBERTY	272 - 2	GUIDED INTO TRUTH AND LIBERTY
LIBERTY	340 - 3	LIBERTY IN THE EVOLVING PRINCIPLE
LIBERTY	418 - 4	INTO LIBERTY UNDER LAW
LIBERTY	481 - 4	LAW IS ONE OF LIBERTY
LIBERTY	481 - 4	LIBERTY COMES ONLY THROUGH
LIBERTY	486 - 3	LIBERTY OF THE SONS OF THE MOST HIGH
LIBERTY	488 - 4	LIBERTY OF THE SONS OF GOD
LICENSE	268 - 2	BUT NOT A LAW OF LICENSE
LICENSE	481 - 4	NEVER ONE OF LICENSE
LIE	379 - 2	LIE IN THE FACE OF HUMAN THOUGHT
LIE	464 - 5	TRUTH CAN NEVER PRODUCE A LIE
LIFE	026 - 1	A LIFE WONDERFUL IN SCOPE
LIFE	027 - 4	THE NATURAL LAWS OF LIFE
LIFE	027 - 5	THE STUDY OF LIFE
LIFE	029 - 4	EACH IS DRAWING FROM LIFE WHAT HE THINKS
LIFE	032 - 1	THE LAW OF OUR LIFE
LIFE	035 - 3	UNIVERSAL LIFE AND ENERGY
LIFE	035 - 4	THE LIFE WHICH WE LIVE
LIFE	036 - 4	THIS ORIGINAL LIFE IS INFINITE
LIFE	036 - 4	IT IS LIFE
LIFE	043 - 1	EITHER VIEWING LIFE

LIFE	044 - 3	IMMERSED IN A PERFECT LIFE
LIFE	044 - 3	ONLY AS MUCH OF THIS LIFE
LIFE	056 - 4	RIGHT ACTION IN MY LIFE
LIFE	067 - 3	POINTS TO ONE CENTRAL LIFE
LIFE	067 - 3	VALUE TO THE INDIVIDUAL LIFE
LIFE	068 - 3	LIFE CANNOT BE DIVIDED
LIFE	068 - 4	PLAY OF LIFE UPON ITSELF
LIFE	069 - 3	SPIRIT IS CONSCIOUS LIFE
LIFE	072 - 1	LIFE WAITS UPON MAN'S DISCOVERY
LIFE	072 - 3	CONSCIOUS UNION WITH LIFE
LIFE	082 - 1	SPIRIT IS ALL LIFE
LIFE	082 - 2	THE LIFE IN EVERYTHING
LIFE	082 - 4	THAT THEY MIGHT HAVE LIFE
LIFE	087 - 1	THE MEANING OF INHERENT LIFE
LIFE	103 - 2	SEPARATE LIFE FROM LIVING
LIFE	126 - 3	LIFE ACTING THROUGH LAW
LIFE	151 - 4	LIFE MUST REVEAL ITSELF TO US THROUGH OUR
LIFE	154 - 1	ETERNAL REALITIES OF LIFE
LIFE	189 - 1	POSSIBLE EXPRESSION OF LIFE
LIFE	190 - 3	MAN'S LIFE IN REALITY IS SPIRITUAL
LIFE	191 - 1	IT IS WITHIN EVERY MAN'S LIFE
LIFE	191 - 3	MAN'S LIFE IS A DRAMA
LIFE	216 - 2	THE GREAT LAW OF ALL LIFE
LIFE	219 - 1	THE HEALING CURRENTS OF LIFE
LIFE	229 - 2	HUMAN LIFE IS THE INCARNATION
LIFE	233 - 3	LOVE FULFILLS ALL THE LAWS OF LIFE
LIFE	233 - 4	LAY HOLD OF LIFE IN
LIFE	239 - 3	LIFE CANNOT GROW OLD
LIFE	239 - 3	CO-OPERATE MENTALLY WITH THIS LAW OF LIFE
LIFE	240 - 4	LIFE IS FOREVER PRESENT IN ITS FULLNESS
LIFE	246 - 2	THE ONE UNBROKEN CHAIN OF LIFE
LIFE	249 - 2	THE TRUTH THAT GOD'S LIFE FLOWS
LIFE	256 - 5	VERY LIFE OF GOD VITALIZES
LIFE	256 - 5	THE INFINITE LIFE
LIFE	262 - 3	THAT MAKES LIFE WORTH WHILE
LIFE	268 - 5	GOD TO BE THE PRINCIPLE OF LIFE
LIFE	269 - 1	US TO EXPRESS GREATER LIFE
LIFE	271 - 5	SEE HIS LIFE AS HE WISHES
LIFE	280 - 2	HOW MUCH LIFE CAN ANY MAN
LIFE	284 - 3	THE LIFE OF MAN IS GOD
LIFE	284 - 4	GOD IS ALSO THE LIFE OF MAN
LIFE	295 - 2	PEACE, POWER, LIFE AND TRUTH
LIFE	298 - 3	THE LIFE THAT HAS NOT LOVED
LIFE	303 - 4	IT IS FILLING YOU WITH LIFE AND LOVE
LIFE	307 - 2	RADIATE LIFE
LIFE	323 - 3	THERE IS ONE LIMITLESS LIFE
LIFE	358 - 2	PERFECT LIFE FLOW THROUGH US
LIFE	372 - 3	TO INQUIRE WHY LIFE ITSELF IS
LIFE	383 - 3	WHAT MORE CAN LIFE DEMAND
LIFE	384 - 4	WHEN WE ENTER THE LARGER LIFE
LIFE	385 - 2	PERSONAL LIFE BEYOND THE GRAVE
LIFE	385 - 2	MY LIFE HAPPY WHILE ON EARTH
LIFE	386 - 3	KNOWS THAT LIFE ITSELF MOVES
LIFE	386 - 4	TO ANOTHER LIFE ON THIS PLANE
LIFE	387 - 1	THE SPIRAL OF LIFE IS UPWARD

LIFE	387 - 2	RECONCILIATION BETWEEN THIS LIFE
LIFE	388 - 2	LIFE IS GOOD AND GOD IS GOOD
LIFE	405 - 3	SOMETHING OTHER THAN LIFE
LIFE	412 - 2	LIFE IS A MOTION PICTURE
LIFE	412 - 3	EXPRESSES LIFE AND HAPPINESS
LIFE	453 - 2	LIFE IS WHAT CONSCIOUSNESS MAKES
LIFE	463 - 2	LIFE WITHOUT WHICH NOTHING CAN LIVE
LIFE	474 - 6	LIFE IS FROM SPIRIT, NOT FROM MATTER
LIFE	475 - 6	FATHER HAS LIFE SO THE SON HAS LIFE
LIFE	484 - 3	SPIRITUALLY MINDED IS LIFE
LIFE	487 - 7	LIFE IS NEITHER SEPARATE
LIFE-FORCE	226 - 2	FLOW OF LIFE-FORCE TO THE BRAIN
LIFE FORCES	245 - 2	LIFE FORCES FLOW FREELY
LIFE PRINCIPLE	473 - 1	LIFE PRINCIPLE SYMBOLIZED BY THE SERPENT
LIFE PRINCIPLE	474 - 5	SERPENT MEANS THE LIFE PRINCIPLE
LIFETIMES	349 - 4	MANY LIFETIMES OF HARD STUDY
LIFTED	056 - 1	AND I, IF I BE LIFTED UP
LIFTED	282 - 3	BE LIFTED OUT OF HIS CONDITION
LIFTED	474 - 5	MOSES LIFTED UP THE SERPENT
LIFTS	238 - 1	LIFTS HIM UP MENTALLY AND SPIRITUALLY
LIFTS	278 - 4	LIFTS ONE OUT OF HIS ENVIRONMENT
LIGHT	041 - 2	WE STAND IN THE LIGHT
LIGHT	042 - 1	LIGHT OF LOVE
LIGHT	042 - 2	ALL MEN RECEIVE SOME LIGHT
LIGHT	042 - 2	ALWAYS THE SAME LIGHT
LIGHT	060 - 3	A NEW LIGHT IS COMING
LIGHT	067 - 3	ONLY LIGHT ON RELIGION
LIGHT	079 - 3	WILL EITHER LIGHT OUR HOUSE
LIGHT	114 - 4	LIGHT OF RECENT INVESTIGATIONS
LIGHT	151 - 1	LIGHT ON AN IMPORTANT LAW
LIGHT	158 - 4	THE BEACON LIGHT
LIGHT	158 - 5	FAITH WILL LIGHT THE PLACE
LIGHT	158 - 5	FAITH WILL LIGHT THE WAY
LIGHT	158 - 5	FAITH IS EVER THE LIGHT
LIGHT	164 - 4	LETS IN THE LIGHT
LIGHT	183 - 2	LIGHT HAS THE POWER TO OVERCOME
LIGHT	183 - 2	EXACTLY WHAT IT IS: LIGHT
LIGHT	183 - 2	LIGHT SHINETH IN THE DARKNESS
LIGHT	191 - 4	MORE LIGHT WILL BE GIVEN
LIGHT	200 - 4	ABSENCE OF LIGHT
LIGHT	208 - 1	MIGHT APPEAR AS LIGHT
LIGHT	208 - 1	LIGHT DURING A TREATMENT
LIGHT	229 - 2	LIGHT OF GOD
LIGHT	229 - 5	LIGHT OF THE BODY IS THE EYE
LIGHT	230 - 1	SHALL BE FULL OF LIGHT
LIGHT	230 - 2	LIGHT OF UNDERSTANDING DAWNS
LIGHT	230 - 5	LIGHT OF SPIRITUAL UNDERSTANDING
LIGHT	231 - 2	LIGHT OF LOVE
LIGHT	235 - 5	LIGHT OF SPIRIT DISSIPATES
LIGHT	238 - 4	IN THE LIGHT OF EXPERIENCE
LIGHT	247 - 2	FAITH IN GOD AS THE LIGHT
LIGHT	264 - 5	WONDERFUL PEACE AND LIGHT
LIGHT	274 - 3	AND LETS IN THE LIGHT
LIGHT	281 - 4	THE LIGHT HE THROWS ON OTHERS
LIGHT	332 - 4	I AM THE LIGHT OF THE WORLD

LIGHT	345 – 1	BECAME CONSCIOUS OF THIS LIGHT
LIGHT	345 – 1	AN ATMOSPHERE OF LIGHT
LIGHT	345 – 2	ACCOMPANIED BY A GREAT LIGHT
LIGHT	345 – 2	WE SHALL CALL A LESSER LIGHT
LIGHT	345 – 3	THE LIGHT SHINES IN THE DARKNESS
LIGHT	345 – 3	AS A PATHWAY OF LIGHT
LIGHT	345 – 4	HAVE BEEN BLINDED BY THE LIGHT
LIGHT	362 – 4	YE ARE THE LIGHT OF THE WORLD
LIGHT	388 – 3	GIVES LIGHT AND COLOR TO OUR EVERYDAY
LIGHT	411 – 1	THE LIGHT IS GREATER THAN THE DARKNESS
LIGHT	415 – 1	THE LIGHT CANNOT BE BORROWED
LIGHT	430 – 2	LIGHT OF THE WORLD
LIGHT	430 – 2	LIGHT BE KEPT TRIMMED
LIGHT	432 – 2	SHALL BE FILLED WITH LIGHT
LIGHT	446 – 2	BORROW ITS LIGHT
LIGHT	468 – 1	LIGHT INSTANTLY ILLUMINATES IT
LIGHT	501 – 4	ENTER HIS LIGHT WE ARE HEALED
LIGHTS	270 – 1	ARE BUT FEEBLE LIGHTS
LIGHTS	435 – 2	LIGHTS LIGHTING THE WAY
LIKE	338 – 3	WE SHALL BE LIKE HIM
LIKELY	417 – 4	LIKELY TO FALL INTO THE ERROR
LIKENESS	340 – 2	LIKENESS WHICH EXACTLY BALANCES
LIKENESS	411 – 4	LIKENESS OF THIS EMBODIMENT
LIKENESS	478 – 3	HIS EXPRESSED LIKENESS
LIKES	350 – 3	EXPLAIN OUR LIKES AND DISLIKES
LILIES	432 – 2	LILIES OF THE FIELD
LIMIT	037 – 4	IS WITHOUT LIMIT
LIMIT	050 – 2	THERE CAN BE NO LIMIT
LIMIT	087 – 2	NO LIMIT CAN BE PLACED UPON
LIMIT	102 – 4	NO LIMIT SHOULD BE PLACED
LIMIT	118 – 2	NO LIMIT TO WHAT IT CAN OR WOULD DO FOR US
LIMIT	125 – 4	LIMIT OF OUR ABILITY TO USE THIS POWER IS
LIMIT	188 – 1	PLACE NO LIMIT ON PRINCIPLE
LIMIT	197 – 5	NO LIMIT TO THE POWER TO HEAL
LIMIT	197 – 5	LIMIT OF OUR ABILITY TO CONCEIVE
LIMIT	215 – 1	LIMIT TO ITS POWER
LIMIT	267 – 4	THERE APPEARS TO BE A LIMIT
LIMIT	306 – 2	LIMIT OF OUR ABILITY TO
LIMIT	403 – 4	CAN IN NO WAY LIMIT MIND
LIMITATION	032 – 3	ENTIRE PROBLEM OF LIMITATION
LIMITATION	038 – 5	IDEA OF LIMITATION
LIMITATION	038 – 5	IS A PICTURE OF LIMITATION
LIMITATION	055 – 2	THESE IMAGES OF LIMITATION
LIMITATION	118 – 2	LIMITATION IS NOT IN PRINCIPLE NOR IN LAW
LIMITATION	133 – 2	LIMITATION IS NOT INHERENT IN THE LAW
LIMITATION	147 – 4	NO LIMITATION OUTSIDE OUR
LIMITATION	180 – 4	LIMITATION IS A MISTAKE
LIMITATION	185 – 2	LIMITATION APPEARS AT ALL SIDES
LIMITATION	186 – 2	IN REALITY THERE IS NO LIMITATION
LIMITATION	195 – 2	HERE IS NO REAL LIMITATION
LIMITATION	204 – 2	SUBJECTIVE IDEA OF LIMITATION
LIMITATION	208 – 5	OUTLINE BUT NOT OF LIMITATION
LIMITATION	223 – 2	ANY SENSE OF LIMITATION
LIMITATION	231 – 5	A BELIEF IN LIMITATION
LIMITATION	264 – 1	FROM THE THOUGHT OF LIMITATION

LIMITATION	267 - 2	FREEDOM FROM SUCH LIMITATION
LIMITATION	301 - 3	THOUGHTS OF FAILURE, LIMITATION
LIMITATION	303 - 3	A BELIEF IN A LIMITATION
LIMITATION	317 - 2	FROM ANY FORM OF LIMITATION
LIMITATION	319 - 2	TO VIEW LIMITATION IS TO IMPRESS IT
LIMITATION	321 - 1	BOUND NOT BY A LIMITATION
LIMITATION	322 - 4	TALK ABOUT LIMITATION OR POVERTY
LIMITATION	402 - 4	LIMITATION IS THE RESULT OF AN IGNORANT USE
LIMITATION	403 - 1	LIMITATION INTO FREEDOM
LIMITATION	403 - 2	LIMITATION IS A CONDENSATION OF THE IDEA
LIMITATION	404 - 1	LIMITATION IS UNREAL TO MIND
LIMITATIONS	038 - 4	LIMITATIONS, OTHER BELIEFS WILL CHANGE THEM
LIMITATIONS	054 - 3	SPIRIT IMPOSES NO LIMITATIONS
LIMITATIONS	406 - 2	EXCEPT THE LIMITATIONS THAT WE SET
LIMITED	279 - 2	ONLY REASON MAN IS LIMITED
LIMITED	280 - 2	LIMITED ONLY A LITTLE CAN COME
LIMITED	302 - 3	LIMITED POOR OR MISERABLE
LIMITED	321 - 1	BUT BY LIMITED THOUGHT
LIMITED	394 - 2	OUR CONSCIOUS MIND IS LIMITED
LIMITED	401 - 2	TO THAT WHICH IS LIMITED
LIMITED	459 - 3	TOO LIMITED A CONCEPT OF GOD
LIMITED	484 - 3	A LIMITED CONCEPT OF TRUTH
LIMITED	488 - 3	LIMITED TO OUR PRESENT UNDERSTANDING
LIMITING	405 - 2	STOP LIMITING GOD
LIMITLESS	029 - 3	A POWER THAT SEEMS TO BE LIMITLESS
LIMITLESS	045 - 1	DIFFERENTIATING IS LIMITLESS
LIMITLESS	067 - 1	SPIRIT IS THE LIMITLESS
LIMITLESS	086 - 4	WHICH IS LIMITLESS
LIMITLESS	165 - 1	LIMITLESS MEDIUM OF SUBJECTIVITY
LIMITLESS	267 - 3	WITHIN ITSELF A LIMITLESS POSSIBILITY
LIMITLESS	271 - 2	OF USING IT ARE LIMITLESS
LIMITLESS	283 - 1	LIMITLESS SEA OF RECEPTIVITY
LIMITLESS	300 - 2	THE LIMITLESS AND THE CONDITIONED
LIMITLESS	302 - 3	IT IS LIMITLESS KNOWS NO BOUNDS
LIMITLESS	364 - 2	THE SPIRIT ARE LIMITLESS
LIMITLESS	397 - 4	SUBJECTIVE MEDIUM IS LIMITLESS
LIMITLESS	399 - 4	WITH LIMITLESS POWER AND ENERGY
LIMITS	030 - 2	UNIVERSAL WHICH HAS NO LIMITS
LINE	436 - 2	IN LINE WITH TRUTH
LINK	371 - 2	LINK WHICH BINDS ONE EVENT
LIONS	158 - 2	STOPPED THE MOUTHS OF LIONS
LIPS	350 - 3	WHAT THE LIPS MAY BE SAYING
LIQUID	047 - 5	SOLID BECOMES LIQUID
LIQUID	048 - 2	CREATED FROM THE GENERAL LIQUID
LIQUID	184 - 2	THE SOLID AND THE LIQUID
LIQUOR	223 - 1	LIQUOR HABIT COMES TO YOU
LIQUOR	223 - 2	THE LIQUOR HABIT HAS NO POWER
LISTEN	275 - 2	TO THE DEGREE THAT WE LISTEN
LISTEN	367 - 1	LEARN TO LISTEN FOR THIS VOICE
LISTEN	401 - 3	LISTEN TO THOSE WHO DENY US
LISTEN	470 - 3	TO LISTEN TO THE INNER VOICE OF TRUTH
LISTENED	217 - 2	LISTENED TO THE WAILING OF
LISTENING	258 - 1	LISTENING ATTITUDE
LITERALLY	041 - 1	NOT TOO LITERALLY
LITERALLY	473 - 3	LITERALLY WOULD BE RIDICULOUS

LITERALLY	481 - 3	LITERALLY ABIDE IN THE MAN JESUS
LITTLE	086 - 4	KNOWING NO BIG AND NO LITTLE
LITTLE	087 - 1	MAN IS A LITTLE WORLD
LITTLE	287 - 3	ANSWERS THE BIG AND THE LITTLE
LITTLE	312 - 1	GOD KNOWS BIG AND LITTLE
LITTLE	393 - 2	MAN IN THE LITTLE WORLD
LITTLENESS	418 - 4	A NO LONGER USEFUL LITTLENESS
LIVE	029 - 5	IS TO LEARN HOW TO LIVE
LIVE	035 - 3	IN HIM WE LIVE
LIVE	076 - 3	IN HIM WE LIVE
LIVE	082 - 2	WITHIN THIS ONE ALL LIVE
LIVE	123 - 1	HOW TO THINK IS TO LEARN HOW TO LIVE
LIVE	270 - 4	WHILE WE LIVE, WE LIVE
LIVE	274 - 3	ALREADY LIVE IN A PERFECT UNIVERSE
LIVE	313 - 3	FOR ALL LIVE UNTO HIM
LIVE	384 - 3	TO LIVE AFTER THIS DIVINE LAW
LIVE	386 - 1	I WANT TO LIVE AND KEEP ON LIVING
LIVE	388 - 2	ACCEPT THIS AND BEGIN TO LIVE
LIVE	388 - 4	PREPARE NOT TO DIE, BUT TO LIVE
LIVE	410 - 3	LIVE IN OBEDIENCE TO THE POWER
LIVE	481 - 5	LIVE IN CONSCIOUS UNITY WITH GOOD
LIVED	384 - 3	IF WE HAVE LIVED ANY OTHER WAY
LIVER	255 - 4	LIVER, THE GREAT LABORATORY OF THE BODY
LIVER	255 - 5	DISTURBANCES ARISE IN THE LIVER
LIVES	032 - 3	LIVES AND MOVES AND HAS HIS BEING
LIVES	140 - 4	LAW IN OUR INDIVIDUAL LIVES
LIVES	151 - 3	EACH LIVES IN MIND
LIVES	152 - 5	WHICH LIVES AND MOVES AND HAS ITS BEING
LIVES	307 - 2	OUR LIVES ARE THE RESULT OF
LIVES	396 - 3	LIVES ONLY THROUGH MAN
LIVES	448 - 1	SINCE NO ONE LIVES BY PROXY
LIVING	072 - 2	WE EXPERIENCE LIVING
LIVING	103 - 2	SEPARATE LIFE FROM LIVING
LIVING	139 - 4	ARE LIVING IN AN INTELLIGENT UNIVERSE
LIVING	183 - 1	LIVING IN A UNIVERSE
LIVING	270 - 4	FROM HERE WE SHALL KEEP ON LIVING
LIVING	272 - 2	CHANGE OUR MODE OF LIVING
LIVING	311 - 1	DEAD BUT OF THE LIVING
LIVING	311 - 1	LIVING IN A SPIRITUAL UNIVERSE
LIVING	335 - 3	OF THE DEAD BUT OF THE LIVING
LIVING	436 - 2	LIVING NOR GOD FROM HIS CREATION
LIVING	443 - 1	LIVING IS THE ONLY EXPLANATION
LIVING	443 - 4	LIVING SUCH A GOD-LIKE LIFE
LIVINGNESS	082 - 4	OTHER THAN IN LIVINGNESS
LIVINGNESS	188 - 4	EXPRESS A GREATER DEGREE OF LIVINGNESS
LIVINGNESS	336 - 3	CONTEMPLATE THE SPIRIT OF LIVINGNESS
LIVINGNESS	336 - 3	LIVINGNESS PERSONIFIES ITSELF AS PHYSICAL
LIVINGNESS	404 - 2	A GREATER DEGREE OF LIVINGNESS
LIVINGNESS	450 - 5	BOUNDLESS SEA OF LIVINGNESS
LIVING PRESENCE	334 - 4	FORGET THE LIVING PRESENCE
LO	124 - 1	LO HERE NOR LO THERE
LO	150 - 4	LO HERE NOR LO THERE
LOAD	438 - 2	UNDER A LOAD OF CONDEMNATION
LOAD	457 - 4	LOAD IS DROPPED FROM THE SHOULDERS
LOAVES	341 - 1	MULTIPLY THE LOAVES AND FISHES

LOCATED	362 - 1	HE LOCATED GOD
LOCATED	363 - 3	LOCATED GOD IN HIS OWN SOUL
LOCKED	033 - 2	LOCKED TO THE IGNORANT
LOCOMOTION	340 - 4	THE INEVITABLE END OF LOCOMOTION
LODGE	094 - 2	SIR OLIVER LODGE IN WHICH HE WRITES
LOGIC	355 - 3	ITS POWER OF LOGIC
LOGIC	376 - 4	UNABLE TO FOLLOW THE LOGIC
LOGICAL	053 - 2	LOGICAL REACTIONS OF THE UNIVERSE
LOGICAL	069 - 2	THIS IS LOGICAL TO SUPPOSE
LOGICAL	110 - 1	LOGICAL RESULT OF OUR THOUGHT AND ACT
LOGICAL	173 - 2	LOGICAL ARGUMENT IN THE MIND
LOGICAL	178 - 1	LOGICAL OUTCOME OF WHAT HE THINKS
LOGICAL	269 - 1	THIS SEEMS TO BE A FAIR LOGICAL
LOGICAL	292 - 4	LOGICAL RESULT OF INVOLUTION
LOGICAL	339 - 2	IT IS THE LOGICAL
LOGICAL	355 - 4	BY DRAWING A LOGICAL CONCLUSION
LOGICAL	372 - 1	LOGICAL SEQUENCE OF PERSONALITY
LOGICAL	377 - 2	IT IS LOGICAL
LOGICAL	382 - 3	LOGICAL AND SCIENTIFIC EXPLANATION
LOGICAL	420 - 4	CREATION IS THE LOGICAL RESULT
LOGICAL	433 - 3	LOGICAL EFFECT OF HIS ACTIONS
LOGICAL	437 - 4	BUT ONE LOGICAL EXPLANATION
LOGICAL	448 - 1	LOGICAL OUTCOME OF HIS INNER VISION
LOGICALLY	183 - 2	LOGICALLY FOLLOWS THAT
LOGOS	113 - 1	LOGOS, WHICH MEANS THE WORD
LONG	153 - 1	WE LONG FOR AND NEED
LONG	261 - 4	DOES NOT LONG FOR ANYTHING
LONG	263 - 6	TO LONG FOR THE GOOD
LONG	468 - 1	HOW LONG WE MAY HAVE BEEN AWAY
LONG RUN	429 - 2	LONG RUN OF THE ADVENTURE OF THE SOUL
LONG RUN	429 - 3	LONG RUN, THE MERCIFUL WILL OBTAIN
LONG RUN	434 - 2	LONG RUN, NOTHING JUDGES US BUT
LOOK	044 - 2	LOOK TO THE MIND
LOOK	053 - 5	LOOK AT A WRONG CONDITION
LOOK	185 - 3	LOOK UNTO ME
LOOK	189 - 2	ABLE TO LOOK A FACT
LOOK	265 - 1	LOOK AT THE PRESENT
LOOK	459 - 5	LOOK FOR GOD IN EACH OTHER
LOOK	466 - 3	LOOK AT GOD, GOD LOOKS AT US
LOOKING	036 - 3	LOOKING AT IT THROUGH OUR OWN EYES
LOOKING	124 - 2	LOOKING FOR, WE ARE LOOKING
LOOKING	266 - 3	LOOKING AWAY FROM THE CONDITIONS
LOOKING	364 - 2	STOPPED LOOKING FOR THE SPIRIT
LOOKING	364 - 2	THE THING WE HAVE BEEN LOOKING FOR
LOOKING	435 - 1	LOOKING UPON ALL WITH LOVE
LOOKING	466 - 3	LOOKING THROUGH US AT HIMSELF
LOOKS	303 - 3	LOOKS AS IF ONE WERE NOT TELLING
LOOK WITH	364 - 2	LOOK WITH IS THE THING
LOOSE	291 - 1	LOOSE HIM AND LET HIM GO
LOOSE	457 - 1	LOOSE ON EARTH SHALL BE LOOSED IN HEAVEN
LOOSE	501 - 6	LOOSE OUR TROUBLES AND ARE HEALED
LOOSED	489 - 4	GOD IS LOOSED IN YOUR WORK
LOOSES	179 - 2	HE LOOSES THOUGHT
LORD, LORD	436 - 3	NOT EVERYONE WHO SAYS "LORD, LORD"
LORD, LORD	499 - 5	LORD, LORD BUT THOSE WHO DO

LORD'S	286 - 1	LORD'S PRAYER IS SPIRITUAL
LOS ANGELES	094 - 1	THIS PRINCIPLE IN LOS ANGELES
LOS ANGELES	165 - 2	PRACTITIONER IN LOS ANGELES
LOSE	381 - 2	TO LOSE THE SELF-CONSCIOUSNESS
LOSE	454 - 3	LOSE IS THE SENSE OF LIVING
LOSE	454 - 5	LOSE A PERSONAL SENSE OF RESPONSIBILITY
LOSE	454 - 5	WE LOSE THE PERSONAL
LOSING	456 - 3	LOSING HIS SENSE OF THAT INNER GUIDE
LOSS	239 - 2	TO A FEELING OF LOSS FROM FINANCIAL
LOSS	358 - 3	LOSS OF HIS INDIVIDUALITY
LOSS	387 - 3	THE LOSS OF DEAR ONES
LOST	152 - 4	SOUL IS NEVER LOST
LOST	228 - 1	HAVING LOST HIS MIND
LOST	335 - 3	IMPOSSIBLE THAT ANY SOUL CAN BE LOST
LOST	367 - 2	LOST IN THE MIGHTY DEPTHS OF THY
LOST	383 - 3	CAN NO MORE BE LOST
LOST	429 - 2	PERSPECTIVE OF REALITY IS LOST
LOST	463 - 2	FEELING LOST AND IN WANT
LOUDLY	492 - 3	EFFECT LOUDLY AFFIRMS THE NATURE
LOVE	026 - 1	OF A LOVE BEYOND OUR FONDEST DREAM
LOVE	026 - 2	BUT THE GREAT LOVE OF THE UNIVERSE
LOVE	026 - 2	WE APPROACH LOVE THROUGH THE LAW
LOVE	026 - 2	THIS, THEN, IS THE TEACHING, LOVE AND LAW
LOVE	026 - 2	AS THE LOVE OF GOD IS PERFECT SO THE LAW
LOVE	032 - 2	LIFE DOMINATED BY LOVE
LOVE	042 - 1	LIGHT OF LOVE RUNNING THROUGH LIFE
LOVE	043 - 1	ALL IS LOVE
LOVE	043 - I	LOVE RULES THROUGH LAW
LOVE	043 - 1	LOVE IS SPONTANEOUS
LOVE	043 - 2	LOVE POINTS THE WAY
LOVE	043 - 3	THIS IS THE WAY OF LOVE
LOVE	082 - I	LOVE BEING CAUSE AND EFFECT
LOVE	082 - 2	LOVE THROUGH EVERYTHING
LOVE	157 - 2	VERITIES LIKE TRUTH AND LOVE, BEAUTY
LOVE	179 - 1	DIVINE LIFE, LOVE, LAW
LOVE	184 - 3	HAVE A CONSCIOUSNESS OF LOVE
LOVE	190 - 2	MOTION THE LAW OF LOVE
LOVE	196 - 2	LOVE AS WELL AS A UNIVERSE
LOVE	205 - 2	REALIZATION OF LIFE AND LOVE
LOVE	231 - 3	PRISM OF GOD'S LOVE
LOVE	233 - 3	LOVE IS ALWAYS HEALING
LOVE	233 - 3	LOVE FULFILLS ALL THE LAWS OF LIFE
LOVE	238 - 3	CENTER OF DIVINE LOVE
LOVE	238 - 3	LOVE IS AT THE CENTER OF MAN'S BEING
LOVE	238 - 3	GOVERNED BY LOVE
LOVE	238 - 4	PARTICULARLY LOSS OF LOVE
LOVE	238 - 4	REMEDY FOR THIS IS LOVE
LOVE	238 - 4	LOVE CASTETH OUT FEAR
LOVE	239 - 2	HEART TROUBLE IS LOVE
LOVE	243 - 2	ONLY THOUGHTS OF PEACE, LOVE
LOVE	246 - 1	FILLED WITH LOVE
LOVE	248 - 1	LOVE, HARMONY, AND PEACE REIGN
LOVE	249 - 2	TREATED BY THOUGHTS OF LOVE
LOVE	249 - 2	LOVE IS STRONGER
LOVE	253 - 1	GOD'S LOVE, CARE AND SUBSTANCE

LOVE	255 - 3	ANGER CAN BE TURNED INTO LOVE
LOVE	256 - 5	REMEDY FOR STOMACH TROUBLE IS LOVE
LOVE	265 - 2	I AM POISED IN LOVE
LOVE	284 - 6	LOVE IS THE IMPULSION
LOVE	285 - 4	MANIFEST LOVE
LOVE	297 - 4	LEARNED TO LOVE ALL PEOPLE
LOVE	298 - 1	UNTIL WE LEARN TO LOVE
LOVE	298 - 1	NOT SENDING OUT LOVE VIBRATIONS
LOVE	298 - 1	WE RECEIVE LOVE IN RETURN
LOVE	298 - 2	SEND IT FULL OF LOVE
LOVE	298 - 3	IS TO LOVE EVERYBODY
LOVE	298 - 3	LOVE IS THE GRANDEST HEALING
LOVE	298 - 3	LOVE IS THE SOLE IMPULSE
LOVE	298 - 3	LOVE AS THE GREATEST INCENTIVE
LOVE	298 - 4	WHO HATH LOVED MUCH
LOVE	299 - 1	LOVE CANNOT HEAR THE PRAYER
LOVE	303 - 4	IT IS FILLING YOU WITH LIFE AND LOVE
LOVE	323 - 2	ALL IS LOVE
LOVE	323 - 2	LOVE IS THE IMPELLING FORCE
LOVE	330 - 4	COMMON LAW OF LOVE
LOVE	330 - 4	LOVE IS THE SELF-GIVINGNESS OF SPIRIT
LOVE	368 - 3	TO KNOW GOD IS TO LOVE
LOVE	405 - 4	LOVE ALONE CAN OVERCOME FEAR
LOVE	408 - 2	ITS GOVERNMENT IS ONE OF LOVE
LOVE	408 - 2	LOVE IS THE FULFILLING OF THE PERFECT LAW
LOVE	408 - 2	LOVE AND LAW GO HAND IN HAND
LOVE	412 - 1	WITH LOVE AND BEAUTY
LOVE	415 - 2	WINGED WITH LOVE AND REASON
LOVE	428 - 2	LOVE MASTERS EVERYTHING
LOVE	430 - 1	THE TABLE OF LOVE
LOVE	430 - 5	LOVE WHICH IS GOD
LOVE	430 - 5	DIVINE LOVE ENCOMPASSES EVERYTHING
LOVE	430 - 6	FOR THE PURE LOVE OF GOOD
LOVE	431 - 4	LOVE ALONE CAN BEGET LOVE
LOVE	433 - 5	ON THE SHOULDERS OF LOVE
LOVE	438 - 3	THE ETERNAL HEART IS ONE OF LOVE
LOVE	449 - 5	LOVE MUST BECOME UNIVERSAL
LOVE	459 - 3	LOVE IS A COMPLETE UNITY
LOVE	459 - 5	LOVE THE RIGHT ALONE
LOVE	460 - 3	LOVE ALONE OVERCOMES ALL
LOVE	460 - 6	LOVE OF GOD IS OMNIPRESENT
LOVE	465 - 2	IT GIVES. IT IS LOVE
LOVE	467 - 1	LOVE AND KNOWS NOTHING ABOUT HATE
LOVE	469 - 3	ALL IS LOVE AND YET ALL IS LAW
LOVE	469 - 3	LOVE AND LAW ARE PERFECT
LOVE	478 - 3	LOVE IS THE CENTRAL FLAME
LOVE	478 - 3	LOVE IS SELF-GIVINGNESS
LOVE	478 - 4	LOVE IS AN ESSENCE
LOVE	478 - 5	ONLY LOVE KNOWS LOVE
LOVE	478 - 5	LOVE IS GOD
LOVE	482 - 3	LOVE KNOWS NO BOUNDS
LOVE	491 - 4	LOOK AT LOVE LONG ENOUGH
LOVE	503 - 7	WITH LOVE, ALL THINGS ARE POSSIBLE
LOVE	504 - 2	LOVE IS GREATER THAN ALL ELSE
LOVE	504 - 2	LOVE IS GOD

LOVE	560 - 2	LOVE CASTS OUT FEAR
LOVED	380 - 3	LOVED ARE STILL CONSCIOUS OF US
LOVELY	226 - 1	WHATSOEVER THINGS ARE LOVELY
LOVELY	491 - 4	WE SHALL BECOME LOVELY
LOVERS	056 - 1	LOVERS OF THE RACE
LOVES	225 - 3	THE LOVES AND PASSIONS
LOVING-KINDNESS	039 - 4	LOVING-KINDNESS SHALL FOLLOW ME
LOWELL	280 - 3	LOWELL SAID, "THE GIFT WITHOUT THE GIVER
LOWELL	496 - 5	LOWELL TELLS US THAT
LOWEST	124 - 1	WE CALL THE HIGHEST AND THE LOWEST
LUKEWARM	159 - 4	NOT BE LUKEWARM IN OUR CONVICTION
LUNG	228 - 2	LUNG ITSELF IS UNIVERSAL AND PERFECT
LUNGS	229 - 2	LUNGS ARE CONSTANTLY RENEWED
LUNGS	232 - 4	IF THE LUNGS HOARDED THE AIR
LUST	428 - 1	PASSION AND LUST FOR POWER HAVE STREWN
LUST	460 - 2	SWORD IN HATE, AVARICE, OR LUST
LUSTERLESS	231 - 2	HOPELESSNESS MAKE THE EYES LUSTERLESS
LYING	176 - 2	LYING TO OURSELVES OR OTHERS

M

MACHINE	412 - 2	THE PROJECTING MACHINE FIRMLY
MACHINES	273 - 4	NO FLYING MACHINES UNTIL MAN
MACHINES	328 - 3	MACHINES TO DO THE WORK OF THOUSANDS
MACROCOSM	113 - 1	MICROCOSM WITHIN THE MACROCOSM
MADE	305 - 5	DEMONSTRATIONS SHOULD BE MADE
MADE	384 - 3	WILL BE WHAT WE HAVE MADE IT
MAGNETISM	179 - 3	MAGNETISM HAS NOTHING TO DO WITH MENTAL
MAGNIFIED	164 - 3	PERPETUATED AND MAGNIFIED
MAGNIFY	337 - 1	SHADES TO MAGNIFY ITS GLORY
MAGNITUDE	306 - 5	DWELL UPON THE MAGNITUDE
MAIN	392 - 1	MAIN POINTS WE SHOULD REMEMBER
MAINTAINED	229 - 4	MAINTAINED BY THE ALL-POWERFUL ESSENCE
MAINTAINED	348 - 2	MAINTAINED BETWEEN ALL PEOPLE
MAINTAINS	123 - 1	INDIVIDUAL MAINTAINS HIS IDENTITY
MAINTAINS	318 - 3	EVERY MAN MAINTAINS HIS IDENTITY
MAINTAINS	422 - 2	EACH MAINTAINS A STREAM
MAJESTY	456 - 1	MAJESTY AND MIGHT
MAJESTY	493 - 7	MAJESTY OF OUR BEING
MAJORITY	184 - 3	CONSTITUTES A COMPLETE MAJORITY
MAJORITY	302 - 3	THE MAJORITY OF THE RACE
MAJORITY	417 - 1	LIFE OF THE MAJORITY
MAKE	272 - 1	HAVE TO MAKE THE LAW WORK
MAKE	292 - 2	MAKE CONSCIOUSNESS PERCEIVE
MAKE	501 - 3	MAKE THE GIFT OF HEALTH
MAKES	295 - 1	OUR THOUGHT MAKES OUR WORLD
MAKES	403 - 2	MAKES IT TRUE IN OUR EXPERIENCE
MAKES	416 - 4	IT MAKES ALL THE DIFFERENCE
MAKE UP	398 - 1	YOU MAKE UP ITS MIND FOR IT
MAKE UP	402 - 3	WE MAKE UP ITS MIND
MALICE	240 - 3	HATRED, MALICE OR SELFISHNESS
MALICIOUS	383 - 3	VINDICTIVE OR MALICIOUS POWER
MALPRACTICE	121 - 1	IMMUNE FROM MALPRACTICE

MALPRACTICE	211 - 1	INNOCENT MALPRACTICE
MALPRACTICE	211 - 1	MALPRACTICE BECAUSE IT IS THE WRONG
MAN	032 - 3	MAN LIVES AND MOVES
MAN	036 - 3	A HIGHER STANDARD FOR MAN
MAN	036 - 3	INTERPRET HIMSELF TO MAN
MAN	079 - 4	KNOW GOD EXCEPT BY STUDYING MAN
MAN	106 - 1	MAN IS EVOLVED FROM THE UNIVERSE
MAN	107 - 2	MAN IS MADE OUT OF AND FROM LIFE
MAN	112 - 2	MAN IS A SELF-CONSCIOUS THINKING
MAN	112 - 3	MAN IS ONE WITH EVERYTHING PHYSICAL
MAN	130 - 2	MAN NEVER CREATES, HE DISCOVERS AND USES
MAN	130 - 3	IT CAN AUTOMATICALLY DO FOR MAN
MAN	170 - 5	CONTEMPLATING THE PERFECT MAN
MAN	186 - 1	PERFECT GOD, PERFECT MAN
MAN	196 - 3	MAN IS CONSCIOUS MIND
MAN	201 - 4	PERFECT GOD, PERFECT MAN, PERFECT BEING
MAN	202 - 4	TREAT MAN NOT AS A PHYSICAL BODY
MAN	228 - 3	PERFECT GOD, PERFECT MAN
MAN	247 - 1	MAN IS THE TRUTH
MAN	250 - 2	NO MAN OUTSIDE OF GOD
MAN	254 - 6	MAN IS PURE SPIRIT RIGHT NOW
MAN	267 - 5	MAN MUST BECOME MORE IF HE WISHES
MAN	275 - 3	THE SPIRIT WITHIN MAN IS GOD
MAN	333 - 5	TAUGHT THE DIVINITY OF MAN
MAN	338 - 3	GOD-INTENDED MAN, A PERFECT BEING
MAN	359 - 3	THE MAN GAVE WAY TO GOD
MAN	359 - 4	WAS A MAN LIKE AS WE ARE
MAN	363 - 4	PUT OFF THE OLD MAN
MAN	372 - 2	WHAT OF THE MAN
MAN	377 - 2	LIVING MAN NEVER DIES
MAN	386 - 2	A MAN ROSE FROM THE DEAD
MAN	388 - 3	GOD AS MAN, IN MAN, IS MAN
MAN	390 - 4	THE MIND OF MAN IS SOME PART
MAN	390 - 6	THE MIND OF GOD IN MAN
MAN	391 - 4	FULL-ORBED IN MAN ALONE
MAN	394 - 4	THROUGH THE MEDIUM OF MIND, MAN
MAN	396 - 3	MAN IS ITS DESIRE WILL
MAN	401 - 2	THINK OF IT AS IN MAN OR IN GOD
MAN	407 - 5	SPIRIT IS CONSCIOUS OF MAN
MAN	409 - 1	NO MATERIAL MAN TO SUFFER PAIN
MAN	421 - 4	MAN AS A DIVINE REALITY
MAN	459 - 4	MAN AS AN EXPRESSION OF GOD
MAN	461 - 2	MAN IS A CONSCIOUS SELF-KNOWING
MAN	477 - 1	MAN IS A THREEFOLD PRINCIPLE
MAN	478 - 1	MAN IS HIS IMAGE AND LIKENESS
MAN	478 - 2	MAN THE ONLY SELF-CONSCIOUS BEING
MAN	482 - 3	GOD AS MAN, IN MAN, IS MAN
MANDATE	442 - 1	BY ANY DIVINE MANDATE
MANDATORY	365 - 3	SORT OF A MANDATORY POWER
MANIFEST	052 - 2	MANIFEST FOR US
MANIFEST	063 - 1	MANIFEST LIFE OF OURS
MANIFEST	070 - 2	MADE MANIFEST ON SOME PLANE
MANIFEST	100 - 2	SPIRIT MUST BE MANIFEST
MANIFEST	132 - 4	MANIFEST UNIVERSE IS A RESULT
MANIFEST	221 - 5	MANIFEST IN A PEACEFUL MANNER

MANIFEST	240 - 3	MANIFEST GOD OR PERFECTION
MANIFEST	311 - 2	MADE MANIFEST THROUGH VIBRATION
MANIFEST	337 - 3	COMPLETELY MANIFEST THE WHOLE IDEA
MANIFESTATION	032 - 3	SOME PART OR MANIFESTATION
MANIFESTATION	057 - 4	A CONCRETE MANIFESTATION
MANIFESTATION	072 - 2	HAVE SEEN IS THE MANIFESTATION
MANIFESTATION	080 - 1	BODY MEANS THE MANIFESTATION
MANIFESTATION	083 - 5	MANIFESTATION HENCE SOUL AND BODY
MANIFESTATION	098 - 1	THE ENTIRE MANIFESTATION OF SPIRIT
MANIFESTATION	100 - 2	THERE MUST BE A MANIFESTATION
MANIFESTATION	102 - 1	OF THOUGHT INTO MANIFESTATION
MANIFESTATION	132 - 5	LAW AND MANIFESTATION ARE AUTOMATIC
MANIFESTATION	157 - 1	BRINGS INTO MANIFESTATION THE THING
MANIFESTATION	163 - 3	INTO ACTUAL MANIFESTATION THE HEALTH
MANIFESTATION	165 - 1	MANIFESTATION WHICH WE CALL FORM
MANIFESTATION	166 - 2	OBSTRUCTION IN MANIFESTATION
MANIFESTATION	172 - 4	MANIFESTATION OF PURE SPIRIT
MANIFESTATION	174 - 2	DEMONSTRATION IS A MANIFESTATION
MANIFESTATION	208 - 5	CONSCIOUS OF MANIFESTATION
MANIFESTATION	264 - 4	MANIFESTATION OF LOVE WITHIN ME
MANIFESTATION	300 - 1	THE RESULT OR MANIFESTATION
MANIFESTATION	339 - 2	MANIFESTATION IN EVERY FORM
MANIFESTATION	373 - 4	BODY IS A CONCRETE MANIFESTATION
MANIFESTATION	373 - 4	MANIFESTATION OF SPIRIT IS NECESSARY
MANIFESTATION	388 - 1	A MANIFESTATION IN THE FINITE
MANIFESTATION	420 - 4	OF SPIRIT INTO MANIFESTATION
MANIFESTATION	420 - 4	A STATE OF PERFECT MANIFESTATION
MANIFESTATION	433 - 4	MANIFESTATION OF OUR MOTIVES
MANIFESTATION	485 - 3	MANIFESTATION OF OUR OWN INNER DIVINITY
MANIFESTATIONS	064 - 1	MANIFESTATIONS COME INTO BEING
MANIFESTATIONS	085 - 2	SEE ONLY THEIR MANIFESTATIONS
MANIFESTATIONS	100 - 3	LIKE OTHER PHYSICAL MANIFESTATIONS
MANIFESTATIONS	183 - 3	WITH IMPERFECT MANIFESTATIONS
MANIFESTATIONS	189 - 2	ALL MANIFESTATIONS ARE EFFECTS
MANIFESTATIONS	377 - 3	PHYSICAL MANIFESTATIONS EXPERIENCED
MANIFESTED	296 - 2	MANIFESTED THROUGH EVERY LIVING SOUL
MANIFESTING	492 - 7	MANIFESTING HIMSELF IN TIME
MANIFESTS	042 - 5	GOD MANIFESTS THROUGH EVERYTHING
MANIFESTS	245 - 2	MANIFESTS AS PERFECT HARMONY
MANIFESTS	361 - 5	IT MANIFESTS THE CHRIST NATURE
MANIFESTS	475 - 6	MANIFESTS THROUGH US AS WE BELIEVE
MANIFESTS	480 - 2	WHEN ONE MANIFESTS GOODNESS
MANIFESTS	499 - 7	PURE RELIGION MANIFESTS ITSELF
MANIPULATES	207 - 2	HE NEVER MANIPULATES
MAN IS	373 - 1	SIMPLE STATEMENT THAT MAN IS
MANKIND	462 - 4	MANKIND IS TO RETURN TO THE FATHER'S
MANKIND'S	163 - 3	MANKIND'S NORMAL AND DIVINE HERITAGE
MAN-MADE	211 - 3	EVERY MAN-MADE LAW AND CASTS IT OUT
MAN-MADE	336 - 4	MAN-MADE THROUGH IGNORANCE
MANNA	428 - 4	MANNA FROM HEAVEN
MANNA	428 - 5	MANNA WHICH HAS SUSTAINED
MANNER	188 - 3	IN THIS MANNER THINK RIGHT BACK
MANNER	284 - 1	IN SUCH A MANNER THAT REALITY
MANNER	495 - 6	MANNER IN WHICH THE EXPRESSION IS USED
MAN'S	164 - 1	MAN'S LIFE IS ROOTED IN THE

MAN'S	322 - 1	MAN'S WORLD OF AFFAIRS
MANSIONS	098 - 2	HOUSE ARE MANY MANSIONS
MANSIONS	098 - 2	WE DO NOT SEE ALL THESE MANSIONS
MANSIONS	479 - 4	FATHER'S HOUSE ARE MANY MANSIONS
MANY	092 - 1	AS MANY FOR US AS WE ASK
MANY	407 - 1	TREAT FOR AS MANY CONDITIONS
MARBLES	314 - 4	IT BE MILLIONS OR MARBLES
MARCHED	158 - 3	MARCHED BOLDLY ON WITH IT
MARK	039 - 6	MARK IN MIND AND SPIRIT
MARK	469 - 1	MISSED THE MARK
MARKETED	305 - 2	MARKETED UNDER A UNIVERSAL PLAN
MARRED	387 - 2	MARRED BY INCOMPLETENESS
MARRIED	381 - 3	HAD BEEN MARRIED FIVE TIMES
MARVELED	437 - 3	JESUS MARVELED AT THIS FAITH
MARVELOUS	122 - 4	MARVELOUS AS THIS CONCEPT
MARVELOUS	140 - 3	MARVELOUS THOUGHT TO BEAR IN MIND
MARVELOUS	369 - 2	TELL THEE OF MARVELOUS THINGS
MARVELOUS	384 - 2	MARVELOUS MIND AND SUBTLE BODY
MARVELOUS	419 - 4	US OF THE MARVELOUS RELATIONSHIP
MARVELOUS	443 - 1	OF THIS MARVELOUS MAN
MASCULINE	082 - 1	MASCULINE AND THE FEMININE PRINCIPLES
MASTER	344 - 2	DECLARATION OF THE GREAT MASTER
MASTER	436 - 3	ONE MASTER WHICH IS TRUTH
MATERIA	199 - 3	FIELD OF MATERIA MEDICA
MATERIA	216 - 4	MATERIA MEDICA IS USING THE TERM INCURABLE
MATERIAL	051 - 2	OVER APPARENT MATERIAL RESISTANCE
MATERIAL	056 - 3	OVER APPARENT MATERIAL RESISTANCE
MATERIAL	159 - 4	APPARENT MATERIAL RESISTANCE
MATERIAL	236 - 6	CAUSE IS NEVER MATERIAL OR PHYSICAL
MATERIAL	286 - 1	MATERIAL PRESENTATION OF A SPIRITUAL
MATERIAL	317 - 1	REMAKING THE MATERIAL OR PHYSICAL MAN
MATERIAL	362 - 1	MATERIAL SURFACE OF CREATION
MATERIAL	409 - 1	THERE IS NO MATERIAL BODY
MATERIAL	413 - 5	NO MATERIAL CAUSE OR EFFECT
MATERIAL	452 - 6	MATERIAL STANDS THE SPIRITUAL
MATERIAL	452 - 6	THERE COULD BE NO MATERIAL
MATERIAL	463 - 4	LEAGUE HIMSELF WITH MATERIAL FORCES
MATERIALIST	442 - 3	HE IS A MATERIALIST AND A GLUTTON
MATERIALIST	456 - 5	LET NOT THE MATERIALIST DENY US
MATERIALISTIC	473 - 2	ISOLATED AND MATERIALISTIC BASIS
MATERIALIZE	355 - 1	IF IT IS EVER GOING TO MATERIALIZE
MATERIAL MAN	317 - 1	NOT DEAL WITH THE MATERIAL MAN
MATERIAL SENSE	502 - 7	MATERIAL SENSE CANNOT RECOGNIZE
MATERIAL WORLD	448 - 1	MATERIAL WORLD WHICH APPEARS IMPERFECT
MATHEMATICAL	096 - 4	MATHEMATICAL CERTAINTY
MATHEMATICALLY	078 - 3	DOES SO MATHEMATICALLY INEXORABLY
MATHEMATICALLY	085 - 4	THINKING MATHEMATICALLY
MATHEMATICALLY	086 - 2	THINKER THINKING MATHEMATICALLY
MATHEMATICALLY	124 - 3	IT ACTS ACCURATELY AND MATHEMATICALLY
MATHEMATICIAN	053 - 2	PUNISH THE MATHEMATICIAN
MATHEMATICIAN	072 - 2	MATHEMATICIAN SOLVES A PROBLEM
MATHEMATICIANS	408 - 3	BY UNNUMERABLE MATHEMATICIANS
MATHEMATICS	072 - 2	THE PRINCIPLE OF MATHEMATICS
MATTER	060 - 3	VEIL BETWEEN SPIRIT AND MATTER
MATTER	081 - 1	ENERGY AS DISTINCT FROM MATTER

MATTER	091 – 2	IMMATERIAL AS WE THINK OF MATTER
MATTER	091 – 2	THE MATTER OF SPIRIT
MATTER	091 – 2	MATTER IN THE PHYSICAL WORLD
MATTER	091 – 3	FINAL ANALYSIS OF MATTER
MATTER	091 – 3	ALREADY DONE AWAY WITH MATTER
MATTER	091 – 3	MATTER COMES FROM SOMEWHERE
MATTER	094 – 2	THE CEMENT OF MATTER
MATTER	099 – 3	MATTER AND PHYSICAL FORM
MATTER	103 – 2	SPIRIT FROM MATTER
MATTER	103 – 3	MIND AND MATTER ARE THE
MATTER	104 – 3	MORE SOLID THAN MATTER
MATTER	116 – 3	MATTER IS NOT A SOLID STATIONARY THING
MATTER	116 – 4	LAST ANALYSIS OF MATTER
MATTER	117 – 3	LATENT MASS OF MATTER
MATTER	286 – 1	UNIVERSE IS EITHER ALL MATTER
MATTER	286 – 1	FORMERLY CALLED MATTER IS SPIRIT
MATTER	335 – 1	SEEN THROUGH THE VEIL OF MATTER
MATTER	338 – 1	IT IS ALL A MATTER OF BELIEF
MATTER	373 – 5	BUT WHAT IS MATTER
MATTER	373 – 5	MATTER IS AN AGGREGATION OF SMALL PARTICLES
MATTER	375 – 3	EACH HAVING ITS OWN MATTER
MATTER	473 – 1	VIEWED ONLY AS MATTER IS DEATH
MAYA	093 – 2	CALLED BY THE ANCIENTS MAYA
ME	077 – 1	GOD EXISTS IN ME
MEADOW	451 – 3	THERE IS NO MEADOW
MEAGERLY	404 – 3	THROUGH THE ONE WHO LIVES MEAGERLY
MEAN	397 – 4	WE MEAN BY THE LAW OF MIND
MEANING	034 – 1	MEANING OF THE WORD CHRIST
MEANING	132 – 3	ALL HAVE THE SAME MEANING
MEANING	385 – 2	LIFE WOULD HAVE NO MEANING
MEANING	427 – 1	FULL MEANING OF HIS SAYINGS
MEANING	465 – 2	MEANING OF COMING TO ONE'S SELF
MEANING	474 – 1	MEANING OF GOD SAYING HE SHALL
MEANS	080 – 1	LAW MEANS THE WAY
MEANS	157 – 4	IT IS A MEANS TO AN END
MEANS	305 – 1	MEANS FOR MY GREATER EXPRESSION
MEANS	466 – 3	THIS MEANS THAT GOD TURNS TO US
MEANS AND METHODS	161 – 4	MEANS AND METHODS WILL BE FOUND
MEANT	417 – 2	MEANT BY ENTERING THE ABSOLUTE
MEASLES	316 – 3	MEASLES, POVERTY OR UNHAPPINESS
MEASURE	101 – 2	THE MEASURE OF EXPERIENCE
MEASURE	156 – 4	NOT IN SOME MEASURE UNDERSTAND
MEASURE	161 – 4	THE MEASURE OF OUR EXPERIENCE
MEASURE	433 – 2	WITH WHAT MEASURE YE METE
MEASURED	067 – 1	EXPERIENCE IS MEASURED BY TIME
MEASURED	280 – 2	BE MEASURED OUT TO US
MEASURES	436 – 5	MEASURES CAUSES BY EFFECTS
MEASURES	455 – 2	MEASURES EVERYTHING EXACTLY AS IT IS
MEASURING	280 – 2	ACCORDING TO OUR OWN MEASURING
MEASURING	450 – 4	MEASURING BACK TO THEM THE LOGICAL
MEAT	476 – 4	MEAT WHICH PERISHETH
MECHANICAL	038 – 2	THE MECHANICAL SIDE OF NATURE
MECHANICAL	044 – 3	MECHANICAL TO THE VOLITIONAL
MECHANICAL	064 – 4	THE LAW IS MECHANICAL
MECHANICAL	065 – 3	GOD MADE THE MECHANICAL

MECHANICAL	071 - 2	MAKE A MECHANICAL INDIVIDUAL
MECHANICAL	086 - 4	MECHANICAL FIELD AND MUST OPERATE
MECHANICAL	143 - 2	WORK WITH A MECHANICAL PROCESS
MECHANICAL	340 - 1	THIS NATURE IS MECHANICAL
MECHANICAL	415 - 4	LIVING IN A MECHANICAL WORLD
MECHANICAL	415 - 5	UNIVERSE IS ALWAYS MECHANICAL
MECHANICAL	416 - 1	TO MECHANICAL LAWS
MECHANICALLY	143 - 2	CONSCIOUSNESS MAY BE MECHANICALLY
MECHANICALLY	307 - 1	MECHANICALLY IF NECESSARY
MECHANICS	416 - 1	MECHANICS OF THE UNIVERSE
MECHANISTIC	143 - 4	AS A MECHANISTIC INDIVIDUALITY
MEDIATOR	272 - 4	THERE IS NO MEDIATOR
MEDICA	199 - 3	MEDICA TO DO ITS OWN WORK
MEDICAL	236 - 5	MEDICAL PRACTICE TAKES INTO
MEDICAL	242 - 4	MANY MEDICAL MEN BELIEVE
MEDICAL	316 - 1	NOT OPPOSED TO THE MEDICAL PRACTITIONER
MEDICINE	216 - 4	IN THE FIELD OF MEDICINE
MEDICINE	320 - 1	THE PATIENT IS TAKING MEDICINE
MEDICINE	320 - 1	NO LONGER NEEDS MEDICINE
MEDITATE	057 - 4	TIME TO MEDITATE
MEDITATE	185 - 2	DAILY MEDITATE ON THE PERFECT LIFE
MEDITATE	246 - 4	MEDITATE UPON THOSE
MEDITATE	306 - 4	WE MEDITATE DAILY
MEDITATE	306 - 4	MEDITATE UPON THIS INDWELLING GOD
MEDITATE	458 - 7	MEDITATE UPON ITS ACTUAL BEING
MEDITATE	488 - 5	SCIENTIFIC TO MEDITATE ON PLENTY
MEDITATE	489 - 1	MEDITATE ON THE THINGS YOU
MEDITATE	489 - 2	MEDITATE UPON THIS LIFE
MEDITATED	068 - 2	MEDITATED LONG AND EARNESTLY
MEDITATED	365 - 3	HAVE MEDITATED UPON THE VASTNESS
MEDITATING	220 - 4	MEDITATING UPON THE SPIRITUAL SIGNIFICANCE
MEDITATING	358 - 3	MEDITATING UPON THE IMMENSITY
MEDITATION	028 - 2	ALONG A DEFINITE LINE OF MEDITATION
MEDITATION	047 - 3	PASSIVE MEDITATION WILL NEVER
MEDITATION	168 - 1	FROM SUCH DAILY MEDITATION HE SHOULD
MEDITATION	229 - 2	GOOD MEDITATION FOR PRACTITIONER
MEDITATION	292 - 5	FOLLOWING MEDITATION MIGHT BE USED
MEDITATION	299 - 1	OUR MEDITATION FOR FRIENDSHIP
MEDITATION	304 - 5	A GOOD MEDITATION FOR OPPORTUNITY
MEDITATION	346 - 2	MEDITATION FOR PRACTICAL WORK
MEDITATION	455 - 6	MEDITATION BEFORE HIS PROBLEM
MEDITATION	488 - 4	NOT BY MEDITATION UPON LIMITATION
MEDITATION	489 - 4	MEDITATION IS CENTERED ON WHAT
MEDITATIONS	291 - 2	REFLECTIONS OF OUR MEDITATIONS
MEDITATIONS	358 - 4	DAILY PRACTICE IN OUR MEDITATIONS
MEDIUM	030 - 1	THOUGHTS GO INTO A MEDIUM THAT IS INFINITE
MEDIUM	076 - 5	EXISTS IN THE SAME MEDIUM
MEDIUM	077 - 2	MEDIUM WHICH IS UNIVERSAL
MEDIUM	077 - 4	OPERATIVE THROUGH A UNIVERSAL MEDIUM
MEDIUM	078 - 1	MEDIUM IS AUTOMATIC
MEDIUM	080 - 2	CREATIVE MEDIUM OF THE SOIL
MEDIUM	083 - 2	RECEPTIVE MEDIUM INTO WHICH
MEDIUM	083 - 2	MEDIUM OF THE THOUGHT
MEDIUM	083 - 5	MEDIUM THROUGH WHICH SPIRIT
MEDIUM	084 - 1	MEDIUM THROUGH WHICH THE SPIRIT

MEDIUM	088 - 1	MEDIUM THROUGH WHICH EXPERIENCES COME
MEDIUM	088 - 3	MEDIUM OF SOUL
MEDIUM	092 - 2	TO THE UNIVERSAL SOUL OR CREATIVE MEDIUM
MEDIUM	092 - 3	THE CREATIVE MEDIUM OF SPIRIT
MEDIUM	101 - 5	THE CREATIVE MEDIUM
MEDIUM	120 - 1	MEDIUM IN WHICH WE ALL LIVE
MEDIUM	165 - 1	LIMITLESS MEDIUM OF SUBJECTIVITY
MEDIUM	165 - 1	WE CALL THE MEDIUM
MEDIUM	200 - 1	THE MEDIUM OF A LAW
MEDIUM	217 - 1	NEITHER CAUSE MEDIUM NOR EFFECT
MEDIUM	264 - 3	CAUSE MEDIUM AND EFFECT
MEDIUM	272 - 4	THERE IS NO MEDIUM
MEDIUM	351 - 2	THE MEDIUM READS THE BOOK OF REMEMBRANCE
MEDIUM	390 - 3	MEDIUM FOR ALL THOUGHT ACTION
MEDIUM	390 - 3	MEDIUM BY WHICH MAN MAY
MEDIUM	421 - 5	TAKES PLACE THROUGH THE MEDIUM
MEDIUM	445 - 4	NO MEDIUM BETWEEN GOD AND MAN
MEDIUM	475 - 4	SOLE MEDIUM BETWEEN THE ABSOLUTE
MEEK	427 - 5	MEEK SHALL INHERIT THE EARTH
MEETING	409 - 2	HE IS MEETING AND NEUTRALIZING
MELODY	258 - 1	ITS MELODY, RHYTHM AND BEAUTY
MEMBERS	318 - 4	ALL MEMBERS OF ONE ANOTHER
MEMBERS	357 - 3	MEMBERS OF THAT ONE BODY
MEMORIES	122 - 2	MEMORIES WE HAVE
MEMORY	073 - 2	RETURNED TO HIM AS MEMORY
MEMORY	073 - 3	MEMORY WAS AN ACTIVE THING
MEMORY	073 - 3	MEMORY MUST BE THE STOREHOUSE
MEMORY	074 - 1	SINCE MEMORY IS ACTIVE
MEMORY	074 - 1	MEMORY IS THE RESULT OF CONSCIOUS
MEMORY	114 - 3	SOUL CONTAINS THE MEMORY
MEMORY	255 - 5	FROM THE MEMORY
MEMORY	347 - 4	IS THE SEAT OF MEMORY
MEMORY	349 - 2	MIND IS THE STOREHOUSE OF MEMORY
MEMORY	371 - 2	IDENTITY OF COURSE POSTULATES MEMORY
MEMORY	372 - 1	YOU WILL NEVER FIND MEMORY
MEN	042 - 5	IS INCARNATED IN ALL MEN
MEN	076 - 2	ONE MIND COMMON TO ALL MEN
MEN	286 - 1	FOUR MEN ARE ALL WITHOUT POSITIONS
MENTAL	029 - 2	WITHIN US IS A MENTAL LAW
MENTAL	039 - 1	NO MENTAL COERCION IN THIS
MENTAL	077 - 3	UNCONSCIOUS MENTAL CONVERSATION
MENTAL	126 - 3	THIS LAW IS MENTAL
MENTAL	144 - 3	MENTAL IN THEIR NATURE
MENTAL	168 - 1	HE IS A MENTAL AND SPIRITUAL PRACTITIONER
MENTAL	190 - 3	IS SPIRITUAL AND MENTAL
MENTAL	217 - 2	RECOGNITION IS A MENTAL ACT
MENTAL	220 - 6	THE MENTAL AND SPIRITUAL WORLD
MENTAL	253 - 3	MENTAL AGENCIES WHICH CONTRIBUTE
MENTAL	257 - 1	A DISTURBED MENTAL CONDITION
MENTAL	308 - 2	TREAT BY A MENTAL PROCESS
MENTAL	320 - 2	WORK ON THE MENTAL PLANE
MENTAL	379 - 1	SOME POWER WHICH IS MENTAL
MENTAL	379 - 4	COMMUNICATION MUST BE MENTAL
MENTAL	435 - 4	PRAYER IS A MENTAL
MENTAL	446 - 5	MENTAL ATTENTION TO AN IDEAL

MENTAL	458 - 5	TAKE THE MENTAL IMAGES
MENTAL	465 - 4	ONE OF OUR WORST MENTAL DISEASES
MENTAL	470 - 1	MENTAL CONDITION TO RECEIVE
MENTAL ACT	458 - 4	PRAYER WHICH IS A MENTAL ACT
MENTAL ACTION	382 - 3	EXPLAIN ALL MENTAL ACTION
MENTAL AFFAIRS	395 - 1	IN OUR MENTAL AFFAIRS
MENTAL ATMOSPHERE	350 - 3	EACH PERSON HAS A MENTAL ATMOSPHERE
MENTAL ATTENTION	308 - 2	MENTAL ATTENTION WE SHOULD HAVE
MENTAL AVENUE	269 - 2	A MENTAL AVENUE MUST BE PROVIDED
MENTAL BURDENS	479 - 2	MENTAL BURDENS OFTEN BECOME UNBEARABLE
MENTAL CAUSE	226 - 3	MENTAL CAUSE WILL BE DISCOVERED
MENTAL CONFLICTS	252 - 2	MENTAL CONFLICTS ALSO CAUSE CONFUSION
MENTAL CONTROL	266 - 1	MENTAL CONTROL OF CONDITIONS
MENTAL EQUIVALENT	118 - 2	PROVIDE A MENTAL EQUIVALENT OF OUR DESIRE
MENTAL EQUIVALENT	161 - 1	MENTAL EQUIVALENT OF DIVINE AUTHORITY
MENTAL EQUIVALENT	281 - 4	WE MUST HAVE A MENTAL EQUIVALENT
MENTAL EQUIVALENT	306 - 2	A GREATER MENTAL EQUIVALENT
MENTAL EQUIVALENTS	269 - 2	MENTAL EQUIVALENTS MUST NEVER BE
MENTAL HEALER	192 - 2	MENTAL HEALER WILL DO ALL OF HIS WORK
MENTAL HEALING	142 - 3	MENTAL HEALING IS INSISTENTLY ON GOD
MENTAL HEALING	409 - 4	VERY ESSENCE OF MENTAL HEALING
MENTAL HEALING	413 - 3	IS TO PRACTICE MENTAL HEALING
MENTAL HEALING	486 - 5	MENTAL HEALING IS A CONSCIOUS
MENTAL HEALING	487 - 1	MENTAL HEALING IS SUBJECT
MENTAL INFLUENCE	348 - 2	MEANING OF MENTAL INFLUENCE
MENTALITIES	040 - 1	OUR OWN RECEPTIVE MENTALITIES
MENTALITIES	044 - 4	MIND INTO OUR MENTALITIES
MENTALITIES	190 - 3	WE SEEK TO HEAL MEN'S MENTALITIES
MENTALITIES	408 - 3	LIMITLESS NUMBERS OF MENTALITIES
MENTALITIES	501 - 6	BALANCE OUR MENTALITIES
MENTALITY	170 - 5	MENTALITY OF THE PRACTITIONER
MENTALITY	178 - 5	MENTALITY OF THE PRACTITIONER
MENTALITY	197 - 1	MENTALITY AWAY FROM A BODY
MENTALITY	224 - 2	REACHES THE MENTALITY OF HIS PATIENT
MENTALITY	274 - 3	IT CLARIFIES THE MENTALITY
MENTALITY	328 - 5	ANOTHER'S SUBJECTIVE MENTALITY
MENTALITY	422 - 1	THE POINT OF ANYONE'S MENTALITY
MENTALITY	450 - 3	MENTALITY OF A SUCCESSFUL MAN
MENTALITY	463 - 2	RAN THROUGH HIS PERSONAL MENTALITY
MENTAL LAW	030 - 1	THERE IS ONE MENTAL LAW IN THE UNIVERSE
MENTAL LAW	092 - 3	MENTAL LAW OF THE UNIVERSE
MENTALLY	222 - 1	TO MENTALLY SEE THE SPIRITUAL PERFECTION
MENTALLY	223 - 2	MENTALLY SEE HIM FREE
MENTALLY	295 - 3	AS THEY MENTALLY HELD THEMSELVES
MENTALLY	418 - 3	MENTALLY UNCOVER AND REVEAL
MENTALLY	421 - 5	TO MENTALLY RECEIVE A MESSAGE
MENTALLY ACCEPT	398 - 3	MENTALLY ACCEPT A HOME
MENTAL MAKE-UP	294 - 2	BECOME A PART OF OUR MENTAL MAKE-UP
MENTAL MEDIUM	077 - 5	THINK OF THE MENTAL MEDIUM
MENTAL MEDIUM	130 - 6	HE DISCOVERS A MENTAL MEDIUM
MENTAL PICTURE	271 - 5	A MENTAL PICTURE OF HIS IDEAL
MENTAL PICTURE	300 - 4	MAKE A MENTAL PICTURE
MENTAL PRACTICE	051 - 2	MENTAL PRACTICE IN THE SAME LIGHT
MENTAL PRACTICE	344 - 2	MENTAL PRACTICE IS TO LISTEN
MENTAL PRACTITIONER	316 - 1	THE MENTAL PRACTITIONER SHOULD REMAIN

MENTAL PROCESS	327 - 2	WITHOUT MENTAL PROCESS
MENTAL QUALITIES	322 - 2	REPULSION ARE MENTAL QUALITIES
MENTAL QUALITIES	398 - 2	REALIZATION ARE MENTAL QUALITIES
MENTAL SCIENCE	161 - 5	MENTAL SCIENCE DOES NOT DENY
MENTAL SCIENCE	192 - 5	ALL TRUE MENTAL SCIENCE IS BUILT
MENTAL SCIENCE	308 - 2	SPIRITUAL TREATMENT TO A MENTAL SCIENCE
MENTAL SCIENCE	400 - 1	GREAT SECRETS OF MENTAL SCIENCE
MENTAL STATE	045 - 3	MENTAL STATE A DIFFERENT MANIFESTATION
MENTAL STATES	139 - 4	RESPONDS TO OUR MENTAL STATES
MENTAL TREATMENT	159 - 2	MENTAL TREATMENT IS PERFECT
MENTAL TREATMENT	163 - 1	MENTAL TREATMENT IS PROPELLED BY
MENTAL TREATMENT	178 - 6	MENTAL TREATMENT BEGINS AND ENDS WITHIN
MENTAL TREATMENT	413 - 4	MENTAL TREATMENT WE SHOULD FEEL
MENTAL TREATMENT	476 - 1	MENTAL TREATMENT IS FOR THE PURPOSE
MENTAL WORK	045 - 4	MENTAL WORK IS DEFINITE
MENTAL WORK	094 - 1	MENTAL WORK IS DONE IN OUR BEING
MENTAL WORK	168 - 5	MENTAL WORK IS BASED ON PERFECT GOD
MENTAL WORK	290 - 2	MENTAL WORK WE MUST REALIZE
MENTAL WORK	435 - 3	SPIRITUAL AND MENTAL WORK
MENTAL WORLD	320 - 4	NATURAL LAW IN THE MENTAL WORLD
MENTAL WORLD	333 - 2	OF THE UNIVERSE IN THE MENTAL WORLD
MERCY	122 - 2	ACTS OF KINDNESS AND MERCY
MERCY	429 - 1	FOR THEY SHALL OBTAIN MERCY
MERELY	108 - 3	MERELY TO THINK AND DREAM
MERELY	372 - 2	MERELY THE RESULT OF ONE'S LIFE
MERGED	489 - 7	SOUL IS MERGED WITH GOD
MERGES	087 - 2	MERGES WITH THE UNIVERSAL SPIRIT
MERGES	115 - 2	SOUL LIFE OF ALL PEOPLE MERGES
MERGES	358 - 3	WHERE THE INDIVIDUAL MERGES
MERIT	442 - 1	MERIT IS AN OBJECTIVE OUTCOME
MERITS	434 - 2	MERITS REWARD WILL FIND THAT IT
MERRY	466 - 6	AND THEY BEGAN TO BE MERRY
MESSAGE	119 - 3	MESSAGE IN ALL OF THIS IS
MESSAGE	379 - 4	CAUSE ITS MESSAGE TO COME UP
MESSAGE	421 - 5	VIBRATION OF THAT MESSAGE
MESSAGE	440 - 6	NOT ALWAYS RECEIVE THEIR MESSAGE
MET	384 - 4	MET BY LOVING FRIENDS
METABOLISM	247 - 3	METABOLISM REPRESENTS THE INTELLIGENCE
METAPHYSICAL	027 - 5	MEANING OF TRUE METAPHYSICAL TEACHING
METAPHYSICAL	027 - 5	THE METAPHYSICAL VIEWPOINT
METAPHYSICAL	051 - 2	IT IS IN THE METAPHYSICAL FIELD
METAPHYSICAL	085 - 3	METAPHYSICAL WORK RESTS UPON THE THEORY
METAPHYSICAL	199 - 2	REAL METAPHYSICAL HEALING
METAPHYSICAL	199 - 2	METAPHYSICAL HEALING WE ARE CONSCIOUS
METAPHYSICAL	209 - 1	OF THE METAPHYSICAL PRACTITIONER
METAPHYSICAL	330 - 4	SECRET OF SUCCESSFUL METAPHYSICAL WORK
METAPHYSICAL	380 - 2	PSYCHOLOGICAL AND METAPHYSICAL LAWS
METAPHYSICAL	455 - 3	METAPHYSICAL ACT OF PRAYER
METAPHYSICAL	458 - 2	THE VERY DEPTHS OF THE METAPHYSICAL
METAPHYSICALLY	087 - 3	METAPHYSICALLY WE RECOGNIZE
METAPHYSICIAN	316 - 2	BETWEEN PHYSICIAN AND METAPHYSICIAN
METAPHYSICIAN	316 - 3	METAPHYSICIAN TURNS ENTIRELY AWAY
METAPHYSICS	026 - 5	IN DEALING WITH METAPHYSICS
METAPHYSICS	027 - 1	ANY MORE IN METAPHYSICS
METAPHYSICS	027 - 2	WE THINK OF METAPHYSICS

METAPHYSICS	051 - 2	THE PRINCIPLE OF METAPHYSICS
METAPHYSICS	085 - 2	PHILOSOPHY OF APPLIED METAPHYSICS
METAPHYSICS	086 - 2	METAPHYSICS BEGINS WHERE PHYSICS
METAPHYSICS	100 - 1	PSYCHOLOGY AND METAPHYSICS ARE BUT TWO
METAPHYSICS	125 - 1	PSYCHOLOGY AND METAPHYSICS SEPARATE
METAPHYSICS	125 - 3	STUDENT OF METAPHYSICS
METAPHYSICS	174 - 2	IN THE LANGUAGE OF METAPHYSICS
METAPHYSICS	319 - 1	THERE IS A LAW OF METAPHYSICS
METAPHYSICS	332 - 5	METAPHYSICS UNIVERSALIZES IT
METHOD	119 - 3	MOST DIRECT METHOD IMAGINABLE
METHOD	172 - 2	IS NOT THE BEST METHOD
METHOD	225 - 1	ONLY METHOD WE KNOW
METHOD	274 - 3	THIS IS A GOOD METHOD
METHOD	277 - 2	JESUS' METHOD OF APPROACH
METHOD	331 - 5	THE METHOD IS PERFECT
METHOD	331 - 5	THIS METHOD CAN BE USED IN ALL
METHOD	334 - 3	METHOD IS BY FAR THE MOST EFFECTIVE
METHOD	346 - 2	BY A METHOD A PROCEDURE
METHOD	367 - 4	HIS METHOD WAS DIRECT
METHODIST	275 - 4	ELECTRICIAN MAY BE A METHODIST
METHODS	058 - 2	WHAT METHODS TO USE
METHODS	101 - 5	SPIRIT NEVER THINKS OF METHODS
METHODS	170 - 3	SEVERAL METHODS OF TREATMENT ARE USED
METHODS	192 - 2	LEGITIMATE TO USE ALL METHODS
METHODS	201 - 3	METHODS OF APPROACH
METHODS	417 - 4	MENTAL AND SPIRITUAL METHODS
MICROCOSM	113 - 1	MICROCOSM WITHIN THE MACROCOSM
MICROCOSM	314 - 1	MICROCOSM THE LITTLE WORLD
MIDDLE-AGE	226 - 3	AT WHAT WE TERM MIDDLE-AGE
MIDDLE AGES	357 - 2	GREAT MYSTICS OF THE MIDDLE AGES
MIDST	413 - 3	IN THE MIDST OF THEE
MIDST	428 - 2	MIDST OF THIS DRAMA OF HUMAN EXISTENCE
MIDST	469 - 2	LIVE IN THE MIDST OF ETERNAL GOOD
MIGHT	277 - 2	MIGHT BE ABLE TO GET UP
MIGHT	364 - 1	COMES WITH POWER AND MIGHT
MIGHT	406 - 1	NOR THROUGH OBJECTIVE MIGHT
MIGHTY	253 - 4	MIGHTY TO HEAL
MILLION	282 - 2	MILLION DOLLARS TOMORROW
MILLIONS	105 - 3	MANY MILLIONS OF FORMS
MILLIONS	152 - 5	COUNTLESS MILLIONS OF PEOPLE TO HIGHER
MILLIONS	178 - 2	STIMULATED COUNTLESS MILLIONS
MILLIONS	314 - 4	WHETHER IT BE MILLIONS OF MARBLES
MILLIONS	407 - 2	COUNTLESS MILLIONS OF YEARS
MILLS OF GOD	429 - 2	MILLS OF GOD WILL GRIND THE CHAFF
MIND	026 - 3	SCIENCE OF MIND IS A STUDY OF MIND
MIND	028 - 2	WITHIN THE MIND OF THE ONE PRAYING
MIND	028 - 3	WHAT IS THE MIND
MIND	028 - 3	BY MIND WE MEAN CONSCIOUSNESS
MIND	028 - 3	WE CANNOT ISOLATE MIND
MIND	029 - 3	FALLING INTO HIS SUBJECTIVE MIND
MIND	030 - 2	DEPTHS OF THE INDIVIDUAL MIND
MIND	033 - 2	IN THE MIND OF INTELLIGENCE
MIND	034 - 3	THE MIND THAT GOVERNS EVERYTHING
MIND	035 - 3	UNIVERSAL MIND, SPIRIT, INTELLIGENCE
MIND	039 - 4	MIND THE FUNDAMENTAL PROPOSITION

MIND	040 - 1	MIND THAT KNOWS ALL THINGS
MIND	040 - 2	MIND OF GOD
MIND	040 - 3	SURROUNDED BY A MIND
MIND	040 - 3	MIND IS WILLING TO REVEAL
MIND	043 - 4	IT IS THE MIND WHICH DISCOVERS
MIND	043 - 4	IS NOT THIS MIND THE SPIRIT IN US
MIND	044 - 2	THROUGH SOMEONE'S MIND
MIND	076 - 1	THERE IS ONE MIND COMMON TO ALL
MIND	076 - 2	IN ONE AND THE SAME MIND
MIND	076 - 3	MIND IS BOTH UNIVERSAL AND INDIVIDUAL
MIND	078 - 2	UNIVERSAL MIND AND UNIVERSAL SPIRIT
MIND	081 - 4	SPIRIT IS CONSCIOUS MIND
MIND	087 - 3	MIND OF MAN IS AN EXTENSION
MIND	087 - 4	YOUR MIND, MY MIND
MIND	087 - 4	THERE IS ONLY MIND
MIND	087 - 6	OUR IDENTITY IN INFINITE MIND
MIND	090 - 3	MIND NEVER COULD BE UNCONSCIOUS
MIND	094 - 2	MIND MUST OPERATE UPON MIND
MIND	094 - 2	MIND AND ETHER INTERACT
MIND	099 - 4	MIND COMPLETELY CONTROLS THE BODY
MIND	099 - 4	BUT A REFLECTION OF THE MIND
MIND	102 - 4	ONE MIND CONCEIVES ALL THINGS
MIND	112 - 3	MIND IS THE SPIRITUAL MIND
MIND	120 - 4	MIND CANNOT ACT AGAINST ITSELF
MIND	126 - 2	MIND LIKE A SEED PLANTED
MIND	155 - 1	APPROACH IT THROUGH THE MIND
MIND	163 - 3	MIND FROM EVERY FORM OF BONDAGE
MIND	169 - 2	IN HIS OWN MIND
MIND	188 - 1	KNOW YOUR OWN MIND
MIND	192 - 2	DO ALL OF HIS WORK IN MIND
MIND	205 - 4	IS IN THE SAME MIND
MIND	216 - 3	DISEASE IS LARGELY A STATE OF MIND
MIND	218 - 3	TRANSFORMED BY THE RENEWING OF THE MIND
MIND	219 - 1	LAW OF MIND DO THE REST
MIND	227 - 4	THE ONLY MIND THERE IS
MIND	228 - 1	HAVING LOST HIS MIND
MIND	232 - 5	THE WASTE PRODUCTS OF THE MIND
MIND	237 - 3	THAT NOTHING MOVES BUT MIND
MIND	245 - 1	OF A FIRM UNWAVERING MIND
MIND	273 - 4	MIND OF THE UNIVERSE
MIND	279 - 1	MIND IS THE ONLY ACTOR
MIND	284 - 2	BOTH THE MIND OF MAN
MIND	284 - 2	WE USE THE MIND OF GOD
MIND	298 - 1	A RELIGIOUS ATTITUDE OF MIND
MIND	301 - 3	WE LIVE IN MIND
MIND	305 - 5	NOTHING MOVES BUT MIND
MIND	310 - 2	MIND IS ONE THING AND MATTER
MIND	312 - 4	MIND IS INDIVIDUALIZED
MIND	323 - 3	THIS MIND IS THROUGH, IN, AND AROUND
MIND	364 - 3	LET THIS MIND BE IN YOU
MIND	390 - 1	THE MIND OF MAN IS SOME PART
MIND	390 - 6	IS THE MIND OF GOD IN MAN
MIND	391 - 1	MIND OF MAN IS CONSCIOUS
MIND	396 - 2	MIND IS THE CONSCIOUSNESS
MIND	397 - 1	MIND IN THE ABSTRACT

MIND	407 - 3	MIND IS ALSO ALL EFFECT
MIND	409 - 1	ONLY PERSON'S MIND HE CAN
MIND	409 - 1	IN HIS OWN MIND
MIND	409 - 3	WORKS WITHIN HIS OWN MIND
MIND	443 - 1	CHILD-LIKE MIND IS MORE PERCEPTIVE
MIND	447 - 3	CONSCIOUS UNITY MAKES OUR MIND
MIND	487 - 1	MIND WHICH KNOWS THE TRUTH
MIND	495 - 6	MIND WHICH WAS IN CHRIST JESUS
MIND	496 - 4	MIND IS THE CREATOR OF THE HEAVENS
MIND-ACTIVITY	278 - 3	THROUGH AVENUES OF MIND-ACTIVITY
MINDED	217 - 2	TO BE SPIRITUALLY MINDED
MIND HEALING	250 - 6	MIND HEALING THE UNDERLYING
MIND OF CHRIST	496 - 3	MAN HAS THE MIND OF CHRIST
MIND OF TRUTH	495 - 7	CHRIST JESUS WAS THE MIND OF TRUTH
MINDS	501 - 6	MINDS ARE BURDENED WITH MANY THINGS
MIND WITHIN	169 - 2	GET AWAY FROM THE MIND WITHIN
MINERALS	117 - 1	MINERALS, SOLIDS AND LIQUIDS ARE
MINGLE	348 - 2	MINGLE AND RECEIVE SUGGESTION
MINIATURE	165 - 1	ITSELF ON A MINIATURE SCALE
MINUTE	117 - 1	MINUTE PARTICLES WHICH TAKE
MINUTES	200 - 2	MINUTES MORE OR LESS
MINUTES	225 - 1	IF IT TAKES FIVE MINUTES
MIRACLE	166 - 3	MIRACLE HAS HAPPENED
MIRACLE	166 - 3	MIRACLE AS EVERYTHING ELSE IN LIFE IS
MIRACLE	171 - 2	NO MIRACLE HAS BEEN ENACTED
MIRACLES	162 - 3	FEW MIRACLES RESULT
MIRACLES	162 - 4	MIRACLES MERELY PROVED THE DIVINITY
MIRACLES	358 - 3	THE MENTALITY PERFORMS SEEMING MIRACLES
MIRACULOUS	162 - 3	MIRACULOUS RESULTS FOLLOW
MIRROR	093 - 2	THE MIRROR OF THE MIND
MIRROR	114 - 5	SOUL IS THE SEAT OF MEMORY THE MIRROR
MIRROR	297 - 2	THE MIRROR OF KING AND SLAVE
MIRROR	320 - 4	LIFE IS A MIRROR
MIRROR	322 - 4	LIFE IS A MIRROR AND WILL REFLECT
MIRROR	396 - 1	A MIRROR AND A PERFECT ONE
MIRROR	449 - 2	MIRROR OF LIFE CANNOT HELP REFLECTING
MISCONCEPTION	200 - 4	THOUGHT FORCE A MISCONCEPTION
MISCONCEPTION	210 - 1	THIS IS A MISCONCEPTION
MISCONSTRUED	436 - 4	MISCONSTRUED TO MEAN OR EVEN TO SUGGEST
MISERABLE	209 - 4	MISERABLE CAN MAKE US HAPPY
MISERABLE	467 - 1	MISERABLE SINNER YOU ARE NO MORE
MISERY	288 - 2	BECAUSE OF YOUR MISERY
MISFORTUNE	133 - 1	BRINGING ON HIMSELF MISFORTUNE
MISFORTUNE	295 - 2	WHERE THERE IS NO MISFORTUNE
MISFORTUNE	336 - 2	TRUE MEANING OF MISFORTUNE
MISPLACED	156 - 4	FAITH MISPLACED
MISPLACED	211 - 3	MISPLACED, MISLAID, NEUTRALIZED
MISSED THE MARK	469 - 1	ELDER SON HAD MISSED THE MARK
MISSHAPEN	244 - 2	MISSHAPEN BY THE CREATIVE POWER
MISSING	383 - 3	NOT ONE WILL BE MISSING
MISSING	387 - 3	CANNOT HELP MISSING THEM
MISSION	367 - 4	HIS MISSION AND PURPOSE IN LIFE
MIST	147 - 2	MIST DISAPPEARS BEFORE THE SUN
MISTAKE	059 - 4	MISTAKE CAN HINDER
MISTAKE	099 - 4	BODY IS UNREAL IS A MISTAKE

MISTAKE	110 - 4	NO SIN BUT A MISTAKE
MISTAKE	180 - 4	LIMITATION IS A MISTAKE
MISTAKE	192 - 3	WILL TO INFLUENCE PEOPLE IS A MISTAKE
MISTAKE	209 - 3	WOULD NEVER MAKE MISTAKE
MISTAKE	267 - 5	IT IS A GREAT MISTAKE TO SAY
MISTAKE	334 - 4	MISTAKE TO SO ABSTRACT
MISTAKE	342 - 3	MISTAKE A PSYCHIC IMPRESSION
MISTAKE	367 - 3	MISTAKE TO SUPPOSE THAT HE WAS DIFFERENT
MISTAKE	410 - 2	MISTAKE OF USING ONLY ONE
MISTAKE	453 - 5	MISTAKE TO ACCEPT EVERY MAN'S PHILOSOPHY
MISTAKE	465 - 4	IT IS ALWAYS A MISTAKE
MISTAKE	477 - 3	NO GREATER MISTAKE COULD BE MADE
MISTAKEN	413 - 5	OF ITS MISTAKEN IDEA
MISTAKES	043 - 1	AVOID TWO GRAVE MISTAKES
MISTAKES	114 - 1	THE GREATEST POSSIBLE MISTAKES
MISTAKES	290 - 2	NO MISTAKES
MISTAKES	292 - 3	IT NEVER MAKES MISTAKES
MISTAKES	383 - 1	IF WE MAKE MISTAKES WE SUFFER
MISTAKES	502 - 2	MISTAKES CAN BE BLOTTED OUT
MISUNDERSTAND	298 - 2	MISUNDERSTAND OR BE MISUNDERSTOOD
MISUSE	037 - 1	THE MISUSE OF THIS POWER
MISUSE	111 - 3	MISUSE OF THE LAW OF FREEDOM
MISUSE	120 - 4	SOME CLAIM THAT WE CANNOT MISUSE
MISUSE	121 - 2	NO FEAR OF THE MISUSE OF THIS LAW
MISUSE	138 - 2	MISUSE OF MENTAL AND SPIRITUAL LAWS
MISUSE	276 - 1	LEST WE MISUSE IT
MISUSE	313 - 3	IN OUR IGNORANCE WE MISUSE OUR DIVINITY
MISUSE	335 - 2	SIMPLY A MISUSE OF POWER
MISUSE	434 - 5	BUT A MISUSE OF A POWER
MISUSE	471 - 2	MISUSE OF OUR TRUE NATURE
MODE	272 - 2	CHANGE OUR MODE OF LIVING
MODELS	273 - 4	LITTLE FLYING MACHINE MODELS
MOLD	030 - 3	THOUGHT CREATES A MOLD
MOLD	048 - 2	WE MAKE THE MOLD
MOLD	048 - 2	THIS IDEA IS THE MOLD
MOLD	057 - 4	MOLD FORMED IN THE SUBJECTIVE
MOLD	065 - 1	THE WORD IS THE MOLD
MOLD	145 - 1	MOLD THE BODY IN HEALTH OR SICKNESS
MOLD	174 - 2	GIVEN A SUBJECTIVE MOLD
MOLD	268 - 1	WE PROVIDE THE MOLD
MOLD	268 - 1	UNLESS THE MOLD IS INCREASED
MOLD	397 - 1	FIRST CREATE THE THOUGHT MOLD
MOLD	432 - 2	MOLD OUR PURPOSES WHEN WE
MOLD	476 - 1	WORD IS A MOLD
MOLD	490 - 7	MOLD IT INTO A PRESENT ACTUALITY
MOLDED	117 - 1	READY TO BECOME MOLDED
MOLDED	375 - 2	INSTINCTIVE MAN HAS MOLDED
MOLDED	392 - 2	MOLDED INTO ANY OR ALL FORMS
MOLDS	047 - 5	THEN POURED INTO MOLDS
MOLDS	048 - 1	PLACE IT IN THE PROPER MOLDS
MOLDS	048 - 2	MOLDS ARE MADE IN OUR OWN
MOLDS	048 - 2	DEFINITE MOLDS OR CONCEPTS DECIDE
MOLDS	410 - 2	THE LETTER MOLDS
MOLEHILL	123 - 3	MOUNTAIN AND THE MOLEHILL
MOLEHILL	312 - 2	MOLEHILL BUT NOT AS BIG AND LITTLE

MOLTEN	410 - 2	CONVICTION IS THE MOLTEN SUBSTANCE
MOMENT	282 - 4	SUPREME MOMENT TO DEMONSTRATE
MOMENT	315 - 3	IT IS AN EXPERIENCE OF THE MOMENT
MOMENTS	470 - 3	OUR MOMENTS OF QUIETNESS AND SOLITUDE
MONEY	128 - 2	CONDITIONS, MONEY, HAPPINESS, FRIENDS
MONEY	235 - 5	MONEY AND MEN
MONEY	263 - 5	AN ABUNDANCE OF MONEY
MONEY	263 - 5	OF SUPPLY, OF MONEY, OF ALL THAT I NEED
MONEY	398 - 3	IF WE WISH MONEY WE SHOULD ASK FOR
MONOPOLY	304 - 2	NO MONOPOLY IN MY EXPERIENCE
MONTHS	374 - 1	MONTHS AGO THEY HAVE COMPLETELY
MOORINGS	283 - 1	CUT LOOSE FROM ALL APPARENT MOORINGS
MORBID	124 - 2	ABODE OF OUR MORBID IMAGINATIONS
MORBID	145 - 2	MORBID MENTAL STATE PROJECTS ITSELF
MORBID	160 - 3	MORBID SENSE THAT THE WILL OF GOD
MORBID	465 - 4	IT IS MORBID AND DETRIMENTAL
MORBID	470 - 5	NOT WITH A MORBID MIND
MORBIDITIES	434 - 4	RESULT OF RELIGIOUS MORBIDITIES
MORBIDITY	270 - 5	FREE FROM MORBIDITY
MORBIDNESS	501 - 6	MORBIDNESS ON THE SUBJECTIVE SIDE
MORE	170 - 2	MORE COMPLETELY THE PRACTITIONER
MORE	314 - 3	LESS MISERY, MORE GOOD
MORE	321 - 2	MORE THAN WE APPEAR TO PUT
MORE	362 - 4	GOD IS MORE THAN ALL WE ARE
MORE	396 - 1	NO MORE AND NO LESS
MORE	471 - 1	MORE COULD NOT BE GIVEN
MORE	493 - 7	INFINITELY MORE THAN WE ARE
MORE THAN	403 - 3	SPIRIT ITSELF IS MORE THAN
MORNING	457 - 5	SWEET AS THE MORNING DEW
MORTAL	484 - 4	SPIRIT QUICKENS OUR MORTAL BODIES
MORTAL	484 - 4	QUICKENS THE MORTAL PART OF US
MORTAL	484 - 4	MORTAL IS ALWAYS AN EFFECT
MOSES	064 - 3	THOUGHT TO HAVE BEEN MOSES
MOSES	071 - 2	MOSES LED THE CHILDREN OF ISRAEL
MOSES	071 - 2	MOSES NOR ANY OF HIS FOLLOWERS
MOSES	152 - 2	BY MOSES HAD HE UNDERSTOOD THIS LAW
MOSES	158 - 2	ABRAHAM, MOSES, GIDEON
MOSES	329 - 2	MOSES READING GOD'S LAW
MOSES	344 - 3	MOSES COMING DOWN FROM THE MOUNTAIN
MOSES	453 - 6	THE TEACHINGS OF MOSES THAT "GOD IS ONE"
MOSES	461 - 2	MOSES REFERRED TO THE SAME
MOSES	472 - 5	MOSES LIFTED UP THE SERPENT
MOSES	477 - 6	MOSES TAUGHT THAT I AM
MOSES	495 - 1	WITH MOSES WE CAN SAY
MOST	194 - 5	MOST IMPORTANT THINGS FOR US
MOST HIGH	333 - 5	CHILDREN OF THE MOST HIGH
MOST HIGH	431 - 5	SECRET PLACE OF THE MOST HIGH
MOTHER	041 - 3	MOTHER HAS CLASPED
MOTHER	430 - 2	COSMIC MOTHER OF ALL
MOTHER	449 - 4	WHO IS MY MOTHER
MOTHER SOUL	360 - 2	MOTHER SOUL BROODING OVER HER UNBORN
MOTION	030 - 3	MOTION IN ACCORDANCE WITH THE THOUGHT
MOTION	069 - 3	WHICH SETS POWER IN MOTION
MOTION	070 - 2	SETTING IN MOTION THE LAW
MOTION	078 - 3	TENDENCY SET IN MOTION

MOTION	127 - 3	VERY POWER SET IN MOTION
MOTION	133 - 5	MOTION BY THE CONSCIOUS THOUGHT
MOTION	141 - 3	UPON ITSELF CREATES A MOTION
MOTION	152 - 3	LIFE IN MOTION FOR US
MOTION	166 - 3	MOTION IN THE SUBJECTIVE WORLD
MOTION	178 - 5	SETTING SUBJECTIVE LAW IN MOTION
MOTION	179 - 5	SET THAT BELIEF IN MOTION
MOTION	190 - 2	SETS IN MOTION THE LAW
MOTION	194 - 5	CAUSE WE HAVE SET IN MOTION
MOTION	221 - 5	UNIVERSAL LAW IN MOTION
MOTION	267 - 3	SETS A LAW IN MOTION
MOTION	286 - 2	HE HAS SET A LAW IN MOTION
MOTION	300 - 1	TO SET THE WORD IN MOTION
MOTION	305 - 5	SETTING THE LAW IN MOTION IS OURS
MOTION	318 - 2	MOTION IS AN ACTIVE THING
MOTION	322 - 3	WE SET THE POWER IN MOTION
MOTION	392 - 3	SET IN MOTION BY MIND IN A CONSCIOUS STATE
MOTION	433 - 3	LAW ALREADY SET IN MOTION
MOTIVATION	269 - 3	THIS IS A SELFISH MOTIVATION
MOTIVE	047 - 3	DEFINITE MOTIVE IN MIND
MOTIVES	433 - 4	MANIFESTATION OF OUR MOTIVES
MOUNT	389 - 1	SPIRIT FREED SHALL MOUNT THE AIR
MOUNTAIN	076 - 3	IS NOT IN THE MOUNTAIN
MOUNTAIN	150 - 4	NEITHER IN THE MOUNTAIN NOR AT THE TEMPLE
MOUNTAIN	162 - 2	MOUNTAIN REMOVE HENCE
MOUNTAIN	312 - 2	GOD CANNOT KNOW THE MOUNTAIN
MOUTH	146 - 1	IN THINE OWN MOUTH
MOUTH	212 - 2	GOETH FORTH OUT OF MY MOUTH
MOUTH	449 - 2	MOUTH SPEAKS FROM THE HEART
MOVE	128 - 2	NOTHING TO MOVE SAVE MIND
MOVE	339 - 3	MOVE IS BY AN INTERIOR MOVEMENT
MOVE	368 - 4	WE LIVE, MOVE AND HAVE OUR BEING
MOVED	231 - 5	ALWAYS MOVED UPON
MOVED	281 - 1	NOT BECAUSE GOD HAS BEEN MOVED
MOVEMENT	028 - 2	A MOVEMENT OF THOUGHT
MOVEMENT	085 - 4	IN MOVEMENT IS PRINCIPLE
MOVEMENT	171 - 3	A CONSCIOUS MOVEMENT OF THOUGHT
MOVEMENT	263 - 5	MOVEMENT TOWARD ME OF SUPPLY
MOVEMENT	339 - 3	MOVEMENT OF CONSCIOUSNESS
MOVEMENT	407 - 2	THIS INITIAL MOVEMENT STARTS
MOVER	305 - 5	MIND THAT IS THE MOVER
MOVES	032 - 3	LIVES AND MOVES AND HAS HIS BEING
MOVES	197 - 4	NOTHING MOVES BUT MIND
MOVES	304 - 5	NOTHING MOVES BUT MIND
MOVES	318 - 2	A TREATMENT MOVES IN THOUGHT
MOVES	458 - 4	MOVES FROM THE THOUGHT TO THE THING
MUCH	450 - 3	AS MUCH GATHERS MORE
MULTIPLICATION	269 - 1	MULTIPLICATION IN THE DIVINE PLAN
MULTIPLICITY	045 - 4	MULTIPLICITY PROCEEDING FROM UNITY
MULTIPLICITY	069 - 2	THE WORLD OF MULTIPLICITY
MULTIPLICITY	102 - 4	MULTIPLICITY IS MANIFESTED
MULTIPLICITY	103 - 1	MULTIPLICITY IS DEEP ROOTED
MULTIPLICITY	116 - 2	TAKE FORM IN MULTIPLICITY
MULTIPLICITY	116 - 3	UNITY IS EXPRESSED IN MULTIPLICITY
MULTIPLICITY	131 - 2	MULTIPLICITY COMES FROM UNITY

MULTIPLICITY	321 - 2	MULTIPLICITY BUT NEVER DIVISION
MULTIPLICITY	493 - 4	MULTIPLICITY OR MANY WITHIN UNITY
MULTIPLIED	396 - 1	CASTS THEM BACK MULTIPLIED
MULTIPLIES	270 - 6	MULTIPLIES ITS OWN EXPERIENCE
MULTIPLY	270 - 6	TENDS TO MULTIPLY OUR GIFTS
MULTIPLY	341 - 1	MULTIPLY THE LOAVES AND FISHES
MULTITUDE	504 - 2	COVERS A MULTITUDE OF MISTAKES
MUMBLING	283 - 5	QUIBBLING OR MUMBLING OF WORDS
MUSIC	328 - 2	GREATEST MUSIC EVER COMPOSED
MUST	046 - 5	MUST DO THIS CONSCIOUSLY
MUST	047 - 4	MIND MUST CONCEIVE BEFORE
MUST	052 - 4	MUST AND WILL RESPOND
MUST	110 - 1	WE MUST EXPECT TO EXPERIENCE
MUST	131 - 6	SPIRIT MUST CREATE
MUST	173 - 4	MUST BELIEVE THAT THIS POWER
MUST	202 - 3	MUST COME THROUGH MIND
MUST	207 - 3	MUST EXPERIENCE SOME PHYSICAL
MUST	338 - 4	MAN MUST BE PERFECT
MUST	415 - 1	THERE MUST COME A TIME
MUSTARD	162 - 2	AS A GRAIN OF MUSTARD
MUSTARD	451 - 4	LIKE A GRAIN OF MUSTARD SEED
MUST DO	317 - 3	WHAT IT IS THAT ONE MUST DO
MY	057 - 1	MY WORD IS THE LAW
MY	263 - 3	MY THOUGHT IS GOD
MY BODY	261 - 2	MY BODY IS THE BODY
MY OWN	385 - 3	MY OWN AND OTHER PEOPLES'
MYSELF	446 - 4	MYSELF RIGHT WITH THE UNIVERSE
MYSTERIES	063 - 1	WORLD IS TIRED OF MYSTERIES
MYSTERIOUS	327 - 1	NOTHING MYSTERIOUS IN THE TRUTH
MYSTERY	031 - 2	THERE IS NO MYSTERY HERE
MYSTERY	049 - 1	MYSTERY WITH WHICH MOST PEOPLE
MYSTERY	095 - 2	THE MYSTERY IS THE MYSTERY
MYSTERY	204 - 4	MYSTERY OF THE APPEARANCE
MYSTERY	343 - 2	CONSCIOUSNESS IS NOT A MYSTERY
MYSTERY	402 - 3	THIS IS THE GREAT MYSTERY
MYSTERY	420 - 5	THIS IS NOT A MYSTERY
MYSTERY	484 - 2	THERE IS NO MYSTERY
MYSTIC	327 - 1	A MYSTIC IS NOT A MYSTERIOUS PERSON
MYSTIC	341 - 1	THE MYSTIC INTUITIVELY PERCEIVES TRUTH
MYSTIC	360 - 1	THE MYSTIC CHRIST COMES
MYSTIC	419 - 2	MYSTIC IS ONE WHO INTUITIVELY
MYSTICAL	035 - 3	MEANING OF THAT MYSTICAL SAYING
MYSTICAL	069 - 2	THE MYSTICAL SECRET OF THE AGES
MYSTICAL	289 - 2	THIS IS THE MYSTICAL MEANING
MYSTICAL	357 - 1	MYSTICAL CONCEPTION OF CHRIST
MYSTICAL	454 - 2	MYSTICAL SAYINGS OF JESUS
MYSTICAL	484 - 5	A MYSTICAL AND BEAUTIFUL SAYING
MYSTICAL	493 - 7	MYSTICAL SAYING GOD IS IN ALL
MYSTICAL MARRIAGE	343 - 5	TAUGHT THE MYSTICAL MARRIAGE
MYSTIC CHRIST	361 - 5	THESE IDEAS CONSTITUTE THE MYSTIC CHRIST
MYSTIC CHRIST	368 - 3	MYSTIC CHRIST COMES FROM THE BOSOM
MYSTICISM	327 - 1	MYSTICISM AND PSYCHISM
MYSTICS	306 - 4	MYSTICS CALL THE MAN OF THE HEART
MYSTICS	327 - 2	TEACHINGS OF THE GREAT MYSTICS
MYSTICS	328 - 2	SPIRITUAL PHILOSOPHERS ARE MYSTICS

MYSTICS	328 - 5	MYSTICS HAVE ALL SENSED ONE
MYSTICS	329 - 2	MYSTICS HAVE BEEN PERFECTLY NORMAL PEOPLE
MYSTICS	333 - 6	MYSTICS HAVE CONSCIOUSLY WALKED
MYSTICS	344 - 3	MYSTICS HAVE SEEN THIS COSMIC LIGHT
MYSTICS	419 - 2	MYSTICS INCLUDE THE GREAT PROPHETS
MYSTICS	419 - 4	TRUE MYSTICS HAVE NOT DENIED
MYSTICS	421 - 2	THE GREAT MYSTICS LIKE JESUS
MYTH	217 - 1	THE DEVIL IS A MYTH

N

NAKED	367 - 2	I HAVE STOOD NAKED
NAKED	388 - 4	FATHER'S HOUSE NAKED AND UNAFRAID
NAKED	431 - 2	ENTER THIS SECRET PLACE NAKED
NAKED	497 - 5	SOUL MUST STAND NAKED
NAKEDNESS	474 - 2	SO DOING REVEALS ITS OWN NAKEDNESS
NAME	065 - 5	I WILL LET HIM NAME
NAME	151 - 2	IN MY NAME
NAME	222 - 2	CALL YOUR OWN NAME
NAME	287 - 3	WE NAME IT BIG AND LITTLE
NAME	410 - 3	ADAM WAS PERMITTED TO NAME
NAME	459 - 6	COMES IN THE NAME OF THE LORD
NAME	480 - 4	NAME WHICH IS OUR OWN NAME
NAME	496 - 3	NO OTHER NAME UNDER HEAVEN
NAPOLEON	428 - 2	CAESAR AND A NAPOLEON
NATION	348 - 3	NATION HAS ITS INDIVIDUAL ATMOSPHERE
NATIONS	362 - 2	NATIONS HAVE RISEN
NATIONS	460 - 1	NATIONS WHO HAVE RISEN BY THE SWORD
NATIVE	233 - 4	INTO ITS NATIVE NOTHINGNESS
NATIVE	470 - 6	NATIVE TO THE HEAVENLY HOME
NATIVE	498 - 5	NATIVE TO THE ATMOSPHERE OF GOD
NATIVE STATE	474 - 2	NATIVE STATE OF MAN IS ONE OF PURITY
NATURAL	027 - 5	FOUND SPONTANEOUSLY NATURAL
NATURAL	071 - 2	TRUE OF ALL NATURAL LAWS
NATURAL	075 - 2	WILL BE FOUND SPONTANEOUSLY NATURAL
NATURAL	176 - 2	MORE NATURAL WE CAN BE
NATURAL	192 - 4	NATURAL LAWS ARE IMPERSONAL
NATURAL	220 - 6	DEALING WITH A NORMAL NATURAL LAW
NATURAL	275 - 4	ELECTRICITY BEING A NATURAL LAW
NATURAL	285 - 4	PERFECTLY NATURAL AND NORMAL REALM
NATURAL	308 - 1	SPIRITUALITY IS NATURAL GOODNESS
NATURAL	334 - 2	NATURAL TO TURN TO THE GREAT
NATURAL	341 - 1	NATURAL LAW IN A SPIRITUAL WORLD
NATURAL	376 - 1	THERE IS A NATURAL BODY
NATURAL	481 - 5	GOODNESS IS NATURAL
NATURAL GOODNESS	456 - 3	GOD IS NATURAL GOODNESS
NATURAL LAW	403 - 3	NO NATURAL LAW IS EVER SELECTIVE
NATURE	025 - 3	INHERENT NATURE OF MAN
NATURE	026 - 3	WHATEVER THE NATURE OF ANY PRINCIPLE
NATURE	027 - 5	THE NATURE OF THE LAW
NATURE	030 - 3	ACCORDING TO THE NATURE
NATURE	033 - 2	NATURE SEEMS TO AWAIT
NATURE	034 - 1	NATURE OF THE DIVINE BEING

NATURE	034 - 1	VIOLATE ITS OWN NATURE
NATURE	035 - 2	THE NATURE OF THE THING
NATURE	036 - 4	SANCTUARY OF OUR OWN NATURE
NATURE	037 - 1	SO DEEPLY INTO NATURE
NATURE	037 - 1	IGNORANT OF OUR TRUE NATURE
NATURE	038 - 1	NATURE OBEYS US AS WE FIRST OBEY IT
NATURE	038 - 2	MECHANICAL SIDE OF NATURE
NATURE	040 - 2	SECRETS OF NATURE
NATURE	040 - 4	WE PARTAKE OF ITS NATURE
NATURE	041 - 1	PARTAKE OF THE DIVINE NATURE
NATURE	041 - 2	ITS NATURE IS TO IMPART
NATURE	042 - 2	ONE NATURE DIFFUSED THROUGHOUT
NATURE	042 - 3	INHERENT IN OUR NATURE
NATURE	042 - 4	NATURE OF THE UNIVERSE
NATURE	042 - 5	NATURE HERSELF IS THE BODY OF GOD
NATURE	042 - 5	LAWS OF NATURE ARE SET AND IMMUTABLE
NATURE	043 - 1	STUDY THE NATURE OF REALITY
NATURE	047 - 4	IT IS ITS NATURE TO SPRING
NATURE	048 - 3	ONLY THOSE WHO BY NATURE
NATURE	050 - 1	THE NATURE OF THOUGHT
NATURE	050 - 1	THE NATURE OF BEING
NATURE	050 - 2	IT IS THE NATURE OF BEING TO REACT
NATURE	052 - 4	USE IT ACCORDING TO ITS NATURE
NATURE	058 - 1	PARTAKING OF THIS ORIGINAL NATURE
NATURE	063 - 1	NATURE OF THE INVISIBLE CAUSE
NATURE	064 - 5	NATURE TO CREATE
NATURE	065 - 4	BY IMPARTING HIS OWN NATURE
NATURE	065 - 4	MUST PARTAKE OF THE NATURE
NATURE	068 - 2	NATURE OF THE DIVINE BEING
NATURE	068 - 2	NATURE OF THAT REALITY
NATURE	068 - 4	NATURE OF THIS INNER ACTION
NATURE	071 - 2	DISCOVER HIS TRUE NATURE
NATURE	072 - 4	NATURE WORKS THROUGH HIM
NATURE	075 - 2	NATURE OF THE LAWS OF THOUGHT
NATURE	076 - 5	NATURE MAY BE COHERENT
NATURE	078 - 2	TRUE OF THE LAWS OF NATURE
NATURE	079 - 4	STUDYING THE NATURE OF THOSE THINGS
NATURE	079 - 5	THE TRUE NATURE OF MAN
NATURE	080 - 1	REAL NATURE OF GOD
NATURE	080 - 1	THREEFOLD IN HIS NATURE
NATURE	082 - 4	NATURE OF FIRST CAUSE
NATURE	082 - 5	NATURE OF FIRST CAUSE
NATURE	084 - 2	A PART OF THE CAUSELESS NATURE
NATURE	092 - 2	ACCORDING TO THE LAW OF ITS NATURE
NATURE	092 - 2	TRUE OF THE NATURE OF ALL LAW
NATURE	092 - 2	NATURE OF THE SPIRIT
NATURE	103 - 3	NATURE IS SPIRIT REDUCED
NATURE	104 - 2	A UNITY WITH NATURE AND HER FORCES
NATURE	107 - 2	NATURE FROM WHICH HE SPRINGS
NATURE	107 - 2	WE DID NOT CREATE OUR NATURE
NATURE	110 - 2	FOREVER REMAINS TRUE TO ITS OWN NATURE
NATURE	148 - 2	NATURE OF MENTAL POWERS
NATURE	153 - 1	TO THE NATURE AND INTELLECT OF MAN
NATURE	163 - 1	NATURE OF MAN TO USE IT
NATURE	164 - 1	SPIRITUAL NATURE OF ALL BEING

NATURE	191 - 2	IN THE INNER NATURE OF REAL MAN
NATURE	192 - 4	THERE IS NO LAW OF NATURE
NATURE	192 - 5	IT IS HIS NATURE TO ACT
NATURE	193 - 1	NATURE TO ACT CREATIVELY UPON THE IMAGES
NATURE	194 - 5	BEAT NATURE AT ITS OWN GAME
NATURE	196 - 5	NATURE IS RE-ENACTED IN MAN
NATURE	232 - 2	ACCORDING TO THEIR NATURE
NATURE	239 - 3	HIS OWN NATURE
NATURE	251 - 4	IT IS ITS NATURE TO DO SO
NATURE	256 - 4	IN THE EMOTIONAL NATURE
NATURE	266 - 3	THE NATURE OF OUR OWN EXISTENCE
NATURE	268 - 3	ALL NATURE CONSPIRES TO PRODUCE
NATURE	268 - 3	THE NATURE OF THE UNIVERSE
NATURE	271 - 2	COMPLY WITH ITS NATURE, WORK AS IT WORKS
NATURE	272 - 1	IT IS ITS NATURE TO WORK
NATURE	273 - 2	IN THE NATURE OF THE UNIVERSE
NATURE	279 - 2	SUSTAINS ITSELF IN NATURE
NATURE	280 - 1	IS THE NATURE OF GOD
NATURE	285 - 4	CHANGE ITS OWN NATURE
NATURE	285 - 4	INTO IT IN ITS OWN NATURE
NATURE	305 - 5	INHERENT IN ITS OWN NATURE
NATURE	314 - 2	WE CANNOT CHANGE OUR NATURE
NATURE	328 - 3	MAN HAS COMPELLED NATURE
NATURE	339 - 1	NATURE IS COMPRISED OF ONE
NATURE	358 - 5	EXCEPT THROUGH OUR OWN NATURE
NATURE	364 - 3	INTO OUR OWN DIVINE NATURE
NATURE	378 - 3	WHY HAS NATURE PROVIDED US
NATURE	378 - 3	NATURE IS NOT FOOLISH
NATURE	384 - 4	NATURE PROVIDES FOR HERSELF
NATURE	385 - 1	NATURE DEMANDS THE CHANGE
NATURE	387 - 1	NATURE IS LIMITED TO ONE SPHERE OF ACTION
NATURE	394 - 4	POWER WILL NEVER DENY ITS OWN NATURE
NATURE	395 - 1	NATURE SHALL BE PERFECT
NATURE	405 - 3	WE ARE OF ITS NATURE
NATURE	422 - 3	THROUGH OUR OWN SPIRITUAL NATURE
NATURE	434 - 5	KNOW THE NATURE OF GOOD
NATURE	443 - 4	DEEPLY INTO HIS OWN NATURE
NATURE	447 - 3	LAW OF ITS OWN NATURE
NATURE	461 - 4	NATURE NEVER ARGUES
NATURE	471 - 7	DIVINE NATURE IS MAN
NATURE	496 - 3	NATURE ALWAYS GUARDS HERSELF
NATURE'S	071 - 2	ANY OF NATURE'S FORCES
NATURES	444 - 2	DEEPLY INTO THEIR OWN NATURES
NAUGHT	457 - 4	HOLDS NAUGHT AGAINST ANYONE
NAY	464 - 3	NO GODS TO SAY US NAY
NECESSARY	083 - 5	NECESSARY THAT SOUL AND BODY
NECESSARY	128 - 3	NECESSARY THAT EACH ONE DO THIS
NECESSARY	164 - 4	NECESSARY WHILE WE ARE CONFRONTED
NECESSARY	172 - 2	NOT NECESSARY TO SPECIFY THE TROUBLE
NECESSARY	213 - 2	NECESSARY THAT THE PRACTITIONER
NECESSARY	277 - 3	NECESSARY WHILE WE ARE CONFRONTED
NECESSARY	394 - 1	NECESSARY IN ORDER THAT MIND
NECESSARY	466 - 1	NECESSARY TO BRING US TO OURSELVES
NECESSITY	089 - 2	NECESSITY FOR WARMTH AND COLOR
NECESSITY	109 - 3	IT IS THE NECESSITY OF THE CASE

NECESSITY	139 - 1	NECESSITY OF BEING TRUE TO ITS OWN NATURE
NECESSITY	195 - 3	NECESSITY OF THE UNIVERSE
NECESSITY	213 - 3	TO ADMIT ITS NECESSITY
NECESSITY	224 - 3	NECESSITY OF THE CONDITION
NECESSITY	270 - 1	FIND THAT THE LAWS OF NECESSITY
NECESSITY	280 - 2	IMPLIED THE NECESSITY OF FAITH
NECESSITY	340 - 3	FUNDAMENTAL LAWS OF NECESSITY
NECESSITY	440 - 1	THE NECESSITY OF FAITH AND BELIEF
NEED	141 - 2	NEED IS NOT SOME GREATER POWER
NEED	319 - 4	NEED NO MORE TREATMENT
NEED	364 - 2	NEED FOR GREATER FREEDOM
NEED	375 - 1	WILL STILL NEED AND HAVE A BODY
NEED	445 - 6	WE NEED SPIRITUAL EXPERIENCE
NEED	451 - 3	MEN NEED SPIRITUAL CONVICTIONS
NEED	476 - 4	NEED FOOD TO EAT WHILE IN THE FLESH
NEEDED	410 - 2	SOME NEEDED EXPERIENCE
NEEDING	306 - 4	PERFECT AND COMPLETE, NEEDING NOTHING
NEEDS	390 - 3	HE NEEDS OR ENJOYS ON THE PATHWAY
NEEDS	451 - 3	WORLD NEEDS SPIRITUAL EXPERIENCE
NEEDS	496 - 5	GOD WILL SUPPLY ALL OUR NEEDS
NEEDY	301 - 3	OURSELVES AS POOR AND NEEDY
NEGATION	177 - 5	NOT CONSCIOUSLY THINK NEGATION
NEGATION	207 - 1	CONSCIOUSLY WE THINK NEGATION
NEGATION	218 - 3	ONE OF NEGATION
NEGATION	354 - 2	NEGATION EXISTS IN THE REALM OF SUBJECTIVE
NEGATION	473 - 6	NEGATION EQUALS POSITIVE GOODNESS
NEGATION	495 - 3	THOUGHT OF NEGATION CAN ENTER
NEGATIVE	054 - 2	MADE NEGATIVE IN THE EXPERIENCE
NEGATIVE	058 - 3	OWN TREATMENT NEGATIVE
NEGATIVE	059 - 3	DISSOLVES THE NEGATIVE APPEARANCE
NEGATIVE	110 - 1	UNTIL THROUGH NEGATIVE EXPERIENCES
NEGATIVE	156 - 4	NEGATIVE USE OF FAITH
NEGATIVE	169 - 1	CAUGHT BY NEGATIVE THOUGHT
NEGATIVE	183 - 2	TO NEUTRALIZE NEGATIVE THOUGHT
NEGATIVE	216 - 5	TOO MUCH ON THE NEGATIVE
NEGATIVE	217 - 2	DWELLING TOO MUCH ON THE NEGATIVE
NEGATIVE	217 - 2	NEGATIVE STREAM OF CONSCIOUSNESS
NEGATIVE	251 - 6	IMMUNE TO NEGATIVE EXPERIENCES
NEGATIVE	298 - 2	REFUSE TO SEE THE NEGATIVE SIDE
NEGATIVE	301 - 3	NEGATIVE AND MUST BE COUNTED OUT
NEGATIVE	387 - 2	WORLD HAVE BEEN SO NEGATIVE
NEGATIVE	488 - 6	DROP ALL NEGATIVE
NEITHER	093 - 2	NEITHER SPIRIT NOR THE SOUL
NEITHER	201 - 1	NEITHER PERSON, PLACE NOR THING
NEO-PLATONIC	341 - 4	GREATEST OF THE NEO-PLATONIC
NEPHIRTIS	253 - 3	NEPHRITIS FOLLOWED BY DEATH
NERVE	244 - 5	TREATMENT FOR NERVE DISORDERS
NERVES	244 - 4	NERVES CERTAINLY REPRESENT
NERVES	245 - 1	NERVES ARE SO RESPONSIVE
NERVES	245 - 1	SENSITIVE, QUICKLY-RESPONDING NERVES
NERVOUS	227 - 1	KNOWN AS NERVOUS PROSTRATION
NERVOUS	242 - 2	NERVOUS PERSONS
NERVOUS SYSTEM	247 - 1	NERVOUS SYSTEM IS PURE SPIRIT
NEUTRAL	092 - 2	BEING A NEUTRAL CREATIVE MEDIUM
NEUTRAL	118 - 3	ENTIRELY RECEPTIVE AND NEUTRAL

NEUTRAL	193 - 3	PASS INTO A STATE OF NEUTRAL
NEUTRAL	208 - 3	PLASTIC, NEUTRAL, IMPERSONAL
NEUTRAL	278 - 1	RECEPTIVE, NEUTRAL, IMPERSONAL
NEUTRAL	494 - 5	MENTAL LAW IS NEUTRAL
NEUTRALIZE	048 - 4	CONSCIOUSLY TO OPPOSE, NEUTRALIZE
NEUTRALIZE	055 - 3	THEY WILL NEUTRALIZE THE POSITION
NEUTRALIZE	183 - 2	POWER TO NEUTRALIZE NEGATIVE THOUGHT
NEUTRALIZE	209 - 1	NEUTRALIZE THOSE WHICH CAUSED
NEUTRALIZE	221 - 4	NEUTRALIZE IT BY AN OPPOSITE ONE
NEUTRALIZE	224 - 3	AS TO NEUTRALIZE A BELIEF
NEUTRALIZE	228 - 3	WORD HE SPEAKS WILL NEUTRALIZE
NEUTRALIZE	291 - 4	TO NEUTRALIZE THE BELIEF
NEUTRALIZE	297 - 3	WOULD NEUTRALIZE OUR WORD
NEUTRALIZE	303 - 1	WE OFTEN NEUTRALIZE OUR WORD
NEUTRALIZE	303 - 2	REFUSE TO RECOGNIZE WE NEUTRALIZE
NEUTRALIZE	319 - 3	WILL NEUTRALIZE THE FEAR
NEUTRALIZED	119 - 3	THOUGHT IS TOO OFTEN NEUTRALIZED
NEUTRALIZED	142 - 4	AND DELIBERATELY NEUTRALIZED
NEUTRALIZED	211 - 3	MISLAID, NEUTRALIZED OR DESTROYED
NEUTRALIZED	224 - 2	FIRST NEUTRALIZED THE IDEA
NEUTRALIZED	245 - 2	NEUTRALIZED BY OUR REFUSAL
NEUTRALIZED	353 - 3	UNLESS THE VIBRATION IS NEUTRALIZED
NEUTRALIZES	049 - 4	NOW NEUTRALIZES ALL DOUBT
NEUTRALIZES	179 - 6	NEUTRALIZES THE FALSE THOUGHT
NEUTRALIZES	228 - 2	PRACTITIONER NEUTRALIZES THIS BELIEF
NEUTRALIZES	279 - 1	NEUTRALIZES ITS EFFECT
NEUTRALIZES	501 - 2	NEUTRALIZES FALSE IMAGES
NEUTRALIZES	504 - 2	NEUTRALIZES ALL THAT IS UNLIKE ITSELF
NEUTRALIZING	183 - 2	PURPOSE OF UNCOVERING AND NEUTRALIZING
NEUTRALIZING	197 - 3	BY UNCOVERING, NEUTRALIZING
NEUTRALIZING	204 - 4	OPPOSING, NEUTRALIZING, ERASING
NEUTRALIZING	210 - 2	THE GREAT NEUTRALIZING POWER
NEUTRALIZING	409 - 2	MEETING AND NEUTRALIZING FALSE CLAIMS
NEUTRALIZING	412 - 2	DO ITS NEUTRALIZING WORK
NEVER	167 - 2	NEVER LEARN HOW TO GIVE AN
NEVER	168 - 4	NEVER MENTION THE NAMES
NEVER	171 - 3	NEVER SEND OUT A THOUGHT
NEVER	186 - 2	NEVER LOOK AT THAT WHICH
NEVER	201 - 4	NEVER LOCATE DISEASE
NEVER	203 - 2	NEVER SAY HERE IS A PATIENT
NEVER	209 - 3	NEVER RECEIVED FALSE IMPRESSIONS
NEVER	231 - 4	NEVER THINK A SICK PERSON
NEVER	289 - 2	NEVER TREAT A PROCESS
NEVER	289 - 3	NEVER LOOKING FOR RESULTS
NEVER	289 - 3	NEVER BEING HURRIED NOR WORRIED
NEVER	297 - 3	WE MUST NEVER LOOK TO SEE IF
NEVER	303 - 3	THIS SPIRIT NEVER FAILS
NEVER	304 - 4	NEVER DEPEND UPON PEOPLE
NEVER	312 - 4	IT WILL NEVER BE AN INDIVIDUAL
NEVER	322 - 4	ONE SHOULD NEVER ALLOW HIMSELF
NEVER	334 - 4	MAN WILL NEVER BE SATISFIED
NEVER	381 - 2	NEVER GOOD OR RIGHT
NEVER	382 - 1	NEVER ADMIT ANY MENTAL IMPRESSIONS
NEVER	392 - 1	IT NEVER IS, HOWEVER
NEVER	412 - 3	WILL NEVER DENY US ANYTHING

NEVER SAY	210 - 2	NEVER SAY: I AM NOT GOOD ENOUGH
NEW	051 - 1	NEW ORDER OF THOUGHT
NEW	060 - 3	A NEW SCIENCE
NEW	060 - 3	A NEW RELIGION
NEW	060 - 3	A NEW PHILOSOPHY
NEW	275 - 2	BEHOLD I MAKE ALL THINGS NEW
NEW	281 - 2	THIS IS NOTHING NEW
NEW	281 - 2	WE HAVE NOTHING NEW
NEW	281 - 2	A NEW APPROACH TO AN OLD TRUTH
NEW	406 - 4	NEW THOUGHTS CREATE NEW CONDITIONS
NEW	414 - 1	THINGS NEW IN OUR EXPERIENCE
NEW	417 - 2	LAW WITH A NEW IDEA OF OURSELVES
NEWER	410 - 1	WILL EVER EVOLVE INTO NEWER
NEW MAN	363 - 4	PUT ON THE NEW MAN
NEW MAN	494 - 1	PUT ON THE NEW MAN
NEWNESS	242 - 2	INTO A NEWNESS OF LIFE
NEWNESS	414 - 4	INTO NEWNESS OF ACTION
NEWNESS	489 - 6	THIS IMAGE INTO A NEWNESS
NEW ORDER	481 - 6	SATISFIED IN A NEW ORDER OF LIVING
NEWS	429 - 4	NEWS OF HEAVEN OTHER THAN
NEWS	452 - 3	NEWS WE HAVE OF HEAVEN
NEW TESTAMENT	357 - 2	OUR NEW TESTAMENT
NEWTON	095 - 2	NEWTON SAID, THE FACT THAT WE ARE ABLE TO
NEW YORK	165 - 2	MAN IN NEW YORK
NEW YORK CITY	345 - 1	NEW YORK CITY WAS IN FLAMES
NEXT LIFE	457 - 3	NEXT LIFE IS A LOGICAL CONTINUATION
NIGH	146 - 1	THE WORD IS NIGH THEE
NIGHTMARE	487 - 6	AWAKES FROM A NIGHTMARE
NIRVANA	344 - 1	BUT NOT LOST IN NIRVANA
NO	201 - 1	NO SPIRITUAL LAW TO SUPPORT IT
NO	250 - 2	NO MAN OUTSIDE OF GOD
NO	413 - 5	NO MATERIAL CAUSE OR EFFECT
NO	420 - 2	NO ULTIMATE REALITY TO EVIL
NO BEGINNING	373 - 1	FROM A SOURCE THAT HAD NO BEGINNING
NOBLE	198 - 1	HIGHEST, THE MOST NOBLE
NOBLE	231 - 1	FAITH OR NOBLE PURPOSE
NO BODY	099 - 4	CANNOT SAY THERE IS NO BODY
NO GOOD	458 - 6	CAN BE NO GOOD TO US ALONE
NO GOOD	463 - 4	NO GOOD APART FROM A UNITY
NOISES	351 - 1	NOTHING BUT A LOT OF NOISES
NO LIMIT	267 - 4	THERE IS NO LIMIT TO THE LAW
NO LIMIT	439 - 3	THERE IS NO LIMIT TO THE POSSIBILITY
NO MORE	501 - 6	NO MORE AGAINST US FOREVER
NON-COMBATIVE	441 - 1	NON-COMBATIVE BUT CERTAIN OF THEMSELVES
NON-COMBATIVE	459 - 6	POSITIVE BUT NON-COMBATIVE
NON-EXISTENT	229 - 3	ETERNAL CAN NEVER BE NON-EXISTENT
NON-PHYSICAL	372 - 1	NON-PHYSICAL FACULTY OF PERCEPTION
NON-RECOGNITION	303 - 2	NON-RECOGNITION OF EVIL IS THE ONLY WAY
NON-RESISTANCE	427 - 5	TEACHING OF NON-RESISTANCE
NOONDAY	457 - 5	BRILLIANT AS THE NOONDAY SUN
NO ONE	203 - 2	NO ONE BELIEVES IN DISEASE
NO ONE	408 - 5	NO ONE TO BE HEALED IN THE TRUTH
NO ONE	423 - 2	NO ONE CAN LIVE OUR LIFE FOR US
NO ONE	445 - 3	NO ONE CAN LIVE FOR US
NO OTHER	343 - 4	HE CAN KNOW NO OTHER

NO OTHER	492 - 6	IF WE ADMITTED NO OTHER
NO PART	049 - 4	NO PART IN AN EFFECTIVE
NO PAST	095 - 1	NO PAST, PRESENT OR FUTURE
NO PAST	353 - 3	NO PAST, NO PRESENT AND NO FUTURE
NO RESISTANCE	233 - 2	NO RESISTANCE TO TRUTH
NO RIGHT	309 - 3	HAS NO RIGHT TO EXIST
NORMAL	099 - 5	THE BODY WILL BE NORMAL AND HEALTHY
NORMAL	175 - 4	IT IS REDUCED TO NORMAL
NORMAL	220 - 6	DEALING WITH A NORMAL, NATURAL LAW
NORMAL	231 - 5	ALL ACTION IS NORMAL, HARMONIOUS
NORMAL	249 - 3	BLOOD PRESSURE IS FOUND TO BE NORMAL
NORMAL	250 - 2	THE BLOOD PRESSURE IS NORMAL
NORMAL	285 - 4	NATURAL AND NORMAL REALM
NORMAL	300 - 3	LAW WORKING IN A NORMAL WAY
NORMAL	323 - 1	IS BOTH NATURAL AND NORMAL
NORMAL	329 - 2	HAVE BEEN PERFECTLY NORMAL PEOPLE
NORMAL	329 - 2	NATURAL TO THEM—PERFECTLY NORMAL
NORMAL	334 - 2	NORMAL TO BELIEVE IN THIS POWER
NORMAL	353 - 2	NORMAL STATE OF MIND IS HARMLESS
NORMAL	381 - 2	NORMAL PSYCHIC POWER IS PRODUCED
NORMAL	395 - 1	NORMAL FUNCTIONS OF LIFE
NORMAL	452 - 4	SPIRITUAL EXPERIENCES ARE NORMAL
NORMAL	452 - 5	NORMAL STATE OF MIND
NORMALLY	075 - 1	APPROACH IT NORMALLY
NORMALLY	300 - 3	APPROACH THE LAW NORMALLY
NORMALLY	308 - 1	NORMALLY AS WE GO ABOUT OUR DAILY AFFAIRS
NORMALLY-MINDED	253 - 1	NORMALLY-MINDED PERSON WILL EAT
NORMAL PSYCHICS	353 - 2	MANY NORMAL PSYCHICS WHO CAN
NO SUCH	365 - 3	COULD BE NO SUCH DIVINE BEING
NO SUCH THING	486 - 1	NO SUCH THING AS ETERNAL DAMNATION
NOT	049 - 3	NOT A CORRECT TREATMENT
NOT	049 - 3	NOT THE SCIENTIFIC USE OF THIS
NOT	126 - 4	IT IS NOT AN EXTERNAL ACT
NOT	202 - 4	NOT NEEDING TO BE HEALED
NOT	303 - 3	NOT TELLING THE TRUTH TO HIMSELF
NOT	308 - 1	GOD IS NOT A PERSON
NOT	320 - 2	IT IS NOT A GOOD TREATMENT
NOT	473 - 4	IS NOT FOR OUR BEST GOOD
NOT APART FROM	352 - 5	NOT APART FROM, BUT IS IN, MIND
NOT ENOUGH	393 - 2	CREATIVENESS IS NOT ENOUGH
NOT ENOUGH	459 - 3	TO LOVE GOD ALONE IS NOT ENOUGH
NO THING	097 - 2	NATURE IS THE GREAT NO THING
NOTHING	036 - 2	ONE ORIGINAL CAUSE AND NOTHING
NOTHING	063 - 2	NOTHING BUT THE LIFE PRINCIPLE
NOTHING	075 - 3	NOTHING IS MORE EVIDENT
NOTHING	083 - 3	MAKING SOMETHING OUT OF NOTHING
NOTHING	085 - 3	BEFORE WHICH NOTHING COMES
NOTHING	087 - 5	NOTHING FROM WHICH TO MAKE THINGS
NOTHING	097 - 3	IT IS NOT EXACTLY NOTHING
NOTHING	128 - 2	THERE IS NOTHING ELSE
NOTHING	140 - 4	NOTHING BUT MIND
NOTHING	161 - 3	NOTHING IN THE UNIVERSAL ORDER
NOTHING	199 - 4	NOTHING BUT A THOUGHT
NOTHING	209 - 5	THERE IS NOTHING BUT SPIRIT
NOTHING	239 - 3	NOTHING TO BE BORN, MATURE, DECAY AND DIE

NOTHING	263 - 1	NOTHING IS GREAT
NOTHING	267 - 2	PROMISE SOMETHING FOR NOTHING
NOTHING	283 - 4	NOTHING LEFT IN THE SUBJECTIVE STATE
NOTHING	299 - 4	THEN THERE IS NOTHING IN THIS TEACHING
NOTHING	306 - 4	PERFECT AND COMPLETE, NEEDING NOTHING
NOTHING	313 - 3	GOD HAD NOTHING TO DO WITH IT
NOTHING	346 - 2	NOTHING IS SAID... SOMETHING IS FELT
NOTHING	364 - 2	NOTHING BUT A GREATER REALIZATION
NOTHING	402 - 3	NOTHING IS REALLY THE SUBSTANCE
NOTHING	404 - 1	IN THE ABSOLUTE NOTHING DEPENDS
NOTHING	441 - 3	NOTHING CAN HAPPEN TO
NOTHING	445 - 4	NOTHING BETWEEN LIFE AND LIVING
NOTHING	445 - 5	MEANS NOTHING TO US UNLESS
NOTHING	463 - 4	NOTHING OUTSIDE THE UNITY
NOTHING	465 - 1	NOTHING CAN BE TAKEN FROM
NOTHING	486 - 3	NOTHING CAN KEEP US FROM THE LOVE
NOTHINGNESS	233 - 4	INTO ITS NATIVE NOTHINGNESS
NOTHINGNESS	411 - 1	VANISHED INTO ITS NATIVE NOTHINGNESS
NOTHINGNESS	501 - 4	THOUGHT INTO ITS NATIVE NOTHINGNESS
NOT WORK	052 - 5	APPEARING TO NOT WORK
NOURISH	235 - 2	SOMETHING TO NOURISH IT
NOW	047 - 2	EACH OF US IS NOW DEMONSTRATING
NOW	166 - 2	PERSON IS NOW ALL RIGHT
NOW	175 - 5	THE INSTANTANEOUS NOW
NOW	204 - 2	AND IT IS MY LIFE NOW
NOW	204 - 2	IT IS IN ME NOW
NOW	213 - 3	NOW IN SUCH DEGREE
NOW	261 - 3	NOW TAKE THE TIME
NOW	264 - 5	I LIVE IN AN ETERNAL NOW
NOW	289 - 4	ULTIMATE RIGHT ACTION IS NOW TODAY
NOW	290 - 2	EXPERIENCE OF JOY IS MINE NOW
NOW	291 - 2	THAT MIND IS OUR MIND NOW
NOW	334 - 5	ULTIMATE REALITY IS HERE NOW
NOW	489 - 2	THIS LIFE IS YOUR LIFE NOW
NOW	503 - 1	NOW ARE WE THE SONS OF GOD
NO-WHERE	389 - 1	AFAR IN THAT GREAT NO-WHERE
NOWHERE	396 - 3	IT HAS NOWHERE TO GO
NUMBER	074 - 4	NUMBER OF KNOWN FACTS ABOUT ITS INVISIBLE
NUMBERED	039 - 5	NUMBERED WITH THE THINGS
NUMBERLESS	070 - 1	SUBSTANCE AND NUMBERLESS FORMS
NUMBERS	045 - 2	AS ALL NUMBERS PROCEED
NURTURED	236 - 2	NURTURED BY TRUTH

O

OBEDIENCE	038 - 1	OBEDIENCE TO IT IS OUR ACCEPTANCE
OBEDIENCE	410 - 3	IN OBEDIENCE TO THE POWER
OBEY	064 - 4	THE LAW MUST OBEY
OBEY	130 - 1	READY TO OBEY HIS WILL
OBEY	130 - 4	OBEY NATURE AND SHE WILL THEN OBEY HIM
OBEY	275 - 3	SEEK TO OBEY THIS SPIRIT
OBEY	276 - 1	WHO BELIEVE IN AND OBEY IT
OBEY	334 - 4	COMPELLED TO OBEY HIS WILL

OBEY	397 - 4	OBEY THE CONSCIOUS THOUGHT
OBEY	400 - 1	LAW KNOWS ONLY TO OBEY
OBEYING	122 - 4	A LAW OBEYING HIS WORD
OBEYING	129 - 2	OBEYING THE WILL OF SPIRIT
OBEYING	339 - 1	DIVINE LAW OBEYING THE DICTATES
OBEYING	340 - 1	LAW OBEYING THE WILL
OBEYS	038 - 1	NATURE OBEYS US
OBEYS	191 - 2	SPIRIT KNOWS AND THE LAW OBEYS
OBEYS	382 - 1	ANYTHING THAT OBEYS THE ONE
OBEYS	397 - 3	THE LAW OF MIND OBEYS
OBJECT	076 - 2	NO OBJECT CAN
OBJECTIFICATION	098 - 1	THE OBJECTIFICATION OF SPIRIT
OBJECTIFICATION	240 - 3	OBJECTIFICATION OF THE PERFECT LIFE
OBJECTIFIED	224 - 4	AS IF IT WERE ALREADY OBJECTIFIED
OBJECTIFIES	171 - 1	OBJECTIFIES THROUGH HER BODY
OBJECTIFY	118 - 2	IT CAN OBJECTIFY ANY IDEA
OBJECTIFY	145 - 3	POWER TO OBJECTIFY THEMSELVES
OBJECTIFY	351 - 2	THE ABILITY TO OBJECTIFY
OBJECTIFY	353 - 1	OBJECTIFY PSYCHIC IMPRESSIONS
OBJECTIFY	422 - 2	THIS STREAM MAY OBJECTIFY IT
OBJECTIFY	029 - 1	THE OBJECTIVE OR CONSCIOUS
OBJECTIVE	076 - 5	ACTUALLY ARISE FROM THE OBJECTIVE SIDE
OBJECTIVE	141 - 3	HAPPENS IN THE OBJECTIVE WORLD
OBJECTIVE	169 - 5	OBJECTIVE MIND INTO SUBJECTIVITY
OBJECTIVE	187 - 2	NO ATTENTION TO THE OBJECTIVE EXPRESSION
OBJECTIVE	196 - 3	HIS OBJECTIVE FACULTY
OBJECTIVE	218 - 3	OBJECTIVE MAN IS PERFECT
OBJECTIVE	281 - 4	ANYTHING ELSE IN THE OBJECTIVE LIFE
OBJECTIVE	301 - 1	A PICTURE OF HIS OBJECTIVE CIRCUMSTANCES
OBJECTIVE	338 - 2	OBJECTIVE POINT OF HIS OWN SELF
OBJECTIVE	376 - 4	THE OBJECTIVE FACULTIES DIE
OBJECTIVE	381 - 3	WHILE IN AN OBJECTIVE STATE
OBJECTIVE	400 - 3	FORM OBJECTIVE CIRCUMSTANCES AROUND THEM
OBJECTIVE	402 - 2	OBJECTIVE FORM OF OUR SUBJECTIVE
OBJECTIVE	422 - 1	IN HIS OBJECTIVE STATE
OBJECTIVELY	051 - 2	SCIENCES ARE OBJECTIVELY REAL
OBJECTIVELY	303 - 1	OBJECTIVELY MAKING STATEMENTS
OBJECTIVELY	381 - 3	CONSCIOUSLY AND OBJECTIVELY EXERCISE
OBJECTIVE MIND	112 - 3	OBJECTIVE MIND MUST BE THE SPIRITUAL
OBLIGATION	176 - 2	DISCHARGE THE OBLIGATION
OBLIGATION	200 - 2	OBLIGATION TO TREAT A CASE
OBLIGATION	221 - 6	OBLIGATION WHICH IS TO GIVE THE TREATMENT
OBLIGATION	270 - 5	DUTY OR SOCIAL OBLIGATION
OBLIGATIONS	107 - 2	CERTAIN OBLIGATIONS
OBLITERATE	048 - 4	OBLITERATE THE OPPOSITE MENTAL
OBLITERATE	127 - 3	OBLITERATE THE SPIRIT OF THE ANTICHRIST
OBLITERATING	204 - 4	OBLITERATING SUPPRESSION, FEAR, DOUBT
OBLITERATING	213 - 2	OBLITERATING FALSE THOUGHT
OBLITERATION	186 - 4	LAW OF ELIMINATION AND OBLITERATION
OBLITERATION	239 - 3	OBLITERATION TO ANYTHING
OBLIVION	107 - 4	UNHAPPY AND END IN OBLIVION
OBLIVION	387 - 2	ROPE IS FOR UTTER OBLIVION
OBSERVATION	345 - 3	COMETH NOT BY OBSERVATION
OBSERVATION	374 - 2	BY OBSERVATION I NOTE
OBSERVATION	472 - 2	COMES NOT BY OBSERVATION

OBSERVATIONS	429 - 1	OBSERVATIONS BASED ON A FINITE
OBSERVE	043 - 3	OBSERVE ANY SCIENTIFIC DISCOVERY
OBSESSES	314 - 4	POSSESSES AND OBSESSES US
OBSESSION	456 - 2	EVIL IS BUT AN OBSESSION
OBSTACLES	059 - 3	THERE ARE NO OBSTACLES
OBSTACLES	164 - 4	BY OBSTRUCTIONS OR OBSTACLES
OBSTINATE	233 - 2	PEOPLE ARE OBSTINATE, RESISTANT
OBSTRUCTION	153 - 2	THERE IS NO OBSTRUCTION
OBSTRUCTION	164 - 4	REMOVES THE OBSTRUCTION
OBSTRUCTIONS	219 - 3	THESE MENTAL OBSTRUCTIONS
OBSTRUCTIONS	282 - 4	NO OBSTRUCTIONS TO THE OPERATION OF TRUTH
OBSTRUCTIONS	352 - 5	OBSTRUCTIONS ARE UNKNOWN TO MIND
OBTAINED	445 - 2	OBTAINED THROUGH MAN'S KNOWLEDGE
OCCULT	031 - 3	NOT THROUGH MYSTERIES OR OCCULT
OCCULT	046 - 6	NO OCCULT TRICK
OCCULT	437 - 4	JESUS HAD AN OCCULT POWER
OCCUPATION	168 - 1	NO MATTER WHAT THE OCCUPATION
OCCUPIES	052 - 2	OCCUPIES ALL SPACE
OCCUPY	376 - 1	CAN OCCUPY THE SAME SPACE
OCEAN	121 - 4	WATER IS NOT THE OCEAN
OCEAN	259 - 1	THE DAMPNESS OF THE OCEAN
OCEAN	307 - 1	HOW BIG THE OCEAN IS
OCEAN	312 - 4	IT WILL BE THE OCEAN AS A WAVE
OCEAN	388 - 3	THE OCEAN IN THE DROP OF WATER
OFFICE	194 - 4	THE OFFICE OF THE WILL TO DETERMINE
OFFICE	403 - 3	OFFICE OF THE INNER MIND
OFFICE	418 - 4	THE OFFICE OF THE IMAGINATION
OFFSET	173 - 3	OFFSET THESE APPARENT CONDITIONS
OFFSPRING	372 - 2	HIMSELF IN HIS OFFSPRING
OFFSPRING	391 - 3	HAVE NO INDEPENDENT OFFSPRING
OFFSPRING	484 - 5	SPIRIT AS ITS OWN OFFSPRING
OFF THE TRACK	446 - 3	WE ARE OFF THE TRACK
OIL	311 - 2	COAL AND OIL WE BURN TODAY
OIL	415 - 1	THE OIL OF THE ETERNAL
OIL	430 - 2	BURNING WITH THE OIL OF PURE SPIRIT
OLD	059 - 2	TOO OLD TO FIND MY RIGHTFUL PLACE
OLD	147 - 4	OLD MENTAL REACTIONS
OLD	167 - 2	OLD SYSTEM OF THOUGHT
OLD	239 - 3	LIFE CANNOT GROW OLD
OLD	287 - 1	OLD LAW THAT WE CAN EXPAND
OLD	365 - 3	IN THE OLD ORDER WE THOUGHT
OLD	486 - 5	OLD CONCEPTS OF DISEASE AND FAILURE
OLD AGE	249 - 2	WHAT IS CALLED OLD AGE
OLD AGE	376 - 2	FREE FROM DISEASE, OLD AGE
OLDEN	295 - 3	OLDEN TIMES USED TO INSTRUCT
OLD MAN	363 - 4	PUT OFF THE OLD MAN
OLD NIGHT	053 - 5	CHAOS AND OLD NIGHT
OLD THOUGHT	365 - 4	ERROR AS IN THE OLD THOUGHT
OMNIPOTENT	206 - 4	OMNIPOTENT POWER WHICH IS
OMNIPOTENT	337 - 4	UNIVERSAL SOUL, OMNIPOTENT LAW
OMNIPRESENCE	059 - 2	GOD IS OMNIPRESENCE
OMNIPRESENCE	276 - 2	RECOGNITION OF THE OMNIPRESENCE
OMNIPRESENT	087 - 3	INFINITE IS OMNIPRESENT
OMNIPRESENT	121 - 2	OMNIPRESENT IT IS IN US
OMNIPRESENT	165 - 3	UNIVERSAL MIND BEING OMNIPRESENT

OMNIPRESENT	198 - 5	UNIVERSAL AND OMNIPRESENT
OMNIPRESENT	231 - 1	THE BEAUTY OF THE OMNIPRESENT GOD
OMNIPRESENT	323 - 3	THE ONLY GOD THERE IS, IS OMNIPRESENT
OMNIPRESENT	340 - 4	WE SHALL BE OMNIPRESENT
OMNIPRESENT	422 - 2	CONSCIOUSNESS IS ALWAYS OMNIPRESENT
OMNISCIENCE	156 - 3	OMNISCIENCE, OMNIPOTENCE
OMNISCIENCE	342 - 2	OMNISCIENCE IN THE ANIMAL
OMNISCIENT	066 - 2	IS OMNISCIENT, ALL-KNOWING
ONE	026 - 2	ONE WITH THE GREAT LAW OF ITS OWN BEING
ONE	029 - 3	BECAUSE HE IS ONE WITH THE WHOLE
ONE	029 - 4	USE WE ARE MAKING OF THE ONE LAW
ONE	034 - 2	MAN IS ONE WITH GOD
ONE	034 - 2	ONE WITH THE WHOLE
ONE	068 - 3	ALL THINGS MUST BE ONE
ONE	068 - 3	INFINITE MUST BE ONE
ONE	069 - 2	MANY LIVE IN THE ONE
ONE	076 - 2	ONE AND THE SAME MIND
ONE	076 - 4	THE UNIVERSE HAS TO BE ONE
ONE	082 - 1	FROM THE ONE
ONE	082 - 2	WITHIN THIS ONE ALL LIVE
ONE	087 - 2	FOR THE TWO ARE REALLY ONE
ONE	093 - 4	BUT IN REALITY THEY ARE ONE
ONE	112 - 3	ONE WITH EVERYTHING PHYSICAL
ONE	116 - 3	ONE SUBSTANCE IN THE UNIVERSE
ONE	122 - 3	WE MUST BE ONE WITH THE LAW
ONE	123 - 2	TEACHER HAS KNOWN THAT GOD IS ONE
ONE	133 - 2	HE IS ONE WITH THE WHOLE
ONE	138 - 4	ONE OF ITS ACTIVITIES
ONE	171 - 3	SINCE THERE IS ONLY ONE
ONE	178 - 5	SINCE THERE IS BUT ONE MIND
ONE	184 - 3	ONE ALONE IN CONSCIOUSNESS
ONE	192 - 1	GOD IS THE ONE LIFE
ONE	195 - 3	ONE WITH THE WHOLE
ONE	195 - 3	ONE WITH UNMANIFEST SUBSTANCE
ONE	204 - 2	ONE PRESENCE
ONE	205 - 4	EACH IS IN THE ONE MIND
ONE	205 - 4	UPON THE ONE MIND
ONE	206 - 3	ONE COMMON MIND
ONE	208 - 2	ONE SUBJECTIVE MIND IN THE UNIVERSE
ONE	209 - 5	THERE IS ONLY ONE LAW
ONE	222 - 3	ONE FOR WHOM YOU ARE WORKING
ONE	227 - 4	ONE MIND, WHICH MIND IS GOD
ONE	234 - 4	THERE IS BUT ONE MIND
ONE	236 - 6	ONLY ONE FIRST CAUSE
ONE	237 - 3	ONE FUNDAMENTAL INTELLIGENCE
ONE	237 - 3	ONE MIND MANIFESTS AS PERSON
ONE	241 - 3	CONSCIOUSNESS OF THE ONE INDWELLING
ONE	245 - 1	THE PREMISE OF ONE POWER
ONE	258 - 5	I AM AT ONE WITH ALL
ONE	273 - 4	THE ONE TO ITSELF
ONE	282 - 4	STAY WITH THE ONE AND NEVER DEVIATE
ONE	284 - 2	THERE IS BUT ONE MIND
ONE	290 - 2	THERE IS ONE INFINITE MIND
ONE	291 - 2	THERE IS BUT ONE MIND
ONE	292 - 3	THERE IS ONE LIFE

ONE	295 - 1	EVERYTHING ORIGINATES IN THE ONE
ONE	296 - 4	"I AND MY FATHER ARE ONE"
ONE	296 - 4	ONE WITH THE INFINITE MIND
ONE	296 - 4	ONE WITH THE PERSONALITY OF GOD
ONE	299 - 3	I AM ONE WITH LIFE
ONE	303 - 1	THE ONE PERFECT POWER
ONE	312 - 3	THE PHYSICAL UNIVERSE IS ONE
ONE	328 - 4	ONE AND THE SAME TRUTH
ONE	330 - 4	ONE COMMON LAW OF LOVE
ONE	332 - 2	MAY BE ONE EVEN AS WE ARE ONE
ONE	332 - 3	ONE WITH EACH OTHER
ONE	334 - 2	TURN TOWARD THE ONE AND ONLY POWER
ONE	335 - 2	ONE OF THE MOST ILLUMINATING
ONE	343 - 5	AS WE ENTER INTO THE ONE
ONE	357 - 3	RECOGNIZE IT AS THE ONE
ONE	382 - 1	BELIEVES ONLY IN THE ONE
ONE	388 - 3	IS ONE AND THE SAME GOD
ONE	392 - 1	GOD AND MAN ARE ONE
ONE	393 - 3	NOT TWO MINDS BUT ONE
ONE	396 - 3	SPIRITUAL MAN IS ONE
ONE	401 - 2	THERE IS BUT ONE MIND
ONE	408 - 3	IS REALLY ONLY ONE MAN VIEWED
ONE	412 - 3	THE UNIVERSE IS ONE AND NEVER TWO
ONE	415 - 3	AS ONE ALL-EMBRACING MIND
ONE	420 - 2	ONE OF THE MOST ILLUMINATING
ONE	420 - 4	THE ONE ENCOMPASSES AND FLOWS
ONE	422 - 3	THERE IS ONE FATHER OF ALL
ONE	429 - 1	RANGE OF ONE HUMAN EXPERIENCE
ONE	431 - 2	ONE RETURNS TO ONE
ONE	459 - 4	GOD AND MAN ARE ONE
ONE	476 - 1	AS IT IS ONE WITH POWER
ONE	499 - 4	IT IS ONE AND NEVER TWO
ONE ENERGY	035 - 3	THERE IS ONE ENERGY
ONE LAW	133 - 3	ONE MIND AND ONE LAW
ONE LORD	493 - 5	ONE LORD, ONE FAITH, ONE BAPTISM
ONE LIFE	035 - 3	THERE IS ONE LIFE
ONE MIND	133 - 3	ONE MIND AND ONE LAW
ONENESS	076 - 4	A PERCEPTION OF ONENESS
ONENESS	127 - 4	ONENESS WITH GOD AND LAW
ONENESS	210 - 1	OUR ONENESS WITH GOD
ONENESS	230 - 2	ONENESS WITH ALL GOOD
ONENESS	231 - 3	ONENESS OF GOD AND MAN
ONENESS	239 - 2	ONENESS WITH INFINITE INTELLIGENCE
ONENESS	239 - 3	ONENESS WITH THE GOD LIFE
ONENESS	243 - 2	ONENESS WITH INFINITE LIFE
ONENESS	249 - 1	MY ONENESS IN ESSENCE
ONENESS	251 - 2	MY IMMEDIATE ONENESS WITH GOD
ONENESS	261 - 4	ITS ONENESS WITH SPIRIT
ONENESS	300 - 4	REALIZING OUR ONENESS WITH IT
ONENESS	332 - 2	MAN CLEARLY RECOGNIZES HIS ONENESS
ONENESS	366 - 4	HIS ONENESS WITH GOD
ONE ONE ONE	117 - 2	ONE, ONE, ONE!! NO GREATER UNITY COULD BE
ONE ONE ONE	323 - 3	ONE! ONE! ONE! I AM GOD
ONE ONE ONE	493 - 6	ONE, ONE, ONE…NEVER TWO
ONESELF	369 - 1	ONESELF A DIVINE PRESENCE

ONE SPIRIT	035 - 3	THERE IS ONE SPIRIT
ONE STUFF	105 - 3	THEY ALL COME FROM ONE STUFF
ONE SUBSTANCE	311 - 2	COMES FROM ONE SUBSTANCE
ONLOOK	307 - 3	ONLOOK THOU THE DEITY
ONLY	100 - 2	ONLY THING IN THE UNIVERSE
ONLY	109 - 2	THE ONLY WAY GOD CAN
ONLY	142 - 2	AND THINK OF THIS ONLY
ONLY	188 - 4	ONLY INQUIRIES WE NEED
ONLY	225 - 1	ONLY METHOD WE KNOW
ONLY	286 - 3	CAN HAVE ONLY WHAT WE CAN TAKE
ONLY	301 - 3	RETURN TO US ONLY WHAT WE THINK
ONLY	302 - 3	ONLY WHAT YOU WISH TO EXPERIENCE
ONLY	382 - 2	ONLY REASON FOR INTRODUCING
ONLY	390 - 5	SPIRIT IS REALLY THE ONLY MIND
ONLY	395 - 3	ONLY THE POWER HE DECREES
ONLY	396 - 2	ONLY THE POWER WHICH HE GIVES
ONLY	416 - 4	ONLY THAT WHICH WE KNOW
ONLY	431 - 3	ONLY IN SO DOING CAN WE ENTER
ONLY	463 - 2	ONLY AS WE LIVE IN CONSCIOUS UNION
ONLY LIFE	343 - 4	ONLY LIFE MAN HAS IS FROM WITHIN
OPEN	047 - 1	THE DOOR IS OPEN
OPEN	059 - 3	OPEN TO A NEW INFLUX OF SPIRIT
OPEN	293 - 1	OPEN THE PORTALS OF MY SOUL
OPEN	369 - 1	WE MUST OPEN IF WE ARE TO RECIEVE
OPEN	455 - 3	BECAUSE THEY OPEN UP GREATER
OPENETH	157 - 3	OPENETH HIS HAND AND SATISFIETH
OPEN FACE	489 - 5	OPEN FACE BEHOLDING AS IN A GLASS
OPENS	164 - 4	TREATMENT OPENS UP THE AVENUES
OPERATE	184 - 2	SPIRIT CAN OPERATE FOR THE INDIVIDUAL
OPERATE	205 - 5	SOIL OPERATE ON THE SEED
OPERATE	269 - 2	OPERATE AS A LAW OF LIBERTY
OPERATE	276 - 2	OPERATE ON THAT WHICH IS KNOWN
OPERATE	364 - 3	LIFE OPERATE THROUGH HIM
OPERATE	377 - 2	SOUL CAN OPERATE INDEPENDENTLY
OPERATE	412 - 3	REFUSES TO OPERATE AGAINST ITSELF
OPERATE	421 - 1	TRUTH OPERATE THROUGH LAW
OPERATES	034 - 1	IN SO FAR AS IT OPERATES
OPERATES	084 - 3	SPIRIT OPERATES THROUGH LAW
OPERATES	170 - 5	MIND OPERATES THROUGH THE PATIENT
OPERATES	421 - 4	OPERATES THROUGH THE SUBJECTIVE
OPERATING	117 - 2	INTELLIGENCE OPERATING
OPERATING	170 - 2	OPERATING AS THE TRUTH
OPERATING	184 - 2	ONLY BY OPERATING THROUGH HIM
OPERATING	200 - 5	EXPERIENCE OPERATING THROUGH PEOPLE
OPERATING	391 - 2	OPERATING THROUGH THE THOUGHT
OPERATION	130 - 1	OPERATION WITH HER LAWS
OPERATION	132 - 7	OPERATION OF SPIRIT IS THROUGH
OPERATION	163 - 2	LAW IS ALWAYS IN OPERATION
OPERATIONS	140 - 4	MIND DOES ITS OPERATIONS
OPERATIVE	077 - 4	OPERATIVE THROUGH A UNIVERSAL MEDIUM
OPERATIVE	111 - 1	MUST BE ETERNALLY OPERATIVE
OPERATIVE	141 - 2	OPERATIVE THROUGH OUR OWN THOUGHT
OPERATIVE	171 - 3	WORK IS OPERATIVE THROUGH A FIELD
OPERATIVE	177 - 4	MORE OR LESS OPERATIVE
OPINION	025 - 1	SCIENCE KNOWS NOTHING OF OPINION

OPINION	056 - 2	IS OF THE SAME OPINION STILL
OPINION	113 - 2	OPINION IS OUR ESTIMATE OF REALITY
OPINION	301 - 4	WORLD'S OPINION TO CONTROL OUR THINKING
OPINION	417 - 1	HUMAN OPINION BELIEVES
OPINION	437 - 1	BUILDS HIS HOME ON FALSE OPINION
OPINIONS	418 - 2	SWAYED BY THE OPINIONS OF OTHERS
OPPORTUNITIES	204 - 2	OPPORTUNITIES GOVERN YOU
OPPORTUNITIES	290 - 3	A BELIEF IN LIMITED OPPORTUNITIES
OPPORTUNITIES	291 - 1	EXIST IN LIMITLESS OPPORTUNITIES
OPPORTUNITIES	304 - 6	MY OPPORTUNITIES ARE UNLIMITED
OPPORTUNITY	264 - 2	OPPORTUNITY FOR SELF-EXPRESSION
OPPORTUNITY	264 - 2	OPERATE UPON THIS OPPORTUNITY
OPPORTUNITY	279 - 1	IF WE ARE WITHOUT OPPORTUNITY
OPPORTUNITY	290 - 3	ONE OPPORTUNITY WHICH COMES TO MAN
OPPORTUNITY	291 - 1	POINT OF LIMITLESS OPPORTUNITY
OPPORTUNITY	291 - 1	OPPORTUNITY IS RIGHT HERE TODAY
OPPORTUNITY	292 - 3	THE MIDST OF ETERNAL OPPORTUNITY
OPPORTUNITY	304 - 5	A GOOD MEDITATION FOR OPPORTUNITY
OPPOSED	114 - 1	OPPOSED TO THE SELF-EVIDENT
OPPOSED	161 - 2	UNIVERSE AS OPPOSED TO ITSELF
OPPOSED	209 - 5	AS OPPOSED TO A LAW OF DISEASE
OPPOSED	316 - 1	NOT OPPOSED TO THE MEDICAL PRACTITIONER
OPPOSING	133 - 5	THE OPERATION OF OPPOSING POWERS
OPPOSING	237 - 1	OPPOSING DESIRES WHICH CONFLICT
OPPOSITE	176 - 1	OPPOSITE AND EQUAL REACTION
OPPOSITE	194 - 2	VERY OPPOSITE TO OUR WISHES
OPPOSITE	194 - 2	OPPOSITE TO THE POWER OF GOOD
OPPOSITE	221 - 4	BY AN OPPOSITE ONE
OPPOSITE	461 - 4	GOD HAS NO OPPOSITE
OPPOSITES	082 - 1	NO OPPOSITES AND NO OPPOSITION
OPPOSITES	133 - 5	APPEAR TO BE OPPOSITES ARE NOT REALLY
OPPOSITES	189 - 3	TRUTH KNOWS NO OPPOSITES
OPPOSITES	286 - 1	DEAL WITH THE PAIRS OF OPPOSITES
OPPOSITION	127 - 4	OPPOSITION IS REMOVED
OPPOSITION	160 - 1	NO OPPOSITION TO IT
OPPOSITION	411 - 1	OPPOSITION OR APPARENT SEPARATION
OPPOSITION	412 - 3	GOD COULD BE IN OPPOSITION
OPPOSITION	436 - 1	OPPOSITION TO THE FUNDAMENTAL HARMONY
OPULENT	263 - 5	LIFE HAPPY AND OPULENT
ORATORY	497 - 5	ORATORY WE CALL IT INSPIRATION
ORBED	359 - 3	CHRIST WAS MORE FULLY ORBED
ORDAIN	107 - 4	IT COULD NOT ORDAIN THAT MAN
ORDAINED	260 - 2	SPIRITUAL AND DIVINELY ORDAINED
ORDAINED	395 - 1	SPIRIT HAS ALREADY ORDAINED
ORDAINS	109 - 3	DIVINE DECREE ORDAINS SUFFERING
ORDER	031 - 3	LAW AND OF MECHANICAL ORDER
ORDER	043 - 1	IRRESPECTIVE OF LAW AND ORDER
ORDER	051 - 1	THE NEW ORDER
ORDER	060 - 3	ANY RELIGION SECT OR ORDER
ORDER	085 - 4	A SEQUENCE OF LAW AND ORDER
ORDER	190 - 1	UNIVERSE OF LAW AND ORDER
ORDER	235 - 3	TO THE DIVINE ORDER
ORDER	248 - 3	DIVINE ORDER REIGNS THROUGHOUT
ORDER	254 - 6	PERFECT AND DIVINE ORDER
ORDER	337 - 2	PART OF THIS SPIRITUAL ORDER

ORDER	365 - 4	IN THE NEW ORDER OF THOUGHT
ORDERLY	255 - 4.	ORDERLY BALANCE
ORDERS	397 - 3	ORDERS THAT ARE GIVEN
ORGAN	073 - 1	THE ORGAN OF THOUGHT
ORGAN	198 - 4	ORGAN OF THE BODY SPECIFICALLY
ORGAN	230 - 4	FAIL TO USE ANY ORGAN
ORGAN	256 - 2	NO ORGAN IN THE BODY
ORGANISM	073 - 2	BACK OF THE ORGANISM
ORGANIZATION	162 - 4	IMMERSED IN OBJECTIVE ORGANIZATION
ORGANIZED	312 - 3	ONLY WHEN KNOWLEDGE IS ORGANIZED
ORGANS	232 - 4	THE ORGANS OF OUR BODY
ORIGIN	035 - 3	THAT IS THE ORIGIN OF EVERYTHING
ORIGIN	201 - 5	MENTAL IN THEIR ORIGIN
ORIGINAL	036 - 2	IS ONE ORIGINAL CAUSE
ORIGINAL	085 - 3	AND ORIGINAL CREATIVE ENERGY
ORIGINAL	267 - 3	IN ITS ORIGINAL STATE FILLS ALL SPACE
ORIGINAL	393 - 3	ORIGINAL MIND AND ORIGINAL ENERGY
ORIGINAL	393 - 3	ORIGINAL MIND OF GOD
ORIGINAL STATE	052 - 4	IN ITS ORIGINAL STATE
ORIGINATED	148 - 3	CREATION COULD HAVE ORIGINATED ONLY IN
ORIGINATES	295 - 1	EVERYTHING ORIGINATES IN THE ONE
ORTHODOX	138 - 1	MOST ORTHODOX OF MEDICAL CIRCLES
OTHER	301 - 1	ONE IS THE CAUSE OF THE OTHER
OTHERNESS	358 - 3	THERE IS NO SENSE OF OTHERNESS
OTHERS	028 - 2	AND NOT TO OTHERS
OTHERS	130 - 6	HE CAN THINK FOR OTHERS
OTHERWISE	051 - 3	HE BE WISE OR OTHERWISE
OTHERWISE	385 - 3	FEEL OTHERWISE SEEMS UNTHINKABLE
OUR	052 - 5	OUR OWN PUNISHMENT
OUR	469 - 2	DOWN TO OUR OWN EXPERIENCE
OUR FATHER	343 - 4	OUR FATHER WHICH ART IN HEAVEN
OUR HOPE	503 - 2	CHRIST IN US OUR HOPE
OUR PART	272 - 2	OUR PART IS TO BE READY
OURSELVES	036 - 1	WHICH WE FIND IN OURSELVES
OURSELVES	036 - 3	SEE OURSELVES
OURSELVES	328 - 3	WE MUST LEARN IT FOR OURSELVES
OURSELVES	338 - 2	ALONE TO DISCOVER OURSELVES
OURSELVES	488 - 1	OURSELVES AS GOD KNOWS US
OUR SOUL	034 - 1	OUR SOUL WILL NEVER CHANGE
OUT	060 - 3	THE TRUTH WILL OUT
OUTCOME	339 - 2	OUTCOME OF UNIVERSAL
OUTCOME	354 - 1	WILL SEE THE FINAL OUTCOME
OUTCOME	408 - 2	LAW IS THE OUTCOME OF LOVE
OUTCOME	448 - 1	LOGICAL OUTCOME OF HIS INNER VISION
OUTCOME	474 - 4	LOGICAL OUTCOME OF TASTING OF DUAL
OUTER	126 - 2	HAPPEN IN THE OUTER EXPERIENCE
OUTER	446 - 1	WHEN THE OUTER VOICE IS QUIET
OUTER	475 - 5	IS THE OUTER QUICKENING
OUTER	490 - 3	OUTER MAN BECOMES CHANGED
OUTER	490 - 4	OUTER IS BROUGHT ABOUT BY THE SPIRIT
OUTER MAN	349 - 2	OUTER MAN NEVER CONSCIOUSLY KNEW
OUTER RIM	462 - 3	OUTER RIM OF SPIRITUAL EXISTENCE
OUTER RIM	486 - 2	OUTER RIM OF REALITY
OUTER WORLD	400 - 2	OBJECTIVE FORM IN THE OUTER WORLD
OUT-GOING	229 - 2	WITH EVERY OUT-GOING BREATH

OUTLET	035 – 3	EVERGY FINDS AN OUTLET
OUTLET	040 – 1	MUST HAVE AN OUTLET
OUTLET	218 – 4	CORRESPONDING OUTLET IN THE PHYSICAL MAN
OUTLET	273 – 5	OUTLET IN TWO WAYS
OUTLET	498 – 1	OUTLET AS WELL AS AN INLET
OUTLETS	489 – 7	CONSCIOUSLY BECOME OUTLETS
OUTLINE	101 – 2	THE POSSIBILITY OF OUTLINE
OUTLINE	176 – 3	OUTLINE AS A SCIENTIFIC TREATMENT
OUTLINE	208 – 5	CONSCIOUS OF OUTLINE
OUTLINED	115 – 4	PRODUCE THE THING OUTLINED
OUTLINES	314 – 1	BOUND BY THE OUTLINES OF THE FORMS
OUTLINING	301 – 1	NEVER OUTLINING HOW IT SHALL BE DONE
OUTLIVED	376 – 3	OUTLIVED MANY PHYSICAL BODIES
OUTLOOK	435 – 1	WITH A BRIGHTER OUTLOOK
OUT-PICTURE	140 – 4	INEVITABLY OUT-PICTURE
OUT-POURING	420 – 3	A FOREVER OUT-POURING SPIRIT
OUTPOURING	059 – 2	OUTPOURING OF OUR SUBJECTIVE WORDS
OUTPOURING	460 – 6	ETERNAL OUTPOURING OF SPIRIT
OUTPUSH	420 – 4	OUTPUSH OF LIFE INTO SELF-EXPRESSION
OUT-PUSH	247 – 3	BY THE OUT-PUSH OF SPIRIT
OUTPUSIIER	408 – 2	LOVE IS THE OUTPUSHER
OUTSIDE	144 – 2	OUTSIDE OF THE SAME THING
OUTSIDE	173 – 4	NEVER GET OUTSIDE OURSELVES
OUTSIDE	180 – 3	HEAVEN AS BEING OUTSIDE HIMSELF
OUTSIDE	217 – 2	OUTSIDE OF OURSELVES
OUTSIDE	262 – 1	SOME POWER OUTSIDE MYSELF
OUTSIDE	289 – 2	INSIDE THE OTHER THE OUTSIDE
OUTSIDE	338 – 2	OUTSIDE INFLUENCE TO ENTER
OUTSIDE	399 – 1	OUTSIDE AND THIS IS IMPOSSIBLE
OUTSIDE	447 – 3	IMPOSSIBLE TO EMBODY ANYTHING OUTSIDE
OUTSIDE	463 – 4	CAUSE OUTSIDE OF SPIRIT
OUTSIDE	486 – 2	GOD KNOWS NO OUTSIDE
OUTSTRETCHED	370 – 1	OUTSTRETCHED HAND OF THE UNIVERSE
OUTWARD	039 – 6	OUTWARD MANIFESTATION IN OUR MATERIAL
OUTWARD	115 – 4	OUTWARD LIFE IS A RESULT
OUTWARD	432 – 1	FAST WITHOUT OUTWARD SIGN
OUTWARD	432 – 2	OUTWARD THINGS WHICH ARE NECESSARY
OUTWARD	455 – 7	TOO USED TO THE OUTWARD SIGN
OUTWARDLY	140 – 4	WHAT WE OUTWARDLY ARE
OUTWARDLY	411 – 4	WE OUTWARDLY EXPERIENCE
OUTWARD SIGN	475 – 5	OUTWARD SIGN OF THE INNER BELIEF
OVERACTION	255 – 1	THERE IS NO OVERACTION
OVER AND OVER	233 – 3	THE THOUGHT OVER AND OVER
OVERCOME	048 – 2	OVERCOME HIS DOUBTS
OVERCOME	146 – 2	OVERCOME EVERY OBSTACLE
OVERCOME	164 – 3	WE CANNOT OVERCOME IT
OVERCOME	185 – 3	TO OVERCOME HIS LIMITATION
OVERCOME	448 – 4	THOUGHT OF GOOD MUST EVER OVERCOME
OVERCOME	487 – 3	OVERCOME EVIL WITH GOOD
OVERCOMES	404 – 4	CONFIDENCE OVERCOMES THE DEPRESSION
OVERCOMING	152 – 2	OVERCOMING GOD'S
OVERCOMING	421 – 3	OVERCOMING OF ALL EVIL BY GOOD
OVERCONCERNED	442 – 4	OVERCONCERNED WITH NON-ESSENTIALS
OVEREAT	259 – 3	OVEREAT OR TO EAT THE WRONG THINGS
OVERLOOKED	388 – 3	WE HAVE OVERLOOKED

OVERLOOKED	417 - 3	MUST NEVER BE OVERLOOKED
OVER-MIND	044 - 4	OVER-MIND MUST BE ACCEPTED
OVERSHADOW	413 - 4	OVERSHADOW THE THOUGHTS AND ACTIONS
OVERSHADOWING	435 - 1	OVERSHADOWING ETERNITY MUST ALSO
OVERSHADOWS	153 - 5	A LOVE WHICH OVERSHADOWS
OVER-SHADOWS	038 - 5	OVER-SHADOWS ETERNITY AND FINDS
OVERSOUL	032 - 2	THE OVERSOUL OR ETERNAL SPIRIT
OVERWORKED	226 - 3	I AM OVERWORKED
OWN	092 - 2	OWN ABILITY TO DO
OWN	188 - 1	KNOW YOUR OWN MIND
OWN I	478 - 1	WHEN WE UNDERSTAND OUR OWN I

P

PAEAN	495 - 5	PAEAN OF PRAISE A PSALM OF BEAUTY
PAID	502 - 3	PAID WHEN WE LET GO AND TRUST
PAIN	099 - 2	PAIN AND FEAR ARE IN CONSCIOUSNESS
PAIN	099 - 4	EXPERIENCE OF PAIN AND SICKNESS
PAIN	109 - 3	ETERNAL REALITY TO PAIN
PAIN	213 - 3	NO SUCH THING AS PAIN
PAIN	223 - 3	WHERE PAIN SEEMS TO OPERATE
PAIN	224 - 1	PAIN IS ELIMINATED
PAINSTAKING	378 - 1	YEARS OF PAINSTAKING INVESTIGATION
PAINT	222 - 5	SHALL PAINT THE THING
PANORAMA	103 - 1	VAST OBJECTIVE PANORAMA
PARADISE	491 - 2	WE SHALL ENTER THE PARADISE
PARADISE	504 - 2	PARADISE THROUGH THE GATEWAY OF LOVE
PARALYSIS	240 - 4	THE MANIFESTATION OF PARALYSIS
PARALYSIS	241 - 2	SUFFERING FROM PARALYSIS
PARALYSIS	241 - 3	HEALING OF ANY CASE OF PARALYSIS
PARALYZED	240 - 4	LIFE CANNOT BECOME PARALYZED
PARALYZED	281 - 3	PARALYZED MAN TAKE UP THY BED
PARALYZED	359 - 4	FRONT OF A PARALYZED MAN
PARENTAGE	499 - 3	UNBELIEF HAVING NO PARENTAGE
PARENT MIND	132 - 8	AS HAS THE FATHER OR PARENT MIND
PARENTS	210 - 4	TEACH THE PARENTS HOW TO THINK
PARENTS	449 - 5	PARENTS SYMBOLIZE THIS HEAVENLY PARENTAGE
PART	098 - 2	FOR WE KNOW IN PART
PART	132 - 3	PART OF REALITY WHICH ACTS AS LAW
PART	133 - 2	PART OF HIM WHICH HAS VOLITION
PART	277 - 2	BECOMES A PART OF THE LAW
PART	313 - 4	WE ARE SOME PART OF EACH OTHER
PART	373 - 2	WE ARE SOME PART OF LIFE
PART	392 - 1	LAW OF THE APPARENT PART
PART	397 - 4	MAN IS SOME PART OF GOD
PART	447 - 2	BE HEALED IN PART
PARTAKE	040 - 4	AS WE PARTAKE OF ITS NATURE
PARTAKE	107 - 2	AS EFFECT MUST PARTAKE
PARTAKE	119 - 3	I PARTAKE OF THE NATURE AND BOUNTY
PARTAKE	187 - 2	PARTAKE OF THE NATURE OF ITS CAUSE
PARTAKES	033 - 4	PARTAKES OF THE NATURE
PARTAKES	034 - 1	PARTAKES OF THE NATURE
PARTAKES	357 - 3	EACH PARTAKES OF THE CHRIST

PARTAKING	058 - 1	PARTAKING OF THIS ORIGINAL NATURE
PARTAKING	310 - 3	PARTAKING OF THE SAME NATURE
PARTAKING	497 - 4	PLANE PARTAKING OF THE NATURE
PARTIAL	153 - 2	ONE OF PARTIAL BELIEF
PARTIAL	437 - 4	BELIEVE IN A PARTIAL GOD
PARTICLES	094 - 2	NO TWO PHYSICAL PARTICLES
PARTICLES	373 - 5	AGGREGATION OF SMALL PARTICLES
PARTICLES	374 - 1	NEW PARTICLES HAVE TAKEN
PARTICULAR	045 - 2	THAT PARTICULAR THING
PARTICULAR	046 - 5	DEMONSTRATE SOME PARTICULAR GOOD
PARTICULAR	202 - 2	PARTICULAR KIND OF TROUBLE
PARTICULAR	401 - 2	PARTICULAR EFFECT MAY BE CHANGED
PARTICULAR	417 - 3	GREATER THAN ANY PARTICULAR USE
PARTICULARIZATION	337 - 3	UNITY TO THE POINT OF PARTICULARIZATION
PARTNERSHIP	415 - 2	A DIVINE PARTNERSHIP HAS ALREADY BEEN
PARTS	269 - 1	THE PARTS TO THE WHOLE
PARTS	391 - 2	THAT IS WITHOUT PARTS
PASS	046 - 4	PASS THROUGH OUR CONSCIOUSNESS
PASS	441 - 2	EVERYTHING TO PASS IN DUE TIME
PASS	492 - 2	PASS FROM ONE EXPERIENCE TO ANOTHER
PASSED	379 - 1	PASSED ON MIGHT STILL BE NEAR US
PASSING	385 - 1	PASSING IN A DIFFERENT LIGHT
PASSION	228 - 2	TROUBLE IS A CONSUMING PASSION
PASSION	428 - 1	PASSION AND LUST FOR POWER HAVE STREWN
PASSIONS	225 - 3	PASSIONS AND EVERYTHING WHICH
PASSIVE	047 - 3	PASSIVE MEDITATION WILL NEVER
PASS ON	270 - 4	IF WE SHOULD PASS ON TONIGHT
PASS ON	341 - 1	PASS ON TO ANOTHER PLANE
PAST	059 - 4	PAST MISTAKE CAN HINDER
PAST	095 - 1	NO PAST, PRESENT OR FUTURE
PAST	187 - 1	BY ANY PAST EXPERIENCE
PAST	245 - 4	THE PAST THAT CAN DISTURB ME
PAST	245 - 4	IN THE PAST HAVE CAUSED ANXIETY
PAST	245 - 4	THE SPIRIT KNOWS NO PAST
PAST	246 - 2	NO PAST TO BRING DISCORD INTO THE PRESENT
PAST	246 - 2	I LOVE MY PAST
PAST	264 - 3	NO PAST, PRESENT AND FUTURE TO IT
PAST	264 - 5	NO FEAR AS A RESULT OF MY PAST
PAST	353 - 3	LOOK INTO THE PAST AND SEE
PAST	353 - 3	PAST IS AN ACTIVE THING IN THE PRESENT
PAST	384 - 4	JUDGING THE FUTURE BY THE PAST
PAST	422 - 2	THE PAST AND THE PRESENT ARE ONE
PAST	471 - 4	FORGET THE PAST AND LIVE
PAST AND PRESENT	352 - 5	PAST AND PRESENT ARE ONE
PATH	116 - 3	PATH THROUGH THIS LIFE
PATH	219 - 3	IN YOUR PATH
PATH	270 - 1	INTO THE PATH OF TRUE RIGHTEOUSNESS
PATH	271 - 4	THEN WE ARE ON THE RIGHT PATH
PATHS	185 - 2	INTO THE PATHS OF PERFECTION
PATHWAY	041 - 2	SHADOW ACROSS THE PATHWAY
PATHWAY	059 - 3	PATHWAY OF TRUTH
PATHWAY	133 - 5	PATHWAY TO FREEDOM
PATHWAY	333 - 4	THE SOUL IS ON THE PATHWAY
PATHWAY	335 - 2	EXPERIENCE ON THE PATHWAY
PATHWAY	390 - 3	THE PATHWAY OF HIS EXPERIENCE

PATHWAY	419 - 4	THE PATHWAY OF EXPERIENCE
PATHWAY	439 - 2	THE SOUL IS ON THE PATHWAY
PATHWAY	490 - 7	PATHWAY TO PEACE AND HAPPINESS
PATIENT	059 - 5	PATIENT SHOULD TRY TO BE RECEPTIVE
PATIENT	170 - 5	OPERATES THROUGH THE PATIENT
PATIENT	178 - 6	IN WHICH HIS PATIENT LIVES
PATIENT	192 - 2	WILL LEAVE HIS PATIENT
PATIENT	206 - 4	PATIENT MUST BE RECEPTIVE
PATIENT	262 - 2	PATIENT IS PURE SPIRIT
PATIENT	316 - 2	PATIENT GO BACK TO HIS PHYSICIAN
PATIENT	413 - 5	NOT A PATIENT NOR A DISEASE
PATIENT'S	178 - 5	ACCORDING TO HIS BELIEF AND THE PATIENT'S
PATIENT'S	291 - 3	PATIENT'S MIND AND HIS OWN MIND
PATTERN	092 - 2	LIKENESS OF THE PATTERN GIVEN IT
PATTERN	140 - 2	PATTERN OUR THOUGHT GIVES IT
PATTERN	231 - 3	SUBJECTIVE MIND A NEW PATTERN
PATTERN	231 - 3	ORIGINAL PATTERN FOR PERFECT EYES
PATTERN	235 - 3	AFTER THE PATTERN OF PERFECTION
PATTERN	252 - 4	THEREBY REMOVING A PATTERN
PATTERN	256 - 5	PATTERN OF AN INFINITE
PATTERN	302 - 1	CREATE A NEW PATTERN
PATTERN	303 - 4	PERFECT IS THE PATTERN
PATTERN	491 - 6	PERFECTLY PATTERN THE DIVINE
PATTERN	494 - 2	NEW PATTERN OF THOUGHT
PATTERNS	114 - 5	CREATING FROM THE PATTERNS GIVEN IT
PATTERNS	246 - 4	PATTERNS OF THOUGHT
PATTERNS	400 - 4	IDEAS OR THOUGHT PATTERNS
PATTERNS	411 - 3	THE PATTERNS OF OUR THOUGHT
PAUL	158 - 2	PAUL ENUMERATES AT LENGTH THE EXPERIENCES
PAUSE	410 - 2	WE PAUSE AND TRY TO REALIZE
PAY	268 - 2	EVERY MAN MUST PAY THE PRICE
PEACE	036 - 4	FILLED WITH PEACE
PEACE	151 - 3	BECOMES RECEPTIVE TO THE IDEA OF PEACE
PEACE	160 - 2	POISE, PEACE AND CONFIDENCE
PEACE	165 - 2	THERE IS LACK OF PEACE
PEACE	175 - 3	PEACE WHEN THERE IS NO PEACE
PEACE	180 - 4	PEACE WITHOUT WHICH NO LIFE
PEACE	180 - 4	THE UNION OF PEACE WITH POISE
PEACE	184 - 3	WORK IN PERFECT PEACE AND CALM
PEACE	185 - 2	PEACE WHICH PASSETH UNDERSTANDING
PEACE	193 - 4	DETERMINE TO THINK PEACE
PEACE	202 - 5	REALIZATION OF PEACE
PEACE	221 - 5	A SENSE OF PEACE
PEACE	224 - 1	CALM SENSE OF PEACE AND EASE
PEACE	237 - 4	HOW TO BE AT PEACE
PEACE	246 - 5	PEACE SPOKEN TO THE NERVOUS
PEACE	247 - 1	PEACE I LEAVE WITH YOU
PEACE	248 - 1	LOVE, HARMONY AND PEACE REIGN
PEACE	264 - 3	PEACE UNTIL WE KNOW
PEACE	264 - 4	PRINCIPLE OF PEACE
PEACE	264 - 5	PEACE AND JOY ACCOMPANY ME
PEACE	267 - 2	RESIGNATION AND CALL IT PEACE
PEACE	267 - 2	BUT IT WILL NOT BE PEACE
PEACE	285 - 4	WE CANNOT ENTER INTO PEACE
PEACE	300 - 3	FROM PEACE TO GREATER PEACE

PEACE	323 - 3	ALL THE PEACE THERE IS
PEACE	383 - 2	WHICH IS AT PEACE
PEACE	412 - 1	WITH PEACE AND HAPPINESS
PEACE	430 - 1	PEACE CAN ENTER THE GATES
PEACE	430 - 1	PEACE IN THEIR MINDS AND LOVE IN THEIR
PEACE	435 - 1	RETIRE AT NIGHT IN PEACE
PEACE	440 - 5	LET YOUR PEACE COME UPON
PEACE	440 - 5	LET YOUR PEACE RETURN TO YOU
PEACE	440 - 6	PEACE RETURN UNTO
PEACE	444 - 3	PEACE IS THE POWER AT THE HEART
PEACE	445 - 2	PEACE BUT THE REVELATION
PEACE	445 - 3	PEACE IS BROUGHT ABOUT
PEACE	447 - 1	LET US COME IN PEACE
PEACE	481 - 1	PEACE WHICH THE WORLD CANNOT
PEACE	493 - 2	MAINTAIN A STATE OF PEACE
PEACE	495 - 2	SHOD WITH THE GOSPEL OF PEACE
PEACE	504 - 1	PEACE AND NOT CONFUSION
PEACEFUL	099 - 5	THE MIND PEACEFUL AND HAPPY
PEACEFUL	165 - 2	JOHN IS PEACEFUL
PEACEMAKERS	429 - 5	PEACEMAKERS ARE CALLED THE CHILDREN OF GOD
PEARL	452 - 2	PEARL OF GREAT PRICE
PECULIAR	207 - 3	THERE IS NO PECULIAR SENSATION
PENETRATE	153 - 3	PENETRATE THIS INNER CHAMBER
PENETRATE	367 - 1	SELDOM DOES THIS VOICE PENETRATE
PENETRATE	427 - 1	PENETRATE THE MEANING OF HIS TEACHING
PENETRATED	040 - 2	PENETRATED THE SECRETS OF NATURE
PENETRATED	450 - 1	FIRST PENETRATED THE INVISIBLE CAUSE
PENETRATED	452 - 3	PENETRATED THE VEIL OF ILLUSION
PENETRATES	261 - 2	PENETRATES THE MARROW
PENETRATES	375 - 2	THE ETHER PENETRATES EVERYTHING
PENETRATES	441 - 3	PENETRATES THE DEPTHS OF CREATIVE
PENETRATES	474 - 3	PENETRATES EVEN THE PRISON WALLS
PENETRATES	501 - 2	PENETRATES THE SUBJECTIVE THOUGHT
PENETRATES	503 - 3	PENETRATES ALL SUPPOSITIONAL OPPOSITES
PENETRATING	364 - 3	PENETRATING DEEPER AND YET DEEPER
PENT-UP	151 - 4	THE PENT-UP ENERGY OF LIFE
PEOPLE	133 - 3	WHICH ALL PEOPLE USE
PEOPLE	297 - 3	MUST NEVER THINK OF CERTAIN PEOPLE
PEOPLE	345 - 3	PEOPLE HAVE SENSED THAT TRUTH
PEOPLED	307 - 2	PEOPLED WITH THE PERSONIFICATIONS
PEOPLED	407 - 4	PEOPLED WITH SPIRITUAL FORMS
PEOPLES	295 - 1	PEOPLES IT WITH OUR EXPERIENCES
PERCEIVE	049 - 5	PERCEIVE THIS PERFECTION
PERCEIVE	201 - 2	PERCEIVE THE INDIVIDUAL AS A SPIRITUAL
PERCEIVE	262 - 1	PERCEIVE THIS HABIT
PERCEIVE	432 - 2	WE PERCEIVE THE UNITY OF GOOD
PERCEIVE	448 - 1	WE MENTALLY PERCEIVE
PERCEIVED	076 - 1	CAUSE OF THE OBJECT PERCEIVED
PERCEIVED	122 - 1	PERCEIVED AND PROCLAIMED THIS FACT
PERCEIVED	350 - 3	CONSCIOUSLY OR UNCONSCIOUSLY PERCEIVED
PERCEIVING	076 - 1	WAS NOT THE RESULT OF PERCEIVING
PERCEPTION	030 - 2	POINT OF CONSCIOUS PERCEPTION
PERCEPTION	075 - 4	AN INTUITIVE PERCEPTION WITHIN US
PERCEPTION	076 - 1	THE INTUITIVE PERCEPTION WAS
PERCEPTION	076 - 2	PERCEPTION AND THE PERCEIVER

PERCEPTION	093 - 5	POINT OF CONSCIOUS PERCEPTION
PERCEPTION	125 - 4	PERCEPTION OF LIFE AND HIS REACTION
PERCEPTION	148 - 3	PERCEPTION OF OUR RELATION TO THE INFINITE
PERCEPTION	150 - 5	TRUE PERCEPTION OF SPIRITUAL POWER
PERCEPTION	328 - 2	FROM MEN OF SPIRITUAL PERCEPTION
PERCEPTION	368 - 1	HEIGHTS OF SPIRITUAL PERCEPTION
PERCEPTION	372 - 1	NON-PHYSICAL FACULTY OF PERCEPTION
PERCEPTION	477 - 6	PERCEPTION OF THIS FIRST PRINCIPLE
PERCEPTIONS	287 - 2	PERCEPTIONS OF LIFE HAD PROVIDED
PERENNIALLY	456 - 5	SPRINGS PERENNIALLY FROM THE INNER LIFE
PERFECT	026 - 2	AS THE LOVE OF GOD IS PERFECT
PERFECT	026 - 2	SO THE LAW OF GOD IS ALSO PERFECT
PERFECT	039 - 6	KNOWLEDGE AND PERFECT FAITH
PERFECT	053 - 4	SPIRIT THAT IS COMPLETE AND PERFECT
PERFECT	053 - 5	BE YE THEREFORE PERFECT
PERFECT	059 - 4	WHICH IS PERFECT MAN
PERFECT	060 - 2	GOD'S WORLD IS PERFECT
PERFECT	082 - 1	PERFECT WITHIN ITSELF
PERFECT	102 - 5	THROUGH PERFECT LAW
PERFECT	108 - 4	PERFECT AS IS THE INHERENT GOD
PERFECT	130 - 3	MAN IS POTENTIALLY PERFECT
PERFECT	168 - 5	PERFECT GOD, PERFECT MAN, PERFECT BEING
PERFECT	177 - 2	SPIRITUAL MAN IS PERFECT
PERFECT	179 - 1	GOVERNED BY A PERFECT LAW
PERFECT	179 - 4	THE PERFECT MAN ALWAYS HEALS
PERFECT	179 - 4	MAN'S PERFECT STATE IN SPIRIT
PERFECT	184 - 4	UNIVERSE WERE NOT PERFECT
PERFECT	185 - 1	PEOPLE POTENTIALLY PERFECT
PERFECT	185 - 2	BE YE THEREFORE PERFECT
PERFECT	186 - 1	TREATMENT STARTS WITH PERFECT GOD
PERFECT	191 - 1	SEE A PERFECT MAN, HE WILL APPEAR
PERFECT	191 - 1	REAL MAN IS PERFECT
PERFECT	201 - 4	MAN IS FUNDAMENTALLY PERFECT
PERFECT	202 - 4	REALIZE MAN IS PERFECT
PERFECT	212 - 4	IDEA WHICH IS ALREADY PERFECT
PERFECT	213 - 2	THE PERFECT BODY IS THERE
PERFECT	217 - 2	LIVING IN A PERFECT UNIVERSE
PERFECT	217 - 2	SURROUNDED BY PERFECT SITUATIONS
PERFECT	217 - 2	GOVERNED BY PERFECT LAW
PERFECT	218 - 2	IS COMPLETE AND PERFECT
PERFECT	218 - 3	SPIRITUAL MAN IS PERFECT
PERFECT	224 - 4	IS DONE COMPLETE AND PERFECT
PERFECT	245 - 2	COMPLETE AND PERFECT
PERFECT	274 - 3	LIVE IN A PERFECT UNIVERSE
PERFECT	284 - 3	SYSTEM IS PERFECT
PERFECT	303 - 4	PERFECT IS THE PATTERN
PERFECT	303 - 4	PERFECT WILL BE THE RESULT
PERFECT	310 - 4	GOD MADE MAN PERFECT
PERFECT	317 - 1	THAT GOD IS PERFECT
PERFECT	331 - 5	METHOD IS PERFECT
PERFECT	338 - 4	PERFECT MAN IS THE ONLY MAN GOD KNOWS
PERFECT	390 - 5	COMPLETE AND PERFECT, HAPPY AND WHOLE
PERFECT	395 - 1	NATURE SHALL BE PERFECT
PERFECT	395 - 1	IT MUST BE PERFECT IN ITS NATURE
PERFECT	395 - 1	MUST PRODUCE A PERFECT EFFECT

PERFECT	407 - 4	PERFECT LAWS ON THEIR WAY
PERFECT	408 - 1	PERFECT MANIFESTATION OF THE DIVINE
PERFECT	418 - 2	MAN IS ALREADY COMPLETE AND PERFECT
PERFECT	420 - 4	A STATE OF PERFECT MANIFESTATION
PERFECT	432 - 2	PERFECT LAW WE SHALL FIND
PERFECT	435 - 1	LET US LEARN TO BE PERFECT
PERFECT	446 - 3	SPIRIT MUST BE AND IS PERFECT
PERFECT	466 - 3	PERFECT LESSON EVER TAUGHT
PERFECT	470 - 3	PERFECT BEINGS WITHIN
PERFECT	488 - 3	CONSCIOUS OF THE PERFECT
PERFECT BEING	309 - 3	GOD, PERFECT MAN AND PERFECT BEING
PERFECT GOD	159 - 2	PERFECT GOD, PERFECT MAN AND PERFECT BEING
PERFECT GOD	201 - 4	PERFECT GOD, PERFECT MAN, PERFECT BEING
PERFECT GOD	218 - 2	PERFECT GOD, PERFECT MAN AND PERFECT BEING
PERFECT GOD	309 - 2	PERFECT GOD, PERFECT MAN AND PERFECT BEING
PERFECT IDEA	197 - 3	LETTING THE PERFECT IDEA REFLECT ITSELF
PERFECTION	036 - 4	NESTLES THE SEED PERFECTION
PERFECTION	053 - 5	STANDARD IS ONE OF PERFECTION
PERFECTION	059 - 3	RECOGNIZING ONLY PERFECTION
PERFECTION	060 - 2	LIFE AS ONE OF ABSOLUTE PERFECTION
PERFECTION	184 - 1	THE SPIRITUAL PERFECTION OF THE PERSON
PERFECTION	189 - 2	ONLY PERFECTION STANDS BEFORE HIM
PERFECTION	197 - 5	OWN INABILITY TO SEE PERFECTION
PERFECTION	198 - 1	REFLECTS A GREATER PERFECTION
PERFECTION	199 - 2	REALIZE THE STATE OF PERFECTION
PERFECTION	202 - 5	RECOGNIZE YOUR OWN PERFECTION
PERFECTION	214 - 1	THE APPEARANCE PERFECTION IS
PERFECTION	222 - 1	SPIRITUAL PERFECTION OF YOUR PATIENT
PERFECTION	247 - 3	EQUALIZED BY SPIRITUAL PERFECTION
PERFECTION	254 - 2	NATURAL AND SPIRITUAL PERFECTION
PERFECTION	256 - 5	AN INFINITE AND ETERNAL PERFECTION
PERFECTION	409 - 1	IS HE TO BECOME CONSCIOUS OF PERFECTION
PERFECTION	409 - 4	PART OF ITS ETERNAL PERFECTION
PERFECTION	486 - 1	GOD KNOWS ONLY PERFECTION
PERFECTION	488 - 1	SEES AND KNOWS ONLY PERFECTION
PERFECTLY	345 - 5	TAKES PLACE IN A PERFECTLY NORMAL
PERFECTLY	470 - 4	PERFECTLY DO WE EXPRESS GOD
PERFECT MAN	218 - 2	OF PERFECT GOD, PERFECT MAN
PERFECT PRESENCE	172 - 5	REALIZE THE PERFECT PRESENCE
PERFORM	310 - 1	INTELLIGENCE TO PERFORM A CERTAIN ACT
PERFORMANCE	275 - 2	PRINCIPLE BUT IN PERFORMANCE
PERFORMANCE	359 - 4	PERFORMANCE WERE ENACTED IN THE MIND
PERFORMANCE	477 - 2	FROM PRAYER TO PERFORMANCE
PERFORMS	251 - 4	PERFORMS EVERY RIGHT ACTION
PERFORMS	358 - 3	MENTALITY PERFORMS SEEMING MIRACLES
PERFORMS	372 - 1	PERFORMS ITS FUNCTIONS
PERISH	460 - 1	SHALL PERISH WITH THE SWORD
PERMANENCE	295 - 2	SUBSTANTIALITY AND PERMANENCE CAN COME
PERMANENT	065 - 2	WORD OF GOD IS PERMANENT
PERMANENT	190 - 3	CURE WILL BE PERMANENT
PERMANENT	193 - 2	NO PARTICULAR ONE IS PERMANENT
PERMANENT	216 - 4	STATE OF THOUGHT NEED BE PERMANENT
PERMANENT	393 - 4	NO FORM IS PERMANENT
PERMANENT	396 - 3	NOTHING OF PERMANENT WORTH FOR MAN
PERMANENTLY	197 - 4	NOTHING CAN PERMANENTLY HEAL

PERMEATE	261 - 2	PERMEATE EVERY ATOM OF MY BEING
PERMEATE	451 - 5	GRADUALLY PERMEATE THE MIND
PERMEATES	088 - 2	PERMEATES THE SOUL OF THE UNIVERSE
PERMEATES	125 - 2	PERMEATES AND FLOWS THROUGH US
PERMEATES	126 - 3	PERMEATES AND PENETRATES
PERMEATES	257 - 5	REST PERMEATES MY MIND AND BODY
PERMEATES	296 - 2	PERMEATES EVERYTHING THAT HE DOES
PERMEATES	305 - 1	PERMEATES ME AND FILLS ALL SPACE
PERMEATING	305 - 5	PERFECTION PERMEATING EVERYTHING
PERMIT	194 - 2	THE DESIRE TO PERMIT
PERMITS	310 - 1	PERMITS A CREATIVE INTELLIGENCE
PERMITTED	410 - 3	ADAM WAS PERMITTED TO NAME
PERPETUATE	118 - 4	LAW WHICH CONTINUES TO PERPETUATE
PERPETUATE	406 - 3	AS TO PERPETUATE AN OLD ONE
PERPETUATE	502 - 1	PERPETUATE THEIR DIRE RESULTS
PERPETUATED	164 - 3	IT IS PERPETUATED AND MAGNIFIED
PERPETUATING	207 - 1	PERPETUATING HIS OWN CONDITION
PERSIST	147 - 4	WHILE WE PERSIST IN
PERSIST	303 - 2	WHAT WE PERSIST IN RECOGNIZING
PERSIST	385 - 2	PERSIST BEYOND THE GRAVE
PERSISTED	199 - 3	IS PERSISTED IN OVER A PERIOD
PERSISTENCY	115 - 2	DETERMINED PERSISTENCY OF PURPOSE
PERSISTENT	176 - 3	PERSISTENT ABILITY TO USE THE LAW
PERSISTENT	483 - 5	PERSISTENT CONSTRUCTIVE THOUGHT
PERSISTS	055 - 1	OF HIS LIMITATION PERSISTS
PERSISTS	352 - 5	PERSISTS IT WILL REMAIN PRESENT
PERSON	031 - 3	IT IS NEVER A PERSON
PERSON	045 - 2	NEITHER PERSON, PLACE NOR THING
PERSON	054 - 2	NEITHER PERSON, PLACE NOR THING
PERSON	055 - 2	NEITHER PERSON, PLACE NOR THING
PERSON	088 - 5	THINK OF GOD OR SPIRIT AS PERSON
PERSON	097 - 2	NEVER A PERSON
PERSON	097 - 2	NEITHER PERSON, PLACE NOR THING
PERSON	201 - 1	PERSON, PLACE NOR THING
PERSON	217 - 1	PERSON, PLACE NOR THING
PERSON	224 - 3	PERSON, PLACE NOR THING
PERSON	236 - 2	PERSON, PLACE NOR THING
PERSON	250 - 2	PERSON AS BEING DIVINE
PERSON	253 - 4	NEITHER PERSON, PLACE NOR THING
PERSON	359 - 3	CHRIST IS NOT A PERSON
PERSON	308 - 1	GOD IS NOT A PERSON
PERSON	409 - 1	NEITHER PERSON, PLACE NOR THING
PERSONAL	029 - 4	THROUGH HIS PERSONAL USE OF IT
PERSONAL	050 - 1	PERSONAL AND IMPERSONAL PRINCIPLES
PERSONAL	072 - 3	FIRST DAY OF PERSONAL ATTAINMENT
PERSONAL	123 - 1	HIS PERSONAL USE OF LAW
PERSONAL	123 - 4	COMES A PERSONAL CONSCIOUSNESS
PERSONAL	124 - 1	FROM THE PERSONAL TO THE COSMIC
PERSONAL	179 - 2	THERE IS NO PERSONAL RESPONSIBILITY
PERSONAL	199 - 4	SENSE OF PERSONAL RESPONSIBILITY
PERSONAL	201 - 2	IT IS A PERSONAL
PERSONAL	221 - 6	NO PERSONAL RESPONSIBILITY
PERSONAL	313 - 1	COMES TO A POINT IN THE PERSONAL
PERSONAL	333 - 6	PERSONAL TO ALL WHO BELIEVE
PERSONAL	334 - 4	INFINITE IS PERSONAL TO EVERY SOUL

PERSONAL	336 - 1	PERSONAL AND NOT A COSMIC PROBLEM
PERSONAL	363 - 2	GOD IS PERSONAL TO ALL
PERSONAL	408 - 4	IT IS BOTH PERSONAL AND IMPERSONAL
PERSONAL	408 - 4	IT IS PERSONAL
PERSONAL	421 - 3	PERSONAL TO THE INDIVIDUAL
PERSONAL	423 - 2	TRUTH IS PERSONAL TO EACH
PERSONAL	430 - 3	NEED HAVE NO PERSONAL ANIMOSITY
PERSONAL AFFAIRS	168 - 4	NOR THE PERSONAL AFFAIRS OF THOSE
PERSONALITIES	031 - 3	IMPULSES FOR ACTUAL PERSONALITIES
PERSONALITIES	416 - 1	OURSELVES AS PERSONALITIES
PERSONALITY	055 - 2	NO POWER PERSONALITY NOR PRESENCE
PERSONALITY	085 - 4	ESSENCE OF CONCRETE PERSONALITY
PERSONALITY	089 - 2	INHERENT POSSIBILITY OF PERSONALITY
PERSONALITY	094 - 1	THE VIBRATION OF HIS PERSONALITY
PERSONALITY	127 - 4	PERSONALITY MAINTAINS ITS INDIVIDUALIZED
PERSONALITY	128 - 2	HE IS A POINT OF PERSONALITY
PERSONALITY	172 - 2	AS A PERSONALITY AND GIVE
PERSONALITY	184 - 2	PERSONALITY IS THE INSTRUMENT
PERSONALITY	197 - 2	HE UNFOLDS HIS OWN PERSONALITY
PERSONALITY	203 - 3	THOUGHT AS A PERSONALITY
PERSONALITY	210 - 2	PERSONALITY AND NOT THE LAW
PERSONALITY	279 - 1	PRINCIPLE AND NOT PERSONALITY
PERSONALITY	296 - 2	IT IS THE PERSONALITY
PERSONALITY	296 - 4	ONE WITH THE PERSONALITY OF GOD
PERSONALITY	297 - 1	WE HAVE ALL PERSONALITY
PERSONALITY	332 - 4	INDIVIDUAL CHARACTER AND PERSONALITY
PERSONALITY	333 - 1	MANIFESTATION OF HIS PERSONALITY
PERSONALITY	334 - 2	PERSONALITY IS WHAT ONE DOES
PERSONALITY	362 - 3	INFINITE, LIMITLESS PERSONALITY
PERSONALITY	372 - 1	ALONE GUARANTEES PERSONALITY
PERSONALITY	372 - 1	PERSONALITY FOR WHAT WE ARE IS THE RESULT
PERSONALITY	385 - 2	IF PERSONALITY DOES NOT PERSIST
PERSONALITY	386 - 1	TRULY SAID OF THE PERSONALITY
PERSONALITY	416 - 1	PERSONALITY IS BOUND
PERSONALITY	416 - 1	PERSONALITY USES THESE MECHANICAL
PERSONALITY	419 - 5	PERSONALITY IS WHAT ONE DOES
PERSONALITY	444 - 1	COME UNTO HIS PERSONALITY
PERSONALITY	444 - 1	PERSONALITY WOULD SOON BE DISSOLVED
PERSONALITY	484 - 1	PERSONALITY BUT TO A UNIVERSAL PRINCIPLE
PERSONALIZED	089 - 2	SOMETHING IS PERSONALIZED
PERSONALLY	108 - 3	EXPRESS LIFE AS ONE PERSONALLY DESIRES
PERSONIFICATION	089 - 2	PERSONAL TO ITS OWN PERSONIFICATION
PERSONIFICATION	347 - 3	SUBJECTIVE PERSONIFICATION OF OURSELVES
PERSONIFICATION	368 - 1	TO BE THE PERSONIFICATION OF GOD
PERSONIFICATION	454 - 5	A PERSONIFICATION OF ITSELF
PERSONIFICATIONS	307 - 2	PERSONIFICATIONS OF OUR THOUGHTS
PERSONIFIED	076 - 3	MIND WHICH IS PERSONIFIED
PERSONIFIED	108 - 1	PERSONIFIED SPIRIT, COMPLETE FREEDOM
PERSONIFIED	118 - 4	PERSONIFIED A LAW
PERSONIFIED	141 - 2	BEING PERSONIFIED THROUGH US
PERSONIFIED	308 - 1	PERSONIFIED IN US
PERSONIFIED	332 - 5	PERSONIFIED SPIRIT, COMPLETE FREEDOM
PERSONIFIED	408 - 4	IT IS PERSONIFIED THROUGH US
PERSONIFIED	470 - 4	GOD BECOME PERSONIFIED
PERSONIFIES	132 - 8	PERSONIFIES THE TRINITY OF BEING

PERSONIFY	041 - 1	PERSONIFY ITSELF THROUGH MAN
PERSONIFY	341 - 3	PERSONIFY IN OUR PERSON
PERSONS	041 - 2	NO RESPECTER OF PERSONS
PERSONS	052 - 4	LAW IS NO RESPECTER OF PERSONS
PERSONS	284 - 2	NO RESPECTER OF PERSONS
PERSPECTIVE	429 - 2	PERSPECTIVE OF REALITY IS LOST WHEN
PERSPECTIVE	429 - 2	LIFE FROM THE GREAT PERSPECTIVE
PERVADES	257 - 5	PERVADES MY ROOM AND MY BED
PERVADES	478 - 5	LOVE WHILE ELUSIVE PERVADES
PETITION	180 - 2	PETITION IS TRANSMUTED INTO ACCEPTANCE
PETTY	457 - 4	RISE FROM HIS PETTY VIRTUES
PHASES	397 - 4	ITS PHASES IS SOME PART OF GOD
PHASES	414 - 1	PHASES OF HUMAN BELIEF
PHENOMENA	138 - 1	PHENOMENA AND MENTAL PROCESSES
PHENOMENA	347 - 1	PHENOMENA OF THE SOUL
PHENOMENA	378 - 1	COULD BE PRODUCING THE PHENOMENA
PHENOMENON	402 - 2	SHOULD WE DOUBT THIS PHENOMENON
PHILOSOPHERS	068 - 2	THE PHILOSOPHERS OF ALL AGES
PHILOSOPHERS	092 - 2	SOME OF THE EARLIER PHILOSOPHERS
PHILOSOPHERS	328 - 2	SPIRITUAL PHILOSOPHERS ARE MYSTICS
PHILOSOPHY	037 - 1	PHILOSOPHY IN THIS SIMPLE STATEMENT
PHILOSOPHY	060 - 3	A NEW PHILOSOPHY
PHILOSOPHY	066 - 2	IN PHILOSOPHY, THE WORD REALITY
PHILOSOPHY	066 - 2	THE REALITY OF PHILOSOPHY
PHILOSOPHY	080 - 3	EVERY GREAT SPIRITUAL PHILOSOPHY
PHILOSOPHY	085 - 2	THE PHILOSOPHY OF APPLIED METAPHYSICS
PHILOSOPHY	113 - 2	LITERATURE, PHILOSOPHY AND RELIGION
PHILOSOPHY	124 - 4	IT IS HELD IN OUR PHILOSOPHY
PHILOSOPHY	183 - 1	PHILOSOPHY OF SPIRITUAL MIND
PHILOSOPHY	273 - 2	IN PHILOSOPHY THIS IDEA
PHILOSOPHY	327 - 2	PHILOSOPHY OF THE WORLD
PHILOSOPHY	382 - 2	PHILOSOPHY WHICH DEALS WITH MIND
PHILOSOPHY	417 - 3	BASED UPON A FALSE PHILOSOPHY
PHILOSOPHY	423 - 3	ALL TRUE RELIGIOUS PHILOSOPHY
PHILOSOPHY	427 - 1	EXPLANATION OF OUR OWN PHILOSOPHY
PHILOSOPHY	433 - 1	TAUGHT HIS MARVELOUS PHILOSOPHY
PHILOSOPHY	436 - 4	PHILOSOPHY OF LIFE FOR TIME
PHILOSOPHY	444 - 4	PROBLEM OF PHILOSOPHY IS TO UNITE
PHILOSOPHY	444 - 4	PHILOSOPHY LEADS TO TRUE RELIGION
PHILOSOPHY OF JESUS	363 - 4	PHILOSOPHY OF JESUS IN A DIFFERENT
PHONOGRAPH	349 - 1	PHONOGRAPH DISC OR THE SOUND FILM
PHYSICAL	064 - 1	PHYSICAL MANIFESTATIONS
PHYSICAL	095 - 1	MEDIUM FOR PHYSICAL ACTION
PHYSICAL	111 - 4	CALLED THE PHYSICAL UNIVERSE
PHYSICAL	117 - 3	MAN IS ONE WITH THE PHYSICAL
PHYSICAL	145 - 2	CREATE ITS PHYSICAL CORRESPONDENT
PHYSICAL	190 - 3	MENTAL AS WELL AS A PHYSICAL STATE
PHYSICAL	191 - 3	ON THREE PLANES: THE PHYSICAL
PHYSICAL	207 - 3	EXPERIENCE SOME PHYSICAL SENSATION
PHYSICAL	218 - 4	OUTLET IN THE PHYSICAL MAN
PHYSICAL	218 - 4	NEVER TO TREAT THE PHYSICAL
PHYSICAL	236 - 6	CAUSE IS NEVER MATERIAL OR PHYSICAL
PHYSICAL	260 - 1	PHYSICAL BODY ARE BOTH SPIRITUAL
PHYSICAL	316 - 2	PHYSICIAN FOR A PHYSICAL CHECK-UP
PHYSICAL	382 - 3	REPRODUCTIONS OF MAN'S PHYSICAL

PHYSICAL	415 - 5	PHYSICAL UNIVERSE IS ALWAYS MECHANICAL
PHYSICAL	427 - 4	PHYSICAL BENEFITS OF THE HUMAN
PHYSICAL	476 - 6	LIVE ONLY ON THE PHYSICAL
PHYSICAL DEATH	352 - 5	SHALL HAVE SUFFERED PHYSICAL DEATH
PHYSICAL MAN	116 - 2	PHYSICAL MAN IS IN UNITY WITH ALL OTHER
PHYSICAL UNIVERSE	098 - 3	PHYSICAL UNIVERSE IS THE BODY OF GOD
PHYSICAL UNIVERSE	141 - 4	PHYSICAL UNIVERSE IS SPIRIT IN FORM
PHYSICAL WORLD	333 - 2	WITH THE BODY OF THE PHYSICAL WORLD
PHYSICIAN	168 - 3	PHYSICIAN WHO CARES FOR
PHYSICIAN	175 - 3	CAN BE CHECKED BY A PHYSICIAN
PHYSICIAN	199 - 3	PHYSICIAN IS IN HIS OWN FIELD
PHYSICIANS	138 - 1	PHYSICIANS OF HIGHEST REPUTE ARE
PHYSICIANS	144 - 3	PHYSICIANS NOW TESTIFY
PHYSICIANS	236 - 5	EMINENT PHYSICIANS PROBE DEEPLY
PHYSICIANS	240 - 2	SOME PHYSICIANS NOW CLAIM
PHYSICIST	085 - 4	ONE LEARNED PHYSICIST
PHYSICIST	095 - 2	PHYSICIST WHO HAS STUDIED
PHYSICS	068 - 4	AS WE UNDERSTAND PHYSICS
PHYSICS	086 - 2	BEGINS WHERE PHYSICS LEAVES OFF
PHYSICS	309 - 5	PHYSICS BEGINS WITH ENERGY AND INTELLIGENCE
PHYSICS	310 - 2	PHYSICS HAS CHASED THIS FORM
PHYSIQUE	490 - 3	PHYSIQUE TAKE ON A NEWNESS
PICKS UP	351 - 2	JUST AS HE PICKS UP RADIO MESSAGES
PICTURE	038 - 5	PICTURE OF LIMITATION
PICTURE	084 - 4	THOUGHT CANNOT PICTURE A TIME
PICTURE	105 - 3	DIVINE MENTAL PICTURE
PICTURE	186 - 4	PICTURE OF UNDESIRABLE CONDITIONS
PICTURE	267 - 1	FURNISHES BUT A MENTAL PICTURE
PICTURE	271 - 5	MAKE A MENTAL PICTURE OF HIS IDEAL
PICTURE	272 - 1	PASS THIS PICTURE
PICTURE	282 - 1	HAVING A STRONG PICTURE
PICTURE	297 - 2	FOR ONE IS THE PICTURE
PICTURE	300 - 4	MAKE A MENTAL PICTURE OF IT ALL
PICTURE	301 - I	TAKE A PICTURE OF HIS OBJECTIVE
PICTURE	301 - 1	A PICTURE OF HIS SUBJECTIVE MENTALITY
PICTURE	380 - 2	PSYCHIC SEES THE PICTURE
PICTURE	380 - 2	THAT WHICH IS ONLY A PICTURE
PICTURE	399 - 2	COMPLETE MENTAL PICTURE OF HIMSELF
PICTURE	399 - 2	A MENTAL PICTURE IN MIND
PICTURE	412 - 2	LIFE IS A MOTION PICTURE
PICTURE	422 - 2	A MENTAL PICTURE OF HIMSELF
PICTURE	422 - 2	WE SEE GENERALLY IS THE PICTURE
PICTURES	348 - 1	SENSE AS MENTAL PICTURES
PICTURES	351 - 2	THESE PICTURES OR VIBRATIONS
PICTURES	351 - 3	PICTURES EXIST AT ANY AND EVERY POINT
PICTURES	422 - 2	THESE PICTURES ARE OFTEN SEEN
PICTURING	260 - 2	PICTURING AND MANIFESTATION
PIG PEN	464 - 5	GOD CANNOT ENTER THE PIG PEN
PILL	191 - 3	WHETHER IT BE A PILL OR A PRAYER
PILL	220 - 3	PILL DOES ANY GOOD
PILL	316 - 1	TREAT THIS MAN IF HE TAKES A PILL
PILL	316 - 1	NEED TO TAKE A PILL
PILL	320 - 1	DISHONOR GOD WHEN THEY TAKE A PILL
PINT	287 - 1	WILL A PINT DIPPER EVER HOLD MORE
PLACATE	149 - 3	PLACATE GOD OR PERSUADE HIM

PLACE	097 - 2	NEITHER PERSON, PLACE NOR THING
PLACE	151 - 3	EACH HAS A UNIQUE PLACE
PLACE	151 - 4	THERE IS A PLACE IN US
PLACE	152 - 1	THE PLACE IS WHERE WE ARE
PLACE	224 - 3	PERSON, PLACE NOR THING
PLACE	253 - 4	NEITHER PERSON, PLACE NOR THING
PLACE	262 - 1	PERSON, PLACE NOR THING
PLACE	263 - 6	MY PLACE IN THE UNIVERSE
PLACE	275 - 2	CONDUCT US TO A PLACE
PLACE	295 - 2	HIMSELF TO THE PLACE IN MIND
PLACE	303 - 1	NOT CONTINGENT UPON ANY PLACE
PLACE	332 - 4	IT IS THE PLACE WHERE GOD
PLACE	364 - 3	NO PLACE EXCEPT WITHIN
PLACE	385 - 1	ANY ONE PLACE TOO LONG
PLACE	395 - 3	NEITHER PERSON, PLACE NOR THING
PLACE	397 - 4	MAN'S MIND IS SIMPLY THE PLACE
PLACED	391 - 3	THE ETERNAL HAS PLACED HIMSELF
PLACES	352 - 5	MAY BE KNOWN IN ALL PLACES
PLACES	406 - 1	IN ALL PLACES IT FOLLOWS
PLAIN	429 - 1	WORLD AS ONE VAST PLAIN
PLAINLY	132 - 7	IT CANNOT BE TOO PLAINLY STATED
PLAN	290 - 3	ARE NONE IN THE DIVINE PLAN
PLAN	290 - 3	NO PLAN FOR MAN OTHER THAN THE DIVINE
PLANE	070 - 2	MADE MANIFEST ON SOME PLANE
PLANE	099 - 3	TO FUNCTION ON THIS PLANE
PLANE	099 - 3	BODY IS NECESSARY TO THIS PLANE
PLANE	104 - 3	NOW FROM ONE PLANE
PLANE	104 - 5	WAS ON ANOTHER PLANE
PLANE	120 - 1	TAKES PLACE ON EVERY PLANE
PLANE	125 - 5	IT IS ON A HIGHER PLANE
PLANE	207 - 4	PLANE IS TRUE ON ALL
PLANE	230 - 6	PLANE OF EXPRESSION
PLANE	251 - 4	ON ANY PLANE OF EXPRESSION
PLANE	330 - 5	INVISIBLE TO A VISIBLE PLANE
PLANE	351 - 2	PLANE REMAINS WITHIN ITS SUBJECTIVE
PLANE	374 - 5	WHEN WE PASS FROM THIS PLANE
PLANE	375 - 3	ONLY ONE PLANE OF EXPRESSION
PLANE	380 - 2	LAWS ARE THE SAME ON EVERY PLANE
PLANE	382 - 3	EACH PLANE REPRODUCES THE ONE
PLANE	382 - 3	ONE PLANE IS TRUE ON ALL
PLANE	386 - 2	PASSED FROM THIS PLANE TO THE NEXT
PLANE	387 - 1	LIFE ON THIS PLANE
PLANE	437 - 3	AUTHORITY ON THE PHYSICAL PLANE
PLANE	492 - 2	EXPRESS THE SOUL ON THAT PLANE
PLANE	497 - 4	PLANE IS TRUE ON ALL
PLANE	497 - 4	PLANE PARTAKING OF THE NATURE
PLANES	098 - 2	MANIFESTATION OF SPIRIT ON ALL PLANES
PLANES	104 - 5	PLANES ARE NOT PLACES
PLANES	104 - 5	PLANES ARE STATES OF CONSCIOUSNESS
PLANES	191 - 3	TAKES PLACE ON THREE PLANES
PLANES	387 - 1	BELIEVE IN PLANES BEYOND THIS ONE
PLANES	437 - 3	MENTAL AND SPIRITUAL PLANES
PLANES	476 - 6	WE LIVE ON THREE PLANES
PLANET	103 - 2	ACTIVITIES ON THIS PLANET
PLANET	120 - 3	PSYCHIC ATMOSPHERE OF THIS PLANET

PLANET	186 - 2	MAKE A PLANET AS AN ACORN
PLANET	348 - 4	HAPPENED ON THIS PLANET
PLANET	351 - 3	TRANSPIRED ON THIS PLANET
PLANET	404 - 3	MANIFESTATION ON THIS PLANET
PLANETS	063 - 2	NO SYSTEM OF PLANETS
PLANETS	125 - 4	POWER THAT MOLDS THE PLANETS
PLANETS	227 - 3	HOLDS THE PLANETS IN SPACE
PLANETS	279 - 2	THE PLANETS ARE ETERNALLY FALLING
PLANT	078 - 2	PLANT FROM IT
PLANT	090 - 2	FROM WHICH PLANT LIFE COMES
PLANT	205 - 5	MIND PRODUCES THE PLANT
PLANT	234 - 5	PLANT WHICH MY HEAVENLY FATHER
PLANT	271 - 4	WE CAN PLANT AN IDEA IN MIND
PLANTING	453 - 4	PLANTING SHALL BE ROOTED UP
PLANTS	478 - 4	RESPONSE OF PLANTS
PLASTIC	083 - 2	PLASTIC, PASSIVE AND RECEPTIVE
PLASTIC	098 - 1	PLASTIC AND RECEPTIVE MEDIUM
PLASTIC	105 - 3	IS A RECEPTIVE OR PLASTIC SUBSTANCE
PLASTIC	125 - 2	PLASTIC MEDIUM WHICH SURROUNDS US
PLASTIC	126 - 3	IMPERSONAL, NEUTRAL, PLASTIC
PLASTIC	207 - 1	RECEPTIVE PLASTIC SUBSTANCE
PLASTIC	494 - 5	LAW IS NEUTRAL, PLASTIC, RECEPTIVE
PLATO	314 - 1	PLATO MEANT WHEN HE GAVE US
PLATO	329 - 4	BUDDHA, PLATO, SOCRATES, EMERSON
PLAUSIBLE	453 - S	BECAUSE IT SOUNDS PLAUSIBLE
PLAY	131 - 6	PLAY OF LIFE UPON ITSELF
PLAY	394 - 1	PLAY OF LIFE UPON ITSELF
PLAY	465 - 1	THE PLAY OF LIFE UPON ITSELF
PLEASANTNESS	495 - 2	HER WAYS ARE WAYS OF PLEASANTNESS
PLEASE	269 - 2	NOT MEAN WE MUST PLEASE THE LAW
PLEASE	430 - 3	WE CANNOT ALWAYS PLEASE
PLEASED	288 - 2	PLEASED BY A LIFE OF SACRIFICE
PLEASES	464 - 4	ALWAYS DO AS HE PLEASES
PLEASING	147 - 2	THINGS BEAUTIFUL AND PLEASING
PLEASING	377 - 2	PLEASING AND SATISFACTORY
PLEASURE	109 - 1	YOUR FATHER'S GOOD PLEASURE
PLEASURE	270 - 6	ITS OWN PLEASURE
PLEASURE	300 - 4	LOOKING AT AND FINDING PLEASURE
PLEASURE	403 - 2	PRODUCE PLENTY INSTEAD OF LACK
PLEASURE	404 - 4	MIDST OF PLENTY, HUMANITY LIVES IN WANT
PLEASURE	405 - 1	IT IS GOD'S PLEASURE
PLEASURE	454 - 4	GIVING UP OF ALL PLEASURE
PLEASURE	486 - 3	THE FATHER'S GOOD PLEASURE
PLENTY	055 - 2	REALIZATION OF PLENTY
PLENTY	164 - 3	POISE, POWER, PLENTY
PLENTY	488 - 5	SCIENTIFIC TO MEDITATE ON PLENTY
PLOTINUS	079 - 2	PLOTINUS SPEAKS OF IT AS A DOER
PLOTINUS	097 - 2	PLOTINUS HAD A CLEAR CONCEPT
PLOTINUS	113 - 2	PLOTINUS TELLS US THAT THERE ARE THREE
PLOTINUS	115 - 5	PLOTINUS, PERHAPS THE GREATEST
PLOTINUS	341 - 4	PLOTINUS HAD SEVEN DISTINCT PERIODS
PLOTINUS	461 - 1	PLOTINUS TELLS US
PLOTINUS	489 - 7	PLOTINUS SAYS THAT WHEN
PLUMB	093 - 4	PLUMB THE DEPTHS OF THE INDIVIDUAL MIND
PLUMBED	031 - 5	NO MAN HAS PLUMBED THE DEPTHS OF

PLUMBED	095 - 2	NO ONE HAS EVER PLUMBED
PLUMBED	479 - 1	ALREADY PLUMBED THE DEPTHS
PLUNDERERS	427 - 5	PLUNDERERS OF HUMAN POSSESSIONS
PLUNGED	362 - 1	PLUNGED BENEATH THE MATERIAL SURFACE
PNEUMONIA	252 - 2	DRAFT MAY PRODUCE PNEUMONIA
POET	455 - 6	POET WAITING IN THE SILENCE
POETRY	328 - 1	POETRY WHICH IS IMMORTAL
POETS	327 - 4	POETS HAVE BEEN TRUE MYSTICS
POETS	386 - 2	POETS HAVE SUNG OF THE ETERNALITY
POINT	056 - 4	A POINT OF GOD CONSCIOUS
POINT	067 - 3	POINT A WAY TO ETERNAL VALUES
POINT	093 - 5	POINT OF CONSCIOUS PERCEPTION
POINT	093 - 5	WITHIN THE INDIVIDUALIZED POINT
POINT	094 - 1	KNOWN AT ONE POINT
POINT	105 - 3	INITIAL STARTING POINT
POINT	121 - 3	REPRESENT A POINT WHERE
POINT	127 - 4	POINT IN UNIVERSAL MIND
POINT	130 - 3	EVOLVED HIM TO A POINT
POINT	187 - 3	POINT WHERE WE ARE NOT DISTURBED
POINT	208 - 2	POINT THAT PEOPLE OFTEN DO NOT
POINT	224 - 2	SIMPLY A POINT
POINT	228 - 1	IS A POINT IN UNIVERSAL MIND
POINT	236 - 6	IMPORTANT POINT IN HEALING
POINT	237 - 3	POINT WHERE THIS ONE MIND
POINT	272 - 2	POINT THE WAY
POINT	291 - 1	STANDS AT THE POINT OF LIMITLESS
POINT	330 - 3	EVERY POINT WITHIN GOD
POINT	358 - 2	POINT OF OUR OWN CONSCIOUSNESS
POINT	358 - 3	POINT OF OUR OWN CONSCIOUSNESS
POINT	400 - 1	IS THE STARTING POINT
POINT	403 - 4	STARTING POINT FOR A CREATIVE PATTERN
POINT	409 - 5	AT THIS POINT THE MOST EFFECTIVE
POINT	419 - 3	A POINT IN UNIVERSAL CONSCIOUSNESS
POINT	422 - 1	POINT OF ANYONE'S MENTALITY
POINTING	369 - 3	POINTING THE WAY TO A GREATER
POINTS	067 - 3	POINTS TO ONE CENTRAL LIFE
POINTS	094 - 1	KNOWN AT ALL POINTS INSTANTLY
POISE	151 - 3	IDEA OF PEACE, POISE AND CALM
POISE	180 - 4	POISE WHICH IS FOUNDED
POISE	180 - 4	UNION OF PEACE WITH POISE
POISE	244 - 5	PEACE, POISE AND POWER
POISED	194 - 4	EMOTIONS ARE RIGHTLY POISED
POISED	228 - 1	RATIONAL AND POISED
POISED	249 - 1	I AM CALM, POISED AND AT PEACE
POISED	264 - 4	POISED IN PEACE AND BEAUTY
POISED	321 - 2	TREAT TO KNOW THAT HE IS POISED
POISED	447 - 3	BECOME POISED AND POWERFUL
POISON	240 - 3	ALL CASES OF POISON
POISONOUS	434 - 4	POISONOUS SECRETIONS IN THE BODY
POISONS	255 - 3	POISONS IN THE MAKING
POLLEN	242 - 4	POLLEN OF CERTAIN FLOWERS OR PLANTS
POLLEN	243 - 2	POLLEN WHICH YOU HAVE THOUGHT
PONDER	431 - 4	WE SHOULD PONDER DEEPLY
PONDERED	068 - 2	THEY HAVE PONDERED
PONDEROSITY	042 - 4	DO AWAY WITH A PONDEROSITY

POOR	119 - 2	I AM LIKELY TO REMAIN POOR
POOR	168 - 5	GOD IS NOT POOR
POOR	169 - 1	WHO IS NEVER POOR
POOR	279 - 1	IF WE ARE POOR
POPULAR	309 - 1	POPULAR IDEA OF MENTAL CONCENTRATION
POPULAR	337 - 2	THIS REVERSES THE POPULAR
POPULAR	436 - 4	THE POPULAR CONCEPT OF HELL
PORTALS	293 - 1	PORTALS OF MY SOUL AND ACCEPT
PORTALS	305 - 3	OPEN THE PORTALS OF MY SOUL
PORTALS	447 - 1	ENTERING THE PORTALS OF REALITY
PORTALS	491 - 4	ENTER ITS PORTALS AND BE HAPPY
POSITION	055 - 3	ACCEPT THE FALSE POSITION
POSITION	231 - 6	LOSS OF POSITION
POSITIONS	286 - 1	ALL WITHOUT POSITIONS
POSITIVE	053 - 4	THAT IS POSITIVE
POSITIVE	054 - 1	POSITIVE UNDERSTANDING
POSITIVE	146 - 1	TO MAN IS EQUALLY POSITIVE
POSITIVE	279 - 1	MAINTAIN A CONSISTENT POSITIVE
POSITIVE	450 - 3	POSITIVE CONVICTION OF THE INNER POWER
POSITIVE	451 - 1	POSITIVE THOUGHTS OF ACHIEVEMENT
POSITIVE	473 - 6	NEGATION EQUALS POSITIVE GOODNESS
POSITIVITY	046 - 6	POSITIVITY SHOULD ACCOMPANY ALL STATEMENTS
POSSESS	072 - 4	SEEMED TO POSSESS THE EARTH
POSSESSED	448 - 2	POSSESSED OF UNCLEAN THOUGHTS
POSSESSES	314 - 4	POSSESS, POSSESSES AND OBSESSES US
POSSESSES	338 - 2	PRECIOUS THING A MAN POSSESSES
POSSESSIONS	315 - 1	POSSESSIONS WHICH POSSESS YOU
POSSESSIONS	315 - 1	ADVISABILITY OF USING POSSESSIONS
POSSIBILITIES	032 - 3	POWERS AND HIGHER POSSIBILITIES
POSSIBILITIES	266 - 1	ABLE TO BRING GREATER POSSIBILITIES
POSSIBILITIES	271 - 2	THE POSSIBILITIES OF THE LAW
POSSIBILITIES	271 - 2	POSSIBILITIES OF USING IT ARE LIMITLESS
POSSIBILITIES	305 - 2	POSSIBILITIES OF MY EXPERIENCE ARE
POSSIBILITY	045 - 3	UNIVERSAL POSSIBILITY
POSSIBILITY	109 - 3	POSSIBILITY OF LIMITLESS FREEDOM
POSSIBILITY	124 - 1	THE POTENTIAL POSSIBILITY
POSSIBILITY	177 - 1	POSSIBILITY OF SPIRITUAL MIND HEALING
POSSIBILITY	179 - 3	POSSIBILITY OF MENTAL HEALING
POSSIBILITY	244 - 4	POSSIBILITY OF COMPLETELY HEALING
POSSIBILITY	267 - 3	ITSELF A LIMITLESS POSSIBILITY
POSSIBILITY	336 - 4	POSSIBILITY OF EXPERIENCING IT
POSSIBILITY	461 - 2	POSSIBILITY OF EXPERIENCING GOOD
POSSIBILITY	468 - 2	COMPREHEND SUCH AN INFINITE POSSIBILITY
POSSIBLE	044 - 5	ALL THINGS ARE POSSIBLE
POSSIBLE	315 - 3	WITH GOD ALL THINGS ARE POSSIBLE
POSTULATE	129 - 2	POSTULATE A THREE-FOLD NATURE OF
POSTULATED	074 - 3	THEORIES ARE POSTULATED
POSTULATES	371 - 2	OF COURSE POSTULATES MEMORY
POTENTIAL	040 - 3	POTENTIAL KNOWLEDGE OF ALL THINGS
POTENTIAL	108 - 4	POTENTIAL MAN IS JUST AS PERFECT AS
POTENTIAL	144 - 2	EFFECT IS POTENTIAL IN CAUSE
POTENTIAL	243 - 3	POTENTIAL PERFECTION OF THE UNIVERSE
POTENTIAL	267 - 4	A LIMITLESS POTENTIAL
POTENTIAL	271 - 1	THE POTENTIAL OF ALL THINGS
POTENTIAL	289 - 2	EFFECT IS ALREADY POTENTIAL IN ITS CAUSE

POTENTIAL	309 - 5	UNBORN BUT POTENTIAL POSSIBILITY
POTENTIAL	392 - 2	POTENTIAL WITH ALL POSSIBLE FORM
POTENTIAL	409 - 5	SPIRIT IS THE LIMITLESS POTENTIAL
POTENTIAL	473 - 6	POTENTIAL IN ALL OF US
POTENTIALITIES	085 - 3	BEING WITH POTENTIALITIES
POTENTIALITY	027 - 2	IS A POWER AND POTENTIALITY
POTENTIALITY	112 - 4	SPIRIT IS POTENTIALLY FOCUSED
POTENTIALLY	185 - 1	AMONG PEOPLE POTENTIALLY PERFECT
POUNDS	499 - 6	WORTH MANY POUNDS OF AFFIRMATION
POUR	165 - 2	POUR THE UPLIFTING TRUTH
POUR	301 - 4	READY TO POUR INTO OUR EXPERIENCE
POUR	307 - 3	POUR YOU OUT A BLESSING
POURED	030 - 3	IDEA IS ACCEPTED AND POURED
POURED	165 - 3	PRACTITIONER HAS POURED INTO SUBJECTIVE
POURED	204 - 5	CONSTANTLY POURED INTO CONSCIOUSNESS
POURING	150 - 1	POURING HIMSELF INTO HIS CREATION
POURING	151 - 4	BY POURING ITSELF THROUGH US
POURING	279 - 1	POURING IN AN OPPOSITE THOUGHT
POURS	257 - 4	POURS THROUGH ME NOW
POURS	486 - 5	CONSCIOUS THOUGHT POURS TRUTH
POVERTY	055 - 4	SICKNESS, POVERTY AND UNHAPPINESS
POVERTY	097 - 2	DISEASE, POVERTY UNHAPPINESS
POVERTY	118 - 4	THOUGHT POVERTY YEAR AFTER YEAR
POVERTY	187 - 1	POVERTY, DEGRADATION AND MISERY
POVERTY	264 - 1	FEAR OF POVERTY
POVERTY	288 - 2	EXPRESSED THROUGH POVERTY
POVERTY	292 - 3	NO LIMITATION, POVERTY, WANT NOR LACK
POVERTY	320 - 4	LIMITATION AND POVERTY ARE NOT THINGS
POVERTY	402 - 3	THOUGHTS OF LACK, POVERTY
POVERTY	416 - 4	IF WE THINK POVERTY
POWER	025 - 3	AIR IS VIBRANT WITH POWER
POWER	026 - 3	THE POWER BACK OF CREATION
POWER	027 - 2	HERE IS A POWER AND POTENTIALITY
POWER	029 - 3	A POWER THAT SEEMS TO BE LIMITLESS
POWER	030 - 2	WE ALL USE THE CREATIVE POWER
POWER	030 - 3	SETS POWER IN MOTION
POWER	032 - 2	BY THE POWER TO CREATE
POWER	032 - 3	THERE IS A POWER IN THE UNIVERSE
POWER	032 - 3	POWER BEHIND EVERYTHING IS GOOD
POWER	036 - 4	IT IS POWER
POWER	036 - 5	MISUSED THE HIGHEST POWER
POWER	036 - 5	AND SO GREAT IS THIS POWER
POWER	037 - 1	MISUSE OF THIS POWER
POWER	037 - 1	THE ONLY POWER IN THE UNIVERSE
POWER	037 - 2	RECOGNIZE IT AS POWER
POWER	039 - 1	POWER OF THE SELF-ASSERTIVE TRUTH
POWER	039 - 4	POWER OF EVIL
POWER	039 - 4	POWER OF GOOD
POWER	042 - 5	POWER TO BRING THEM INTO PRACTICAL USE
POWER	047 - 2	GIVES CONSCIOUS POWER TO HIS THOUGHT
POWER	047 - 2	THE MORE POWER ONE GIVES TO HIS THOUGHT
POWER	048 - 4	SPECIFIC STATEMENT HAS POWER
POWER	053 - 3	SUBTLE POWER OF MIND AND SPIRIT
POWER	055 - 2	HAVE NO POWER
POWER	058 - 2	EQUIPPED WITH POWER AND VOLITION

POWER	058 - 2	THE POWER INTO THIS WORD
POWER	058 - 2	POWER OF THE LAW FLOW
POWER	058 - 3	NOT A POWER OF WILL
POWER	058 - 3	BUT A POWER OF CHOICE
POWER	060 - 4	POWER BACK OF CREATION
POWER	063 - 2	POWER DID IT EMPLOY
POWER	064 - 4	POWER OF HIS WORD
POWER	067 - 2	POWER THAT KNOWS ITSELF
POWER	068 - 5	POWER OF SPIRIT
POWER	069 - 3	SETS POWER IN MOTION
POWER	070 - 2	SETS POWER IN MOTION
POWER	078 - 2	THE POWER THAT KNOWS ITSELF
POWER	082 - 1	ONLY POWER IN THE UNIVERSE
POWER	083 - 2	POWER AND ACTION OF SPIRIT
POWER	086 - 5	POWER THAT KNOWS ITSELF
POWER	092 - 2	IT HAS THE INTELLIGENCE AND POWER
POWER	101 - 2	THE POWER THAT CREATED IT
POWER	108 - 1	POWER TO BACK UP THAT FREEDOM
POWER	125 - 4	POWER THAT MOLDS THE PLANETS
POWER	128 - 4	POWER OF RIGHT THINKING THAT IT CANCELS
POWER	139 - 4	STUDYING THE POWER OF THOUGHT
POWER	145 - 4	OUR OWN WORD HAS THE POWER
POWER	146 - 1	ALL WORDS HAVE POWER
POWER	146 - 4	POWER THAT MAKES THINGS DIRECTLY OUT OF
POWER	150 - 5	THE POWER IS NO LONGER I
POWER	153 - 2	DISSIPATE BY THE POWER OF TRUTH
POWER	155 - 2	HAS POWER OVER THE VISIBLE
POWER	156 - 1	FAITH HAVE GREAT POWER
POWER	156 - 4	A POWER OPPOSED TO GOD
POWER	170 - 2	CONVINCED OF THE POWER OF HIS OWN WORD
POWER	173 - 4	POWER IS IN THE REALIZATION
POWER	173 - 4	POWER IN THE ARGUMENT
POWER	173 - 4	A POWER AND A PRESENCE
POWER	176 - 2	THE MORE POWER WE SHALL HAVE
POWER	183 - 2	POWER TO NEUTRALIZE NEGATIVE THOUGHT
POWER	185 - 2	IN A POWER APART FROM GOD
POWER	186 - 4	THE MORE POWER IT WILL HAVE
POWER	188 - 3	THE POWER OF RIGHT THINKING
POWER	188 - 4	ALL THE POWER IN THE UNIVERSE
POWER	189 - 3	REMIND OURSELVES OF THE POWER
POWER	191 - 5	POWER OF GOOD
POWER	191 - 5	POWER OF EVIL
POWER	192 - 3	CONSCIOUS, DIRECTIVE POWER
POWER	192 - 4	INFLUENCE OTHERS BY WILL POWER
POWER	192 - 4	EFFECTS OF WILL POWER
POWER	192 - 4	GREATER POWER OF WILL
POWER	192 - 5	USE OF WILL POWER CONTRADICTS
POWER	193 - 2	WITHIN OUR POWER TO CAUSE IT
POWER	193 - 3	USE THE CREATIVE POWER OF MIND
POWER	193 - 3	THE CREATIVE POWER HAS TIME
POWER	194 - 2	THE POWER OF GOOD
POWER	197 - 5	THOUGHT OPERATES THROUGH A POWER
POWER	209 - 5	POWER TO OPPOSE
POWER	215 - 1	POWER OF A THOUGHT
POWER	216 - 1	IS THE PRESENCE POWER

POWER	218 - 3	SECRET POWER OF OUR WORK
POWER	218 - 4	POWER IS GIVEN UNTO HIM
POWER	219 - 2	SHALL DEMONSTRATE ITS POWER
POWER	220 - 6	ENOUGH POWER TO TREAT
POWER	221 - 1	POWER AND THAT SUCH POWER KNOWS
POWER	221 - 1	SUCH POWER KNOWS DEGREES OF DISCOMFORT
POWER	221 - 1	THERE IS BUT ONE POWER
POWER	221 - 1	THAT POWER KNOWS ONLY PERFECTION
POWER	221 - 2	THE POWER THAT MADE EVERYTHING
POWER	224 - 2	WE ARE USING A POWER
POWER	225 - 2	VITALIZING POWER OF SPIRIT
POWER	227 - 3	THE POWER BACK OF YOUR WORD
POWER	228 - 3	IT IS POWER
POWER	236 - 2	NO VITALITY, NO SUBSTANCE AND NO POWER
POWER	238 - 4	THE POWER TO BUILD UP OR DESTROY
POWER	241 - 2	FURTHER POWER IS GIVEN TO THE BELIEF
POWER	242 - 5	HAY FEVER HAS NO POWER
POWER	243 - 2	YOU HAVE THE POWER
POWER	244 - 2	CREATIVE POWER OF OUR OWN THOUGHT
POWER	245 - 1	THE PREMISE OF ONE POWER
POWER	245 - 1	INFINITE POWER FOR GOOD
POWER	245 - 2	POWER AND DECISION OF SPIRIT
POWER	247 - 2	POWER AND INSPIRATION OF OUR LIFE
POWER	250 - 6	TO CLAIM OUR POWER
POWER	276 - 2	THE GREATEST POWER OVER THAT LAW
POWER	279 - 1	POWER WITH WHICH WE ARE DEALING
POWER	279 - 1	INTELLIGENCE, TRUTH AND POWER
POWER	280 - 3	THE ESSENCE OF THE POWER
POWER	283 - 3	FAITH IS THE POWER OF PRAYER
POWER	292 - 1	POWER WITH WHICH HE IS DEALING
POWER	292 - 2	IMPLANTED IN THE CREATIVE POWER
POWER	296 - 4	DRAWING POWER OF ATTRACTION
POWER	296 - 4	ONE POWER THAT CREATES ALL
POWER	300 - 4	RECOGNIZE THE POWER
POWER	301 - 3	GOD HAS GIVEN US A POWER
POWER	301 - 4	SILENT POWER BEHIND ALL THINGS
POWER	302 - 3	IT IS ALL POWER
POWER	302 - 3	MIND IS THE POWER
POWER	304 - 1	FROM THIS WORD THE POWER OF THE INFINITE
POWER	310 - 4	THIS POWER OF THE WORD
POWER	322 - 2	A POWER ALWAYS AT WORK
POWER	334 - 3	IT GIVES A SENSE OF POWER
POWER	334 - 4	POWER OF JESUS LAY IN HIS RECOGNITION
POWER	357 - 3	TO BE THE PRESENCE POWER
POWER	364 - 1	CHRIST ALWAYS COMES WITH POWER
POWER	377 - 3	DIRECT POWER OF THOUGHT OPERATING
POWER	379 - 1	OUR REASONING POWER IS CORRECT
POWER	379 - 1	SOME POWER WHICH IS MENTAL
POWER	379 - 4	THE POWER OF ITS THOUGHT
POWER	388 - 2	NO POWER IN THE UNIVERSE
POWER	392 - 2	IT IS UNEXPRESSED POWER, SUBSTANCE
POWER	394 - 3	CAN USE THIS POWER FOR THE HEALING
POWER	396 - 1	POWER THAT WE GIVE
POWER	396 - 2	UNIVERSAL MIND HAS UNLIMITED POWER
POWER	397 - 3	SEE WHAT A TREMENDOUS POWER

POWER	398 - 4	CREATIVE POWER RESPONDS TO FEELING MORE
POWER	398 - 5	CREATIVE POWER IN OUR THOUGHT
POWER	399 - 4	INNER RECEPTIVITY WITH POWER
POWER	399 - 5	THE GREATEST POWER OF ALL
POWER	401 - 1	POWER OF REAL SELF-EXPRESSION
POWER	401 - 3	WE CAN USE CREATIVE POWER
POWER	401 - 3	USE THIS POWER FOR DEFINITE PURPOSES
POWER	406 - 1	IT IS NOT BY EXTERNAL POWER
POWER	410 - 3	LIVE IN OBEDIENCE TO THE POWER
POWER	410 - 4	THE POWER TO CREATE RESIDES
POWER	410 - 4	WE HAVE POWER OVER CONDITIONS
POWER	412 - 1	TO BE IDENTIFIED WITH POWER
POWER	413 - 4	THE WHOLE POWER OF THE UNIVERSE
POWER	414 - 2	THIS POWER IS SUPERIOR TO THE INTELLECT
POWER	414 - 3	A SPIRITUAL POWER IS RELEASED
POWER	417 - 4	OUR HUMAN WILL POWER WILL
POWER	418 - 2	USING AN ISOLATED POWER
POWER	419 - 1	POWER OVER HIS OBJECTIVE WORLD
POWER	431 - 3	POWER IN THE OUTWARD LIFE DEPENDS
POWER	434 - 6	POWER OF THAT THOUGHT
POWER	437 - 4	POWER OF JESUS
POWER	440 - 1	DEMONSTRATION OF SPIRITUAL POWER
POWER	463 - 2	POWER WITHOUT WHICH
POWER	476 - 1	POWER ONLY AS IT IS ONE WITH POWER
POWER	483 - 3	POWER WITHIN THEMSELVES TO BE
POWERFUL	145 - 3	MOST POWERFUL HEALING AGENCY
POWERFUL	178 - 5	THE MORE POWERFUL THE TREATMENT
POWERFUL	188 - 2	POWERFUL AS THE WORDS WHICH JESUS SPOKE
POWERFUL	209 - 1	IS FAR MORE POWERFUL THAN UNTRAINED
POWERFUL	256 - 1	DIVINE, POWERFUL, VITAL ESSENCE
POWERFUL	415 - 1	WE LIVE IS REAL AND POWERFUL
POWERFUL	447 - 3	WE BECOME POISED AND POWERFUL
POWERFUL	454 - 4	POWERFUL ONLY AS WE UNITE WITH POWER
POWER LINE	454 - 3	BINDS US TO THE MAIN POWER LINE
POWERS	032 - 3	NEW POWERS AND HIGHER POSSIBILITIES
POWERS	053 - 3	WITH SUCH POWERS AND FORCES
POWERS	378 - 3	US WITH SUCH SUBTLE POWERS
POWERS	402 - 3	NOT DEALING WITH TWO POWERS
PRACTICAL	042 - 5	PRACTICAL USE IN EVERYDAY LIFE
PRACTICAL	051 - 2	PRACTICAL APPLICATION IS NECESSARY
PRACTICAL	086 - 3	PRACTICAL LIFE OF THE INDIVIDUAL
PRACTICAL	140 - 1	PRACTICAL APPLICATION OF THIS SCIENCE
PRACTICAL	314 - 2	A PRACTICAL USE OF THE TRUTH
PRACTICAL	318 - 2	WE MAKE PRACTICAL APPLICATION
PRACTICAL	336 - 3	FOR A PRACTICAL APPLICATION
PRACTICAL	346 - 2	PRACTICAL WORK FOR HEALING
PRACTICAL	393 - 2	SPIRITUAL WORK FROM A PRACTICAL
PRACTICAL	444 - 4	MAKE PRACTICAL USE OF ITS KNOWLEDGE
PRACTICAL	475 - 3	LESSON IN THE PRACTICAL
PRACTICAL	476 - 6	PRACTICAL WAY OF MAKING HIS DREAMS
PRACTICAL	500 - 1	WOULD LIKE A PRACTICAL DEMONSTRATION
PRACTICE	051 - 1	TOO LITTLE PRACTICE
PRACTICE	054 - 1	PRACTICE OF THE SCIENCE OF MIND
PRACTICE	086 - 4	FUNDAMENTAL TO OUR PRACTICE
PRACTICE	185 - 2	BY THIS PRACTICE THE SOUL

PRACTICE	206 - 2	PRACTICE WE MAKE NO ATTEMPT
PRACTICE	277 - 2	PRACTICE IS A DEFINITE STATEMENT
PRACTICE	358 - 4	DAILY PRACTICE IN OUR MEDITATIONS
PRACTICE	410 - 2	IN PRACTICE WE STATE CLEARLY
PRACTICE	413 - 2	TO PRACTICE THE PRESENCE OF GOD
PRACTICE	419 - 1	PART OF OUR EVERYDAY PRACTICE
PRACTICE	423 - 1	TRUTH THAN IT IS TO PRACTICE IT
PRACTICE	423 - 2	PRACTICE OF TRUTH
PRACTICED	487 - 2	MAY BE PRACTICED BY ANYONE
PRACTICING	094 - 1	PRACTICING THIS PRINCIPLE IN LOS ANGELES
PRACTITIONER	053 - 3	PRACTITIONER OF THIS SCIENCE
PRACTITIONER	059 - 3	PRACTITIONER MUST KNOW
PRACTITIONER	097 - 2	FIRST THINGS A PRACTITIONER
PRACTITIONER	163 - 1	PRACTITIONER DOES NOT FEEL
PRACTITIONER	165 - 2	PRACTITIONER BEGINS TO THINK PEACE
PRACTITIONER	165 - 2	PRACTITIONER DOES NOT SEND OUT THOUGHTS
PRACTITIONER	165 - 2	PRACTITIONER TREATS THE PRACTITIONER
PRACTITIONER	166 - 2	PRACTITIONER WORKS THROUGH THE LAW
PRACTITIONER	167 - 3	IS A MENTAL OR SPIRITUAL PRACTITIONER
PRACTITIONER	168 - 3	THIS CONFIDENCE A PRACTITIONER SHOULD KEEP
PRACTITIONER	169 - 2	PRACTITIONER NEVER TRIES TO GET AWAY
PRACTITIONER	169 - 4	PRACTITIONER REALIZES THAT MAN IS BORN
PRACTITIONER	169 - 5	PRACTITIONER THEN IS ONE WHO
PRACTITIONER	169 - 6	PRACTITIONER REALLY DOES IS TO TAKE
PRACTITIONER	171 - 3	PRACTITIONER MUST DO THE WORK
PRACTITIONER	176 - 1	PRACTITIONER DOES NOT TRY TO CREATE
PRACTITIONER	178 - 5	PRACTITIONER IS ONE WHO RECOGNIZES MAN
PRACTITIONER	199 - 2	PRACTITIONER IS TRYING TO REALIZE
PRACTITIONER	200 - 1	PRACTITIONER MUST TREAT HIMSELF
PRACTITIONER	205 - 4	PRACTITIONER IS IN THE SAME MIND
PRACTITIONER	205 - 5	PRACTITIONER REALIZES A CERTAIN TRUTH
PRACTITIONER	216 - 1	THE PRACTITIONER REALIZES
PRACTITIONER	218 - 4	THE PRACTITIONER MUST REALIZE
PRACTITIONER	238 - 2	PRACTITIONER MUST BE FILLED
PRACTITIONER	262 - 2	PRACTITIONER MUST REALIZE
PRACTITIONER	262 - 2	PRACTITIONER MUST KNOW THAT
PRACTITIONER	286 - 2	PRACTITIONER TAKES THE THOUGHT
PRACTITIONER	291 - 3	AS FAR AS THE PRACTITIONER IS CONCERNED
PRACTITIONER	291 - 3	THE PRACTITIONER TREATS HIMSELF
PRACTITIONER	316 - 1	PRACTITIONER SHOULD DEAL WITH HIS FIELD
PRACTITIONER	317 - 2	PRACTITIONER MUST NOT DEAL WITH TIME
PRACTITIONER	335 - 5	SPIRITUAL PRACTITIONER SHOULD SENSE
PRACTITIONER	408 - 5	PRACTITIONER DEALS WITH THOUGHT
PRACTITIONER	409 - 1	PRACTITIONER MUST TRY TO BECOME
PRACTITIONER	409 - 1	MAN TO BE HEALED IS THE PRACTITIONER
PRACTITIONER	409 - 3	PRACTITIONER WORKS WITHIN HIS OWN
PRACTITIONER	413 - 5	PRACTITIONER TREATS NOT A PATIENT
PRACTITIONER	418 - 3	PRACTITIONER KNOWS THAT THE SPIRITUAL
PRACTITIONERS	168 - 4	PRACTITIONERS DO MEET OCCASIONALLY
PRACTITIONER'S	168 - 5	PRACTITIONER'S BUSINESS TO UNCOVER GOD
PRAISE	230 - 5	PRAISE OUR VISION
PRAISE	434 - 2	LAW RESPONDING TO PRAISE
PRAISE	434 - 3	PRAISE AND NOT CONDEMN
PRAISE	434 - 7	WHEN WE CONSTRUCTIVELY PRAISE
PRAISE	438 - 5	WE MIGHT PRAISE

PRAISES	361 - 2	HOSTS OF HEAVEN SING PRAISES
PRAY	217 - 2	PRAY TO THE FATHER WHO
PRAY	280 - 1	WE DO NOT HAVE TO PRAY GOD
PRAY	283 - 2	PRAY RIGHT AND GOD CANNOT HELP RESPONDING
PRAY	290 - 1	WHEN YE PRAY BELIEVE THAT YE HAVE
PRAY	398 - 3	PRAY WE SHOULD BELIEVE
PRAY	497 - 1	PRAY WITHOUT CEASING
PRAYER	027 - 6	OR PHYSICAL DISEASE THROUGH PRAYER
PRAYER	028 - 1	ANSWER THE PRAYER OF ONE ABOVE ANOTHER
PRAYER	028 - 2	THEIR PRAYER (THEIR THOUGHT) HAS RESPONDED
PRAYER	028 - 2	ANSWER TO PRAYER IS IN THE PRAYER
PRAYER	028 - 2	A PRAYER IS A MOVEMENT OF THOUGHT
PRAYER	149 - 2	PRAYER IS A RECOGNITION OF SPIRIT'S
PRAYER	149 - 2	PRAYER IS A SPIRITUAL TREATMENT
PRAYER	150 - 2	MEN WHO BELIEVE IN GOD BELIEVE IN PRAYER
PRAYER	151 - 2	PRAYER WE SHOULD NOT DWELL UPON EVIL
PRAYER	152 - 2	PRAYER IS NOT AN ACT OF OVERCOMING GOD'S
PRAYER	152 - 3	PRAYER IS CONSTRUCTIVE BECAUSE IT ENABLES
PRAYER	152 - 4	PRAYER IS ESSENTIAL NOT TO THE SALVATION
PRAYER	153 - 4	PRAYER IS ITS OWN ANSWER
PRAYER	154 - 1	OUR PRAYER IS ANSWERED
PRAYER	155 - 2	PRAYER IS A MENTAL APPROACH
PRAYER	155 - 2	THE IDEA SYMBOLIZED THAT MAKES PRAYER
PRAYER	157 - 4	PRAYER IS NOT AN END OF ITSELF
PRAYER	178 - 2	PRAYER IS ESSENTIAL TO HAPPINESS
PRAYER	178 - 2	PRAYER IS ESSENTIAL TO THE CONSCIOUS
PRAYER	178 - 2	PRAYER IS ITS OWN ANSWER
PRAYER	190 - 1	HEALED THROUGH PRAYER AND FAITH
PRAYER	190 - 1	ALL PRAYER IS MENTAL
PRAYER	190 - 2	PRAYER IS IN THE PRAYER WHEN IT IS PRAYED
PRAYER	191 - 3	WHETHER IT BE A PILL OR A PRAYER
PRAYER	268 - 4	TRUE PRAYER MUST BE
PRAYER	280 - 1	PRAYER DOES SOMETHING TO THE MIND
PRAYER	280 - 3	UNCOVER THE SCIENCE OF PRAYER
PRAYER	283 - 2	BELIEVES MORE IN PRAYER
PRAYER	431 - 3	PRAYER HAS POWER NOT THROUGH REPETITION
PRAYER	435 - 3	TEACHING REGARDING PRAYER
PRAYER	435 - 4	PRAYER IS A MENTAL
PRAYER	435 - 4	PRAYER SHOULD BE DIRECT AND SPECIFIC
PRAYER	436 - 1	TEACHING OF JESUS RELATIVE TO PRAYER
PRAYER	455 - 3	METAPHYSICAL ACT OF PRAYER
PRAYER	458 - 4	PRAYER WHICH IS A MENTAL ACT
PRAYER	500 - 5	PRAYER OF FAITH IS AN UNCONDITIONAL BELIEF
PRAYER OF FAITH	501 - 2	PRAYER OF FAITH PENETRATES THE SUBJECTIVE
PRAYERS	149 - 1	ARE PRAYERS AND TREATMENTS IDENTICAL
PRAYERS	156 - 3	ANSWER OUR PRAYERS
PRAYERS	190 - 1	PRAYERS FALL SHORT OF THIS STATE
PRAYERS	431 - 2	PRAYERS ARE TO BE MADE TO GOD
PRAYERS	436 - 1	PRAYERS WHICH HAVE NO MEANING
PRAYERS	481 - 4	PRAYERS TO THE ONE WILL BE ANSWERED
PRAYERS	503 - 7	PRAYERS ARE ANSWERED
PRAYING	280 - 1	TO THE MIND OF THE ONE PRAYING
PREACH	162 - 4	CEASED TO PREACH THE NECESSITY
PRECEDENT	162 - 3	PRINCIPLE IS NOT BOUND BY PRECEDENT
PRECEDENT	275 - 2	NOT BOUND BY PRECEDENT

PRECIOUS	338 - 2	MOST PRECIOUS THING A MAN POSSESSES
PREDESTINATE	485 - 6	HE ALSO DID PREDESTINATE
PREDESTINED	359 - 3	NO ONE PARTICULAR MAN PREDESTINED TO
PREDETERMINED	486 - 1	PREDETERMINED BY THE DIVINE MIND
PREEMINENTLY	329 - 3	PREEMINENTLY SANE PEOPLE
PRE-EXISTS	345 - 3	IT IS SOMETHING WHICH PRE-EXISTS
PREMISE	082 - 3	FUNDAMENTAL PREMISE
PREMISE	096 - 2	AN ALREADY ESTABLISHED PREMISE
PREMISE	159 - 2	ORGANIZED TO FIT THIS PREMISE
PREMISE	166 - 4	BASED UPON THE PREMISE
PREMISE	179 - 3	PREMISE THAT WE ALL LIVE IN ONE
PREMISE	201 - 4	THIS IS OUR WHOLE PREMISE
PREMISE	245 - 1	THE PREMISE OF ONE POWER
PREMISE	317 - 1	THE PREMISE THAT GOD IS PERFECT
PREMISE	355 - 4	ALREADY ESTABLISHED PREMISE
PREMISES	400 - 4	BUILT ON ALREADY ACCEPTED PREMISES
PREMIUM	458 - 2	A PREMIUM UPON WRONG-DOING
PREPARE	388 - 2	PREPARE TO MEET HIS GOD
PREPARE	479 - 5	PREPARE A PLACE FOR YOU
PREROGATIVE	143 - 4	NO INDIVIDUALITY WITHOUT PREROGATIVE
PRESENCE	041 - 4	THERE IS A SPIRITUAL PRESENCE
PRESENCE	045 - 1	COURTED THE PARTICULAR PRESENCE
PRESENCE	055 - 2	PERSONALITY NOR PRESENCE
PRESENCE	059 - 2	IN THIS PRESENCE
PRESENCE	060 - 3	EVOLUTION OF THE GREAT PRESENCE
PRESENCE	094 - 1	UNIVERSAL SIMULTANEOUS PRESENCE
PRESENCE	094 - 1	IN THIS PRESENCE ALL LIVE
PRESENCE	150 - 1	GOD IS A UNIVERSAL PRESENCE
PRESENCE	152 - 5	DISCONNECTED FROM THIS INFINITE PRESENCE
PRESENCE	153 - 1	GOD AS AN INDWELLING PRESENCE
PRESENCE	153 - 3	A PRESENCE THERE THAT KNOWS
PRESENCE	164 - 4	REALIZATION OF THE PRESENCE
PRESENCE	173 - 4	TO APPROACH THIS PRESENCE SIMPLY
PRESENCE	178 - 7	NO ABSENCE IN THE ONE PRESENCE
PRESENCE	183 - 2	THE DIVINE PRESENCE
PRESENCE	186 - 4	RECOGNITION OF THE PRESENCE OF GOD
PRESENCE	202 - 4	PRESENCE AND THE POWER
PRESENCE	204 - 2	PRESENCE CANNOT CHANGE
PRESENCE	205 - 2	PRESENCE IN AND THROUGH
PRESENCE	216 - 1	HIS WORD IS THE PRESENCE
PRESENCE	217 - 1	AFFIRM THE PRESENCE OF GOD
PRESENCE	217 - 1	ALWAYS AN INDWELLING PRESENCE
PRESENCE	218 - 3	REALIZATION OF THE PRESENCE
PRESENCE	219 - 4	SPIRIT IS AN ACTIVE PRESENCE
PRESENCE	221 - 4	PRESENCE OF SPIRIT IN YOUR PATIENT
PRESENCE	223 - 3	THE PRESENCE OF GOD IS
PRESENCE	224 - 1	PRESENCE THERE IS NO TENSION
PRESENCE	234 - 5	IS ETERNAL PRESENCE
PRESENCE	240 - 1	RECOGNIZE ITS PRESENCE
PRESENCE	240 - 4	REALIZE THE PRESENCE OF LIFE
PRESENCE	241 - 3	ONE INDWELLING PRESENCE
PRESENCE	245 - 3	SPIRIT IS THE ONLY PRESENCE
PRESENCE	263 - 1	REALIZATION OF THE PRESENCE
PRESENCE	275 - 3	HEAVENLY FATHER IS A DIVINE PRESENCE
PRESENCE	276 - 1	DIVINE PRESENCE AS A UNIVERSAL SPIRIT

PRESENCE	276 - 2	GREATEST SENSE OF THE DIVINE PRESENCE
PRESENCE	276 - 3	REALIZATION OF THE PRESENCE OF SPIRIT
PRESENCE	285 - 1	A CONSCIOUSNESS OF THE DIVINE PRESENCE
PRESENCE	308 - 1	A PRESENCE PERSONIFIED IN US
PRESENCE	314 - 2	PRESENCE IN THE UNIVERSE
PRESENCE	323 - 3	ALL THE PRESENCE THERE IS
PRESENCE	327 - 4	REVEALED THE PRESENCE OF GOD
PRESENCE	329 - 3	COURTING OF THE DIVINE PRESENCE
PRESENCE	330 - 4	SENSE THIS MARVELOUS PRESENCE
PRESENCE	333 - 6	WHO BELIEVE IN ITS PRESENCE
PRESENCE	334 - 4	THAT WE FORGET THE LIVING PRESENCE
PRESENCE	344 - 2	TO DECLARE ITS PRESENCE
PRESENCE	357 - 3	THAT LIVING PRESENCE WITHIN
PRESENCE	357 - 3	TO BE THE PRESENCE POWER
PRESENCE	363 - 4	THE DIVINE PRESENCE WITHIN HIM
PRESENCE	378 - 1	PRESENCE OF AN UNKNOWN AGENCY
PRESENCE	380 - 3	VAGUE SENSE OF THEIR PRESENCE
PRESENCE	388 - 3	FEEL THAT SUBTLE PRESENCE
PRESENCE	388 - 3	DO WE NOT SENSE ANOTHER PRESENCE
PRESENCE	398 - 5	CONSCIOUS OF ITS PRESENCE WITHIN US
PRESENCE	413 - 2	TO PRACTICE THE PRESENCE OF GOD
PRESENCE	413 - 3	TO PRACTICE THE PRESENCE
PRESENCE	418 - 3	INDWELLING PRESENCE IS ALREADY PERFECT
PRESENCE	420 - 1	ONLY PRESENCE IN THE ENTIRE UNIVERSE
PRESENCE	422 - 3	THE DIVINE PRESENCE WITHIN HIM
PRESENCE	423 - 3	THE PRESENCE OF PERFECTION WITHIN
PRESENCE	431 - 3	ENTER THE PRESENCE OF SPIRIT
PRESENCE	439 - 5	PRESENCE OF WHICH HEALS
PRESENT	095 - 1	NO PAST, PRESENT OR FUTURE
PRESENT	178 - 7	ABSENT AND A PRESENT TREATMENT
PRESENT	241 - 3	PRESENT IN THE ORGANS
PRESENT	246 - 1	THE VICTORY OF A PERFECT PRESENT
PRESENT	246 - 2	NO PAST TO BRING DISCORD INTO THE PRESENT
PRESENT	289 - 4	CAN NEVER BECOME PRESENT
PRESENT	330 - 3	GOD IS PRESENT AT ANY AND EVERY POINT
PRESENT	335 - 1	KINGDOM OF GOD IS NOW PRESENT
PRESENT	353 - 3	NO PAST, NO PRESENT AND NO FUTURE
PRESENT	399 - 2	WHOLE THING AS A PRESENT REALITY
PRESENT	422 - 2	THE PAST AND THE PRESENT ARE ONE
PRESENT	488 - 3	LIMITED TO OUR PRESENT UNDERSTANDING
PRESENTATION	341 - 3	MYSTICAL PRESENTATION OF CHRIST
PRESENT TREATMENT	171 - 3	OPPOSED TO A PRESENT TREATMENT
PRESENT TREATMENTS	178 - 7	ABSENT AND PRESENT TREATMENTS ARE THE
PRESS	439 - 2	WE SHOULD PRESS BOLDLY FORWARD
PRESS	439 - 3	PRESS BRAVELY ON
PRESSING	445 - 3	PRESSING EVER OUTWARD
PRESSURE	247 - 3	HIGH PRESSURE NOR LOW PRESSURE
PRESSURE	249 - 3	HIGH BLOOD PRESSURE
PRESSURE	249 - 4	PRESSURE AND ALL THAT GOES WITH IT
PRESSURE	340 - 3	AN IRRESISTIBLE PRESSURE
PRETENSE	500 - 1	IT IS SICK OF PRETENSE
PREVENTION	225 - 4	FOR THE PREVENTION OF HEADACHE
PREVIOUS	110 - 3	FROM HIS PREVIOUS EXPERIENCES
PREVIOUS	265 - 1	BACK OVER ALL PREVIOUS
PRICE	268 - 2	MUST PAY THE PRICE

PRICE	268 - 2	THAT PRICE IS PAID IN MENTAL
PRIDE	033 - 1	CONGEALED BY PRIDE
PRIEST	042 - 3	THE PRIEST AND THE PROFESSOR
PRIEST	168 - 3	PRIEST WHO OFFICIATES AT THE CONFESSIONAL
PRIESTS	448 - 2	PRIESTS HAD REASONED WITHIN
PRIMAL	316 - 2	UNITY IN ONE PRIMAL PRINCIPLE
PRIMARILY	164 - 4	PROBLEM IS PRIMARILY MENTAL
PRIMARILY	203 - 2	PRIMARILY A THING OF THOUGHT
PRIMARILY MENTAL	277 - 3	EVERY PROBLEM IS PRIMARILY MENTAL
PRIMORDIAL	058 - 1	PRIMORDIAL WORD OF THE CREATOR
PRIMORDIAL	091 - 3	SOUL-STUFF REFERS TO THE PRIMORDIAL
PRIMORDIAL	117 - 1	MADE FROM THIS PRIMORDIAL SUBSTANCE
PRIMORDIAL	310 - 2	A PRIMORDIAL UNITY OF ENERGY
PRINCIPLE	026 - 3	WHATEVER THE NATURE OF ANY PRINCIPLE
PRINCIPLE	026 - 4	DEALING WITH A DEFINITE PRINCIPLE
PRINCIPLE	026 - 6	DEALING WITH A PRINCIPLE
PRINCIPLE	032 - 3	MANIFESTATION OF THIS ETERNAL PRINCIPLE
PRINCIPLE	040 - 1	ITS PRINCIPLE DOES NOT CONTAIN
PRINCIPLE	043 - 3	PRINCIPLE GOVERNING THE SCIENCE
PRINCIPLE	043 - 3	WAY THE PRINCIPLE WORKS
PRINCIPLE	045 - 4	THOUGHT TAPS THE SAME PRINCIPLE
PRINCIPLE	045 - 5	FIRST PRINCIPLE IS GOODNESS
PRINCIPLE	046 - 4	LET US RESTATE OUR PRINCIPLE
PRINCIPLE	047 - 3	IN ACCORD WITH THE PRINCIPLE
PRINCIPLE	048 - 3	HIS ABILITY IN THE PRINCIPLE
PRINCIPLE	048 - 3	PROVING THE PRINCIPLE
PRINCIPLE	049 - 3	SCIENTIFIC USE OF THIS PRINCIPLE
PRINCIPLE	049 - 5	PRINCIPLE THAT WE HAVE
PRINCIPLE	051 - 2	OF ANY SCIENTIFIC PRINCIPLE
PRINCIPLE	051 - 2	PRINCIPLE OF OTHER SCIENCES
PRINCIPLE	052 - 1	ANNOUNCE A PRINCIPLE
PRINCIPLE	052 - 5	ACCORDING TO THE PRINCIPLE
PRINCIPLE	053 - 2	APPLIES THE RIGHT PRINCIPLE
PRINCIPLE	060 - 2	PRINCIPLE WE HAVE TO DEMONSTRATE
PRINCIPLE	063 - 2	NOTHING BUT THE LIFE PRINCIPLE
PRINCIPLE	064 - 2	SPIRIT TO BE THE LIFE PRINCIPLE
PRINCIPLE	066 - 2	IN SCIENCE, THE WORD PRINCIPLE
PRINCIPLE	066 - 3	WE STATE OUR FIRST PRINCIPLE
PRINCIPLE	067 - 2	ETERNAL CREATIVE PRINCIPLE
PRINCIPLE	071 - 1	HAD TO HAVE A PRINCIPLE
PRINCIPLE	072 - 2	PRINCIPLE OF ANY SCIENCE
PRINCIPLE	074 - 2	UPON SOME PROVEN PRINCIPLE
PRINCIPLE	074 - 3	PRINCIPLE IS ANNOUNCED
PRINCIPLE	074 - 4	ABOUT ITS INVISIBLE PRINCIPLE
PRINCIPLE	075 - 3	ETERNAL PRINCIPLE IS FOREVER HIDDEN
PRINCIPLE	079 - 3	THIS IS THE PRINCIPLE
PRINCIPLE	081 - 4	SELF-CONSCIOUS PRINCIPLE
PRINCIPLE	082 - 1	PRINCIPLE OF UNITY BACK
PRINCIPLE	083 - 4	PRINCIPLE IS SPIRIT
PRINCIPLE	086 - 4	NOT IN THE PRINCIPLE
PRINCIPLE	088 - 4	GOD NOT ONLY AS PRINCIPLE
PRINCIPLE	092 - 2	SAME PRINCIPLE HOLDS GOOD
PRINCIPLE	098 - 3	INVISIBLE PRINCIPLE OF LIFE
PRINCIPLE	102 - 4	UPON THE CREATIVE PRINCIPLE
PRINCIPLE	118 - 2	LIMITATION IS NOT IN PRINCIPLE

PRINCIPLE	138 - 3	PRINCIPLE FUNDAMENTAL TO THE UNDERSTANDING
PRINCIPLE	146 - 4	PRINCIPLE SCIENTIFICALLY CORRECT
PRINCIPLE	157 - 4	PRINCIPLE GOVERNING FAITH IS
PRINCIPLE	160 - 1	SPIRITUAL PRINCIPLE INCARNATED IN
PRINCIPLE	162 - 3	PRINCIPLE IS NOT BOUND BY PRECEDENT
PRINCIPLE	167 - 2	THE PRINCIPLE OF SPIRITUAL TREATMENT
PRINCIPLE	184 - 3	AN IMPERSONAL PRINCIPLE
PRINCIPLE	188 - 3	THINK RIGHT BACK TO PRINCIPLE
PRINCIPLE	195 - 3	PRINCIPLE OF SUBJECTIVE LAW
PRINCIPLE	197 - 5	WE ARE LIMITED NOT BY PRINCIPLE
PRINCIPLE	201 - 3	PRINCIPLE NO MATTER HOW
PRINCIPLE	205 - 3	PRINCIPLE MAKES LITTLE DIFFERENCE
PRINCIPLE	201 - 3	PRINCIPLE WORKS INDEPENDENTLY
PRINCIPLE	219 - 3	PRINCIPLE IS INFINITE
PRINCIPLE	221 - 2	PRINCIPLE IS THE POWER
PRINCIPLE	221 - 5	THE LAW GOVERNING THIS PRINCIPLE
PRINCIPLE	235 - 4	THE ACTIVITY OF PERFECT PRINCIPLE
PRINCIPLE	268 - 5	THE PRINCIPLE OF LIFE
PRINCIPLE	275 - 2	LIMITATION IN PRINCIPLE BUT IN PERFORMANCE
PRINCIPLE	275 - 2	PRINCIPLE IS NOT BOUND BY PRECEDENT
PRINCIPLE	278 - 4	PRINCIPLE IS ABSOLUTE
PRINCIPLE	279 - 1	PRINCIPLE AND NOT PERSONALITY
PRINCIPLE	281 - 2	A PRINCIPLE WHICH RESPONDS
PRINCIPLE	299 - 4	THERE IS A DIVINE PRINCIPLE
PRINCIPLE	302 - 3	ON THE PRINCIPLE OF LIFE ITSELF
PRINCIPLE	339 - 2	EVOLUTION IS A PRINCIPLE
PRINCIPLE	359 - 3	NOT A PERSON BUT A PRINCIPLE
PRINCIPLE	365 - 4	THINKING OF GOD AS MERELY PRINCIPLE
PRINCIPLE	388 - 3	FOREVER-EXPANDING PRINCIPLE
PRINCIPLE	415 - 3	A UNIFYING PRINCIPLE OF LIFE
PRINCIPLE	419 - 1	KNOWLEDGE OF UNSEEN PRINCIPLE
PRINCIPLE	423 - 1	PROVE ITS PRINCIPLE
PRINCIPLE	432 - 3	PROVING THE PRINCIPLE
PRINCIPLE	441 - 3	PRINCIPLE INVOLVED IS PLAIN
PRINCIPLE	450 - 2	PRINCIPLE WHICH GOVERNS ALL THINGS
PRINCIPLES	025 - 1	PRINCIPLES ARE UNIVERSAL
PRINCIPLES	026 - 5	PRINCIPLES ARE FOREVER HIDDEN FROM OUR
PRINCIPLES	026 - 5	BUT INVISIBLE PRINCIPLES
PRINCIPLES	027 - 3	PRINCIPLES ARE NEVER RESPECTERS OF PERSONS
PRINCIPLES	043 - 3	BASED UPON PROVEN PRINCIPLES
PRINCIPLES	045 - 1	PRINCIPLES OF HIS SCIENCE
PRINCIPLES	051 - 2	ALL PRINCIPLES ARE AS INTANGIBLE
PRINCIPLES	067 - 3	BASIC PRINCIPLES OF THE RELIGIONS
PRINCIPLES	085 - 2	INVISIBLE PRINCIPLES ARE THEORETICAL
PRINCIPLES	095 - 2	DO NOT CREATE LAWS AND PRINCIPLES
PRINCIPLES	221 - 1	PRINCIPLES IN WHICH I BELIEVE
PRINT	344 - 3	PUT INTO WORDS OR INTO PRINT
PRIOR	064 - 4	PRIOR TO THE CREATION
PRIOR	347 - 3	PRIOR TO OUR USE OF IT
PRISM	231 - 3	PRISM OF GOD'S LOVE
PRISON	456 - 3	PRISON WALLS OF FALSE EXPERIENCE
PRISONER	108 - 3	PRISONER UNDER A LIFE SENTENCE
PRIVILEGE	161 - 4	PRIVILEGE OF GIVING BIRTH TO IT
PRIVILEGE	305 - 3	ETERNAL DAY OF INFINITE PRIVILEGE
PRIVILEGE	415 - 2	IS INDEED A GREAT PRIVILEGE

PRIVILEGES	401 - 3	PRIVILEGES WE WISH TO ENJOY
PROBABILITY	052 - 2	POSSIBILITY OF ALL HUMAN PROBABILITY
PROBLEM	053 - 2	PROBLEM DOES PUNISH HIM
PROBLEM	072 - 2	MATHEMATICIAN SOLVES A PROBLEM
PROBLEM	164 - 4	EVERY PROBLEM IS PRIMARILY MENTAL
PROBLEM	201 - 2	PROBLEM TO THE INDIVIDUAL
PROBLEM	273 - 3	ANSWER TO THAT PROBLEM IS RIGHT THEN
PROBLEM	365 - 2	THE SOLUTION TO EVERY PROBLEM
PROBLEM	383 - 2	PROBLEM OF GOOD AND EVIL
PROBLEM	420 - 2	PROBLEM IS IN MAN'S OWN CONSCIOUSNESS
PROBLEMS	044 - 2	ANSWER TO ALL OUR PROBLEMS
PROBLEMS	078 - 2	DIFFICULT PROBLEMS TO REALIZE
PROBLEMS	164 - 4	ANSWER TO ALL PROBLEMS
PROBLEMS	277 - 3	ANSWERS TO OUR PROBLEMS WILL BE FOUND
PROBLEMS	334 - 3	TRY TO SOLVE ALL OF ITS PROBLEMS
PROBLEMS	388 - 1	TIME TO WORK OUT ALL PROBLEMS
PROBLEMS	456 - 4	PROBLEMS AS THOUGH THEY WERE NOT
PROCEDURE	308 - 2	PROCEDURE IN MENTAL TREATMENT
PROCEED	222 - 2	PROCEED WITH THE TREATMENT
PROCEED	282 - 3	THE WAY TO PROCEED
PROCEED	305 - 3	PROCEED ON MY WAY AS ONE
PROCEED	446 - 4	CANNOT PROCEED FROM THE ETERNAL
PROCEEDETH	427 - 3	WORD THAT PROCEEDETH OUT OF THE MOUTH
PROCEEDS	472 - 2	PROCEEDS FROM THE INNERMOST
PROCESS	057 - 3	NO PROCESS OF HEALING
PROCESS	057 - 3	PROCESS IN HEALING
PROCESS	057 - 3	THIS PROCESS IS THE TIME AND EFFORT
PROCESS	067 - 2	PROCESS OF AN ETERNAL CREATION
PROCESS	069 - 2	AN INNER PROCESS OF CONSCIOUSNESS
PROCESS	083 - 4	PROCESS IN ITS MANIFESTATION
PROCESS	102 - 3	EVOLUTION IS THE PROCESS, THE WAY, THE TIME
PROCESS	119 - 3	UNCONSCIOUS PROCESS OF THOUGHT
PROCESS	160 - 2	THROUGH A PROCESS OF THOUGHT
PROCESS	170 - 5	SPIRITUAL AND MEDITATIVE PROCESS
PROCESS	173 - 3	PROCESS CALLED TREATING
PROCESS	179 - 4	NOT A PROCESS BUT A REVELATION
PROCESS	179 - 4	PROCESS IF THERE IS ONE
PROCESS	187 - 3	DURING THE PROCESS MANY THINGS
PROCESS	190 - 1	AN UPLIFTING PROCESS
PROCESS	203 - 4	PROCESS OF REASONING
PROCESS	208 - 3	PROCESS OF REALIZATION
PROCESS	212 - 4	THE PROCESS IN HEALING
PROCESS	212 - 4	PROCESS OF HEALING
PROCESS	289 - 2	NEVER TREAT A PROCESS
PROCESS	301 - 2	THIS PROCESS GOES ON
PROCESS	338 - 3	THIS PROCESS OF EVOLUTION
PROCESS	409 - 2	PROCESS IS ONE OF THOUGHT
PROCESS	419 - 2	WITHOUT CONSCIOUS MENTAL PROCESS
PROCESS	420 - 3	EVOLUTION IS THE TIME AND THE PROCESS
PROCESSES	053 - 4	CONTROL OUR THOUGHT PROCESSES
PROCESSES	126 - 2	PROCESSES WHICH AFFECT OR IMPRESS US
PROCESSES	388 - 3	SILENT PROCESSES OF THOUGHT
PROCESSES	394 - 5	AUTOMATIC PROCESSES OF NATURE
PROCLAIM	051 - 3	EASY TO PROCLAIM
PROCLAIM	121 - 4	PROCLAIM THEMSELVES THROUGH MAN'S

PROCLAIMED	122 - 1	PERCEIVED AND PROCLAIMED THIS FACT
PROCLAIMING	336 - 2	GOD PROCLAIMING HIS OWN BEING
PROCLAIMING	368 - 1	PROCLAIMING ITSELF AS THE SON
PROCLAIMING	423 - 3	GOD PROCLAIMING I AM THAT WHICH
PROCLAIMING	451 - 3	PROCLAIMING THE FREEDOM OF ALL
PROCLAIMS	122 - 2	PROCLAIMS ITSELF IN EVERY THOUGHT
PROCLAMATION	056 - 2	LOUD IN ITS PROCLAMATION
PROCLAMATION	472 - 2	NOR BY LOUD PROCLAMATION
PROCLAMATION	499 - 6	MORE THAN THE LOUDEST PROCLAMATION
PRODIGAL SON	147 - 3	PRODIGAL SON REMAINED A PRODIGAL
PRODIGAL SON	460 - 4	PRODIGAL SON CONSTITUTES ONE OF THE
PRODIGAL SON	463 - 3	PRODIGAL SON BEGAN TO BE IN WANT
PRODUCE	057 - 4	PRODUCE SPECIFIC RESULTS
PRODUCE	092 - 2	POWER TO PRODUCE BUT NO CHOICE
PRODUCE	115 - 4	AT ONCE SETS TO WORK TO PRODUCE
PRODUCE	120 - 2	PRODUCE ITS LOGICAL RESULT
PRODUCE	126 - 4	CAUSE IT TO PRODUCE
PRODUCE	402 - 3	NECESSARY TO PRODUCE LACK
PRODUCED	086 - 3	PRODUCED UNPLEASANT CONDITIONS
PRODUCED	319 - 2	CONSCIOUSNESS WHICH PRODUCED IT
PRODUCED	377 - 3	PRODUCED BY THOSE NOW IN THE FLESH
PRODUCED	379 - 1	PRODUCED BY EITHER
PRODUCED	472 - 7	PRODUCED A CONSCIOUSNESS OF UNITY
PRODUCES	131 - 5	PRODUCES CREATION
PRODUCES	173 - 2	EACH PRODUCES THE SAME RESULTS
PRODUCES	189 - 3	TRUTH PRODUCES FREEDOM
PRODUCT	493 - 3	PRODUCT OF THE ONE SPIRIT
PRODUCTION	482 - 1	PRINCIPLE OF ABUNDANCE AND PRODUCTION
PRODUCTIVE	152 - 4	PRODUCTIVE OF THE HIGHEST GOOD
PROFANE	056 - 2	MOUTH OF THE PROFANE
PROFOUND	140 - 2	NO MORE PROFOUND STATEMENT
PROFOUND	151 - 2	ANOTHER PROFOUND STATEMENT
PROFOUND	308 - 1	THAT PHILOSOPHY IS PROFOUND
PROFOUND	327 - 2	AT THEIR PROFOUND CONCLUSIONS
PROFOUND	422 - 3	PROFOUND TRUTH JESUS DISCOVERED
PROGRAM	188 - 4	UNIVERSE IS BACK OF OUR PROGRAM
PROGRESS	051 - 2	NO PROGRESS IN ANY SCIENCE
PROGRESS	072 - 3	ALL FURTHER PROGRESS HIMSELF
PROGRESS	139 - 3	PROGRESS OF THE HUMAN RACE
PROGRESS	387 - 1	IN ETERNAL PROGRESS
PROGRESS	387 - 2	PROGRESS AN EVERLASTING EXPANSION
PROGRESSION	250 - 5	IS A HARMONIOUS PROGRESSION
PROGRESSION	378 - 3	TRIUMPHANT PROGRESSION OF THE SOUL
PROGRESSIVE	387 - 1	ETERNAL AND PROGRESSIVE EXPANSION
PROJECT	097 - 3	METHODS OF PROJECT ITSELF
PROJECT	235 - 1	PROJECT HEALING POWER
PROJECT	314 - 3	TO PROJECT INTO OUR EXPERIENCE
PROJECT	416 - 1	PROJECT AN IDEA OF OURSELVES
PROJECTED	165 - 1	PROJECTED OUT OF ITSELF
PROJECTED	273 - 3	PROJECTED THROUGH HIS INTELLECT
PROJECTED	416 - 4	PROJECTED INTO OUR EXPERIENCE
PROJECTING	102 - 3	INTELLIGENCE IS PROJECTING EVOLUTION
PROJECTING	251 - 4	PROJECTING INTO THE OBJECTIVE
PROJECTING	273 - 4	PROJECTING ITSELF INTO CREATION
PROJECTING	314 - 1	PROJECTING THE EXPERIENCES FROM IT

PROJECTING	412 - 2	THE PROJECTING MACHINE FIRMLY
PROJECTS	315 - 2	PROJECTS THE FORM OF HAVE-NOT
PROLIFIC	176 - 2	MOST PROLIFIC FIELD FOR DELUSION
PROLONGED	145 - 2	PROLONGED DISCORDANT MENTAL STATE
PROMISE	146 - 1	PROMISE TO MAN IS EQUALLY POSITIVE
PROMISE	232 - S	PROMISE WE HAVE ALL PROVEN
PROMISE	248 - 3	PROMISE YE SHALL KNOW THE TRUTH
PROMISE	267 - 2	DOES NOT PROMISE SOMETHING
PROMISE	268 - 1	DOES NOT PROMISE ANYTHING
PROMISES	414 - 4	GOD HIMSELF FULFILLS ITS PROMISES
PROMOTE	047 - 3	PROMOTE A SALUTARY ATMOSPHERE
PROMULGATED	193 - 5	IDEAS HAVE BEEN PROMULGATED
PRONE	501 - 4	WE ARE PRONE TO LINGER WITH THEM
PRONOUNCEMENT	336 - 2	ITS PRONOUNCEMENT OF ITSELF
PROOF	059 - 1	COMPLETE PROOF OUR FAITH
PROOF	073 - 1	IT WAS PROOF THAT HE EXISTED
PROOF	075 - 3	PROOF WE HAVE OF MIND
PROOF	148 - 2	PROOF THAT WE HAVE LIMITED OURSELVES
PROOF	377 - 2	FURNISHES PROOF OF THE POSSIBILITY
PROOF	441 - 4	PROOF OF THIS DOCTRINE
PROPELLED	163 - 1	PROPELLED BY A CONSCIOUSNESS OF LOVE
PROPELLED	420 - 4	PROPELLED BY THE COSMIC URGE
PROPER	162 - 3	FAITH FINDS ITS PROPER PLACE
PROPER	393 - 2	KEY TO ALL PROPER MENTAL
PROPERTY	392 - 1	PROPERTY OF THE INDIVIDUAL
PROPHECY	354 - 2	IN THE WAY OF A PROPHECY
PROPHECY	355 - 3	PROPHECY IS THE READING OF SUBJECTIVE
PROPHECY	356 - 1	ANY RELIABLE SPIRIT OF PROPHECY
PROPHESY	355 - 4	PROPHESY THAT THE WINDOW
PROPHET	442 - 1	PROPHET IN THE NAME OF A PROPHET
PROPHETS	122 - 1	SAVIOURS AND CHRISTS, THE PROPHETS
PROPHETS	328 - 2	THE OLD PROPHETS WERE MYSTICS
PROPHETS	383 - 3	BY THE WAILING OF PROPHETS
PROPHETS	395 - 2	HANGS ALL THE LAW AND THE PROPHETS
PROPHETS	419 - 2	INCLUDE THE GREAT PROPHETS
PROPOSITION	036 - 1	WE HAVE THIS PROPOSITION
PROPOSITION	074 - 2	A COLD-BLOODED PROPOSITION
PROPOSITION	274 - 2	UP AGAINST A PROPOSITION
PROPOSITION	309 - 2	START WITH THIS SIMPLE PROPOSITION
PROPOSITION	411 - 4	PROPOSITION OF THE CREATIVE POWER
PROPOSITION	483 - 3	DEPENDS UPON THIS PROPOSITION
PROPOSITIONS	085 - 2	SIMPLE THEORETICAL PROPOSITIONS
PROSPER	307 - 3	IT SHALL PROSPER
PROSPERED	323 - 2	ALREADY SAVED, HEALED AND PROSPERED
PROSPERITY	143 - 2	A CONSCIOUSNESS OF PROSPERITY
PROSPERITY	187 - 1	PLENTY, PROSPERITY, PEACE
PROSPERITY	266 - 1	LESSONS ON PROSPERITY
PROSPERITY	282 - 2	A TREATMENT TODAY FOR PROSPERITY
PROSPERITY	287 - 4	BEGIN TO DEMONSTRATE PROSPERITY
PROSPERITY	291 - 3	TREATMENT FOR PROSPERITY
PROSPEROUS	033 - 3	BE HAPPY, PROSPEROUS AND WELL
PROSPEROUS	364 - 3	HELP US TO BECOME PROSPEROUS
PROSPERS	167 - 4	EVERYTHING HE DOES PROSPERS
PROSTRATION	227 - 1	KNOWN AS NERVOUS PROSTRATION
PROTECTED	257 - 4	I AM DIVINELY PROTECTED

PROTECTION	494 - 6	ARMOR OF GOD SUGGEST PROTECTION
PROTOTYPE	202 - 2	PROTOTYPE IN SUBJECTIVE MIND
PROTOTYPE	340 - 2	IS THE PROTOTYPE OF THE FORM
PROUD	368 - 1	PROUD OF HIS DIVINITY
PROVE	048 - 2	THIS SHOULD PROVE TO US
PROVE	051 - 1	PROVE BY ACTUAL DEMONSTRATION
PROVE	051 - 1	THAT WHICH WE CAN PROVE
PROVE	052 - 1	PROVE SUCH STATEMENTS
PROVE	066 - 1	HOW MUCH OF IT WE MAY PROVE
PROVE	176 - 3	USE IT UNTIL WE PROVE IT
PROVE	185 - 1	PROVE TO HIMSELF THAT HIS POSITION
PROVE	263 - 2	PROVE THE LAW
PROVE	266 - 3	BE ABLE TO PROVE THIS
PROVE	307 - 3	PROVE ME NOW HEREWITH
PROVE	314 - 3	TO DEMONSTRATE MEANS TO PROVE
PROVE	316 - 1	UNLESS THE PRACTITIONER CAN PROVE
PROVE	423 - 1	SCIENCE PROVE ITS PRINCIPLE
PROVE	438 - 1	IN ORDER TO PROVE HIS POSITION
PROVE	489 - 3	PROVE YOUR PRINCIPLE BY ALLOWING
PROVE	498 - 2	PROVE ALL THINGS, HOLD FAST
PROVED	052 - 3	PROVED THAT BY THINKING CORRECTLY
PROVED	067 - 2	CREATION IS PROVED BY THE FACT
PROVED	367 - 4	PROVED HIS WAY TO BE A CORRECT
PROVEN	246 - 3	PROVEN BY DEMONSTRATION
PROVEN	488 - 3	PROVEN IN MENTAL AND SPIRITUAL
PROVEN FACT	386 - 3	BUT AS A PROVEN FACT
PROVES	059 - 2	UNTIL HE PROVES HIS PRINCIPLE
PROVES	289 - 4	PROVES THAT IT IS UNCONSCIOUS OF TIME
PROVES	334 - 3	PROVES THAT IT IS A REALITY
PROVES	378 - 1	PROVES THAT ALL OF THE MANIFESTATIONS
PROVIDE	118 - 2	PROVIDE A MENTAL EQUIVALENT
PROVIDE	119 - 3	PROVIDE A HIGHER CONTEMPLATION
PROVIDE	141 - 2	ABLE TO PROVIDE THE CONSCIOUSNESS
PROVIDE	431 - 3	WILL PROVIDE FOR AND BLESS US
PROVIDENCE	467 - 3	GOD'S LOVE AND PROVIDENCE
PROVIDING	358 - 3	PROVIDING THE MENTAL EQUIVALENTS
PROVINCE	193 - 2	PROVINCE TO USE IT
PROVINCE	438 - 4	OUTSIDE THE PROVINCE OF REALITY
PROVING	048 - 3	PROVING THE PRINCIPLE
PROVING	271 - 2	ARE TODAY PROVING THIS LAW
PROVING	301 - 3	SAVING THE WORLD BY PROVING THIS LAW
PROVING	432 - 3	THEORY ARE PROVING THE PRINCIPLE
PROVISION	385 - 1	THIS IS A WISE PROVISION
PROXY	445 - 3	CAN NEVER COME BY PROXY
PROXY	448 - 1	NO ONE LIVES BY PROXY
PSALMS	364 - 2	OF THE MOST HIGH PSALMS
PSYCHE	378 - 2	THE PSYCHE, THE SUBJECTIVE SOUL LIFE
PSYCHIC	120 - 3	WHO CAME TO UNDERSTAND THE PSYCHIC
PSYCHIC	328 - 4	PSYCHIC EXPERIENCES REAR THE EXACT OPPOSITE
PSYCHIC	328 - 4	PSYCHIC SEES A DIFFERENT KIND
PSYCHIC	342 - 1	PSYCHIC MAY OR MAY NOT BE TRUE
PSYCHIC	342 - 3	PSYCHIC IMPRESSIONS MAY CONTROL
PSYCHIC	346 - 1	TO DO WITH THE PSYCHIC STATE
PSYCHIC	351 - 2	ALL PEOPLE ARE REALLY PSYCHIC
PSYCHIC	352 - 3	THE PSYCHIC IS MERELY READING

PSYCHIC	353 - 1	SINCE WE ARE ALL PSYCHIC
PSYCHIC	378 - 1	HUDSON IN HIS LAW OF PSYCHIC PHENOMENA
PSYCHIC	380 - 2	A PSYCHIC SEES THE PICTURE
PSYCHIC	381 - 2	WE ALL HAVE PSYCHIC CAPACITIES
PSYCHIC	381 - 2	PSYCHIC CAPACITY IS NORMAL ONLY
PSYCHIC	381 - 2	PSYCHIC POWER IS PRODUCED
PSYCHIC	381 - 3	A NORMAL PSYCHIC CAPACITY
PSYCHIC	382 - 2	UNDERSTANDING OF PSYCHIC PHENOMENA
PSYCHIC	382 - 2	OF PSYCHIC PHENOMENA
PSYCHIC	382 - 3	LAW OF PSYCHIC PHENOMENA
PSYCHICAL	099 - 5	PSYCHICAL OR SUBJECTIVE DISTURBANCES
PSYCHIC LAWS	354 - 2	CREATED GREAT PSYCHIC LAWS FOR ITSELF
PSYCHICS	328 - 5	NO TWO PSYCHICS SEE THE SAME THING
PSYCHICS	329 - 4	DISCLOSURES OF MOST PSYCHICS
PSYCHICS	341 - 6	MOST PSYCHICS ARE CONTRADICTORY
PSYCHICS	351 - 2	THESE PEOPLE WE CALL PSYCHICS
PSYCHISM	327 - 1	MYSTICISM AND PSYCHISM
PSYCHISM	329 - 4	WHILE PSYCHISM IS A MOST INTERESTING FIELD
PSYCHISM	342 - 1	BETWEEN PSYCHISM AND MYSTICISM
PSYCHO-ANALYSIS	236 - 6	PSYCHO-ANALYSIS IS ANALYSIS OF THE SOUL
PSYCHO-ANALYSIS	236 - 6	PSYCHO-ANALYSIS FROM PSYCHE OR SOUL
PSYCHO-ANALYSIS	501 - 5	PSYCHO-ANALYSIS WHICH IS THE ANALYSIS OF
PSYCHO-ANALYZE	167 - 2	LEARN HOW TO PSYCHO-ANALYZE
PSYCHOLOGICAL	114 - 4	IN BOTH THE PSYCHOLOGICAL
PSYCHOLOGICAL	194 - 4	A GOOD PSYCHOLOGICAL BALANCE
PSYCHOLOGICAL	345 - 3	NOT A PSYCHOLOGICAL EXPLOSION
PSYCHOLOGICAL	372 - 3	OUR PHYSIOLOGICAL AND PSYCHOLOGICAL
PSYCHOLOGICAL	380 - 2	THE PSYCHOLOGICAL AND METAPHYSICAL LAWS
PSYCHOLOGICAL	438 - 2	A GREAT PSYCHOLOGICAL LAW
PSYCHOLOGICAL	458 - 3	PSYCHOLOGICAL LAW OF OUR BEING
PSYCHOLOGICAL	473 - 5	AS A PSYCHOLOGICAL BEING
PSYCHOLOGICAL	501 - 2	PSYCHOLOGICAL CHANGE TAKES PLACE
PSYCHOLOGICAL	501 - 5	PSYCHOLOGICAL TRUTHS OF THE INNER NATURE
PSYCHOLOGICAL	502 - 2	IN A BETTER PSYCHOLOGICAL POSITION
PSYCHOLOGY	027 - 4	SCIENCE OF SPIRITUAL PSYCHOLOGY
PSYCHOLOGY	093 - 3	NEXT GREAT BRIDGE THAT PSYCHOLOGY
PSYCHOLOGY	099 - 5	PSYCHOLOGY HAS SHOWN THAT
PSYCHOLOGY	100 - 1	PSYCHOLOGY AND METAPHYSICS ARE BUT TWO
PSYCHOLOGY	122 - 3	PSYCHOLOGY HAS DETERMINED THE FACT
PSYCHOLOGY	125 - 1	HERE IS WHERE PSYCHOLOGY AND METAPHYSICS
PSYCHOLOGY	144 - 4	PSYCHOLOGY AFFIRMS THAT ALL THE THOUGHTS
PSYCHOLOGY	332 - 5	PSYCHOLOGY TEACHES THE PERSONIFICATION
PSYCHOLOGY	347 - 3	PSYCHOLOGY TEACHES ABOUT THE MIND
PSYCHOLOGY	348 - 3	THE PSYCHOLOGY OF THAT PEOPLE
PSYCHOLOGY	404 - 4	PSYCHOLOGY OF ECONOMIC CYCLES
PSYCHOLOGY	489 - 7	PSYCHOLOGY HAS PROVEN BEYOND
PSYCHOLOGY	497 - 3	PSYCHOLOGY WE LEARN THAT CONGESTED
PUBLICANS	442 - 2	FRIEND OF PUBLICANS AND SINNERS
PUFFED UP	469 - 1	PUFFED UP WITH SELF-RIGHTEOUSNESS
PULSATING	196 - 2	PULSATING WITH FEELING
PULSATIONS	238 - 3	THE PULSATIONS OF LIFE ARE STEADY
PULSATIONS	238 - 3	CONTINUOUS PULSATIONS OF LIFE
PUNISH	053 - 2	GOD DOES NOT PUNISH
PUNISHED	111 - 2	PUNISHED AS LONG AS HE CONTINUED
PUNISHES	149 - 4	THEN ETERNALLY PUNISHES

PUNISHES	383 - 1	NEITHER PUNISHES NOR REWARDS
PUNISHMENT	052 - 5	THIS IS OUR OWN PUNISHMENT
PUNISHMENT	053 - 1	NOT A PUNISHMENT IMPOSED
PUNISHMENT	053 - 2	THUS SIN AND PUNISHMENT
PUNISHMENT	111 - 1	NO PUNISHMENT BUT AN INEVITABLE CONSEQUENCE
PUNISHMENT	111 - 2	SIN IS ITS OWN PUNISHMENT
PUNISHMENT	337 - 1	NO PUNISHMENT OUTSIDE OF THAT
PUNISHMENT	382 - 4	WHAT OF REWARD AND PUNISHMENT
PUNISHMENT	383 - 1	PUNISHMENT A CONSEQUENCE
PUNISHMENT	383 - 1	REWARD AND OUR OWN PUNISHMENT
PUNISHMENT	434 - 2	DESERVES PUNISHMENT WILL RECEIVE IT
PURCHASED	383 - 3	PURCHASED A SEAT IN HEAVEN
PURE	226 - 1	WHATSOEVER THINGS ARE PURE
PURE	240 - 2	BLESSED ARE THE PURE
PURE	402 - 3	WILT SHOW THYSELF PURE
PURE	406 - 2	PURE SPIRIT IS AT THE CENTER
PURE	430 - 6	GOOD FOR THE PURE LOVE OF GOOD
PURE	442 - 1	TO THE PURE ALL IS PURE
PURE IN HEART	429 - 4	PURE IN HEART SHALL SEE GOD
PURELY	148 - 1	PURELY MENTAL ACTION
PURE WATERS	469 - 2	THE PURE WATERS OF REALITY
PURIFIED	249 - 2	PURIFIED AND REFRESHED
PURIFY	204 - 5	EVENTUALLY PURIFY IT
PURITY	254 - 5	PURITY AND STRENGTH
PURITY	429 - 4	PURITY SEES IT AND IS BEHOLDING
PURPOSE	028 - 2	FOR A SPECIFIC PURPOSE
PURPOSE	048 - 2	PURPOSE AND DIRECTION
PURPOSE	059 - 5	PURPOSE OF THE UNIVERSE
PURPOSE	100 - 1	PURPOSE OF MENTAL HEALING
PURPOSE	100 - 2	NO PURPOSE OTHER THAN TO EXECUTE
PURPOSE	130 - 1	PURPOSE WHICH IS GOODNESS
PURPOSE	183 - 2	PURPOSE OF UNCOVERING
PURPOSE	195 - 2	A DEFINITE PURPOSE
PURPOSE	221 - 3	CLEAR PURPOSE IN MIND
PURPOSE	231 - 2	FAITH OR NOBLE PURPOSE
PURPOSE	239 - 1	PURPOSE A DETERMINATION TO
PURPOSE	243 - 2	LIFE IN ITS SPIRITUAL PURPOSE
PURPOSE	270 - 1	VERY PURPOSE FOR WHICH FREEDOM EXISTS
PURPOSE	270 - 4	DOES NOT EXIST FOR THE PURPOSE
PURPOSE	340 - 2	THE PURPOSE AND THE EXECUTION
PURPOSE	394 - 2	WHATSOEVER PURPOSE WE WILL
PURPOSE	397 - 1	PURPOSE OF BEING USED
PURPOSE	440 - 4	TO ANY LEGITIMATE PURPOSE
PURPOSE	448 - 1	PURPOSE OF THE SCIENCE OF MIND
PURPOSE	476 - 1	MENTAL TREATMENT IS FOR THE PURPOSE
PURPOSES	054 - 2	DEFINITELY AND FOR SPECIFIC PURPOSES
PURPOSES	393 - 2	KNOWLEDGE FOR DEFINITE PURPOSES
PURPOSES	398 - 2	THOUGHT FOR DEFINITE PURPOSES
PURPOSES	432 - 2	SPIRIT WILL MOLD OUR PURPOSES
PURPOSES	477 - 4	PURPOSES ARE ANIMATED
PUSH	058 - 5	NOT HAVE TO DRIVE OR PUSH
PUSH	157 - 3	PUSH FORWARD AND TAKE THAT WHICH
PUSHING	088 - 4	PUSHING FORWARD INTO EXPRESSION
PUSHING	301 - 2	OR PUSHING THEM AWAY
PUSHING	364 - 3	PUSHING FURTHER AND FURTHER BACK

PUSHING	469 - 3	PUSHING US FORWARD TO THE GOAL
PUT	058 - 3	PUT THE POWER INTO THE TREATMENT
PUT	331 - 2	PUT INTO IT NO MORE AND NO LESS
PUZZLED	311 - 4	STUDENTS ARE PUZZLED WHEN

Q

QUALITITES	386 - 2	THOSE QUALITIES AND ATTRIBUTES
QUEER	402 - 2	SHOULD BE THOUGHT QUEER
QUENCH	495 - 3	ABLE TO QUENCH ALL THE FIERY DARTS
QUENCH	497 - 3	QUENCH NOT THE SPIRIT
QUENCH	498 - 1	QUENCH NOT THE SPIRIT
QUEST	033 - 3	CAUSES THE ETERNAL QUEST
QUESTION	037 - 4	NOT A QUESTION OF ITS WILLINGNESS
QUESTION	037 - 4	QUESTION OF OUR OWN RECEPTIVITY
QUESTION	190 - 1	NO QUESTION THAT PEOPLE
QUESTION	307 - 2	ACCEPT THIS WITHOUT QUESTION
QUESTION	365 - 2	THE ANSWER TO EVERY QUESTION
QUESTION	422 - 3	QUESTION IS WITHIN MAN
QUESTION	446 - 4	QUESTION EACH SHOULD ASK HIMSELF
QUESTIONED	446 - 3	UNIVERSE CANNOT BE QUESTIONED
QUIBBLING	283 - 5	IT IS BEYOND THE MERE QUIBBLING
QUICKEN	414 - 4	DOES NOT QUICKEN THE FLESH
QUICKENING	168 - 1	QUICKENING INTO RIGHT ACTION
QUICKENING	242 - 1	QUICKENING IT INTO LIFE AND ACTION
QUICKENING	428 - 2	INSPIRATION AND THAT QUICKENING
QUICKENS	242 - 2	QUICKENS EVERY PART OF ME
QUICKENS	484 - 4	QUICKENS OUR MORTAL BODIES
QUICKLY	184 - 3	JUST AS QUICKLY AS FOR ANOTHER
QUICKLY	398 - 4	RESPONDS TO FEELING MORE QUICKLY
QUICKLY	411 - 3	LAW OF MIND AS QUICKLY CREATES
QUIETNESS	361 - 3	QUIETNESS AND CONFIDENCE ARE MINE

R

RACE	040 - 2	HAS COME TO THE RACE
RACE	044 - 2	RACE MUST FIRST FIND AN AVENUE
RACE	056 - 1	THE GREATEST LOVERS OF THE RACE
RACE	085 - 1	INTELLIGENCE OF THE HUMAN RACE
RACE	088 - 1	INHERITED TENDENCIES AND RACE SUGGESTIONS
RACE	091 - 4	INTELLIGENCE OF THE RACE
RACE	111 - 3	SOLVED FOR THE ENTIRE RACE
RACE	113 - 2	RACE IS GROWING INTO A BROADER DIVINITY
RACE	119 - 2	RACE BELIEVES MORE IN GOOD THAN IN EVIL
RACE	177 - 4	RACE ALREADY SUBJECTIFIED WITHIN HIM
RACE	198 - 1	RACE CONSCIOUSNESS
RACE	226 - 3	LAW OF RACE SUGGESTION
RACE	237 - 2	CONDEMNATION WHICH THE RACE HOLDS
RACE	272 - 4	RUN THROUGH EVERY AGE AND RACE
RACE	302 - 3	THE MAJORITY OF THE RACE
RACE	335 - 2	RACE TO TURN FROM EVIL

RACE	348 - 1	FAMILY AND RACE CHARACTERISTICS
RACE	348 - 4	THE HISTORY OF THE RACE
RACE	349 - 2	MUCH OF THE RACE KNOWLEDGE
RACE	402 - 4	WHICH BINDS THE RACE
RACE-EMOTION	349 - 3	PICK UP THE ENTIRE RACE-EMOTION
RACE-MENTALITY	349 - 4	SUBJECTIVE SIDE OF THE RACE-MENTALITY
RACES	067 - 3	MORE VITAL RACES OF THE WORLD
RACE SUGGESTION	096 - 3	OF ALL RACE SUGGESTION
RACE-SUGGESTION	114 - 3	CONTAINS THE RACE-SUGGESTION
RACE-SUGGESTION	115 - 2	A POWERFUL RACE-SUGGESTION
RACE-SUGGESTION	119 - 3	NO RACE-SUGGESTION OPERATING
RACE-SUGGESTION	177 - 4	WITHIN HIM THROUGH RACE-SUGGESTION
RACE-SUGGESTION	204 - 2	RACE-SUGGESTION BELIEF IN LIMITATION
RACE-SUGGESTION	239 - 3	RACE-SUGGESTION CARRIES A STRONG
RACE-SUGGESTION	249 - 2	WHICH RACE-SUGGESTION SAYS
RACE-SUGGESTION	348 - 2	RACE-SUGGESTION IS A VERY REAL THING
RACE-SUGGESTION	421 - 4	IN THE FORM OF RACE-SUGGESTION
RACE-THOUGHT	177 - 4	WORKS THROUGH SUBJECTIVE RACE-THOUGHT
RACE-THOUGHT	349 - 3	VIBRATES TO THE RACE-THOUGHT
RACE-THOUGHT	421 - 5	IS RETAINED IN THE RACE-THOUGHT
RACIAL	417 - 1	AFTER THE MOLD OF RACIAL BELIEF
RADIANCE	368 - 3	OTHER SOULS BY THE RADIANCE
RADIANT	184 - 3	A RADIANT FEELING FLOWING
RADIANT	246 - 2	FOR RADIANT SELF-EXPRESSION
RADIATE	292 - 3	I RADIATE LIFE, I AM LIFE
RADIATE	302 - 2	HE SHOULD RADIATE JOY
RADIATE	307 - 2	RADIATE LIFE
RADIO	077 - 4	RADIO MESSAGES ARE OPERATIVE
RADIO	077 - 5	THE MEDIUM OF RADIO TRANSMISSION
RADIO	213 - 4	BROADCAST OVER A RADIO
RADIO	214 - 1	RADIO AND TALK
RADIO	351 - 1	THERE MUST BE IN RADIO
RAFT	340 - 3	FROM THE RAFT TO MODERN SHIPS
RAIN	028 - 1	SENDETH RAIN ON THE JUST
RAIN	258 - 4	IN RAIN AND IN CLOUDS
RAIN	258 - 5	THE RAIN AND THE SUNSHINE
RAIN	430 - 5	RAIN TO FALL AND HIS SUN TO SHINE
RAISE	315 - 2	SPIRITUAL POWER TO RAISE THE DEAD
RANGE	281 - 4	ACCORDING TO ITS RANGE
RANGE	282 - 2	THE RANGE OF OUR POSSIBILITIES
RANGE	282 - 2	RANGE OF OUR PRESENT CONCEPTS
RANGE	429 - 1	RANGE OF ONE HUMAN EXPERIENCE
RAPIDLY	423 - 2	IN A RAPIDLY CHANGING WORLD
RATIONAL	228 - 1	ALL PERSONS ARE RATIONAL AND POISED
RATIONAL	285 - 3	MORE RATIONAL IT WILL APPEAR TO BE
RATIONAL	443 - 1	DEMAND TOO RATIONAL AN EXPLANATION
RATIONAL	452 - 4	NORMAL, NATURAL AND RATIONAL
RATIONAL	452 - 4	RATIONAL INTELLECTS AND WELL-BALANCED
RATIONALLY	040 - 1	STUDY OF THIS SCIENCE RATIONALLY
RAYS	388 - 3	SUN IN ITS RAYS
REACT	033 - 1	REACT AND CAUSE PHYSICAL DISORDERS
REACT	211 - 2	REACT TO THESE EMOTIONS SUBJECTIVELY
REACTION	031 - 3	REACTION, AN EFFECT, A WAY
REACTION	044 - 3	REACTION OF THE MECHANICAL
REACTION	079 - 3	FROM SUCH A SUPERSTITIOUS REACTION

REACTION	122 - 2	REACTION OF THE SELF-KNOWING MIND
REACTION	130 - 5	REACTION TO HIS THOUGHT
REACTION	176 - 1	OPPOSITE AND EQUAL REACTION
REACTION	253 - 3	EVERY MENTAL AND EMOTIONAL REACTION
REACTION	266 - 3	ENVIRONMENT ITS REACTION TO US
REACTION	336 - 4	DIFFERENCE IN OUR REACTION
REACTION	347 - 3	REACTION OF OUR THOUGHT
REACTION	416 - 1	REACTION OF THE MECHANICS
REACTIONS	053 - 2	LOGICAL REACTIONS OF THE UNIVERSE
REACTIONS	099 - 5	PHYSICAL REACTIONS
REACTIONS	372 - 3	REACTIONS CAN BE ANALYZED
REACTS	032 - 1	ONE REACTS TO THE OTHER
REACTS	032 - 1	REACTS TO OUR SPIRITUAL OR MATERIAL
REACTS	138 - 3	REACTS TO OUR THOUGHT ACCORDING
REACTS	177 - 1	REACTS TO OUR THOUGHT
REACTS	271 - 4	LAW AUTOMATICALLY REACTS TO HIM
READ	049 - 1	READ INTO IT
READ	055 - 4	READ OR THINK ABOUT
READ	328 - 4	DOES NOT READ HUMAN THOUGHT
READ	351 - 2	READ IT MORE OR LESS ACCURATELY
READING	350 - 5	READING SUBJECTIVE THOUGHT
READING	438 - 1	READING THEIR THOUGHTS AND KNOWING
READY	037 - 4	READY TO FILL EVERYTHING
READY	272 - 2	OUR PART IS TO BE READY
READY	273 - 3	READY TO RECEIVE
READY	392 - 2	READY BUT HAVING NO INITIATIVE
READY	418 - 2	NOT YET READY TO HELP OTHERS
REAL	101 - 2	TIME IS REAL
REAL	111 - 2	BONDAGE IS NOT REAL
REAL	153 - 3	GOD IS REAL TO THE ONE
REAL	191 - 1	REAL MAN IS PERFECT
REAL	220 - 6	REAL AS ANY OTHER KNOWN LAW
REAL	284 - 1	BECOMES REAL TO THE BELIEVER
REAL	291 - 4	REAL MAN KNOWS NO DISCOURAGEMENT
REAL	350 - 3	MENTAL ATMOSPHERE IS VERY REAL
REAL	404 - I	OUTLINE IS REAL
REAL	412 - 2	REAL AS FIGURES BUT NOT SELF-CREATED
REAL	470 - 2	WHICH REMEMBERS THE REAL STATE
REALITIES	151 - 3	EMBODIES THESE DIVINE REALITIES
REALITIES	154 - 1	ETERNAL REALITIES IN LOVE
REALITY	030 - 2	IN REALITY THEY ARE ONE
REALITY	033 - 2	TRUE NATURE OF REALITY
REALITY	041 - 3	LOOK TOO FAR AWAY FOR REALITY
REALITY	042 - 3	REALITY ARE WE GOING TO EXPRESS
REALITY	043 - 1	STUDY THE NATURE OF REALITY
REALITY	043 - 2	ETERNAL EXISTENCE IN REALITY
REALITY	053 - 3	GOES WITH ULTIMATE REALITY
REALITY	053 - 4	BRING THEM INTO LINE WITH REALITY
REALITY	053 - 5	DENY ITS REALITY
REALITY	054 - 3	IN ACCORD WITH ULTIMATE REALITY
REALITY	063 - 1	WHAT IS REALITY
REALITY	063 - 1	LONGS FOR REALITY
REALITY	066 - 2	IN PHILOSOPHY THE WORD REALITY IS USED
REALITY	066 - 2	AS GOD, SPIRIT, REALITY, TRUTH
REALITY	068 - 2	ONE ULTIMATE REALITY

REALITY	068 - 2	TO THE NATURE OF THAT REALITY
REALITY	071 - 2	ELECTRICITY WAS A REALITY
REALITY	073 - 2	PROOF OF THIS REALITY
REALITY	076 - 2	ON THE OUTSIDE OF REALITY
REALITY	076 - 2	REALITY MUST BE AN INFINITE
REALITY	076 - 3	REALITY NOT IN THE MOUNTAIN
REALITY	084 - 5	THREE IN REALITY ARE ONE
REALITY	085 - 2	WE REASON THAT THE REALITY EXISTS
REALITY	086 - 4	CONVINCE OURSELVES OF THE REALITY
REALITY	089 - 1	ARISES OUT OF REALITY
REALITY	090 - 1	THE THREEFOLD NATURE OF REALITY
REALITY	108 - 2	REALITY TO WHICH BONDAGE IS NOT
REALITY	155 - 2	MENTAL APPROACH TO REALITY
REALITY	156 - 2	AFFIRMATIVE MENTAL APPROACH TO REALITY
REALITY	177 - 3	SICKNESS IS NOT A SPIRITUAL REALITY
REALITY	184 - 2	SPIRIT IS CHANGELESS REALITY
REALITY	186 - 2	IN REALITY THERE IS NO LIMITATION
REALITY	188 - 2	AN ANNOUNCEMENT OF REALITY
REALITY	189 - 3	THE SAME AS THE INNER REALITY
REALITY	190 - 3	MAN'S LIFE IN REALITY IS SPIRITUAL
REALITY	204 - 3	CLEAR CONCEPT OF REALITY
REALITY	213 - 2	THE APPEARANCE IS THE REALITY
REALITY	213 - 2	UNCOVER THIS REALITY
REALITY	213 - 2	BUT NOT A SPIRITUAL REALITY
REALITY	213 - 4	NOT A DIVINE REALITY
REALITY	233 - 4	AND LAY HOLD OF REALITY
REALITY	234 - 2	GRASP REALITY
REALITY	234 - 5	IS THE REALITY OF MAN
REALITY	244 - 2	BUT ONE FINAL TRUTH OR REALITY
REALITY	264 - 3	THE EXPERIENCE OF REALITY
REALITY	268 - 1	THIS IS TRUE IN REALITY
REALITY	272 - 1	PEACEFUL SENSE OF REALITY
REALITY	274 - 3	LETS REALITY THROUGH
REALITY	275 - 2	PARTAKES OF THE NATURE OF REALITY
REALITY	284 - 3	DEATHLESS REALITY OF ALL BEING
REALITY	284 - 4	GAZE UPON A SOLID REALITY
REALITY	285 - 4	IS IN LINE WITH REALITY
REALITY	296 - 3	INNER RECOGNITION OF REALITY
REALITY	297 - 3	NOT AS AN ILLUSION BUT AS A REALITY
REALITY	300 - 3	NATURAL UNFOLDMENT OF REALITY
REALITY	304 - 5	AND THE THING ARE ONE IN REALITY
REALITY	313 - 3	WE CAN NEVER CHANGE REALITY
REALITY	334 - 5	THERE IS BUT ONE ULTIMATE REALITY
REALITY	381 - 4	THE SHADOW FOR THE REALITY
REALITY	396 - 2	THE NATURE OF REALITY
REALITY	398 - 4	THIS REALITY IS FELT
REALITY	409 - 5	SILENT SENSE OF DIVINE REALITY
REALITY	411 - 1	POWER OF REALITY OVER SEEMING OPPOSITION
REALITY	415 - 4	A UNIVERSAL STANDARD OF REALITY
REALITY	420 - 2	THERE IS NO ULTIMATE REALITY TO EVIL
REALITY	428 - 5	THIRST AFTER REALITY ARE ALWAYS FED
REALITY	430 - 1	ENTER THE GATES OF REALITY
REALITY	430 - 4	REALITY TO US UNLESS WE RECOGNIZE
REALITY	435 - 2	REALITY UNTIL OUR EYES ARE
REALITY	436 - 2	CERTAIN ESTIMATE OF REALITY

REALITY	436 - 5	EFFECTS AND ESTIMATES REALITY
REALITY	438 - 4	OUTSIDE THE PROVINCE OF REALITY
REALITY	465 - 2	THAT SUCH A STATE IS A REALITY
REALITY	480 - 4	REALITY WAS NOT EXHAUSTED
REALIZATION	035 - 1	REALIZATION THAT GOOD IS UNIVERSAL
REALIZATION	048 - 2	REALIZATION OF THIS SPECIFIC GOOD
REALIZATION	055 - 2	THE REALIZATION OF PLENTY
REALIZATION	055 - 2	REALIZATION OF THIS TRUTH
REALIZATION	086 - 4	A REALIZATION OF THE MEANING
REALIZATION	099 - 5	TRUE SPIRITUAL REALIZATION
REALIZATION	121 - 2	REALIZATION THAT THERE IS BUT ONE
REALIZATION	122 - 2	ALONE COMES REALIZATION
REALIZATION	142 - 3	REALIZATION OF THE ESSENTIAL DIVINITY
REALIZATION	145 - 3	REALIZATION OF THE PRESENCE OF GOD IS
REALIZATION	149 - 2	REALIZATION OF MAN'S UNITY
REALIZATION	163 - 1	REALIZATION THAT THE CREATIVE SPIRIT
REALIZATION	164 - 4	FOUND IN SPIRITUAL REALIZATION
REALIZATION	167 - 4	REALIZATION IN EVERYDAY AFFAIRS
REALIZATION	170 - 3	ARGUMENTATIVE AND THE OTHER REALIZATION
REALIZATION	170 - 5	REALIZATION METHOD IS ONE WHEREBY THE
REALIZATION	170 - 5	INDUCING AN INNER REALIZATION
REALIZATION	170 - 5	REALIZATION ACTING THROUGH MIND
REALIZATION	172 - 5	USING THE METHOD OF REALIZATION
REALIZATION	173 - 2	PURE REALIZATION WE WILL HAVE ATTAINED
REALIZATION	173 - 4	A STATE OF REALIZATION AND ACCEPTANCE
REALIZATION	173 - 4	IS IN THE REALIZATION
REALIZATION	179 - 1	IN HIS OWN MIND THE REALIZATION
REALIZATION	183 - 2	IS BUILT UPON A REALIZATION
REALIZATION	184 - 1	REALIZATION IN THE MIND OF THE PRACTITIONER
REALIZATION	186 - 1	TO THE REALIZATION OF HEALTH
REALIZATION	192 - 1	REALIZATION OF GOD
REALIZATION	202 - 4	THAN THE REALIZATION OF THE PRESENCE
REALIZATION	205 - 2	REALIZATION OF LIFE AND LOVE
REALIZATION	218 - 3	OUR STATEMENTS TO A REALIZATION
REALIZATION	218 - 3	REALIZATION BECOMES A SUBJECTIVE EMBODIEMENT
REALIZATION	220 - 2	BECOMES A SUBJECTIVE REALIZATION
REALIZATION	223 - 3	REALIZATION OF A PERFECT PRESENCE
REALIZATION	223 - 3	THE PERFECT REALIZATION
REALIZATION	233 - 3	PRACTITIONER HAS A FULL REALIZATION
REALIZATION	263 - 1	REALIZATION OF THE PRESENCE
REALIZATION	270 - 5	THIS REALIZATION DOES NOT LESSEN
REALIZATION	276 - 2	THE HIGHEST REALIZATION
REALIZATION	277 - 3	REALIZATION OF THE PRESENCE OF SPIRIT
REALIZATION	283 - 5	THE PLANE OF REALIZATION
REALIZATION	295 - 2	HELP US ON THE ROAD TO REALIZATION
REALIZATION	305 - 5	IN A REALIZATION OF DIVINE LOVE
REALIZATION	318 - 3	THIS IS THE THIRD STEP: REALIZATION
REALIZATION	319 - 4	FOR A REALIZATION OF PERFECTION
REALIZATION	327 - 2	ARRIVES AT SPIRITUAL REALIZATION
REALIZATION	330 - 5	PROCESS OF SPIRITUAL REALIZATION
REALIZATION	337 - 3	REALIZATION OF THE UNITY OF SPIRIT
REALIZATION	346 - 2	TECHNIQUE AND A REALIZATION
REALIZATION	357 - 2	REALIZATION OF ITS OWN PERFECTION
REALIZATION	358 - 2	DEEP INNER REALIZATION
REALIZATION	362 - 2	THE REALIZATION THAT GOD IS INDWELLING

REALIZATION	364 - 2	NOTHING BUT A GREATER REALIZATION
REALIZATION	364 - 3	SIMPLY NEED A GREATER REALIZATION
REALIZATION	398 - 2	ACCEPTANCE AND REALIZATION
REALIZATION	398 - 2	REALIZATION ARE MENTAL QUALITIES
REALIZATION	409 - 2	ONE OF THOUGHT AND REALIZATION
REALIZATION	409 - 5	THIS IS WHAT WE MEAN BY REALIZATION
REALIZATION	409 - 5	WHERE REALIZATION BEGINS
REALIZATION	413 - 3	BUILDING UP THE REALIZATION
REALIZATION	416 - 1	DEPENDS UPON A REALIZATION
REALIZATION	423 - 3	IS AN INNER REALIZATION
REALIZATION	444 - 1	REALIZATION OF LIFE TRUTH AND BEAUTY
REALIZATION	452 - 2	REALIZATION OF THEIR RELATIONSHIP
REALIZATION	481 - 4	CONSCIOUS REALIZATION THAT WE ARE ONE
REALIZATION	503 - 1	AWAKENING TO THE REALIZATION THAT GOD
REALIZATIONS	044 - 3	OUR FUTURE AND PRESENT REALIZATIONS
REALIZATIONS	057 - 3	OUR REALIZATIONS OF TRUTH
REALIZATIONS	164 - 3	REALIZATIONS OF PEACE POISE POWER PLENTY
REALIZATIONS	218 - 2	STATEMENTS AND REALIZATIONS
REALIZATIONS	277 - 3	FOUND IN SPIRITUAL REALIZATIONS
REALIZATIONS	358 - 3	HEIGHTS OF ITS GREATEST REALIZATIONS
REALIZE	134 - 1	REALIZE HIS RELATION TO THE WHOLE
REALIZE	172 - 5	REALIZE THE PERFECT PRESENCE
REALIZE	173 - 3	TIMES REALIZE MAN'S PERFECTION
REALIZE	184 - 4	TO REALIZE THE SPIRITUAL UNIVERSE
REALIZE	199 - 2	REALIZE THE STATE OF PERFECTION
REALIZE	211 - 3	REALIZE THE PATIENT
REALIZE	264 - 3	TO REALIZE ALL THESE TRUTHS
REALIZE	297 - 2	REALIZE THAT IT IS A LAW OF REFLECTION
REALIZE	332 - 1	REALIZE THAT DIVINE POWER IS
REALIZE	369 - 1	TO REALIZE WITHIN ONESELF
REALIZE	388 - 3	MORE TO US THAN WE REALIZE
REALIZE	410 - 2	TRY TO REALIZE THE PRESENCE
REALIZE	446 - 4	REALIZE HIS SPIRIT IN MY LIFE
REALIZE	472 - 6	REALIZE OUR DIVINE NATURE
REALIZE	489 - 3	ALL YOU NEED DO IS TO REALIZE
REALIZES	130 - 6	REALIZES HIMSELF TO BE A THINKING CENTER
REALIZES	170 - 5	PRACTITIONER REALIZES WITHIN HIMSELF
REALIZES	180 - 2	PRACTITIONER FIRST REALIZES HIS OWN BEING
REALIZES	216 - 1	THE PRACTITIONER REALIZES
REALIZES	332 - 3	TO THE DEGREE THAT MAN REALIZES
REALIZING	271 - 4	WE ARE REALIZING MORE OF TRUTH
REALIZING	320 - 1	ENTIRE ATTENTION TO REALIZING
REAL LIFE	065 - 3	REAL LIFE WITHIN HIMSELF
REALM	100 - 3	THE REALM OF EFFECT
REALM	285 - 4	COME INTO THE SPIRITUAL REALM
REALM	342 - 1	PSYCHIC REALM IS THE REALM
REALM	414 - 1	ELSE IT WILL NOT ENTER THE REALM
REAL MAN	132 - 9	REAL MAN IS IN AN ETERNAL STATE OF COMPLETE
REAL MAN	388 - 3	REAL MAN IS BIRTHLESS, DEATHLESS
REALMS	220 - 3	HIGHER REALMS OF CONSCIOUSNESS
REAP	039 - 3	SO SHALL HE REAP
REAP	195 - 2	SO WE MUST REAP
REAP	269 - 2	THAT SHALL HE ALSO REAP
REAP	340 - 2	SOWS SO ALSO SHALL HE REAP
REAP	429 - 3	REAP AS WE HAVE SOWN

REAP	433 - 3	REAP AS HE HAS SOWN
REAP	458 - 5	BEFORE WE CAN REAP A HARVEST
REASON	032 - 2	BY LOVE BY REASON
REASON	095 - 2	CAN BE NO REASON GIVEN
REASON	095 - 2	THE REASON FOR ITS ACTION
REASON	113 - 1	REASON BOTH INDUCTIVELY
REASON	125 - 5	ITS OWN REASON FOR BEING
REASON	210 - 3	REASON PEOPLE DO NOT GET BETTER
REASON	233 - 2	BY REASON OR BY CHANCE
REASON	237 - 3	REASON PEOPLE DO NOT REALIZE
REASON	265 - 2	POISED IN LOVE AND REASON
REASON	298 - 1	REASON IS THIS AS ALL IS MIND
REASON	307 - 1	RECOGNIZE TRUTH THROUGH REASON
REASON	330 - 2	REASON DECLARES THAT
REASON	373 - 2	KEEP FAITH WITH REASON
REASON	397 - 4	REASON OTHER THAN DEDUCTIVELY
REASON	416 - 2	REASON ONLY FROM A DEDUCTIVE VIEW
REASONING	096 - 2	TWO WAYS OF REASONING
REASONING	096 - 3	NO INDUCTIVE REASONING IN SPIRIT
REASONING	170 - 4	PROCESS OF MENTAL REASONING
REASONING	203 - 4	REASONING WHICH PRESENTS ITSELF
REASONING	203 - 4	SYSTEMATIC PROCESS OF REASONING
REASONING	341 - 2	ANY PROCESS OF REASONING
REASONING	358 - 2	MANY ABSTRACT PROCESSES OF REASONING
REASONING	378 - 1	ELABORATE PROCESS OF REASONING
RE-BUILDS	032 - 1	RE-BUILDS ACCORDING TO OUR BELIEFS
REBUKED	456 - 1	JESUS REBUKED THE DEVIL
RECAPITULATE	033 - 4	BRIEFLY LET US RECAPITULATE
RECEDING	330 - 3	NOR RECEDING FROM IT
RECEIVE	273 - 3	READY TO RECIEVE IT
RECEIVE	290 - 1	HE SAID YE SHALL RECEIVE
RECEIVE	380 - 1	RECEIVE A COHERENT MESSAGE
RECEIVE	435 - 3	RECEIVE THAT FOR WHICH WE ASK
RECEIVE	450 - 1	RECEIVE MORE SOUNDS UNFAIR
RECEIVE	470 - 1	A MENTAL CONDITION TO RECEIVE THE GIFT
RECEIVED	363 - 3	HE RECEIVED A DEFINITE REPLY
RECEIVED	462 - 1	RECEIVED EXACTLY WHAT HE ASKED
RECEIVER	280 - 3	CAN BE NO GIFT WITHOUT A RECEIVER
RECEIVES	092 - 2	IT RECEIVES ALL IDEAS GIVEN IT
RECEIVES	433 - 2	EVERYONE RECEIVES HIS JUST DUE
RECEIVING	154 - 1	BELIEVING AND RECEIVING
RECEIVING	351 - 1	RECEIVING CONSCIOUS THOUGHT
RECEIVING	431 - 3	SIMPLE DIRECT AND RECEIVING
RECEPTACLE	114 - 3	RECEPTACLE FOR THE SEEDS
RECEPTACLE	349 - 2	RECEPTACLE OF MUCH OF THE RACE
RECEPTION	233 - 4	TO THE RECEPTION OF TRUTH
RECEPTIVE	032 - 2	REVEALS ITSELF TO WHOEVER IS RECEPTIVE
RECEPTIVE	040 - 1	OUR OWN RECEPTIVE MENTALITIES
RECEPTIVE	046 - 5	MAKE HIS MIND RECEPTIVE
RECEPTIVE	059 - 5	PATIENT SHOULD TRY TO BE RECEPTIVE
RECEPTIVE	083 - 2	IS THAT RECEPTIVE MEDIUM
RECEPTIVE	088 - 2	SOUL AS RECEPTIVE TO INTELLIGENCE
RECEPTIVE	096 - 3	IT IS RECEPTIVE AND CREATIVE
RECEPTIVE	105 - 3	IS A RECEPTIVE OR PLASTIC SUBSTANCE
RECEPTIVE	118 - 1	ENTIRELY RECEPTIVE TO OUR THOUGHT

RECEPTIVE	142 - 3	RECEPTIVE TO THIS HEALING PRESENCE
RECEPTIVE	151 - 3	RECEPTIVE TO THE IDEA OF LOVE HE BECOMES
RECEPTIVE	165 - 1	RECEPTIVE OR CREATIVE LAW
RECEPTIVE	165 - 3	RECEPTIVE TO THE HARMONY OF
RECEPTIVE	193 - 3	BECOME ACTIVE OR RECEPTIVE
RECEPTIVE	206 - 4	PATIENT MUST BE RECEPTIVE
RECEPTIVE	206 - 5	THINKING INTO A RECEPTIVE
RECEPTIVE	208 - 3	IT IS DEDUCTIVE RECEPTIVE
RECEPTIVE	234 - 4	BY A RECEPTIVE INTELLIGENCE
RECEPTIVE	258 - 1	RECEPTIVE CAPACITY OF MIND
RECEPTIVE	258 - 3	RECEPTIVE TO THE TRUTH
RECEPTIVE	278 - 1	CREATIVE CONSCIOUSNESS WHICH IS RECEPTIVE
RECEPTIVE	301 - 4	PROVIDE A RECEPTIVE AVENUE FOR IT
RECEPTIVE	363 - 2	RECEPTIVE TO THE DIVINE INFLUX
RECEPTIVE	397 - 3	RECEPTIVE AS WELL AS INTELLIGENT
RECEPTIVE	398 - 1	WITH A COMPLETELY RECEPTIVE ONE
RECEPTIVE	403 - 3	IT IS RECEPTIVE WITHOUT CARING
RECEPTIVE	447 - 1	AN OPEN AND RECEPTIVE MIND
RECEPTIVE	447 - 3	MIND RECEPTIVE TO COMPLETION
RECEPTIVITY	037 - 4	QUESTION OF OUR OWN RECEPTIVITY
RECEPTIVITY	041 - 1	ACCORDING TO MAN'S RECEPTIVITY TO IT
RECEPTIVITY	041 - 4	OUR RECEPTIVITY TO IT
RECEPTIVITY	045 - 1	HAS A DIFFERENT RECEPTIVITY
RECEPTIVITY	058 - 5	RECOGNITION AND RECEPTIVITY
RECEPTIVITY	206 - 3	RECEPTIVITY IN THE THOUGHT
RECEPTIVITY	243 - 3	CHANNELS OF PURE RECEPTIVITY
RECEPTIVITY	283 - 1	LIMITLESS SEA OF RECEPTIVITY
RECEPTIVITY	329 - 3	A CONSCIOUS RECEPTIVITY TO IT
RECEPTIVITY	406 - 1	SPIRIT IS BOTH RECEPTIVITY
RECEPTIVITY	436 - 1	A POSITIVE RECEPTIVITY
RECEPTIVITY	442 - 1	RESULT OF HIS OWN RECEPTIVITY
RECEPTIVITY	455 - 3	FIELDS OF RECEPTIVITY IN OUR MINDS
RECIPROCAL	460 - 4	RECIPROCAL ACTION BETWEEN THE UNIVERSAL
RECIPROCAL	466 - 3	ALWAYS A RECIPROCAL ACTION
RECITING	352 - 2	RECITING THE THINGS THAT ENGAGED
RECOGNITION	042 - 5	SPONTANEOUS RECOGNITION OF THESE LAWS
RECOGNITION	058 - 5	A STATE OF CONSCIOUS RECOGNITION
RECOGNITION	059 - 2	NO RECOGNITION OF AGE IN THE TRUTH
RECOGNITION	149 - 2	RECOGNITION OF SPIRIT'S
RECOGNITION	164 - 2	CONSCIOUS RECOGNITION THAT HEALTH
RECOGNITION	167 - 3	RECOGNITION OF THE CREATIVE POWER
RECOGNITION	170 - 2	RECOGNITION THAT THE POWER OF THE WORD
RECOGNITION	178 - 5	RECOGNITION WITHIN HIS OWN MIND
RECOGNITION	186 - 4	RECOGNITION OF THE PRESENCE OF GOD
RECOGNITION	187 - 2	THE RIGHT SUBJECTIVE RECOGNITION
RECOGNITION	196 - 3	HIS RECOGNITION OF LIFE
RECOGNITION	206 - 3	TRUE RECOGNITION OF PERFECTION
RECOGNITION	216 - 2	THE SPONTANEOUS RECOGNITION
RECOGNITION	217 - 2	RECOGNITION IS A MENTAL ACT
RECOGNITION	220 - 1	AT THE LEVEL OF OUR RECOGNITION
RECOGNITION	232 - 3	A RECOGNITION OF THE UNITY
RECOGNITION	276 - 2	RECOGNITION OF THE OMNIPRESENCE
RECOGNITION	296 - 3	INNER RECOGNITION OF REALITY
RECOGNITION	303 - 1	THE RECOGNITION OF THE ONE PERFECT POWER
RECOGNITION	318 - 3	FIRST RECOGNITION, SECOND UNIFICATION

RECOGNITION	319 - 1	BY ITS OWN RECOGNITION
RECOGNITION	331 - 2	A RECOGNITION OF THE ABSOLUTE UNITY
RECOGNITION	331 - 2	RECOGNITION WHICH JESUS HAD
RECOGNITION	331 - 4	TO THE POINT OF OUR RECOGNITION
RECOGNITION	331 - 5	THANKS THIS WAS RECOGNITION
RECOGNITION	334 - 4	POWER OF JESUS LAY IN HIS RECOGNITION
RECOGNITION	336 - 2	OUR RECOGNITION OF TRUTH
RECOGNITION	336 - 3	AT THE LEVEL OF OUR RECOGNITION OF IT
RECOGNITION	342 - 3	AND WAITS FOR RECOGNITION
RECOGNITION	371 - 1	A FULL RECOGNITION OF OURSELVES
RECOGNITION	379 - 4	TO AN OBJECTIVE STATE OF RECOGNITION
RECOGNITION	390 - 4	UNFOLDING INTO A GREATER RECOGNITION
RECOGNITION	411 - 4	FROM THIS INNER RECOGNITION
RECOGNITION	413 - 3	A RECOGNITION OF THIS DIVINE PRESENCE
RECOGNITION	437 - 3	WITHOUT THIS RECOGNITION
RECOGNITION	444 - 3	RECOGNITION OF THE UNITY
RECOGNITION	471 - 7	RECOGNITION OF THIS IS BEING BORN
RECOGNITION	472 - 4	RECOGNITION THAT HEAVEN IS
RECOGNIZE	034 - 3	RECOGNIZE ITS SIMPLICITY
RECOGNIZE	037 - 2	WE RECOGNIZE IT AS POWER
RECOGNIZE	121 - 2	RECOGNIZE SUBCONSCIOUS MIND
RECOGNIZE	152 - 2	WE RECOGNIZE A SPIRITUAL LAW
RECOGNIZE	160 - 1	RECOGNIZE THE PURE ESSENCE
RECOGNIZE	202 - 5	RECOGNIZE YOUR OWN PERFECTION
RECOGNIZE	211 - 3	RECOGNIZE THE WORD AS POWER
RECOGNIZE	240 - 1	RECOGNIZE ITS PRESENCE
RECOGNIZE	276 - 3	RECOGNIZE THE SPIRIT IN EVERYTHING
RECOGNIZE	303 - 2	WE REFUSE TO RECOGNIZE WE NEUTRALIZE
RECOGNIZE	307 - 1	RECOGNIZE TRUTH THROUGH REASON
RECOGNIZE	327 - 2	TO RECOGNIZE THAT SPIRIT ALONE
RECOGNIZE	336 - 3	RECOGNIZE NO LOW VITALITY BUT REAL
RECOGNIZE	337 - 1	RECOGNIZE THE APPEARANCE OF EVIL
RECOGNIZE	357 - 3	RECOGNIZE IT AS THE ONE
RECOGNIZE	369 - 1	TO RECOGNIZE THE CHRIST
RECOGNIZE	415 - 3	COULD NOT RECOGNIZE EACH OTHER
RECOGNIZE	430 - 4	UNLESS WE RECOGNIZE IT
RECOGNIZE	503 - 2	RECOGNIZE HIM FOR WE SHALL SEE HIM
RECOGNIZED	419 - 3	RECOGNIZED THE ABSOLUTE UNITY OF GOD
RECOGNIZES	120 - 3	RECOGNIZES THE LAW AND USES IT
RECOGNIZES	178 - 5	ONE WHO RECOGNIZES MAN
RECOGNIZES	179 - 6	RECOGNIZES THAT ALL
RECOGNIZES	180 - 1	RECOGNIZES THE TRUE
RECOGNIZES	220 - 3	THE SOUL RECOGNIZES ITS OWN I-AM-NESS
RECOGNIZES	291 - 1	IT RECOGNIZES HIM AS HE RECOGNIZES
RECOGNIZING	077 - 2	RECOGNIZING THAT WE ARE
RECOGNIZING	231 - 3	RECOGNIZING THE CONDITION
RECOGNIZING	303 - 2	WHAT WE PERSIST IN RECOGNIZING
RECOLLECTION	377 - 2	A CONSTANT STREAM OF RECOLLECTION
RECONCILE	123 - 2	TRYING TO RECONCILE THE WORLD
RECONCILE	123 - 3	RECONCILE SUFFERING AND LACK
RECONCILE	448 - 1	SCIENCE OF MIND IS TO RECONCILE
RECONCILED	285 - 4	FIRST BE RECONCILED TO THY BROTHER
RECONCILIATION	468 - 2	RECONCILIATION WITH THE UNIVERSE
RECORD	115 - 2	CONTAINS A RECORD OF EVERYTHING
RECORD	427 - 1	RECORD OF HIS SAYINGS

RECORDS	158 - 3	BELIEVED THESE RECORDS
RECORDS	341 - 5	RECORDS OF PEOPLE
RECOVERY	221 - 6	RECOVERY OF YOUR PATIENT
RECREATES	260 - 3	AS EASILY RECREATES
RE-DIRECT	078 - 3	WE CAN RE-DIRECT ITS MOVEMENT
REDUCE	036 - 1	REDUCE ALL THAT IS TO A FUNDAMENTAL
REED	302 - 3	A REED SHAKEN BY THE WIND
RE-EDUCATED	211 - 2	RE-EDUCATED JUST AS DO ADULTS
RE-ENACTED	106 - 2	RE-ENACTED THROUGH MAN
RE-ENACTED	196 - 5	DIVINE NATURE IS RE-ENACTED IN MAN
RE-ENACTS	097 - 4	MAN RE-ENACTS THE NATURE OF GOD
RE-ENACTS	132 - 8	MAN RE-ENACTS THE DIVINE NATURE
REFER	067 - 2	DOES NOT REFER TO A TIME
REFERRING	444 - 2	REFERRING TO HIS UNDERSTANDING
REFERRING	477 - 5	JESUS WAS NOT REFERRING
REFERRING	479 - 3	REFERRING TO THE INDIVIDUAL I
REFLECT	140 - 2	REFLECT WHATEVER IS CAST INTO IT
REFLECT	218 - 4	MUST REFLECT SPIRITUAL IDEAS
REFLECT	396 - 2	REFLECT THIS LIMITED CONCEPT
REFLECT	467 - 2	REFLECT ITSELF IN THE DIVINE
REFLECT	490 - 2	REFLECT THE DIVINE GLORY
REFLECTED	299 - 3	IS REFLECTED BACK TO ME FROM ALL
REFLECTED	414 - 4	REFLECTED THROUGH MAN'S CONSCIOUSNESS
REFLECTING	295 - 2	REFLECTING HIS STATMENTS INTO CONSCIOUSNESS
REFLECTING	449 - 2	LIFE CANNOT HELP REFLECTING
REFLECTION	099 - 4	REFLECTION OF THE MIND
REFLECTION	176 - 1	A REFLECTION WHICH NOTHING CAN STOP
REFLECTION	176 - 1	TO CREATE THE REFLECTION
REFLECTION	217 - 1	IMAGINATION, IDEA, NOR REFLECTION
REFLECTION	297 - 2	LAW OF REFLECTION
REFLECTION	301 - 1	REFLECTION OF THAT IMAGE
REFLECTION	320 - 4	LAW IS A LAW OF REFLECTION
REFLECTION	411 - 2	MIND IS ONE OF REFLECTION
REFLECTION	412 - 2	REFLECTION OF THE SUBJECTIVE STATE
REFLECTION	417 - 1	REFLECTION OF WHAT THE CONSENSUS
REFLECTION	456 - 5	REFLECTION OF HIS BLINDNESS BEFORE
REFLECTION	484 - 4	BODY IS A REFLECTION
REFLECTIONS	291 - 2	REFLECTIONS OF OUR MEDITATIONS
REFLECTS	144 - 3	REFLECTS ITSELF IN A HEALTHY BODY
REFLECTS	196 - 5	AS HE CONTEMPLATES HE REFLECTS
REFLECTS	198 - 1	REFLECTS A GREATER PERFECTION
REFLECTS	199 - 1	THINKING AND REFLECTS THEM
REFLECTS	296 - 1	REFLECTS INTO MIND TENDS TO TAKE FORM
REFLECTS	492 - 4	OUTER MAN REFLECTS
REFRAIN	485 - 5	REFRAIN FROM MAKING MORE MISTAKES
REFRAINS	174 - 1	REFRAINS FROM WILL POWER
REFUSE	055 - 3	REFUSE MENTALLY TO ACCEPT THE FALSE
REFUSE	055 - 4	REFUSE TO TALK ABOUT
REFUSE	185 - 1	REFUSE TO BELIEVE IN ITS OPPOSITE
REFUSE	209 - 4	CANNOT REFUSE MAN ANYTHING
REFUSE	298 - 2	REFUSE TO SEE THE NEGATIVE SIDE
REFUSE	302 - 3	REFUSE TO THINK OF FAILURE
REFUSE	303 - 2	WE REFUSE TO RECOGNIZE WE NEUTRALIZE
REFUSE	307 - 3	REFUSE TO HAVE THE FEELINGS HURT
REFUSE	307 - 3	REFUSE TO RECIEVE ANYONE'S CONDEMNATION

REFUSE	432 - 4	REFUSE TO CARRY THE CORPSE
REFUSES	167 - 3	REFUSES TO ALLOW NEGATIVE THOUGHTS
REFUSES	169 - 3	MIND REFUSES TO SEE
REFUTED	186 - 2	IT MUST BE REFUTED
REFUTED	354 - 2	IT SHOULD BE DIRECTLY REFUTED
REGAIN	230 - 4	TO REGAIN THIS ONE MUST USE THE INNER SIGHT
REGAIN	446 - 4	REGAIN THE LOST PARADISE
REGARDLESS	184 - 3	REGARDLESS OF WHAT CONDITIONS EXIST
REGARDLESS	200 - 5	REGARDLESS OF ITS PARTICULAR SOURCE
REGARDLESS	268 - 4	HOW TO GET WHAT THEY WANT REGARDLESS
REGARDLESS	282 - 1	REGARDLESS OF CIRCUMSTANCES
REGULATE	185 - 1	HE WILL REGULATE HIS THINKING
REHEARSE	353 - 4	PAST CONTINUALLY REHEARSE THEMSELVES
REIGN	248 - 1	LOVE HARMONY AND PEACE REIGN
REINSTATE	475 - 5	REINSTATE THE OUTER MAN IN PEACE
REITERATE	374 - 5	REITERATE THERE CAN BE NO
REJECT	092 - 2	IF IT COULD CHOOSE IT COULD REJECT
REJECT	096 - 3	SUBJECTIVITY CAN NEVER REJECT
REJECT	198 - 2	IT CAN NEVER REJECT
REJECT	390 - 2	MAY ACCEPT OR REJECT
REJECTS	315 - 2	MIND CANNOT ACCEPT WHAT IT REJECTS
REJOICE	259 - 2	IN THIS FREEDOM I REJOICE
REJOICE	496 - 6	WE ARE TO REJOICE
REJOICING	251 - 6	I REST IN MIND REJOICING
RELATE	410 - 2	THEN WE RELATE THESE STATEMENTS
RELATED	155 - 1	RELATED MENTAL ATTITUDES
RELATIONSHIP	032 - 2	SOME RELATIONSHIP TO THE UNIVERSAL MIND
RELATIONSHIP	075 - 1	RELATIONSHIP TO THE UNIVERSAL
RELATIONSHIP	115 - 3	RELATIONSHIP TO THE UNIVERSAL
RELATIONSHIP	134 - 1	RELATIONSHIP IS ONE OF COMPLETE UNITY
RELATIONSHIP	180 - 3	HIS RELATIONSHIP TO THE UNIVERSE
RELATIONSHIP	186 - 3	RELATIONSHIP TO THE DIVINE
RELATIONSHIP	191 - 2	TRUE RELATIONSHIP TO THE WHOLE
RELATIONSHIP	281 - 1	A RIGHT RELATIONSHIP WITH THE SPIRIT
RELATIONSHIP	283 - 4	IN RELATIONSHIP TO ONE'S ABILITY
RELATIONSHIP	330 - 1	THE RELATIONSHIP OF MAN TO GOD
RELATIONSHIP	331 - 1	RELATIONSHIP OF THE INDIVIDUAL
RELATIONSHIP	333 - 6	OF THE MARVELOUS RELATIONSHIP
RELATIONSHIP	367 - 3	HIS DIRECT RELATIONSHIP TO THE WHOLE
RELATIONSHIP	390 - 4	TRUE RELATIONSHIP TO GOD OR SPIRIT
RELATIONSHIP	401 - 2	ALTERING OUR THOUGHT RELATIONSHIP
RELATIONSHIP	406 - 3	RELATIONSHIP TO ITSELF ALONE
RELATIONSHIP	416 - 1	ITS RIGHT RELATIONSHIP TO GOD
RELATIONSHIP	419 - 4	THE MARVELOUS RELATIONSHIP WHICH EXISTS
RELATIONSHIP	443 - 3	DIRECT RELATIONSHIP BETWEEN GOD AND MAN
RELATIONSHIP	472 - 6	RELATIONSHIP TO THE TRUTH
RELATIVE	169 - 3	WE TURN ENTIRELY AWAY FROM THE RELATIVE
RELATIVE	179 - 1	THOUGHT RELATIVE TO THIS PERSON
RELATIVE	274 - 4	WITHDRAW FROM THE RELATIVE
RELATIVE	275 - 1	RELATIVE AND NECESSARILY CONDITIONED
RELATIVE	275 - 2	THE FACTS ARE RELATIVE
RELATIVE	300 - 2	THE RELATIVE AND THE ABSOLUTE
RELATIVE	315 - 3	WITHDRAW FROM THE RELATIVE
RELATIVE	319 - 2	WE TURN FROM THE RELATIVE
RELATIVE	342 - 1	SUBCONSCIOUS OR RELATIVE FIRST CAUSE

RELATIVE	405 - 3	HAVE TO EXPAND THE RELATIVE
RELATIVE	436 - 1	TEACHING OF JESUS RELATIVE TO PRAYER
RELATIVE CAUSE	197 - 2	A PART OF THE RELATIVE CAUSE
RELAX	233 - 4	RELAX YOUR THOUGHT
RELAXATION	225 - 2	A SENSE OF RELAXATION TO THE BODY
RELAXATION	232 - 2	TREATMENT FOR COMPLETE RELAXATION
RELAXES	256 - 5	RELAXES ALL THE MUSCLES
RELEASE	140 - 4	RELEASE OUR MINDS FROM THE THOUGHT
RELEASE	232 - 4	RELEASE ALL THOUGHTS
RELEASE	232 - 4	RELEASE THAT WHICH IS NOT NEEDED
RELEASE	257 - 5	I RELEASE ALL RESPONSIBILITY
RELEASE	282 - 3	RELEASE WRONG SUBJECTIVE TENDENCIES
RELEASE	501 - 4	RELEASE OUR TROUBLES
RELEASED	176 - 3	SHOULD BE SO RELEASED FROM OUTLINE
RELEASED	257 - 3	ALL TENSION IS RELEASED
RELEASED	414 - 3	SPIRITUAL POWER IS RELEASED
RELEASES	257 - 3	RELEASES ALL SENSE OF BURDEN
RELIABLE	356 - 2	ANY RELIABLE SPIRIT OF PROPHECY
RELIANCE	323 - 1	BELIEF IN AND RELIANCE UPON TRUTH
RELIANCE	408 - 4	SPONTANEOUS RELIANCE ON TRUTH
RELIANCE	432 - 3	RELIANCE UPON GOD
RELIANCE	432 - 3	ABSOLUTE RELIANCE MAY BE PLACED
RELIANCE	455 - 5	RELIANCE UPON THE LAW
RELIEF	320 - 1	ALL THE RELIEF WE CAN GET
RELIEVE	288 - 2	RELIEVE THE GREATER DEMANDS OF NECESSITY
RELIEVED	160 - 3	HE HAS RELIEVED HIS MIND
RELIEVED	302 - 3	WE ARE RELIEVED OF ALL THOUGHT
RELIGHT	218 - 3	RELIGHT THE TORCH OF
RELIGION	025 - 1	SCIENCE AND RELIGION SHALL WALK
RELIGION	060 - 3	A NEW RELIGION
RELIGION	060 - 3	ANY RELIGION SECT OR ORDER
RELIGION	066 - 2	THE GOD OF RELIGION
RELIGION	067 - 3	THE ONLY LIGHT ON RELIGION
RELIGION	269 - 3	A PREACHER FOR HIS RELIGION
RELIGION	308 - 1	RELIGION IS A LIFE, A LIVING
RELIGION	308 - 1	THAT RELIGION IS SPIRITUAL
RELIGION	444 - 4	SAME PROBLEM CONFRONTS RELIGION
RELIGION	499 - 7	PURE RELIGION MANIFESTS ITSELF
RELIGIONS	067 - 3	THE RELIGIONS OF THE WORLD
RELIGIONS	445 - 5	GREAT RELIGIONS HAVE TAUGHT TRUTH
RELIGIOUS	155 - 3	TO DO WITH OUR RELIGIOUS EXPERIENCE
RELIGIOUS	276 - 1	SEEM TO BE RELIGIOUS AND SPIRITUAL
RELIGIOUS	434 - 4	RESULT OF RELIGIOUS MORBIDITIES
RELIGIOUS	439 - 2	A LESSON IN RELIGIOUS DEVELOPMENT
RELIGIOUS	449 - 1	RELIGIOUS BELIEF MAY OR MAY NOT BE
RELIGIOUS EDUCATION	460 - 4	IN THE HISTORY OF RELIGIOUS EDUCATION
RELUCTANCE	152 - 2	OVERCOMING GOD'S RELUCTANCE
RELUCTANT	397 - 5	YOU ARE NOT DEALING WITH A RELUCTANT
REMAIN	316 - 1	REMAIN IN HIS OWN FIELD
REMAINING	202 - 5	REMAINING FOR A FEW MOMENTS
REMAKING	317 - 1	REMAKING THE MATERIAL OR PHYSICAL MAN
REMARKABLE	366 - 4	TO THIS REMARKABLE MAN
REMEDY	238 - 4	REMEDY FOR THIS IS LOVE
REMEDY	256 - 5	REMEDY FOR STOMACH TROUBLE
REMEDY	483 - 5	WE KNOW THE REMEDY

REMEDY	483 - 5	ALWAYS THE REMEDY
REMEMBER	392 - 1	POINTS WE SHOULD REMEMBER
REMEMBER	502 - 2	REMEMBER THEM NO LONGER AGAINST OURSELVES
REMEMBERED	460 - 3	BEEN BEST REMEMBERED BY IT
REMEMBERS	372 - 1	REMEMBERS WHAT IT HAS DONE
REMEMBRANCE	303 - 3	BOOK OF MY REMEMBRANCE
REMEMBRANCE	347 - 4	CONTAINS A REMEMBRANCE OF EVERYTHING
REMEMBRANCE	348 - 3	SUBJECTIVE ATMOSPHERE OR REMEMBRANCE
REMEMBRANCE	372 - 1	REMEMBRANCE ALONE GUARANTEES PERSONALITY
REMEMBRANCE	376 - 2	REMEMBRANCE LINKS EVENTS TOGETHER
REMEMBRANCE	462 - 3	NO REMEMBRANCE OF GOD
REMIIND	401 - 4	SHOULD AGAIN REMIND OURSELVES
REMISSION	269 - 3	REMISSION OF SINS
RE-MOLD	074 - 1	RE-MOLD HIS AFFAIRS
REMOLDING	317 - 1	REMOLDING AND REMAKING THE MATERIAL
RE-MOLDS	490 - 4	RE-MOLDS CONDITIONS
REMOVE	054 - 2	REMOVE FALSE CONDITIONS
REMOVE	058 - 4	REMOVE THIS DOUBT
REMOVE	293 - 2	REMOVE MY FEAR OF LACK AND NEGATION
REMOVED	438 - 2	THIS REMOVED THE WEIGHT
REMOVES	166 - 2	REMOVES ANY OBSTRUCTION IN MIND
RENEW	229 - 4	NOW RENEW AND REBUILD ME
RENEWAL	257 - 1	SECRET OF RELAXATION REST AND RENEWAL
RENEWED	229 - 3	NOW RENEWED BY THE VERY LIFE
RENEWED	247 - 3	STREAM OF LIFE IS RENEWED DAILY
RENEWED	248 - 1	BLOOD STREAM IS CONTINUOUSLY RENEWED
RENEWED	249 - 2	TO HIM WHERE IT IS RENEWED
RENEWED	486 - 5	BODY IS AUTOMATICALLY RENEWED
RENEWED	494 - 1	RENEWED IN MIND BY THE SPIRIT
RENEWING	415 - 1	EVER RENEWING SUBSTANCE OF FAITH
RENEWING	218 - 3	RENEWING OF THE MIND
RENEWING	248 - 2	FOREVER INVIGORATING FOREVER RENEWING
RENEWING	486 - 5	RENEWING OF THE MIND IS A SCIENTIFIC ACT
RENEWS	235 - 3	CLEANSES, HEALS AND RENEWS EVERY ORGAN
RENUNCIATION	454 - 4	IDEA OF A FALSE RENUNCIATION
REPAY	487 - 4	I WILL REPAY SAITH THE LORD
REPEAT	318 - 3	REPEAT THIS TREATMENT TWO OR THREE TIMES
REPEAT	380 - 1	I REPEAT HOW DIFFICULT IT
REPEAT	423 - 1	REPEAT ALL THE WORDS OF WISDOM
REPEATED	225 - 1	REPEATED DAILY UNTIL A HEALING
REPEATING	220 - 4	REASON FOR REPEATING TREATMENTS
REPELLING	294 - 2	WE ARE EITHER ATTRACTING OR REPELLING
REPELS	142 - 2	REPELS WHAT IS UNLIKE
REPETITION	290 - 3	THERE IS BOUND TO BE A REPETITION
REPETITION	431 - 3	POWER NOT THROUGH REPETITION
REPLY	200 - 2	REPLY DO YOU MEAN
REPOSE	033 - 3	STRETCHED IN SMILING REPOSE
REPOSE	388 - 1	STRETCHED IN SMILING REPOSE
REPRESENT	354 - 3	REPRESENT THE TYPE OF MANIFESTATION
REPRESENTATION	395 - 1	GOD IS WILL AND REPRESENTATION
REPRESENTATION	477 - 3	REAL REPRESENTATION OF THE DIVINE
REPRESENTS	365 - 3	REPRESENTS THE WHOLE
REPRESSED	238 - 4	REPRESSED OR SUPPRESSED
REPROACH	457 - 4	BEYOND REPROACH
REPROACHES	466 - 7	GOD NEVER REPROACHES

REPRODUCE	106 - 1	REPRODUCE THE UNIVERSE
REPRODUCE	183 - 1	TEND TO REPRODUCE THEMSELVES
REPRODUCE	211 - 2	NOT REPRODUCE FALSE IMPRESSIONS
REPRODUCE	314 - 1	WE REPRODUCE THE COSMOS
REPRODUCE	349 - 1	STILL REPRODUCE THESE VIBRATIONS
REPRODUCED	116 - 1	THE SAME PRINCIPLE REPRODUCED IN MAN
REPRODUCES	167 - 1	MAN REPRODUCES THE UNIVERSAL
REPRODUCES	224 - 2	MIND REPRODUCES THIS IDEA
REPRODUCES	483 - 4	REPRODUCES THE DIVINE NATURE
REPRODUCES	497 - 4	EACH REPRODUCES FROM THE LOWEST
REPRODUCTIONS	382 - 3	REPRODUCTIONS OF MAN'S PHYSICAL
REPUDIATE	049 - 5	REPUDIATE THE FALSEHOOD
REPUDIATE	191 - 4	REPUDIATE ANY BELIEF
REPUDIATED	039 - 2	NO LONGER REPUDIATED
REPUDIATES	409 - 2	REPUDIATES THIS BELIEF
REPULSION	119 - 1	LAWS OF ATTRACTION AND REPULSION ARE
REPULSION	126 - 2	ATTRACTION AND REPULSION
REPULSION	322 - 2	ATTRACTION AND REPULSION ARE MENTAL
REPUTE	138 - 1	PHYSICIANS OF HIGHEST REPUTE
REQUEST	142 - 3	GOD WILL HONOR HIS REQUEST
REQUIRE	447 - 2	WHAT WE REQUIRE IS MONEY FRIENDS
REQUISITE	168 - 3	FIRST REQUISITE FOR THE MENTAL
REQUISITES	440 - 1	AS SUPREME REQUISITES
RESCUE	464 - 4	COME TO THE RESCUE OF HIS BELOVED
RESEARCH	074 - 3	THROUGH RESEARCH AND INVESTIGATION
RESEARCH	309 - 5	RESEARCH IN THE FIELD OF PHYSICS
RESENT	241 - 2	RESENT SO THOROUGHLY THE BONDAGE
RESENTMENT	145 - 2	DEEP AND CONTINUED RESENTMENT
RESENTMENT	248 - 4	RESENTMENT AGAINST PERSONS
RESENTMENT	249 - 1	RESENTMENT IN MY LIFE
RESENTMENT	255 - 3	HATRED AND RESENTMENT
RESERVOIR	463 - 1	INEXHAUSTIBLE RESERVOIR OF ETERNAL
RESERVOIRS	394 - 3	WE CAN TAP THE RESERVOIRS
RESIDENT	138 - 1	RESIDENT IN THE DYNAMIC FORCES
RESIDES	397 - 1	RESIDES WITHIN US FOR THE PURPOSE
RESIDES	410 - 4	THE POWER TO CREATE RESIDES
RESIDING	435 - 1	RESIDING IN THE HEART OF ALL
RESIGNATION	267 - 2	RESIGNATION AND CALL IT PEACE
RESIST	303 - 2	JESUS SAID RESIST NOT
RESIST	430 - 5	RESIST NOT EVIL TO LOVE OUR ENEMIES
RESISTANCE	056 - 3	APPARENT MATERIAL RESISTANCE
RESISTANCE	159 - 4	APPARENT MATERIAL RESISTANCE
RESISTANCE	226 - 3	RESISTANCE TO CONDITIONS
RESOLUTELY	167 - 4	SHOULD BE RESOLUTELY DENIED
RESOLUTELY	315 - 4	WE MUST RESOLUTELY TURN AWAY
RESOLUTELY	317 - 2	MUST RESOLUTELY TURN AWAY
RESOLVABLE	310 - 3	RESOLVABLE INTO A UNIVERSAL ENERGY
RESOLVE	091 - 2	RESOLVE INTO THE ETHER
RESOLVE	123 - 2	RESOLVE THE MATERIAL UNIVERSE
RESOLVE	197 - 1	RESOLVE INTO THE UNIVERSAL SUBSTANCE
RESOLVE	224 - 3	RESOLVE THINGS INTO THOUGHT
RESOLVE	453 - 3	RESOLVE TO BE TRUE TO HIMSELF
RESPECTER	034 - 1	NO RESPECTER OF PERSONS
RESPECTER	041 - 2	NO RESPECTER OF PERSONS
RESPECTER	052 - 4	LAW IS NO RESPECTER OF PERSONS

RESPECTER	284 - 2	IT IS NO RESPECTER OF PERSONS
RESPECTER	500 - 4	RESPECTER OF PERSONS AND WILL
RESPECTERS	027 - 3	NEVER RESPECTERS OF PERSONS
RESPIRATION	229 - 2	RENEWED BY EVERY RESPIRATION
RESPOND	052 - 4	RESPOND TO EVERYONE
RESPOND	139 - 1	ABLE TO RESPOND TO EACH OTHER
RESPOND	281 - 3	SOMETHING TO RESPOND TO HIM
RESPOND	438 - 5	RESPOND TO THE THOUGHT OF OTHERS
RESPONDED	028 - 2	GOD HAS RESPONDED
RESPONDING	139 - 1	INFINITE INTELLIGENCE RESPONDING TO FINITE
RESPONDING	283 - 2	GOD CANNOT HELP RESPONDING
RESPONDING	406 - 2	ALWAYS RESPONDING TO OUR THOUGHT
RESPONDING	434 - 2	DIRECT LAW RESPONDING TO PRAISE
RESPONDS	052 - 3	RESPONDS TO OUR ADVANCE
RESPONDS	157 - 4	RESPONDS MORE QUICKLY
RESPONDS	173 - 4	PRESENCE THAT RESPONDS
RESPONDS	174 - 4	LAW IS AND RESPONDS
RESPONDS	281 - 2	WHICH RESPONDS
RESPONDS	293 - 4	LAW RESPONDS TO MY THOUGHT
RESPONDS	396 - 1	RESPONDS BY CORRESPONDENCE
RESPONDS	398 - 5	THAT SPIRIT RESPONDS TO US
RESPONDS	412 - 1	LIFE RESPONDS TO US
RESPONSE	060 - 2	A READY RESPONSE FROM THE INVISIBLE
RESPONSE	435 - 3	THERE IS A DIRECT RESPONSE
RESPONSE	437 - 3	RESPONSE FROM A HEART OF LOVE
RESPONSIBILITY	107 - 2	OBLIGATION AND RESPONSIBILITY
RESPONSIBILITY	176 - 2	WITHOUT TAKING ON THE RESPONSIBILITY OF
RESPONSIBILITY	179 - 2	RESPONSIBILITY IN HEALING
RESPONSIBILITY	199 - 4	SENSE OF PERSONAL RESPONSIBILITY
RESPONSIBILITY	199 - 4	RESPONSIBILITY DOWN TO ITS LAST
RESPONSIBILITY	203 - 1	YOUR ONLY RESPONSIBILITY
RESPONSIBILITY	221 - 6	RESPONSIBILITY FOR THE RECOVERY
RESPONSIBILITY	305 - 4	NEVER LET ONE MOMENT'S RESPONSIBILITY
RESPONSIBILITY	318 - 3	WE TAKE NO RESPONSIBILITY
RESPONSIBILITY	454 - 5	PERSONAL SENSE OF RESPONSIBILITY
RESPONSIBLE	200 - 1	RESPONSIBLE FOR THE LAW
RESPONSIBLE	395 - 1	WE ARE RESPONSIBLE
RESPONSIVE	042 - 6	RESPONSIVE TO EACH AND ALL
RESPONSIVE	362 - 3	RESPONSIVE TO EVERYTHING THAT WE DO
RESPONSIVENESS	374 - 2	RESPONSIVENESS HAVE FLED
RESPONSIVENESS	406 - 1	AND CREATIVE RESPONSIVENESS
REST	189 - 3	RESULTS REST IN THE ETERNAL LAW
REST	251 - 6	I REST IN MIND
REST	257 - 5	REST PERMEATES MY MIND
REST	289 - 3	REST IN PERFECT CONFIDENCE PEACE
RESTATE	046 - 4	RESTATE OUR PRINCIPLE
RESTORE	439 - 6	ABLE TO RESTORE THEIR VISION
RESTORING	250 - 1	RESTORING HIM TO COMPLETE WHOLENESS
RESTRICTED	320 - 4	RESTRICTED WAYS OF THINKING
RESTRICTED	321 - 1	CAUSES US TO FEEL RESTRICTED
RESTRICTION	110 - 2	TEMPORARY RESTRICTION OF BONDAGE
RESTRICTION	231 - 5	THERE IS NO RESTRICTION
RESTRICTION	240 - 4	RESTRICTION BACK OF THE MANIFESTATION
RESTRICTION	288 - 2	FROM A STANDPOINT OF RESTRICTION
RESTS	138 - 3	RESTS ENTIRELY ON THE THEORY

RESTS	433 - 5	UNIVERSE RESTS ON THE SHOULDERS OF LOVE
RESTS	434 - 6	OUR THOUGHT RESTS UPON
RESULT	026 - 4	CAN PRODUCE A CERTAIN RESULT
RESULT	026 - 6	WILL GET THE SAME RESULT
RESULT	033 - 2	RESULT OF OUR IGNORANCE
RESULT	057 - 4	RESULT OF RIGHT TREATMENT
RESULT	068 - 5	RESULT OF THE SELF-CONTEMPLATION
RESULT	080 - 1	GOD IS RESULT OR BODY
RESULT	088 - 3	RESULT OF THE THOUGHT OF SPIRIT
RESULT	098 - 1	THE BODY BEING THE RESULT
RESULT	115 - 4	MAN'S OUTWARD LIFE IS A RESULT
RESULT	126 - 1	RESULT OF THE USE HE HAS MADE OF
RESULT	132 - 4	RESULT OF THE KNOWINGNESS OF SPIRIT
RESULT	140 - 1	RESULT OF THIS MENTAL WORK
RESULT	188 - 3	RESULT OF YOUR TREATMENT
RESULT	208 - 3	YOU WILL GET A RESULT
RESULT	299 - 4	IN AS THE RESULT OF CONSCIOUS THOUGHT
RESULT	300 - 1	THE RESULT OR MANIFESTATION
RESULT	304 - 5	IS THE RESULT OF THE SUBJECTIVE
RESULT	307 - 2	THE RESULT OF THE SELF-CONTEMPLATION
RESULT	445 - 7	RESULT OF ACTUALLY REALIZING
RESULT	471 - 2	THE RESULT OF IGNORANCE
RESULT	489 - 4	CULMINATES IN THE DESIRED RESULTS
RESULTS	026 - 5	TANGIBLE OTHER THAN RESULTS
RESULTS	058 - 2	WILL PRODUCE THE BEST RESULTS
RESULTS	059 - 2	TREAT UNTIL WE GET RESULTS
RESULTS	060 - 2	LEAVE THE RESULTS TO THAT LAW
RESULTS	173 - 2	EACH PRODUCES THE SAME RESULTS
RESULTS	191 - 3	METHOD WHICH PRODUCES RESULTS
RESULTS	192 - 2	GET THE BEST RESULTS
RESULTS	225 - 1	TREAT UNTIL YOU GET RESULTS
RESULTS	225 - 4	OFTEN BRINGS QUICK RESULTS
RESULTS	237 - 4	PRODUCE CERTAIN PHYSICAL RESULTS
RESULTS	402 - 2	BE SURPRISED AT THE RESULTS
RESULTS	443 - 1	JUDGING HIS WORK BY ITS RESULTS
RESURRECTION	104 - 5	JESUS AFTER HIS RESURRECTION
RESURRECTION	310 - 4	DEATH AND RESURRECTION ARE INVENTIONS
RESURRECTION	377 - 2	FOLLOWERS AFTER HIS RESURRECTION
RESURRECTION	413 - 2	RESURRECTION IS THE DEATH OF
RESURRECTION BODY	376 - 2	RESURRECTION BODY THEN WILL NOT
RETAIN	354 - 3	RETAIN ALL THE SUGGESTIONS
RETAINED	088 - 1	RETAINED ALL OF THE IMAGES
RETAINING	386 - 2	RETAINING AND CARRYING WITH HIM
RETARDED	434 - 6	EITHER RETARDED OR QUICKENED BY
RETARDED	440 - 2	LAW OF CIRCULATION IS RETARDED
RETARDS	232 - 1	FEAR THOUGHT RETARDS
RETENTION	377 - 2	COMPLETE RETENTION OF OUR FACULTIES
RETIRE	114 - 1	RETIRE FROM THE WORLD TO BE SPIRITUAL
RETIRE	435 - 1	WE MAY RETIRE AT NIGHT IN PEACE
RETURN	123 - 2	MODERN THOUGHT IS TO RETURN
RETURN	269 - 2	RETURN TO THE THINKER
RETURN	297 - 4	PEOPLE WHO WILL RETURN THAT LOVE
RETURN	386 - 4	NOT BELIEVE IN THE RETURN OF THE SOUL
RETURN	456 - 4	WE MUST RETURN THE WAY WE CAME
RETURN	503 - 4	RETURN IS A CONSCIOUS ACT ON OUR PART

RETURNS	433 - 3	RETURNS TO THE THINKER
REVEAL	040 - 1	IT CAN REVEAL ITS SECRETS
REVEAL	040 - 3	WILLING TO REVEAL OR IMPART TO US
REVEAL	131 - 1	REVEAL THE PERFECT IDEA
REVEAL	151 - 4	LIFE MUST REVEAL ITSELF TO US THROUGH OUR
REVEAL	262 - 2	ABILITY TO REVEAL THE REAL MAN
REVEAL	418 - 3	REVEAL THAT WHICH NEEDS NO HEALING
REVEAL	443 - 2	SON WILL REVEAL HIM
REVEAL	443 - 4	REVEAL GOD TO HIS FELLOWMEN
REVEAL	479 - 5	INWARD GAZE ALONE CAN REVEAL
REVEALED	162 - 1	REVEALED THROUGH YOU AND ME
REVEALED	327 - 4	REVEALED THE PRESENCE OF GOD
REVEALED	418 - 3	HAS NOT YET BECOME REVEALED
REVEALED	443 - 3	REVEALED THROUGH THE SON
REVEALED	449 - 2	HE STANDS REVEALED AS HE IS
REVEALED	492 - 3	REVEALED BY WHAT HE DOES
REVEALERS	330 - 1	THE GREAT REVEALERS TO MAN
REVEALING	079 - 4	ONLY BY REVEALING HIMSELF
REVEALING	179 - 4	REVEALING OF THE PERFECT MAN ALWAYS HEALS
REVEALING	212 - 4	REVEALING AN IDEA WHICH IS
REVEALING	480 - 2	HE IS REVEALING THE FATHER
REVEALS	032 - 2	LIFE REVEALS ITSELF
REVEALS	079 - 4	GOD REVEALS HIMSELF TO US
REVEALS	474 - 2	SO DOING REVEALS ITS OWN NAKEDNESS
REVEALS	480 - 3	REVEALS BUT DOES NOT ABSORB
REVEALS	503 - 4	REVEALS US TO OURSELVES
REVELATION	025 - 1	REVELATION MUST KEEP FAITH WITH REASON
REVELATION	035 - 1	NOT A SPECIAL REVELATION
REVELATION	098 - 2	REVELATION HAS SHOWN
REVELATION	179 - 4	HEALING IS NOT A PROCESS BUT A REVELATION
REVELATION	212 - 4	IT IS A REVELATION
REVELATION	332 - 3	UNITY OF GOOD IS A REVELATION
REVELATION	339 - 1	COME TO IT FOR INSPIRATION AND REVELATION
REVELATION	366 - 4	A DIRECT REVELATION OF HIS SONSHIP
REVELATION	381 - 4	THE HOLLOW VOICE FOR REVELATION
REVELATION	386 - 3	THE REVELATION OF ANYONE BUT MYSELF
REVELATION	444 - 3	REVELATION OF THE SELF TO THE SELF
REVELATION	445 - 2	REVELATION OF THE INDIVIDUAL
REVELATION	475 - 1	REVELATION OF THE SELF TO THE SELF
REVELATION	480 - 5	REVELATION OF THE SELF TO THE SELF
REVELATION	503 - 4	REVELATION OF THE SELF TO THE SELF
REVELATIONS	035 - 1	THE CULMINATION OF ALL REVELATIONS
REVELATIONS	341 - 5	PSYCHIC REVELATIONS AND COSMIC CONSCIOUSNESS
REVELATIONS	346 - 1	PERIODS THAT REAL REVELATIONS COME
REVELATIONS	386 - 3	IN OTHER MEN'S REVELATIONS
REVELATIONS	439 - 2	REVELATIONS OF OLD TRUTHS
REVERSE	055 - 3	REVERSE HIS PREVIOUS AFFIRMATIONS
REVERSE	148 - 2	REVERSE OUR THINKING
REVERSE	403 - 4	REVERSE THE THOUGHT
REVERSE	404 - 2	REVERSE MENTAL ATTITUDE TO FAITH
REVERSE	405 - 5	LEARN TO REVERSE THE THOUGHTS
REVERSE	455 - 3	CANNOT REVERSE ITS OWN NATURE
REVERSE	483 - 5	REVERSE THE PROCESS OF THOUGHT
REVERSED	211 - 3	IT CANNOT BE REVERSED
REVERSES	322 - 1	REVERSES THE CONDITION ATTENDANT

REVERSES	337 - 2	THIS REVERSES THE POPULAR BELIEF
REVITALIZING	248 - 2	FOREVER RENEWING, FOREVER REVITALIZING
REVITALIZING	250 - 1	CLEANSING, REVITALIZING
REWARD	111 - 2	RIGHTEOUSNESS IS ITS OWN REWARD
REWARD	217 - 2	SHALL REWARD US OPENLY
REWARD	283 - 1	RECEIVE THE GREATEST REWARD
REWARD	382 - 4	REWARD AND PUNISHMENT
REWARD	383 - 1	WE ARE OUR OWN REWARD
REWARD	431 - 1	WILL REWARD US OPENLY
REWARD	434 - 2	WHOEVER MERITS REWARD
REWARD	442 - 1	A RIGHTEOUS MAN'S REWARD
REWARD	442 - 1	REWARD OF HIS OWN VISIONING
REWARD	442 - 1	REWARD OF MERIT IS AN OBJECTIVE
REWARDED	111 - 1	RIGHT ACTS ARE REWARDED
REWARDS	383 - 1	GOD NEITHER PUNISHES NOR REWARDS
RHEUMATISM	260 - 2	CONGESTION WHICH APPEAR AS RHEUMATISM
RHYTHM	233 - 4	IN THE RHYTHM AND HARMONY
RHYTHM	242 - 2	PERFECT RHYTHM AND HARMONY
RHYTHM	258 - 1	RHYTHM AND BEAUTY
RHYTHMIC	242 - 3	THE RHYTHMIC EASE OF MIND
RHYTHMIC	248 - 3	THE RHYTHMIC HARMONY OF LIFE
RHYTHMICALLY	249 - 2	RHYTHMICALLY THE LIFE OF GOD
RIB	473 - 5	MADE FROM A RIB OF ADAM
RICH	305 - 3	LIFE LIES OPEN TO ME RICH FULL ABUNDANT
RICHES	025 - 3	THE EARTH CONTAINS UNTOLD RICHES
RID	478 - 2	WISHING TO RID ITSELF OF A BODY
RIDDLE	030 - 2	THE RIDDLE IS SOLVED
RIDDLE	041 - 4	RIDDLE OUT OF SIMPLICITY
RIDDLE	194 - 3	RIDDLE IS SOLVED
RIDDLE	445 - 1	SOLUTION OF ITS GREAT RIDDLE
RIDDLE	445 - 1	UNTIL THIS RIDDLE IS SOLVED
RIDDLES	194 - 3	ONE OF THOSE DIVINE RIDDLES
RIGHT	046 - 2	TO KNOW WHAT IS RIGHT
RIGHT	046 - 2	KNOWS RIGHT FROM WRONG
RIGHT	060 - 3	HOLD IT AS A VESTED RIGHT
RIGHT	166 - 2	HAS NO RIGHT TO BE
RIGHT	263 - 4	SURROUNDED BY RIGHT ACTION
RIGHT	270 - 2	WHAT IS RIGHT OR WRONG FOR HIM
RIGHT	270 - 2	IF IT DOES IT IS RIGHT
RIGHT	310 - 4	TO SHOW US THE RIGHT USE
RIGHT	354 - 3	NEVER DOES IT CONTRADICT THE RIGHT
RIGHT	428 - 3	JESUS WAS RIGHT WHEN
RIGHT	447 - 2	RIGHT RELATIONSHIPS TO LIFE
RIGHT	451 - 1	KNOW THAT RIGHT IS MIGHT
RIGHT	494 - 5	RIGHT AND A WRONG USE OF THIS LAW
RIGHT	500 - 3	RIGHT IT REWARDS
RIGHT	503 - 5	WE DO RIGHT WE ARE RIGHT
RIGHT ACTION	055 - 2	RIGHT ACTION IN HIS LIFE
RIGHT ACTION	187 - 1	RIGHT ACTION UNTIL THEY APPEAR
RIGHT ACTION	251 - 3	KNOW THAT RIGHT ACTION PREVAILS
RIGHT ACTION	274 - 4	WE TREAT FOR RIGHT ACTION
RIGHTEOUS	152 - 3	RIGHTEOUS PRAYER SETS THE LAW
RIGHTEOUS	442 - 1	RECEIVE A RIGHTEOUS MAN'S REWARD
RIGHTEOUS	442 - 2	RIGHTEOUS, ALL IS RIGHTEOUS
RIGHTEOUS	496 - 3	RIGHTEOUS ALONE MAY ENTER

RIGHTEOUSNESS	053 - 2	RIGHTEOUSNESS AND SALVATION
RIGHTEOUSNESS	223 - 2	THRIST AFTER RIGHTEOUSNESS
RIGHTEOUSNESS	270 - 1	PATH OF TRUE RIGHTEOUSNESS
RIGHT HERE	358 - 5	RIGHT HERE THROUGH OUR OWN NATURE
RIGHT LIVING	223 - 2	RIGHT LIVING FOR THEY SHALL
RIGHT MOTIVE	500 - 4	RIGHT MOTIVE THEN WE SHALL BE MADE FREE
RIGHT THINKING	197 - 4	ACCOMPANIED BY RIGHT THINKING
RIGHT TO CHOOSE	143 - 4	RIGHT TO CHOOSE WHAT WE WISH TO EXPERIENCE
RING	297 - 1	LET THIS RING THROUGH OUR MIND
RING	467 - 3	RING IS WITHOUT BEGINNING
RISE	302 - 1	WE RISE SUPERIOR TO THE WORLD
RISE	318 - 4	WORD OF THE PRACTITIONER WILL RISE
RISE	401 - 2	RISE TO LESSER CAUSES AND EFFECTS
RISE	403 - 2	NOR IS IT EASY TO RISE ABOVE IT
RISE	435 - 1	RISE IN THE MORNING RENEWED
RIVER	374 - 1	OUR BODIES ARE LIKE A RIVER
ROAD	109 - 3	ROAD TO SELF-DISCOVERY
ROAD	434 - 1	ON THE ROAD OF EXPERIENCE
ROB	188 - 4	ROB NO ONE
ROB	245 - 4	ROB US OF TODAY"S HAPPINESS
ROB	372 - 2	DEATH CANNOT ROB HIM
ROB	464 - 3	NO ONE CAN ROB
ROB	486 - 3	ROB US OF OUR BIRTHRIGHT
ROBBING	036 - 1	NOT ROBBING GOD IS A SELF-EVIDENT FACT
ROBE	466 - 5	ROBE AND PUT IT ON HIM
ROBE	467 - 3	ROBE IS SEAMLESS
ROBED	420 - 4	ROBED IN NUMBERLESS FORMS
ROBERT BROWNING	103 - 3	ROBERT BROWNING WRITES OF THE SPARK
ROBS	376 - 4	SOME THINK THAT DEATH ROBS US
ROBS	383 - 2	NO ONE ROBS US BUT OURSELVES
ROCK	436 - 5	SOLID ROCK OF TRUTH
ROLLED	039 - 5	ROLLED UP LIKE A SCROLL
ROMAN	352 - 1	YEARS AGO IN SOME ROMAN ARENA
ROOT	138 - 2	ROOT OF MANY UNHAPPY CONDITIONS
ROOT	175 - 2	EXTRACT THE CUBE ROOT
ROOTED	121 - 3	YET ALL PEOPLE ARE ROOTED
ROOTED	123 - 3	ROOTED IN THE ONE CREATIVE SOUL
ROOTED	164 - 1	ROOTED IN THE UNIVERSAL
ROOTED	413 - 1	ROOTED IN ONE COMMON CREATIVE MIND
ROSE	388 - 2	IN THE BUDDING ROSE
ROSEBUD	141 - 1	COULD NOT MAKE A SINGLE ROSEBUD
ROSES	096 - 4	REGARDING THE PLANTING OF ROSES
ROSES	103 - 1	TO A GARDEN OF ROSES
ROUT	209 - 1	PUTS TO ROUT THAT WHICH IS WRONG
ROYAL	185 - 2	A ROYAL ROAD TO FREEDOM
RULES	232 - 2	INTELLIGENCE WITHIN ME RULES ME
RUN	395 - 1	NOT RUN ON THE SCALE OF MAN'S
RUNNING	064 - 2	RUNNING THROUGH ALL MANIFESTATION
RUNNING	413 - 4	RUNNING THROUGH THE WORDS

S

| SACRED BOOKS | 167 - 2 | ANY OF THESE SACRED BOOKS |

SACREDNESS	168 - 3	THE SACREDNESS OF HIS TRUST
SACREDNESS	168 - 3	SACREDNESS OF THE CONFIDENCE
SACRIFICE	288 - 2	PLEASED BY A LIFE OF SACRIFICE
SADNESS	496 - 6	THERE IS NO SADNESS IN THE SPIRIT
SAFE	146 - 2	SAFE, SATISFIED AND AT PEACE
SAFE	387 - 3	GOD'S KEEPING AND THEY ARE SAFE
SAGES	330 - 4	THE SAINTS AND SAGES OF THE PAST
SAGES	386 - 2	SAINTS AND SAGES OF THE AGES
SAID	350 - 3	HE HAS THOUGHT SAID AND DONE
SAID	421 - 5	EVER BEEN THOUGHT SAID OR DONE
SAILING	450 - 5	SAILING ON THAT BOUNDLESS SEA
SAINT	045 - 1	THE SAINT DRAWS CHRIST INTO
SAINT	103 - 1	TO THE SAINT AND THE SINNER
SAINT	492 - 5	SAINT SIMPLY MEANS AN UNUSUALLY
SAINTS	386 - 2	SAINTS AND SAGES OF THE AGES
SALUTARY	109 - 3	SUFFERING MAY BE SALUTARY
SALUTARY	253 - 1	CAN HAVE ANY SALUTARY EFFECT
SALUTARY	452 - 5	NO EXPERIENCE IS SALUTARY UNLESS
SALUTARY	491 - 2	SALUTARY LEADING THE SOUL
SALUTE	440 - 5	COME INTO A HOUSE SALUTE IT
SALVATION	033 - 1	SALVATION OF OUR OWN SOULS
SALVATION	053 - 2	SALVATION ARE LOGICAL REACTIONS
SALVATION	152 - 4	THE SALVATION OF THE SOUL
SALVATION	217 - 1	THE SURE SALVATION OF THE LORD
SALVATION	268 - 3	OUR OWN SALVATION MAY BE
SALVATION	269 - 3	SALVATION OF THE INDIVIDUAL SOUL
SALVATION	335 - 3	ULTIMATE SALVATION OF ALL PEOPLE
SALVATION	337 - 1	NO SALVATION OUTSIDE OF CONSCIOUS
SALVATION	383 - 2	CONSTITUTES TRUE SALVATION
SALVATION	384 - 1	WORK OUT OUR OWN SALVATION
SALVATION	420 - 2	NO SALVATION OUTSIDE OF CONSCIOUS
SALVATION	453 - 3	SALVATION WILL COME TO THE WORLD
SALVATION	457 - 2	SALVATION OF THE SOUL
SALVATION	488 - 1	SALVATION WILL COME TO US
SALVATION	503 - 1	DAY OF COMPLETE SALVATION
SAMARIA	081 - 2	THE WOMAN OF SAMARIA
SAME	066 - 2	HAVE MUCH THE SAME MEANING
SAME	107 - 5	SAME AS GOD'S NATURE
SAME	124 - 1	SAME THING FUNCTIONING
SAME	148 - 3	SAME IN KIND WITH THE CREATIVENESS
SAME	310 - 2	THEY ARE THE SAME THING
SAME	374 - 1	HAS PROVIDED THE SAME MOLD
SAME	391 - 2	OF MAN IS THE SAME MIND
SAME	434 - 2	SAME LAW USED IN DIFFERENT WAYS
SAMUEL	158 - 2	GIDEON SAMUEL AND THE PROPHETS
SANCTUARY	036 - 4	IN THAT INNER SANCTUARY
SANCTUARY	495 - 2	SANCTUARY TO THE HEART OF HEARTS
SAND	025 - 3	COUNT THE GRAINS OF SAND
SANDS	429 - 3	SHIFTING SANDS OF TIME
SANDWICHED	432 - 4	SANDWICHED BETWEEN THESE TWO
SANE	042 - 2	TO RETURN TO A SANE SIMPLICITY
SANE	044 - 3	HAPPY, SANE, HARMONIOUS
SANE	175 - 4	INTELLIGENCE OF ANY SANE INDIVIDUAL
SANE	269 - 1	LOGICAL SANE AND INTELLIGENT CRITERION
SANE	329 - 3	SANE PEOPLE SOUND PEOPLE

SANE	502 - 4	SANE PERSON TO BELIEVE THAT GOD DELIGHTS
SANELY	447 - 1	NATURALLY SANELY AND EXPECTANTLY
SATISFACTION	222 - 4	SOMETHING THAT WILL GIVE SATISFACTION
SATISFIED	265 - 1	WHOLE, COMPLETE AND SATISFIED
SATISFIED	334 - 4	MAN WILL NEVER BE SATISFIED
SATISFIED	390 - 5	SATISFIED AND AT PEACE
SATISFIED	409 - 3	UNTIL HE IS MENTALLY SATISFIED
SATISFIED	428 - 4	SATISFIED WITH SPIRITUAL FOOD
SATISFIED	492 - 6	SATISFIED, HAPPY, PROSPEROUS
SATISFY	065 - 3	THIS DID NOT SATISFY HIM
SATISFY	414 - 3	WILL IT SATISFY US
SATURATED	490 - 8	WORLD IS SATURATED WITH DIVINITY
SAUL	344 - 3	SAUL ON HIS RETURN TO DAMASCUS
SAVAGE	417 - 1	THE SAVAGE THINKS AFTER THE MODE
SAVED	323 - 2	HE IS ALREADY SAVED
SAVED	472 - 5	IN THIS SON WE ARE SAVED
SAVED	486 - 1	BE SAVED FROM THEMSELVES
SAVING	301 - 3	TOWARD SAVING THE WORLD
SAVIOR	186 - 4	TEACHER BECAME THE SAVIOR
SAVIOURS	122 - 1	SAGES THE SAVIOURS AND CHRISTS
SAVOR	459 - 5	WHICH DOES NOT SAVOR OF RIGHT
SAW	330 - 1	THEY SAW AND KNEW
SAY	036 - 1	SAY THAT THE MIND SPIRIT
SAY	117 - 3	IT IS ONE THING TO SAY
SAY	268 - 1	TO SAY THAT EVERYTHING IS OURS
SAY	310 - 2	DO NOT SAY THAT MIND IS ONE THING
SAY	420 - 3	SAY THAT HE IS
SAY	467 - 1	HE DID NOT SAY
SAYING	086 - 4	THE SAYING OF PEACE
SAYING	175 - 3	NOT A PROCESS OF SAYING
SAYING	419 - 1	MORE THAN A SAYING
SAYINGS	427 - 1	SAYINGS CAN NEVER BE CLEAR
SCALE	124 - 1	UP A SCALE OF UNITY
SCALE	167 - 1	UNIVERSAL ON AN INDIVIDUAL SCALE
SCALE	395 - 1	THE SCALE OF MAN'S IGNORANCE
SCALE	483 - 4	ON THE SCALE OF THE INDIVIDUAL
SCARCELY	149 - 4	WE CAN SCARCELY COMPREHEND
SCHEME	106 - 2	SHALL SEE THAT THE WHOLE SCHEME
SCIENCE	025 - 1	SCIENCE AND RELIGION SHALL WALK HAND
SCIENCE	025 - 1	SCIENCE KNOWS NOTHING OF OPINION
SCIENCE	026 - 5	WE ACCEPT THE DEDUCTIONS OF SCIENCE
SCIENCE	040 - 1	STUDY OF THIS SCIENCE RATIONALLY
SCIENCE	043 - 3	ALL SCIENCE IS BASED UPON
SCIENCE	049 - 1	THIS STUDY IS A SCIENCE
SCIENCE	053 - 3	A PRACTITIONER OF THIS SCIENCE
SCIENCE	060 - 3	A NEW SCIENCE
SCIENCE	060 - 4	SCIENCE IS THE STUDY OF FIRST CAUSE
SCIENCE	066 - 2	THE PRINCIPLE OF SCIENCE
SCIENCE	066 - 2	SCIENCE THE WORD PRINCIPLE
SCIENCE	072 - 2	PRINCIPLE OF ANY SCIENCE IS INVISIBLE
SCIENCE	074 - 2	SCIENCE IS THE KNOWLEDGE OF FACTS
SCIENCE	074 - 2	FACTS OF SCIENCE ARE DEMONSTRABLE
SCIENCE	074 - 4	SCIENCE IS GRADUALLY FORMULATED
SCIENCE	074 - 4	SCIENCE CONSISTS OF THE NUMBER OF KNOWN
SCIENCE	098 - 2	SCIENCE HAS REVEALED

SCIENCE	113 - 2	SCIENCE IS SPIRIT INDUCING ITS OWN LAWS
SCIENCE	113 - 2	IN THE STUDY OF THIS SCIENCE
SCIENCE	123 - 2	MODERN SCIENCE
SCIENCE	140 - 1	PRACTICAL APPLICATION OF THIS SCIENCE
SCIENCE	160 - 2	THIS SCIENCE OF FAITH
SCIENCE	164 - 3	TREATMENT IS THE SCIENCE OF INDUCING
SCIENCE	189 - 2	A CAREFUL STUDY OF THE SCIENCE OF MIND
SCIENCE	191 - 3	IN THIS SCIENCE WE BELIEVE
SCIENCE	192 - 5	ALL TRUE MENTAL SCIENCE
SCIENCE	194 - 1	IN MENTAL SCIENCE IT MEANS
SCIENCE	198 - 4	THE SCIENCE OF INDUCING THOUGHT
SCIENCE	275 - 2	THE STANDPOINT OF SPIRITUAL SCIENCE
SCIENCE	280 - 3	UNCOVER THE SCIENCE OF PRAYER
SCIENCE	291 - 4	IN PHYSICAL SCIENCE WE KNOW
SCIENCE	299 - 4	OUR WHOLE SCIENCE IS A MISTAKE
SCIENCE	311 - 2	SCIENCE TELLS US THAT ALL FORM
SCIENCE	311 - 3	UNTIL SCIENCE AT LAST RESOLVES
SCIENCE	312 - 3	WE BELIEVE IN SCIENCE
SCIENCE	312 - 3	SCIENCE IS LEADING US SURELY
SCIENCE	362 - 2	SCIENCE HAS SOLVED MANY PROBLEMS
SCIENCE	373 - 5	SCIENCE TELLS US THAT MATTER
SCIENCE	375 - 2	SCIENCE IS RAPIDLY PROVING
SCIENCE	402 - 4	EVERY ADVANCE IN ANY SCIENCE
SCIENCE	407 - 2	ALL ADVANCE IN SCIENCE
SCIENCE	407 - 2	AS SCIENCE POSTULATES
SCIENCE	423 - 1	SCIENCE PROVE ITS PRINCIPLE
SCIENCE	444 - 4	TRUE OF SCIENCE
SCIENCE	444 - 4	SCIENCE SEEKS TO JOIN CAUSES
SCIENCE	444 - 4	SCIENCE IS REALLY SPIRITUAL
SCIENCE	444 - 4	SCIENCE IS THE HANDMAID OF RELIGION
SCIENCE OF MIND	025 - 3	THE SCIENCE OF MIND DEALS WITH THESE
SCIENCE OF MIND	026 - 3	STUDY OF THE SCIENCE OF MIND
SCIENCE OF MIND	027 - 4	APPROACH THE SCIENCE OF MIND
SCIENCE OF MIND	035 - 1	SCIENCE OF MIND IS NOT A SPECIAL REVELATION
SCIENCE OF MIND	048 - 3	PRINCIPLE OF THE SCIENCE OF MIND
SCIENCE OF MIND	054 - 1	THE PRACTICE OF THE SCIENCE OF MIND
SCIENCE OF MIND	075 - 1	APPROACH THE SCIENCE OF MIND
SCIENCE OF MIND	075 - 2	THE SCIENCE OF MIND THEN IS THE STUDY
SCIENCE OF MIND	107 - 3	SCIENCE OF MIND AND SPIRIT
SCIENCE OF MIND	149 - 1	ASKED ABOUT THE SCIENCE OF MIND
SCIENCE OF MIND	157 - 4	SCIENCE OF MIND IT IS A WAY
SCIENCE OF MIND	160 - 2	A GOOD STUDENT OF THE SCIENCE OF MIND
SCIENCE OF MIND	160 - 3	DAILY THE SCIENCE OF MIND
SCIENCE OF MIND	160 - 4	STUDENTS OF THE SCIENCE OF MIND
SCIENCE OF MIND	189 - 2	STUDY OF THE SCIENCE OF MIND
SCIENCE OF MIND	266 - 1	SCIENCE OF MIND IS NOT A GET RICH QUICK
SCIENCE OF MIND	267 - 3	THE SCIENCE OF MIND IS BASED ENTIRELY
SCIENCE OF MIND	448 - 1	SCIENCE OF MIND IS TO RECONCILE
SCIENCE OF MIND	483 - 5	IN THE SCIENCE OF MIND WE LEARN
SCIENCE OF MIND	494 - 1	SCIENCE OF MIND TEACHES HOW TO
SCIENCE OF MIND	495 - 3	SCIENCE OF MIND WE LEARN
SCIENCES	130 - 2	ALL SCIENCES ARE EVOLVED
SCIENCES	159 - 3	SCIENCES ARE BUILT UPON FAITH PRINCIPLES
SCIENCES	193 - 1	IN THE NATURAL SCIENCES WE KNOW
SCIENTIFIC	049 - 3	NOT THE SCIENTIFIC USE OF THIS PRINCIPLE

SCIENTIFIC	049 - 4	SCIENTIFIC USE OF A MENTAL
SCIENTIFIC	079 - 3	THEOLOGICAL RATHER THAN A SCIENTIFIC
SCIENTIFIC	138 - 2	SCIENTIFIC STUDY OF MIND IS STILL
SCIENTIFIC	173 - 3	AFRAID OF THIS SCIENTIFIC APPROACH
SCIENTIFIC	201 - 1	SCIENTIFIC DYNAMIC SPIRITUAL
SCIENTIFIC	203 - 4	SCIENTIFIC MENTAL HEALING
SCIENTIFIC	220 - 4	MENTAL HEALING IS SCIENTIFIC
SCIENTIFIC	282 - 3	NOT SCIENTIFIC TO ATTEMPT
SCIENTIFIC	290 - 3	SCIENTIFIC PRACTICE TO DECLARE
SCIENTIFIC	298 - 1	IT IS A DEEP SCIENTIFIC FACT
SCIENTIFIC	378 - 2	SCIENTIFIC RESEARCH IN THE REALM
SCIENTIFIC	476 - 6	LEARNED AND A SCIENTIFIC MAN
SCIENTIFIC	486 - 5	OF THE MIND IS A SCIENTIFIC
SCIENTIFIC	488 - 5	SCIENTIFIC TO MEDITATE ON PLENTY
SCIENTIFIC	502 - 3	SCIENTIFIC TO CONSCIOUSLY LET GO
SCIENTIFIC	502 - 6	SCIENTIFIC FOR ONE TO CONSCIOUSLY
SCIENTIFICALLY	057 - 4	SCIENTIFICALLY TO WORK OUT
SCIENTIFICALLY	146 - 4	PRINCIPLE SCIENTIFICALLY CORRECT
SCIENTIFICALLY	169 - 3	PRACTICING SCIENTIFICALLY WHEN THE MIND
SCIENTIFICALLY	275 - 2	WISH TO HANDLE IT SCIENTIFICALLY
SCIENTIFICALLY	338 - 1	BELIEF IS SCIENTIFICALLY INDUCED
SCIENTIFIC TREATMENT	176 - 3	THAN A SCIENTIFIC TREATMENT
SCIENTIST	042 - 3	SCIENTIST AND THE PHILOSOPHER
SCIENTIST	045 - 1	THE SCIENTIST DISCOVERS THE PRINCIPLES
SCIENTIST	103 - 2	THE SCIENTIST FINDS
SCIENTIST	455 - 6	SCIENTIST IN PROFOUND THOUGHT
SCIENTISTS	091 - 3	THAT SCIENTISTS IN THEORY
SCIENTISTS	219 - 2	ANNOUNCEMENT FROM SCIENTISTS
SCOPE	390 - 4	ITS OWN POWER OR SCOPE
SCORN	457 - 4	TO POINT THE FINGER OF SCORN
SCORN	457 - 4	POINT THE FINGER OF SCORN AT YOUR BROTHER
SCREEN	314 - 1	THE SCREEN OF OUR OBJECTIVE LIVES
SCREEN	412 - 2	WHAT IS THE SCREEN
SCRIBES	437 - 5	SCRIBES WHO HEARD JESUS
SCRIPTURE	120 - 3	IN EVERY SACRED SCRIPTURE
SCRIPTURES	196 - 1	THE SCRIPTURES SAY
SCRIPTURES	229 - 5	ACCORDING TO THE SCRIPTURES
SCROLL	039 - 5	ROLLED UP LIKE A SCROLL
SCROLL	329 - 4	ROLLED UP LIKE A SCROLL
SCROLL	486 - 1	SCROLL AND NUMBERED WITH PAST ILLUSIONS
SCULPTOR	455 - 6	SCULPTOR CHISELLING AT HIS MARBLE
SEA	246 - 4	A SEA OF PERFECT LIFE
SEA	246 - 4	SEA OF UNTROUBLED WATERS OF LIFE
SEAMLESS	055 - 5	SEAMLESS GARMENT OF TRUTH
SEAMLESS	467 - 3	WAS A SEAMLESS GARMENT
SEARCH	049 - 1	THE SEARCH FOR TRUTH
SEARCH	362 - 2	ENGAGED IN THIS SEARCH
SEARCHING	362 - 2	NEVER SUCH A SEARCHING AFTER GOD
SEAT	383 - 3	PURCHASED A SEAT IN HEAVEN
SEATED	140 - 4	SEATED CONVICTIONS
SEAT OF MEMORY	114 - 3	SEAT OF MEMORY IT CONTAINS
SECOND	143 - 3	EVERY SECOND THERE IS CHOICE
SECOND	311 - 1	SECOND MAN IS THE LORD FROM HEAVEN
SECOND	318 - 3	FIRST RECOGNITION, SECOND UNIFICATION
SECOND	403 - 3	SECOND THOUGHT WE FIND THAT ALL

SECRET	047 - 1	THE SECRET OF SUCCESS
SECRET	069 - 2	MYSTICAL SECRET OF THE AGES
SECRET	176 - 3	SECRET IN THIS BUSINESS
SECRET	176 - 3	SECRET IS THE PERSISTENT ABILITY TO USE
SECRET	187 - 3	WE HAVE FOUND THE SECRET
SECRET	217 - 2	SECRET AND THE FATHER WHO SEETH
SECRET	217 - 2	FATHER WHO SEETH IN SECRET
SECRET	218 - 1	SECRET PLACE OF THE MOST HIGH
SECRET	218 - 3	SECRET POWER OF OUR WORK
SECRET	257 - 1	SECRET OF RELAXATION REST AND RENEWAL
SECRET	276 - 2	THE SECRET OF THE POWER OF JESUS
SECRET	367 - 3	THE SECRET OF HIS SUCCESS
SECRET	398 - 3	THIS IS THE WHOLE SECRET
SECRET	431 - 1	SECRET WILL REWARD US OPENLY
SECRET	431 - 2	SECRET PLACE OF OUR OWN BEING
SECRET	431 - 3	SECRET OF PRAYER AND ITS POWER
SECRET	431 - 5	FATHER WHO SEEST IN SECRET
SECRET	493 - 6	THIS IS TO KNOW A SECRET
SECRET	494 - 2	SECRET OF THE CREATIVE LAW OF MIND
SECRET	498 - 1	SECRET OF A WELL-BALANCED LIFE
SECRET PLACE	169 - 3	SECRET PLACE OF THE MOST HIGH
SECRETS	040 - 1	BEFORE IT CAN REVEAL ITS SECRETS
SECRETS	040 - 2	PENETRATED THE SECRETS OF NATURE
SECRETS	400 - 1	GREAT SECRETS OF MENTAL SCIENCE
SECT	060 - 3	ANY RELIGION SECT OR ORDER
SECURE	257 - 4	I AM SECURE AND SAFE
SECURELY	366 - 1	INNER POWER THAT HOLDS SECURELY
SECURITY	180 - 4	A SENSE OF SECURITY WHICH KNOWS NO FEAR
SEE	036 - 3	SEE IT AS IT IS
SEE	101 - 4	EVERYTHING WE SEE TOUCH TASTE
SEE	144 - 2	WE CANNOT ALWAYS SEE
SEE	185 - 2	SEE AS GOD MUST
SEE	189 - 2	SEE BEYOND THE APPEARANCE
SEE	271 - 5	TO SEE HIS LIFE AS HE WISHES IT
SEE	281 - 4	AS HE CHOOSES TO SEE THEM
SEE	300 - 4	HE SHOULD SEE HIS PLACE FILLED
SEE	378 - 4	SEE WITHOUT THE AGENCY
SEE	422 - 2	DOES NOT MEAN THAT WE REALLY SEE
SEE	422 - 2	WE SEE GENERALLY IS THE PICTURE
SEE	451 - 2	LOOKING SEE OR LISTENING HEAR
SEE	480 - 1	SEE ONLY WHAT IT DOES
SEE	503 - 2	SEE ONLY IN PART
SEED	036 - 4	NESTLES THE SEED PERFECTION
SEED	038 - 2	A FARMER PLANTS A SEED
SEED	078 - 2	HOW TO TAKE A SEED
SEED	103 - 2	IDEA CONCEALED IN THE SEED
SEED	148 - 4	SEED OF THOUGHT IN THE ABSOLUTE
SEED	205 - 5	SEED IN THE GROUND
SEED	206 - 1	SEED IS PUT INTO THE GROUND
SEED	206 - 1	UNLESS A SEED IS PLANTED
SEED	207 - 4	SEED PLANTED IN THE CREATIVE
SEED	292 - 1	A SEED OF THOUGHT IN SUBJECTIVITY
SEED	354 - 3	SEED ARE BOTH CAUSE AND EFFECT
SEEDS	039 - 3	IN FAITH TO SOW HIS SEEDS
SEEDS	090 - 2	IN WHICH SEEDS ARE PLANTED

SEEDS	295 - 3	WITHIN IT SEEDS OF THOUGHT
SEEDS	321 - 2	SEEDS WHICH CAN PRODUCE MORE
SEEING	230 - 3	ONE PERFECT SEEING
SEEING	230 - 3	NOW SEEING THROUGH ME
SEEING	352 - 2	REALLY BE SEEING THE PERSON
SEEK	185 - 2	LET US SEEK THE GOOD
SEEK	269 - 3	NATURALLY SEEK TO FREE HIMSELF
SEEK	314 - 2	WE SEEK A PRACTICAL USE
SEEK	380 - 1	THEY DO SEEK TO COMMUNICATE
SEEK	432 - 5	SEEK THE KINGDOM FIRST
SEEK	447 - 2	SEEK WHOLENESS ABOVE ALL ELSE
SEEK	463 - 4	SEEK THE CAUSE IN THE EFFECT
SEEK	486 - 4	SEEK WITHIN FOR THE CAUSE
SEEKING	048 - 3	SEEKING TO DEMONSTRATE
SEEKS	202 - 4	PRACTITIONER SEEKS TO REALIZE
SEEKS	413 - 5	SEEKS TO HEAL THE THOUGHT
SEEM	306 - 4	WHAT WE SEEM TO BE
SEEN	072 - 2	NO ONE HAS SEEN GOD
SEEN	072 - 2	NO ONE HAS SEEN INTELLIGENCE
SEEN	074 - 3	SEEN ANY OF THESE PRINCIPLES
SEEN	159 - 3	NO MAN HAS SEEN GOD
SEEN	164 - 4	IT NEEDS TO BE SEEN MENTALLY
SEEN	274 - 3	NEEDS TO BE MENTALLY SEEN
SEEN	345 - 4	HAVE ALSO SEEN SUBSTANCE
SEEN	480 - 1	SEEN ME, HATH SEEN THE FATHER
SEES	055 - 2	HE SENSES AND MENTALLY SEES
SEES	104 - 3	SEES ONLY ON ONE PLANE
SEES	230 - 3	GOD SEES AND HIS IS THE ONLY MIND
SEES	474 - 3	SEES THROUGH EVERYTHING
SELDOM	367 - 1	SELDOM DOES THIS VOICE
SELECTIVE	403 - 3	LAW OF MIND IS NOT SELECTIVE
SELECTIVE	403 - 3	IS EVER SELECTIVE OF ITSELF
SELECTIVE	403 - 3	HAVING ANY SELECTIVE QUALITY
SELECTIVITY	107 - 2	SELECTIVITY THAT IS VOLITION AND CHOICE
SELECTIVITY	403 - 3	SELECTIVITY IS THE OFFICE OF THE CONSCIOUS
SELF	332 - 4	SELF IS GOD-GIVEN
SELF	406 - 3	SELF IS THE IMMEDIATE CONNECTION BETWEEN
SELF	408 - 4	OF GOD IS OUR REAL SELF
SELF	444 - 3	OF THE SELF TO THE SELF
SELF	475 - 1	REVELATION OF THE SELF TO THE SELF
SELF-ANALYSIS	248 - 5	HONEST SELF-ANALYSIS
SELF-ANALYSIS	446 - 4	BY CAREFUL SELF-ANALYSIS
SELF-ASSERTIVE	039 - 1	POWER OF THE SELF-ASSERTIVE TRUTH
SELF-ASSERTIVE	132 - 7	ONLY SELF-ASSERTIVE PRINCIPLE
SELF-ASSERTIVE	390 - 2	SELF-KNOWING SELF-ASSERTIVE
SELF-ASSERTIVE	445 - 7	DEEP CALM AND SELF-ASSERTIVE
SELF-CHOICE	065 - 5	GIVE HIM SELF-CHOICE
SELF-CHOICE	071 - 2	A POINT OF SELF-CHOICE
SELF-CHOICE	071 - 2	SELF-CHOICE AND FREE WILL
SELF-CHOICE	130 - 3	SELF-CHOICE CAUSE HIM TO APPEAR IMPERFECT
SELF-CHOICE	332 - 5	INDIVIDUALITY MEANS SELF-CHOICE
SELF-CHOICE	461 - 2	MAN HAS THE RIGHT OF SELF-CHOICE
SELF-CHOOSING	210 - 1	THE MATTER OF SELF-CHOOSING
SELF-COMPREHENSION	139 - 1	SELF-COMPREHENSION WE KNOW
SELF-CONDEMNATION	465 - 4	SELF-CONDEMNATION AND PERSONAL DISTRUST

SELF-CONDEMNATION	465 - 4	SELF-CONDEMNATION IS ALWAYS DESTRUCTIVE
SELF-CONSCIOUS	070 - 2	SPIRIT BEING SELF-CONSCIOUS
SELF-CONSCIOUS	079 - 3	NOT SELF-CONSCIOUS AWARENESS
SELF-CONSCIOUS	086 - 5	TO BE SELF-CONSCIOUS
SELF-CONSCIOUS	086 - 5	MIND IN ITS SELF-CONSCIOUS FORM
SELF-CONSCIOUS	091 - 1	IT IS NOT SELF-CONSCIOUS
SELF-CONSCIOUS	103 - 2	THE PRODUCTION OF SELF-CONSCIOUS LIFE
SELF-CONSCIOUS	106 - 1	SELF-CONSCIOUS THINKING CENTER
SELF-CONSCIOUS	132 - 5	SPIRIT ALONE IS SELF-CONSCIOUS
SELF-CONSCIOUS	347 - 2	WE WOULD NOT BE SELF-CONSCIOUS
SELF-CONSCIOUS	371 - 1	AS A SELF-CONSCIOUS PERSONALITY
SELF-CONSCIOUS	381 - 2	WHILE IN A SELF-CONSCIOUS STATE
SELF-CONSCIOUS	392 - 3	NOT A SELF-CONSCIOUS KNOWER
SELF-CONSCIOUSNESS	227 - 4	LOSE ITS SELF-CONSCIOUSNESS
SELF-CONSCIOUSNESS	373 - 3	TO SELF-CONSCIOUSNESS HE HAD A BODY
SELF-CONSCIOUSNESS	381 - 2	TO LOSE THE SELF-CONSCIOUSNESS
SELF-CONTEMPLATION	064 - 2	SELF-CONTEMPLATION OF GOD
SELF-CONTEMPLATION	102 - 2	SELF-CONTEMPLATION OF SPIRIT
SELF-CONTEMPLATION	307 - 2	THE SELF-CONTEMPLATION OF GOD
SELF-CONTEMPLATION	322 - 1	THE SELF-CONTEMPLATION
SELF-CONTEMPLATIVE	198 - 3	IN HIS OWN SELF-CONTEMPLATIVE
SELF-CREATED	412 - 2	AS FIGURES BUT NO SELF-CREATED
SELF-DECEPTION	176 - 2	SELF-DECEPTION ABOUT THE TRUTH
SELF-DELUSION	457 - 4	LIVES A LIFE OF SELF-DELUSION
SELF-DEPENDENCE	446 - 2	OWN SELF-DEPENDENCE ON SPIRIT
SELF-DESTRUCTIVE	412 - 3	AS BEING SELF-DESTRUCTIVE
SELF-DETERMINATION	117 - 3	UNIVERSE HAS NO SELF-DETERMINATION
SELF-DETERMINATION	338 - 2	POINT OF HIS OWN SELF-DETERMINATION
SELF-DISCOVERY	108 - 1	SUFFERS ON HIS ROAD TO SELF-DISCOVERY
SELF-DISCOVERY	333 - 4	OF EXPERIENCE OF SELF-DISCOVERY
SELF-DISCOVERY	419 - 4	OF SELF-DISCOVERY ON THE WAY
SELF-EFFACEMENT	454 - 4	SELF-EFFACEMENT THE NEGLECT OF THE BODY
SELF-EVIDENT	129 - 1	ACCEPT AS BEING SELF-EVIDENT
SELF-EVIDENT	443 - 1	THE SELF-EVIDENT FACT OF LIVING
SELF-EVIDENT	453 - 5	DIRECT AND ALWAYS SELF-EVIDENT
SELF-EXISTENT	064 - 2	SELF-EXISTENT CONSCIOUSNESS
SELF-EXISTENT	064 - 2	SELF-EXISTENT SUBSTANCE
SELF-EXISTENT	069 - 3	FIRST CAUSE MUST BE SELF-EXISTENT
SELF-EXISTENT	069 - 3	GOD MUST BE SELF-EXISTENT
SELF-EXISTENT	085 - 3	THIS INTELLIGENCE IS SELF-EXISTENT
SELF-EXISTENT	090 - 3	EACH BEING SELF-EXISTENT
SELF-EXISTENT	125 - 5	IN ORDER TO BE AT ALL MUST BE SELF-EXISTENT
SELF-EXISTENT	372 - 3	LIFE IS SELF-EXISTENT
SELF-EXPRESSED	195 - 3	UNIVERSE TO BECOME SELF-EXPRESSED
SELF-EXPRESSED	267 - 2	IN SO GIVING LIFE IS SELF-EXPRESSED
SELF-EXPRESSION	076 - 5	COME INTO SELF-EXPRESSION
SELF-EXPRESSION	108 - 3	MAN'S WORLD IS ONE OF SELF-EXPRESSION
SELF-EXPRESSION	161 - 3	INDIVIDUAL'S GOOD OR SELF-EXPRESSION
SELF-EXPRESSION	226 - 2	PASS INTO SELF-EXPRESSION
SELF-EXPRESSION	246 - 2	OPPORTUNITY FOR RADIANT SELF-EXPRESSION
SELF-EXPRESSION	264 - 2	OPPORTUNITY FOR SELF-EXPRESSION
SELF-EXPRESSION	269 - 3	THIS IS LEGITIMATE SELF-EXPRESSION
SELF-EXPRESSION	269 - 4	TO ATTEMPT THIS SELF-EXPRESSION
SELF-EXPRESSION	270 - 3	EXISTS FOR SELF-EXPRESSION
SELF-EXPRESSION	388 - 1	OF GOD INTO SELF-EXPRESSION

SELF-EXPRESSION	393 - 2	FOR PERSONAL SELF-EXPRESSION
SELF-EXPRESSION	401 - 1	POWER OF REAL SELF-EXPRESSION
SELF-EXPRESSION	404 - 3	IN THE DESIRE FOR SELF-EXPRESSION
SELF-EXPRESSION	412 - 3	ALWAYS SEEKING SELF-EXPRESSION
SELF-EXPRESSION	413 - 1	THE SELF-EXPRESSION OF MAN
SELF-EXPRESSION	416 - 1	THERE COULD BE NO SELF-EXPRESSION
SELF-EXPRESSION	420 - 4	OUTPUSH OF LIFE INTO SELF-EXPRESSION
SELF-EXPRESSION	482 - 2	TO A POINT OF SELF-EXPRESSION
SELF-FRUITION	101 - 2	NEVER COME TO SELF-FRUITION
SELF-FULFILLMENT	269 - 3	ARE BUT WAYS OF SELF-FULFILLMENT
SELF-GOVERNING	408 - 2	SELF-GOVERNING AND SELF-PROPELLING
SELF-HYPNOSIS	446 - 5	NOT A PROCESS OF SELF-HYPNOSIS
SELF-IMPOSED	395 - 1	IGNORANT AND SELF-IMPOSED BONDAGE
SELF-INFLICTED	337 - 1	SELF-INFLICTED THROUGH IGNORANCE
SELFISH	269 - 3	THIS IS A SELFISH MOTIVATION
SELFISH	270 - 2	IT IS NOT SELFISH
SELFISH	299 - 1	FROM SELFISH
SELFISHNESS	232 - 5	CONGESTIVE THOUGHTS SELFISHNESS
SELFISHNESS	240 - 3	SELFISHNESS CAN LODGE IN CONSCIOUSNESS
SELFISHNESS	255 - 3	SELFISHNESS AND JEALOUSY
SELFISHNESS	256 - 4	AN EXPRESSION OF SELFISHNESS
SELF-KNOWING	069 - 1	IT IS THE SELF-KNOWING MIND
SELF-KNOWING	069 - 4	SPIRIT OR THE SELF-KNOWING MIND
SELF-KNOWING	078 - 1	SPIRIT MUST BE SELF-KNOWING
SELF-KNOWING	100 - 3	IT IS NOT SELF-KNOWING
SELF-KNOWING	121 - 4	SELF-KNOWING MIND HIS UNITY
SELF-KNOWING	122 - 2	THE SELF-KNOWING MIND
SELF-KNOWING	132 - 2	REALITY WHICH IS SELF-KNOWING
SELF-KNOWING	132 - 8	SELF-KNOWING IN HIS CONSCIOUS MIND
SELF-KNOWING	285 - 2	MENTAL PROCESS OF SELF-KNOWING
SELF-KNOWING	312 - 2	THROUGH ITS SELF-KNOWING
SELF-KNOWING	390 - 2	MIND OF MAN IS SELF-KNOWING
SELF-KNOWING	391 - 2	THE SELF-KNOWING MIND OF GOD
SELF-KNOWING	391 - 2	MIND IN ITS SELF-KNOWING STATE IS SPIRIT
SELF-KNOWING	393 - 2	BY THE SELF-KNOWING MIND
SELF-KNOWING	393 - 2	IT IS NOT SELF-KNOWING
SELF-KNOWING	478 - 2	MAN IS THE ONLY SELF-KNOWING
SELF-KNOWINGNESS	064 - 2	OF SELF-KNOWINGNESS
SELF-KNOWINGNESS	087 - 3	AN INFINITE SELF-KNOWINGNESS
SELF-KNOWINGNESS	100 - 2	WHICH HAS SELF-KNOWINGNESS
SELF-KNOWINGNESS	101 - 5	SELF-KNOWINGNESS IS IN SPIRIT
SELF-KNOWINGNESS	101 - 5	THE SELF-KNOWINGNESS OF GOD
SELF-KNOWINGNESS	205 - 5	SELF-KNOWINGNESS RISES INTO
SELF-KNOWINGNESS	285 - 2	THE SELF-KNOWINGNESS OF GOD
SELF-KNOWINGNESS	342 - 4	HE CAME TO A POINT OF SELF-KNOWINGNESS
SELF-KNOWINGNESS	343 - 2	THE SELF-KNOWINGNESS OF GOD THROUGH MAN
SELF-KNOWINGNESS	373 - 3	NECESSARY OUTCOME OF SELF-KNOWINGNESS
SELF-KNOWINGNESS	391 - 2	SELF-KNOWINGNESS OF THE MIND
SELF-KNOWINGNESS	391 - 2	MAN IS THE SELF-KNOWINGNESS
SELF-KNOWINGNESS	391 - 4	DIVINE SELF-KNOWINGNESS IN MAN
SELF-KNOWINGNESS	396 - 3	THROUGH MAN AS SELF-KNOWINGNESS
SELF-KNOWINGNESS	421 - 1	SELF-KNOWINGNESS OF GOD THROUGH MAN
SELF-MASTERY	130 - 1	TO ATTAIN SELF-MASTERY
SELF-OPERATING	073 - 2	BODY AS SELF-OPERATING
SELF-PERCEPTION	064 - 2	OF SELF-PERCEPTION

SELF-PERPETUATING	412 - 2	SELF-CREATED NOT SELF-PERPETUATING
SELF-PRONOUNCEMENT	157 - 4	EXISTS BY ITS OWN SELF-PRONOUNCEMENT
SELF-PROPELLING	081 - 5	THE SPIRIT IS SELF-PROPELLING
SELF-PROPELLING	408 - 2	SELF GOVERNING AND SELF-PROPELLING
SELF-REALIZATION	083 - 5	NEVER COMING TO SELF-REALIZATION
SELF-REALIZATION	101 - 1	NEVER ARRIVE AT SELF-REALIZATION
SELF-REALIZATION	108 - 3	NEVER COME TO SELF-REALIZATION
SELF-REALIZATION	196 - 4	SELF-REALIZATION OF THE INFINITE MIND
SELF-REALIZATION	366 - 2	IN THE ECSTASY OF SELF-REALIZATION
SELF-REALIZATION	367 - 5	SELF-REALIZATION AND I-AM-NESS
SELF-REALIZATION	373 - 4	TO COME INTO SELF-REALIZATION
SELF- RECOGNITION	247 - 3	SPIRIT IN JOYOUS SELF-RECOGNITION
SELF-RECOGNITION	331 - 4	TO THE POINT OF SELF-RECOGNITION
SELF-RIGHTEOUSNESS	469 - 1	PUFFED UP WITH SELF-RIGHTEOUSNESS
SELF-UNFOLDMENT	335 - 2	ON THE PATHWAY OF SELF-UNFOLDMENT
SELF-UNFOLDMENT	368 - 3	ITS OWN SELF-UNFOLDMENT
SELL	452 - 2	MAN WILL SELL ALL THAT HE HAS
SELVES	263 - 6	SELF IS UNITED WITH ALL SELVES
SENDER	351 - 2	SENDER KNOW THAT THIS IS TAKING
SENDING	281 - 4	GETTING BACK WHAT HE IS SENDING OUT
SEND OUT	165 - 2	DOES NOT SEND OUT THOUGHTS
SEND OUT	199 - 2	SEND OUT A THOUGHT
SEND OUT	206 - 4	SEND OUT A THOUGHT
SENSATION	177 - 3	KNOW NOR EXPERIENCE SENSATION
SENSATION	207 - 3	SOME PHYSICAL SENSATION
SENSATION	207 - 3	SENSATION WHICH ACCOMPANIES A TREATMENT
SENSATION	207 - 4	HAVE A GREAT SENSATION
SENSATION	208 - 1	SENSATION OUT OF THE ORDINARY
SENSE	077 - 2	PEOPLE SHOULD SENSE OUR THOUGHTS
SENSE	090 - 2	SENSE OF A UNIVERSAL SOUL
SENSE	138 - 4	SENSE THE PRESENCE
SENSE	148 - 3	SENSE EVEN THOUGH DIMLY
SENSE	148 - 4	SENSE OF THAT INDWELLING GOD
SENSE	153 - 3	TO COMMUNE WITH SPIRIT-TO SENSE AND FEEL
SENSE	212 - 5	SENSE BODY AS A SPIRITUAL IDEA
SENSE	328 - 2	THE SENSE OF A LIVING PRESENCE
SENSE	333 - 6	THE MYSTIC SENSE REVEALS
SENSE	358 - 3	SENSE OF THE ONENESS OF ALL LIFE
SENSE	409 - 5	SILENT SENSE OF DIVINE REALITY
SENSE	437 - 1	LIVING ONLY IN SENSE PERCEPTION
SENSE	445 - 6	UNLESS WE SENSE HIM WITHIN
SENSE	489 - 2	SENSE THE INFINITE LIFE
SENSES	085 - 2	APPRAISE THEM WITH OUR PHYSICAL SENSES
SENSES	101 - 4	WITH THE PHYSICAL SENSES
SENSES	328 - 4	HE SENSES THE ATMOSPHERE OF GOD
SENSES	378 - 2	SENSES HAS BEEN DUPLICATED
SENSING	047 - 3	SENSING KNOWING SOME SPECIFIC GOOD
SENSITIVE	243 - 2	SENSITIVE ONLY TO GOOD
SENSITIVE	244 - 1	MY THOUGHT IS NOT SENSITIVE
SENSITIVE	397 - 3	ENTIRELY SENSITIVE TO OUR THOUGHT
SENSITIVE	403 - 3	THE LAW OF MIND IS SENSITIVE
SENSITIVE	416 - 2	LAW IS THAT IT IS SENSITIVE
SENSITIVENESS	242 - 4	RESULT OF AN UNDUE SENSITIVENESS
SENSITIVENESS	247 - 3	NO SENSITIVENESS, NO STRAIN
SENT	176 - 1	WHEREUNTO IT WAS SENT

SENT	188 - 2	WHEREUNTO IT WAS SENT
SENTIMENT	244 - 1	DISCORDANT OR DISAGREEABLE SENTIMENT
SENTIMENT	297 - 4	THIS IS NOT MERE SENTIMENT
SEPARATE	077 - 1	IT IS OBJECTIVELY SEPARATE
SEPARATE	090 - 3	SPIRIT AS SEPARATE FROM EACH OTHER
SEPARATE	103 - 2	WE SHOULD NOT SEPARATE LIFE
SEPARATE	113 - 4	NEITHER SEPARATE SPIRIT FROM MATTER
SEPARATE	201 - 2	SEPARATE THE BELIEF
SEPARATE	201 - 4	SEPARATE THE BELIEF FROM THE BELIEVER
SEPARATE	234 - 4	CANNOT SEPARATE OURSELVES
SEPARATE	316 - 2	WORKING IN TWO SEPARATE FIELDS
SEPARATE	422 - 1	MAN IS SEPARATE AND DISTINCT
SEPARATE	436 - 2	NOT TO SEPARATE LIFE FROM LIVING
SEPARATE	477 - 3	SEPARATE LIFE FROM WHAT IT DOES
SEPARATE	490 - 6	NOT TO SEPARATE LIFE FROM LIVING
SEPARATED	114 - 3	A SEPARATED OR ISOLATED SUBJECTIVE MIND
SEPARATED	127 - 4	OURSELVES AS BEING SEPARATED
SEPARATED	337 - 1	SEPARATED THE APPEARANCE FROM
SEPARATED	391 - 3	WITHOUT BECOMING SEPARATED FROM
SEPARATED	392 - 1	NOT SEPARATED FROM THE UNIVERSAL
SEPARATED	413 - 2	BELIEF THAT WE ARE SEPARATED
SEPARATED	419 - 3	NOT AS A SEPARATED BUT AS A SEPARATE
SEPARATED	462 - 3	TO BE SEPARATED AND ENTIRELY APART
SEPARATING	221 - 3	SEPARATING THE FALSE FROM THE TRUE
SEPARATION	128 - 1	BELIEF IN SEPARATION FROM GOD
SEPARATION	240 - 3	NO SEPARATION FROM GOD
SEPARATION	321 - 1	A SENSE OF SEPARATION FROM GOOD
SEPARATION	411 - 1	OPPOSITION OR APPARENT SEPARATION
SEPARATION	448 - 1	APPARENT SEPARATION OF THE SPIRITUAL WORLD
SEQUENCE	085 - 4	SEQUENCE OF LAW AND ORDER
SEQUENCE	101 - 2	SEQUENCE OF EVENTS
SEQUENCE	290 - 1	A LAW OF LOGICAL SEQUENCE
SEQUENCE	340 - 2	THIS IS THE SEQUENCE
SEQUENCE	354 - 1	SEQUENCE OF THIS MOVEMENT
SEQUENCE	355 - 3	POWER OF LOGIC AND SEQUENCE
SEQUENCE	371 - 2	SEQUENCE THE OLD LIFE AND THE NEW
SEQUENCE	472 - 4	SEQUENCE BUT NOT TIME
SEQUENTIAL	057 - 2	LOGICAL AND SEQUENTIAL EVOLUTION
SERENE	252 - 1	I AM SERENE
SERENITY	218 - 3	SERENITY OF THOUGHT
SERIES	067 - 2	BEGINNING OF ANY CREATIVE SERIES
SERIES	309 - 2	SERIES OF THOUGHTS OR STATEMENTS
SERIOUS	308 - 1	RELIGION IS SPIRITUAL AND LIFE SERIOUS
SERMONS	042 - 1	SERMONS WRITTEN IN STONES
SERPENT	055 - 3	TALE OF THE SERPENT
SERPENT	472 - 5	MOSES LIFTED UP THE SERPENT
SERPENT	473 - 2	SERPENT MEANT THE OUTER RIM
SERVANT	029 - 2	THE SERVANT OF HIS SPIRIT
SERVANT	029 - 2	THE SERVANT OF THE ETERNAL SPIRIT
SERVANT	031 - 1	A SERVANT TO THE WISE
SERVANT	080 - 1	SERVANT OF THE SPIRIT
SERVANT	083 - 2	SERVANT OF THE ETERNAL SPIRIT
SERVANT	084 - 1	LAW IS THE SERVANT OF THE SPIRIT
SERVANT	088 - 3	THE SERVANT OF THE ETERNAL
SERVANT	091 - 3	IS THE SERVANT OF SPIRIT

SERVANT	100 - 2	SERVANT OF THE SPIRIT
SERVANT	121 - 2	GREAT SERVANT OF OUR THOUGHT
SERVANT	161 - 1	HEAL HIS SERVANT AND JESUS SAID
SERVANT	332 - 1	SERVANT OF THE ETERNAL SPIRIT
SERVANT	358 - 1	LAW IS THE SERVANT OF THE SPIRIT
SERVANT	437 - 3	MY SERVANT SHALL BE HEALED
SERVICE	258 - 2	IDEAS HAVE A SERVICE TO RENDER
SERVICE	398 - 3	SERVICE IN GAINING A COMPLETE
SET	300 - 1	SET THE WORD IN MOTION
SET	385 - 1	WE WOULD BECOME TOO SET
SET	406 - 2	LIMITATIONS THAT WE SET
SETS	140 - 2	HE SETS MIND IN ACTION
SETS	475 - 3	SETS THE TENDENCY OF THE OUTWARD LIFE
SEVENTY	457 - 4	FORGIVE UNTIL SEVENTY TIMES SEVEN
SEVERAL	170 - 3	SEVERAL METHODS OF TREATMENT
SEX	237 - 1	NOT NECESSARILY SEX EMOTIONS
SHACKLES	406 - 4	THE SHACKLES OF BONDAGE
SHADE	411 - 3	WE CAN SIT IN THE SHADE
SHADES	337 - 1	SHADES TO MAGNIFY ITS GLORY
SHADOW	041 - 3	SHADOW OF A MIGHTY MIND
SHADOW	153 - 2	SLIGHTEST SHADOW OF
SHADOW	368 - 4	THE ONLY SHADOW WE CAST
SHADOW	381 - 4	SHADOW FOR THE REALITY
SHADOW	411 - 3	SITTING IN THE SHADOW WE MAY
SHADOW	495 - 1	SHADOW OF THE EVERLASTING TRUTH
SHADOWS	314 - 1	SAW THE SHADOWS OF BONDAGE
SHADOWS	355 - 3	CAST THEIR SHADOWS BEFORE
SHAKESPEARE	103 - 3	SHAKESPEARE PERCEIVED SERMONS IN STONES
SHAKESPEARE	137 - 1	SHAKESPEARE IS ACCREDITED WITH
SHALL	429 - 4	SHALL SEE GOD BUT DO SEE HIM
SHAM	435 - 2	WINNOWING FROM THE SOUL OF SHAM
SHAPE	476 - 1	ASSUMES SHAPE AND BECOMES
SHAPING	460 - 5	SHAPING A DIVINE INDIVIDUALITY
SHARP	138 - 2	STANDS OUT CLEAR AND SHARP
SHE	473 - 5	SHE WAS TAKEN FROM HIS BEING
SHELTER	342 - 2	TO FIND FOOD AND SHELTER
SHIELD	495 - 3	SHIELD OF FAITH
SHIELD	495 - 3	TRUTH IS A SHIELD
SHIFTING	436 - 5	SHIFTING SANDS OF INSTABILITY
SHIFTY	231 - 2	SUSPICION MAKE THE EYES SHIFTY
SHINE	435 - 1	LET GOODNESS SHINE FORTH
SHINES	487 - 3	GOODNESS SHINES TO ETERNITY
SHIPS	328 - 3	PASS AS SHIPS IN THE NIGHT
SHIPS	340 - 3	FROM THE RAFT TO MODERN SHIPS
SHOCK	253 - 3	CAUSED BY SUDDEN SHOCK AND GRIEF
SHOCK	257 - 1	SHOCK, GRIEF OR ANXIETY
SHOE STRINGS	188 - 4	SHOE STRINGS ALL OF WHICH
SHOOT	480 - 6	EVERY INDIVIDUAL SHOOT SPRINGS
SHORT	466 - 1	FALLEN SHORT OF THE DIVINE CALLING
SHORTCOMINGS	298 - 4	MAN MAY HAVE MANY SHORTCOMINGS
SHOULDERS	457 - 4	SHOULDERS OF PERSONAL RESPONSIBILITY
SHOUTED	431 - 2	ARE NOT TO BE SHOUTED
SHOUTING	051 - 3	RUSH ABOUT SHOUTING
SHOUTS	037 - 2	SHOUTS AT US FROM EVERY ANGLE
SHUNNED	435 - 2	A THING TO BE SHUNNED

SHUT OUT	431 - 3	WE ARE TO SHUT OUT ALL ELSE
SICK	168 - 5	GOD IS NOT SICK
SICK	189 - 2	LOOK AT THE SICK MAN
SICK	209 - 3	NEVER BE SICK, POOR, OR UNHAPPY
SICK	209 - 4	FORCE WHICH MAKES US SICK
SICK	211 - 1	THE POOR LITTLE SICK THING
SICK	225 - 1	PATIENT IS NO LONGER SICK
SICK	231 - 4	MERELY HAS A SICK BODY
SICK	408 - 5	NOT DEALING WITH A SICK BODY
SICKNESS	055 - 4	REFUSE TO LOOK AT SICKNESS
SICKNESS	107 - 3	SICKNESS, POVERTY AND UNHAPPINESS
SICKNESS	138 - 1	SICKNESS BY MENTAL AND SPIRITUAL MEANS
SICKNESS	177 - 3	SICKNESS IS NOT A SPIRITUAL REALITY
SICKNESS	191 - 2	DELIVER HIMSELF FROM SICKNESS
SICKNESS	417 - 2	WHOLENESS INSTEAD OF SICKNESS
SIFT	199 - 4	SIFT THAT SENSE OF RESPONSIBILITY
SIFTED	418 - 3	THOUGHT IS SIFTED
SIGHT	229 - 5	PERFECT ABIDING SIGHT
SIGHT	230 - 4	ONE MUST USE THE INNER SIGHT
SIGHT	230 - 5	SIGHT DECLARE THAT SPIRITUAL VISION
SIGHT	472 - 5	FROM THE SIGHT OF HUMANITY
SIGN	175 - 5	BE SOME SIGN OF IMPROVEMENT
SIGN	471 - 6	SIGN OF AN INNER CONVICTION
SIGNIFICANCE	044 - 3	FRAUGHT WITH TREMENDOUS SIGNIFICANCE
SIGNIFICANCE	220 - 4	MEDITATING UPON THE SPIRITUAL SIGNIFICANCE
SIGNIFICANCE	226 - 2	SPIRITUAL SIGNIFICANCE IS ASSIMILATED
SIGNIFICANT	043 - 4	SIGNIFICANT FACT THAT IT IS THE MIND
SIGNIFICANT	068 - 2	IT IS SIGNIFICANT
SIGNIFICANT	467 - 2	MOST SIGNIFICANT THING IN THIS
SILENCE	257 - 3	RESTS IN THE STILL SILENCE
SILENCE	366 - 4	THE SILENCE OF HIS OWN SOUL
SILENCE	388 - 2	IN THE SILENCE OF HIS OWN SOUL
SILENCE	458 - 7	INTO THE SILENCE AND MEDITATE
SILENT	077 - 3	AT ALL TIMES A SILENT COMMUNICATION
SILENT	202 - 5	FEW MOMENTS IN SILENT RECOGNITION
SILENT	219 - 1	SILENT ASSURANCE THAT MAN
SILENT	367 - 1	THOUGHT AND SILENT CONTEMPLATION
SILENT	388 - 3	SILENT PROCESSES OF THOUGHT
SILENT	421 - 4	SILENT INFLUENCE IS ALWAYS GOING ON
SILENTLY	057 - 4	WORKING SILENTLY IN THE LAW
SILENTLY	077 - 3	UNCONSCIOUSLY AND SILENTLY PERCEIVED
SILENTLY	342 - 4	SILENTLY AWAITS HIS RECOGNITION
SILL	328 - 1	SILL AND OTHERS OF LIKE NATURE
SIMPLE	076 - 3	MAKE THE SIMPLE STATEMENT
SIMPLE	123 - 4	THEN A SIMPLE CONSCIOUSNESS
SIMPLE	124 - 1	FROM THE SIMPLE TO THE PERSONAL
SIMPLE	140 - 2	NO MORE SIMPLE
SIMPLE	195 - 4	SIMPLE RULES ARE FOLLOWED
SIMPLE	367 - 4	EASY AND SIMPLE TO COMPREHEND
SIMPLE	373 - 1	SIMPLE STATEMENT THAT MAN IS
SIMPLE	411 - 4	SIMPLE PROPOSITION OF THE CREATIVE
SIMPLE	431 - 3	PRAYER IS TO BE SIMPLE
SIMPLE	453 - 5	TRUTH IS SIMPLE, DIRECT AND ALWAYS
SIMPLEST	040 - 3	SIMPLEST WAY TO STATE
SIMPLEST	091 - 3	SIMPLEST WAY WOULD BE

SIMPLEST	205 - 4	SIMPLEST WAY IS TO SAY
SIMPLEST	296 - 1	WHOLE THING TO ITS SIMPLEST FORM
SIMPLICITY	034 - 3	SHOULD RECOGNIZE ITS SIMPLICITY
SIMPLICITY	037 - 1	FUNDAMENTAL SIMPLICITY TO HIM
SIMPLICITY	041 - 4	RIDDLE OUT OF SIMPLICITY
SIMPLICITY	042 - 2	RETURN TO A SANE SIMPLICITY
SIMPLICITY	045 - 2	THE ESSENCE OF SIMPLICITY
SIMPLICITY	046 - 6	SIMPLICITY SHOULD MARK
SIMPLICITY	086 - 4	SIMPLICITY OF OUR OWN LANGUAGE
SIMPLIFIES	129 - 2	SIMPLIFIES THE WHOLE MATTER
SIMPLY	042 - 4	THE THING SIMPLY AND QUIETLY
SIMPLY	054 - 3	IS SIMPLY AN EXPERIENCE
SIMPLY	079 - 1	WE HAVE SIMPLY DETERMINED
SIMPLY	079 - 3	IS SIMPLY A LAW OF NATURE
SIMPLY	085 - 5	TO EXPRESS THIS MORE SIMPLY
SIMPLY	364 - 3	SIMPLY NEED A GREATER REALIZATION
SIMPLY	390 - 3	SIMPLY THE LAW OF MIND
SIMPLY	412 - 3	SIMPLY THAT THE UNIVERSE IS ONE
SIMPLY	498 - 5	THE LESSON IS SIMPLE ENOUGH
SIMULTANEOUS	086 - 4	BOTH SIMULTANEOUS AND INSTANTANEOUS
SIN	053 - 2	THUS SIN AND PUNISHMENT
SIN	110 - 4	THERE IS NO SIN BUT A MISTAKE
SIN	111 - 2	SIN IS NOT REAL TO GOD
SIN	111 - 2	NOT SAY THAT MAN CANNOT SIN
SIN	123 - 2	SIN WHICH IS NOTHING MORE THAN A MISTAKE
SIN	365 - 2	THE FORGIVENESS OF ALL SIN
SIN	383 - 1	THAT SIN IS A MISTAKE
SIN	438 - 4	GOD KNOWS NOTHING OF HIS SIN
SIN	467 - 2	IF GOD COULD KNOW SIN
SIN	486 - 1	IS NO SIN BUT IGNORANCE
SIN	498 - 4	NOT OF FAITH IS SIN
SIN	500 - 3	SIN BUT A MISTAKE AND NO PUNISHMENT
SIN	501 - 7	SIN MEANS MAKING MISTAKES
SINCERITY	430 - 6	THE LESSON OF SINCERITY
SINCERITY	459 - 6	LOVES SINCERITY
SINGERS	428 - 3	THEME OF OUR GREATEST SINGERS
SINGLE	229 - 5	SINGLE TO THE GOOD
SINGLE	229 - 5	THINE EYE BE SINGLE
SINGLE	432 - 2	IF OUR EYE BE SINGLE
SINGS	033 - 3	FOREVER SINGS AND SINGS
SINK	399 - 4	SINK INTO THIS INNER RECEFFIVITY
SINLESS	467 - 2	GOD IS SINLESS
SINNED	466 - 4	SINNED AGAINST HEAVEN
SINNER	103 - 1	TO THE SAINT AND THE SINNER
SINNER	438 - 4	HE WOULD BE A SINNER
SINNER	467 - 2	TALKED ABOUT BEING A SINNER
SINNERS	456 - 3	TOLD THAT THEY ARE SINNERS
SINS	237 - 2	JESUS FORGAVE THE MAN HIS SINS
SINS	237 - 2	THY SINS BE FORGIVEN THEE
SINS	269 - 3	THE REMISSION OF SINS
SINS	438 - 1	THY SINS BE FORGIVEN THEE
SIT	146 - 3	POWER TO SIT IN THE MIDST
SIT	470 - 2	SIT IN QUIET CONTEMPLATION OF GOOD
SITS	287 - 4	BECAUSE HE SITS AROUND AND THINKS
SITTING	047 - 3	NOT SITTING AROUND

SITUATIONS	217 - 2	SURROUNDED BY PERFECT SITUATIONS
SIZE	208 - 5	BUT NOT OF SIZE
SIZE	286 - 1	THE SIZE OF THE LOAF WOULD BE
SIZE	311 - 4	KNOW FORM BUT NOT SIZE
SIZE	312 - 2	GOD KNOWS FORM BUT NOT SIZE
SIZE	404 - 1	IT KNOWS FORM BUT NOT SIZE
SKEPTICISM	137 - 2	DAY FOR INCREDULOUS SKEPTICISM
SKIN	234 - 1	THE SKIN REPRESENTS A TEMPORARY
SKIN	248 - 3	TROUBLES AND SKIN DISEASES
SKIN	248 - 3	SKIN DISEASES AND BLOOD DISORDERS
SLEEP	257 - 5	I ACCEPT RESTFUL SLEEP
SLEEP	487 - 5	AWAKE OUT OF SLEEP
SLEEPING	247 - 2	WHETHER WAKING OR SLEEPING
SLIGHT	201 - 3	SLIGHT YOU FEEL YOUR KNOWLEDGE
SLIGHT	204 - 1	SLIGHT POINT WHICH IS NOT CLEAR
SUGHTEST	263 - 1	EVEN IN THE SLIGHTEST THINGS
SLIP	388 - 4	THOUGHT OF DEATH SHOULD SLIP
SLOGAN	137 - 2	SLOGAN HE CAN WHO THINKS
SLUMBERING	415 - 2	LATENT IN THE SLUMBERING THOUGHT
SMALL	263 - 1	NOTHING IS SMALL TO THE DIVINE
SMALL	311 - 4	NO GREAT AND NO SMALL
SMILE	470 - 5	SMILE FROM THE UNIVERSE
SMILING	388 - 1	LIES STRETCHED IN SMILING REPOSE
SNATCHED	376 - 2	SNATCHED FROM SOME COSMIC SHELF
SO	244 - 2	BECAUSE IT ALREADY IS SO
SO BE IT	127 - 1	SO BE IT DONE UNTO THEE
SO-CALLED	313 - 1	SO-CALLED MIND IS NOT ANOTHER MIND
SO-CALLED	377 - 3	CAUSED BY THE SO-CALLED DEAD
SOCIAL	270 - 5	WE SHOULD DO IN A SOCIAL STATE
SOCIETY	431 - 4	INDIVIDUAL MEMBERS OF SOCIETY
SOCIETY	433 - 4	NECESSARY TO THE WELL-BEING OF SOCIETY
SOCIETY	433 - 4	WHO SEEK TO DESTROY SOCIETY
SOCRATES	066 - 3	BRAIN OF A SOCRATES OR AN EINSTEIN
SOCRATES	311 - 3	MEN LIKE SOCRATES ANNOUNCED
SOCRATES	329 - 4	BUDDHA, PLATO, SOCRATES, EMERSON
SOCRATES	342 - 1	PLATO, SOCRATES, ARISTOTLE
SOIL	078 - 2	SOIL KNOWS HOW TO TAKE A SEED
SOIL	092 - 2	JUST ONCE THE SOIL FAILED
SOIL	354 - 3	IN THE CREATIVE SOIL
SOIL	354 - 3	SOIL DOES NOT ARGUE
SOLACE	109 - 3	IT IS A SOLACE TO THE MIND
SOLE	057 - 2	IT IS THE SOLE CAUSE
SOLE	132 - 7	SOLE AND ONLY OPERATION OF SPIRIT
SOLE	392 - 4	SOLE AND ONLY CREATIVE AGENCY
SOLE	475 - 4	SOLE MEDIUM BETWEEN THE ABSOLUTE
SOLELY	175 - 1	SOLELY UPON OUR BELIEF
SOLELY	207 - 2	PRACTITIONER DEALS SOLELY WITH IDEAS
SOLELY	395 - 1	LAW AS THOUGH IT EXISTED SOLELY
SOLID	047 - 5	SOLID BECOMES LIQUID
SOLID	184 - 2	SOLID AND THE LIQUID ARE ONE SUBSTANCE
SOLID	375 - 2	ETHER IS MORE SOLID THAN MATTER
SOLITUDE	470 - 3	MOMENTS OF QUIETNESS AND SOLITUDE
SOLOMON	232 - 3	SOLOMON TELLS US THAT
SOLOMON	238 - 4	SOLOMON IS ACCREDITED WITH MANY WORDS
SOLOMON	495 - 2	SOLOMON WE ARE HAPPY

SOLUTION	072 - 2	THE SOLUTION OF THE PROBLEM
SOLUTION	128 - 4	THE SOLUTION TO EVERY DIFFICULTY
SOLUTION	188 - 3	THE SOLUTION TO EVERY DIFFICULTY
SOLUTION	365 - 2	SOLUTION TO EVERY PROBLEM IS WITHIN MAN
SOLUTION	445 - 1	SEEKS A SOLUTION OF ITS GREAT RIDDLE
SOLVE	194 - 3	SOLVE ONE OF THOSE DIVINE RIDDLES
SOLVED	111 - 3	PROBLEM OF EVIL BE SOLVED
SOLVED	123 - 3	THE DIFFICULTY IS SOLVED
SOLVES	188 - 3	SOLVES ALL PROBLEMS
SOMEDAY	336 - 4	SOMEDAY WE SHALL DECIDE
SOMEONE	054 - 2	SOMEONE TO EXPERIENCE THEM
SOMEONE	295 - 2	SOMEONE MAY HELP US ON THE ROAD
SOMEONE	298 - 3	SOMETHING OR SOMEONE TO LOVE
SOMETHING	038 - 3	THROUGH US A CREATIVE SOMETHING
SOMETHING	083 - 2	SOMETHING THAT IS COMPELLED
SOMETHING	083 - 3	NOT SOMETHING OUT OF NOTHING
SOMETHING	266 - 1	PROMISE SOMETHING FOR NOTHING
SOMETHING	267 - 2	PROMISE SOMETHING FOR NOTHING
SOMETHING	296 - 3	WHAT IS THAT SOMETHING
SOMETHING	377 - 3	SOMETHING MUST MAKE THEM HAPPEN
SOMETHING	402 - 3	THE SUBSTANCE OF EVERY SOMETHING
SOMETHING	405 - 3	SOMETHING OTHER THAN LIFE
SOMETIMES	399 - 1	SOMETIMES WE SHALL BE TRYING
SON	088 - 3	SON IS THE OFFSPRING OF THE FATHER
SON	106 - 3	SON TO HAVE LIFE WITHIN HIMSELF
SON	132 - 8	SON WITHIN THE FATHER
SON	132 - 8	SON HAS THE SAME LIFE ESSENCE
SON	265 - 2	SON OF THE LIVING GOD
SON	367 - 1	THIS IS MY BELOVED SON
SON	443 - 2	AND NO MAN KNOWETH THE SON
SON	468 - 1	SON FOUND EVERYTHING
SON	479 - 5	SON IS THE WAY TO THE FATHER
SONG	385 - 1	AND A SONG IN THE HEART
SON OF GOD	036 - 2	CALLED THE SON OF GOD
SON OF GOD	503 - 5	SON OF GOD IN ALL HIS BEAUTY
SON OF MAN	442 - 2	SON OF MAN CAME EATING
SON OF MAN	474 - 6	THE SON OF MAN IS EVERY MAN
SONS	338 - 3	NOW ARE WE THE SONS OF GOD
SONS	469 - 1	BOTH SONS WERE FOOLISH
SONS	502 - 7	SONS OF FREEDOM AND NOT OF BONDAGE
SONSHIP	443 - 3	SONSHIP MUST BE PURE
SONS OF GOD	162 - 1	ALL MEN ARE THE SONS OF GOD
SOONER	140 - 4	SOONER WE SHALL BE ABLE
SOONER	400 - 3	SOONER WE KNOW JUST WHAT
SOUL	037 - 3	SOUL THAT MAKETH ALL
SOUL	081 - 3	SPIRIT, SOUL AND BODY
SOUL	083 - 2	SOUL OF THE UNIVERSE IS
SOUL	083 - 2	THE SOUL OF THE UNIVERSE
SOUL	090 - 2	SOUL IS THE CREATIVE SOIL
SOUL	090 - 2	SOUL THROUGH WHICH SPIRIT OPERATES
SOUL	090 - 2	SOUL IS THE HOLY GHOST
SOUL	091 - 1	SOUL IS SUBJECTIVE TO SPIRIT
SOUL	091 - 1	THE SUBJECTIVE MIND WHICH WE CALL SOUL
SOUL	091 - 1	BUSINESS OF SOUL
SOUL	091 - 2	SOUL IS IMMATERIAL

SOUL	091 - 3	SOUL IS SUBJECTIVE INTELLIGENCE
SOUL	091 - 4	SOUL MAY NOT CHOOSE
SOUL	092 - 2	THE SOUL OF THE UNIVERSE
SOUL	092 - 3	SOUL IS THE MEDIUM
SOUL	096 - 4	SOUL IS WITHOUT CONSCIOUS CONSCIOUSNESS
SOUL	105 - 2	THE SOUL OR SUBJECTIVITY
SOUL	111 - 4	SOUL OF THE UNIVERSE AND UNIVERSAL SPIRIT
SOUL	114 - 4	WE TREAT OF SOUL AS BEING
SOUL	114 - 5	SOUL IS THE SEAT OF MEMORY
SOUL	131 - 4	SOUL AND UNIVERSAL SUBJECTIVE MIND
SOUL	152 - 4	THE SOUL FOR THE SOUL IS NEVER LOST
SOUL	185 - 2	HAPPINESS TO THE SOUL OF MAN
SOUL	220 - 3	SOUL RECOGNIZES ITS OWN I-AM-NESS
SOUL	230 - 2	THE WINDOWS OF THE SOUL
SOUL	230 - 4	EYES ARE THE ORGANS OF THE SOUL
SOUL	269 - 3	OF THE INDIVIDUAL SOUL
SOUL	299 - 1	ANYTHING AGAINST ANY LIVING SOUL
SOUL	327 - 3	NO LIVING SOUL COULD HAVE TAUGHT
SOUL	328 - 3	CONQUERED HIS OWN SOUL
SOUL	347 - 1	THE SOUL IS REALLY THE SUBJECTIVE PART
SOUL	363 - 3	LOCATED GOD IN HIS OWN SOUL
SOUL	374 - 4	THE SOUL NEEDS A PHYSICAL BODY HERE
SOUL	376 - 2	AS THE SOUL SOARS ALOFT
SOUL	378 - 2	SOUL CAN OPERATE INDEPENDENTLY
SOUL	383 - 3	THE SOUL CAN NO MORE BE LOST
SOUL	388 - 4	GREAT EVENT OF THE SOUL TAKES PLACE
SOUL	401 - 3	A LIVING SOUL IN A DEAD BODY
SOUL	405 - 4	SOUL MUST MAKE A COMPLETE SURRENDER
SOUL	413 - 2	CHRIST IS GOD IN THE SOUL OF MAN
SOUL	419 - 4	THE SOUL IS ON THE PATHWAY OF EXPERIENCE
SOUL	431 - 1	SOUL SHALL BE THROWN BACK UPON ITSELF
SOUL	439 - 2	THE SOUL IS ON THE PATHWAY
SOUL	457 - 3	SOUL TURNS FROM THAT WHICH HURTS
SOUL	476 - 5	WISDOM FOR THE SOUL
SOUL	477 - 1	SOUL HE FINDS A PERFECT LAW
SOUL	477 - 2	SOUL WHICH IS THE SUBJECTIVE MENTALITY
SOUL	503 - 1	SOUL INTO THE LIGHT OF SPIRIT IS
SOUL AND SPIRIT	090 - 3	SOUL AND SPIRIT
SOUL CULTURE	446 - 4	ONLY THROUGH SOUL CULTURE
SOUL HUNGER	428 - 4	WHO DOES NOT HAVE A SOUL HUNGER
SOUL LIFE	100 - 1	CONTROLLED BY THE SOUL LIFE
SOULS	383 - 3	OUR SOULS BOTH HERE AND HEREAFTER
SOULS	434 - 4	WE ARE FREE SOULS
SOUL SIDE	114 - 3	SOUL SIDE MAN IS SUBCONSCIOUS
SOUL-STUFF	091 - 2	FINALLY BECOMES SOUL-STUFF
SOUL-STUFF	091 - 3	SOUL-STUFF IS THE SOURCE
SOUL-STUFF	091 - 3	SOUL-STUFF REFERS TO THE PRIMORDIAL
SOUND	039 - 6	WORK WITH THIS SOUND KNOWLEDGE
SOUND	329 - 4	PHILOSOPHY OF JESUS WILL REMAIN SOUND
SOURCE	045 - 1	ALL FROM THE SAME SOURCE
SOURCE	189 - 1	COME FROM THE SAME SOURCE
SOURCE	295 - 1	COMES FROM THE SAME SOURCE
SOURCE	304 - 4	FROM THIS OR THAT SOURCE
SOURCE	446 - 4	I MUST FIND THE SOURCE
SOW	195 - 2	AS WE SOW SO WE MUST REAP

SOWETH	269 - 2	WHATSOEVER A MAN SOWETH
SOWS	039 - 3	AS HE SOWS SO SHALL HE REAP
SOWS	205 - 5	PRACTITIONER SOWS THE SEED
SPACE	052 - 2	IT OCCUPIES ALL SPACE
SPACE	094 - 2	SPACE BETWEEN THE PLANETARY
SPACE	095 - 1	AS THE ETHER OF SPACE
SPACE	101 - 2	SPACE WHICH IS NEVER A THING OF ITSELF
SPACE	208 - 5	BUT NOT OF SPACE
SPACE	267 - 3	ORIGINAL STATE FILLS ALL SPACE
SPACE	279 - 2	ETERNALLY FALLING THROUGH SPACE
SPACE	307 - 1	THE IMMENSITY OF SPACE
SPACE	373 - 4	EXISTING IN TIME AND SPACE
SPACE	375 - 2	THROUGHOUT ALL SPACE
SPACE	375 - 3	OCCUPY THE SAME SPACE SIMULTANEOUSLY
SPACE	376 - 1	SAME SPACE WHICH OUR BODY DOES
SPACE	422 - 2	TIME AND SPACE ARE UNKNOWN
SPAKE	068 - 5	SPAKE AND IT WAS DONE
SPAN	460 - 3	EXISTENCE FROM THIS SHORT SPAN
SPARE	293 - 3	ENOUGH AND TO SPARE
SPARK	103 - 3	THE SPARK WHICH WE MAY DESECRATE
SPARK	169 - 1	SPARK WHICH A MAN MAY DESECRATE
SPARK	368 - 3	AWAKENS THE DIVINE SPARK
SPARK	414 - 3	SPARK WHICH BURNS AT THE CENTER
SPARK	463 - 1	BECOMES AN ISOLATED SPARK
SPEAK	059 - 2	SPEAK THE NAME OF THIS PERSON
SPEAK	160 - 1	AS WE SPEAK THE TRUTH
SPEAK	184 - 3	DARE TO SPEAK AND TO KNOW
SPEAK	306 - 1	SPEAK THE WORD CONSCIOUSLY
SPEAK	332 - 1	SPEAK THE WORD AS ONE
SPEAK	343 - 3	SPEAK TO HIM THOU FOR HE HEARS
SPEAK	3S8 - 1	SPEAK THE WORD WITH BELIEF
SPEAK	369 - 1	LET THE TRUTH SPEAK THROUGH US
SPEAK	415 - 1	SPEAK THE CONVICTION THAT IS
SPEAK	437 - 2	SPEAK THE WORD ONLY
SPEAK	441 - 1	FOR IT IS NOT YE THAT SPEAK
SPEAK	476 - 3	WE SPEAK IT INTO FORM
SPEAKING	069 - 1	SPEAKING ITSELF INTO MANIFESTATION
SPEAKING	094 - 1	THE SPEAKING OF HIS NAME
SPEAKING	368 - 1	THIS WAS THE CHRIST SPEAKING
SPEAKS	055 - 2	HE DEFINITELY SPEAKS IT INTO BEING
SPEAKS	064 - 4	HE SPEAKS HIS WORD BECOMES
SPEAKS	069 - 3	SPEAKS AND IT IS DONE
SPEAKS	084 - 1	FIRST CAUSE SPEAKS AND IT IS DONE
SPEAKS	169 - 5	SPEAKS FROM HIS OBJECTIVE MIND
SPEAKS	171 - 1	HE SPEAKS HER NAME
SPEAKS	229 - 1	HE SPEAKS INTO INTELLIGENCE
SPECIAL	410 - 2	WHICH EVERY SPECIAL GOOD COMES
SPECIALIZED	417 - 2	SPECIALIZED USE OF THE LAW
SPECIALIZING	273 - 3	GOD IS SPECIALIZING
SPECIFIC	028 - 2	FOR A SPECIFIC PURPOSE
SPECIFIC	038 - 4	CERTAIN SPECIFIC WAYS OF THOUGHT
SPECIFIC	038 - 4	AND IT SHOULD BE SPECIFIC
SPECIFIC	048 - 2	CONSCIOUS AND SPECIFIC THOUGHT
SPECIFIC	048 - 2	SPECIFIC TECHNIQUE IN MENTAL TREATMENT
SPECIFIC	049 - 2	THEY MUST BE SPECIFIC

SPECIFIC	054 - 2	DEFINITELY AND FOR SPECIFIC PURPOSES
SPECIFIC	057 - 4	MUST PRODUCE SPECIFIC RESULTS
SPECIFIC	105 - 3	A SPECIFIC CAUSE
SPECIFIC	113 - 3	SPECIFIC KNOWLEDGE MUST COME
SPECIFIC	145 - 2	SPECIFIC DISEASE IS ALWAYS THE RESULT
SPECIFIC	145 - 2	NO SPECIFIC THOUGHT OF SICKNESS
SPECIFIC	176 - 3	SPECIFIC THAN A SCIENTIFIC TREATMENT
SPECIFIC	198 - 2	TANGIBLE SPECIFIC OPERATION
SPECIFIC	198 - 4	THAT EVERY SPECIFIC IDEA
SPECIFIC	200 - 2	DO SPECIFIC MENTAL WORK
SPECIFIC	200 - 3	TREATMENT IS A SPECIFIC THING
SPECIFIC	200 - 3	EACH CASE IS SPECIFIC
SPECIFIC	211 - 3	BE SPECIFIC IN TREATING
SPECIFIC	224 - 3	A TREATMENT IS A SPECIFIC THING
SPECIFIC	254 - 4	NO REAL SPECIFIC TREATMENT
SPECIFIC	254 - 4	ATTENTION TO THE SPECIFIC IDEA
SPECIFIC	301 - 1	WE MUST BE SPECIFIC
SPECIFIC	318 - 2	BE DEFINITE SPECIFIC CONCRETE
SPECIFIC	397 - 1	USED FOR SPECIFIC PURPOSES
SPECIFIC	397 - 5	SPECIFIC MENTAL ATTENTION
SPECIFIC	398 - 3	WHEN WE TREAT WE SHOULD BE SPECIFIC
SPECIFIC	435 - 4	SHOULD BE DIRECT AND SPECIFIC
SPECIFICALLY	049 - 5	SPECIFICALLY TURN TO THAT THOUGHT
SPECIFICALLY	058 - 4	SHOULD SPECIFICALLY TREAT HIMSELF
SPECIFICALLY	169 - 5	POWER OF MIND DEFINITELY SPECIFICALLY
SPECIFICALLY	198 - 4	ORGAN OF THE BODY SPECIFICALLY
SPECIFICALLY	201 - 2	DEFINITELY SPECIFICALLY AND CONSCIOUSLY
SPECIFICALLY	202 - 5	SPECIFICALLY MENTION EVERYTHING
SPECIFICALLY	236 - 4	SPECIFICALLY GO OVER
SPECIFICALLY	290 - 3	DENIED COMPLETELY AND SPECIFICALLY
SPECIFIES	199 - 1	THE DIRECTION HE SPECIFIES
SPECIFY	172 - 2	SPECIFY THE TROUBLE
SPEECH	418 - 5	WITH RIGHT SPEECH
SPEND	219 - 4	SPEND OUR ENTIRE TIME TRYING TO FIND
SPHERE	377 - 2	PASSING TO A HIGHER SPHERE
SPHERE	387 - 1	LIMITED TO ONE SPHERE OF ACTION
SPILLING	420 - 4	SPILLING ITSELF INTO NUMBERLESS FORMS
SPIN	432 - 2	TOIL NOT, NOR DO THEY SPIN
SPINOZA	103 - 3	SPINOZA SAYS THAT MIND AND MATTER ARE
SPINOZA	310 - 2	WHAT SPINOZA HAD IN MIND
SPIRAL	387 - 1	THE SPIRAL OF LIFE IS UPWARD
SPIRALS	443 - 4	LADDER WHICH EVER SPIRALS UPWARD
SPIRIT	026 - 3	SCIENCE OF MIND IS A STUDY OF SPIRIT
SPIRIT	029 - 2	THE ETERNAL SPIRIT THROUGHOUT THE AGES
SPIRIT	031 - 4	THE CONSCIOUS MIND IS SPIRIT
SPIRIT	032 - 1	FILLED WITH SPIRIT
SPIRIT	032 - 1	WE ARE SPIRIT AND WE ARE LAW
SPIRIT	032 - 2	ETERNAL SPIRIT WHICH WE CALL GOD
SPIRIT	034 - 2	SPIRIT MAN IS ONE WITH GOD
SPIRIT	036 - 2	SPIRIT PLUS NOTHING LEAVES SPIRIT
SPIRIT	040 - 4	SPIRIT CAN GIVE US ONLY
SPIRIT	043 - 2	THERE IS AN INFINITE SPIRIT
SPIRIT	043 - 4	IS NOT THIS MIND THE SPIRIT IN US
SPIRIT	045 - 4	INSPIRED BY THE SAME SPIRIT
SPIRIT	053 - 1	BY THE SPIRIT OF GOD

SPIRIT	053 - 3	THE ORIGINAL SPIRIT IS HARMONY
SPIRIT	054 - 1	INNER SPIRIT GUIDE US
SPIRIT	057 - 1	IN THE SPIRIT OF TRUTH
SPIRIT	064 - 4	GOD IS NOT ONLY PURE SPIRIT
SPIRIT	066 - 2	AS GOD, SPIRIT, REALITY
SPIRIT	066 - 5	SPIRIT BEING ALL AND ONLY
SPIRIT	069 - 3	GOD IS SPIRIT
SPIRIT	075 - 3	GOD IS SPIRIT
SPIRIT	077 - 1	SPIRIT IS THE MEDIUM
SPIRIT	078 - 1	SPIRIT MUST BE SELF-KNOWING
SPIRIT	078 - 2	INFINITE SELF-KNOWING SPIRIT
SPIRIT	079 - 2	MEANT BY THE SPIRIT OF GOD
SPIRIT	080 - 1	GOD IS SPIRIT
SPIRIT	081 - 2	GOD IS SPIRIT AND THEY THAT WORSHIP
SPIRIT	081 - 2	WORSHIP HIM IN SPIRIT
SPIRIT	081 - 3	SPIRIT, SOUL AND BODY
SPIRIT	081 - 4	SPIRIT IS FIRST CAUSE
SPIRIT	081 - 5	SPIRIT IS SELF-PROPELLING
SPIRIT	082 - 1	SPIRIT IS ALL
SPIRIT	082 - 3	SPIRIT IS ONE
SPIRIT	083 - 4	THE SPIRIT IS CONSCIOUS
SPIRIT	084 - 1	SPIRIT KNOWS ITSELF
SPIRIT	084 - 4	SPIRIT AND AN INFINITE LAW
SPIRIT	085 - 3	SPIRIT WAS NOT CREATED
SPIRIT	087 - 1	IS THE LAW OF SPIRIT
SPIRIT	087 - 1	MAN IS A SPIRIT
SPIRIT	087 - 1	WHILE GOD IS THE SPIRIT
SPIRIT	088 - 2	SPIRIT, SOUL, AND BODY
SPIRIT	124 - 1	SPIRIT IS NOT SOMETHING APART FROM MATTER
SPIRIT	132 - 2	CONSCIOUS MIND AND SPIRIT HAVE THE SAME
SPIRIT	153 - 4	SPIRIT FLOWS THROUGH US
SPIRIT	194 - 1	SPIRIT OF THE THING IS
SPIRIT	201 - 2	SPIRIT WHATEVER HE CHOOSES
SPIRIT	217 - 2	SPIRIT IS EVER AVAILABLE
SPIRIT	217 - 2	OUTSIDE OF OURSELVES TO FIND THIS SPIRIT
SPIRIT	219 - 4	SPIRIT IS AN ACTIVE PRESENCE
SPIRIT	238 - 2	SPIRIT OF DIVINE COMPASSION
SPIRIT	247 - 3	SPIRIT IS NEVER ANAEMIC
SPIRIT	250 - 3	SPIRIT IS ALREADY IN HIS PATIENT
SPIRIT	250 - 3	SPIRIT OF PERFECT CIRCULATION
SPIRIT	252 - 5	SPIRIT IS NOT SUBJECT TO HEAT
SPIRIT	254 - 3	SPIRIT CANNOT MAKE A MISTAKE
SPIRIT	264 - 3	SPIRIT IS THE ONLY CAUSE
SPIRIT	275 - 3	THE SPIRIT WITHIN MAN IS GOD
SPIRIT	275 - 3	THE SPIRIT OF THE UNIVERSE
SPIRIT	277 - 3	LAW IS SUBJECT TO SPIRIT
SPIRIT	283 - 2	THE SPIRIT OF THE LAW
SPIRIT	286 - 1	TO CALL SPIRIT IS MATTER
SPIRIT	338 - 2	SPIRIT DOES NOT SEEK TO CONTROL US
SPIRIT	340 - 1	WE AS CONSCIOUS SPIRIT
SPIRIT	379 - 2	POSSIBILITY OF SPIRIT COMMUNICATION
SPIRIT	379 - 3	SPIRIT COMMUNICATION MUST BE POSSIBLE
SPIRIT	390 - 5	SPIRIT IS REALLY THE ONLY
SPIRIT	397 - 4	GOD OR SPIRIT IS A COMPLETE
SPIRIT	401 - 1	PART OF MIND THE SPIRIT OF MAN

SPIRIT	401 – 2	CONSCIOUS STATE IS SPIRIT
SPIRIT	406 – 1	SPIRIT IS PRESENT IN ITS ENTIRETY
SPIRIT	407 – 5	SPIRIT IS CONSCIOUS OF MAN
SPIRIT	410 – 2	SPIRIT TO THE LETTER OF THE LAW
SPIRIT	412 – 3	SPIRIT AS BEING SELF-DESTRUCTIVE
SPIRIT	418 – 3	THE SPIRIT OF MAN IS GOD
SPIRIT	422 – 3	SPIRIT IS AN INDIVISIBLE
SPIRIT	430 – 2	SPIRIT THROUGH THE WICK OF PEACE
SPIRIT	435 – 4	SPIRIT A CONSCIOUS ACT OF THE MIND
SPIRIT	463 – 2	SPIRIT WITHOUT WHICH NOTHING
SPIRIT	477 – 1	SPIRIT HE RECEIVES INSPIRATION
SPIRIT	477 – 2	SPIRIT FIRES THE SOUL
SPIRIT	484 – 2	SPIRIT MAKES US FREE FROM SIN
SPIRIT	485 – 1	THE SPIRIT OF FREEDOM
SPIRIT	503 – 6	SPIRIT WHICH GAVE THE HEART
SPIRIT AGENCIES	379 – 1	ARGUMENT AGAINST SPIRIT AGENCIES
SPIRIT AND SOUL	088 – 2	SPIRIT AND SOUL INTERSPHERE EACH OTHER
SPIRIT OF CHRIST	120 – 3	SPIRIT OF CHRIST MEANS THAT MENTALITY
SPIRIT OF GOD	112 – 2	ONE WITH THE SPIRIT OF GOD
SPIRIT OF GOD	391 – 2	IS THE SPIRIT OF GOD
SPIRIT OF MAN	418 – 3	SPIRIT OF MAN NEEDS NO HEALING
SPIRIT OF PROPHECY	355 – 3	THE AVERAGE SPIRIT OF PROPHECY
SPIRITS	252 – 5	COLDS RESULT FROM DAMP SPIRITS
SPIRITS	374 – 5	SHALL WE BECOME SPIRITS
SPIRITS	375 – 1	WE ARE SPIRITS NOW
SPIRITS	377 – 3	SPIRITS OF THE SUPPOSED DEAD
SPIRITS	379 – 3	IF SPIRITS REALLY EXIST
SPIRITS	381 – 4	AGAINST HAVING FAMILIAR SPIRITS
SPIRIT SOUL AND BODY	090 – 1	TRINITY OF BEING AS SPIRIT, SOUL AND BODY
SPIRIT SOUL AND BODY	129 – 2	WE SHALL CALL SPIRIT, SOUL AND BODY
SPIRITUAL	031 – 2	IN THE SPIRITUAL WORLD
SPIRITUAL	032 – 2	LIVING IN A SPIRITUAL UNIVERSE
SPIRITUAL	042 – 5	SPIRITUAL WISDOM
SPIRITUAL	057 – 4	A SPIRITUAL ENTITY
SPIRITUAL	067 – 2	TO BE SPIRITUAL IS TO CREATE
SPIRITUAL	103 – 4	DISCLOSING A SPIRITUAL UNIVERSE
SPIRITUAL	114 – 1	FROM THE WORLD TO BE SPIRITUAL
SPIRITUAL	139 – 4	SUBJECT OF SPIRITUAL MIND HEALING
SPIRITUAL	160 – 2	SPIRITUAL UNDERSTANDING IS NOT MEANT
SPIRITUAL	167 – 4	SPIRITUAL REALIZATION IN EVERYDAY AFFAIRS
SPIRITUAL	168 – 2	SPIRITUAL MEANS AND METHODS
SPIRITUAL	170 – 5	SPIRITUAL AND MEDITATIVE
SPIRITUAL	178 – 5	THE MORE SPIRITUAL OR GODLIKE
SPIRITUAL	190 – 3	IN REALITY IS SPIRITUAL AND MENTAL
SPIRITUAL	191 – 3	MENTAL AND THE SPIRITUAL
SPIRITUAL	192 – 2	A SPIRITUAL PRACTITIONER
SPIRITUAL	218 – 4	BELIEVE THAT MAN IS SPIRITUAL
SPIRITUAL	218 – 4	ENTIRE BEING AS SPIRITUAL
SPIRITUAL	219 – 1	MAN BEING SPIRITUAL
SPIRITUAL	220 – 4	MEDITATING UPON THE SPIRITUAL SIGNIFICANCE
SPIRITUAL	229 – 3	I EXPRESS THROUGH A SPIRITUAL BODY
SPIRITUAL	247 – 3	SPIRITUAL FLOW OF LIFE
SPIRITUAL	259 – 4	MY SYSTEM IS SPIRITUAL
SPIRITUAL	259 – 4	SPIRITUAL AND HARMONIOUS WITH MY SYSTEM
SPIRITUAL	268 – 2	MENTAL AND SPIRITUAL COIN

SPIRITUAL	270 - 6	SPIRITUAL MAN IS ALREADY A SUCCESS
SPIRITUAL	312 - 3	SPIRITUAL DEDUCTIONS OF THE AGES
SPIRITUAL	313 - 3	WE LIVE IN A SPIRITUAL SYSTEM
SPIRITUAL	313 - 3	SPIRITUAL BEINGS BUT WE DO NOT KNOW IT
SPIRITUAL	316 - 1	MENTAL AND SPIRITUAL PRACTITIONER
SPIRITUAL	322 - 4	THE MORE SPIRITUAL THE THOUGHT
SPIRITUAL	342 - 1	SPIRITUAL IS THE REALM OF FIRST CAUSE
SPIRITUAL	376 - 1	THERE IS A SPIRITUAL BODY
SPIRITUAL	407 - 4	UNIVERSE IS A SPIRITUAL SYSTEM
SPIRITUAL	407 - 4	PEOPLED WITH SPIRITUAL FORMS
SPIRITUAL	417 - 4	MENTAL AND SPIRITUAL METHODS
SPIRITUAL	427 - 1	SPIRITUAL REALIZATION FAR BEYOND THAT
SPIRITUAL	427 - 1	SPIRITUAL THINGS MUST BE SPIRITUALLY
SPIRITUAL	445 - 6	WE NEED SPIRITUAL EXPERIENCE
SPIRITUAL	451 - 3	SPIRITUAL CONVICTIONS COME ALL ELSE
SPIRITUAL	452 - 4	SPIRITUAL EXPERIENCES ARE NORMAL NATURAL
SPIRITUAL	452 - 6	JESUS LIVED IN THE SPIRITUAL WORLD
SPIRITUAL	476 - 6	LIVE ONLY ON THE SPIRITUAL
SPIRITUAL	483 - 1	COUNTERPART OF THE SPIRITUAL
SPIRITUAL	497 - 4	UNEXPRESSED SPIRITUAL EMOTIONS
SPIRITUAL BEINGS	448 - 1	SPIRITUAL BEINGS GOVERNED BY MENTAL LAW
SPIRITUAL EMOTION	497 - 3	SPIRITUAL EMOTION IS COMMON
SPIRITUAL EXPERIENCE	445 - 7	SPIRITUAL EXPERIENCE IS DEEP
SPIRITUAL EYE	503 - 3	SPIRITUAL EYE THAT DIMS NOT
SPIRITUAL FOOD	428 - 4	SATISFIED WITH SPIRITUAL FOOD
SPIRITUAL GENIUS	315 - 1	SPIRITUAL GENIUS HAS TAUGHT US
SPIRITUAL HEALING	484 - 4	MENTAL AND SPIRITUAL HEALING
SPIRITUALITY	308 - 1	SPIRITUALITY IS NATURAL GOODNESS
SPIRITUALITY	308 - 1	SPIRITUALITY IS NOT A THING
SPIRITUALITY	446 - 2	SPIRITUALITY MAY BE DEFINED
SPIRITUALIZATION	104 - 5	RESULT OF THE SPIRITUALIZATION
SPIRITUAL LAW	362 - 2	SPIRITUAL LAW IN THE MENTAL WORLD
SPIRITUALLY	060 - 2	MUST BE SPIRITUALLY DISCERNED
SPIRITUALLY	094 - 1	MENTALLY, PHYSICALLY, SPIRITUALLY
SPIRITUALLY	108 - 4	WE ARE SPIRITUALLY COMPLETE
SPIRITUALLY	476 - 5	PEOPLE ARE STARVED SPIRITUALLY
SPIRITUALLY	502 - 7	MUST BE SPIRITUALLY UNDERSTOOD
SPIRITUALLY MINDED	428 - 5	SPIRITUALLY MINDED AND THE QUESTION
SPIRITUAL MAN	169 - 1	SPIRITUAL MAN WHO IS NEVER SICK
SPIRITUAL MAN	201 - 4	SPIRITUAL MAN HAS NO DISEASE
SPIRITUAL MAN	203 - 1	SPIRITUAL MAN NEEDS NO HEALING
SPIRITUAL MAN	218 - 3	SPIRITUAL MAN IS PERFECT
SPIRITUAL MAN	317 - 1	SPIRITUAL MAN IS PERFECT
SPIRITUAL MAN	318 - 3	TRUTH ABOUT THE SPIRITUAL MAN
SPIRITUAL MAN	320 - 2	SPIRITUAL MAN IS ALREADY PERFECT
SPIRITUAL MAN	418 - 2	SPIRITUAL MAN IS ALREADY COMPLETE
SPIRITUAL MIND	294 - 1	SPIRITUAL MIND HEALING IS A RESULT
SPIRITUAL MIND	423 - 3	ESSENCE OF SPIRITUAL MIND HEALING
SPIRITUAL PHILOSOPHY	341 - 4	SPIRITUAL PHILOSOPHY WAS A RESULT
SPIRITUAL POWER	151 - 2	SPIRITUAL POWER LIES IN A CONSCIOUSNESS
SPIRITUAL QUALITY	178 - 3	FAITH IN GOD IS A SPIRITUAL QUALITY
SPIRITUAL SCIENCE	448 - 1	SINCERE STUDENTS OF SPIRITUAL SCIENCE
SPIRITUAL SENSE	343 - 3	DEGREE AS ONE HAS SPIRITUAL SENSE
SPIRITUAL SYSTEM	155 - 1	UNIVERSE IS A SPIRITUAL SYSTEM
SPIRITUAL SYSTEM	336 - 1	UNIVERSE IS NOW A SPIRITUAL SYSTEM

SPIRITUAL TREATMENT	149 - 2	PRAYER IS A SPIRITUAL TREATMENT
SPIRITUAL TREATMENT	163 - 3	SPIRITUAL TREATMENT SHOULD BRING INTO
SPIRITUAL TREATMENT	345 - 3	SPIRITUAL TREATMENT COULD BE SEEN
SPIRITUAL TREATMENT	406 - 1	MENTAL AND SPIRITUAL TREATMENT
SPIRITUAL WORLD	341 - 1	LAW IN A SPIRITUAL WORLD
SPITE	119 - 2	IN SPITE OF ALL CONDITIONS
SPITE	174 - 4	DEMONSTRATE IN SPITE OF OURSELVES
SPOKE	286 - 3	PRACTITIONER SPOKE THE SAME
SPOKE	479 - 2	SPOKE WORDS OF COMFORT TO THOSE
SPOKEN	065 - 1	SPOKEN WITHIN HIMSELF
SPOKEN	160 - 1	THE ALMIGHTY HAS SPOKEN
SPOKEN	169 - 3	WHERE UNTO IT IS SPOKEN
SPOKEN	184 - 3	LAW UNTO THE THING SPOKEN
SPOKEN	203 - 3	THING UNTO WHICH IT IS SPOKEN
SPOKEN	216 - 2	THING WHERE UNTO IT IS SPOKEN
SPOKEN	233 - 2	THE WORD OF HEALING IS SPOKEN
SPOKEN	262 - 2	WHERE TO THEY ARE SPOKEN
SPOKEN	262 - 2	SPOKEN UNTO YOU ARE SPIRIT
SPOKEN	263 - 3	WHERE UNTO IT IS SPOKEN
SPOKEN	303 - 4	HAS BEEN SPOKEN IN CALM
SPOKEN	304 - 1	THE THING FOR WHICH IT IS SPOKEN
SPOKEN	475 - 6	WHEN OUR WORD IS SPOKEN
SPOKEN	476 - 3	THEN A SPOKEN WORD
SPOKEN WORD	115 - 1	HEALING POWER OF THE SPOKEN WORD
SPONTANEITY	143 - 2	SPONTANEITY PUT INTO THE MECHANICAL WORD
SPONTANEOUS	025 - 2	INDIVIDUALITY MUST BE SPONTANEOUS
SPONTANEOUS	042 - 5	SPONTANEOUS RECOGNITION
SPONTANEOUS	043 - 3	THE SPONTANEOUS ELEMENT
SPONTANEOUS	064 - 4	THE WORD IS SPONTANEOUS
SPONTANEOUS	065 - 5	BE SPONTANEOUS NOT AUTOMATIC
SPONTANEOUS	086 - 1	THE ONLY THING THAT IS SPONTANEOUS
SPONTANEOUS	104 - 1	UNIVERSE IS A SPONTANEOUS EMERGENCE
SPONTANEOUS	143 - 4	INDIVIDUALS IS TO BE SPONTANEOUS
SPONTANEOUS	176 - 2	THE MORE SPONTANEOUS WE CAN BE
SPONTANEOUS	195 - 3	ORDER IS ONE OF SPONTANEOUS BEING
SPONTANEOUS	195 - 3	SPONTANEOUS MANIFESTATION
SPONTANEOUS	196 - 1	IT MUST BE SPONTANEOUS
SPONTANEOUS	362 - 3	SPONTANEOUS SENSE
SPONTANEOUS	408 - 4	SPONTANEOUS RELIANCE ON TRUTH
SPONTANEOUS	415 - 5	SPIRIT IS ALWAYS SPONTANEOUS
SPONTANEOUS	416 - 1	THIS ACTION IS SPONTANEOUS
SPREAD	496 - 5	SPREAD WITH BLESSEDNESS AND PEACE
SPREADS	037 - 2	SPREADS ITSELF OVER THE WHOLE
SPRING	047 - 4	SPRING INTO BEING THROUGH
SPRINGS	107 - 1	UNIVERSE FROM WHICH HE SPRINGS
SPRINGS	446 - 2	IT SPRINGS FROM WITHIN
SQUARELY	204 - 4	HITS FAIRLY AND SQUARELY
STAGNATION	067 - 2	NO STAGNATION IN SPIRIT
STAGNATION	440 - 2	STAGNATION RESULTS
STAGNATION	497 - 3	THE RESULT IS STAGNATION
STAND	292 - 3	I STAND IN THE MIDST OF ETERNAL
STAND	358 - 2	IF WE COULD STAND ASIDE
STANDARD	036 - 3	AT A HIGHER STANDARD FOR MAN
STANDARD	053 - 5	OUR STANDARD IS ONE OF PERFECTION
STANDARD	415 - 4	A UNIVERSAL STANDARD OF REALITY

STANDPOINT	097 - 2	STANDPOINT OF THE SPIRITUAL MAN
STANDPOINT	107 - 2	STANDPOINT OF THE ABSOLUTE
STANDPOINT	109 - 3	STANDPOINT OF THE DIVINITY
STANDPOINT	160 - 1	THE STANDPOINT OF THE SPIRIT
STANDPOINT	387 - 3	FROM THE HIGHER STANDPOINT
STANDS	449 - 2	STANDS REVEALED AS HE IS
STAR	096 - 4	THE MOST BEAUTIFUL PICTURE STAR
STAR	222 - 5	EACH IN HIS SEPARATE STAR
STARS	204 - 2	STARS GOVERN YOU
STARS	306 - 5	THINK HOW MANY STARS
START	309 - 2	START WITH THIS SIMPLE PROPOSITION
START	407 - 2	WE START WITH THE PREMISE
STARTING	117 - 2	WORD AS THE STARTING POINT
STARTING	148 - 2	STARTING POINT THE INHERENT NATURE
STARTING	339 - 4	STARTING POINT OF CREATION
STARTING	400 - 1	STARTING POINT OF EVERY NEW CREATION
STARTING POINT	314 - 2	SPIRIT IS THE STARTING POINT
STARVATION	476 - 5	STARVATION TAKES PLACE
STATE	180 - 2	SPIRITUAL STATE OF HIS PATIENT'S
STATE	216 - 3	STATE OF MIND
STATE	234 - 4	THE SUBJECTIVE STATE OF OUR THOUGHT
STATE	364 - 2	SUBJECTIVE STATE OF OUR THOUGHT
STATE	399 - 3	WE DO NOT DREAM WE STATE
STATE	420 - 3	HIGHER STATE OF MANIFESTATION
STATE	422 - 1	IN HIS OBJECTIVE STATE
STATE	462 - 3	RATHER A STATE OF CONSCIOUSNESS
STATE	472 - 4	A STATE OF CONSCIOUSNESS
STATEMENT	049 - 3	ANY DEFINITE STATEMENT
STATEMENT	431 - 4	STATEMENT OF THE LAW OF CAUSE
STATEMENTS	178 - 5	STATEMENTS RISE TO OBJECTIVE CONDITIONS
STATES	144 - 4	MENTAL AND SPIRITUAL STATES
STATIC	232 - 4	STATIC CONDITION WE WOULD HAVE
STATIC	233 - 4	THE STATIC FIXED INFLEXIBLE
STATING	044 - 4	BY STATING AND FEELING THAT OUR MIND
STATING	047 - 3	ACTIVELY STATING SENSING
STATING	107 - 3	STATING IN NO UNCERTAIN TERMS
STATING	166 - 2	STATING THAT THIS PERSON IS
STATING	302 - 4	STATING THAT THERE ARE NO FAILURES
STATIONARY	116 - 3	MATTER IS NOT A SOLID STATIONARY THING
STATURE	194 - 3	ADD ONE CUBIT TO HIS STATURE
STAY	278 - 4	HE SHOULD STAY WHERE HE IS
STAY	385 - 1	NATURE WILL NOT LET US STAY
STAY-AT-HOME	469 - 1	HOW HUMAN THE STAY-AT-HOME
STEADFAST	455 - 5	STEADFAST DETERMINATION TO ATTAIN
STEADFASTLY	162 - 5	STEADFASTLY TO THE KNOWLEDGE
STEADFASTLY	423 - 2	STEADFASTLY TO THE CONSTRUCTIVE
STEADFASTLY	490 - 5	LOOK STEADFASTLY INTO THIS REALITY
STEADY	178 - 4	OUR MIND MUST BE STEADY IN ITS CONVICTION
STEAM	072 - 4	STEAM TO DO HIS BIDDING
STEAM	328 - 3	CAUGHT THE WIND TRAPPED STEAM
STEP	247 - 2	EVERY STEP OF THE WAY GOD GOES
STEP BY STEP	170 - 5	STEP BY STEP BUILDING UP A CONCLUSION
STEPS	199 - 3	ONE OF THE GREATEST STEPS
STICK	403 - 4	TWO ENDS OF ONE STICK
STICKING	187 - 1	OF STICKING TO AN IDEA

STILL	217 - 1	STAND STILL AND WATCH
STILL	264 - 4	BE STILL AND KNOW THAT I AM GOD
STILL	369 - I	TO BE STILL AND KNOW
STILLNESS	257 - 2	BEING WITH PEACE AND STILLNESS
STILLNESS	445 - 7	EXPERIENCE COMES IN THE STILLNESS
STILL SMALL VOICE	364 - 1	AWAKENED BY THE STILL SMALL VOICE
STIMULATED	056 - 4	STIMULATED BY THE TRUTH
STIMULATED	152 - 5	PRAYER HAS STIMULATED
STIMULATES	369 - 1	STIMULATES ALL OF OUR ACTIONS
STIMULATES	484 - 4	STIMULATES IT INTO NEWNESS OF ACTION
STING	385 - 1	EXPERIENCE LOSES ITS STING
STOMACH	232 - 4	THE STOMACH RETAINED THE FOOD
STOMACH	256 - 2	CONDITION THAN IS THE STOMACH
STOMACH	256 - 4	DISTURBED CONDITION OF THE STOMACH
STOMACH	256 - 5	REMEDY FOR STOMACH TROUBLE IS LOVE
STOMACH	476 - 5	A FULL STOMACH WILL NEVER APPEASE
STONE	217 - 2	ROLL AWAY THE STONE
STONE	428 - 5	STONE WHEN THEY ASKED FOR BREAD
STONE	435 - 3	WE SHALL NOT RECEIVE A STONE
STONES	042 - 1	SERMONS WRITTEN IN STONES
STONES	103 - 3	SERMONS IN STONES
STOP	204 - 1	STOP AT ONCE GO BACK
STOP	304 - 1	STOP AT ONCE AND MEET
STOP	338 - 3	PERHAPS NEVER WILL STOP
STOP	394 - 1	HE CANNOT STOP DOING THIS THEREBY
STOPPED	364 - 2	STOPPED LOOKING FOR THE SPIRIT
STORE	260 - 2	STORE UP WASTE MATTER
STORE	428 - 5	WHAT STORE THEY BOUGHT THEIR GOODS
STOREHOUSE	073 - 3	MEMORY MUST BE THE STOREHOUSE
STOREHOUSE	146 - 3	STOREHOUSE OF NATURE IS FILLED
STOREHOUSE	349 - 2	THE STOREHOUSE OF MEMORY
STORES	468 - 1	WELCOME TO ALL THE DIVINE STORES
STORM	033 - 3	WHAT OUR EMOTIONAL STORM
STORY	068 - 1	WEAVE THE STORY OF TRUTH
STORY	342 - 1	ALL TELL THE SAME STORY OF REALITY
STORY	428 - 2	STORY OF JESUS OR BUDDHA
ST. PAUL	273 - 5	ST. PAUL SAID WE HAVE
STRAIGHT	303 - 1	STRAIGHT THROUGH FROM THE TRUTH
STRAIGHT	496 - 5	STRAIGHT FROM THE CENTER
STRAIGHTEN	401 - 4	WILL STRAIGHTEN OUR THOUGHT
STRAIGHTENS	236 - 4	TREATMENT STRAIGHTENS OUT CONSCIOUSNESS
STRAIN	226 - 2	STRAIN AS THEY PASS INTO SELF-EXPRESSION
STRAIN	239 - 2	TO THOUGHTS OF STRAIN
STRAIN	244 - 5	NO STRAIN OR STRUGGLE
STRAIN	247 - 3	NO SENSITIVENESS NO STRAIN
STRAIN	322 - 1	STRAIN IN KNOWING THE TRUTH
STRANGE	057 - 5	THIS WILL NOT SEEM STRANGE
STRANGE	276 - 1	DOES NOT SEEM STRANGE TO US
STRANGE	403 - 3	STRANGE THAT THE FIRST THING
STRANGE	498 - 2	STRANGE IDEAS OR DOCTRINES
STRANGLES	458 - 1	STRANGLES ITS OWN LIFE
STREAM	125 - 3	CONSCIOUSLY CONTROL THE STREAM
STREAM	217 - 2	NEGATIVE STREAM OF CONSCIOUSNESS
STREAM	246 - 3	NEGATIVE STREAM OF CAUSATION
STREAM	353 - 1	ENTER THE STREAM OF THOUGHT

STREAM	371 - 2	MAKING LIFE A CONTINUOUS STREAM
STREAM	374 - 2	INDIVIDUALIZED STREAM OF CONSCIOUSNESS
STREAM	376 - 2	CONTINUOUS STREAM OF CONSCIOUSNESS
STREAM	377 - 2	A CONSTANT STREAM OF RECOLLECTION
STREAM	384 - 2	INDIVIDUAL STREAM OF CONSCIOUSNESS
STREAM	385 - 2	INDIVIDUAL STREAM OF CONSCIOUSNESS
STREAM	386 - 2	PERSONAL STREAM OF CONSCIOUSNESS
STREAM	388 - 2	IN THE FLOWING STREAM
STREAM	422 - 2	STREAM OF CONSCIOUSNESS
STREAM	422 - 2	CONTACTING THIS STREAM MAY OBJECTIFY
STRENGTH	227 - 3	AN INFINITE STRENGTH
STRENGTH	343 - 3	STRONGER IN ITS STRENGTH
STRENGTH	418 - 1	STRENGTH TO KEEP ON WORKING
STRESS	144 - 3	STRESS PARTICULARLY ANGER
STRETCH	212 - 3	STRETCH FORTH THINE HAND
STREWN	428 - 1	STREWN THE EARTH WITH DESTRUCTION
STRIFE	146 - 3	STRIFE AND STRUGGLE ARE UNNECESSARY
STRIFE	429 - 5	STRIFE ARE OUTSIDE THE KINGDOM
STRIFE	460 - 1	STRIFE BEGETS STRIFE
STRIFE	464 - 5	STRIFE THEN HE WOULD NOT BE GOD
STRIVE	148 - 4	STRIVE TOWARD A PERFECT VISION
STRIVEN	344 - 2	CONSTANTLY STRIVEN TO LET
STRONG	463 - 1	STRONG ONLY WHEN UNITED
STRONG	475 - 2	STRONG ONLY AS WE ARE IN UNITY
STRONG	494 - 3	STRONG IN THE LORD
STRUCTURE	207 - 2	STRUCTURE OF OUR OWN THOUGHT
STRUGGLE	221 - 5	SENSE OF STRUGGLE
STRUGGLE	224 - 1	NO TENSION NO STRUGGLE
STRUGGLE	278 - 4	STRUGGLE JUST AS BEFORE
STUBBORNNESS	241 - 1	STUBBORNNESS AND RESISTANCE TO HEAL
STUBBORNNESS	260 - 2	STUBBORNNESS AND UNBELIEF
STUDENT	125 - 3	STUDENT OF METAPHYSICS
STUDENT	160 - 2	GOOD STUDENT OF THE SCIENCE OF MIND
STUDENT	184 - 5	THE STUDENT OF TRUTH
STUDENT	423 - 1	RATHER SEE A STUDENT
STUDENTS	310 - 3	ANSWER THE QUESTION OF THE STUDENTS
STUDENTS	440 - 6	SINCERE STUDENTS OF TRUTH
STUDENTS	448 - 4	SINCERE STUDENTS OF SPIRITUAL SCIENCE
STUDIED	111 - 4	STUDIED UNIVERSAL SPIRIT
STUDY	040 - 1	STUDY OF THIS SCIENCE RATIONALLY
STUDY	075 - 2	THE STUDY OF LIFE
STUDY	079 - 4	AS WE STUDY OUR OWN BEING
STUDY	246 - 4	WE SHOULD READ, STUDY
STUDY	359 - 4	STUDY HIS LIFE AS A LIVING EXAMPLE
STUDY	434 - 4	MADE A STUDY OF SOUL ANALYSIS
STUDYING	079 - 4	KNOW GOD EXCEPT BY STUDYING MAN
STUFF	026 - 3	THAT ULTIMATE STUFF
STUFF	045 - 2	OF ONE FORMLESS STUFF
STUFF	060 - 4	THAT ULTIMATE STUFF AND INTELLIGENCE
STUFF	065 - 4	THE STUFF OF ETERNITY
STUFF	100 - 3	THIS ONE STUFF IS AN INANIMATE
STUFF	116 - 2	STUFF FROM WHICH A BRICK IS MADE
STUFF	117 - 1	STUFF WHICH MAY BE OPERATED
STUFF	117 - 2	STUFF WHICH HAS NO MIND
STUFF	129 - 1	FORMLESS STUFF IN THE UNIVERSE

STUFF	129 - 2	STUFF FROM WHICH FORM
STUFF	208 - 3	STUFF FROM WHICH ALL THINGS
STUFF	242 - 3	THE VERY STUFF OF WHICH
STUFF	310 - 2	STUFF OF WHICH NO ONE KNOWS THE NATURE
STUFF	345 - 4	A FINE WHITE BRILLIANT STUFF
STUFF	370 - 3	WE ARE MADE OF ETERNAL STUFF
STUFF	393 - 3	AN UNFORMED STUFF AN ENERGY
STUFF	396 - 1	STUFF THAT FORMS THE UNIVERSE
STUPENDOUS	332 - 5	TO MAKE THIS STUPENDOUS DISCOVERY
SUBCONSCIOUS	029 - 1	THE SUBCONSCIOUS OR SUBJECTIVE STATE
SUBCONSCIOUS	030 - 4	GREAT AS THE SUBCONSCIOUS IS
SUBCONSCIOUS	090 - 3	THE TERM SUBCONSCIOUS MIND
SUBCONSCIOUS	101 - 5	IS ENTIRELY SUBCONSCIOUS
SUBCONSCIOUS	114 - 3	SUBCONSCIOUS DOES NOT MEAN UNCONSCIOUS
SUBCONSCIOUS	320 - 3	MAY BE A SUBCONSCIOUS THOUGHT
SUBCONSCIOUS	322 - 2	THOUGHT CONTROLS THE SUBCONSCIOUS
SUBCONSCIOUS	342 - 1	SUBCONSCIOUS OR RELATIVE FIRST CAUSE
SUBJECT	034 - 1	SUBJECT TO THE USE OF THE LEAST
SUBJECT	109 - 3	SUBJECT TO THE LAW OF REALITY
SUBJECT	115 - 1	SUBJECT TO THE CONSCIOUS SPIRIT
SUBJECT	132 - 7	EVERYTHING ELSE IS SUBJECT TO SPIRIT
SUBJECT	196 - 2	MAN IS SUBJECT TO THE LAW
SUBJECT	416 - 1	AT THE SAME TIME SUBJECT TO
SUBJECT	469 - 3	WE ARE SUBJECT TO THE CAUSES
SUBJECTIFIED	124 - 4	THOUGHT THEN BECOMES SUBJECTIFIED
SUBJECTIFIES	133 - 4	AS MAN THINKS HE SUBJECTIFIES
SUBJECTIFYING	304 - 5	KEEP ON SUBJECTIFYING THOUGHT
SUBJECTIVE	029 - 1	AND THE SUBJECTIVE OR UNCONSCIOUS
SUBJECTIVE	029 - 2	IN THE SUBJECTIVE MIND OF MAN
SUBJECTIVE	029 - 3	WHAT HE CALLS HIS SUBJECTIVE MIND
SUBJECTIVE	030 - 2	WE CALL THE SUBJECTIVE MIND
SUBJECTIVE	030 - 4	SUPERIOR TO THE SUBJECTIVE
SUBJECTIVE	031 - 3	THE SUBJECTIVE IS A WORLD OF LAW
SUBJECTIVE	077 - 4	WE CALL OUR SUBJECTIVE MIND
SUBJECTIVE	078 - 2	AS WE EXAMINE THE SUBJECTIVE
SUBJECTIVE	083 - 2	SUBJECTIVE TO THE SPIRIT
SUBJECTIVE	091 - 3	SOUL IS SUBJECTIVE INTELLIGENCE
SUBJECTIVE	093 - 3	MY SUBJECTIVE MIND
SUBJECTIVE	119 - 2	SUBJECTIVE TENDENCY TOWARD CONDITIONS
SUBJECTIVE	197 - 2	SUBJECTIVE TO THE RACE CONCIOUSNESS
SUBJECTIVE	218 - 3	REALIZATION BECOMES SUBJECTIVE
SUBJECTIVE	220 - 4	IF THERE WERE NO SUBJECTIVE DOUBTS
SUBJECTIVE	234 - 4	THE SUBJECTIVE STATE OF OUR THOUGHT
SUBJECTIVE ·	237 - 3	BUT ONE SUBJECTIVE MIND
SUBJECTIVE	287 - 2	SUBJECTIVE REMEMBRANCE ALREADY SET
SUBJECTIVE	300 - 2	SUBJECTIVE STATE OF A MAN'S THOUGHT
SUBJECTIVE	303 - 1	HIS SUBJECTIVE THOUGHT MAY BE DENYING
SUBJECTIVE	350 - 3	ALMOST ENTIRELY SUBJECTIVE
SUBJECTIVE	354 - 2	REALM OF SUBJECTIVE CAUSATION
SUBJECTIVE	376 - 4	IN A PURELY SUBJECTIVE STATE
SUBJECTIVE	391 - 5	ON THE SUBJECTIVE SIDE OF LIFE
SUBJECTIVE	392 - 1	THOUGH HIS SUBJECTIVE MIND
SUBJECTIVE	396 - 4	ALWAYS SUBJECTIVE TO MAN'S DESIRE
SUBJECTIVE	397 - 2	GOD AS SUBJECTIVE MIND IS LAW
SUBJECTIVE	401- 2	UNCONSCIOUS OR SUBJECTIVE STATE

SUBJECTIVE	405 - 4	UNDER SUBJECTION TO THE SPIRIT
SUBJECTIVE	412 - 2	REFLECTION OF THE SUBJECTIVE STATE
SUBJECTIVE	416 - 2	CHARACTERISTIC OF THE SUBJECTIVE LAW
SUBJECTIVE	422 - 1	SUBJECTIVE SIDE OF LIFE HE IS UNIVERSAL
SUBJECTIVE	489 - 7	SUBJECTIVE STATE OF THOUGHT
SUBJECTIVE	490 - 3	SUBJECTIVE STATE OF OUR THOUGHT
SUBJECTIVELY	077 - 1	IT IS SUBJECTIVELY UNIFIED
SUBJECTIVE MIND	029 - 2	USE OF THAT GREATER SUBJECTIVE MIND
SUBJECTIVE MIND	029 - 4	THERE ARE NOT TWO SUBJECTIVE MINDS
SUBJECTIVE MIND	029 - 4	BUT ONE SUBJECTIVE MIND
SUBJECTIVE MIND	029 - 4	WHAT WE CALL OUR SUBJECTIVE MIND
SUBJECTIVE MIND	031 - 4	THE SUBJECTIVE MIND IS LAW
SUBJECTIVE MIND	088 - 1	SUBJECTIVE MIND IS THE MEDIUM
SUBJECTIVE MIND	093 - 3	NO SUCH THING AS YOUR SUBJECTIVE MIND
SUBJECTIVE MIND	112 - 2	SUBJECTIVE MIND REPRODUCES ALL
SUBJECTIVE MIND	112 - 2	BELONGING TO UNIVERSAL SUBJECTIVE MIND
SUBJECTIVE MIND	208 - 3	SUBJECTIVE MIND IN THE UNIVERSE
SUBJECTIVE MIND	391 - 5	THE SUBJECTIVE MIND OF MAN
SUBJECTIVE NATURE	112 - 2	IS CALLED THE SUBJECTIVE NATURE
SUBJECTIVE TENDENCY	119 - 2	SUBJECTIVE TENDENCY TOWARD ULTIMATE GOOD
SUBJECTIVE WORLD	112 - 3	UNIVERSE IN THE SUBJECTIVE WORLD
SUBJECTIVITY	077 - 4	OF A UNIVERSAL SUBJECTIVITY
SUBJECTIVITY	079 - 1	DEALING WITH SUBJECTIVITY
SUBJECTIVITY	096 - 3	SUBJECTIVITY CAN NEVER REJECT
SUBJECTIVITY	118 - 3	SUBJECTIVITY IS ENTIRELY RECEPTIVE
SUBJECTIVITY	196 - 5	INTO THE UNIVERSAL SUBJECTIVITY
SUBJECTIVITY	224 - 2	KIND OF THOUGHTS INTO SUBJECTIVITY
SUBJECTIVITY	355 - 2	TEACHES US A LESSON IN SUBJECTIVITY
SUBJECTIVITY	380 - 3	COMMUNICATE WITH THE SUBJECTIVITY
SUBLIMATE	253 - 1	WHICH HE IS TRYING TO SUBLIMATE
SUBLIMATING	455 - 4	SUBLIMATING AN OLD IDEA
SUBLIME	141 - 2	MORE SUBLIME CONCEPT OF BEING
SUBLIME	160 - 2	THE SUBLIME MINDS OF ALL AGES
SUBLIME	388 - 4	SUBLIME A GLORIOUS EXPERIENCE
SUBMERGED	381 - 4	FACULTIES TO BECOME SUBMERGED
SUBMISSION	268 - 4	NOT A SUBMISSION
SUBSCRIBED	383 - 3	HAVE SUBSCRIBED TO SOME CREED
SUBSISTS	415 - 3	LIVES AND EVERYTHING SUBSISTS
SUBSTANCE	048 - 2	WE MUST CREATE THE SUBSTANCE
SUBSTANCE	052 - 2	AN INTELLIGENT FORCE AND SUBSTANCE
SUBSTANCE	064 - 2	IT HAS SUBSTANCE WITHIN ITSELF
SUBSTANCE	064 - 2	ALSO SELF-EXISTENT SUBSTANCE
SUBSTANCE	070 - 1	GOD DID NOT MAKE SUBSTANCE
SUBSTANCE	070 - 1	OF INFINITE SUBSTANCE
SUBSTANCE	084 - 4	SUBSTANCE INTO FORM
SUBSTANCE	091 - 2	THINK OF THE SUBSTANCE OF SOUL
SUBSTANCE	097 - 3	WE CALL UNDIFFERENTIATED SUBSTANCE
SUBSTANCE	114 - 2	INVISIBLE BUT THE SUBSTANCE
SUBSTANCE	116 - 2	ONE UNIVERSAL SUBSTANCE WHOSE BUSINESS
SUBSTANCE	116 - 3	SUBSTANCE IN THE UNIVERSE
SUBSTANCE	157 - 2	OUT OF THE ONE SUBSTANCE
SUBSTANCE	228 - 3	BURNING UP OF SUBSTANCE
SUBSTANCE	230 - 5	YOUR FAITH IN SPIRITUAL SUBSTANCE
SUBSTANCE	235 - 5	THERE IS ONLY ONE SUBSTANCE
SUBSTANCE	236 - 2	NO VITALITY NO SUBSTANCE AND NO POWER

SUBSTANCE	240 - 3	BODY IS PURE SPIRIT SUBSTANCE
SUBSTANCE	242 - 3	AN ETERNAL AND PERFECT SUBSTANCE
SUBSTANCE	247 - 1	BODY IS PURE SPIRITUAL SUBSTANCE
SUBSTANCE	248 - 2	PURE SPIRITUAL SUBSTANCE
SUBSTANCE	254 - 1	THE GOD SUBSTANCE OF MY BODY
SUBSTANCE	259 - 4	A SPIRITUAL IDEA OF SUBSTANCE
SUBSTANCE	262 - 3	SPIRIT IS SUBSTANCE
SUBSTANCE	268 - 1	SUBSTANCE CANNOT INCREASE
SUBSTANCE	279 - 1	SUBSTANCE, INTELLIGENCE, TRUTH AND POWER
SUBSTANCE	284 - 4	FAITH IS NOT HOPE, IT IS SUBSTANCE
SUBSTANCE	292 - 2	BRING OUT THE IDEA OF SUBSTANCE
SUBSTANCE	292 - 2	THAT SUBSTANCE IS SPIRIT
SUBSTANCE	305 - 5	DEALING WITH THE SUBSTANCE
SUBSTANCE	323 - 3	THERE IS ONE INFINITE SUBSTANCE
SUBSTANCE	345 - 4	HAVE ALSO SEEN SUBSTANCE
SUBSTANCE	345 - 4	A SUBSTANCE INDESTRUCTIBLE
SUBSTANCE	393 - 3	ESSENCE OF MIND IS SUBSTANCE
SUBSTANCE	402 - 3	ITS NOTHING IS REALLY THE SUBSTANCE
SUBSTANCE	415 - 1	SUBSTANCE OF FAITH IN ONESELF
SUBSTANCE	462 - 5	HIS SUBSTANCE WITH RIOTOUS LIVING
SUBSTANCE	470 - 6	SUBSTANCE AND SUPPLY EXIST
SUBSTANTIATE	385 - 3	SUBSTANTIATE THE CLAIM OF IMMORTALITY
SUB-STRATUM	143 - 1	SUB-STRATUM OF OUR MENTAL LIFE
SUBTLE	048 - 2	THE SUBTLE ENERGY OF SPIRIT
SUBTLE	049 - 4	IT IS A SUBTLE ILLUSION
SUBTLE	053 - 3	SUBTLE POWER OF MIND
SUBTLE	207 - 1	SUBTLE THOUGHTS ARE
SUBTLE	296 - 2	FILLED WITH THAT SUBTLE SOMETHING
SUBTLE	304 - 1	THOUGHT IS VERY SUBTLE
SUBTLE	374 - 4	THROUGH A MORE SUBTLE ONE
SUBTLE	378 - 3	ETHERIC AND SUBTLE QUALITIES OF THE SOUL
SUBTLE	450 - 2	SUBTLE REALITY WHICH LIES HIDDEN
SUCCEED	275 - 3	WE REALLY SUCCEED
SUCCEED	380 - 1	THAT THEY OFTEN SUCCEED
SUCCEEDS	282 - 1	HE SUCCEEDS IN BEING A FAILURE
SUCCESS	047 - 1	THE SECRET OF SUCCESS
SUCCESS	207 - 1	TO A GREATER SUCCESS
SUCCESS	254 - 4	POSSIBILITY OF SUCCESS
SUCCESS	262 - 3	SUCCESS IN FINANCIAL MATTERS
SUCCESS	263 - 1	SHOULD BE A SUCCESS
SUCCESS	263 - 3	THAT I DO SHALL BE A SUCCESS
SUCCESS	263 - 4	RIGHT ACTION IS SUCCESS
SUCCESS	270 - 6	MAN IS ALREADY A SUCCESS
SUCCESS	277 - 4	SUCCESS AND HAPPINESS ARE OURS
SUCCESS	296 - 2	SUCCESSFUL PEOPLE THINK ABOUT SUCCESS
SUCCESS	300 - 4	IN HIS BUSINESS MORE SUCCESS
SUCCESS	301 - 2	SO OUR SUCCESS IN BUSINESS
SUCCESS	302 - 2	YOU ARE A SUCCESS NOW
SUCCESS	400 - 2	SUCCESS WILL BECOME HABITUAL
SUCCESS	400 - 3	TREAT HIMSELF FOR GENERAL SUCCESS
SUCCESS	403 - 4	FAILURE AND SUCCESS ARE BUT TWO ENDS
SUCCESS	412 - 1	ABUNDANCE AND WITH SUCCESS
SUCCESS	450 - 5	FROM SUCCESS TO GREATER SUCCESS
SUCCESSFUL	262 - 3	WE SHOULD BE SUCCESSFUL
SUCCESSFUL	263 - 4	SUCCESSFUL IN ALL MY UNDERTAKINGS

SUCCESSFUL	296 - 2	YOU NEVER SAW A SUCCESSFUL MAN
SUCCESSFUL	302 - 2	THAT THE SUCCESSFUL BUSINESS MAN
SUCCESSFUL	400 - 2	IDEA OF A SUCCESSFUL LIFE
SUCCESSFUL	450 - 3	SUCCESSFUL MAN IS SURE
SUFFER	037 - 1	CONDITIONS FROM WHICH WE SUFFER
SUFFER	109 - 3	GOD NEVER INTENDED MAN TO SUFFER
SUFFER	160 - 3	SUFFER BECAUSE WE ARE NOT
SUFFER	244 - 4	DO NOT DENY THAT PEOPLE SUFFER
SUFFER	253 - 4	COMPELLED TO SUFFER
SUFFER	409 - 1	MAN TO SUFFER PAIN OR ANGUISH
SUFFER	499 - 2	SUFFER FROM OUR OWN FOOLISHNESS
SUFFER	502 - 3	IT IS RIGHT THAT WE SHOULD SUFFER
SUFFER	502 - 3	SUFFER FOR OUR PAST MISTAKES
SUFFER	502 - 5	SUFFER AS LONG AS WE MAKE MISTAKES
SUFFERED	033 - 3	ALONE HAS WROUGHT AND SUFFERED
SUFFERING	032 - 3	EVIL SUFFERING AND UNCERTAINTY
SUFFERING	107 - 4	THROUGH SUFFERING AND PAIN
SUFFERING	108 - 1	SUFFERING IS NOT GOD-ORDAINED
SUFFERING	109 - 3	SUFFERING UNIVERSE, A SUFFERING GOD
SUFFERING	109 - 3	SUFFERING MAY BE SALUTARY IN THAT IT LEADS
SUFFERING	109 - 3	SUFFERING IS THE RESULT
SUFFERING	156 - 3	WORLD IS SUFFERING FROM ONE BIG FEAR
SUFFERING	160 - 3	IF THERE WERE A SUFFERING GOD
SUFFERING	160 - 3	SUFFERING GOD IS AN IMPOSSIBILITY
SUFFERING	185 - 2	FILLED WITH SUFFERING
SUFFERING	191 - 3	OVERCOME SUFFERING IS GOOD
SUFFERING	203 - 2	SUFFERING IT CAUSES
SUFFERING	336 - 4	SUFFERING IS MAN-MADE
SUFFERING	336 - 4	WE HAVE HAD ENOUGH SUFFERING
SUFFERING	412 - 1	BELIEVE IN SUFFERING WE SHALL SUFFER
SUFFERING	459 - 5	SUFFERING FOR RIGHTEOUSNESS' SAKE
SUFFERING	485 - 5	SUFFERING SHOULD TEACH US
SUFFICIENT	346 - 2	CONCEPT OF GOD IS SUFFICIENT
SUFFICIENT	431 - 3	PRESENCE IS SUFFICIENT FOR ALL
SUFFICIENT	432 - 4	WHICH WE LIVE IS SUFFICIENT
SUGGEST	199 - 2	SUGGEST A THOUGHT
SUGGEST	262 - 1	IT CANNOT SUGGEST
SUGGESTION	029 - 2	SUGGESTION HAS PROVED
SUGGESTION	056 - 5	SUGGESTION OF AGE POVERTY
SUGGESTION	120 - 2	SUGGESTION HELD IN CREATIVE MIND
SUGGESTION	120 - 2	SUGGESTION OF GOOD IT WOULD CONSTRUCT
SUGGESTION	194 - 2	AN ADVERSE SUGGESTION
SUGGESTION	199 - 2	DIFFERENTIATE BETWEEN SUGGESTION
SUGGESTION	226 - 3	LAW OF RACE SUGGESTION
SUGGESTION	309 - 5	NOT WITH MENTAL SUGGESTION
SUGGESTION	319 - 3	SUGGESTION WHICH HAS NO POWER
SUGGESTION	421 - 4	MENTAL SUGGESTION OPERATES THROUGH
SUGGESTIONS	088 - 1	INHERITED TENDENCIES AND RACE SUGGESTIONS
SUGGESTIONS	251 - 2	EVEN TO NEGATIVE SUGGESTIONS
SUGGESTIVE	262 - 1	ANY SUGGESTIVE POWER
SUM	300 - 2	SUM TOTAL OF HIS THINKING
SUM TOTAL	038 - 3	SUM TOTAL OF THAT BELIEF
SUM TOTAL	322 - 2	THE SUM TOTAL OF ALL BELIEFS
SUM TOTAL	361 - 5	SUM TOTAL OF ALL THESE IDEAS
SUN	028 - 1	SUN TO RISE ON THE EVIL

SUN	388 - 1	SPIRITUAL SUN SHALL NEVER SET
SUN	388 - 2	MEETS HIM IN THE RISING SUN
SUN	430 - 5	HIS SUN TO SHINE ALIKE UPON ALL
SUNLIGHT	128 - 4	SUNLIGHT OF ETERNAL TRUTH
SUNLIGHT	188 - 3	THE SUNLIGHT OF ETERNAL TRUTH
SUNSHINE	152 - 4	SUNSHINE RAISES OUR SPIRITS
SUNSHINE	258 - 4	THE DIVINE IN SUNSHINE
SUNSHINE	258 - 5	WITH SUNSHINE AND SHADOW
SUNSHINE	261 - 2	SUNSHINE OF ETERNAL TRUTH
SUNSHINE	411 - 3	MOVE INTO THE SUNSHINE
SUPERFICIAL	457 - 2	SUPERFICIAL READING OF THIS PASSAGE
SUPERIMPOSED	442 - 1	NOT A THING SUPERIMPOSED
SUPERINTENDETH	418 - 5	SUPERINTENDETH THE ANIMATE
SUPERIOR	030 - 4	CONSCIOUS MIND IS SUPERIOR
SUPERIOR	159 - 5	SUPERIOR TO THE CONDITION
SUPERIOR	302 - 1	WE RISE SUPERIOR TO THE WORLD
SUPERIOR	414 - 2	IS SUPERIOR TO THE INTELLECT
SUPERLATIVE	312 - 1	THE SUPERLATIVE CANNOT BE
SUPERNATURAL	027 - 5	THERE IS NOTHING SUPERNATURAL
SUPERNATURAL	027 - 5	TODAY SEEMS SUPERNATURAL
SUPERNATURAL	075 - 2	NOTHING SUPERNATURAL ANYWHERE
SUPERNATURAL	075 - 2	TODAY SEEMS TO US SUPERNATURAL
SUPER-SENSITIVENESS	256 - 4	SUPER-SENSITIVENESS IS NOTHING
SUPERSTITION	075 - 1	CERTAINLY WITH NO SUPERSTITION
SUPERSTITION	272 - 4	GREAT DEAL OF SUPERSTITION
SUPERSTITION	316 - 2	ALL SUPERSTITION IS IGNORANCE
SUPERSTITION	437 - 4	THIS WOULD BE SUPERSTITION
SUPERSTITION	442 - 4	SWALLOWING MOUNTAINS OF SUPERSTITION
SUPERSTITION	494 - 4	FALSE BELIEF AND SUPERSTITION
SUPERSTITION	499 - 3	IS AN ILLEGITIMATE CHILD OF SUPERSTITION
SUPERSTITIOUS	028 - 1	IT IS SUPERSTITIOUS TO BELIEVE THAT GOD
SUPERSTITIOUS	079 - 3	SUPERSTITIOUS ABOUT OUR USE OF THE LAW
SUPERSTITIOUS	079 - 3	SUCH A SUPERSTITIOUS REACTION
SUPERSTITIOUS	192 - 1	IN ANY WAY SUPERSTITIOUS ABOUT THIS
SUPERSTITIOUS	220 - 6	SUPERSTITIOUS FOR YOU ARE DEALING
SUPERSTITIOUS	316 - 1	WE SHOULD NOT BE SUPERSTITIOUS
SUPERSTITIOUS	316 - 2	THIS IS A SUPERSTITIOUS REACTION
SUPERSTRUCTURE	147 - 5	OUR ENTIRE SUPERSTRUCTURE RESTS
SUPER-TENSION	248 - 2	NO TENSION NOR SUPER-TENSION
SUPPLICATING	150 - 5	SUPPLICATING AS THOUGH GOD
SUPPLIED	496 - 5	SUPPLIED IN EVERY NEED
SUPPLY	047 - 4	SUPPLY THE AVENUE THROUGH WHICH
SUPPLY	138 - 3	DEMONSTRATING SUPPLY
SUPPLY	205 - 2	SUPPLY A SPIRITUAL CONSCIOUSNESS
SUPPLY	228 - 1	FLOWS IN UNLIMITED SUPPLY
SUPPLY	259 - 3	SUBSTANCE AND SUPPLY
SUPPLY	263 - 4	ALWAYS TAKING THE FORM OF SUPPLY
SUPPLY	405 - 1	HE IS SUBSTANCE AND SUPPLY
SUPPLY	470 - 6	SUPPLY EXIST ETERNALLY
SUPPLY	496 - 5	GOD WILL SUPPLY
SUPPLY AND DEMAND	174 - 2	SUPPLY AND DEMAND ARE ONE
SUPPLYING	303 - 4	SPIRIT IS SUPPLYING YOU
SUPPORTING	452 - 6	STANDS THE SPIRITUAL SUPPORTING IT
SUPPOSE	064 - 2	SUPPOSE THAT IT HAS SUBSTANCE
SUPPOSE	346 - 1	SUPPOSE A LARGE GROUP OF PEOPLE

SUPPOSE	436 - 4	TO SUPPOSE AN UNEXPRESSED EXISTENCE
SUPPOSE	457 - 2	SUPPOSE THAT THIS EARTH PROVIDES
SUPPOSE	499 - 5	WHAT WE CANNOT DO WE ONLY SUPPOSE
SUPPOSED	377 - 3	SPIRITS OF THE SUPPOSED DEAD
SUPPOSES	126 - 2	SUPPOSES THAT HE LETS GO OF THOSE THOUGHTS
SUPPOSITION	175 - 6	ENTIRELY UPON THE SUPPOSITION
SUPPOSITION	267 - 3	BASED ENTIRELY UPON THE SUPPOSITION
SUPPOSITIONAL	051 - 2	THEY ARE SUPPOSITIONAL
SUPPOSITIONAL	453 - 6	THAT A SUPPOSITIONAL DEVIL DIVIDES
SUPPOSITIONAL	499 - 1	SUPPOSITIONAL OPPOSITE TO GOOD
SUPPOSITIONAL	499 - 5	UNUSED KNOWLEDGE IS SUPPOSITIONAL
SUPPRESS	501 - 6	SUPPRESS THEM AND CREATE MORBIDNESS
SUPPRESSED	237 - 1	RESULT OF SUPPRESSED EMOTIONS
SUPPRESSED	238 - 4	REPRESSED OR SUPPRESSED
SUPREMACY	051 - 2	SUPREMACY OF SPIRITUAL THOUGHT
SUPREMACY	056 - 3	THE SUPREMACY OF SPIRITUAL THOUGHT
SUPREME	358 - 3	SUPREME MOMENT OF REALIZATION
SUPREME	365 - 1	SUPREME INTELLIGENCE OF THE UNIVERSE
SUPREME	478 - 4	LOVE REIGNS SUPREME
SUPREME GUEST	495 - 3	ENTHRONED AS THE SUPREME GUEST
SUPREME MIND	285 - 2	LIKE NATURE TO THE SUPREME KIND
SUPREME PERSONALITY	330 - 5	SUPREME PERSONALITY OF THAT WHICH
SURE	268 - 3	WE MAY BE SURE GOD IS FOR US
SURE	386 - 3	SURE ONLY OF MY OWN
SURE	486 - 2	MAY BE SURE HE IS EVER WITH US
SURE	494 - 3	SURE OF THE PRINCIPLE OF LIFE
SURENESS	110 - 3	SLOWNESS BUT ALWAYS WITH SURENESS
SURFACE	077 - 3	THIS ARISES TO THE SURFACE
SURFACE	351 - 2	SURFACE OF CONSCIOUS THOUGHT
SURFACE	353 - 1	NEVER COME TO THE SURFACE
SURGE	319 - 3	SURGE OF FEAR COMES OVER HIM
SURGEON	219 - 2	WE CALL IN A SURGEON
SURGES	184 - 2	SURGES AROUND THEM
SURGING	306 - 1	SURGING TO EXPRESS ITSELF
SURPASSES	349 - 2	SURPASSES THE OBJECTIVE FACULTIES
SURPRISED	402 - 2	SHALL BE SURPRISED AT THE RESULTS
SURRENDER	222 - 3	WILLING TO SURRENDER THAT CAUSE
SURRENDER	222 - 3	HE WILL NOT SURRENDER
SURRENDER	405 - 4	SURRENDER OF ITSELF TO THE SPIRIT
SURRENDERS	405 - 4	LOVE SURRENDERS ITSELF
SURROUNDED	052 - 4	SURROUNDED BY AN INTELLIGENT FORCE
SURROUNDED	177 - 1	SURROUNDED BY A UNIVERSAL MIND
SURROUNDED	246 - 4	SURROUNDED BY PERFECT LIFE
SURROUNDED	267 - 3	SURROUNDED BY A UNIVERSAL MIND
SURROUNDED	294 - 2	SURROUNDED BY A THOUGHT ATMOSPHERE
SURROUNDED	439 - 5	ARE SURROUNDED BY AN ATMOSPHERE
SURROUNDED	458 - 4	SURROUNDED BY A UNIVERSAL LAW
SURROUNDED	476 - 3	SURROUNDED BY A SPIRITUAL CONSCIOUSNESS
SUSPICION	231 - 2	SUSPICION MAKE THE EYES SHIFTY
SUSPICIOUS	033 - 1	SUSPICIOUS OF PEOPLE AROUND US
SUSTAIN	056 - 4	SUSTAIN ME WITHOUT EFFORT
SUSTAINED	255 - 1	SUSTAINED IN A DEEP INNER CALM
SUSTAINER	404 - 5	GOD IS THE GIVER AND THE SUSTAINER
SUSTAINING	158 - 2	PROVING ITS SUSTAINING POWER
SUSTAINING	168 - 1	GUIDING AND SUSTAINING

SUSTENANCE	232 - 4	NECESSARY TO THEIR SUSTENANCE
SWALLOWED	246 - 1	PAST IS SWALLOWED UP
SWALLOWED	491 - 8	BE SWALLOWED UP OF LIFE
SWALLOWING	442 - 4	SWALLOWING MOUNTAINS OF SUPERSTITION
SWAYED	418 - 2	SWAYED BY THE OPINIONS OF OTHERS
SWEDENBORG	341 - 2	WITH WHAT SWEDENBORG CALLED
SWINE	463 - 4	HIS FIELDS TO FEED SWINE
SWINE	464 - 1	FEED THE DESPISED SWINE
SWING	477 - 2	SWING FROM INSPIRATION TO ACTION
SWORD	127 - 3	TAKE THE SWORD SHALL PERISH
SWORD	460 - 2	SWORD IN HATE AVARICE OR LUST
SWORD	495 - 4	SWORD OF THE SPIRIT IS
SYMBOL	155 - 2	IT IS NOT THE SYMBOL
SYMBOL	253 - 1	FOOD IS A SYMBOL
SYMBOL	483 - 1	SYMBOL POINTS TO THE SPIRITUAL
SYMBOLIC	064 - 3	AN ALLEGORY OR SYMBOLIC STORY
SYMBOLISM	463 - 4	SYMBOLISM HERE IS MOST INTERESTING
SYMBOLIZE	037 - 1	SYMBOLIZE HEAVEN AND HELL
SYMBOLIZE	449 - 5	PARENTS SYMBOLIZE THIS HEAVENLY PARENTAGE
SYMBOLIZED	155 - 2	THE IDEA SYMBOLIZED
SYMBOLIZED	473 - 1	SYMBOLIZED BY THE SERPENT
SYMBOLIZES	410 - 3	ADAM SYMBOLIZES EVERYMAN'S EXPERIENCE
SYMBOLIZES	462 - 3	IT SYMBOLIZES THE DESCENT OF THE SOUL
SYMBOLIZES	471 - 6	WATER SYMBOLIZES OUR RECOGNITION
SYMBOLIZES	484 - 3	THE CARNAL MIND SYMBOLIZES
SYMBOLS	063 - 1	DOES NOT UNDERSTAND SYMBOLS
SYMBOLS	313 - 4	JESUS' WORDS WERE SYMBOLS OF
SYMPATHETIC	238 - 4	SYMPATHETIC NATURE OF MAN
SYMPATHETIC	348 - 2	SYMPATHETIC VIBRATION WITH EACH OTHER
SYMPATHETICALLY	349 - 3	SYMPATHETICALLY INCLINED TOWARD
SYMPATHETICALLY	353 - 1	WE SYMPATHETICALLY VIBRATE TOWARD
SYMPATHIES	055 - 4	BECAUSE OF OUR SYMPATHIES
SYMPATHY	199 - 4	THE PRACTITIONER, THROUGH SYMPATHY
SYMPATHY	238 - 2	SYMPATHY ELSE HE WILL DO
SYMPATHY	238 - 2	SYMPATHY WITH THE DISEASE
SYMPATHY	238 - 2	SYMPATHY AND EXERCISES IT
SYMPATHY	434 - 1	SYMPATHY AND HELPFULNESS TOWARD ALL
SYMPTOMS	249 - 4	NOT DEALING WITH OBJECTIVE SYMPTOMS
SYNCHRONIZES	251 - 4	SYNCHRONIZES ALL IMPULSES
SYSTEM	064 - 4	ANY SPECIAL WORLD SYSTEM
SYSTEM	166 - 4	UNIVERSE IS A SPIRITUAL SYSTEM
SYSTEM	260 - 2	SYSTEM IS SPIRITUAL AND DIVINELY
SYSTEM	284 - 3	SYSTEM IS PERFECT
SYSTEM	317 - 1	SPIRITUAL SYSTEM IS PERFECT
SYSTEMATIC	281 - 2	A MORE INTELLIGENT, A MORE SYSTEMATIC
SYSTEMATIC	282 - 3	SYSTEMATIC USE OF THE LAW
SYSTEMATIZED	312 - 3	ORGANIZED, SYSTEMATIZED KNOWLEDGE
SYSTEMS	167 - 2	THE OLD SYSTEMS OF THOUGHT

T

TABLE	033 - 3	NATURE'S TABLE IS EVER FILLED
TABLE	374 - 3	THE TABLE HAS FOUR LEGS

TACTICS	232 - 4	AVERAGE TACTICS OF MAN
TAGORE	344 - 1	TAGORE IN SEEKING TO EXPLAIN THIS
TAKE	040 - 4	GIVE US ONLY WHAT WE CAN TAKE
TAKE	042 - 4	GIVE US WHAT WE ARE ABLE TO TAKE
TAKE	217 - 2	ARISE, O SON, AND TAKE
TAKE	384 - 3	TAKE ANYTHING WITH US
TAKE	445 - 6	BUT WE MUST TAKE
TAKE	461 - 1	TAKE ONLY THAT TO WHICH
TAKEN	449 - 6	FROM HIM SHALL BE TAKEN
TAKES HOLD	309 - 3	TAKES HOLD OF OUR CONSCIOUSNESS
TAKING	151 - 4	THIS TAKING IS MENTAL
TAKING	460 - 6	TAKING IS A MENTAL AND SPIRITUAL
TAKING	498 - 3	TAKING IS A MENTAL ACT
TALE	055 - 3	TALE OF WOE ABOUT HARD TIMES
TALE	394 - 1	THE TALE OF GOOD AND EVIL
TALENT	305 - 2	TALENT IS DIVINELY SUSTAINED
TALK	055 - 3	THEN HE CAN TALK WITH ANYONE
TALK	055 - 4	REFUSE TO TALK ABOUT
TALK	291 - 2	TALK TO YOURSELF NOT TO THE WORLD
TALK	322 - 4	TALK ABOUT LIMITATION OR POVERTY
TALK	333 - 6	GOD MUST BE, CAN TALK WITH MAN
TALK	467 - 2	WE TALK ABOUT SIN OR EVIL
TALK	499 - 5	IDLE TALK ABOUT OUR UNDERSTANDING
TANGIBIE	026 - 5	WHAT IS TANGIBLE OTHER THAN RESULTS
TANGIBLE	051 - 2	METAPHYSICS SEEMS LESS TANGIBLE
TANGIBLE	187 - 1	IT BECOMES A TANGIBLE REALITY
TANGIBLE	198 - 2	TANGIBLE SPECIFIC OPERATION
TANGIBLE	309 - 4	TANGIBLE THINGS COULD BE MADE
TANGIBLE	374 - 5	SHALL WE HAVE TANGIBLE BODIES
TAP	394 - 3	WE CAN TAP THE RESERVOIRS
TAPS	045 - 1	CONSCIOUSNESS TAPS THE SAME SOURCE
TAPS	045 - 4	TAPS THE SAME PRINCIPLE
TASKMASTER	031 - 1	TASKMASTER TO THE UNWISE
TASTE	101 - 4	TOUCH, TASTE, FEEL, HEAR
TASTE	487 - 5	TASTE THE WATERS OF REALITY
TASTING	474 - 4	LOGICAL OUTCOME OF TASTING OF DUAL
TAUGHT	090 - 1	TAUGHT BY MOST
TAUGHT	306 - 4	TAUGHT THAT THERE ARE ALWAYS TWO
TAUGHT	327 - 2	WHO COULD HAVE TAUGHT SUCH MEN
TAUGHT	327 - 2	INDEED TAUGHT OF GOD
TEACH	167 - 2	DO NOT TEACH HOW TO GIVE A TREATMENT
TEACH	266 - 2	TEACH THAT YOU CAN GET WHAT YOU WANT
TEACH	423 - 1	EASIER TO TEACH THE TRUTH
TEACH	427 - 3	WHAT DID JESUS TEACH
TEACHER	186 - 3	THE GREATEST TEACHER WHO EVER LIVED
TEACHER	186 - 4	GREATEST TEACHER BECAME THE SAVIOR
TEACHER	327 - 2	SPIRIT ALONE WAS THEIR TEACHER
TEACHER	362 - 2	LOOKING FOR ANOTHER GREAT TEACHER
TEACHES	237 - 4	TEACHES HIM HOW TO BE HARMONIOUS
TEACHING	121 - 3	OUR TEACHING IS THAT MAN
TEACHING	268 - 4	THIS TEACHING SHOULD NOT BE CONFUSED
TEACHING	361 - 5	HIS WHOLE TEACHING WAS
TEACHING	428 - 2	IF HIS TEACHING IS A TRUE ONE
TEACHING	435 - 3	DEFINITE TEACHING REGARDING PRAYER
TEACHING	450 - 3	TEACHING OF JESUS IS TO HAVE FAITH

TEACHINGS	068 - 1	COMBINED TEACHINGS WEAVE THE STORY
TEACHINGS	194 - 3	TEACHINGS OF JESUS
TEACHINGS	310 - 4	CHRIST AND HIS SPIRITUAL TEACHINGS
TEACHINGS	433 - 1	WHO HAVE FOLLOWED HIS TEACHINGS
TEACHINGS	481 - 3	TEACHINGS IS TO THE EFFECT
TECHNIQUE	048 - 2	SPECIFIC TECHNIQUE IN MENTAL TREATMENT
TECHNIQUE	160 - 2	TECHNIQUE THAT WILL CONDUCT OUR MINDS
TECHNIQUE	308 - 2	TREAT BY A TECHNIQUE
TECHNIQUE	308 - 2	THERE IS A METHOD A TECHNIQUE
TECHNIQUE	317 - 1	HAS A TECHNIQUE FOR THIS
TELEPATHY	077 - 3	CALLED MENTAL TELEPATHY
TELEPATHY	350 - 4	THOUGHT-TRANSFERENCE OR TELEPATHY
TELEPATHY	350 - 5	TELEPATHY IS THE ACT OF READING SUBJECTIVE
TELEPATHY	382 - 2	POWERS OF CLAIRVOYANCE TELEPATHY
TELEPATHY	421 - 4	IT IS CALLED MENTAL TELEPATHY
TELEPATHY	421 - 5	TELEPATHY WHICH IS THE ACT
TELL	277 - 1	LAW AND TELL IT WHAT TO DO
TELLING	194 - 3	ALWAYS TELLING HIS FOLLOWERS
TELLS	194 - 3	TELLS US NOT TO TAKE THOUGHT
TEMPERAMENT	497 - 5	CALL THIS EMOTION TEMPERAMENT
TEMPEST	446 - 1	TEMPEST OF HUMAN STRIFE IS ABATED
TEMPLE	227 - 3	TEMPLE OF THE LIVING GOD
TEMPLE	243 - 2	DOOR-KEEPER TO THE TEMPLE
TEMPLE	248 - 3	TEMPLE OF THE LIVING GOD
TEMPLE	436 - 3	TEMPLE OF TRUTH IS APPROACHED
TEMPLE	444 - 2	TEMPLE OF GOD AS GOD
TEMPORAL	428 - 1	STRUGGLE FOR TEMPORAL SUPREMACY
TEMPORAL	479 - 3	THE TEMPORAL IMPERFECTION
TEMPORARY	101 - 2	FORM IS TEMPORARY
TEMPORARY	315 - 1	YOU MAY UNDERSTAND THEIR TEMPORARY
TEMPORARY	390 - 3	MAN MAY CALL INTO TEMPORARY BEING
TEMPORARY	393 - 4	ALL FORM IS TEMPORARY
TEMPORARY	394 - 1	CALL TEMPORARY FORMS INTO BEING
TEMPORARY	407 - 2	ALL FORM IS TEMPORARY
TEMPTED	498 - 6	GOD CANNOT BE TEMPTED
TEMPTS	498 - 6	GOD NEVER TEMPTS
TEN	104 - 3	FROM TEN DIFFERENT PLANES
TEN	329 - 3	SPEAK TEN WORDS
TEN	387 - 2	NINE OUT OF TEN PEOPLE
TEND	045 - 5	TEND TOWARD A CONSTRUCTIVE PROGRAM
TEND	268 - 3	TEND TO TAKE FORM
TEND	269 - 1	TEND TO EXPANSION AND MULTIPLICATION
TEND	399 - 2	TEND TO AND FINALLY DOES
TEND	501 - 1	TEND TO APPEAR IN THE BODY OR IN THE BODY
TENDENCIES	088 - 1	INHERITED TENDENCIES
TENDENCIES	115 - 1	TENDENCIES SET IN MOTION IN THE SOUL
TENDENCIES	282 - 3	RELEASE WRONG SUBJECTIVE TENDENCIES
TENDENCIES	355 - 3	MENTAL TENDENCIES SET IN MOTION
TENDENCY	030 - 4	ITS TENDENCY IS SET IN MOTION
TENDENCY	031 - 2	THE SUBJECTIVE TENDENCY
TENDENCY	038 - 3	CREATES A TENDENCY IN THIS LAW
TENDENCY	078 - 2	ITS TENDENCY CAN BE CHANGED
TENDENCY	078 - 3	TENDENCY SET IN MOTION
TENDENCY	115 - 2	TENDENCY CAN BE CHANGED
TENDENCY	133 - 5	TENDENCY IS SET IN MOTION

TENDENCY	153 - 2	A TENDENCY TOWARD ITS ANSWER
TENDENCY	177 - 4	TENDENCY OF THE RACE
TENDENCY	306 - 3	TENDENCY WHICH OUR THOUGHT IS TAKING
TENDENCY	349 - 1	THERE IS A TENDENCY
TENDENCY	356 - 1	A TENDENCY SET IN MOTION
TENDENCY	475 - 3	TENDENCY OF THIS INNER THOUGHT
TENDERNESS	368 - 1	COMPASSIONATE IN HIS TENDERNESS
TENDS	116 - 1	TENDS TO TAKE OBJECTIVE FORM
TENDS	270 - 6	LAW OF LIFE WHICH TENDS
TENDS	320 - 4	WHATEVER ONE THINKS TENDS TO TAKE FORM
TENET	038 - 1	IS A FUNDAMENTAL TENET
TENNYSON	103 - 3	TENNYSON EXCLAIMS
TENNYSON	327 - 4	BROWNING, TENNYSON, WORDSWORTH
TENSE	225 - 2	TENSE THOUGHTS CAN PRODUCE
TENSE	255 - 5	HARD TENSE THOUGHT FROM THE MIND
TENSENESS	240 - 2	FOR ALL WILL REMOVE TENSENESS
TENSION	224 - 1	PRESENCE THERE IS NO TENSION
TENSION	225 - 2	QUICKLY REMOVES TENSION
TENSION	231 - 6	PRODUCES A MENTAL TENSION
TENSION	248 - 2	TENSION NOR SUPER-TENSION
TEN THOUSAND	353 - 4	WALL FOR THE NEXT TEN THOUSAND
TERRESTRIAL	376 - 1	BODIES TERRESTRIAL
TERRIBLE	152 - 5	THINKING WOULD BE A TERRIBLE
TEST	448 - 1	INDIVIDUAL MUST MAKE THE TEST
TEST	453 - 5	TEST ALL IDEAS TO SEE
TESTIMONY	329 - 1	TESTIMONY IS IN NO WAY CONFUSING
TESTIMONY	344 - 3	TESTIMONY WERE COMPLETE
TEXTBOOK	029 - 2	IN THE BODY OF THIS TEXTBOOK
THANKFUL	447 - 1	THANKFUL HEART IS IN HARMONY
THANKS	174 - 2	THANKS AS HE MAKES HIS DEMAND
THANKS	224 - 4	GIVE THANKS FOR THE ANSWER
THANKS	251 - 2	THANKS THAT I AM DIVINE
THANKS	277 - 2	WAS TO GIVE THANKS
THANKS	497 - 2	IN EVERYTHING GIVES THANKS
THANKSGIVING	253 - 1	EATEN WITH THANKSGIVING
THANKSGIVING	256 - 3	LIFT THOUGHT IN THANKSGIVING
THANKSGIVING	447 - 1	COME WITH THANKSGIVING
THANKSGIVING	452 - 3	THOSE OF APPRECIATION AND THANKSGIVING
THAT LIFE	292 - 4	THAT LIFE IS MY LIFE NOW
THEME	428 - 3	THEME OF OUR GREATEST SINGERS
THEOLOGICAL	079 - 3	THEOLOGICAL RATHER THAN A SCIENTIFIC
THEOLOGICAL	436 - 4	ANYTHING LIKE THE THEOLOGICAL HELL
THEOLOGICAL	465 - 4	THEOLOGICAL STATE OF MIND
THEOLOGICAL	465 - 4	THEOLOGICAL STATE OF INTROSPECTIVE
THEOLOGICAL	469 - 1	WHAT A THEOLOGICAL ATTITUDE
THEOLOGY	204 - 2	FATALISM THEOLOGY OR HELL
THEOLOGY	269 - 3	THEOLOGY MAY SAY THAT THIS IS A SELFISH
THEOLOGY	270 - 1	NOT OF THEOLOGY
THEOLOGY	343 - 3	THEOLOGY WITH ALL ITS WEAKNESS
THEOLOGY	383 - 3	THE ANATHEMAS OF THEOLOGY
THEORETICAL	085 - 2	TWO OR THREE THEORETICAL PROPOSITIONS
THEORETICAL	085 - 2	PRINCIPLES ARE THEORETICAL
THEORETICAL	117 - 1	THEORETICAL BEGINNING OF CREATION
THEORETICALLY	310 - 3	FORMS ARE THEORETICALLY RESOLVABLE
THEORIES	074 - 3	CERTAIN THEORIES ARE POSTULATED

THEORIES	246 - 3	TEST OF ALL THEORIES
THEORY	048 - 3	BY EXPLAINING THE THEORY
THEORY	051 - 1	INDULGE IN TOO MUCH THEORY
THEORY	051 - 2	THEORY OF ANY SCIENTIFIC PRINCIPLE
THEORY	085 - 3	RESTS UPON THE THEORY
THEORY	094 - 1	OUR THEORY IS
THEORY	103 - 2	THE THEORY THAT WE LIE IN THE LAP
THEORY	138 - 3	THEORY THAT WE ARE SURROUNDED
THEORY	175 - 6	THEORY RESTS ENTIRELY
THEORY	177 - 1	THEORY THAT WE ARE SURROUNDED BY A
THEORY	283 - 2	OUR WHOLE THEORY IS BASED
THEORY	376 - 1	THIS THEORY IS ACCEPTED
THEORY	432 - 3	POSITION TO CONTRADICT THIS THEORY
THE OVER-SOUL	032 - 2	THE OVER-SOUL OR THE ETERNAL SPIRIT
THE THING	033 - 4	THIS IS THE THING ITSELF
THE THING	490 - 6	THE THING AND THE WAY IT WORKS
THING	026 - 4	WE ACCEPT THIS THING AND BELIEVE IN IT
THING	028 - 4	THE THING SPIRIT CAUSATION
THING	036 - 1	ORIGINAL CREATIVE THING
THING	036 - 2	WE ARE MADE FROM THIS THING
THING	037 - 2	THE THING THEN WORKS FOR US
THING	045 - 2	PERSON, PLACE, NOR THING
THING	054 - 2	NEITHER PERSON, PLACE, NOR THING
THING	055 - 2	NEITHER PERSON, PLACE, NOR THING
THING	060 - 4	THE THING ITSELF
THING	080 - 3	THING IS ABSOLUTE INTELLIGENCE
THING	097 - 2	NEITHER PERSON, PLACE, NOR THING
THING	099 - 4	NOT A THING OF ITSELF
THING	134 - 1	THING IN THE UNIVERSE WHICH CAN FREE
THING	203 - 3	THING UNTO WHICH IT IS SPOKEN
THING	216 - 2	THING WHEREUNTO IT IS SPOKEN
THING	217 - 1	NEITHER PERSON, PLACE, NOR THING
THING	224 - 3	EVERYTHING IS A THING OF THOUGHT
THING	224 - 3	NEITHER PERSON, PLACE, NOR THING
THING	242 - 2	AS THE THOUGHT BECOMES THE THING
THING	250 - 3	THAT THING WHICH MUST AUTOMATICALLY
THING	274 - 3	THE THING ONE DOES TO HIMSELF
THING	275 - 2	THE THING ITSELF
THING	281 - 4	THE THING WE DESIRE
THING	304 - 1	THE THING FOR WHICH IT IS SPOKEN
THING	304 - 5	OUR THOUGHT BECOMES THE THING
THING	319 - 3	THING TO DO IS TO TREAT
THING	338 - 2	ONLY THING HE REALLY HAS
THING	340 - 2	THOUGHT AND THE THING
THING	364 - 2	THING THAT WE LOOK WITH
THING	410 - 4	NEVER WAS A THING OF ITSELF
THING	411 - 4	THOUGHT BECOMES A THING
THING ITSELF	026 - 3	POWER BACK OF CREATION-THE THING ITSELF
THING ITSELF	463 - 2	THING ITSELF THAT ENERGY WITHOUT
THING ITSELF	474 - 5	DIFFERENCE IS NOT IN THE THING ITSELF
THINGS	059 - 3	THINGS INTO THOUGHTS
THINGS	070 - 2	THINGS MAY COME
THINGS	084 - 5	BY BECOMING THE THINGS IT MAKES
THINGS	087 - 5	THINGS ARE IDEAS IN FORM
THINGS	105 - 2	MUST MANIFEST AS THINGS

THINGS	144 - 3	THOUGHTS ARE THINGS
THINGS	145 - 3	THOUGHTS ARE THINGS
THINGS	178 - 4	THE EVIDENCE OF THINGS NOT SEEN
THINGS	183 - 1	THAT THOUGHTS ARE THINGS
THINGS	187 - 3	NOT MADE OF THINGS WHICH DO APPEAR
THINGS	236 - 1	THINGS WHICH ARE IMPLANTED
THINGS	254 - 5	THOUGHTS ARE THINGS
THINGS	273 - 4	FOREVER DOING NEW THINGS
THINGS	301 - 2	EITHER DRAWING THINGS TO US
THINGS	302 - 3	THINGS ARE STEADILY COMING OUR WAY
THINGS	304 - 4	THINGS MUST COME FROM THIS
THINGS	340 - 1	MAKES THINGS FROM IDEAS
THINGS	414 - 2	THINGS HAVE NO INDEPENDENT EXISTENCE
THINK	029 - 5	TO LEARN HOW TO THINK
THINK	072 - 3	THAT HE COULD THINK
THINK	073 - 1	DISCOVERY OF HIS ABILITY TO THINK
THINK	073 - 2	CONSCIOUSLY THINK AND DECIDE
THINK	123 - 1	TO LEARN HOW TO THINK
THINK	125 - 2	WE THINK INTO A UNIVERSAL
THINK	188 - 1	TRAIN YOURSELF TO THINK
THINK	276 - 3	IN EVERYTHING WE DO, SAY OR THINK
THINK	301 - 3	WHAT WE THINK INTO IT
THINK	380 - 1	THINK A LECTURE TO AN AUDIENCE
THINK	406 - 4	LEARN TO THINK IN THE ABSOLUTE
THINKER	073 - 2	WHERE IS THE THINKER
THINKER	073 - 2	THE THINKER AND THE DOER
THINKER	085 - 4	AN INFINITE THINKER
THINKER	085 - 4	THINKER IS A SPONTANEOUS THINKER
THINKER	115 - 4	THINKER IS CONSCIOUS MIND
THINKER	269 - 2	RETURN TO THE THINKER EXACTLY
THINKER	374 - 3	IT IS THE THINKER USING THE BRAIN
THINKER	377 - 1	THE THINKER ALONE CAN THINK
THINKER	449 - 3	THINKER BEFORE THERE CAN BE
THINKER	449 - 3	THINKER CONDEMNS OR JUSTIFIES
THINKERS	027 - 2	THE MOST PROFOUND THINKERS
THINKERS	032 - 2	DEEPEST THINKERS OF EVERY AGE
THINKERS	068 - 2	THINKERS OF ANTIQUITY
THINKERS	068 - 2	GREAT THINKERS HAVE ARRIVED
THINKERS	083 - 5	GREAT THINKERS OF ALL TIME
THINKETH	137 - 1	AS A MAN THINKETH IN HIS HEART
THINKING	030 - 1	MAN BY THINKING CAN BRING INTO HIS
THINKING	085 - 4	THINKER THINKING MATHEMATICALLY
THINKING	177 - 1	THE POWER OF RIGHT THINKING
THINKING	178 - 1	CONSTRUCTIVE BASIS FOR OUR THINKING
THINKING	185 - 1	THINKING TO MEET THIS NECESSITY
THINKING	185 - 3	THINKING OF HIS WEAKNESS
THINKING	188 - 3	THE POWER OF RIGHT THINKING
THINKING	202 - 1	COMBINATIONS OF THINKING
THINKING	204 - 4	YOU ARE THINKING
THINKING	236 - 4	BY CLEAR THINKING
THINKING	300 - 2	SUM TOTAL OF HIS THINKING AND KNOWING
THINKING STUFF	126 - 3	THINKING STUFF FROM WHICH ALL THINGS COME
THINKS	029 - 4	FROM LIFE WHAT HE THINKS INTO IT
THINKS	030 - 1	IF HE THINKS CORRECTLY
THINKS	137 - 2	HE CAN WHO THINKS HE CAN

THINKS	237 - 2	COMEDY TO HIM WHO THINKS
THINKS	267 - 3	THINKS INTO THIS UNIVERSAL MIND
THINKS	376 - 4	THE THINKER THINKS THROUGH THE BRAIN
THIRD STEP	318 - 3	THE THIRD STEP REALIZATION
THIRST	428 - 4	THIRST AFTER KNOWLEDGE
THIRST	446 - 2	QUENCHES EVERY THIRST
THIRTY	200 - 2	THIRTY MINUTES MORE OR LESS
THISTLES	431 - 4	NOT GATHER ROSES FROM THISTLES
THOMAS	479 - 5	THOMAS WHO WAS A DISCIPLE
THOU	161 - 1	THOU HAST BELIEVED SO BE IT
THOU	423 - 3	THOU ART THAT WHICH I AM
THOU	468 - 7	SON THOU ART EVER WITH ME
THOU ART	366 - 3	THOU ART MY WHOLE BEING
THOUGHT	027 - 5	DIRECTED BY THOUGHT
THOUGHT	029 - 3	MAN'S THOUGHT FALLING INTO HIS SUBJECTIVE
THOUGHT	030 - 3	ALL THOUGHT IS CREATIVE
THOUGHT	030 - 3	THOUGHT CREATES A MOLD
THOUGHT	038 - 5	SHAPE THE BASIS OF HIS THOUGHT
THOUGHT	041 - 1	THIS IS A FAR-REACHING THOUGHT
THOUGHT	041 - 3	BEAUTIFUL AND TRUE THOUGHT
THOUGHT	042 - 4	PONDEROSITY OF THOUGHT
THOUGHT	047 - 2	TRAINED THOUGHT IS FAR MORE POWERFUL
THOUGHT	049 - 5	SPECIFICALLY TURN TO THAT THOUGHT
THOUGHT	050 - 2	SOMETHING HAPPENS TO THOUGHT
THOUGHT	050 - 2	TO THOUGHT THERE CAN BE NO LIMIT
THOUGHT	051 - 1	NEW ORDER OF THOUGHT
THOUGHT	053 - 4	CONTROL OUR THOUGHT
THOUGHT	054 - 2	PRACTITIONER USES THOUGHT DEFINITELY
THOUGHT	056 - 3	SUPREMACY OF SPIRITUAL THOUGHT
THOUGHT	069 - 2	THOUGHT SEEMS TO MEAN
THOUGHT	069 - 2	THOUGHT IS AN INNER PROCESS
THOUGHT	070 - 2	THE SLIGHTEST THOUGHT OF INTELLIGENCE
THOUGHT	073 - 2	THOUGHTS AFTER HE THOUGHT THEM
THOUGHT	094 - 1	ALL THOUGHT IS CREATIVE
THOUGHT	097 - 3	SUBJECT TO THE CONSCIOUS THOUGHT
THOUGHT	116 - 1	THE OBJECT THOUGHT ABOUT
THOUGHT	122 - 4	MAN'S THOUGHT BECOMES THE LAW
THOUGHT	125 - 4	THOUGHT IS AN INNER MOVEMENT
THOUGHT	141 - 3	THOUGHT FORCE IS A MOVEMENT OF
THOUGHT	142 - 4	THAT WHICH THOUGHT HAS DONE
THOUGHT	145 - 3	THOUGHT IS THE CONSCIOUS ACTIVITY
THOUGHT	147 - 5	BE CERTAIN IN OUR OWN MINDS THAT THOUGHT
THOUGHT	179 - 1	OWN THOUGHT RELATIVE TO THIS PERSON
THOUGHT	188 - 3	YOUR THOUGHT BECOMES PERFECTLY CLEAR
THOUGHT	194 - 1	THE THING IS IN THE THOUGHT
THOUGHT	194 - 2	CONCENTRATION OF THOUGHT
THOUGHT	194 - 3	TELLS US NOT TO TAKE THOUGHT
THOUGHT	194 - 3	WE PLACE THOUGHT IMAGINATION
THOUGHT	195 - 2	THOUGHT FIXED UPON THE IDEA
THOUGHT	197 - 5	THOUGHT OPERATES THROUGH A POWER
THOUGHT	199 - 4	IT IS ONLY A THOUGHT
THOUGHT	200 - 2	HOLDING A GOOD THOUGHT
THOUGHT	201 - 1	FEAR COME INTO YOUR THOUGHT
THOUGHT	202 - 2	FREQUENTLY HAS NEVER THOUGHT
THOUGHT	205 - 3	UNTIL A THOUGHT IS CREATED

THOUGHT	205 - 4	SIMPLY REALIZES A THOUGHT
THOUGHT	206 - 3	IN THE THOUGHT OF THE PATIENT
THOUGHT	208 - 4	THINK OF GOD'S THOUGHT
THOUGHT	209 - 1	SMALL AMOUNT OF RIGHT THOUGHT
THOUGHT	210 - 4	THE THOUGHT OF THE PARENTS
THOUGHT	213 - 2	OBLITERATING FALSE THOUGHT
THOUGHT	215 - 1	THE POWER OF A THOUGHT
THOUGHT	216 - 4	DISTURBED STATE OF THOUGHT BE PERMANENT
THOUGHT	218 - 1	ATMOSPHERE OF PURE THOUGHT
THOUGHT	218 - 3	THOUGHT IS TO A GREAT EXTENT
THOUGHT	219 - 4	COMPLETELY OPEN THEIR THOUGHT
THOUGHT	223 - 1	UNLESS WE CONTROL THOUGHT
THOUGHT	224 - 3	RESOLVE THINGS INTO THOUGHT
THOUGHT	224 - 3	EVERYTHING IS A THING OF THOUGHT
THOUGHT	224 - 3	RESOLVED EVERYTHING INTO THOUGHT
THOUGHT	225 - 1	DO NOT CARRY THE THOUGHT OF THE PATIENT
THOUGHT	231 - 4	A SICK THOUGHT AS WELL AS A SICK BODY
THOUGHT	234 - 4	WITHOUT THOUGHT COULD NOT MANIFEST
THOUGHT	242 - 2	AS THE THOUGHT BECOMES THE THING
THOUGHT	246 - 4	OUR PATTERNS OF THOUGHT
THOUGHT	247 - 3	THE CIRCULATION OF PURE THOUGHT
THOUGHT	256 - 2	THOUGHT CONTROLS THE BODY
THOUGHT	256 - 3	LIFT THOUGHT IN THANKSGIVING
THOUGHT	267 - 5	WHICH IS LIKE OUR THOUGHT
THOUGHT	274 - 3	ACTION IN THOUGHT ALONE
THOUGHT	274 - 3	OPENS UP THE AVENUES OF THOUGHT
THOUGHT	278 - 3	THOUGHT SETS DEFINITE FORCES IN MOTION
THOUGHT	279 - 1	POURING IN AN OPPOSITE THOUGHT
THOUGHT	295 - 1	BY THE ACTIVITY OF OUR THOUGHT
THOUGHT	302 - 3	ALL THOUGHT OF CLINGING TO ANYBODY
THOUGHT	303 - 1	SUBJECTIVE THOUGHT MAY BE DENYING
THOUGHT	304 - 1	THOUGHT IS VERY SUBTLE
THOUGHT	304 - 5	THOUGHT AND THE THING ARE ONE
THOUGHT	310 - 3	THOUGHT CAN BECOME A THING
THOUGHT	322 - 4	SPIRITUAL THOUGHT MEANS
THOUGHT	340 - 5	THOUGHT WILL TAKE US
THOUGHT	355 - 2	THOUGHT SETS THE FULFILLMENT
THOUGHT	381 - 3	READ THAT OUT OF HER THOUGHT
THOUGHT	393 - 1	THOUGHT CALLS THINGS FORTH
THOUGHT	399 - 5	HOLDING THINGS IN THOUGHT
THOUGHT	400 - 1	TRAINED THOUGHT IS FAR MORE POWERFUL
THOUGHT	400 - 4	IDEAS OR THOUGHT PATTERNS
THOUGHT	400 - 4	THESE THOUGHT PATTERNS
THOUGHT	403 - 2	TO CONTROL OUR THOUGHT PATTERNS
THOUGHT	403 - 4	REVERSE THE THOUGHT
THOUGHT	408 - 5	DEALS WITH THOUGHT ALONE
THOUGHT	409 - 2	THE WHOLE PROCESS IS ONE OF THOUGHT
THOUGHT	409 - 5	A PLACE IN THOUGHT
THOUGHT	410 - 2	THE THOUGHT IS A MOLD
THOUGHT	410 - 4	THE IMAGE OF THOUGHT IS SET
THOUGHT	411 - 2	THAT WE HAVE CREATIVE THOUGHT
THOUGHT	411 - 3	THE PATTERNS OF OUR THOUGHT
THOUGHT	411 - 4	THE THOUGHT BECOMES A THING
THOUGHT	411 - 4	CREATIVE POWER OF THOUGHT
THOUGHT	412 - 2	IN HIS CONSCIOUS THOUGHT

THOUGHT	413 - 5	HEAL THE THOUGHT OF ITS MISTAKEN IDEA
THOUGHT	414 - 2	OUR ENTIRE EQUIPMENT IS THOUGHT
THOUGHT	415 - 2	THE SLUMBERING THOUGHT
THOUGHT	440 - 4	THOUGHT RESTS ENTIRELY UPON HIMSELF
THOUGHT	449 - 3	COMPLETE THOUGHT AND ACT OF MAN
THOUGHT	461 - 1	THOUGHT IS EVER FATHER TO THE ACT
THOUGHT	478 - 1	THIS THOUGHT BROUGHT OUT
THOUGHT	483 - 5	THOUGHT IS THE GREATEST POWER KNOWN
THOUGHT	494 - 2	THOUGHT IS HELD IN THE MIND
THOUGHT-FORCE	221 - 3	AN IMPERSONAL THOUGHT-FORCE
THOUGHT FORM	352 - 2	THOUGHT FORM OF THAT PERSON
THOUGHTS	030 - 1	NOT DONE BY HOLDING THOUGHTS
THOUGHTS	059 - 3	HE RESOLVES THINGS INTO THOUGHTS
THOUGHTS	144 - 3	THOUGHTS ARE THINGS
THOUGHTS	172 - 2	THOUGHTS BACK OF CERTAIN THINGS
THOUGHTS	183 - 1	THAT THOUGHTS ARE THINGS
THOUGHTS	194 - 1	THOUGHTS WERE THINGS
THOUGHTS	195 - 2	THE RESULTS OF OUR THOUGHTS
THOUGHTS	201 - 4	BECAUSE THOUGHTS ARE THINGS
THOUGHTS	206 - 2	THOUGHTS TO OUR PATIENTS
THOUGHTS	207 - 1	HOW SUBTLE THOUGHTS ARE
THOUGHTS	224 - 2	THE RIGHT KIND OF THOUGHTS
THOUGHTS	244 - 2	THOUGHTS ARE THINGS
THOUGHTS	255 - 3	THOUGHTS OF ANGER
THOUGHTS	353 - 2	READ PEOPLE'S THOUGHTS
THOUGHTS	402 - 3	THOUGHTS OF LACK POVERTY
THOUGHTS	403 - 4	THOUGHTS OF LACK MANIFEST AS LIMITATION
THOUGHTS	403 - 4	THOUGHTS OF ABUNDANCE MANIFEST AS SUCCESS
THOUGHTS	406 - 4	NEW THOUGHTS CREATE
THOUGHTS	409 - 2	RESOLVES THEM INTO THOUGHTS
THOUGHTS	414 - 2	THOUGHTS ARE MORE THAN THINGS
THOUGHT-TRANSFERENCE	350 - 4	THOUGHT-TRANSFERENCE OR MENTAL TELEPATHY
THOUGHT-TRANSFERENCE	379 - 4	IT WOULD BE THOUGHT-TRANSFERENCE
THOUSAND	272 - 3	TEN THOUSAND YEARS AGO
THOUSAND	311 - 3	FIVE THOUSAND YEARS AGO
THOUSAND	353 - 4	THE NEXT TEN THOUSAND YEARS
THOUSANDS	341 - 6	THOUSANDS OF YEARS
THOUSANDS	379 - 2	THOUSANDS OF CASES ON RECORD
THREAD	330 - 3	THAT THREAD OF THE ALL-SUSTAINING BEAUTY
THREAD	495 - 1	THREAD OF UNITY RUNNING THROUGH ALL
THREE	084 - 5	THREE IN REALITY ARE ONE
THREE	113 - 2	THREE WAYS BY WHICH WE GATHER
THREE	121 - 3	THREE SEPARATE MINDS
THREE	191 - 3	WHICH TAKES PLACE ON THREE PLANES
THREE	333 - 2	THREE SIDES OF LIFE
THREE	476 - 6	WE LIVE ON THREE PLANES
THREE-FOLD	165 - 1	THREE-FOLD NATURE OF BOTH MAN
THREEFOLD	080 - 1	MAN IS THREEFOLD IN HIS NATURE
THREEFOLD	080 - 1	GOD IS THREEFOLD IN HIS NATURE
THREEFOLD	083 - 5	THREEFOLD UNIVERSE
THREEFOLD	477 - 1	MAN IS A THREEFOLD
THREE-FOLD NATURE	129 - 2	POSTULATE A THREE-FOLD NATURE
THREE PLANES	111 - 4	GOD AND MAN ON ALL THREE PLANES
THREE PLANES	132 - 8	THE DIVINE NATURE ON ALL THREE PLANES
THRESHOLD	293 - 1	THRESHOLD OF ALL GOOD WISDOM

THRESHOLD	351 - 2	THRESHOLD OF THE OUTER MIND
THRESHOLD	479 - 2	THRESHOLD OF HIS GREATEST EXPERIENCE
THRILLED	242 - 2	THRILLED WITH THE ALMIGHTY
THRONE OF GRACE	455 - 3	THRONE OF GRACE TO A KINDNESS
THROUGH	037 - 2	BY WORKING THROUGH US
THROUGH	052 - 2	IT MUST BE IN AND THROUGH US
THROUGH	072 - 4	NATURE WORKS THROUGH HIM
THROUGH	079 - 4	REVEALING HIMSELF THROUGH US
THROUGH	112 - 3	THROUGH THAT WHICH WE CALL
THROUGH	121 - 4	THROUGH THE SELF-KNOWING MIND
THROUGH	128 - 2	HAPPEN THROUGH HIM
THROUGH	184 - 2	BY OPERATING THROUGH HIM
THROUGH	212 - 4	THROUGH THE THOUGHT OF
THROUGH	299 - 4	IT MUST DO THROUGH US
THROUGH	422 - 3	THROUGH OUR OWN SPIRITUAL NATURE
THROUGH	429 - 4	THROUGH OUR OWN THOUGHT
THROUGH	444 - 2	WORKING THROUGH
THROUGH	470 - 1	IT DOES THROUGH US
THROUGHOUT	066 - 3	MANIFEST THROUGHOUT THE UNIVERSE
THROUGH US	141 - 2	ONLY WHAT IT CAN DO THROUGH US
THROWING OFF	185 - 3	THROWING OFF SOME WEAKNESS
THROWN	431 - 1	SOUL SHALL BE THROWN BACK UPON ITSELF
THYSELF	072 - 4	MAN KNOW THYSELF
TIDE	386 - 3	MOVES WITH A TIDE AS IRRESISTIBLE
TIED UP	395 - 2	HEAVEN AND HELL ARE TIED UP
TILL	473 - 3	TILL THE SOIL AND ENJOY
TIME	039 - 5	THE TIME MUST COME
TIME	049 - 6	WASTE MUCH TIME IN ARGUING
TIME	057 - 2	SUCH TIME IN ITS UNFOLDMENT
TIME	057 - 3	PROCESS IS THE TIME AND EFFORT
TIME	057 - 4	DAILY TAKE THE TIME
TIME	058 - 3	SPEND MUCH TIME IN CONVINCING OURSELVES
TIME	067 - 1	WITHIN WHICH IS ALL TIME
TIME	067 - 2	A TIME WHEN THERE WAS NO CREATION
TIME	073 - 2	GREATEST DISCOVERY OF ALL TIME
TIME	075 - 3	SEEN GOD AT ANY TIME
TIME	084 - 2	IMPOSSIBLE TO THINK OF A TIME
TIME	101 - 2	IN WHAT WE CALL TIME
TIME	101 - 2	TIME IS A SEQUENCE OF EVENTS
TIME	101 - 2	OF COURSE TIME IS REAL
TIME	102 - 3	EVOLUTION IS THE PROCESS, THE WAY, THE TIME
TIME	151 - 4	THE TIME IS NOW
TIME	153 - 3	SHOULD TAKE THE TIME
TIME	158 - 4	BEEN ANY MAN'S AT ANY TIME
TIME	179 - 4	IS THE TIME AND THOUGHT
TIME	179 - 5	TAKE THE TIME TO SET THAT BELIEF IN MOTION
TIME	200 - 2	A DEFINITE TIME
TIME	203 - 1	THERE ALL THE TIME
TIME	205 - 1	A DROP AT A TIME
TIME	212 - 4	MENTAL WORK AND THE TIME
TIME	212 - 4	TIME IT TAKES THE PATIENT
TIME	219 - 4	ARGUING IS OFTEN A WASTE OF TIME
TIME	233 - 4	TIME ONCE A DAY AT LEAST
TIME	243 - 1	NO TIME FOR ANY FEAR THOUGHTS
TIME	246 - 3	BETTER SPEND OUR TIME USING THE LAW

TIME	246 - 4	TAKE TIME TO UNDERSTAND
TIME	251 - 3	ALWAYS AT THE CORRECT TIME
TIME	267 - 2	WHOSE ENTIRE TIME IS SPENT
TIME	271 - 2	AND IN TIME ALL WILL COME
TIME	271 - 3	IN TIME WE SHALL BE MADE FREE
TIME	271 - 5	SHOULD TAKE TIME EVERY DAY
TIME	274 - 2	CONCENTRATE FOR ANY LENGTH OF TIME
TIME	282 - 4	IS THE BEST TIME TO WORK
TIME	289 - 4	KNOWS NEITHER TIME NOR PROCESS
TIME	290 - 2	TIME COMES WE WILL KNOW
TIME	303 - 1	PLACE, PERSON, CONDITION, TIME OF YEAR
TIME	317 - 2	WHAT WE CALL TIME ELAPSES
TIME	317 - 2	SPIRIT THERE IS NO TIME
TIME	317 - 2	HE MUST TRANSCEND TIME
TIME	339 - 1	THE TIME HAS COME
TIME	340 - 2	EVOLUTION IS THE TIME
TIME	348 - 4	IMPRINT ON THE WALLS OF TIME
TIME	352 - 5	TIME SPACE AND OBSTRUCTIONS
TIME	352 - 5	TIME IS ONLY THE MEASURE OF AN EXPERIENCE
TIME	373 - 4	EXISTING IN TIME AND SPACE
TIME	387 - 3	AS A CONTINUITY OF TIME
TIME	387 - 4	TIME HEALS ALL WOUNDS
TIME	387 - 4	TIME ALONE SATISFIES THE EXPANDING SOUL
TIME	388 - 1	TIME TO WORK OUT ALL PROBLEMS
TIME	388 - 1	THERE WILL BE TIME ENOUGH
TIME	407 - 2	GOES IN A PROCESS OF TIME
TIME	407 - 2	ANY GIVEN TIME IS TEMPORARY
TIME	420 - 3	EVOLUTION IS THE TIME AND THE PROCESS
TIME	422 - 2	TIME AND SPACE ARE UNKNOWN
TIME	433 - 4	MUST IN TIME
TIME	436 - 4	WITHOUT THE ELEMENT OF TIME
TIMELESS	067 - 1	SPIRIT IS TIMELESS
TIMELESS	084 - 3	LAW MUST BE AS TIMELESS AS THE SPIRIT
TIMELESS	317 - 2	THE SPIRIT IS TIMELESS
TIMES	055 - 3	TALE OF WOE ABOUT HARD TIMES
TIMES	297 - 1	MANY TIMES EACH DAY
TIMES	318 - 3	TREATMENT TWO OR THREE TIMES
TIMID	439 - 3	TIMID SOUL PUTS ITS COMPLETE TRUST
TIRE	179 - 2	TREATMENT DOES NOT TIRE
TIRED	219 - 4	TIRED OF LOOKING FOR THINGS
TIRED	288 - 2	HE WOULD NEVER BECOME TIRED
TIRED	418 - 1	THAT IT IS TIRED
TIRELESS	288 - 2	THE UNIVERSE IN PLACE IS TIRELESS
TIRES	193 - 4	IF OUR MENTAL WORK TIRES US
TISSUE	229 - 4	EVERY TISSUE ATOM AND FUNCTION
TITANIC	428 - 1	TITANIC STRUGGLE
TO BE	306 - 1	CAUSE OF ALL THAT IS OR IS TO BE
TODAY	084 - 4	SAME YESTERDAY, TODAY AND FOREVER
TODAY	126 - 1	TODAY IS THE RESULT OF
TODAY	432 - 4	WE ARE TO LIVE TODAY
TODAY	462 - 4	AS REAL A MEANING TODAY AS IT HAD
TODAY	471 - 4	TODAY IS GOOD
TODAY	503 - 1	TODAY IS THE DAY OF COMPLETE SALVATION
TOIL	432 - 2	TOIL NOT NOR DO THEY SPIN
TOMATO	078 - 2	TOMATO OR A POTATO

TOMB	359 - 4	THE TOMB OF A DEAD MAN
TOMB	369 - 3	TOMB OF HUMAN LIMITATION
TOMORROWS	246 - 2	TOMORROWS WILL BE HAPPY
TOMORROWS	384 - 2	ALL OF THE TOMORROWS
TOMORROWS	432 - 4	BITTER PROSPECTS OF OUR TOMORROWS
TONGUE	345 - 1	STUCK ITS FORKED TONGUE
TONGUE	374 - 3	NOR DOES THE TONGUE WAG
TONGUE	490 - 6	NOR CAN TONGUE TELL THE GREATER
TOOL	192 - 2	TOOL OF A SPIRITUAL PRACTITIONER
TOOLS	169 - 2	TOOLS OF THOUGHT
TOO PURE	438 - 3	TOO PURE TO BEHOLD EVIL
TOO PURE	499 - 1	TOO PURE TO BEHOLD EVIL
TOP	402 - 1	NO ONE EVER STARTED AT THE TOP
TORCH	218 - 3	MUST RELIGHT THE TORCH
TORCH	415 - 1	FURNISHED WITH A DIVINE TORCH
TORCH	454 - 1	TORCH WHICH FLICKERS NOT NOR FAILS
TORN	033 - 1	TORN BY CONFUSION
TOTAL	038 - 3	TOTAL OF ALL OUR THOUGHT
TOTAL	300 - 2	THE SUM TOTAL OF HIS THINKING
TOTALITY	128 - 3	THERE IS NOTHING BUT TOTALITY
TOTALITY	486 - 2	THE TRUTH IS A TOTALITY
TOUCH	094 - 2	REALLY TOUCH EACH OTHER
TOUCH	094 - 2	NEVER ONCE TOUCH EACH OTHER
TOUCH	128 - 2	TOUCH, TASTE, HANDLE AND SMELL
TOUCH	307 - 3	UNLESS WE LET IT TOUCH
TOUCH	439 - 4	I MAY BUT TOUCH HIS GARMENT
TOUCHES	158 - 1	PRAYER IN FAITH TOUCHES REALITY
TOUCHING	055 - 5	TOUCHING THE SEAMLESS GARMENT
TOWARD	141 - 5	MOVEMENT TOWARD THE THING
TOWARD	334 - 2	TOWARD THE ONE AND ONLY POWER
TOWARD	412 - 3	TOWARD THAT WHICH EXPRESSES LIFE
TOWARD	458 - 4	NOTHING FOR IT TO MOVE TOWARD
TOWNS	348 - 3	SOME TOWNS ARE BUSTLING WITH LIFE
TRACHEA	228 - 3	PERFECT TRACHEA PERFECT LUNGS
TRAGEDY	195 - 1	BE A COMEDY OR A TRAGEDY
TRAGEDY	237 - 2	TRAGEDY TO HIM WHO FEELS
TRAGEDY	438 - 4	TRAGEDY WOULD BE IF GOD DID
TRAIN	188 - 1	TRAIN YOURSELF TO THINK
TRAIN	245 - 2	TRAIN OUR MIND TO
TRAIN	258 - 1	WE CAN SO TRAIN OUR EARS
TRAIN	276 - 3	WE SHOULD DAILY TRAIN OUR THOUGHT
TRAIN	319 - 2	WILL TRAIN HIMSELF TO DO IT
TRAIN	450 - 5	EACH SHOULD TRAIN HIMSELF
TRAIN	470 - 3	TRAIN OURSELVES TO LISTEN
TRAINED	047 - 2	TRAINED THOUGHT IS FAR MORE
TRAINED	209 - 1	TRAINED THOUGHT IS FAR MORE
TRAINED	400 - 1	TRAINED THOUGHT IS FAR MORE
TRANQUIL	218 - 1	TRANQUIL ATMOSPHERE OF PURE THOUGHT
TRANQUILLITY	257 - 2	TRANQUILLITY FILL ME
TRANSCEND	127 - 3	COSMIC LIFE WILL ALWAYS TRANSCEND
TRANSCEND	147 - 4	WE ALL HAVE THE ABILITY TO TRANSCEND
TRANSCEND	155 - 2	WHILE OTHERS TRANSCEND CONDITIONS
TRANSCEND	213 - 3	TRANSCEND THE APPEARANCE
TRANSCEND	260 - 3	IF WE WISH TO TRANSCEND IT
TRANSCEND	317 - 2	MUST TRANSCEND TIME

TRANSCEND	336 - 2	TO TRANSCEND SOME PREVIOUS ONE
TRANSCENDENT	329 - 6	JESUS TAUGHT A POWER TRANSCENDENT
TRANSCENDS	433 - 3	TRANSCENDS THE LAW ALREADY SET IN MOTION
TRANSFORMED	218 - 3	TRANSFORMED BY THE RENEWING OF THE MIND
TRANSFORMED	338 - 3	TRANSFORMED FROM GLORY TO GLORY
TRANSFORMED	448 - 1	TRANSFORMED BY THE RENEWING OF OUR MINDS
TRANSFORMED	486 - 5	TRANSFORMED BY THE RENEWING OF
TRANSFORMED	487 - 2	INNER MIND IS TRANSFORMED
TRANSFORMS	418 - 4	INNER LIFE TRANSFORMS THE IMAGE
TRANSFUSION	152 - 4	IS A SUBTLE TRANSFUSION
TRANSGRESS	500 - 3	WE TRANSGRESS AND ARE PUNISHED
TRANSGRESSIONS	412 - 2	BLOT OUT THEIR TRANSGRESSIONS
TRANSGRESSORS	500 - 2	CONVINCED WE ARE TRANSGRESSORS
TRANSITION	123 - 4	TRANSITION FROM THE ATOMIC TO THE SIMPLE
TRANSITION	317 - 3	TRANSITION WILL GRADUALLY TAKE PLACE
TRANSMISSION	077 - 5	THE MEDIUM RADIO TRANSMISSION
TRANSMISSION	351 - 2	IS THE TRANSMISSION OF THOUGHT
TRANSMIT	400 - 2	TRANSMIT ITSELF INTO A SUBJECTIVE
TRANSMUTE	405 - 5	TRANSMUTE THEM INTO FAITH
TRANSMUTED	180 - 2	TRANSMUTED INTO ACCEPTANCE
TRANSPIRE	056 - 2	WHAT WOULD TRANSPIRE
TRANSPIRED	353 - 3	SEE WHAT HAS TRANSPIRED
TRANSPOSE	249 - 4	TRANSPOSE IT FOR THE SPIRITUAL SENSE
TRAVEL	495 - 2	CAN TRAVEL AND NOT BECOME WEARY
TREASURE	432 - 1	TREASURE IS ALREADY IN HEAVEN
TREASURE	432 - 1	THOUGHT CAN TAKE US TO THIS TREASURE
TREAT	057 - 4	MENTALLY TREAT THE CONDITION
TREAT	059 - 2	TREAT UNTIL WE GET RESULTS
TREAT	114 - 4	WE TREAT OF SOUL AS BEING
TREAT	169 - 4	WE TREAT MAN NOT AS A PATIENT
TREAT	169 - 4	NEITHER DO WE TREAT THE DISEASE
TREAT	200 - 2	OBLIGATION TO TREAT A CASE
TREAT	209 - 6	A DRAIN ON ONE TO TREAT
TREAT	225 - 1	TREAT UNTIL YOU GET RESULTS
TREAT	291 - 3	THERE IS BUT ONE THING TO TREAT
TREAT	309 - 4	TO LEARN HOW TO TREAT IS TO TREAT
TREAT	318 - 3	AGREED TO TREAT THE MAN
TREAT	400 - 3	TREAT HIMSELF FOR GENERAL SUCCESS
TREAT	402 - 1	TREAT OURSELVES UNTIL WE DO BELIEVE
TREATED	319 - 4	TREATED A PATIENT LONG ENOUGH
TREATED	319 - 4	AS IF YOU HAD NEVER TREATED
TREAT HIMSELF	199 - 4	TREAT HIMSELF AGAINST THIS THOUGHT
TREATING	166 - 2	PERSON WHOM HE IS TREATING
TREATING	173 - 3	THIS PROCESS CALLED TREATING
TREATING	284 - 6	KNOWING IS CORRECT MENTAL TREATING
TREATING	304 - 2	WERE TREATING HIS BUSINESS
TREATMENT	046 - 5	HOCUS-POCUS IN A MENTAL TREATMENT
TREATMENT	047 - 1	TREATMENT IS A STATEMENT IN THE LAW
TREATMENT	047 - 3	TREATMENT IS AN ACTIVE THING
TREATMENT	047 - 3	WHEN ONE GIVES A TREATMENT
TREATMENT	049 - 4	AN EFFECTIVE MENTAL TREATMENT
TREATMENT	057 - 4	TREATMENT IS AN INTELLIGENT ENERGY
TREATMENT	058 - 2	A TREATMENT IS A SPIRITUAL
TREATMENT	097 - 3	TREATMENT IS A SPIRITUAL ENTITY
TREATMENT	119 - 3	THIS IS WHAT TREATMENT DOES

TREATMENT	121 - 2	MEDIUM THROUGH WHICH ALL TREATMENT
TREATMENT	163 - 2	TREATMENT SHOULD BE GIVEN IN A CALM
TREATMENT	164 - 2	TREATMENT SHOULD INCORPORATE
TREATMENT	164 - 3	TREATMENT WE TURN ENTIRELY AWAY FROM
TREATMENT	164 - 3	TREATMENT IS THE SCIENCE OF INDUCING
TREATMENT	164 - 4	TREATMENT IS NOT WILLING THINGS TO HAPPEN
TREATMENT	164 - 4	TREATMENT OPENS UP THE AVENUES
TREATMENT	166 - 2	A FORMED TREATMENT STATED DEFINITELY
TREATMENT	167 - 2	BIBLE DOES NOT TELL US HOW TO GIVE A TREATMENT
TREATMENT	167 - 2	LEARN HOW TO GIVE A TREATMENT
TREATMENT	167 - 2	DO NOT TEACH HOW TO GIVE A TREATMENT
TREATMENT	170 - 5	TREATMENT IS FOR THE PURPOSE OF INDUCING
TREATMENT	171 - 3	TREATMENT IS A CONSCIOUS MOVEMENT
TREATMENT	174 - 1	TREATMENT HAS NOTHING TO DO
TREATMENT	179 - 2	TREATMENT DOES NOT TIRE THE ONE
TREATMENT	179 - 6	TREATMENT RECOGNIZES THAT ALL IS MIND
TREATMENT	183 - 2	THIS SYSTEM OF TREATMENT
TREATMENT	183 - 3	TREATMENT DOES NOT CONCERN ITSELF
TREATMENT	186 - 1	TREATMENT STARTS WITH PERFECT GOD
TREATMENT	192 - 1	TREATMENT MUST CARRY WITH IT
TREATMENT	192 - 1	IT IS TO BE A GOOD TREATMENT
TREATMENT	198 - 4	TREATMENT IS THE ACT, THE ART
TREATMENT	198 - 4	TREATMENT DOES NOT NECESSARILY
TREATMENT	205 - 2	TREATMENT IS NOT COMPLETE WITHOUT
TREATMENT	220 - 4	TREATMENT WOULD HEAL
TREATMENT	220 - 4	NO ROOM FOR DOUBT IN TREATMENT
TREATMENT	224 - 3	TREATMENT IS A SPECIFIC THING
TREATMENT	224 - 4	CONCLUSION WHEN GIVING A TREATMENT
TREATMENT	236 - 4	TREATMENT STRAIGHTENS
TREATMENT	244 - 5	TREATMENT FOR NERVE DISORDERS
TREATMENT	254 - 4	NO REAL SPECIFIC TREATMENT
TREATMENT	274 - 2	TREATMENT IS NOT FOR THE PURPOSE
TREATMENT	274 - 2	TREATMENT IS NOT MENTAL COERCION
TREATMENT	274 - 3	TREATMENT IS NOT SOMETHING ONE DOES
TREATMENT	274 - 3	TREATMENT IS AN ACTION IN THOUGHT
TREATMENT	277 - 3	TREATMENT REMOVES DOUBT
TREATMENT	281 - 2	THIS IS WHAT TREATMENT IS FOR
TREATMENT	285 - 3	TREATMENT WILL FIND AN OUTWARD
TREATMENT	287 - 2	TREATMENT WILL LEVEL ITSELF
TREATMENT	304 - 3	TREATMENT IS A THING OF ITSELF
TREATMENT	308 - 2	TREATMENT MUST NOT BE CONFUSED
TREATMENT	308 - 2	TREATMENT IS AN ACTIVE THING
TREATMENT	309 - 2	TREATMENT BE A MOVING THING
TREATMENT	315 - 2	WHAT IS A TREATMENT
TREATMENT	318 - 2	TREATMENT SHOULD ALWAYS BE
TREATMENT	318 - 3	THIS IS WHAT A TREATMENT IS
TREATMENT	321 - 2	TREATMENT IS A DEFINITE CONSCIOUS
TREATMENT	331 - 2	IN TREATMENT THERE SHOULD ALWAYS BE
TREATMENT	399 - 3	DYNAMIC AND CREATIVE TREATMENT
TREATMENT	404 - 1	THIS IS WHAT A TREATMENT
TREATMENT	414 - 1	TREATMENT MUST BE INDEPENDENT
TREATMENT	476 - 3	IN TREATMENT THERE SHOULD BE FIRST
TREATMENTS	046 - 6	GIVING SCIENTIFIC TREATMENTS
TREATMENTS	149 - 1	ARE PRAYERS AND TREATMENTS IDENTICAL
TREATMENTS	220 - 4	REPEATED TREATMENTS

TREE	448 – 5	TREE PRODUCES FOOD FRUIT
TREE	472 – 6	THOUGHT OF AS THE TREE OF UNITY
TREE OF LIFE	472 – 6	CROSS REPRESENTS THE TREE OF LIFE
TREE OF LIPE	473 – 4	TREE OF LIFE IS OUR REAL BEING
TREMBLING	384 – 1	FEAR OR EVEN WITH TREMBLING
TRIAL	108 – 2	MIDST OF THE GREATEST TRIAL
TRIBE	417 – 1	MODE OF HIS TRIBE
TRICK	046 – 6	THERE IS NO OCCULT TRICK
TRICK	345 – 3	NOT A TRICK OF CONCENTRATION
TRIED	432 – 3	UNTIL WE HAVE TRIED
TRIED	471 – 3	NO ONE WHO HAS TRIED THIS HAS FAILED
TRIES	499 – 1	GOD TRIES NO MAN
TRIFLES	225 – 2	THOSE WHO WORRY OVER TRIFLES
TRINITY	080 – 1	TEACHING OF THE TRINITY
TRINITY	080 – 2	THIS TRINITY OF BEING
TRINITY	080 – 3	NECESSITY OF A TRINITY OF BEING
TRINITY	080 – 3	TRINITY HAS BEEN TAUGHT
TRINITY	084 – 5	ARE ONE THE TRINITY
TRINITY	090 – 1	THE TRINITY OF BEING
TRINITY	090 – 2	OF THE CHRISTIAN TRINITY
TRINITY	480 – 6	TRINITY IS A UNITY
TRIUMPH	147 – 4	WE SHALL NEVER TRIUMPH
TRIUMPHANT	147 – 4	RISE TRIUMPHANT ABOVE THEM
TRIUMPHANT	369 – 3	THE CHRIST IS ALWAYS TRIUMPHANT
TRIUMPHANT	422 – 3	THE CHRIST IS ALWAYS TRIUMPHANT
TRIUMPHS	369 – 3	CHRIST TRIUMPHS OVER DEATH AND THE GRAVE
TRIUNE	098 – 1	TRIUNE UNITY OF SPIRIT
TRIUNE	106 – 2	REALIZE THAT GOD IS TRIUNE
TRIUNE NATURE	088 – 2	TRIUNE NATURE OF THE ONE GOD
TROUBLE	172 – 2	NOT NECESSARY TO SPECIFY THE TROUBLE
TROUBLE	315 – 2	WHERE THE TROUBLE COMES IN
TROUBLE	498 – 4	ALL TROUBLE COMES FROM DISBELIEF
TROUBLED	478 – 6	YOUR HEART BE TROUBLED
TROUBLES	464 – 3	ALL OF OUR TROUBLES COME FROM
TROUBLES	486 – 1	TROUBLES WILL BE ROLLED UP
TROUBLES	491 – 1	TROUBLES WE ARE NOT CAST DOWN
TROWARD	269 – 1	AS TROWARD SAID AS THIS IS THE TRUE
TROWARD	274 – 4	TROWARD SAYS THAT WE ENTER THE ABSOLUTE
TROWARD	409 – 5	TROWARD TELLS US THAT THE DIVINE
TRUE	095 – 2	TRUTH IS TRUE
TRUE	106 – 1	TRUE OF THE UNIVERSE
TRUE	110 – 1	TRUE LAW IS A LAW OF LIBERTY
TRUE	129 – 3	TRUE INDIVIDUALITY FUNCTIONS
TRUE	193 – 4	TRUE SPIRITUAL WORK
TRUE	195 – 3	WHAT IS TRUE OF IT IS
TRUE	254 – 6	SEPARATES THE FALSE FROM THE TRUE
TRUE	268 – 1	ONLY AS TRUE AS WE CAN MAKE IT
TRUE	272 – 3	TRUE TEN THOUSAND YEARS
TRUE	280 – 3	TRUE THAT THERE CAN BE NO GIFT
TRUE	342 – 1	SPIRITUAL IS ALWAYS TRUE
TRUE	363 – 4	WHATEVER IS TRUE OF MAN
TRUE	396 – 2	WHICH IS NOT TRUE OF GOD
TRUE	416 – 4	AS BEING TRUE ABOUT OURSELVES
TRUE	422 – 3	WHATEVER IS TRUE OF MAN
TRUE	444 – 2	TRUE ESTIMATE OF VALUE ON THE LIFE

TRUE	495 - 1	TRUE ESTIMATES OF LIFE AND REALITY
TRUE	497 - 4	TRUE ON ONE PLANE IS TRUE ON ALL
TRUE PRAYER	268 - 4	TRUE PRAYER MUST BE THY WILL BE DONE
TRUE PRAYER	455 - 6	TRUE PRAYER TO THE PRINCIPLE OF HIS SCIENCE
TRUE PRAYER	458 - 6	TRUE PRAYER IS ALWAYS UNIVERSAL
TRUE SELF	343 - 2	REALIZATION OF THE TRUE SELF
TRUST	033 - 3	TO TRUST THE UNIVERSE
TRUST	055 - 2	TRUST IN THE LAW OF GOOD
TRUST	057 - 2	WE MUST COME TO TRUST
TRUST	057 - 2	WE MUST TRUST THE INVISIBLE
TRUST	168 - 3	SACREDNESS OF HIS TRUST
TRUST	235 - 4	TRUST IN THE PERFECTION
TRUST	257 - 1	TRUST IN GOD WITHIN
TRUST	264 - 4	I REST IN CALM TRUST
TRUST	276 - 1	TRUST ITS IMPERSONAL ACTION
TRUST	303 - 4	SPOKEN IN CALM TRUST
TRUST	323 - 2	AND IN ABSOLUTE TRUST
TRUST	388 - 2	LEARN TO TRUST LIFE
TRUST	432 - 2	TRUST ABSOLUTELY IN THE LAW
TRUST	432 - 3	COMPLETELY TRUST IN GOD
TRUST	443 - 1	TRUST IN THE GOODNESS OF GOD
TRUST	455 - 5	UNQUALIFIED TRUST IN SPIRIT
TRUST	456 - 3	TRUST IN LIFE WHICH CHILDREN HAVE
TRUST	481 - 6	TRUST IN THE LAW OF GOOD
TRUST	496 - 2	TRUST IMPLICITLY IN THE UNIVERSE
TRUST	497 - 1	TRUST IN THE LAW OF GOOD
TRUSTED	414 - 3	IS TO BE IMPLICITLY TRUSTED
TRUTH	025 - 3	THE TRUTH POINTS TO FREEDOM UNDER LAW
TRUTH	031 - 6	WHY THE TRUTH IS TRUE
TRUTH	032 - 3	TRUTH SHALL MAKE US FREE
TRUTH	033 - 2	TRUTH WILL AUTOMATICALLY FREE HIM
TRUTH	042 - 3	MAN HAS SPOKEN THE TRUTH
TRUTH	044 - 4	TRUTH IS ALREADY KNOWN IN MIND
TRUTH	051 - 1	MUST BE AND IS THE TRUTH
TRUTH	054 - 1	THE SPIRIT OF TRUTH
TRUTH	055 - 5	SEAMLESS GARMENT OF TRUTH
TRUTH	056 - 2	MEN WOULD SPEAK THE TRUTH
TRUTH	057 - 2	TRUTH IS INSTANTANEOUS
TRUTH	058 - 3	THE TRUTH OF OUR TREATMENTS
TRUTH	060 - 3	TRUTH WILL OUT
TRUTH	068 - 1	THE STORY OF TRUTH
TRUTH	086 - 4	TRUTH KNOWN IS DEMONSTRATED
TRUTH	159 - 5	TRUTH WHICH WE ANNOUNCE IS SUPERIOR
TRUTH	165 - 2	POUR THE UPLIFTING TRUTH
TRUTH	166 - 2	THAT THIS NOW IS THE TRUTH
TRUTH	171 - 3	SAME TIME KNOWING THE TRUTH
TRUTH	172 - 1	KNOW THE TRUTH WITHIN HIMSELF
TRUTH	184 - 5	TRUTH IS INDIVISIBLE AND WHOLE
TRUTH	186 - 3	THROUGH THE RECOGNITION OF TRUTH
TRUTH	189 - 3	TRUTH KNOWS NO OPPOSITES
TRUTH	189 - 3	KNOW THAT TRUTH PRODUCES FREEDOM
TRUTH	189 - 3	TRUTH IS FREEDOM
TRUTH	191 - 4	TRUTH IS INFINITE
TRUTH	191 - 4	ALL OF TRUTH HAS BEEN GIVEN
TRUTH	192 - 2	TRUTH ALONE WILL ANSWER

TRUTH	201 - 1	NOTHING BUT THE TRUTH
TRUTH	203 - 4	TRUTH ABOUT MAN'S BEING
TRUTH	206 - 4	TRUTH SHALL MAKE YOU FREE
TRUTH	210 - 2	TRUTH BECAUSE OF THE GREAT NEUTRALIZING
TRUTH	210 - 3	TRUTH DEMONSTRATES ITSELF
TRUTH	213 - 2	A FACT BUT NOT A TRUTH
TRUTH	213 - 4	A FACT BUT NOT A TRUTH
TRUTH	216 - 1	ACTIVITY OF TRUTH
TRUTH	220 - 4	CONCEPT OF AN ALREADY ESTABLISHED TRUTH
TRUTH	223 - 2	COMPLETE EXPRESSION OF TRUTH
TRUTH	232 - 5	TRUTH SHALL MAKE YOU FREE
TRUTH	234 - 3	GUIDED INTO ALL TRUTH
TRUTH	236 - 2	CANNOT TAKE ROOT IN TRUTH
TRUTH	244 - 2	ONE FINAL TRUTH OR REALITY
TRUTH	247 - 1	MAN IS THE TRUTH
TRUTH	248 - 3	THE TRUTH SHALL MAKE YOU FREE
TRUTH	264 - 1	TRUTH MAKES ME FREE
TRUTH	272 - 4	CHRIST MEANS THE TRUTH
TRUTH	276 - 3	REALIZE THIS TRUTH AND MAKE USE OF IT
TRUTH	279 - 1	INTELLIGENCE TRUTH AND POWER
TRUTH	282 - 4	TO DESERT THE TRUTH
TRUTH	295 - 1	WE HAVE NOT KNOWN THE TRUTH
TRUTH	296 - 1	KNOW THE TRUTH
TRUTH	303 - 3	NOT TELLING THE TRUTH TO HIMSELF
TRUTH	328 - 4	ONE AND THE SAME TRUTH
TRUTH	362 - 2	HAS COME THE REAL TRUTH
TRUTH	373 - 1	INQUIRY INTO TRUTH STARTS
TRUTH	391 - 3	THE GREATEST TRUTH ABOUT MAN
TRUTH	418 - 3	REVEAL THE TRUTH OF BEING
TRUTH	418 - 3	THE TRUTH OF OUR BEING
TRUTH	419 - 2	PERCEIVES TRUTH
TRUTH	421 - 1	TRUTH OPERATE THROUGH HIM
TRUTH	423 - 1	EASIER TO TEACH THE TRUTH
TRUTH	436 - 2	THE TRUTH BY ITS FRUITS
TRUTH	437 - 1	TRUTH ALONE ENDURES TO ETERNAL
TRUTH	445 - 5	BECOMES OUR TRUTH
TRUTH	445 - 6	UNTIL WE BECOME TRUTH
TRUTH	453 - 4	TRUTH ALONE CAN ENDURE
TRUTH	453 - 5	TRUTH IS SIMPLE DIRECT
TRUTH	459 - 6	TRUTH IS POSITIVE BUT NON-COMBATIVE
TRUTH	472 - 4	TRUTH KNOWS NEITHER YESTERDAY
TRUTH	474 - 6	TRUTH ALONE MAKES FREE
TRUTH	478 - 2	TRUTH HE WILL NEVER SEE DEATH
TRUTH	483 - 5	THE TRUTH IS ALWAYS THE REMEDY
TRUTH	488 - 2	TRUTH IS SELF-EXISTENT
TRUTHS	420 - 2	TRUTHS WHICH MYSTICISM HAS REVEALED
TRY	334 - 3	TRY TO SOLVE ALL OF ITS PROBLEMS
TRY	346 - 1	TRY TO TELL
TUBERCULOSIS	172 - 4	I HAVE TUBERCULOSIS
TUMORS	235 - 2	TREATING CANCERS AND TUMORS
TUNE	421 - 5	TUNE WITH THE VIBRATION
TUNED	094 - 1	TUNED INTO THE KEYNOTE
TUNE IN	351 - 2	ABILITY TO TUNE IN ON THOUGHT
TUNING IN	351 - 1	THERE MUST BE A MENTAL TUNING IN
TURN	169 - 3	TURN ENTIRELY AWAY FROM THE RELATIVE

TURN	186 - 1	TURN ENTIRELY FROM THE CONDITION
TURN	357 - 3	TURN TO THAT LIVING PRESENCE
TURN	420 - 1	WE DO TURN TOWARD THE ONE
TURN AWAY	317 - 2	RESOLUTELY TURN AWAY FROM ANY
TURNS	173 - 5	MIND TURNS AWAY FROM LACK
TURNS	460 - 4	TURNS TO US AS WE TURN TO HIM
TURNS	466 - 3	TURNS TO US AS WE TURN TO HIM
TURN WITHIN	419 - 5	TURN WITHIN AND FIND GOD
TWO	043 - 2	TWO FUNDAMENTAL CHARACTERISTICS
TWO	068 - 3	NOT BE TWO INFINITE BEINGS
TWO	156 - 4	A BELIEF IN TWO POWERS
TWO	170 - 3	TWO DISTINCT METHODS
TWO	176 - 1	TWO WILL EXACTLY BALANCE
TWO	260 - 4	TWO POSSIBILITIES OF OUR USE
TWO	280 - 3	THESE ARE THE TWO GREAT LAWS
TWO	306 - 4	THERE ARE ALWAYS TWO
TWO	316 - 2	WORKING IN TWO SEPARATE FIELDS
TWO	347 - 2	DO NOT HAVE TWO MINDS
TWO	393 - 3	NOT TWO MINDS BUT ONE
TWO	412 - 3	IS ONE AND NEVER TWO
TWO	459 - 3	TWO GREAT COMMANDMENTS ARE TO LOVE
TWO	476 - 2	TWO TO MAKE A COMPLETE THING
TWO	499 - 4	IT IS ONE AND NEVER TWO
TWO BODIES	375 - 3	TWO BODIES CANNOT OCCUPY
TWO SIDES	321 - 2	TWO SIDES OF THE SAME THING
TWO THOUSAND	362 - 2	IT IS NOW NEARLY TWO THOUSAND
TYPE	045 - 1	ONE TYPE OF KNOWLEDGE
TYPE	123 - 3	TYPE MAINTAINS ITS INTEGRITY
TYPE	288 - 1	TYPE OF OBJECTIVE EXPERIENCE
TYPE	387 - 2	SOME TYPE OF IMMORTALITY
TYPES	254 - 5	DIFFERENT TYPES OF MANIFESTATION
TYPIFIES	467 - 3	TYPIFIES A STATE OF COMPLETE
TYPIFIES	485 - 2	CHRIST TYPIFIES THE UNIVERSAL SON
TYPIFY	230 - 2	TYPIFY THE ABILITY OF THE MIND

U

ULCER	256 - 4	HEMORRHAGE OR STOMACH ULCER
ULTIMATE	044 - 5	ULTIMATE OF ALL THINGS
ULTIMATE	050 - 1	WE HAVE ARRIVED AT THE ULTIMATE
ULTIMATE	050 - 1	THAT IS THE ULTIMATE
ULTIMATE	052 - 4	THE ULTIMATE ESSENCE
ULTIMATE	119 - 2	TENDENCY TOWARD ULTIMATE GOOD
ULTIMATE	289 - 2	CONCEIVE OF THE ULTIMATE OF THE IDEA
ULTIMATE	289 - 2	THE ULTIMATE OF EFFECT
ULTIMATE	289 - 4	ULTIMATE RIGHT ACTION IS NOW TODAY
ULTIMATELY	333 - 4	ULTIMATELY REACH ITS HEAVENLY HOME
ULTIMATELY	434 - 1	ULTIMATELY FIND HIS HOME IN HEAVEN
ULTIMATE REALITY	334 - 5	ULTIMATE REALITY IS HERE NOW
UNACCEPTABLE	430 - 3	ARE UNACCEPTABLE WHILE THERE IS
UNAFRAID	370 - 1	WALKS UNAFRAID THROUGH LIFE
UNALTERABLY	433 - 3	IT IS TRUE UNALTERABLY TRUE
UNANSWERED	373 - 1	MUST FOREVER REMAIN UNANSWERED

UNAWARE	248 - 4	MAY BE UNAWARE OF THE CAUSE
UNBALANCED	380 - 2	PEOPLE SOMETIMES BECOME UNBALANCED
UNBEARABLE	479 - 2	BURDENS OFTEN BECOME UNBEARABLE
UNBELIEF	037 - 3	NOT IN BECAUSE OF UNBELIEF
UNBELIEF	037 - 3	WHILE THERE IS UNBELIEF
UNBELIEF	057 - 1	NO UNBELIEF, NO DOUBT, NO UNCERTAINTY
UNBELIEF	304 - 3	ITS OPERATION BUT UNBELIEF
UNBELIEF	304 - 3	NOT ENTER IN BECAUSE OF UNBELIEF
UNBELIEF	405 - 2	BECAUSE OF THEIR UNBELIEF
UNBELIEVABLE	417 - 1	SO SIMPLE THAT IT SEEMS UNBELIEVABLE
UNBIDDEN	369 - 1	HE DOES NOT COME UNBIDDEN
UNBORN	161 - 4	UNBORN POSSIBILITY
UNBORN	309 - 5	UNBORN BUT POTENTIAL POSSIBILITY
UNBOUNDED	211 - 3	WITHIN ITSELF IT IS UNBOUNDED
UNBROKEN	245 - 4	UNBROKEN STREAM OF GOOD
UNCERTAIN	380 - 2	SPIRITS ARE PRESENT IS UNCERTAIN
UNCERTAINTY	032 - 3	UNCERTAINTY IS NOT GOD-ORDAINED
UNCERTAINTY	057 - 1	NO UNBELIEF, NO DOUBT, NO UNCERTAINTY
UNCERTAINTY	239 - 2	SET FREE FROM UNCERTAINTY
UNCERTAINTY	264 - 5	THERE IS NO UNCERTAINTY
UNCHARITABLENESS	469 - 1	UNCHARITABLENESS TOWARD OTHERS
UNCLEAN	448 - 2	POSSESSED OF UNCLEAN THOUGHTS
UNCLOTHED	491 - 7	DO NOT WISH TO BE UNCLOTHED
UNCOMPROMISING	274 - 4	UNCOMPROMISING AND ABSOLUTE
UNCONDITIONAL	500 - 5	UNCONDITIONAL BELIEF IN BOTH THE ABILITY
UNCONDITIONED	431 - 3	DEPENDS UPON AN UNCONDITIONED FAITH IN
UNCONDITIONED	471 - 3	ABSOLUTE AND UNCONDITIONED ONE
UNCONINNED	158 - 4	UNCONFINED TO AGE OR STATION
UNCONNECTED	315 - 3	ENERGY UNCONNECTED DOES NOTHING
UNCONSCIOUS	049 - 4	IS AN UNCONSCIOUS COMPROMISE
UNCONSCIOUS	074 - 1	UNCONSCIOUS OPERATION
UNCONSCIOUS	090 - 3	MIND NEVER COULD BE UNCONSCIOUS
UNCONSCIOUS	114 - 3	SUBCONSCIOUS DOES NOT MEAN UNCONSCIOUS
UNCONSCIOUS	125 - 3	MOST CASES IT IS UNCONSCIOUS
UNCONSCIOUS	126 - 2	UNCONSCIOUS PROCESS
UNCONSCIOUS	211 - 1	UNCONSCIOUS BECAUSE THE MOTHER
UNCONSCIOUS	289 - 4	PROVES THAT IT IS UNCONSCIOUS OF TIME
UNCONSCIOUS	294 - 2	RESULT OF HIS CONSCIOUS AND UNCONSCIOUS
UNCONSCIOUS	380 - 3	AN UNCONSCIOUS COMMUNICATION GOES ON
UNCONSCIOUS	396 - 3	LAW IS UNCONSCIOUS INTELLIGENCE
UNCONSCIOUS	397 - 3	UNCONSCIOUS THAT SUCH ORDERS
UNCONSCIOUS	488 - 3	UNCONSCIOUS OF THE IMPERFECT
UNCONSCIOUS	492 - 1	COMPLETELY UNCONSCIOUS OF DEATH
UNCONSCIOUS MEMORY	118 - 4	UNCONSCIOUS MEMORY WORKING
UNCOVER	131 - 1	ABLE TO UNCOVER THE APPEARANCE
UNCOVER	168 - 5	UNCOVER GOD IN EVERY MAN
UNCOVER	191 - 1	SEEK TO UNCOVER THIS PERFECTION
UNCOVER	203 - 1	UNCOVER THE TRUTH
UNCOVER	280 - 3	UNCOVER THE SCIENCE OF PRAYER
UNCOVER	418 - 3	MENTALLY UNCOVER AND REVEAL
UNCOVERING	183 - 2	PURPOSE OF UNCOVERING AND NEUTRALIZING
UNCOVERING	197 - 3	IS ACCOMPLISHED BY UNCOVERING
UNCREATED	392 - 2	UNCREATED STATE OF BEING
UNDER	484 - 2	UNDER ITS LAW OF FREEDOM
UNDERLYING	331 - 4	PURPOSE UNDERLYING ALL THINGS

UNDERLYING	363 - 2	UNDERLYING HIS PHILOSOPHY
UNDERSTAND	120 - 3	DID NOT UNDERSTAND THE HARMONIOUS UNITY
UNDERSTAND	171 - 2	UNDERSTAND AND MAKE CONSCIOUS USE
UNDERSTAND	206 - 2	UNDERSTAND THIS VERY CLEARLY
UNDERSTAND	271 - 2	THE DEGREE THAT WE UNDERSTAND
UNDERSTAND	458 - 2	UNDERSTAND THE FRAILTIES OF HUMAN NATURE
UNDERSTANDING	044 - 4	WE SHOULD GET UNDERSTANDING
UNDERSTANDING	054 - 1	FOR A POSITIVE UNDERSTANDING OF THE SPIRIT
UNDERSTANDING	160 - 2	STATE OF SPIRITUAL UNDERSTANDING
UNDERSTANDING	191 - 4	COMPLETE UNDERSTANDING OF TRUTH
UNDERSTANDING	230 - 5	LIGHT OF SPIRITUAL UNDERSTANDING
UNDERSTANDING	267 - 4	COMPLETE UNDERSTANDING OF HIMSELF
UNDERSTANDING	267 - 4	AS HIS UNDERSTANDING UNFOLDS
UNDERSTANDING	271 - 3	IN KNOWLEDGE AND UNDERSTANDING
UNDERSTANDING	271 - 4	WE HAVE A GREATER UNDERSTANDING
UNDERSTANDING	275 - 3	TO DIVORCE SPIRITUAL UNDERSTANDING
UNDERSTANDING	284 - 5	FAITH SHOULD BE ONE OF UNDERSTANDING
UNDERSTANDING	340 - 5	ARRIVED AT A SUFFICIENT UNDERSTANDING
UNDERSTANDING	368 - 1	UNDERSTANDING THE FRAILTIES
UNDERSTANDING	383 - 2	ENLIGHTENMENT AND UNDERSTANDING
UNDERSTANDING	383 - 2	UNDERSTANDING ALONE CONSTITUTES
UNDERSTANDING	394 - 4	LEVEL OF MAN'S UNDERSTANDING
UNDERSTANDING	401 - 4	ROAD OF FAITH AND UNDERSTANDING
UNDERSTANDING	434 - 1	UNDERSTANDING HEART IS FILLED
UNDERSTANDING	444 - 2	REFERRING TO HIS UNDERSTANDING
UNDERSTANDING	472 - 7	UNDERSTANDING PRODUCED A CONSCIOUSNESS
UNDERSTANDS	107 - 3	UNDERSTANDS THESE CONDITIONS AND OBEYS
UNDERSTANDS	340 - 2	UNDERSTANDS THIS MENTAL LAW
UNDERTAKINGS	450 - 3	THE OUTCOME OF HIS UNDERTAKINGS
UNDESIRABLE	148 - 2	IN AN UNDESIRABLE CONDITION
UNDIFFERENTIATED	091 - 3	UNDIFFERENTIATED SUBSTANCE
UNDIFFERENTIATED	157 - 1	THE UNDIFFERENTIATED SUBSTANCE
UNDIFFERENTIATED	177 - 3	SAME UNDIFFERENTIATED SPIRITUAL SUBSTANCE
UNDISPUTED	458 - 5	UNDISPUTED PLACE OF AGREEMENT
UNDISTURBED	479 - 2	DEPTHS OF AN UNDISTURBED SOUL
UNDIVIDED	082 - 1	IT IS UNDIVIDED, COMPLETE
UNDIVIDED	172 - 1	IT IS AN UNDIVIDED WHOLE
UNDIVIDED	432 - 2	ENTIRETY AN UNDIVIDED WHOLE
UNDIVIDED	447 - 3	UNDIVIDED ATTENTION TO THE SPIRITUAL UNIT
UN-DO	142 - 4	THOUGHT HAS DONE THOUGHT CAN UN-DO
UNEARTH	153 - 3	TO UNEARTH THIS HIDDEN CAUSE
UNEARTHS	203 - 4	UNEARTHS THE MENTAL CAUSE
UNEASY	353 - 1	FEEL UNEASY IN THE PRESENCE
UNERRING	292 - 3	IT IS UNERRING
UNEXPRESSED	253 - 1	WITH UNEXPRESSED LONGINGS
UNEXPRESSED	392 - 2	IT IS UNEXPRESSED MIND
UNFAIR	450 - 1	TO RECEIVE MORE SOUNDS UNFAIR
UNFALTERING	262 - 2	UNFALTERING TRUST IN HIS ABILITY
UNFAMILIAR	200 - 2	UNFAMILIAR WITH THIS WORK
UNFOLD	071 - 1	FROM WHICH TO UNFOLD
UNFOLD	138 - 4	UNFOLD EVERYTHING THAT IS
UNFOLD	282 - 2	CAN UNFOLD OUR CONSCIOUSNESS
UNFOLD	289 - 2	UNFOLD AND PRODUCE A PLANT
UNFOLD	338 - 3	WE SHALL FOREVER UNFOLD
UNFOLDING	191 - 4	UNFOLDING IN THE CONSCIOUSNESS OF MAN

UNFOLDING	267 - 4	UNFOLDING FROM A LIMITLESS POTENTIAL
UNFOLDING	306 - 2	THROUGH THE UNFOLDING OF CONSCIOUSNESS
UNFOLDING	340 - 3	EVOLUTION OF LOCOMOTION THE UNFOLDING
UNFOLDING	385 - 1	NECESSARY TO THE UNFOLDING
UNFOLDING	387 - 1	AN UNFOLDING CONSCIOUSNESS
UNFOLDING	387 - 3	A BECOMING GOD AN UNFOLDING SOUL
UNFOLDING	390 - 4	UNFOLDING INTO A GREATER RECOGNITION
UNFOLDING	420 - 3	GOD IS UNFOLDING THROUGH HIS IDEA
UNFOLDING	485 - 3	WE WAIT FOR THE UNFOLDING
UNFOLDMENT	038 - 2	UNFOLDMENT OF THE WORD
UNFOLDMENT	044 - 1	EVOLUTION IS AN ETERNAL UNFOLDMENT
UNFOLDMENT	051 - 2	UNFOLDMENT OF THAT PRINCIPLE
UNFOLDMENT	057 - 2	SUCH TIME IN ITS UNFOLDMENT
UNFOLDMENT	057 - 2	INVISIBLE LAW OF UNFOLDMENT
UNFOLDMENT	193 - 3	THROUGH THE LAW OF UNFOLDMENT
UNFOLDMENT	271 - 4	A LAW OF UNFOLDMENT IN MAN
UNFOLDMENT	300 - 3	THIS IS THE NATURAL UNFOLDMENT
UNFOLDMENT	339 - 2	THE UNFOLDMENT OF THE IDEA
UNFOLDMENT	364 - 3	THE UNFOLDMENT OF PERSONALITY
UNFOLDMENT	376 - 2	FUTURE UNFOLDMENT OF THE SOUL
UNFOLDMENT	282 - 2	UNFOLDMENT TAKING PLACE
UNFOLDS	172 - 1	THE LAW UNFOLDS
UNFOLDS	197 - 2	HE UNFOLDS HIS OWN PERSONALITY
UNFOLDS	198 - 1	UNFOLDS AND EVOLVES
UNFOLDS	267 - 4	AS HIS UNDERSTANDING UNFOLDS
UNFOLDS	271 - 4	AS MAN UNFOLDS IN HIS MENTALITY
UNFOLDS	340 - 2	PROCESS THROUGH WHICH SPIRIT UNFOLDS
UNFOLDS	420 - 3	AN IDEA UNFOLDS
UNFORMED	131 - 4	THE UNFORMED STUFF
UNFORMED	197 - 1	OPERATES UPON UNFORMED SUBSTANCE
UNFORMED	393 - 2	UNFORMED STATE CAN BE CALLED FORTH
UNFORMED	397 - 1	IN THE UNFORMED
UNFORMED	476 - 2	FORM TO THE UNFORMED
UNGUIDED	367 - 1	NO MAN NEED GO UNGUIDED
UNHAPPINESS	056 - 5	UNHAPPINESS IS UPROOTED
UNHAPPINESS	097 - 2	DISEASE, POVERTY, UNHAPPINESS
UNHAPPINESS	213 - 3	NECESSITY FOR UNHAPPINESS
UNHAPPINESS	236 - 3	ALL IS SICKNESS AND UNHAPPINESS
UNHAPPINESS	267 - 2	PEACE AND CLING TO UNHAPPINESS
UNHAPPINESS	269 - 3	FROM MISERY AND UNHAPPINESS
UNHAPPINESS	336 - 5	THE EXPERIENCE OF UNHAPPINESS
UNHAPPY	110 - 3	ABOUT THEIR UNHAPPINESS BECOME UNHAPPY
UNHAPPY	118 - 3	KEEPS ME UNHAPPY
UNHAPPY	168 - 5	GOD IS NOT UNHAPPY
UNHAPPY	213 - 3	THAT ONE HAS TO BE UNHAPPY
UNHAPPY	213 - 3	NO ONE WILL BE UNHAPPY
UNHAPPY	447 - 2	MOST PEOPLE ARE UNHAPPY
UNIFICATION	331 - 5	THIS WAS UNIFICATION
UNIFICATION	395 - 2	UNIFICATION AND ACQUIESCENCE
UNIFIED	068 - 1	A COMPLETE AND UNIFIED PATTERN
UNIFIED	077 - 1	IT IS SUBJECTIVELY UNIFIED
UNIFIED	195 - 5	IS UNIFIED WITH A LAW
UNIFIED	251 - 6	I AM UNIFIED WITH UNIVERSAL LAW
UNIFIED	299 - 2	GOD IN ME IS UNIFIED WITH GOD IN ALL
UNIFIED	341 - 4	UNIFIED WITH THE UNIVERSE

UNIFIES	394 - 4	MAN UNIFIES WITH THE UNIVERSE
UNIFIES	500 - 1	UNIFIES WITH ALL HUMANITY
UNIFY	330 - 5	WE MUST UNIFY
UNIFY	332 - 1	UNIFY WITH IT
UNIFY	357 - 3	UNIFY WITH IT
UNIFY	444 - 4	TO UNIFY WITH FIRST CAUSE
UNIFY	444 - 4	UNIFY MAN WITH GOD
UNIFY	476 - 3	UNIFY WITH THE SPIRITUAL CONSCIOUSNESS
UNIFY	477 - 3	UNIFY AND NOT DIVIDE
UNIFYING	415 - 3	UNIFYING PRINCIPLE OF LIFE
UNIFYING	475 - 1	UNIFYING HIMSELF WITH REALITY
UNINHIBITED	250 - 2	UNINHIBITED CIRCULATION
UNINTELLIGENT	209 - 2	IT IS UNINTELLIGENT
UNION	072 - 3	CONSCIOUS UNION WITH LIFE
UNION	103 - 3	UNION OF CREATION WITH THE CREATOR
UNION	148 - 4	FEEL A DEEPER UNION WITH LIFE
UNION	151 - 2	ONE'S UNION WITH THE WHOLE
UNION	180 - 4	UNION OF PEACE WITH POISE
UNION	331 - 2	THERE IS A PERFECT UNION
UNION	419 - 4	UNION WHICH CANNOT BE BROKEN
UNION	472 - 1	IT IS CONSCIOUS UNION WITH GOD
UNIQUE	121 - 3	EACH INDIVIDUAL IS A UNIQUE VARIATION
UNIQUE	263 - 6	KNOW THAT IT IS UNIQUE
UNIQUE	263 - 6	I AM UNIQUE
UNIQUE	313 - 2	BUT EACH IS UNIQUE, DIFFERENT
UNIQUE	359 - 4	ENTIRELY UNIQUE AND DIFFERENT FROM US
UNIQUE	363 - 2	THE MOST UNIQUE CHARACTER OF HISTORY
UNIQUE	427 - 2	UNIQUE PLACE IN THE HISTORY OF
UNIQUENESS	332 - 4	THE REALIZATION OF THE UNIQUENESS
UNIT	463 - 2	UNIVERSE IS A UNIT
UNITE	320 - 3	UNITE TO PRODUCE DEFINITE EFFECTS
UNITE	444 - 4	UNITE THE INFINITE WITH THE FINITE
UNITED	118 - 1	UNITED INTELLIGENCE OF THE HUMAN RACE
UNITED	140 - 4	UNITED INTELLIGENCE OF THE HUMAN RACE
UNITED	263 - 6	UNITED WITH ALL SELVES
UNITY	039 - 4	DUALITY RATHER THAN UNITY
UNITY	040 - 3	A UNITY MUST BE ESTABLISHED
UNITY	042 - 6	WE HAVE A DUAL UNITY
UNITY	045 - 4	MULTIPLICITY PROCEEDING FROM UNITY
UNITY	045 - 4	UNITY PASSES INTO VARIETY
UNITY	050 - 1	TWO SIDES OF THE INFINITE UNITY
UNITY	053 - 4	A REAL UNITY WITH SPIRIT
UNITY	069 - 2	THE WORLD OF UNITY
UNITY	069 - 2	THIS CONCEPT OF UNITY
UNITY	077 - 1	IN A STATE OF INNER UNITY
UNITY	081 - 3	NATURE OF BEING IS A UNITY
UNITY	082 - 1	UNITY BACK OF ALL THINGS
UNITY	090 - 1	THREEFOLD UNITY OF REALITY
UNITY	096 - 1	CONSCIOUSNESS IS ALWAYS A UNITY
UNITY	098 - 1	TRIUNE UNITY OF SPIRIT
UNITY	102 - 4	UNITY WHICH IS THE ONE
UNITY	102 - 4	MANY NEVER CONTRADICT THE UNITY
UNITY	102 - 5	UNITY WHICH PERMEATES ALL THINGS
UNITY	104 - 2	SENSE A UNITY WITH NATURE
UNITY	111 - 4	UNITY OF GOD AND MAN ON ALL THREE PLANES

UNITY	116 - 2	PHYSICAL MAN IS IN UNITY
UNITY	116 - 3	UNITY IS EXPRESSED IN MULTIPLICITY
UNITY	117 - 2	NO GREATER UNITY COULD BE
UNITY	124 - 1	UP A SCALE OF UNITY
UNITY	132 - 9	ETERNAL STATE OF COMPLETE UNITY
UNITY	153 - 5	SENSES ITS UNITY WITH THE WHOLE
UNITY	156 - 4	THE UNITY OF ALL LIFE
UNITY	167 - 4	SHOULD FEEL A UNITY OF SPIRIT
UNITY	184 - 2	IN AN ETERNAL STATE OF UNITY
UNITY	184 - 3	HAVE AN INNER SENSE OF UNITY
UNITY	192 - 1	THE UNDERSTANDING OF UNITY
UNITY	192 - 1	REALIZE THIS UNITY WITH GOD
UNITY	211 - 2	UNITY WILL PROVE DISASTROUS
UNITY	232 - 3	UNITY OF ALL MEN
UNITY	238 - 2	SENSE OF UNITY
UNITY	258 - 5	COMPLETE UNITY WITH ALL
UNITY	259 - 1	FEEL MY UNITY WITH
UNITY	261 - 4	CONSCIOUS OF ITS UNITY WITH GOD
UNITY	270 - 1	BACK OF IT ALL IS A UNITY
UNITY	278 - 2	OUR UNITY WITH GOOD
UNITY	285 - 4	NATURE IT IS A UNITY
UNITY	299 - 1	OUR UNITY WITH ALL PEOPLE
UNITY	309 - 5	UNITY EXISTS PAST PRESENT AND FUTURE
UNITY	310 - 2	UNITY IN THIS PHYSICAL WOPLD
UNITY	314 - 1	WE ARE LIVING FROM THIS UNITY
UNITY	316 - 2	UNITY IN ONE PRIMAL PRINCIPLE
UNITY	321 - 1	OUR UNITY WITH GOOD
UNITY	327 - 1	HIS UNITY WITH THE WHOLE
UNITY	331 - 2	ABSOLUTE UNITY OF GOD AND MAN
UNITY	334 - 4	SOUL THAT REALIZES ITS UNITY
UNITY	344 - 1	WHILE SENSING THIS UNITY
UNITY	368 - 1	UNITY OF UNIVERSAL SPIRIT
UNITY	391 - 2	UNIVERSAL UNITY AND WHOLENESS
UNITY	391 - 3	UNITY WITH THE SUPREME SPIRIT
UNITY	407 - 3	BUT TWO ENDS OF ONE UNITY
UNITY	419 - 3	ABSOLUTE UNITY OF GOD AND MAN
UNITY	420 - 5	ONE'S CONSCIOUSNESS OF HIS UNITY
UNITY	421 - 1	HIS UNITY WITH THE WHOLE
UNITY	440 - 3	UNITY UNDERLYING ALL LIFE
UNITY	444 - 3	RECOGNITION OF THE UNITY
UNITY	447 - 3	UNITY WITH LIFE
UNITY	451 - 3	UNITY OF GOD WITH MAN
UNITY	460 - 5	UNITY OF LOVE AND LAW
UNIVERSAL	029 - 3	MERGES WITH THE UNIVERSAL SUBJECTIVE MIND
UNIVERSAL	030 - 2	EVERYONE IS UNIVERSAL ON THE SUBJECTIVE
UNIVERSAL	087 - 1	GOD IS THE UNIVERSAL
UNIVERSAL	093 - 4	A FIELD WHICH WE CALL UNIVERSAL
UNIVERSAL	093 - 4	ONE IS UNIVERSAL THE OTHER INDIVIDUAL
UNIVERSAL	107 - 4	UNIVERSAL INTELLIGENCE IS IMBUED
UNIVERSAL	150 - 2	EMBODY CERTAIN UNIVERSAL PRINCIPLES
UNIVERSAL	267 - 3	SURROUNDED BY A UNIVERSAL MIND
UNIVERSAL	421 - 4	UNIVERSAL ON THE SUBJECTIVE SIDE
UNIVERSAL	449 - 5	LOVE MUST BECOME UNIVERSAL
UNIVERSAL	458 - 6	TRUE PRAYER IS ALWAYS UNIVERSAL
UNIVERSAL	477 - 6	BOTH INDIVIDUAL AND UNIVERSAL

UNIVERSAL I AM	081 - 4	THE GREAT OR UNIVERSAL I AM
UNIVERSALITY	343 - 3	UNIVERSALITY IN HIS OWN SOUL
UNIVERSALITY	344 - 1	UNIVERSALITY OF ALL THINGS
UNIVERSAL LAW	392 - 1	USE OF THE UNIVERSAL LAW
UNIVERSAL MIND	044 - 5	UNIVERSAL MIND CONTAINS ALL KNOWLEDGE
UNIVERSAL MIND	320 - 4	UNIVERSAL MIND ACTING AS LAW
UNIVERSAL SONSHIP	361 - 5	UNIVERSAL SONSHIP THE ENTIRE CREATION
UNIVERSE	026 - 2	LOVE OF THE UNIVERSE MUST BE ONE
UNIVERSE	027 - 3	UNIVERSE HAS NO FAVORITES
UNIVERSE	027 - 5	LIVE IN A SPIRITUAL UNIVERSE
UNIVERSE	032 - 2	MATERIAL OR PHYSICAL UNIVERSE
UNIVERSE	042 - 6	UNIVERSE ARE TO BE TRUSTED
UNIVERSE	046 - 1	WE CANNOT FIGHT THE UNIVERSE
UNIVERSE	063 - 2	NO MANIFEST UNIVERSE
UNIVERSE	068 - 5	AS THE INVISIBLE UNIVERSE
UNIVERSE	089 - 2	THE UNIVERSE IS MORE THAN AN INEXORABLE
UNIVERSE	109 - 4	UNIVERSE IS FOR US AND NOT AGAINST US
UNIVERSE	155 - 1	UNIVERSE IS A SPIRITUAL SYSTEM
UNIVERSE	217 - 2	LIVING IN A PERFECT UNIVERSE
UNIVERSE	322 - 1	THE MANIFEST UNIVERSE IS A RESULT
UNIVERSE	395 - 1	UNIVERSE IS NOT RUN ON THE SCALE
UNIVERSE	401 - 1	CONSCIOUS MIND OF THE UNIVERSE
UNIVERSE	415 - 1	UNIVERSE IN WHICH WE LIVE IS REAL
UNIVERSE	462 - 1	UNIVERSE GIVES US WHAT WE ASK
UNIVERSE	465 - 1	UNIVERSE IS NOT LIMITED
UNIVERSE	483 - 2	THE PHYSICAL UNIVERSE
UNIVERSE	492 - 5	THE UNIVERSE PLAYS NO FAVORITES
UNIVERSE	501 - 7	UNIVERSE HOLDS NOTHING AGAINST US
UNKNOWABLE	072 - 4	BUT NOT THE GREAT UNKNOWABLE
UNKNOWN	072 - 4	IS THE GREAT UNKNOWN
UNKNOWN	378 - 1	PRESENCE OF AN UNKNOWN AGENCY
UNLESS	067 - 2	UNLESS IT IS CONSCIOUS OF SOMETHING
UNLESS	307 - 3	REAL TO US UNLESS WE MAKE IT REAL
UNLESS	433 - 3	UNLESS HE TRANSCENDS THE LAW ALREADY SET
UNLIKE	142 - 2	REPELS WHAT IS UNLIKE
UNLIMITED	161 - 3	UNIVERSE REMAINS UNLIMITED
UNLIMITED	228 - 1	FLOWS IN UNLIMITED SUPPLY
UNLIMITED	390 - 1	WITHIN ITSELF UNLIMITED
UNLOOSE	268 - 3	MAY UNLOOSE ITS OWN ENERGY
UNLOVELINESS	281 - 4	SEES ONLY UNLOVELINESS IN OTHERS
UNMANIFEST	098 - 1	COSMIC STUFF UNMANIFEST FORM
UNMANIFEST	195 - 3	ONE WITH UNMANIFEST SUBSTANCE
UNNATURAL	160 - 2	ANYTHING STRANGE OR UNNATURAL
UNNATURAL	192 - 4	UNNATURAL FORCE IS WITHDRAWN
UNNECESSARY	146 - 3	STRUGGLE ARE UNNECESSARY
UNPLEASANT	183 - 3	CONCERN ITSELF WITH UNPLEASANT
UNPLEASANT	255 - 5	ERASE EVERY UNPLEASANT EXPERIENCE
UNQUALIFIED	458 - 5	OF ACCEPTANCE AN UNQUALIFIED
UNQUALIFIEDLY	315 - 2	THE MIND MUST UNQUALIFIEDLY
UNQUESTIONABLY	049 - 2	UNQUESTIONABLY MUST ACCOMPLISH
UNREAL	099 - 4	BODY IS UNREAL IS A MISTAKE
UNREAL	404 - 1	LIMITATION IS UNREAL TO MIND
UNREALITY	435 - 2	UNREALITY FROM THE SHOULDERS OF HYPOCRISY
UNREMITTING	212 - 1	UNREMITTING AND WILL OPERATE
UNRESERVED	433 - 1	UNRESERVED TRUST IN THE GOODNESS

UNRESPONSIVE	414 - 4	IT IS COLD AND UNRESPONSIVE
UNSATISFIED	428 - 5	UNSATISFIED AND APPETITE UNAPPEASED
UNSCIENTIFIC	488 - 5	UNSCIENTIFIC TO DWELL UPON LACK
UNSEEN	041 - 3	SOFT TREAD OF THE UNSEEN GUEST
UNSEEN	148 - 4	THE SEEN AND OF THE UNSEEN
UNSEEN	392 - 4	THE SEEN AND THE UNSEEN
UNSEEN	407 - 2	HAVING FAITH IN THE UNSEEN
UNSEEN	483 - 2	WE UNDERSTAND THE UNSEEN
UNSOLVED	053 - 2	THE UNSOLVED PROBLEM
UNSPONTANEOUS	108 - 1	UNSPONTANEOUS INDIVIDUALITY
UNSPONTANEOUS	332 - 5	AN UNSPONTANEOUS INDIVIDUALITY
UNSULLIED	151 - 2	UNSULLIED AS THE MIND OF GOD
UNTHINK	086 - 3	THINKS IT CAN UNTHINK
UNTHINKABLE	213 - 3	UNTHINKABLE TO ADMIT THAT ONE
UNTHINKABLE	283 - 4	UNTHINKABLE AND IMPOSSIBLE
UNTHOUGHT	397 - 1	MIND IN AN UNTHOUGHT STATE
UNTIMELY	385 - 2	DEATH COULD NOT BE UNTIMELY
UNTO	140 - 3	IT IS DONE UNTO US
UNTOLD	432 - 4	UNTOLD MISERY IS SUFFERED
UNTO THE THING	146 - 3	BECOMES THE LAW UNTO THE THING
UNTRAINED	400 - 1	THAN UNTRAINED
UNUSUAL	207 - 3	I FELT NOTHING UNUSUAL
UNWAVERING	245 - 1	OF A FIRM UNWAVERING MIND
UNWELCOME	369 - 1	AN UNWELCOME GUEST
UNWISE	031 - 1	TASKMASTER TO THE UNWISE
UNWISE	502 - 3	UNWISE TO HOLD THEM
UNWORTHY	027 - 4	THAT WE ARE UNWORTHY
UNWORTHY	075 - 1	ANY SENSE THAT WE ARE UNWORTHY
UP	491 - 6	OUR THOUGHT REACHES UP AND ON
UPLIFT	256 - 1	HEAL CLEANSE AND UPLIFT
UPLIFT	299 - 3	I UPLIFT THEREFORE I AM UPLIFTED
UPLIFTS	253 - 3	PERFECTION SO UPLIFTS THE THOUGHT
UPON	084 - 5	UPON THE UNIVERSAL STUFF
UPON	339 - 3	WITHIN AND UPON THE ONE
UPRIGHT	196 - 1	GOD HATH MADE MAN UPRIGHT
UPROOTED	056 - 5	UPROOTED FROM MY MIND
UPROOTING	495 - 4	UPROOTING THE THISTLES AND BRIARS
UPWARD	336 - 2	ASCENDING CYCLES UPWARD BOUND
UPWARD	387 - 1	SPIRAL OF LIFE IS UPWARD
UPWARD	429 - 4	UPWARD GLANCE EVER SEES THIS
URGE	089 - 1	URGE ARISES OUT OF REALITY
URGE	222 - 4	URGE TO EXPRESS IN ALL PEOPLE
URGE	288 - 2	THE DIVINE URGE WITHIN YOU
URGE	304 - 6	THERE IS A DIVINE URGE
URGE	420 - 4	URGE WHICH BRINGS THEM INTO BEING
URGED	192 - 5	URGED OR FORCED INTO ACTION
US	087 - 2	IN US AS WE ARE IN GOD
US	109 - 4	FOR US AND NOT AGAINST US
US	239 - 3	IN US AND THROUGH US AS US
US	272 - 1	TO MANIFEST THROUGH US
USE	036 - 1	THE USE WE MAKE
USE	093 - 4	WHERE WE USE IT, IT BECOMES OUR LAW
USE	107 - 2	USE THIS NATURE FOR BETTER OR FOR WORSE
USE	118 - 2	INDIVIDUAL USE WE MAKE OF PRINCIPLE
USE	122 - 4	THE USE WE ARE MAKING OF THIS ONE LAW

USE	148 - 4	USE THIS ALMIGHTY POWER FOR DEFINITE
USE	157 - 2	USE OUR CREATIVE IMAGINATION
USE	201 - 3	BEGIN TO USE THIS PRINCIPLE
USE	271 - 2	WE CAN USE IT IF WE COMPLY
USE	271 - 3	ABILITY TO MAKE USE OF THE LAW
USE	275 - 3	PROPER USE OF MENTAL LAW
USE	284 - 2	WE USE THE MIND OF GOD
USE	291 - 4	WHICH HE MAY CONSCIOUSLY USE
USE	364 - 2	INDIVIDUAL USE OF UNIVERSAL LAW
USE	392 - 1	USE OF THE UNIVERSAL LAW
USE	394 - 2	MAKE USE OF THE MIND OF GOD
USE	401 - 2	YOU USE YOUR SUBJECTIVE MIND
USE	402 - 4	IGNORANT USE OF THE LAW
USE	417 - 1	USE OF IT WILL BE A REFLECTION
USE	496 - 3	USE THIS MIND ONLY
USE	500 - 4	USE OR MISUSE OF IT
USEFUL	478 - 2	A BODY NO LONGER USEFUL
USELESS	385 - 3	USELESS TO SAY THAT THEIR INFLUENCE
USELESS	394 - 4	IT IS USELESS TO SEEK ELSEWHERE
USES	140 - 4	USES HE NEVER CREATES ANYTHING
USING	246 - 3	USING THE LAW
UTILITARIAN	311 - 2	ENERGY FOR UTILITARIAN PURPOSES
UTILIZED	312 - 3	SYSTEMATIZED THAT IT CAN BE UTILIZED
UTILIZED	321 - 1	PROPERLY UNDERSTOOD AND UTILIZED
UTILIZED	322 - 2	CONSCIOUSLY UTILIZED FOR DEFINITE PURPOSES
UTILIZES	414 - 2	POWER WHICH IT UTILIZES
UTTERED	154 - 1	ANSWERED BEFORE IT IS UTTERED
UTTERED	436 - 1	THE PRAYER WHEN IT IS UTTERED
UTTERMOST FARTHING	032 - 3	EXACTS THE UTTERMOST FARTHING

V

VACUUM	311 - 3	NOT VACUUM BUT THAT SUBSTANCE
VAGUE	077 - 3	MORE OR LESS VAGUE
VALUABLE	378 - 2	TAUGHT US MANY VALUABLE LESSONS
VALUATION	166 - 3	IDEAS AT THEIR OWN VALUATION
VALUE	067 - 3	VALUE TO THE INDIVIDUAL LIFE
VALUE	382 - 2	VALUE THAT AN UNDERSTANDING
VALUE	450 - 3	GREATER VALUE ON FAITH AND BELIEF
VALUED	368 - 1	WHO VALUED THE HUMAN SOUL
VALUES	025 - 1	TO ACCEPT INTANGIBLE VALUES
VALUES	041 - 2	IT VALUES EACH ALIKE
VALUES	067 - 3	POINT A WAY TO ETERNAL VALUES
VALUES	429 - 3	VALUES CANNOT BE BUILT ON THE SHIFTING
VANISH	408 - 4	ABILITY TO USE IT WILL VANISH
VANISHED	411 - 1	THE DARKNESS VANISHED INTO
VARIATION	121 - 3	UNIQUE VARIATION IN THE UNIVERSE
VARIATIONS	123 - 3	VARIATIONS OF FORM
VARIATIONS	123 - 4	THESE VARIATIONS OF CONSCIOUSNESS
VARIATIONS	259 - 1	VARIATIONS OF THE ONE LIFE
VARIETY	045 - 4	UNITY PASSES INTO VARIETY
VARIETY	069 - 2	AN INFINITE VARIETY OF IDEAS
VARYING	193 - 2	TAKE VARYING FORMS FOR US

VARYING	244 - 2	VARYING FORMS OF ITSELF
VARYING	402 - 3	PRESENTING ITSELF IN VARYING GUISES
VASTNESS	365 - 3	VASTNESS OF THE UNIVERSE
VEHICLE	373 - 4	PURPOSE OF FURNISHING A VEHICLE
VEIL	060 - 3	VEIL BETWEEN SPIRIT AND MATTER
VEIL	335 - 1	SEEN THROUGH THE VEIL OF MATTER
VEIL	379 - 2	PENETRATED THE VEIL OF FLESH
VEIL	429 - 2	JESUS SAW BEYOND THE VEIL
VEIL	452 - 5	ATTEMPT TO BREAK THROUGH THE VEIL
VEIL	465 - 2	VEIL SEEMS THIN BETWEEN
VENGEANCE	487 - 4	VENGEANCE IS MINE
VERGE	103 - 4	WE ARE ON THE VERGE
VERGE	345 - 2	VERGE OF THIS LIGHT FOR MANY YEARS
VERILY	109 - 2	VERILY BY THE LAW WOULD THIS
VERITIES	159 - 2	ETERNAL VERITIES LIKE TRUTH LOVE BEAUTY
VERITIES	328 - 3	REVEALED ETERNAL VERITIES
VERITY	213 - 4	IT IS NOT AN ETERNAL VERITY
VERY GOOD	065 - 7	IT WAS GOOD, VERY GOOD
VIBRATE	353 - 1	VIBRATE TOWARD EACH OTHER
VIBRATION	086 - 2	CERTAIN RATE OF VIBRATION
VIBRATION	094 - 1	VIBRATION OF HIS PERSONALITY
VIBRATION	118 - 2	IN ITS COMPOSITION ITS VIBRATION
VIBRATION	141 - 3	MOTION OR VIBRATION UPON SUBSTANCE
VIBRATION	207 - 5	PEACE OR ELATION A VIBRATION
VIBRATION	212 - 3	VIBRATION OF SUFFERING
VIBRATION	258 - 3	VIBRATION OF PERFECT HARMONY
VIBRATION	311 - 2	MADE MANIFEST THROUGH VIBRATION
VIBRATION	317 - 1	CAUGHT IN ITS MENTAL VIBRATION
VIBRATION	328 - 5	COLORED BY THE VIBRATION
VIBRATION	350 - 3	ATMOSPHERE OR THOUGHT VIBRATION
VIBRATION	352 - 2	AT HIS RATE OF VIBRATION
VIBRATION	352 - 4	VIBRATION WHICH HE EMANATES
VIBRATION	353 - 1	VIBRATION HE CAN MENTALLY CONTACT
VIBRATION	353 - 3	UNLESS THE VIBRATION IS NEUTRALIZED
VIBRATION	421 - 4	HE IS IN HARMONIOUS VIBRATION
VIBRATION	421 - 5	IN TUNE WITH THE VIBRATION
VIBRATIONS	298 - 1	NOT SENDING OUT LOVE VIBRATIONS
VIBRATIONS	349 - 1	VIBRATIONS OF THE HUMAN VOICE
VIBRATIONS	351 - 1	SURROUNDED BY ALL SORTS OF VIBRATIONS
VIBRATIONS	421 - 5	THE VIBRATIONS ARE EVER-PRESENT
VICE	457 - 5	VIRTUE OR VICE IS BUT WHAT TRUTH IS
VICE	458 - 2	NOT THAT WE FOSTER VICE
VICIOUS	285 - 4	MUST BE NOTHING VICIOUS IN IT
VICIOUS	457 - 5	WOULD IMMEDIATELY BECOME VICIOUS
VICISSITUDES	437 - 1	VICISSITUDES OF FORTUNE UPSET
VICTOR	369 - 3	A VICTOR IS NEVER DEFEATED
VICTORY	246 - 1	THE VICTORY OF A PERFECT PRESENT
VICTORY	385 - 1	THE GRAVE ITS VICTORY
VIEW	056 - 2	WHEN WE VIEW IT CORRECTLY
VIEW	187 - 1	NEVER LIMIT YOUR VIEW OF LIFE
VIEWING	043 - 1	EITHER VIEWING LIFE
VIEWPOINT	043 - 2	AS WE GAIN THE BROADER VIEWPOINT
VIEWPOINT	149 - 3	VIEWPOINT THAT GOD IS SOME FAR OFF
VIEWPOINT	193 - 3	ATTENTION TO THE MENTAL VIEWPOINT
VIEWPOINT	203 - 2	OF HIM FROM THIS VIEWPOINT

VIEWPOINT	446 - 4	VIEWPOINT OF LIFE
VIEWPOINT	466 - 1	VIEWPOINT ALL HAVE BEEN SINNERS
VINDICTIVE	383 - 3	VINDICTIVE OR MALICIOUS POWER
VINE	313 - 4	I AM THE VINE
VINEYARD	362 - 2	VINEYARD OF HUMAN ENDEAVOR
VIOLATE	034 - 1	VIOLATE ITS OWN NATURE
VIOLATED	453 - 2	UNIVERSE CAN BE VIOLATED
VIRTUE	110 - 2	WE ARE FREE ONLY BY VIRTUE
VIRTUE	321 - 1	VIRTUE OF SOME INVISIBLE CAUSE
VIRTUE	442 - 1	VIRTUE BUT THROUGH VIRTUE
VIRTUE	442 - 3	VIRTUE CONSISTS NEITHER IN EATING
VIRTUE	442 - 3	VIRTUE IS INDEPENDENT
VIRTUE	457 - 5	VIRTUE DOES NOT KNOW THAT
VIRTUE	457 - 5	VIRTUE IS SWEET
VIRTUES	382 - 4	REWARDED FOR OUR VIRTUES
VISIBLE	131 - 1	VISIBLE WORLD IS AN EFFECT
VISIBLE	217 - 1	VISIBLE NOR INVISIBLE
VISIBLE	340 - 4	DO AWAY WITH EVERY VISIBLE MEANS
VISIBLE	396 - 1	BELIEFS INTO VISIBLE FORM
VISIBLE	407 - 3	THE PHYSICAL END IS VISIBLE
VISION	126 - 2	VISION IMAGE READ AND TALK
VISION	218 - 3	VISION FOR A REALIZATION
VISION	220 - 2	PERFECT VISION SEEING THROUGH YOU
VISION	230 - 3	THERE IS NO OBSTRUCTION TO VISION
VISION	230 - 3	NO NEAR VISION AND NO FAR VISION
VISION	230 - 3	NO WEAK VISION NOR BLURRED VISION
VISION	230 - 5	SPIRITUAL VISION IS CLEAR
VISION	230 - 5	SHOULD PRAISE THE VISION
VISION	230 - 5	THE CLEARNESS OF SPIRITUAL VISION
VISION	281 - 4	VISION AND POSITIVENESS
VISION	282 - 2	BRING OURSELVES TO A GREATER VISION
VISION	327 - 3	HEIGHTS OF SPIRITUAL VISION
VISION	353 - 3	THE PSYCHIC VISION
VISION	354 - 1	CLAIRVOYANT VISION OPERATES
VISION	374 - 3	USING THE POWER OF VISION
VISION	418 - 4	VISION TOWARD THE SPIRIT BROADENS
VISION	418 - 4	SET OUR VISION IN AN OPPOSITE DIRECTION
VISION	418 - 4	SET THE VISION
VISION	443 - 3	OUR PRESENT LIMITED VISION
VISIONING	442 - 1	REWARD OF HIS OWN VISIONING
VISIONS	370 - 3	FLASH-LIKE VISIONS OF MYSTIC GRANDEUR
VISTA	384 - 2	DOWN THE VISTA OF ETERNITY
VISTA	471 - 4	VISTA OF TOMORROWS THAT STRETCHES
VISUALIZE	126 - 2	VISUALIZE, VISION, IMAGE
VISUALIZE	212 - 5	VISUALIZE THIS SPIRITUAL BODY
VISUALIZE	345 - 3	USELESS TO TRY TO VISUALIZE
VITAL	143 - 2	EMBRACES A MORE VITAL CONCEPT
VITAL	159 - 2	MUST KEEP OUR FAITH VITAL
VITAL	342 - 1	VITAL DIFFERENCE BETWEEN PSYCHISM
VITALITY	152 - 4	VITALITY IN OUR COMMUNION
VITALITY	343 - 3	CAUSE OF MUCH OF THEIR VITALITY
VITALIZATION	243 - 2	VITALIZATION AND EXALTATION
VITALIZE	160 - 1	CONSTANTLY VITALIZE OUR FAITH
VITALIZES	256 - 5	VITALIZES MY EVERY ORGAN
VITALIZES	477 - 2	VITALIZES THE BODY AND ANIMATES

VITALIZING	159 - 2	VITALIZING FAITH
VITALIZING	225 - 2	VITALIZING POWER OF SPIRIT
VITALIZING	255 - 3	INTO CREATIVE ENERGIZING VITALIZING ONES
VOCATION	115 - 3	DESTINY, RICHES, POVERTY, BUSINESS, VOCATION
VOICE	033 - 3	THAT ETERNAL VOICE
VOICE	068 - 4	VOICE OF GOD
VOICE	072 - 4	THAT STILL SMALL VOICE
VOICE	258 - 1	THE VOICE OF SPIRIT
VOICE	366 - 1	INNER VOICE THAT SPEAKS SUPREMELY
VOICE	367 - 3	THE VOICE OF GOD TO HUMANITY
VOICE	381 - 4	HOLLOW VOICE FOR REVELATION
VOICE	423 - 3	VOICE OF GOD
VOICE OF GOD	474 - 3	VOICE OF GOD WALKING IN THE GARDEN
VOICES	381 - 4	NEVER LET ANY VOICES SPEAK
VOW	117 - 1	OUT AGAIN INTO THE VOID
VOID	212 - 2	RETURN UNTO ME VOID
VOID	284 - 4	INSTEAD OF SEEING A VOID
VOLITION	038 - 2	NO VOLITION OF ITS OWN
VOLITION	058 - 2	WITH POWER AND VOLITION
VOLITION	079 - 1	SUBJECT TO THE CONSCIOUS VOLITION
VOLITION	079 - 2	VOLITION IN THE UNIVERSE
VOLITION	079 - 3	CONSCIOUS VOLITION AS SPIRIT
VOLITION	081 - 5	AND THE WORD IS VOLITION
VOLITION	108 - 1	SELF-CHOICE VOLITION
VOLITION	117 - 1	ENERGY WITHOUT VOLITION
VOLITION	197 - 1	HAS NEITHER CONSCIOUSNESS NOR VOLITION
VOLITION	390 - 2	IT HAS VOLITION WILL CHOICE
VOLITION	392 - 2	WILLING BUT HAVING NO VOLITION
VOLITION	401 - 1	TRUE VOLITION
VOLITIONAL	044 - 3	MECHANICAL TO THE VOLITIONAL
VOLITIONAL	069 - 4	ONE VOLITIONAL FACTOR IN THE UNIVERSE
VOLITIONAL	196 - 3	THAT IS VOLITIONAL OR SELF-CHOOSING
VOLITIONAL	381 - 3	VOLITIONAL AND CHOOSING FACULTIES

W

WAGON	340 - 3	IN A WAGON
WAILING	217 - 2	HAD LISTENED TO THE WAILING
WAILING	274 - 2	FEASTING, WAILING NOR PRAISING
WAILING	383 - 3	BY THE WAILING OF PROPHETS
WAIT	174 - 4	WAIT ONLY FOR OUR OWN AWAKENED
WAIT	272 - 1	WAIT UPON THE PERFECT LAW
WAITING	157 - 3	WAITING TO BE FORMED
WAITS	129 - 3	ALL NATURE WAITS ON MAN'S RECOGNITION
WAITS	392 - 2	IT WAITS TO BE CALLED INTO
WAKE	384 - 3	WAKE UP TO THE FACTS OF BEING
WAKE	404 - 2	LACK IN ITS WAKE
WALK	101 - 2	WALK THROUGH EACH OTHER
WALK	219 - 2	WALK ON THE WATER
WALK	234 - 3	TO WALK UPRIGHTLY
WALK	279 - 2	WE WALK BY FALLING FORWARD
WALK	341 - 1	WALK ON THE WATER
WALK	359 - 4	GOING TO GET UP AND WALK

WALKS	369 - 1	EVER WALKS LIFE'S ROAD ALONE
WALL	206 - 2	WALL BETWEEN OUR THOUGHT
WALLOW	055 - 4	WALLOW IN THE MUD
WALLS	348 - 1	WALLS ARE HUNG THE PICTURES
WALLS	449 - 2	THE VERY WALLS HAVE EARS
WANT	266 - 2	CAN GET WHAT YOU WANT
WANT	403 - 2	CONDENSATION OF THE IDEA OF WANT
WANT	465 - 1	WHY DO WE WANT
WANTING	298 - 2	WHO IS WANTING THE SAME
WAR	110 - 3	WORLD ARMS FOR WAR
WAR	428 - 2	NOT TO THE WAR LORDS
WARMTH	088 - 4	LOSE ALL WARMTH AND COLOR
WARMTH	089 - 2	NECESSITY FOR WARMTH AND COLOR
WARMTH	374 - 2	ITS WARMTH, COLOR
WARMTH	398 - 4	WARMTH, COLOR, IMAGINATION
WARNED	381 - 4	THEY WARNED AGAINST THESE THINGS
WARNED	436 - 2	CLEARLY WARNED NOT TO FALL
WARNING	452 - 5	TOO GREAT A WARNING CANNOT BE
WARP	152 - 4	WEAVING ITSELF INTO THE VERY WARP
WARRIORS	429 - 5	WARRIORS WITH THE DIVINE KINGDOM
WASHED	260 - 3	WASHED CLEAN BY THE SPIRIT
WASHING	502 - 1	WASHING AWAY OF ALL MISTAKES
WASTE	049 - 6	WASTE MUCH TIME IN ARGUING
WASTE	232 - 5	WASTE PRODUCTS OF THE MIND
WASTE	246 - 3	WASTE NO TIME ARGUING
WASTE	254 - 6	NO WASTE SUBSTANCE IS ALLOWED
WASTING	229 - 3	NO WASTING OR DESTRUCTION OF ANY PART
WATER	027 - 3	THE WATER OF LIFE FREELY
WATER	125 - 5	WATER REACHES ITS OWN LEVEL
WATER	141 - 4	ICE IS FORMED IN THE WATER
WATER	184 - 2	ICE IS SOME FORM OF WATER
WATER	204 - 5	BOTTLE OF IMPURE WATER
WATER	204 - 5	DROPPING PURE WATER INTO
WATER	205 - 5	WATER REACHES ITS OWN LEVEL
WATER	219 - 2	WATER WE TAKE A BOAT
WATER	219 - 3	WALK ON THE WATER
WATER	267 - 2	JUMP INTO WATER AND REMAIN DRY
WATER	279 - 2	WATER FALLS BY ITS OWN WEIGHT
WATER	287 - 2	WATER WILL REACH ITS OWN LEVEL
WATER	319 - 1	WATER WILL REACH ITS OWN LEVEL
WATER	321 - 2	WATER WILL REACH ITS OWN LEVEL
WATER	331 - 2	DROP OF WATER IS IN THE OCEAN
WATER	340 - 3	EVOLUTION OF TRAVEL BY WATER
WATER	388 - 3	OCEAN IN THE DROP OF WATER
WATER	471 - 6	WATER IS USED TO EXPRESS
WATERMELONS	321 - 2	I WILL GET WATERMELONS
WATERS	063 - 2	MOVED UPON THE WATERS
WATERS	246 - 4	SEA OF UNTROUBLED WATERS OF LIFE
WAVE	312 - 4	WILL NEVER BE A WAVE BY ITSELF
WAVER	245 - 1	NEVER WAVER FROM THE PREMISE OF ONE
WAVER	245 - 3	WAVER NOR FALTER IN MY FAITH
WAVERING	302 - 3	NEVER WAVERING NO MATTER WHAT
WAY	050 - 1	WAY THE THING WORKS
WAY	084 - 4	WAY IT WORKS
WAY	100 - 2	THERE MUST BE A WAY

WAY	100 - 2	SOUL THE WAY OR LAW
WAY	102 - 3	EVOLUTION IS THE PROCESS THE WAY THE TIME
WAY	133 - 5	WAY THE ONE POWER
WAY	144 - 2	WAY IN WHICH OUR THOUGHTS ARE TO BECOME
WAY	157 - 4	SCIENCE OF MIND IT IS A WAY
WAY	193 - 4	THE RIGHT WAY WOULD BE
WAY	221 - 5	WAY IN WHICH YOU SAY IT
WAY	237 - 4	TEACHES HIM THE WAY
WAY	272 - 2	LAW WILL POINT THE WAY
WAY	276 - 3	THERE IS NO OTHER WAY
WAY	309 - 4	WAY TO LEARN HOW TO TREAT
WAY	317 - 1	HE HAS A WAY IN WHICH HE THINKS
WAY	340 - 2	COMPLY WITH THE WAY IT WORKS
WAY	401 - 2	WAY THAT WE USE THE GREAT LAW
WAY	403 - 4	CAN IN NO WAY LIMIT MIND
WAY	443 - 4	WAY TO KNOW GOD IS TO BE LIKE HIM
WAY	495 - 7	HE BECAME THE WAY
WAYS	117 - 2	MANY WAYS OF USING IT
WAYS	201 - 3	TO PERCEIVE NEW WAYS
WAYS	292 - 4	WAYS THAT A GOD WHO ALREADY IS
WAY-SHOWER	367 - 4	HE WAS A WAY-SHOWER
WE	052 - 3	WE CAN CAUSE IT TO
WE	108 - 4	THIS MIND THAT WE THINK
WE	108 - 4	WE ARE ETERNAL
WE	108 - 4	WE ARE SPIRITUALLY COMPLETE
WE	126 - 2	WE ALONE CONTROL OUR DESTINY
WE	314 - 1	WE ARE EACH OTHER
WE	383 - 3	WE BELIEVE IN GOD
WE	415 - 3	WE ARE IN IT AND IT FLOWS
WE	464 - 3	WE ALONE CAN RETURN
WEAK	296 - 4	THIS IS STRENGTH FOR THE WEAK
WEAK	396 - 2	I AM WEAK SICK OR UNHAPPY
WEAK	454 - 4	WEAK WHEN WE DESERT THIS POWER
WEAKNESS	174 - 4	IN SPITE OF ALL WEAKNESS
WEARINESS	226 - 3	BELIEF IN WEARINESS
WEATHER	252 - 2	CHANGES IN THE WEATHER
WEATHER	252 - 2	WEATHER IS A DETERMINING FACTOR
WEATHER	252 - 2	WEATHER BUT IN THEIR THINKING
WEATHER	258 - 4	GOVERNED BY ANY WEATHER
WEATHER	258 - 4	WEATHER IS A MANIFESTATION OF SPIRIT
WEATHER	259 - 1	CHANGES IN WEATHER CONDITIONS
WEAVE	068 - 1	WEAVE THE STORY OF TRUTH
WEIGHS	438 - 4	THOUGHT WEIGHS HIM TO THE DUST
WEIGHT	287 - 2	LEVEL BY ITS OWN WEIGHT
WEIGHT	350 - 2	CARRIES MORE WEIGHT THAN THE SPOKEN
WEIGHT	438 - 2	WEIGHT FROM THE MAN'S CONSCIOUSNESS
WEIGHTS	237 - 2	ABOUT ITSELF WEIGHTS IT DOWN
WEIRD	300 - 3	NOTHING PECULIAR OR WEIRD
WELCOME	299 - 1	ALWAYS WELCOME THE MAN
WELCOME	382 - 1	WELCOME BUT ANYTHING OTHER
WELCOME	385 - 1	SHOULD WELCOME IT WITH A SMILE
WELCOME	468 - 1	WELCOME TO ALL THE DIVINE STORES
WELFARE	465 - 4	DETRIMENTAL TO OUR WELFARE
WELL	099 - 5	IS TO BE PERMANENTLY WELL
WELL	432 - 4	WELL WITH OUR SOULS

WELL	485 - 1	GOD WISHES US WELL
WELL-BALANCED	452 - 4	WELL-BALANCED MENTALITIES
WELL-BALANCED	477 - 2	BE A WELL-BALANCED EXISTENCE
WELL-BALANCED	498 - 1	SECRET OF A WELL-BALANCED LIFE
WELL-BEING	178 - 2	CONSCIOUS WELL-BEING OF THE SOUL
WELL-BEING	266 - 2	THE WELL-BEING OF SOMEONE ELSE
WELL-SPRING	446 - 2	WELL-SPRING OF SELF-EXISTENCE
WE SHALL SEE	503 - 3	WE SHALL SEE HIM AS HE IS
WEST	078 - 2	CAUSE AND EFFECT OF THE WEST
WET FEET	252 - 5	THAN FROM WET FEET
WHAT	215 - 1	WHAT SHOULD WE TRY TO HEAL
WHAT	263 - 3	ALWAYS KNOW WHAT TO DO
WHAT	373 - 2	AS IN WHAT WE ARE
WHAT AM I	188 - 3	WHAT AM I WHO IS SPEAKING
WHATEVER	120 - 1	WHATEVER OUR SUBCONSCIOUS MIND HOLDS
WHATEVER	146 - 4	WE COULD ACCOMPLISH WHATEVER
WHATSOEVER	151 - 2	WHATSOEVER YE SHALL ASK IN MY NAME
WHATSOEVER	226 - 1	WHATSOEVER THINGS ARE JUST
WHATSOEVER	394 - 2	WE MAY USE FOR WHATSOEVER
WHEAT	429 - 2	THE WHEAT OF THE SPIRIT
WHENCE	063 - 2	WHENCE CAME ITS PATTERN
WHENCE	075 - 4	WHENCE DO WE GET OUR MENTAL
WHERE	063 - 2	WHERE DID SPIRIT MOVE
WHERE	207 - 2	WHERE THE PATIENT
WHERE	263 - 3	WHERE AND HOW TO DO IT
WHERE	271 - 4	GOING FROM WHERE HE IS
WHERE	271 - 4	BEGIN RIGHT WHERE WE ARE
WHERE	282 - 3	TO BEGIN RIGHT WHERE WE ARE
WHERE	282 - 3	HE IS WHERE HE IS BECAUSE OF WHAT HE IS
WHERE	384 - 2	WHERE SHALL WE GO WHEN WE DIE
WHEREUNTO	169 - 3	LAW OF THAT WHEREUNTO IT IS SPOKEN
WHETHER	322 - 3	WHETHER HE IS CONSCIOUS OF
WHIT	488 - 1	TO BE MADE EVERY WHIT WHOLE
WHITMAN	327 - 4	WORDSWORTH, HOMER, WALT WHITMAN
WHITMAN	345 - 1	WHITMAN WHO REFERS TO IT
WHO	188 - 3	ASK YOURSELF WHO AM I
WHOLE	029 - 3	WITH THE WHOLE ON THE SUBJECTIVE SIDE
WHOLE	034 - 2	ONE WITH THE WHOLE
WHOLE	072 - 1	RELATIONSHIP TO THE GREAT WHOLE
WHOLE	096 - 2	FROM THE WHOLE TO THE PART
WHOLE	106 - 1	UNIVERSE AS A WHOLE
WHOLE	112 - 4	WHOLE OF SPIRIT IS POTENTIALLY FOCUSED
WHOLE	184 - 5	TRUTH IS INDIVISIBLE AND WHOLE
WHOLE	191 - 2	TRUE RELATIONSHIP TO THE WHOLE
WHOLE	195 - 3	SO ONE WITH THE WHOLE
WHOLE	218 - 2	HARMONIOUS AND WHOLE
WHOLE	241 - 3	VITALIZED AND MADE WHOLE TODAY
WHOLE	269 - 1	THE WHOLE TO THE PARTS
WHOLE	382 - 3	GOVERNING IT IS THE WHOLE ANSWER
WHOLE	392 - 1	WHOLE IS GREATER THAN ITS PARTS
WHOLE	447 - 2	THE WHOLE IS AT HAND
WHOLENESS	034 - 1	OF THE UNIVERSAL WHOLENESS
WHOLENESS	101 - 2	IN A UNITARY WHOLENESS
WHOLENESS	233 - 4	TRUTH AND WHOLENESS
WHOLENESS	264 - 5	WHOLENESS FILL MY ENTIRE BEING

WHOLENESS	271 - 1	IN THE UNIVERSAL WHOLENESS
WHOLENESS	416 - 1	HAPPINESS AND APPARENT WHOLENESS
WHOLENESS	417 - 2	WHOLENESS INSTEAD OF SICKNESS
WHOLENESS	463 - 2	LIFE IS ONE PERFECT WHOLENESS
WHOLESOME	143 - 1	WHOLESOME IDEAS OF LIFE
WHOSOEVER	047 - 1	WHOSOEVER WILL MAY ENTER
WHY	338 - 1	WHY MUST WE BELIEVE IT IS
WHY	373 - 1	QUESTION AS TO WHY HE IS
WICK	430 - 2	WICK OF PEACE AND JOY
WICKEDNESS	494 - 5	WICKEDNESS IN HIGH PLACES MEANS
WIFE	269 - 3	A MAN FOR HIS WIFE
WILL	039 - 1	WE DO NOT WILL THINGS
WILL	056 - 2	MAN CONVINCED AGAINST HIS WILL
WILL	058 - 3	A POWER OF WILL
WILL	081 - 5	IT IS WILL BECAUSE IT CHOOSES
WILL	083 - 4	ALL ELSE IS SUBJECT TO ITS WILL
WILL	091 - 1	IT IS A DOER OR EXECUTOR OF THE WILL
WILL	092 - 3	OBEYING THE WILL OF THE SPIRIT
WILL	100 - 2	OBEY THE WILL OF THE SPIRIT
WILL	150 - 3	THE WILL AND NATURE OF GOD
WILL	151 - 4	WORK THROUGH MAN'S IMAGINATION AND WILL
WILL	155 - 1	TO KNOW, WILL AND ACT
WILL	160 - 1	LET GO OF ALL HUMAN WILL
WILL	160 - 3	SENSE THAT THE WILL OF GOD
WILL	174 - 1	GARDENER DOES NOT WILL POTATOES
WILL	192 - 3	THE WILL IS DIRECTIVE
WILL	192 - 3	WILL IS THE CONSCIOUS DIRECTIVE
WILL	192 - 3	IDEA OF USING THE WILL
WILL	193 - 2	WILL IS DIRECTIVE
WILL	193 - 3	THE WILL HOLDS ATTENTION
WILL	193 - 3	DOES THE WILL BECOME CREATIVE
WILL	193 - 4	WILL IS GIVEN US TO PROTECT OURSELVES
WILL	193 - 4	WILL HAS FIRST ADMITTED IT
WILL	193 - 5	THE PROPER USE OF THE WILL
WILL	194 - 3	IMAGINATION WILL AND CONCENTRATION
WILL	194 - 4	BALANCE IS STRUCK WHEN THE WILL
WILL	194 - 4	WILL TO DETERMINE
WILL	195 - 1	WILL TO DECIDE THE ISSUE
WILL	209 - 5	WILL BINDS US
WILL	232 - 3	OF PEACE AND GOOD WILL
WILL	240 - 2	THAT WILL DOES NOT CONTROL THE HEARTBEAT
WILL	244 - 2	NOT BECAUSE WE WILL IT
WILL	262 - 1	WILL MYSELF FREE FROM
WILL	262 - 1	IT CANNOT WILL
WILL	264 - 1	DO NOT STRAIN, WILL OR COERCE
WILL	268 - 4	THY WILL BE DONE
WILL	268 - 4	RELATIVE TO THE WILL OF GOD
WILL	268 - 4	WILL OF GOD IS ALWAYS GOOD
WILL	268 - 5	WHAT THE WILL OF GOD IS
WILL	269 - 1	WILL OF LIFE HAS ONLY TO BE LIFE
WILL	269 - 1	THE WILL OF THAT WHICH
WILL	269 - 1	THAT IS THE WILL OF GOD
WILL	269 - 1	INTERPRET THE WILL OF GOD
WILL	269 - 1	WILL OF GOD FOR US
WILL	274 - 2	ARE EXERCISING A WILL POWER

WILL	274 - 2	IT IS NOT WILL POWER
WILL	277 - 2	TO FOLLOW THE DIVINE WILL
WILL	340 - 1	OBEYING THE WILL OF SPIRIT
WILL	390 - 2	IT HAS VOLITION WILL CHOICE
WILL	394 - 5	THE WILL OF SPIRIT IS ALREADY
WILL	395 - 1	GOD IS WILL AND REPRESENTATION
WILL	400 - 1	NO WILL OF ITS OWN
WILL	405 - 4	THE WILL OF THE SPIRIT IS PEACE
WILL	405 - 4	COULD HAVE NO OTHER WILL
WILL	412 - 3	THE WILL OF GOD IS ALWAYS
WILL	417 - 4	ERROR THAT IT IS HUMAN WILL
WILL	418 - 4	WILL SHOULD HOLD IT IN PLACE
WILL	437 - 4	WILL WAS EVER IN ACCORD WITH
WILL	449 - 4	WILL OF GOD IS HIS MOTHER
WILL	454 - 2	GOD'S ONLY WILL IS TO BE
WILL	472 - 1	WILL OF THE SPIRIT IF GOODNESS
WILL	489 - 3	DO NOT WILL OR TRY TO COMPEL
WILLING	038 - 3	THINKING WILLING KNOWING
WILLING	040 - 1	WILLING TO RECEIVE THEM
WILLING	164 - 4	NOT WILLING THINGS TO HAPPEN
WILLING	195 - 2	ARE WILLING TO EXPERIENCE THE RESULTS
WILLING	272 - 2	WILLING TO BE GUIDED INTO TRUTH
WILLING	374 - 2	KNOWING WILLING AND THINKING FACTORS
WILLING	392 - 2	WILLING BUT HAVING NO VOLITION
WILLING	446 - 5	DOES NOT COME BY SIMPLY WILLING
WILLINGLY	416 - 4	WILLINGLY CREATE ABUNDANCE
WILLINGNESS	037 - 4	NOT A QUESTION OF ITS WILLINGNESS
WILLINGNESS	054 - 1	WILLINGNESS TO LET THIS INNER SPIRIT GUIDE
WILLINGNESS	152 - 2	OF HIS HIGHEST WILLINGNESS
WILLINGNESS	174 - 1	WILLINGNESS TO COMPLY
WILLINGNESS	175 - 1	WILLINGNESS TO COMPLY WITH THE LAW
WILLINGNESS	288 - 1	IN HIS WILLINGNESS TO HELP US
WILLINGNESS	288 - 1	GOD'S WILLINGNESS TO HELP US
WILLINGNESS	404 - 3	THE WILLINGNESS OF SPIRIT
WILL OF LOVE	323 - 2	LAW EXECUTES THE WILL OF LOVE
WILL POWER	174 - 1	REFRAINS FROM WILL POWER
WILL POWER	192 - 4	INFLUENCE OTHERS BY WILL POWER
WILL POWER	192 - 4	EFFECTS OF WILL POWER
WILL POWER	192 - 5	USE OF WILL POWER
WILL POWER	210 - 1	WILL POWER HAS NOTHING WHATEVER TO DO
WILL POWER	223 - 1	WITH MERE WILL POWER STOP IT
WILL POWER	320 - 2	NOT ACCOMPLISHED THROUGH WILL POWER
WILL-POWER	210 - 1	WILL-POWER WOULD BECOME EXHAUSTED
WILLS	395 - 2	MAN IS FREE TO DO AS HE WILLS
WILLS	465 - 2	WILLS ONLY GOOD TO ALL ALIKE
WILLY NILLY	194 - 5	CREATIVE PROCESS WILL GO ON WILLY NILLY
WILLY NILLY	451 - 1	WISHY WASHY NOR WILLY NILLY
WINDOW	355 - 4	A WINDOW ONE MILE DISTANT
WINDOWS	230 - 2	WINDOWS OF THE SOUL
WINDOWS	307 - 3	OPEN YOU THE WINDOWS OF HEAVEN
WINDOWS	374 - 3	WINDOWS OF THE EYES
WINDS	252 - 5	NOT FROM THE WINDS AND RAIN
WINE	439 - 2	NEW WINE INTO OLD BOTTLES
WINE-BIBBER	442 - 3	WINE-BIBBER A FRIEND OF PUBLICANS
WINGED	415 - 2	WINGED WITH LOVE AND REASON

WINNOWING	435 - 2	WINNOWING FROM THE SOUL OF SHAM
WIPED	290 - 3	THEY ARE NOW WIPED OUT
WISDOM	040 - 1	CONTAINS ALL KNOWLEDGE AND WISDOM
WISDOM	040 - 3	TRUTH AND WISDOM COEXIST
WISDOM	041 - 1	OUR WISDOM ONLY IN SUCH DEGREE
WISDOM	042 - 5	SPIRITUAL WISDOM SAYS
WISDOM	044 - 5	ALL THE WISDOM OF THE UNIVERSE
WISDOM	069 - 2	KEY TO SPIRITUAL WISDOM
WISDOM	238 - 4	ACCREDITED WITH MANY WORDS OF WISDOM
WISDOM	271 - 4	GRADUALLY INCREASE IN WISDOM
WISDOM	423 - 1	WORDS OF WISDOM
WISDOM	427 - 4	SPIRITUAL STRENGTH OF DIVINE WISDOM
WISDOM	442 - 2	WISDOM IS JUSTIFIED OF HER CHILDREN
WISDOM	471 - 2	WISDOM PUTS THE RING OF COMPLETION
WISDOM	476 - 5	WISDOM FOR THE SOUL
WISE	031 - 1	A SERVANT TO THE WISE
WISE	073 - 2	SOME WISE MAN CLAIMED THAT IT
WISE	078 - 2	FREES THE WISE
WISE	385 - 1	THIS IS A WISE PROVISION
WISE	436 - 5	WISE MAN BUILDS HIS HOUSE
WISE	436 - 5	WISE MAN BUILDS HIS HOUSE
WISH	044 - 4	WISH TO KNOW A CERTAIN TRUTH
WISH	092 - 1	WE WISH TO HAVE CREATED
WISH	137 - 1	WHAT WE WISH SAID DEMOSTHENES
WISH	188 - 1	THINK WHAT YOU WISH TO THINK
WISH	267 - 5	TAKE WHAT YOU WISH
WISH	267 - 5	WE DO NOT TAKE WHAT WE WISH
WISH	300 - 4	WHAT WE WISH AND TAKE IT
WISH	397 - 1	WISH IT TO DO PROVIDED
WISH	399 - 3	WE DO NOT WISH WE KNOW
WISH	400 - 3	WE WISH TO DO THE QUICKER
WISH	458 - 6	WISH ONLY FOR THAT WHICH IS
WISHES	046 - 4	WISHES TO EXPRESS THROUGH US
WISHES	056 - 3	WISHES TO DEMONSTRATE
WISHES	107 - 4	WISHES MAN TO BE SICK SUFFER
WISHES	195 - 2	CREATIVE LIFE WISHES US
WISHES	398 - 2	WISHES TO CONSCIOUSLY USE
WISHES	400 - 3	WHAT HE WISHES TO DO
WISHES	469 - 3	WISHES TO EXPRESS ITSELF
WISHING	287 - 5	ALL OUR WISHING AND PRAYING
WISHY WASHY	451 - 1	THE COSMIC MIND IS NEITHER WISHY WASHY
WISTFUL WISHING	399 - 3	WISTFUL WISHING FROM REALLY
WIT	454 - 6	WIT OR THE SHAM OF MAN
WITHDRAW	059 - 2	GOD DOES NOT WITHDRAW
WITHDRAW	274 - 4	AS WE WITHDRAW FROM THE RELATIVE
WITHDRAW	315 - 3	WE WITHDRAW FROM THE RELATIVE
WITHDRAWING	311 - 1	WITHDRAWING FROM ANY PARTICULAR FORM
WITH GOD	169 - 3	WITH GOD ALL THINGS ARE POSSIBLE
WITHHELD	405 - 2	SPIRIT HAS NOT WITHHELD GOOD
WITHHOLDS	405 - 3	WITHHOLDS PLEASURE PEACE SUCCESS
WITHIN	028 - 4	WITHIN, IN THAT WHEREVER WE GRASP
WITHIN	029 - 2	WITHIN US IS A MENTAL LAW
WITHIN	034 - 1	THERE IS THAT WITHIN US
WITHIN	067 - 1	WITHIN WHICH IS ALL SPACE
WITHIN	067 - 1	WITHIN WHICH IS ALL TIME

WITHIN	068 - 3	TAKE PLACE WITHIN THIS ONE
WITHIN	076 - 1	ALREADY EXISTED WITHIN US
WITHIN	076 - 3	NOT AFAR OFF BUT WITHIN US
WITHIN	084 - 5	WITHIN ITSELF UPON THE LAW
WITHIN	093 - 4	WITHIN US THEN THERE IS A CREATIVE FIELD
WITHIN	100 - 2	ETERNAL ACTIVITY OF SPIRIT WITHIN ITSELF
WITHIN	102 - 4	LAW WITHIN THIS INTELLIGENCE
WITHIN	105 - 1	SPIRIT KNOWS WITHIN
WITHIN	121 - 2	WITHIN OURSELVES AND NOWHERE ELSE
WITHIN	131 - 6	THINKS OR KNOWS WITHIN ITSELF
WITHIN	133 - 3	MAN IS WITHIN THE ONE
WITHIN	137 - 2	CAUSATION IS FROM WITHIN
WITHIN	153 - 3	GO DEEPLY WITHIN OURSELVES
WITHIN	157 - 3	THE DIVINE URGE WITHIN US
WITHIN	161 - 4	WITHIN US IS THE UNBORN
WITHIN	173 - 4	FOR IT IS WITHIN US
WITHIN	185 - 2	PERFECT GOD WITHIN ME
WITHIN	185 - 2	PERFECT LIFE WITHIN ME
WITHIN	188 - 2	YOU MUST KNOW THIS WITHIN
WITHIN	205 - 4	WITHIN HIMSELF UPON THE ONE
WITHIN	205 - 5	PATIENT WITHIN HIMSELF
WITHIN	217 - 2	WITHIN OUR OWN CONSCIOUSNESS
WITHIN	227 - 3	KNOWING THAT WE HAVE WITHIN US
WITHIN	227 - 3	THIS POWER WITHIN YOU
WITHIN	230 - 2	THE MIND WITHIN DOES THE REAL SEEING
WITHIN	233 - 3	THE VERY LIFE WITHIN
WITHIN	234 - 1	WITHIN IT IS PERFECT
WITHIN	239 - 3	WITHIN US THAT THIS
WITHIN	242 - 2	THE POWER OF GOD WITHIN ME
WITHIN	245 - 2	THE SPIRIT WITHIN YOU
WITHIN	247 - 1	IN THE SPIRIT WITHIN ME
WITHIN	250 - 6	KNOWLEDGE OF THE KINGDOM WITHIN
WITHIN	251 - 4	THE CREATIVE LAW WITHIN YOU KNOWS
WITHIN	252 - 4	THE GOD WITHIN SUSTAINS US NOW
WITHIN	253 - 4	LIFE OF GOD WITHIN ME
WITHIN	254 - 2	MY LIFE WITHIN ME IS PERFECT
WITHIN	254 - 3	CONTAINS WITHIN ITSELF
WITHIN	256 - 5	LIFE WHICH IS WITHIN ME IS NOW HEALING ME
WITHIN	257 - 4	UNIVERSAL LOVE IS WITHIN ME
WITHIN	261 - 4	THE SPIRIT WITHIN ME
WITHIN	265 - 1	THE LIVING GOD WITHIN ME
WITHIN	273 - 1	SPIRIT WITHIN US KNOWS
WITHIN	274 - 2	PROVIDE WITHIN OURSELVES
WITHIN	284 - 4	IT LOOKS WITHIN ITSELF
WITHIN	291 - 2	ALL EXPERIENCE TAKES PLACE WITHIN
WITHIN	295 - 1	WE HAVE HAD THAT WITHIN
WITHIN	296 - 3	EMANATES FROM WITHIN
WITHIN	299 - 1	FAITHFULLY SEEN IN THE WITHIN
WITHIN	306 - 2	WITHIN OUR POWER TO PROVIDE
WITHIN	306 - 2	THIS GROWTH FROM WITHIN
WITHIN	330 - 3	FOR GOD IS WITHIN MAN
WITHIN	334 - 2	WE SHOULD TURN WITHIN
WITHIN	343 - 4	THAT MAN KNOWS IS WITHIN
WITHIN	362 - 1	THE KINGDOM OF HEAVEN WITHIN HIMSELF
WITHIN	365 - 2	EVERY PROBLEM IS WITHIN MAN

WITHIN	365 - 2	HEAVEN IS WITHIN MAN
WITHIN	366 - 2	HE IS ALWAYS WITHIN US
WITHIN	374 - 1	IS THAT SOMETHING WITHIN
WITHIN	376 - 2	IT IS ALREADY WITHIN
WITHIN	386 - 3	HERE WITHIN MYSELF
WITHIN	398 - 5	ITS PRESENCE WITHIN US
WITHIN	398 - 5	THIS ALLNESS IS WITHIN US
WITHIN	399 - 1	WITHIN IS THE ONLY PLACE WE CAN CONTACT IT
WITHIN	399 - 2	CONTROL OF AFFAIRS IS FROM WITHIN OUT
WITHIN	402 - 3	CONTAIN WITHIN THEMSELVES
WITHIN	411 - 4	A REPLECTION OF THE WITHIN
WITHIN	419 - 5	WE SHOULD TURN WITHIN
WITHIN	423 - 3	PERFECTION WITHIN AND AROUND ABOUT
WITHIN	443 - 3	FATHER WITHIN KNOWS AND UNDERSTANDS
WITHIN	470 - 2	WITHIN WHICH REMEMBERS
WITHIN	470 - 3	WITHIN MAY BECOME THE WITHOUT
WITHIN	472 - 4	HEAVEN IS ALREADY WITHIN
WITHIN	484 - 4	WORKS FROM WITHIN OUT
WITHIN ME	358 - 4	REAL SUBSTANCE WITHIN ME
WITHIN ME	358 - 4	TRUTH WITHIN ME
WITHIN US	415 - 1	CONVICTION THAT IS WITHIN US
WITHOUT	399 - 2	NOT FROM WITHOUT
WITNESS	339 - 1	SPIRIT EVER HAS A WITNESS WITHIN US
WITNESS	370 - 3	WITNESS OF THE ETERNAL
WITNESS	427 - 1	BEARS WITNESS TO OUR OWN BELIEF
WITNESS	465 - 1	WITNESS WHO REMEMBERS THAT
WITNESS	485 - 2	BEARS WITNESS TO THE DIVINE FACT
WOMAN	473 - 5	WOMAN IS MADE FROM THE MAN
WONDER	251 - 4	WONDER OF THIS KNOWING INTELLIGENCE
WONDER	263 - 1	WE SHOULD NEVER WONDER
WONDER	402 - 3	LIMITLESS WONDER OF THE UNIVERSE
WONDERFUL	044 - 3	THE CONCEPT IS WONDERFUL
WONDERFUL	295 - 3	WONDERFUL ME
WONDERFUL	307 - 3	FEEL THAT YOU ARE WONDERFUL
WONDERFUL	307 - 3	WONDERFUL THAN THE MANIFESTATION
WONDERING	049 - 3	SIMPLY WONDERING IF POSSIBLY
WONDERING	309 - 4	WONDERING IF ANYTHING IS REALLY
WONDERS	193 - 3	THE WONDERS OF THE SPIRITUAL LIFE
WONDERS	229 - 1	NEVER WONDERS WHETHER HIS WORD
WOOF	152 - 4	WOOF OF OUR OWN MENTALITIES
WORD	029 - 2	A LAW OBEYING HIS WORD
WORD	038 - 2	THE BIBLE CALLS THE WORD
WORD	050 - 1	THIS LAW EXECUTES THE WORD
WORD	056 - 4	THERE IS POWER IN THIS WORD
WORD	056 - 4	RIGHT WORD AT THE RIGHT TIME
WORD	057 - 1	MY WORD IS THE LAW
WORD	058 - 1	WORD OF THE CREATOR
WORD	058 - 1	S0 EVERY MAN'S WORD
WORD	058 - 2	POWER INTO THIS WORD
WORD	058 - 4	THIS WORD HAS POWER
WORD	059 - 3	MUST KNOW THAT HIS WORD
WORD	064 - 2	CALLED THE WORD OF GOD
WORD	064 - 4	THROUGH THE POWER OF HIS WORD
WORD	064 - 4	GOD CANNOT SPEAK A WORD
WORD	065 - 1	THE WORD IS THE MOLD

WORD	065 - 2	WORD IS EQUIPPED TO PERPETUATE
WORD	068 - 5	WORD WAS WITH GOD
WORD	068 - 5	THE WORD OF GOD MEANS
WORD	069 - 1	IS THE WORD OF SPIRIT
WORD	069 - 1	THE WORD IS THE CONCEPT
WORD	069 - 1	WORD BACK OF EVERYTHING
WORD	069 - 3	WORD OF GOD BEING THAT
WORD	069 - 3	HIS WORD MUST BE LAW
WORD	069 - 3	GOD IS WORD
WORD	079 - 2	THE DOER OF THE WORD
WORD	081 - 5	IT IS THE WORD
WORD	081 - 5	WORD IS VOLITION
WORD	084 - 1	HIS WORD IS LAW
WORD	084 - 1	GOD IS WORD
WORD	084 - 1	SET IN MOTION THROUGH ITS WORD
WORD	084 - 3	WORD OF SPIRIT MOVES THROUGH THE LAW
WORD	084 - 4	IN MOTION BY THE WORD OF SPIRIT
WORD	086 - 4	UNLESS BACK OF THE WORD
WORD	090 - 2	THE WORD OF SPIRIT FALLS
WORD	102 - 2	THIS WORD OF THE BIBLE
WORD	117 - 2	WORD AS THE STARTING POINT OF ALL
WORD	117 - 2	MAN'S WORD IN THE SMALL WORLD
WORD	129 - 2	FORMED BY THE WORD
WORD	145 - 5	OUR OWN WORD HAS THE POWER
WORD	145 - 4	THE WORD WAS WITH GOD
WORD	166 - 2	FREE FROM IT THAT THIS WORD
WORD	166 - 4	THE POWER OF ITS WORD
WORD	169 - 3	THAT HIS WORD IS THE LAW
WORD	170 - 2	POWER OF HIS OWN WORD
WORD	171 - 1	HIS WORD OPERATIVE THROUGH
WORD	174 - 2	WORD OF A PRACTITIONER TAKES FORM
WORD	176 - 1	WORD AND NOT AN EMBODIMENT
WORD	176 - 1	WORD WHICH CARRIES POWER
WORD	176 - 1	THAT OUR WORD HAS ACCOMPLISHED
WORD	179 - 1	HE SPEAKS THE WORD FOR THE OTHER
WORD	186 - 3	CONSCIOUSNESS BACK OF THE WORD
WORD	188 - 2	IF YOU KNEW YOUR WORD WAS THE LAW
WORD	188 - 2	YOUR WORD IS SIMPLY AN ANNOUNCEMENT
WORD	189 - 3	THE POWER OF THE WORD
WORD	195 - 3	THE LAW FOLLOWS THE WORD
WORD	195 - 3	AS THE WORD FOLLOWS THE DESIRE
WORD	195 - 3	WORD GIVES FORM TO SUBSTANCE
WORD	199 - 4	WORD HAS THE POWER TO HEAL
WORD	200 - 1	KNOW THAT THE WORD
WORD	202 - 5	YOUR WORD DESTROYS IT
WORD	203 - 3	YOUR WORD IS THE LAW
WORD	205 - 3	WORD USED HEALS
WORD	206 - 4	WORD OPERATE THROUGH HIS
WORD	211 - 3	RECOGNIZE THE WORD AS POWER
WORD	212 - 2	WORD BE THAT GOETH FORTH OUT
WORD	212 - 3	AS HIS WORD OF HEALING
WORD	216 - 1	HIS WORD IS THE PRESENCE POWER
WORD	216 - 2	WORD IS THE LAW
WORD	216 - 2	THIS WORD BEING
WORD	223 - 2	BY THE POWER OF THIS WORD

WORD	224 - 3	YOUR WORD SHOULD BE SPOKEN
WORD	227 - 3	WORD IS PERFECT LAW
WORD	228 - 3	THE WORD HE SPEAKS IS LAW
WORD	228 - 3	CONSCIOUS THAT THE WORD HE SPEAKS
WORD	229 - 1	THE WORD OF TRUTH IS BEING SPOKEN
WORD	233 - 2	WORD OF HEALING IS SPOKEN
WORD	236 - 4	WORD TO HEAL THEM
WORD	257 - 2	WITH THIS WORD
WORD	261 - 1	THE WORD OF GOD WITHIN ME
WORD	261 - 1	THIS WORD WHICH I SPEAK
WORD	261 - 2	POWER OF MY WORD IS COMPLETE
WORD	289 - 3	YOUR WORD AS BEING THE THING
WORD	291 - 4	A WORD SPOKEN IN MIND
WORD	300 - 1	TO SET THE WORD IN MOTION
WORD	300 - 2	MENTALITY WHICH DENIES OUR WORD
WORD	303 - 1	OFTEN NEUTRALIZE OUR WORD AS FAST
WORD	303 - 4	YOUR WORD WHICH IS ONE WITH
WORD	304 - 1	OUR WORD BECOMES A LAW UNTO THE THING
WORD	304 - 1	GOES FORTH FROM THIS WORD
WORD	306 - 1	SENSE THAT BACK OF THE WORD
WORD	307 - 3	SO SHALL MY WORD BE THAT GOETH FORTH
WORD	310 - 3	IN THE BEGINNING WAS THE WORD
WORD	310 - 3	WITHOUT THE WORD WAS NOT
WORD	311 - 2	SEE THE RELATIONSHIP OF THE WORD
WORD	313 - 2	THE WORD OF GOD
WORD	314 - 2	ITS WORD CREATES AN OBJECTIVE FORM
WORD	318 - 4	THE WORD OF THE PRACTITIONER WILL RISE
WORD	331 - 2	OUR WORD HAS JUST AS MUCH POWER
WORD	337 - 3	THE ABSOLUTENESS OF HIS WORD
WORD	337 - 4	HIS WORD WOULD BE MANIFESTED LIKEWISE
WORD	340 - 2	WORD AND THE LAW
WORD	357 - 3	DECLARE OUR WORD
WORD	358 - 2	KNOW THERE IS NOTHING BUT THE WORD
WORD	431 - 2	THE WORD ONLY
WORD	437 - 3	SPEAK THE WORD ONLY
WORD	437 - 4	POWER OF THIS SPOKEN WORD
WORD	449 - 3	WORD MAY BE CONSIDERED TO
WORD	475 - 6	WHEN OUR WORD IS SPOKEN
WORD	476 - 1	THE WORD IS A MOLD
WORD	476 - 2	WORD GIVES FORM TO THE UNFORMED
WORDS	054 - 1	WORDS SHALL NOT PASS AWAY
WORDS	103 - 3	THE VERY WORDS WHICH HE SPOKE
WORDS	176 - 1	NOT BLITHELY REPEAT WORDS
WORDS	188 - 2	THE WORDS WHICH YOU SPEAK
WORDS	188 - 2	WORDS WHICH JESUS SPOKE
WORDS	207 - 3	THE WORDS THAT HE SPEAKS
WORDS	212 - 2	WORDS SHALL NOT PASS AWAY
WORDS	238 - 4	MANY WORDS OF WISDOM
WORDS	246 - 5	THE WORDS OF PEACE SPOKEN
WORDS	262 - 2	REALIZE THAT THE WORDS HE USES
WORDS	262 - 2	THE WORDS THAT I HAVE SPOKEN
WORDS	304 - 1	SPEAK INTO OUR WORDS THE INTELLIGENCE
WORDS	313 - 4	MY WORDS ABIDE IN YOU
WORDS	318 - 4	CONFORM THE WORDS IN OUR TREATMENT
WORDS	409 - 5	WORDS CARRY THE MIND FORWARD

WORDS	410 - 2	WE STATE CLEARLY IN WORDS
WORDS	410 - 2	WHATEVER WORDS WILL BRING CONVICTION
WORDS	413 - 3	ALL THE WORDS USED
WORDS	413 - 4	THROUGH THE WORDS WE SPEAK
WORDS	423 - 1	REPEAT ALL THE WORDS OF WISDOM
WORDS	437 - 4	HOW SIMPLE THE WORDS
WORDS	441 - 1	WORDS WHICH THEY SHOULD SPEAK
WORDS	449 - 3	WORDS WE ARE JUSTIFIED OR CONDEMNED
WORDSWORTH	103 - 3	WORDSWORTH SINGS THAT HEAVEN IS THE
WORK	058 - 2	KNOWS EXACTLY HOW TO WORK
WORK	169 - 2	WORK IN HIS OWN MIND
WORK	171 - 3	WORK BEGINS AND ENDS IN THE THOUGHT
WORK	219 - 4	WHY IT DOES NOT WORK
WORK	272 - 1	TO MAKE THE LAW WORK
WORK	305 - 5	RESPONSIBILITY OF MAKING IT WORK
WORK	318 - 3	LAW WILL WORK FROM ITS OWN ENERGY
WORK	384 - 1	WORK OUT OUR OWN SALVATION
WORK	401 - 4	WHO DOETH THE WORK
WORK	414 - 2	OUR WORK IS DONE IN MIND ALONE
WORK	414 - 3	BEST INTO OUR SPIRITUAL WORK
WORKER	413 - 5	WORKER IN THIS FIELD WHO JUDGED
WORKING	431 - 4	ONLY BY WORKING THROUGH US
WORKING	491 - 3	WORKING IN TIME AND SPACE
WORKING	496 - 3	GOD WORKING IN AND THROUGH US
WORKINGS	382 - 2	COMPLETE WORKINGS OF THE MIND
WORKS	052 - 4	WORKS FOR US BY FLOWING
WORKS	080 - 3	IT WORKS IS ABSOLUTE LAW
WORKS	166 - 2	WORKS THROUGH THE LAW OF MIND
WORKS	312 - 4	DOETH THE WORKS
WORKS	330 - 4	HE DOETH THE WORKS
WORKS	344 - 2	HE DOETH THE WORKS
WORKS	409 - 3	WORKS WITHIN HIS OWN MIND
WORKS	480 - 4	WORKS THAT I DO SHALL HE DO
WORKS	480 - 4	THROUGH HIS LIFE AND WORKS
WORKS	484 - 4	WORKS FROM WITHIN OUT
WORKS	500 - 1	MADE MANIFEST THROUGH GOOD WORKS
WORLD	031 - 2	NATURAL LAW IN A SPIRITUAL WORLD
WORLD	031 - 3	MEAN BY THE SPIRITUAL WORLD
WORLD	052 - 4	INVISIBLE AND SUBJECTIVE WORLD
WORLD	056 - 2	WORLD IS ALL RIGHT
WORLD	057 - 4	ENERGY IN THE INVISIBLE WORLD
WORLD	060 - 2	GOD'S WORLD IS PERFECT
WORLD	060 - 3	LIGHT IS COMING INTO THE WORLD
WORLD	087 - 1	A LITTLE WORLD WITHIN HIMSELF
WORLD	105 - 3	IN THE SUBJECTIVE WORLD
WORLD	107 - 4	WORLD IS BEGINNING TO REALIZE
WORLD	148 - 3	WORLD CREATED BY OUR CONSCIOUSNESS
WORLD	156 - 3	ENTIRE WORLD IS SUFFERING
WORLD	161 - 3	WHOLE WORLD HAS SUFFERED
WORLD	187 - 2	WHAT HAPPENS IN THE OBJECTIVE WORLD
WORLD	210 - 2	ENTIRE WORLD WILL BELIEVE
WORLD	270 - 5	DO NOT HAVE TO MOVE THE WORLD
WORLD	285 - 3	IN THE OBJECTIVE WORLD
WORLD	295 - 1	OUR THOUGHT MAKES OUR WORLD
WORLD	298 - 2	WHOLE WORLD AS YOUR FRIEND

WORLD	357 - 2	WORLD WITHOUT END
WORLD	415 - 4	PHYSICAL WORLD AROUND US IMPLIES
WORLD	423 - 1	WORLD NEEDS IS SPIRITUAL CONVICTION
WORLD	423 - 2	RAPIDLY CHANGING WORLD
WORLD	427 - 2	WORLD HAS NOT PRODUCED ANOTHER
WORLD	451 - 3	WORLD NEEDS SPIRITUAL EXPERIENCE
WORLD	453 - 3	SALVATION WILL COME TO THE WORLD
WORLD	455 - 7	WORLD IS MUCH BETTER THAN
WORLD	490 - 8	WORLD IS SATURATED WITH DIVINITY
WORLD	492 - 7	WORLD WITHOUT END
WORLD	502 - 7	WORLD DOES NOT KNOW THE SON OF GOD
WORLDS	301 - 4	WORLD'S OPINION TO CONTROL
WORLDS	492 - 7	WORLDS WILL ALWAYS BEGIN
WORM	467 - 1	A WORM OF THE DUST
WORRIED	289 - 3	NEVER BEING HURRIED NOR WORRIED
WORRY	233 - 4	LET GO OF DOUBT DISTRUST WORRY
WORRY	245 - 3	HEAL OURSELVES FROM WORRY
WORRY	253 - 3	TROUBLE ARE WORRY ANXIETY FEAR
WORRY	272 - 1	WORRY ABOUT THIS
WORRY	487 - 4	WORRY HOW THINGS ARE COMING OUT
WORSE	207 - 1	WORSE OR FROM SUCCESS
WORSE	313 - 1	NOT NECESSARILY BETTER OR WORSE
WORSHIP	081 - 2	MUST WORSHIP HIM IN SPIRIT
WORSHIP	150 - 4	THEY THAT WORSHIP HIM
WORSHIP	191 - 4	ALL FORMS OF WORSHIP
WORSHIP	473 - 2	WORSHIP OF MATERIAL EXISTENCE
WORSHIPPER	362 - 4	EVOLVED SOUL IS ALWAYS A WORSHIPPER
WORSHIPS	362 - 4	WORSHIPS GOD IN EVERYTHING
WORST	282 - 4	WORST IS THE BEST TIME TO WORK
WORST	465 - 4	WORST MENTAL DISEASES
WORTH	246 - 2	REALIZATION OF MY OWN WORTH
WORTH	329 - 4	FOR WHAT IT IS WORTH
WORTH WHILE	236 - 3	NOTHING SEEMS WORTH WHILE
WORTH WHILE	264 - 1	RECOGNIZE AS WORTH WHILE
WORTHWHILE	033 - 2	WHAT IS TRULY WORTHWHILE
WRESTLE	494 - 4	WRESTLE NOT AGAINST OUTWARD THINGS
WRITE	412 - 2	CONSCIOUSLY OR UNCONSCIOUSLY WRITE
WRITER	492 - 1	THE BELIEF OF THE WRITER THAT
WRITERS	419 - 2	WRITERS THE ILLUMINED
WRITING	153 - 2	BUT THE WRITING REMAINS
WRITTEN	348 - 2	WRITTEN INTO HIS MENTALITY
WRITTEN	391 - 4	IT IS WRITTEN THAT GOD
WRONG	110 - 2	WRONG USE OF FREEDOM
WRONG	111 - 1	WRONG DOING MUST BE PUNISHED
WRONG	169 - 6	THAT APPEARS TO BE WRONG
WRONG	236 - 3	EVERYTHING IS ALL WRONG
WRONG	236 - 3	PEOPLE ARE WRONG
WRONG	236 - 3	CONDITIONS ARE WRONG
WRONG	270 - 2	MAKING A WRONG USE OF THE LAW
WRONG	404 - 3	NOTHING WRONG IN THE DESIRE
WRONG	475 - 4	WRONG WITH HIS UNCONSCIOUS THINKING
WRONG	494 - 5	RIGHT AND A WRONG USE OF THIS LAW
WRONG	500 - 3	WRONG THE LAW PUNISHES
WRONG-DOING	458 - 2	PLACE A PREMIUM UPON WRONG-DOING
WRONG WAY	193 - 4	THE WILL IN THE WRONG WAY

Y

YE ARE GODS	364 - 2	YE ARE GODS AND ALL OF YOU ARE CHILDREN
YEARN	428 - 4	YEARN FOR TRUTH AND REALITY
YEARS	225 - 1	FIVE DAYS OR FIVE YEARS
YEARS	272 - 3	TRUE TEN THOUSAND YEARS AGO
YEARS	272 - 3	TEN THOUSAND YEARS HENCE
YEARS	362 - 2	NOW NEARLY TWO THOUSAND YEARS
YES	118 - 3	SUBCONSCIOUS MIND SAYS YES
YES	318 - 3	CONSCIOUSNESS WHICH SAYS YES
YESTERDAY	084 - 4	THE SAME YESTERDAY, TODAY
YESTERDAY	150 - 3	YESTERDAY, TODAY AND FOREVER
YESTERDAY	221 - 1	PRESENTED YESTERDAY WAS EASY
YESTERDAY	245 - 4	THE THOUGHTS OF YESTERDAY
YESTERDAY	314 - 3	THAT IS BETTER THAN WE HAD YESTERDAY
YESTERDAY	384 - 2	CONTINUANCE OF YESTERDAY
YESTERDAY	472 - 4	YESTERDAY, TODAY NOR TOMORROW
YESTERDAYS	432 - 4	BURDENS IMPOSED BY OUR YESTERDAYS
YIELD	414 - 1	YIELD TO THE TRUTH AS QUICKLY
YOU	210 - 2	YOU CAN HEAL
YOU	220 - 6	THINK YOU ARE DOING THE HEALING
YOU	260 - 4	YOU CAN IF YOU KNOW
YOU	398 - 1	YOU MAKE UP ITS MIND FOR IT
YOU	401 - 2	YOU USE YOUR SUBJECTIVE MIND
YOUR	289 - 3	YOUR WORD AS BEING THE THING
YOURSELF	221 - 1	AT ONCE HEAL YOURSELF
YOURSELF	221 - 2	CAN DENY GOD IS YOURSELF

About the Authors

DR. AL LOWE was a native of Memphis, Tennessee. Lowe graduated from Auburn University, with degrees in Chemical Engineering and Pharmaceutical Chemistry. Dr. Lowe held an M.S. degree in Psychology and a Ph.D. degree from Florida State University.

Dr. Lowe was a long-time minister of Religious Science, and was at one time the Dean of the School of Ministry of the United Church of Religious Science. Dr. Lowe passed away in 2000.

REV. MARTHA ANN STEWART completed her ministerial studies at the Institute of Religious Science in Los Angeles.

Rev. Stewart received further training as acting Assistant Minister at the Seal Beach Church of Religious Science. She was on the staff at United Church Headquarters in the Education Department and at the New Horizons newsmagazine.